Accomplishments of the Duke's Daughter

2

STORY: Reia
ART: Suki Umemiya
CHARACTER DESIGN: Haduki Futaba

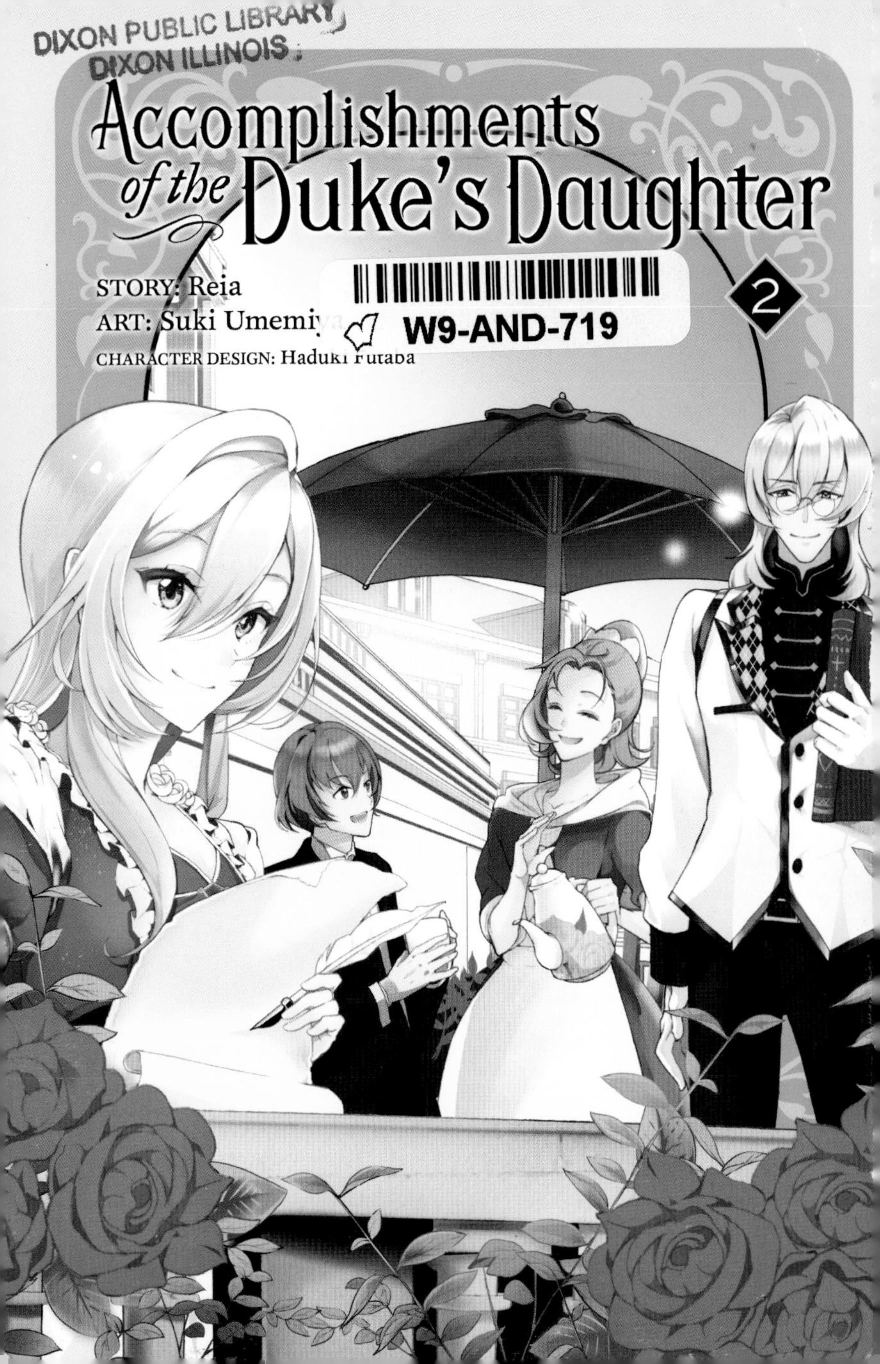

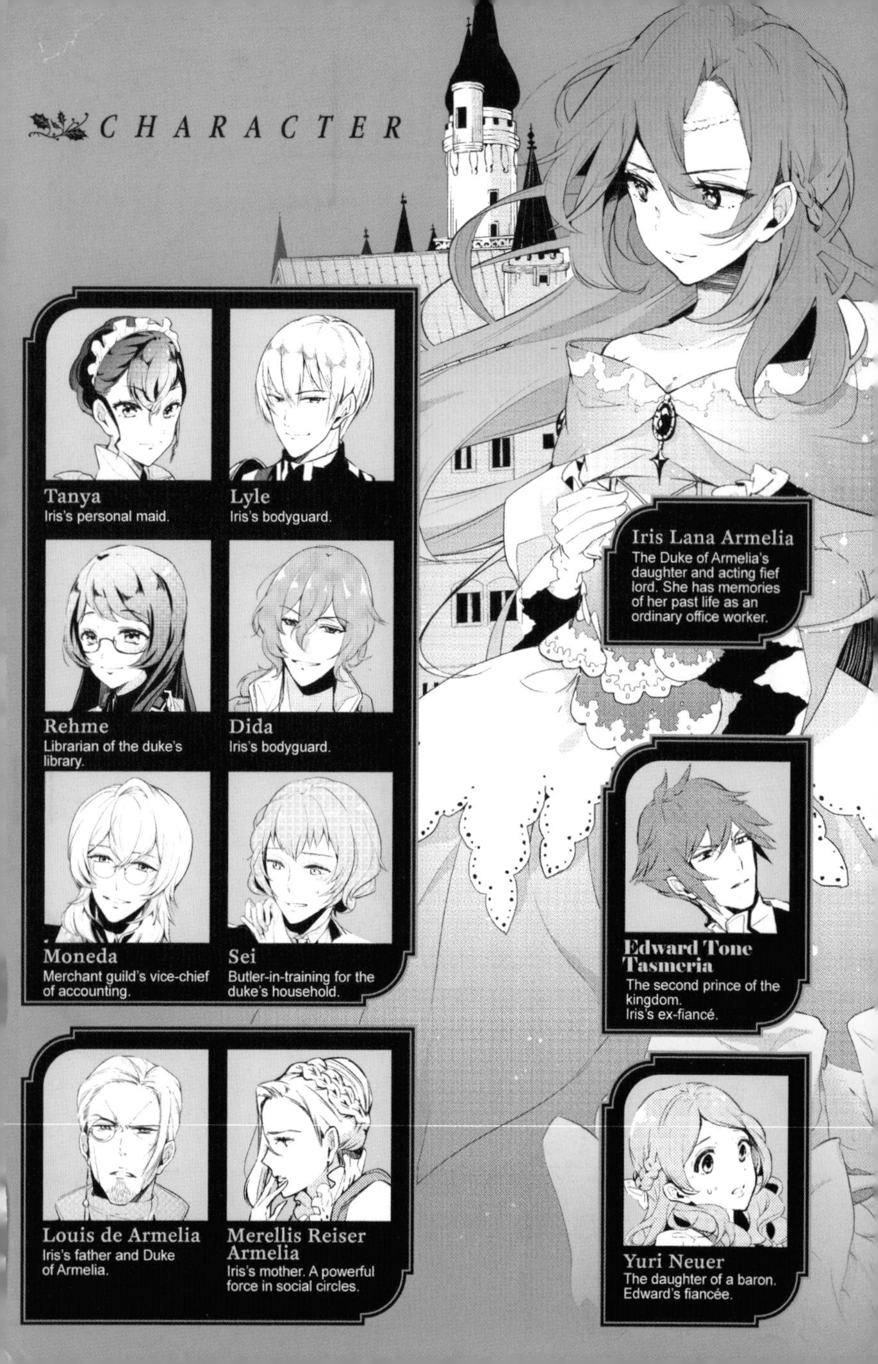
CHARACTER
Iris Lana Armelia
The Duke of Armelia's daughter and acting fief lord. She has memories of her past life as an ordinary office worker.
Edward Tone Tasmeria
The second prince of the kingdom. Iris's ex-fiancé.
Yuri Neuer
The daughter of a baron. Edward's fiancée.
Tanya
Iris's personal maid.
Lyle
Iris's bodyguard.
Rehme
Librarian of the duke's library.
Dida
Iris's bodyguard.
Moneda
Merchant guild's vice-chief of accounting.
Sei
Butler-in-training for the duke's household.
Louis de Armelia
Iris's father and Duke of Armelia.
Merellis Reiser Armelia
Iris's mother. A powerful force in social circles.

SEVEN SEAS ENTERTAINMENT PRESENTS

Accomplishments
of the Duke's Daughter VOLUME 2

story by **REIA**   art by **SUKI UMEMIYA**
character design by **HADUKI FUTABA**

TRANSLATION
Angela Liu

ADAPTATION
Tracy Barnett

LETTERING AND RETOUCH
Alexandra Gunawan

COVER DESIGN
KC Fabellon

PROOFREADER
B. Lana Guggenheim
Janet Houck

EDITOR
Shannon Fay

PRODUCTION ASSISTANT
CK Russell

PRODUCTION MANAGER
Lissa Pattillo

EDITOR-IN-CHIEF
Adam Arnold

PUBLISHER
Jason DeAngelis

KOUSHAKU REIJOU NO TASHINAMI VOL. 2
© Reia, Haduki Futaba 2017
© Suki UMEMIYA 2017
First published in Japan in 2017 by KADOKAWA CORPORATION, Tokyo.
English translation rights arranged with KADOKAWA CORPORATION, Tokyo.

Seven Seas books may be purchased in bulk for promotional, educational, or
business use. Please contact your local bookseller or the Macmillan Corporate
and Premium Sales Department at 1-800-221-7945, extension 5442, or by
e-mail at MacmillanSpecialMarkets@macmillan.com.

Seven Seas and the Seven Seas logo are trademarks of
Seven Seas Entertainment, LLC. All rights reserved.

ISBN: 978-1-626929-66-1

Printed in Canada

First Printing: December 2018

10 9 8 7 6 5 4 3 2 1

FOLLOW US ONLINE: *www.sevenseasentertainment.com*

READING DIRECTIONS

This book reads from *right to left*, Japanese style.
If this is your first time reading manga, you start
reading from the top right panel on each page and
take it from there. If you get lost, just follow the
numbered diagram here. It may seem backwards at
first, but you'll get the hang of it! Have fun!!

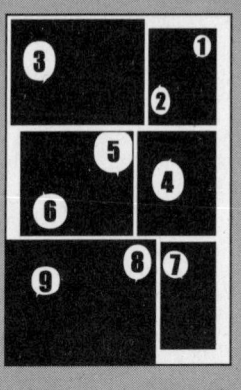

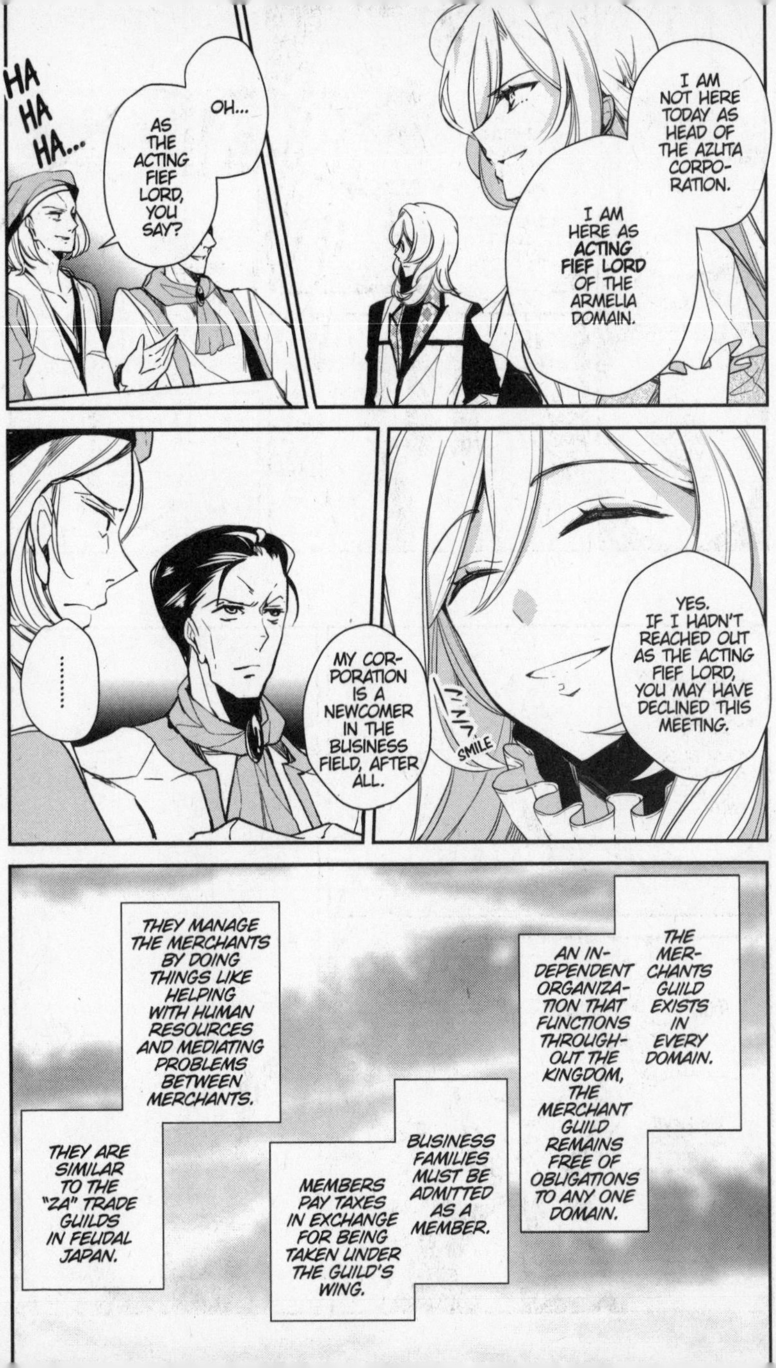
I AM NOT HERE TODAY AS HEAD OF THE AZUTA CORPORATION.
I AM HERE AS ACTING FIEF LORD OF THE ARMELIA DOMAIN.
OH...
AS THE ACTING FIEF LORD, YOU SAY?
HA HA HA...
YES. IF I HADN'T REACHED OUT AS THE ACTING FIEF LORD, YOU MAY HAVE DECLINED THIS MEETING.
SMILE
MY CORPORATION IS A NEWCOMER IN THE BUSINESS FIELD, AFTER ALL.
....
THE MERCHANTS GUILD EXISTS IN EVERY DOMAIN.
AN INDEPENDENT ORGANIZATION THAT FUNCTIONS THROUGHOUT THE KINGDOM, THE MERCHANT GUILD REMAINS FREE OF OBLIGATIONS TO ANY ONE DOMAIN.
BUSINESS FAMILIES MUST BE ADMITTED AS A MEMBER.
MEMBERS PAY TAXES IN EXCHANGE FOR BEING TAKEN UNDER THE GUILD'S WING.
THEY MANAGE THE MERCHANTS BY DOING THINGS LIKE HELPING WITH HUMAN RESOURCES AND MEDIATING PROBLEMS BETWEEN MERCHANTS.
THEY ARE SIMILAR TO THE "ZA" TRADE GUILDS IN FEUDAL JAPAN.

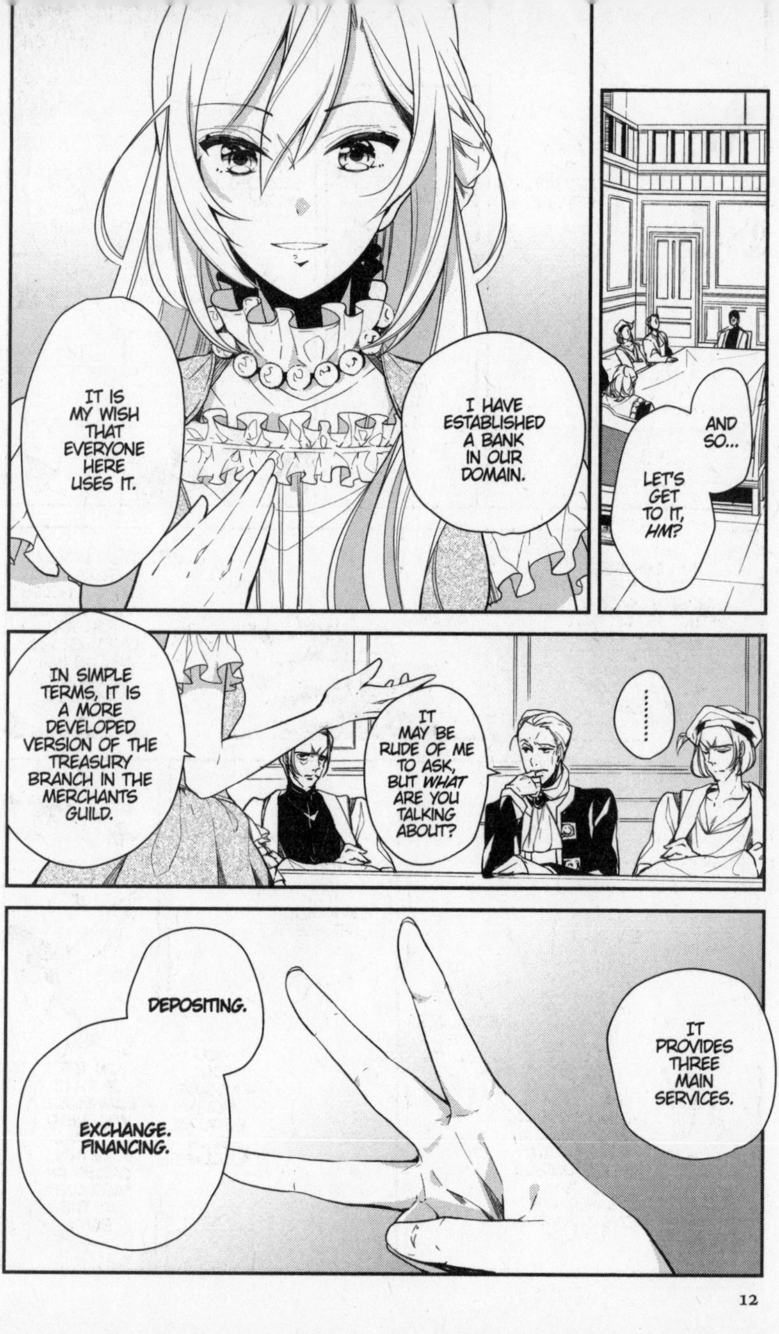
AND SO...
LET'S GET TO IT, *HM?*
I HAVE ESTABLISHED A BANK IN OUR DOMAIN.
IT IS MY WISH THAT EVERYONE HERE USES IT.
......
IT MAY BE RUDE OF ME TO ASK, BUT *WHAT* ARE YOU TALKING ABOUT?
IN SIMPLE TERMS, IT IS A MORE DEVELOPED VERSION OF THE TREASURY BRANCH IN THE MERCHANTS GUILD.
IT PROVIDES THREE MAIN SERVICES.
DEPOSITING.
EXCHANGE. FINANCING.

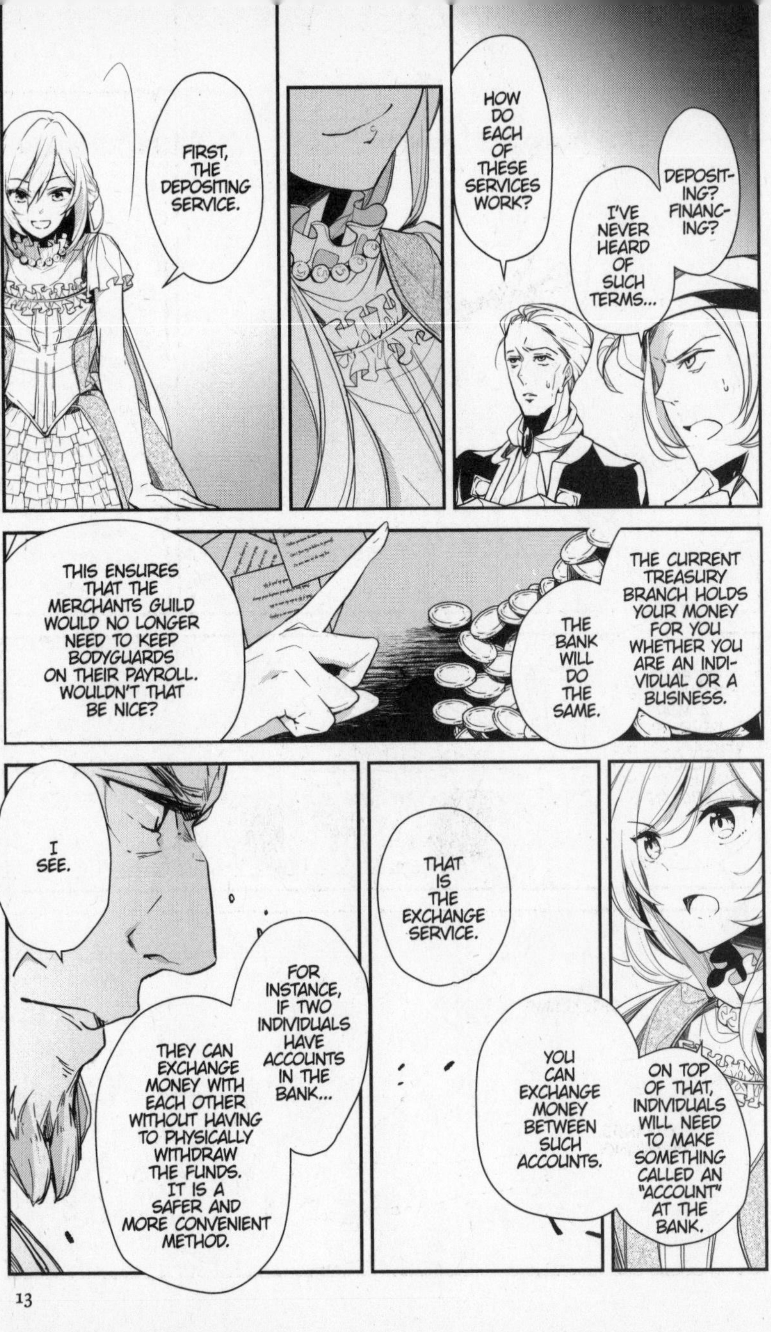
DEPOSITING? FINANCING?
I'VE NEVER HEARD OF SUCH TERMS...
HOW DO EACH OF THESE SERVICES WORK?
FIRST, THE DEPOSITING SERVICE.
THE CURRENT TREASURY BRANCH HOLDS YOUR MONEY FOR YOU WHETHER YOU ARE AN INDIVIDUAL OR A BUSINESS.
THE BANK WILL DO THE SAME.
THIS ENSURES THAT THE MERCHANTS GUILD WOULD NO LONGER NEED TO KEEP BODYGUARDS ON THEIR PAYROLL. WOULDN'T THAT BE NICE?
ON TOP OF THAT, INDIVIDUALS WILL NEED TO MAKE SOMETHING CALLED AN "ACCOUNT" AT THE BANK.
YOU CAN EXCHANGE MONEY BETWEEN SUCH ACCOUNTS.
THAT IS THE EXCHANGE SERVICE.
FOR INSTANCE, IF TWO INDIVIDUALS HAVE ACCOUNTS IN THE BANK...
THEY CAN EXCHANGE MONEY WITH EACH OTHER WITHOUT HAVING TO PHYSICALLY WITHDRAW THE FUNDS. IT IS A SAFER AND MORE CONVENIENT METHOD.
I SEE.

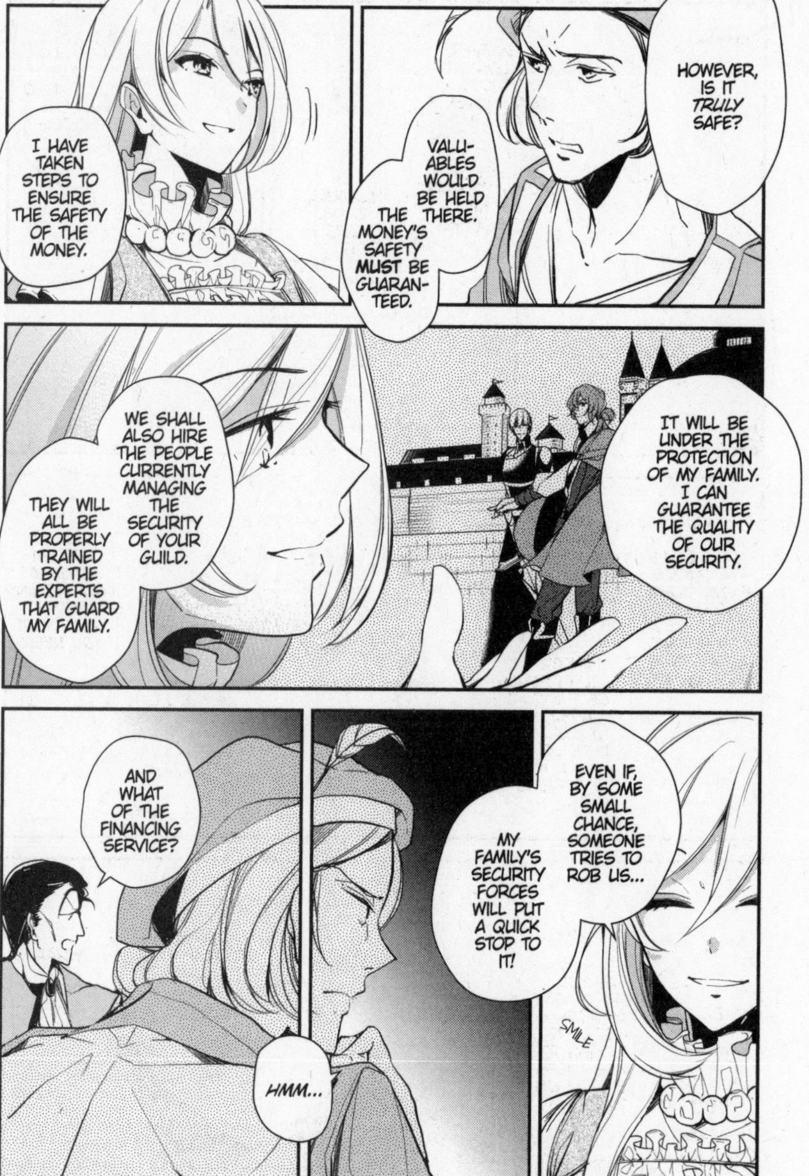
HOWEVER, IS IT TRULY SAFE?
VALUABLES WOULD BE HELD THERE. THE MONEY'S SAFETY MUST BE GUARANTEED.
I HAVE TAKEN STEPS TO ENSURE THE SAFETY OF THE MONEY.
IT WILL BE UNDER THE PROTECTION OF MY FAMILY. I CAN GUARANTEE THE QUALITY OF OUR SECURITY.
WE SHALL ALSO HIRE THE PEOPLE CURRENTLY MANAGING THE SECURITY OF YOUR GUILD.
THEY WILL ALL BE PROPERLY TRAINED BY THE EXPERTS THAT GUARD MY FAMILY.
EVEN IF, BY SOME SMALL CHANCE, SOMEONE TRIES TO ROB US...
MY FAMILY'S SECURITY FORCES WILL PUT A QUICK STOP TO IT!
SMILE
HMM...
AND WHAT OF THE FINANCING SERVICE?

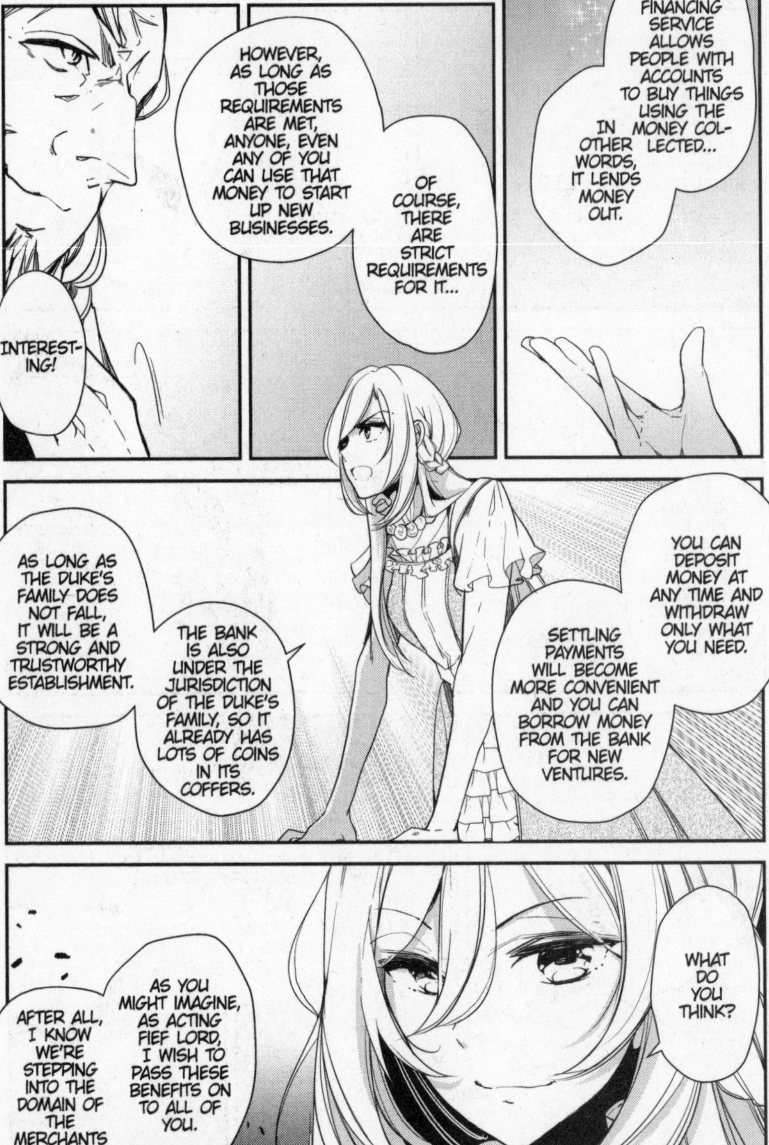
THE FINANCING SERVICE ALLOWS PEOPLE WITH ACCOUNTS TO BUY THINGS USING THE MONEY COL-LECTED...
IN OTHER WORDS, IT LENDS MONEY OUT.
OF COURSE, THERE ARE STRICT REQUIREMENTS FOR IT...
HOWEVER, AS LONG AS THOSE REQUIREMENTS ARE MET, ANYONE, EVEN ANY OF YOU CAN USE THAT MONEY TO START UP NEW BUSINESSES.
INTEREST-ING!
YOU CAN DEPOSIT MONEY AT ANY TIME AND WITHDRAW ONLY WHAT YOU NEED.
SETTLING PAYMENTS WILL BECOME MORE CONVENIENT AND YOU CAN BORROW MONEY FROM THE BANK FOR NEW VENTURES.
THE BANK IS ALSO UNDER THE JURISDICTION OF THE DUKE'S FAMILY, SO IT ALREADY HAS LOTS OF COINS IN ITS COFFERS.
AS LONG AS THE DUKE'S FAMILY DOES NOT FALL, IT WILL BE A STRONG AND TRUSTWORTHY ESTABLISHMENT.
WHAT DO YOU THINK?
AS YOU MIGHT IMAGINE, AS ACTING FIEF LORD, I WISH TO PASS THESE BENEFITS ON TO ALL OF YOU.
AFTER ALL, I KNOW WE'RE STEPPING INTO THE DOMAIN OF THE MERCHANTS GUILD HERE.

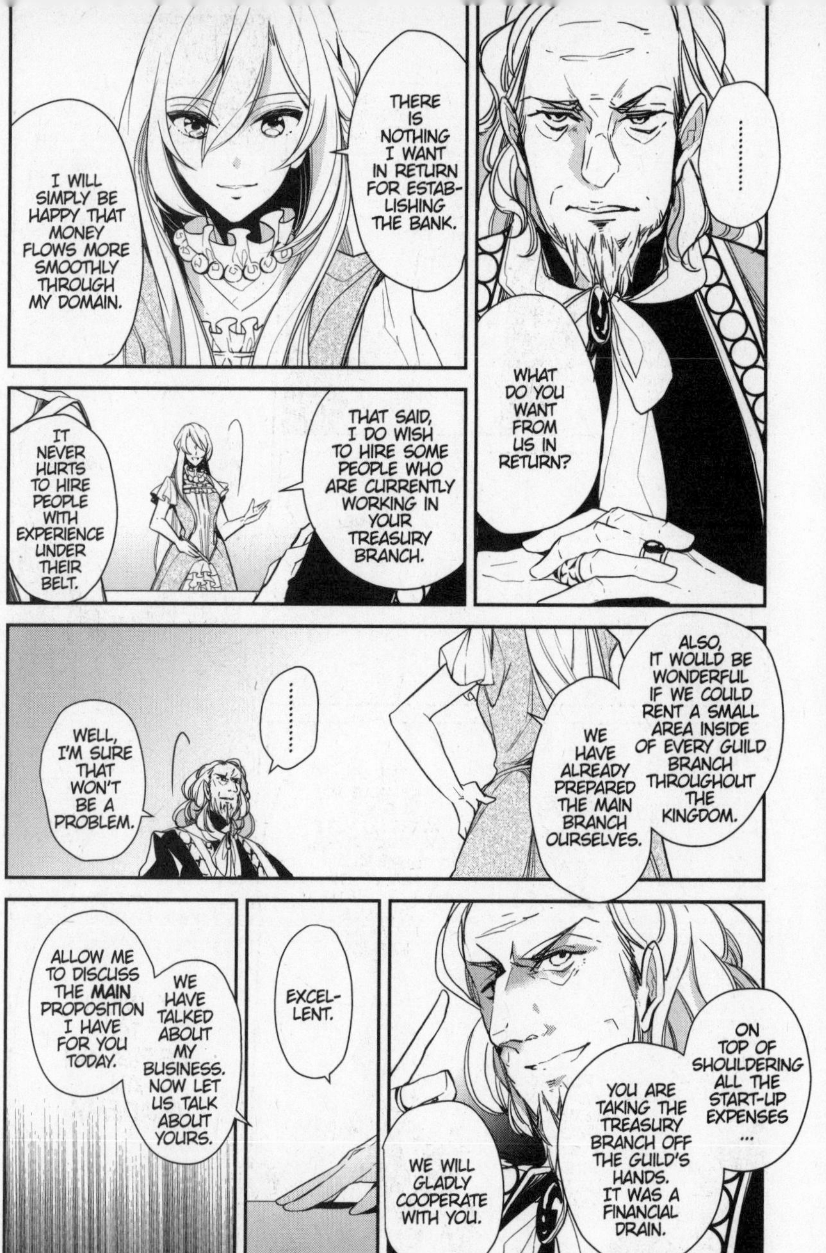
......
WHAT DO YOU WANT FROM US IN RETURN?
THERE IS NOTHING I WANT IN RETURN FOR ESTAB-LISHING THE BANK.
I WILL SIMPLY BE HAPPY THAT MONEY FLOWS MORE SMOOTHLY THROUGH MY DOMAIN.
THAT SAID, I DO WISH TO HIRE SOME PEOPLE WHO ARE CURRENTLY WORKING IN YOUR TREASURY BRANCH.
IT NEVER HURTS TO HIRE PEOPLE WITH EXPERIENCE UNDER THEIR BELT.
ALSO, IT WOULD BE WONDERFUL IF WE COULD RENT A SMALL AREA INSIDE OF EVERY GUILD BRANCH THROUGHOUT THE KINGDOM.
WE HAVE ALREADY PREPARED THE MAIN BRANCH OURSELVES.
......
WELL, I'M SURE THAT WON'T BE A PROBLEM.
ON TOP OF SHOULDERING ALL THE START-UP EXPENSES ...
YOU ARE TAKING THE TREASURY BRANCH OFF THE GUILD'S HANDS. IT WAS A FINANCIAL DRAIN.
WE WILL GLADLY COOPERATE WITH YOU.
EXCEL-LENT.
WE HAVE TALKED ABOUT MY BUSINESS. NOW LET US TALK ABOUT YOURS.
ALLOW ME TO DISCUSS THE MAIN PROPOSITION I HAVE FOR YOU TODAY.

#11 end

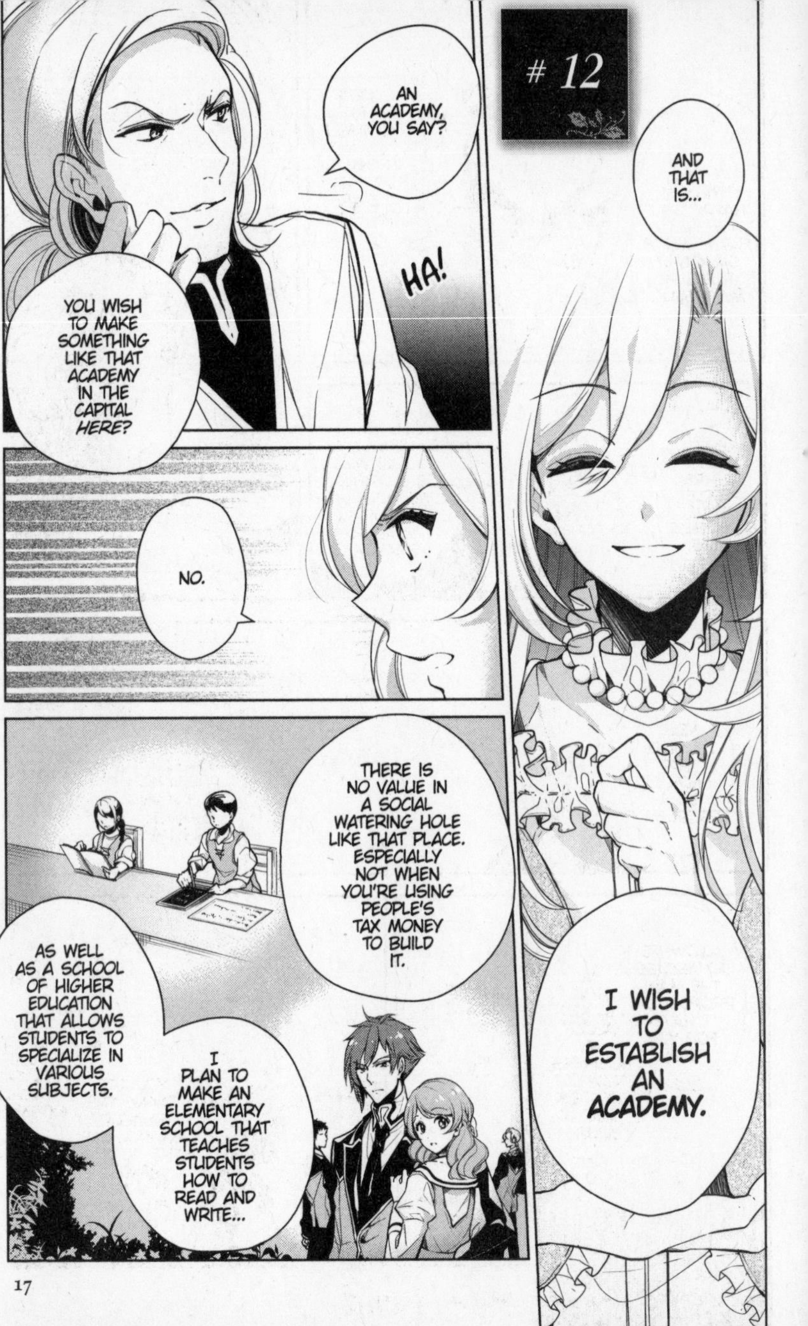

12
AND THAT IS...
I WISH TO ESTABLISH AN ACADEMY.
AN ACADEMY, YOU SAY?
HA!
YOU WISH TO MAKE SOMETHING LIKE THAT ACADEMY IN THE CAPITAL HERE?
NO.
THERE IS NO VALUE IN A SOCIAL WATERING HOLE LIKE THAT PLACE. ESPECIALLY NOT WHEN YOU'RE USING PEOPLE'S TAX MONEY TO BUILD IT.
I PLAN TO MAKE AN ELEMENTARY SCHOOL THAT TEACHES STUDENTS HOW TO READ AND WRITE...
AS WELL AS A SCHOOL OF HIGHER EDUCATION THAT ALLOWS STUDENTS TO SPECIALIZE IN VARIOUS SUBJECTS.

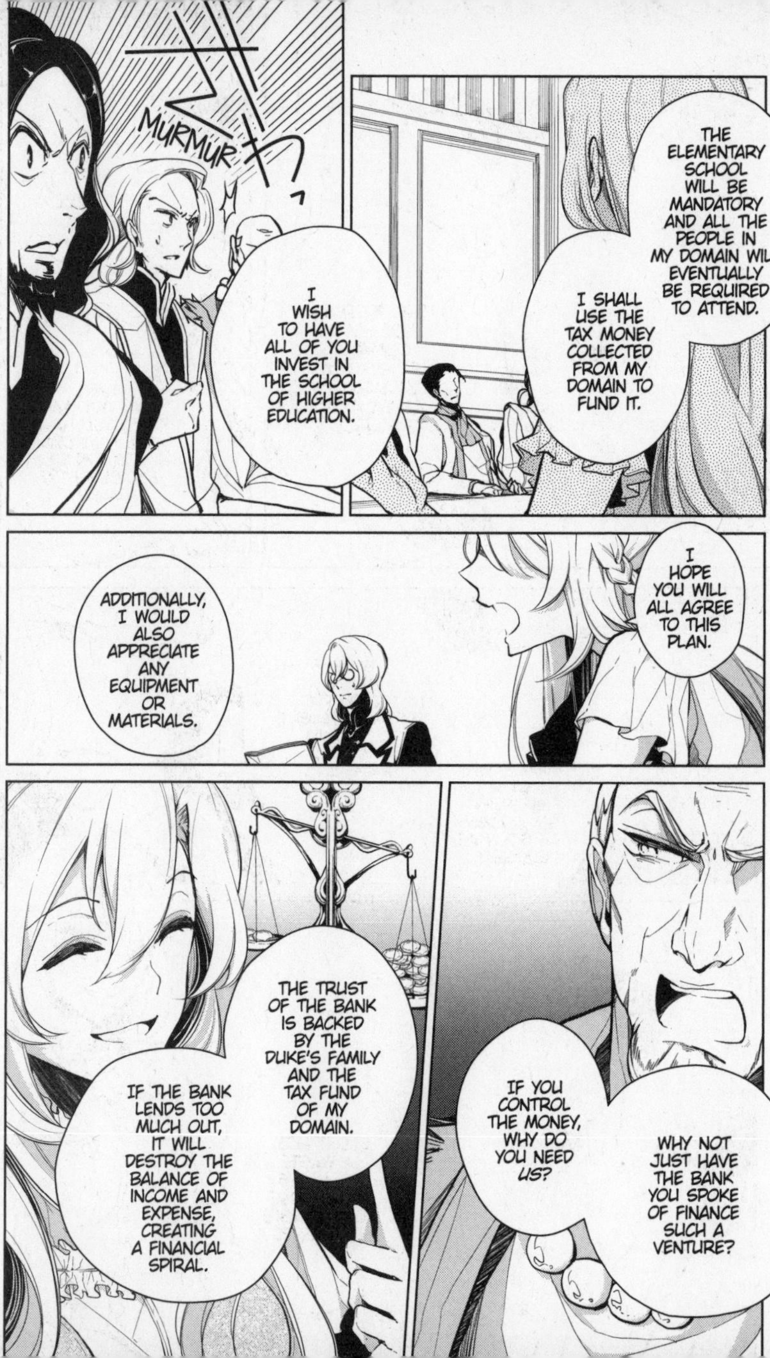
THE ELEMENTARY SCHOOL WILL BE MANDATORY AND ALL THE PEOPLE IN MY DOMAIN WILL EVENTUALLY BE REQUIRED TO ATTEND.
I SHALL USE THE TAX MONEY COLLECTED FROM MY DOMAIN TO FUND IT.
I WISH TO HAVE ALL OF YOU INVEST IN THE SCHOOL OF HIGHER EDUCATION.
MURMUR
I HOPE YOU WILL ALL AGREE TO THIS PLAN.
ADDITIONALLY, I WOULD ALSO APPRECIATE ANY EQUIPMENT OR MATERIALS.
WHY NOT JUST HAVE THE BANK YOU SPOKE OF FINANCE SUCH A VENTURE?
IF YOU CONTROL THE MONEY, WHY DO YOU NEED US?
THE TRUST OF THE BANK IS BACKED BY THE DUKE'S FAMILY AND THE TAX FUND OF MY DOMAIN.
IF THE BANK LENDS TOO MUCH OUT, IT WILL DESTROY THE BALANCE OF INCOME AND EXPENSE, CREATING A FINANCIAL SPIRAL.

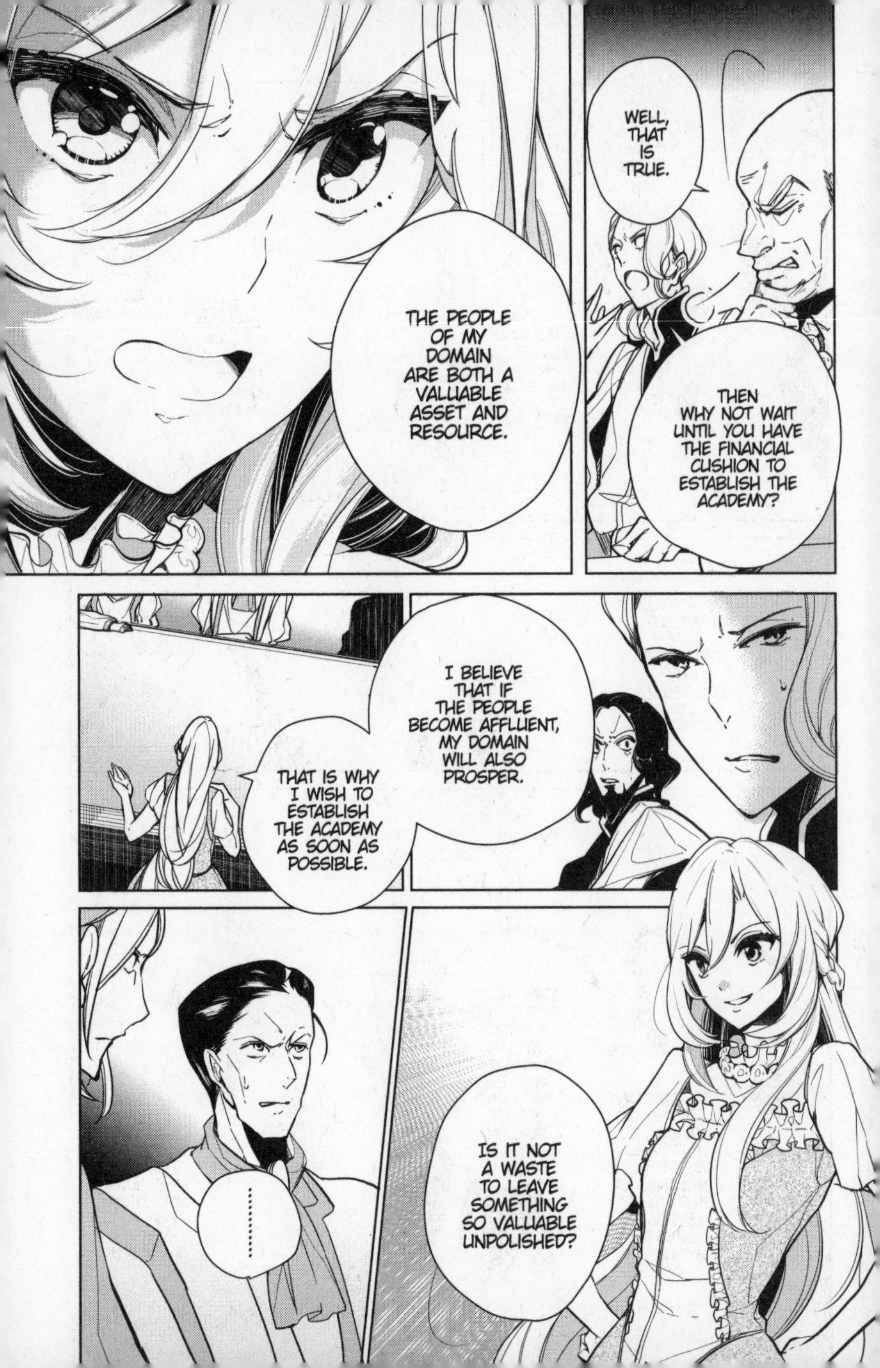
WELL, THAT IS TRUE.
THEN WHY NOT WAIT UNTIL YOU HAVE THE FINANCIAL CUSHION TO ESTABLISH THE ACADEMY?
THE PEOPLE OF MY DOMAIN ARE BOTH A VALUABLE ASSET AND RESOURCE.
I BELIEVE THAT IF THE PEOPLE BECOME AFFLUENT, MY DOMAIN WILL ALSO PROSPER.
THAT IS WHY I WISH TO ESTABLISH THE ACADEMY AS SOON AS POSSIBLE.
IS IT NOT A WASTE TO LEAVE SOMETHING SO VALUABLE UNPOLISHED?
......

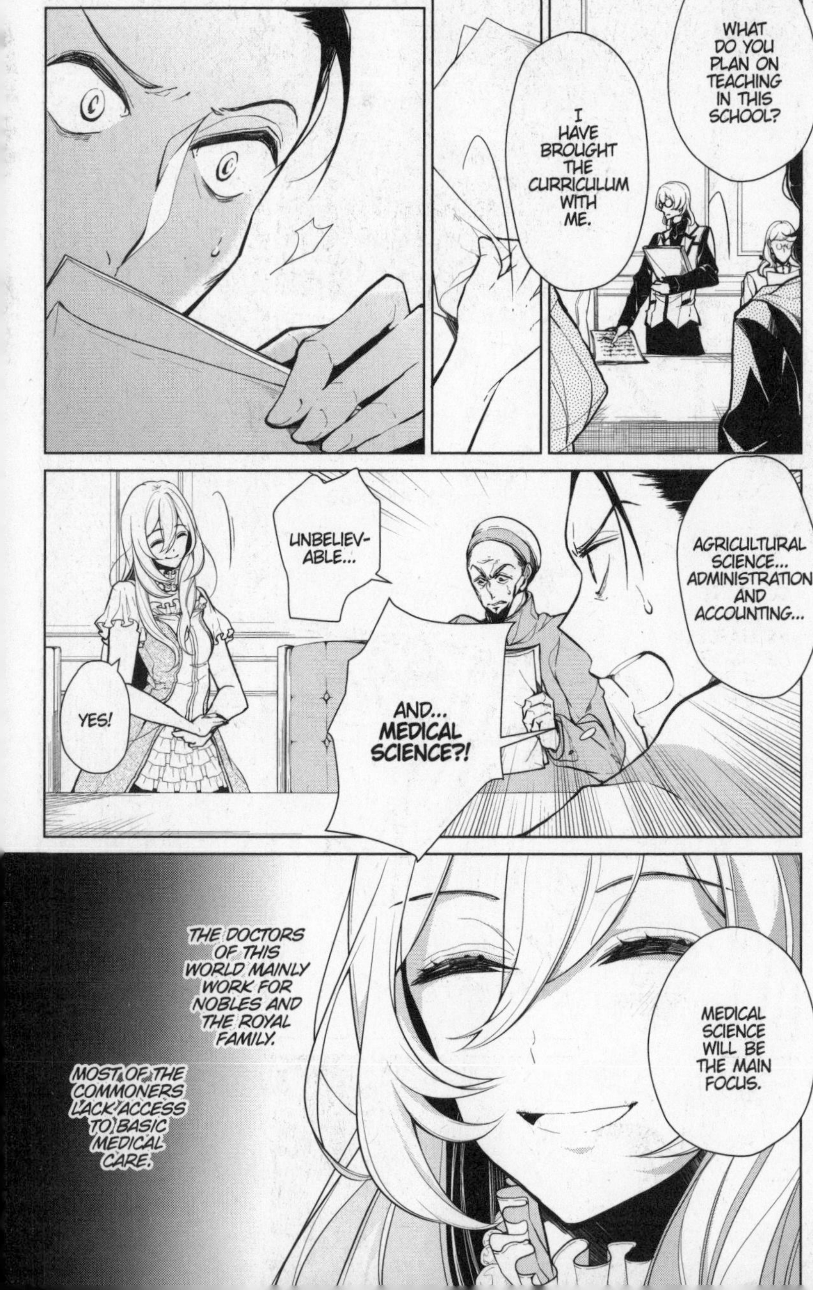
WHAT DO YOU PLAN ON TEACHING IN THIS SCHOOL?
I HAVE BROUGHT THE CURRICULUM WITH ME.
AGRICULTURAL SCIENCE... ADMINISTRATION AND ACCOUNTING...
AND... MEDICAL SCIENCE?!
UNBELIEV-ABLE...
YES!
MEDICAL SCIENCE WILL BE THE MAIN FOCUS.
THE DOCTORS OF THIS WORLD MAINLY WORK FOR NOBLES AND THE ROYAL FAMILY.
MOST OF THE COMMONERS LACK ACCESS TO BASIC MEDICAL CARE.

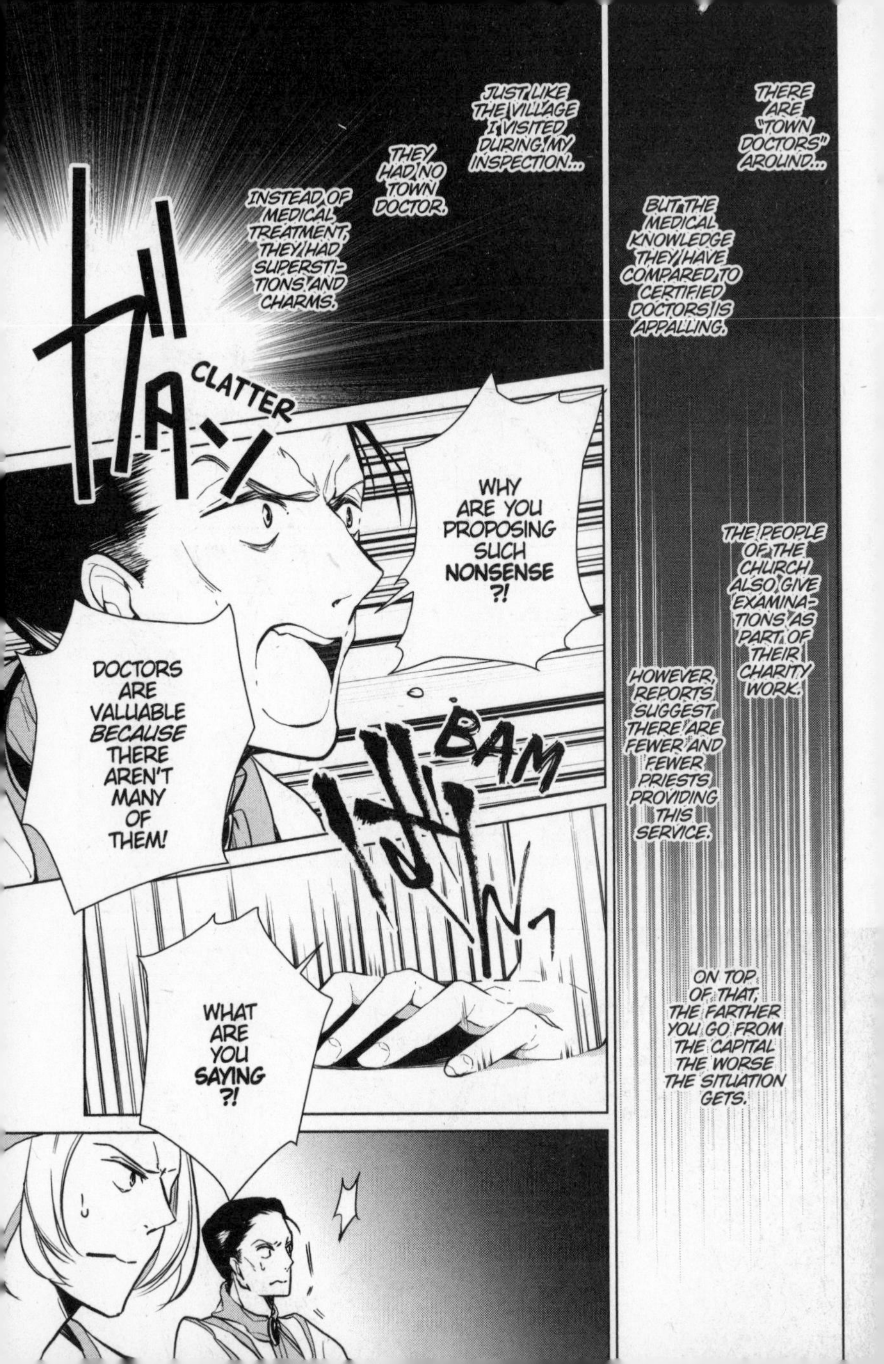
THERE ARE "TOWN DOCTORS" AROUND...
BUT THE MEDICAL KNOWLEDGE THEY HAVE COMPARED TO CERTIFIED DOCTORS IS APPALLING.
THE PEOPLE OF THE CHURCH ALSO GIVE EXAMINA-TIONS AS PART OF THEIR CHARITY WORK.
HOWEVER, REPORTS SUGGEST THERE ARE FEWER AND FEWER PRIESTS PROVIDING THIS SERVICE.
ON TOP OF THAT, THE FARTHER YOU GO FROM THE CAPITAL THE WORSE THE SITUATION GETS.
JUST LIKE THE VILLAGE I VISITED DURING MY INSPECTION...
THEY HAD NO TOWN DOCTOR.
INSTEAD OF MEDICAL TREATMENT, THEY HAD SUPERSTI-TIONS AND CHARMS.
CLATTER
WHY ARE YOU PROPOSING SUCH NONSENSE ?!
DOCTORS ARE VALUABLE BECAUSE THERE AREN'T MANY OF THEM!
BAM
WHAT ARE YOU SAYING ?!

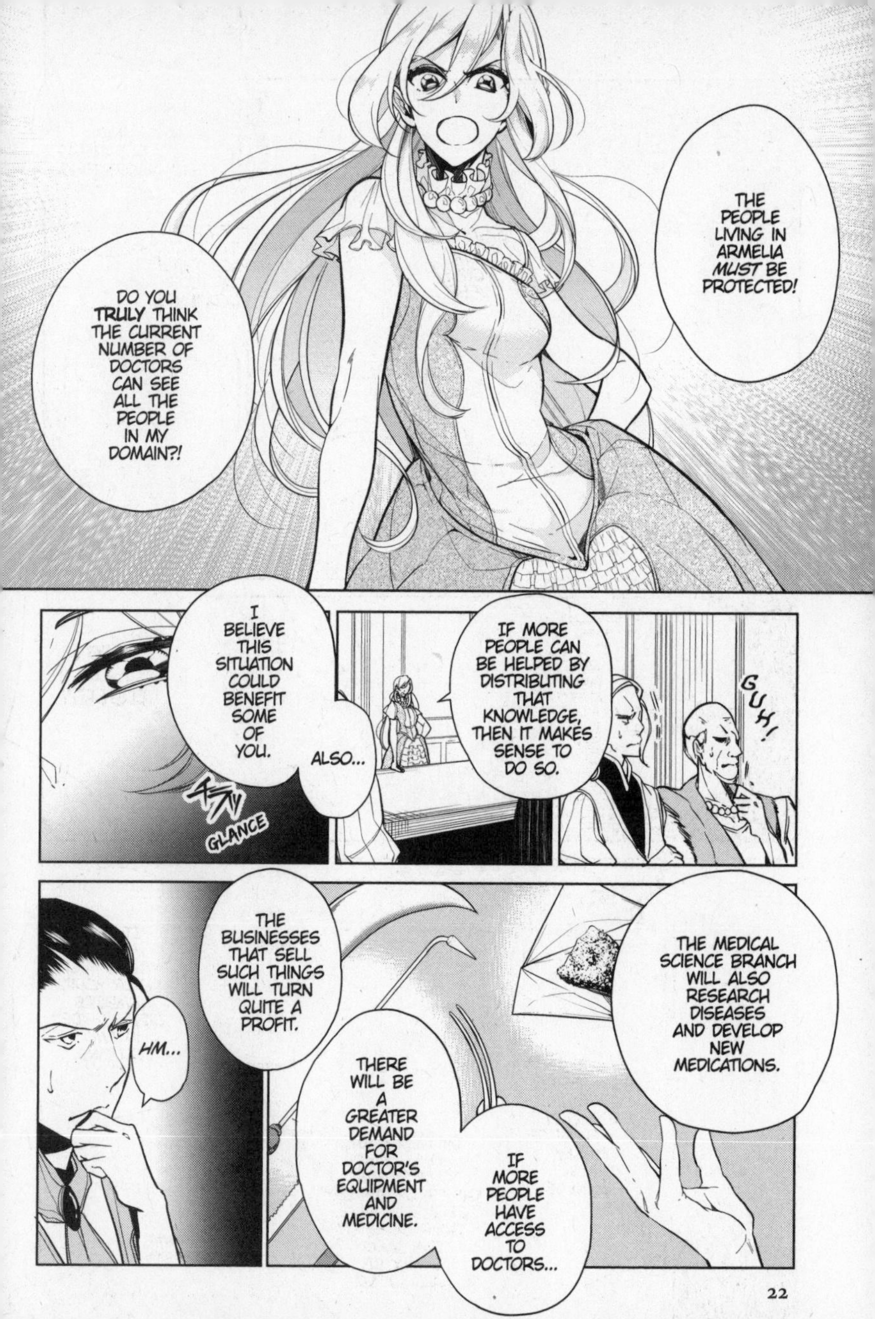
THE PEOPLE LIVING IN ARMELIA *MUST* BE PROTECTED!
DO YOU **TRULY** THINK THE CURRENT NUMBER OF DOCTORS CAN SEE ALL THE PEOPLE IN MY DOMAIN?!
GUH!
IF MORE PEOPLE CAN BE HELPED BY DISTRIBUTING THAT KNOWLEDGE, THEN IT MAKES SENSE TO DO SO.
I BELIEVE THIS SITUATION COULD BENEFIT SOME OF YOU.
ALSO...
GLANCE
THE MEDICAL SCIENCE BRANCH WILL ALSO RESEARCH DISEASES AND DEVELOP NEW MEDICATIONS.
IF MORE PEOPLE HAVE ACCESS TO DOCTORS...
THERE WILL BE A GREATER DEMAND FOR DOCTOR'S EQUIPMENT AND MEDICINE.
THE BUSINESSES THAT SELL SUCH THINGS WILL TURN QUITE A PROFIT.
HM...

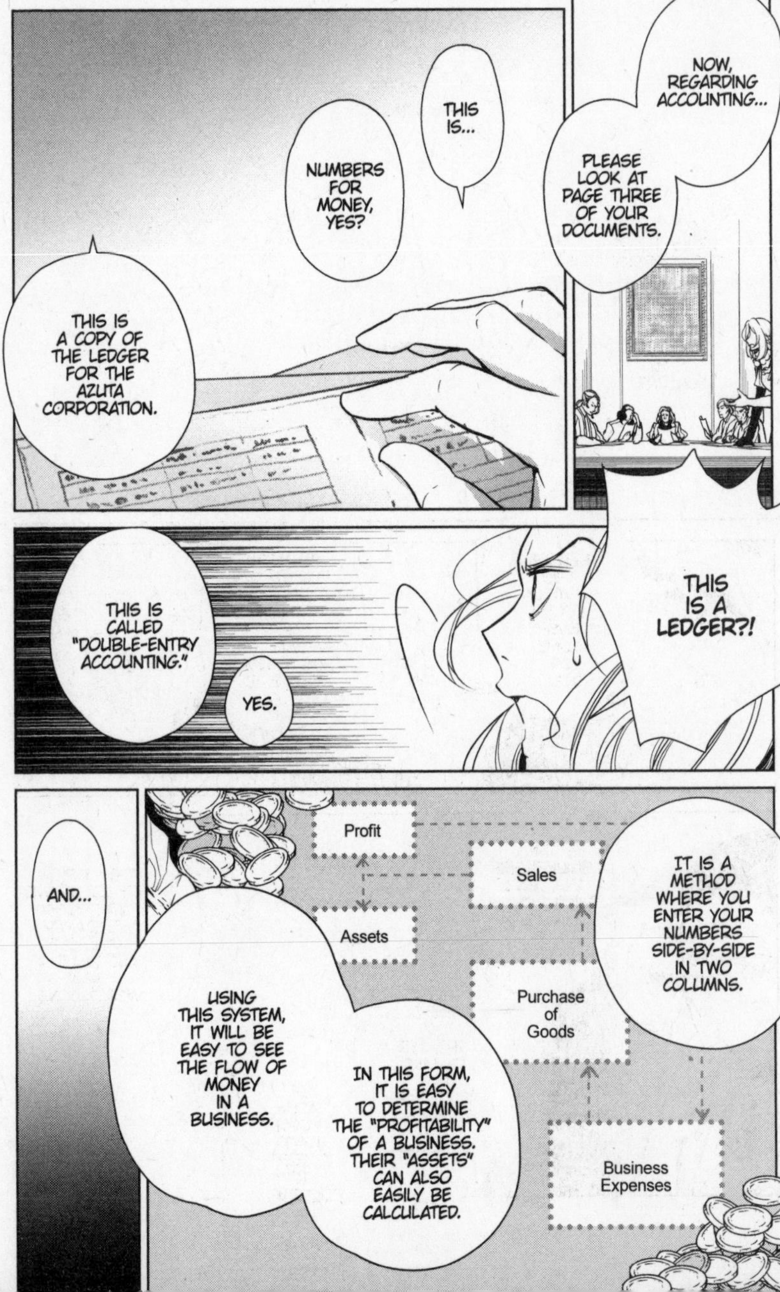
NOW, REGARDING ACCOUNTING...
PLEASE LOOK AT PAGE THREE OF YOUR DOCUMENTS.
THIS IS...
NUMBERS FOR MONEY, YES?
THIS IS A COPY OF THE LEDGER FOR THE AZUTA CORPORATION.
THIS IS A LEDGER?!
THIS IS CALLED "DOUBLE-ENTRY ACCOUNTING."
YES.
IT IS A METHOD WHERE YOU ENTER YOUR NUMBERS SIDE-BY-SIDE IN TWO COLUMNS.
Profit
Sales
Assets
Purchase of Goods
Business Expenses
USING THIS SYSTEM, IT WILL BE EASY TO SEE THE FLOW OF MONEY IN A BUSINESS.
IN THIS FORM, IT IS EASY TO DETERMINE THE "PROFITABILITY" OF A BUSINESS. THEIR "ASSETS" CAN ALSO EASILY BE CALCULATED.
AND...

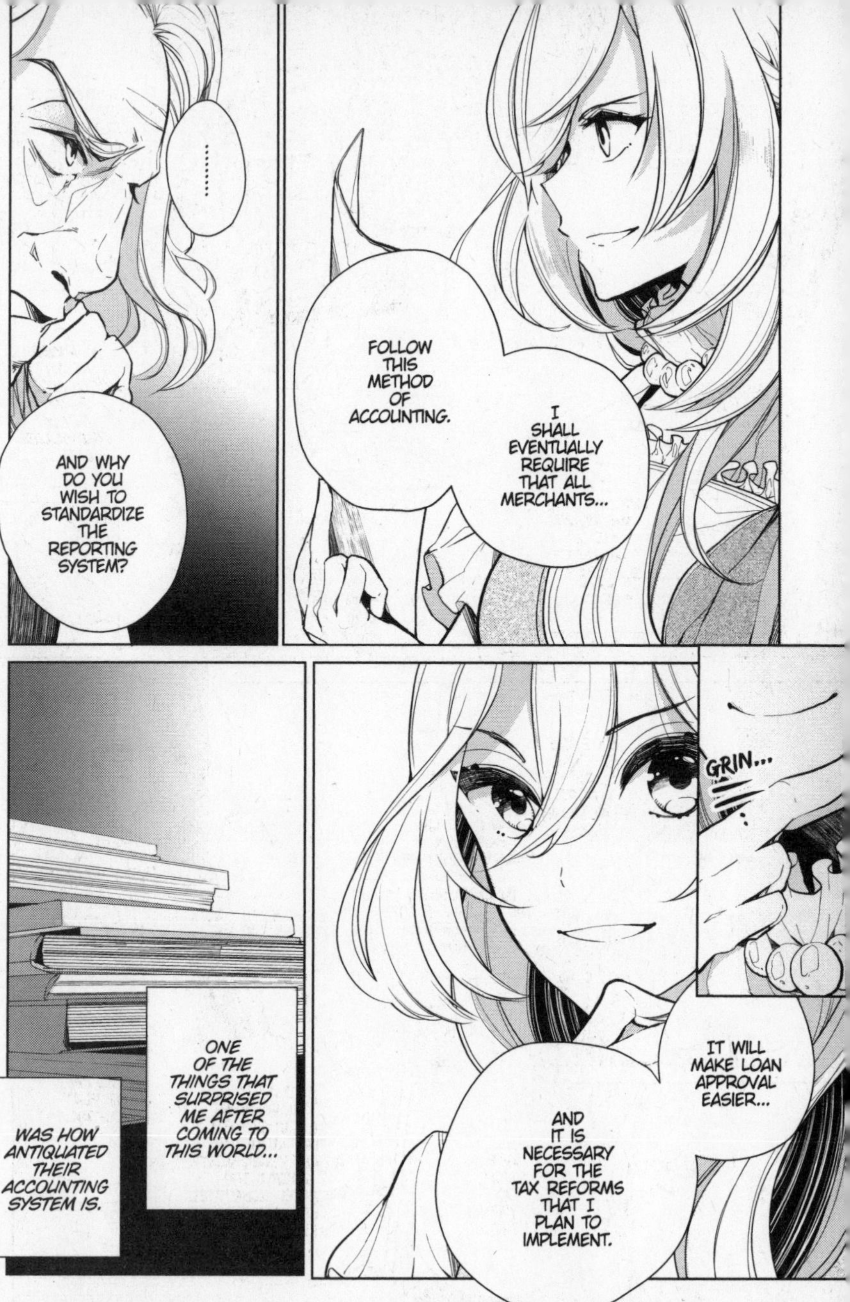
I SHALL EVENTUALLY REQUIRE THAT ALL MERCHANTS...
FOLLOW THIS METHOD OF ACCOUNTING.
......
AND WHY DO YOU WISH TO STANDARDIZE THE REPORTING SYSTEM?
GRIN...
IT WILL MAKE LOAN APPROVAL EASIER...
AND IT IS NECESSARY FOR THE TAX REFORMS THAT I PLAN TO IMPLEMENT.
ONE OF THE THINGS THAT SURPRISED ME AFTER COMING TO THIS WORLD...
WAS HOW ANTIQUATED THEIR ACCOUNTING SYSTEM IS.

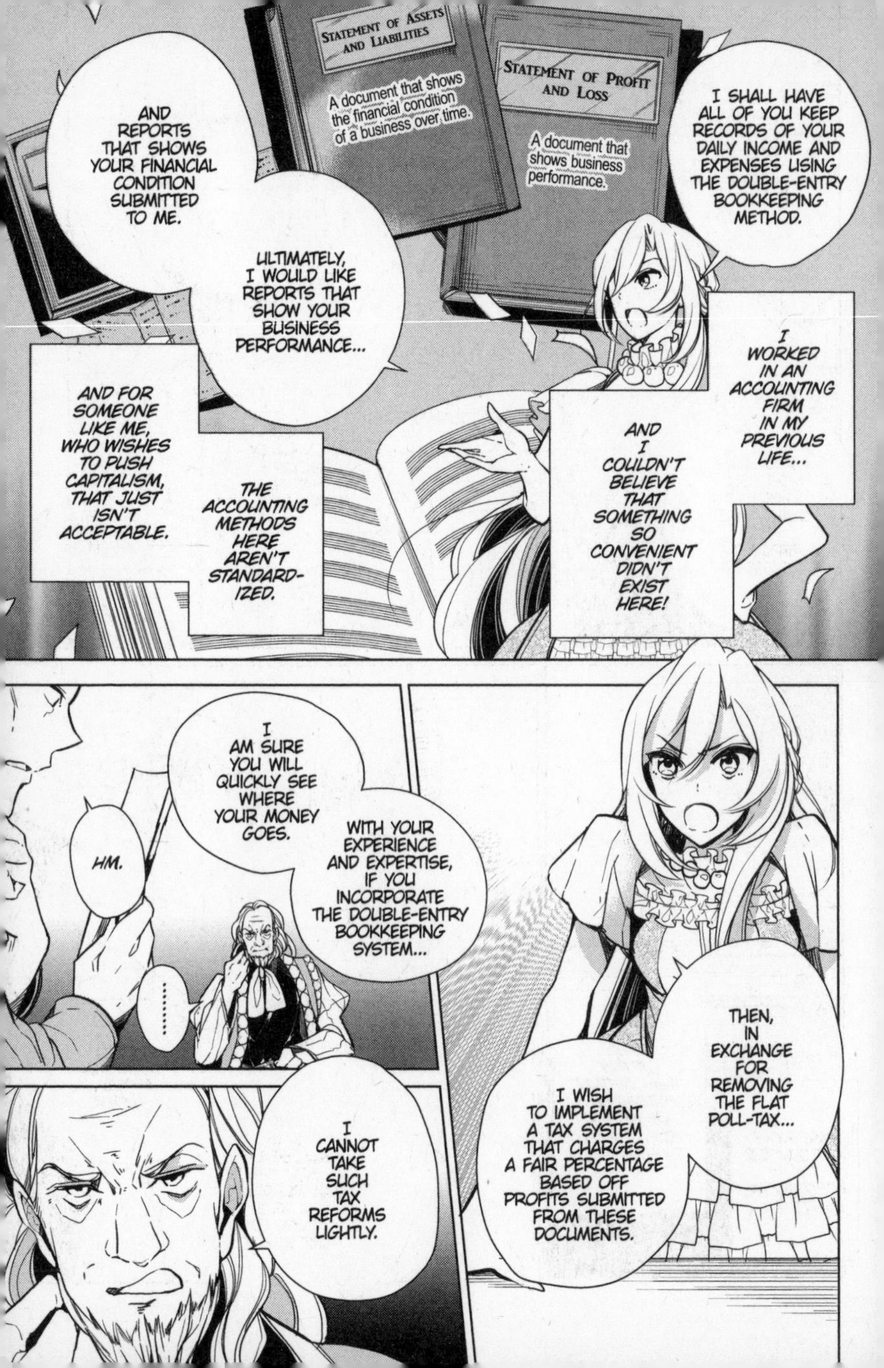
I SHALL HAVE ALL OF YOU KEEP RECORDS OF YOUR DAILY INCOME AND EXPENSES USING THE DOUBLE-ENTRY BOOKKEEPING METHOD.
STATEMENT OF PROFIT AND LOSS
A document that shows business performance.
STATEMENT OF ASSETS AND LIABILITIES
A document that shows the financial condition of a business over time.
ULTIMATELY, I WOULD LIKE REPORTS THAT SHOW YOUR BUSINESS PERFORMANCE...
AND REPORTS THAT SHOWS YOUR FINANCIAL CONDITION SUBMITTED TO ME.
I WORKED IN AN ACCOUNTING FIRM IN MY PREVIOUS LIFE...
AND I COULDN'T BELIEVE THAT SOMETHING SO CONVENIENT DIDN'T EXIST HERE!
THE ACCOUNTING METHODS HERE AREN'T STANDARD-IZED.
AND FOR SOMEONE LIKE ME, WHO WISHES TO PUSH CAPITALISM, THAT JUST ISN'T ACCEPTABLE.
THEN, IN EXCHANGE FOR REMOVING THE FLAT POLL-TAX...
I WISH TO IMPLEMENT A TAX SYSTEM THAT CHARGES A FAIR PERCENTAGE BASED OFF PROFITS SUBMITTED FROM THESE DOCUMENTS.
I AM SURE YOU WILL QUICKLY SEE WHERE YOUR MONEY GOES.
WITH YOUR EXPERIENCE AND EXPERTISE, IF YOU INCORPORATE THE DOUBLE-ENTRY BOOKKEEPING SYSTEM...
HM.
....
I CANNOT TAKE SUCH TAX REFORMS LIGHTLY.

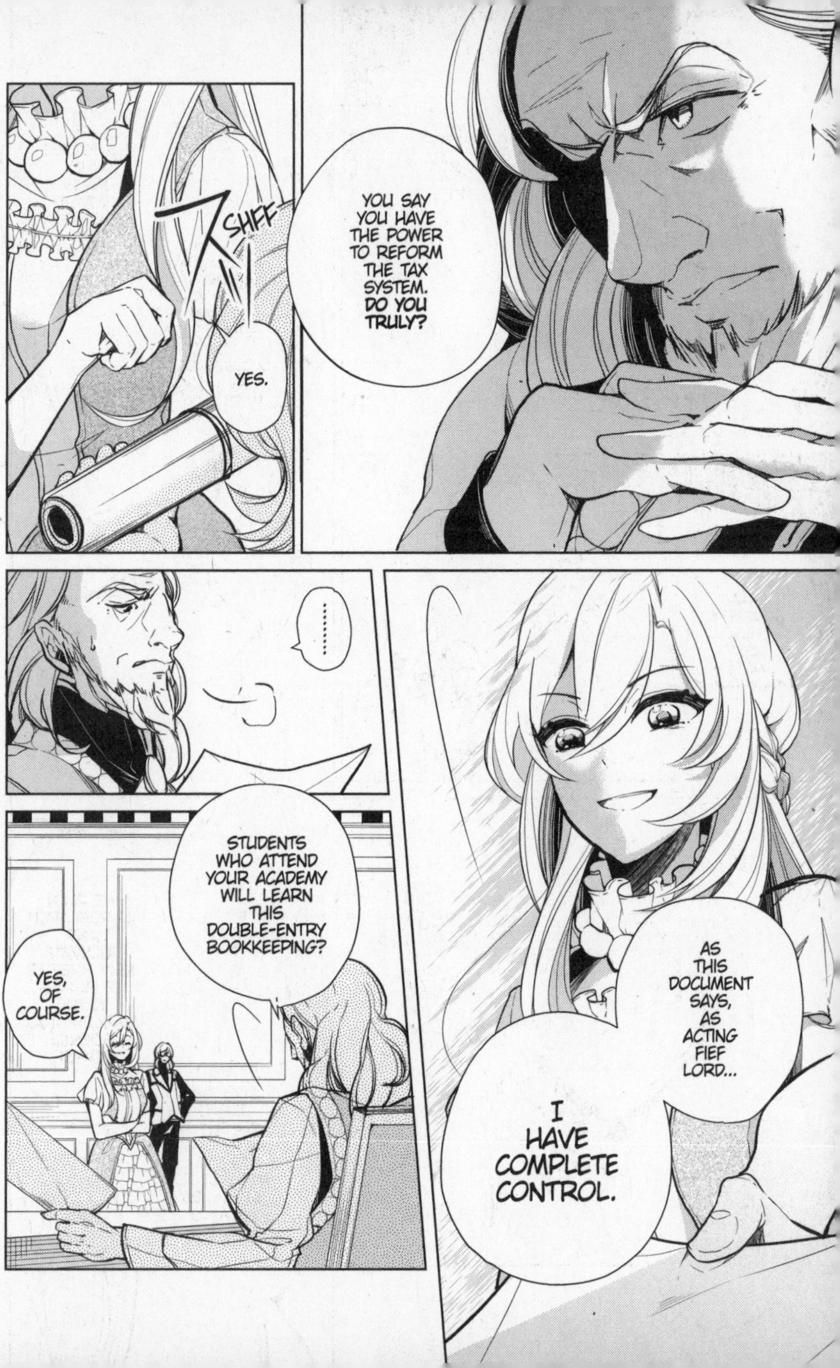
YOU SAY YOU HAVE THE POWER TO REFORM THE TAX SYSTEM. DO YOU TRULY?
SHFF
YES.
AS THIS DOCUMENT SAYS, AS ACTING FIEF LORD...
I HAVE COMPLETE CONTROL.
......
STUDENTS WHO ATTEND YOUR ACADEMY WILL LEARN THIS DOUBLE-ENTRY BOOKKEEPING?
YES, OF COURSE.

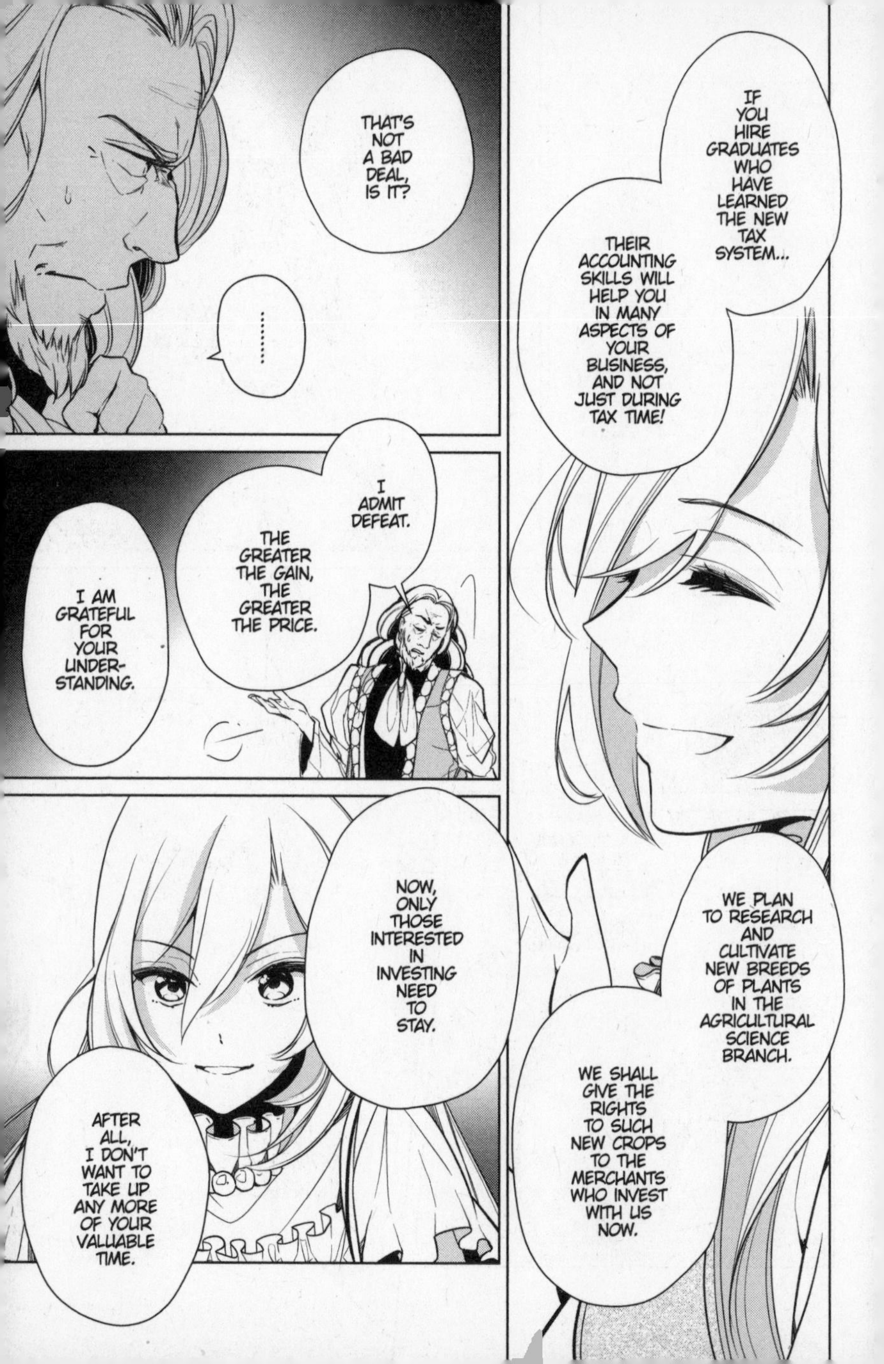
IF YOU HIRE GRADUATES WHO HAVE LEARNED THE NEW TAX SYSTEM...
THEIR ACCOUNTING SKILLS WILL HELP YOU IN MANY ASPECTS OF YOUR BUSINESS, AND NOT JUST DURING TAX TIME!
WE PLAN TO RESEARCH AND CULTIVATE NEW BREEDS OF PLANTS IN THE AGRICULTURAL SCIENCE BRANCH.
WE SHALL GIVE THE RIGHTS TO SUCH NEW CROPS TO THE MERCHANTS WHO INVEST WITH US NOW.
THAT'S NOT A BAD DEAL, IS IT?
......
I ADMIT DEFEAT.
THE GREATER THE GAIN, THE GREATER THE PRICE.
I AM GRATEFUL FOR YOUR UNDER-STANDING.
NOW, ONLY THOSE INTERESTED IN INVESTING NEED TO STAY.
AFTER ALL, I DON'T WANT TO TAKE UP ANY MORE OF YOUR VALUABLE TIME.

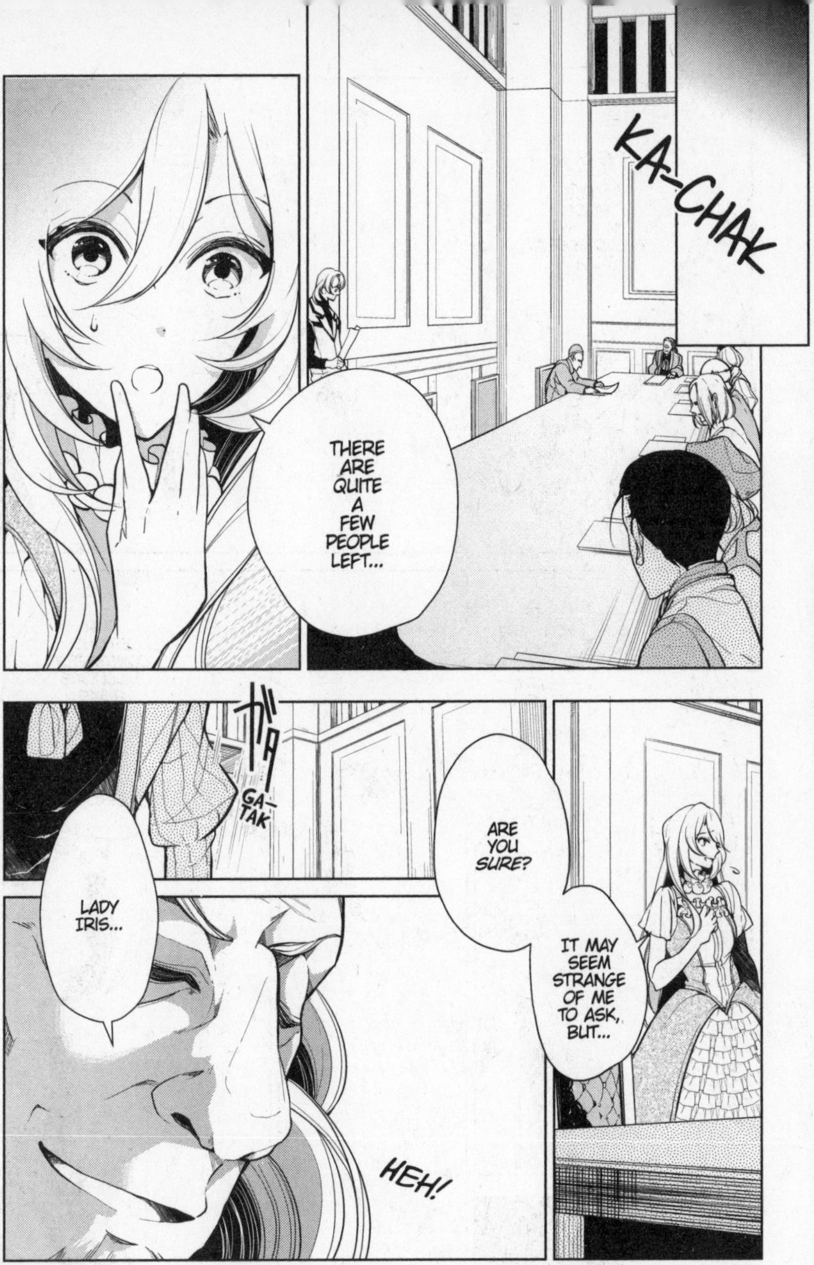
KA-CHAK
THERE ARE QUITE A FEW PEOPLE LEFT...
ARE YOU SURE?
IT MAY SEEM STRANGE OF ME TO ASK, BUT...
GA-TAK
LADY IRIS...
HEH!

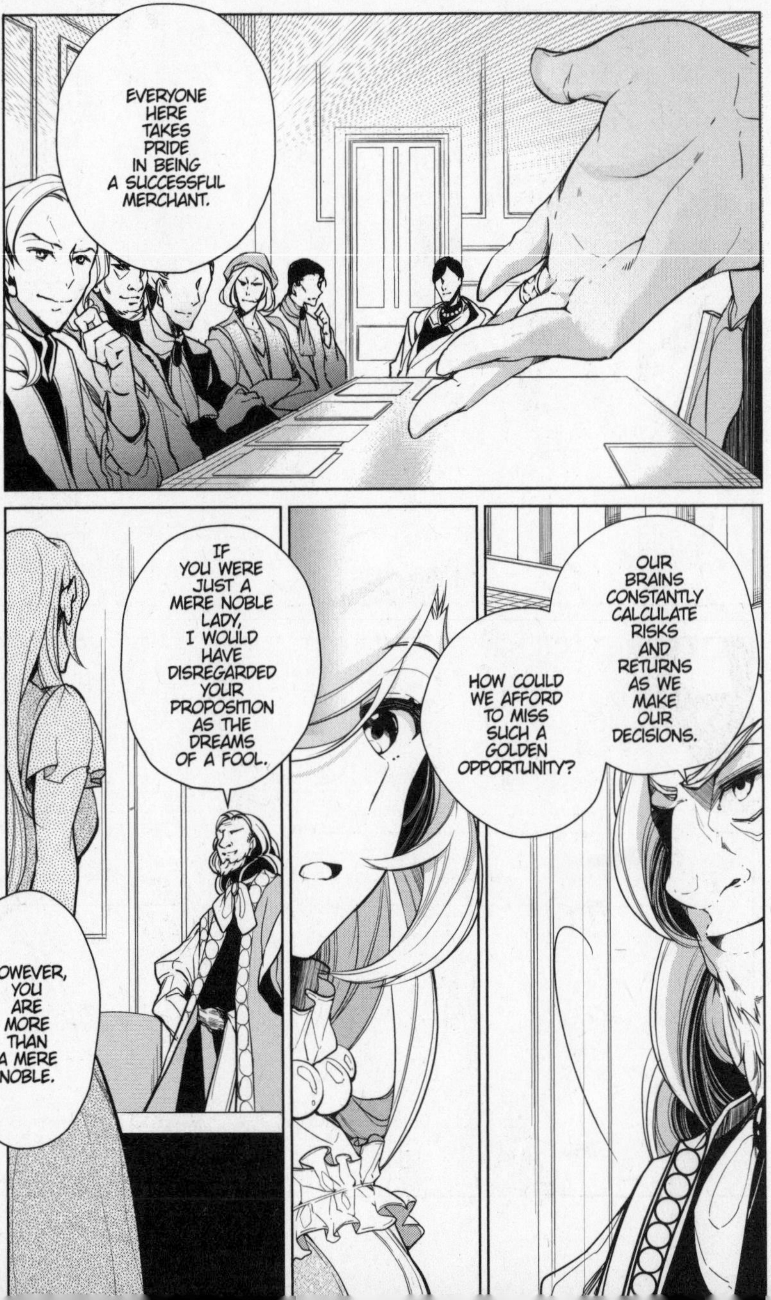
EVERYONE HERE TAKES PRIDE IN BEING A SUCCESSFUL MERCHANT.
OUR BRAINS CONSTANTLY CALCULATE RISKS AND RETURNS AS WE MAKE OUR DECISIONS.
HOW COULD WE AFFORD TO MISS SUCH A GOLDEN OPPORTUNITY?
IF YOU WERE JUST A MERE NOBLE LADY, I WOULD HAVE DISREGARDED YOUR PROPOSITION AS THE DREAMS OF A FOOL.
HOWEVER, YOU ARE MORE THAN A MERE NOBLE.

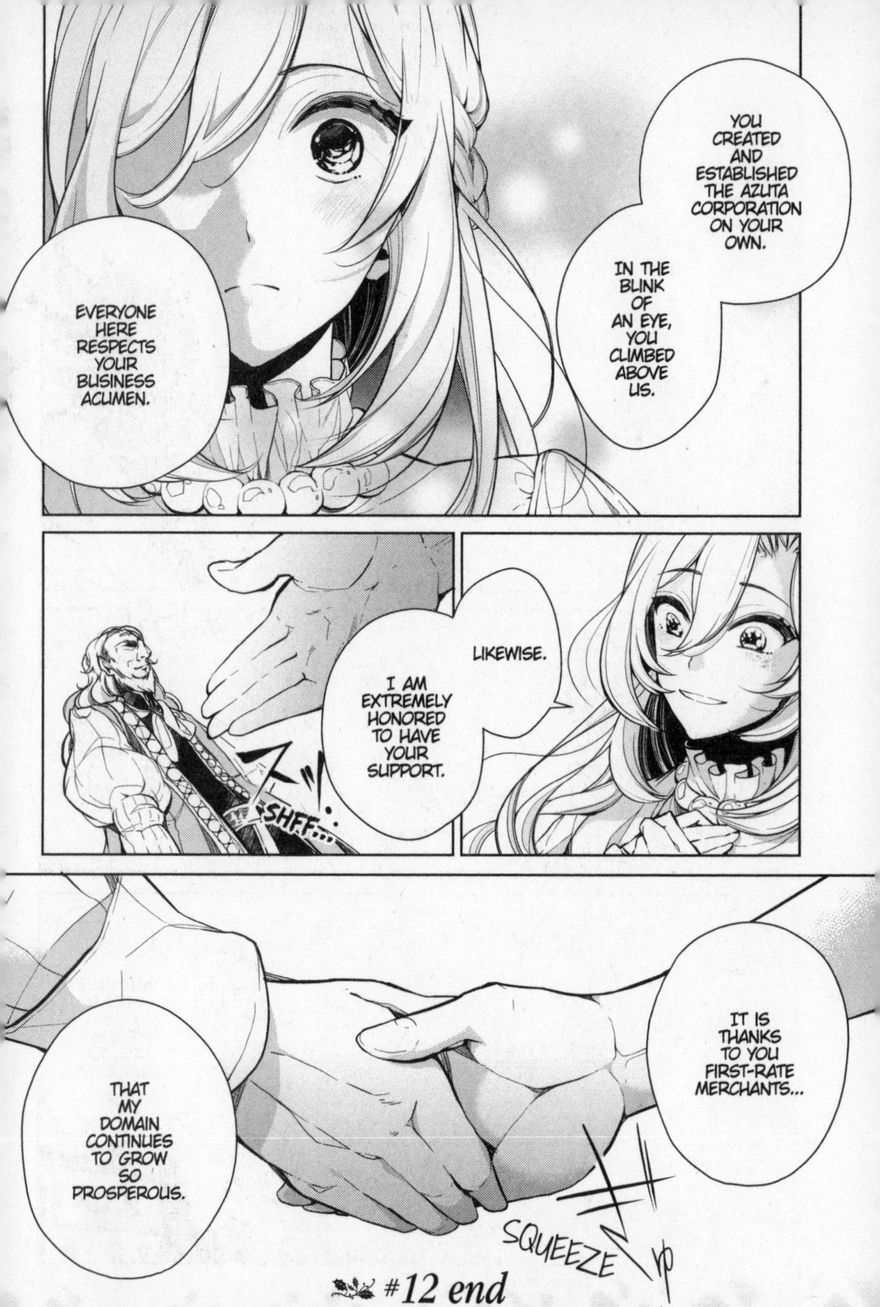
YOU CREATED AND ESTABLISHED THE AZUTA CORPORATION ON YOUR OWN.
IN THE BLINK OF AN EYE, YOU CLIMBED ABOVE US.
EVERYONE HERE RESPECTS YOUR BUSINESS ACUMEN.
LIKEWISE.
I AM EXTREMELY HONORED TO HAVE YOUR SUPPORT.
SHFF...
IT IS THANKS TO YOU FIRST-RATE MERCHANTS...
THAT MY DOMAIN CONTINUES TO GROW SO PROSPEROUS.
SQUEEZE

#12 end

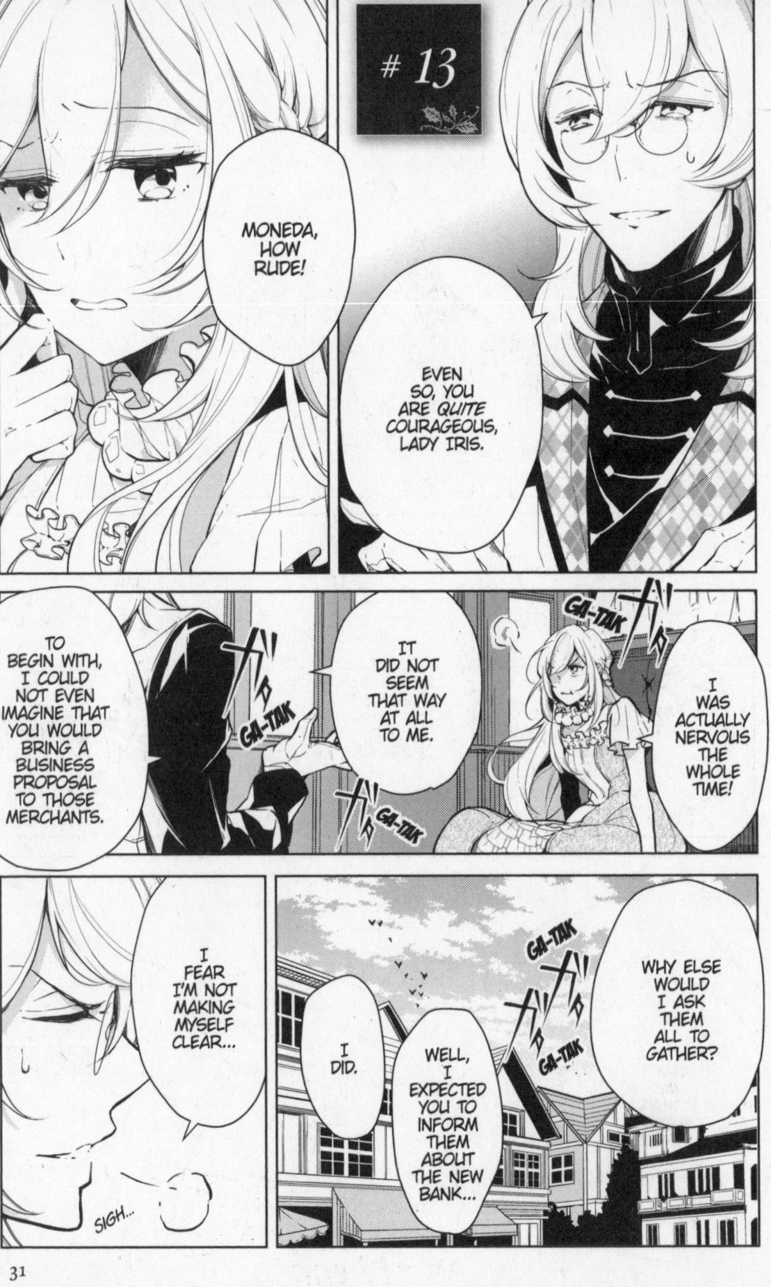

13
EVEN SO, YOU ARE QUITE COURAGEOUS, LADY IRIS.
MONEDA, HOW RUDE!
I WAS ACTUALLY NERVOUS THE WHOLE TIME!
GA-TAK
IT DID NOT SEEM THAT WAY AT ALL TO ME.
GA-TAK
GA-TAK
TO BEGIN WITH, I COULD NOT EVEN IMAGINE THAT YOU WOULD BRING A BUSINESS PROPOSAL TO THOSE MERCHANTS.
WHY ELSE WOULD I ASK THEM ALL TO GATHER?
GA-TAK
GA-TAK
WELL, I EXPECTED YOU TO INFORM THEM ABOUT THE NEW BANK...
I DID.
I FEAR I'M NOT MAKING MYSELF CLEAR...
SIGH...

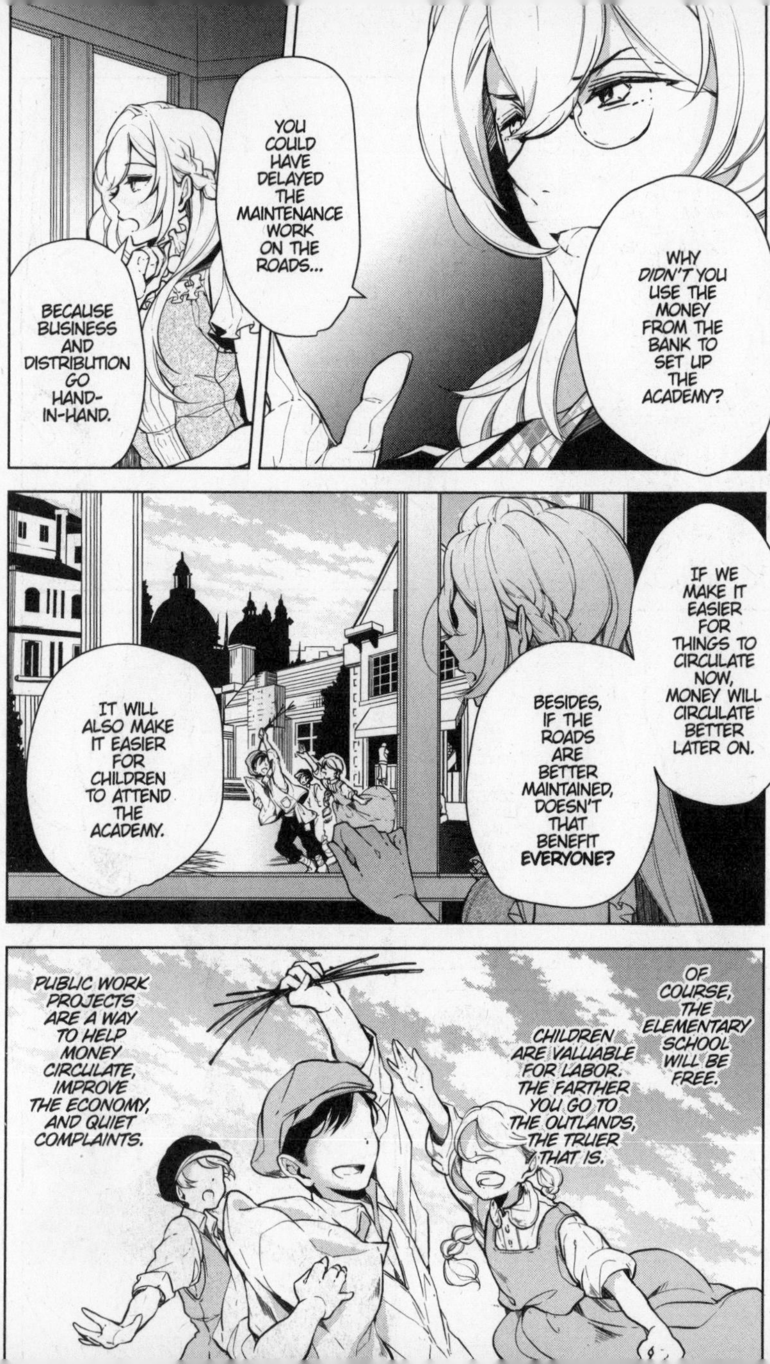
WHY DIDN'T YOU USE THE MONEY FROM THE BANK TO SET UP THE ACADEMY?
YOU COULD HAVE DELAYED THE MAINTENANCE WORK ON THE ROADS...
BECAUSE BUSINESS AND DISTRIBUTION GO HAND-IN-HAND.
IF WE MAKE IT EASIER FOR THINGS TO CIRCULATE NOW, MONEY WILL CIRCULATE BETTER LATER ON.
BESIDES, IF THE ROADS ARE BETTER MAINTAINED, DOESN'T THAT BENEFIT EVERYONE?
IT WILL ALSO MAKE IT EASIER FOR CHILDREN TO ATTEND THE ACADEMY.
OF COURSE, THE ELEMENTARY SCHOOL WILL BE FREE.
CHILDREN ARE VALUABLE FOR LABOR. THE FARTHER YOU GO TO THE OUTLANDS, THE TRUER THAT IS.
PUBLIC WORK PROJECTS ARE A WAY TO HELP MONEY CIRCULATE, IMPROVE THE ECONOMY, AND QUIET COMPLAINTS.

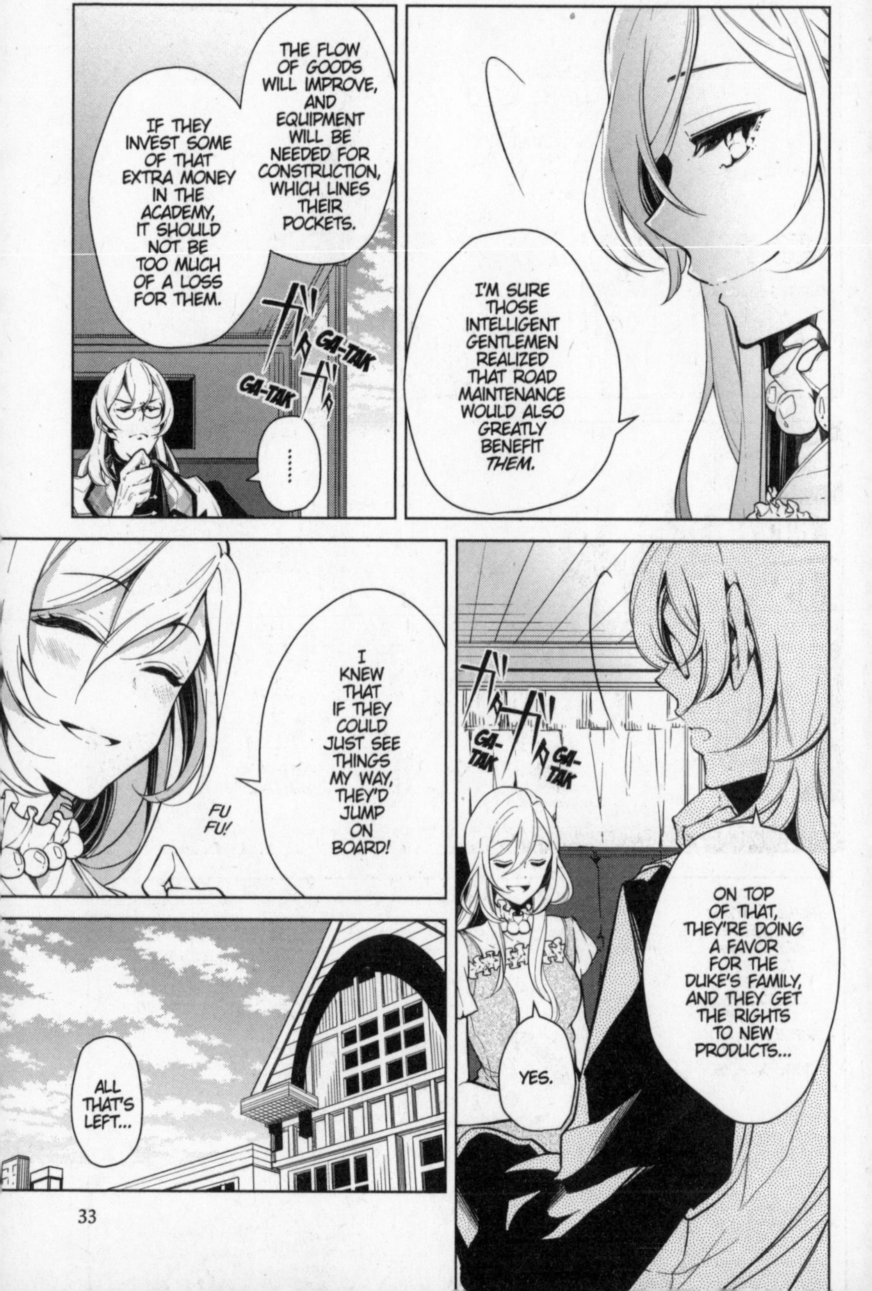
I'M SURE THOSE INTELLIGENT GENTLEMEN REALIZED THAT ROAD MAINTENANCE WOULD ALSO GREATLY BENEFIT *THEM*.
THE FLOW OF GOODS WILL IMPROVE, AND EQUIPMENT WILL BE NEEDED FOR CONSTRUCTION, WHICH LINES THEIR POCKETS.
IF THEY INVEST SOME OF THAT EXTRA MONEY IN THE ACADEMY, IT SHOULD NOT BE TOO MUCH OF A LOSS FOR THEM.
GA-TAK
GA-TAK
......
GA-TAK
GA-TAK
ON TOP OF THAT, THEY'RE DOING A FAVOR FOR THE DUKE'S FAMILY, AND THEY GET THE RIGHTS TO NEW PRODUCTS...
YES.
I KNEW THAT IF THEY COULD JUST SEE THINGS MY WAY, THEY'D JUMP ON BOARD!
FU FU!
ALL THAT'S LEFT...

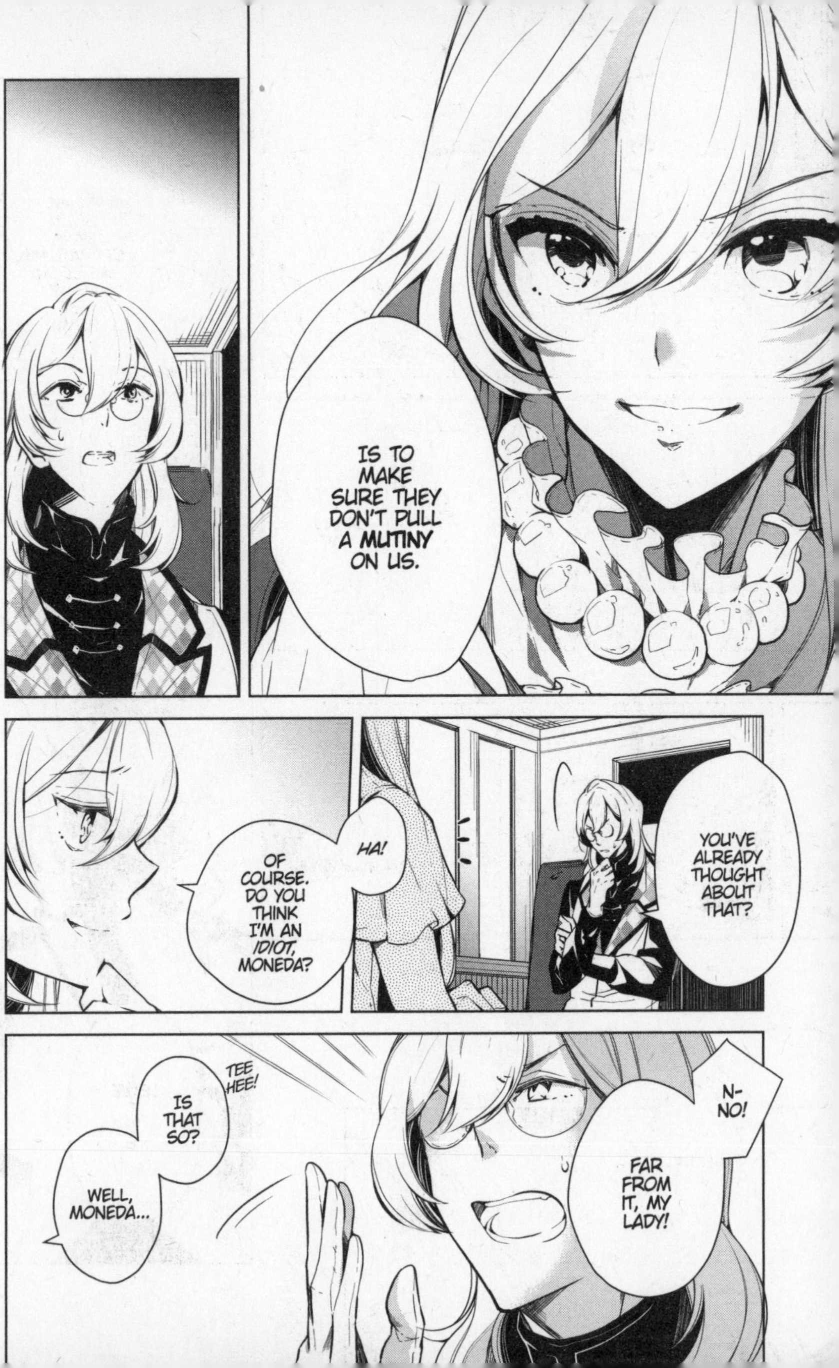
IS TO MAKE SURE THEY DON'T PULL A MUTINY ON US.
YOU'VE ALREADY THOUGHT ABOUT THAT?
HA!
OF COURSE. DO YOU THINK I'M AN *IDIOT,* MONEDA?
N-NO!
FAR FROM IT, MY LADY!
TEE HEE!
IS THAT SO?
WELL, MONEDA...

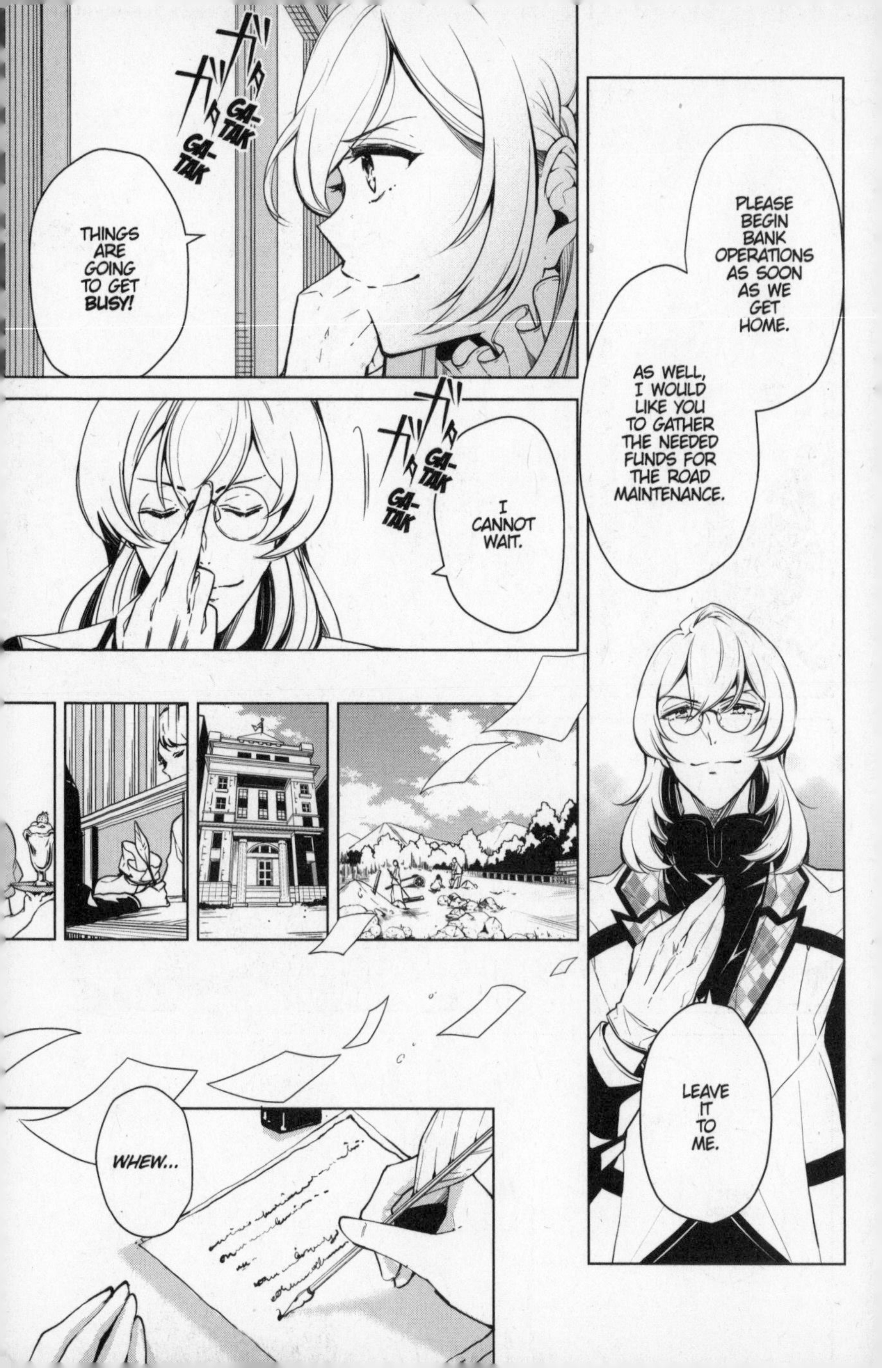
PLEASE BEGIN BANK OPERATIONS AS SOON AS WE GET HOME.
AS WELL, I WOULD LIKE YOU TO GATHER THE NEEDED FUNDS FOR THE ROAD MAINTENANCE.
LEAVE IT TO ME.
GA-TAK GA-TAK
THINGS ARE GOING TO GET BUSY!
GA-TAK GA-TAK
I CANNOT WAIT.
WHEW...

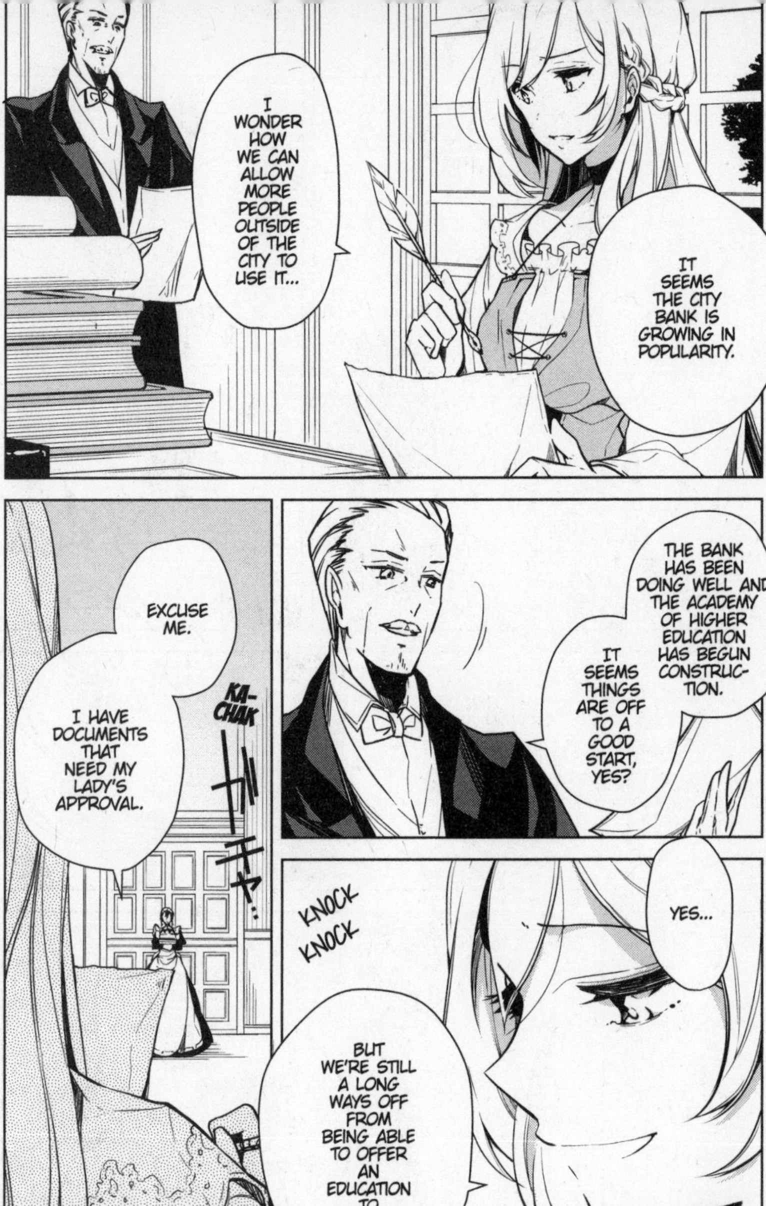
IT SEEMS THE CITY BANK IS GROWING IN POPULARITY.
I WONDER HOW WE CAN ALLOW MORE PEOPLE OUTSIDE OF THE CITY TO USE IT...
THE BANK HAS BEEN DOING WELL AND THE ACADEMY OF HIGHER EDUCATION HAS BEGUN CONSTRUC-TION.
IT SEEMS THINGS ARE OFF TO A GOOD START, YES?
YES...
KNOCK KNOCK
BUT WE'RE STILL A LONG WAYS OFF FROM BEING ABLE TO OFFER AN EDUCATION TO EVERYONE.
KA-CHAK
EXCUSE ME.
I HAVE DOCUMENTS THAT NEED MY LADY'S APPROVAL.

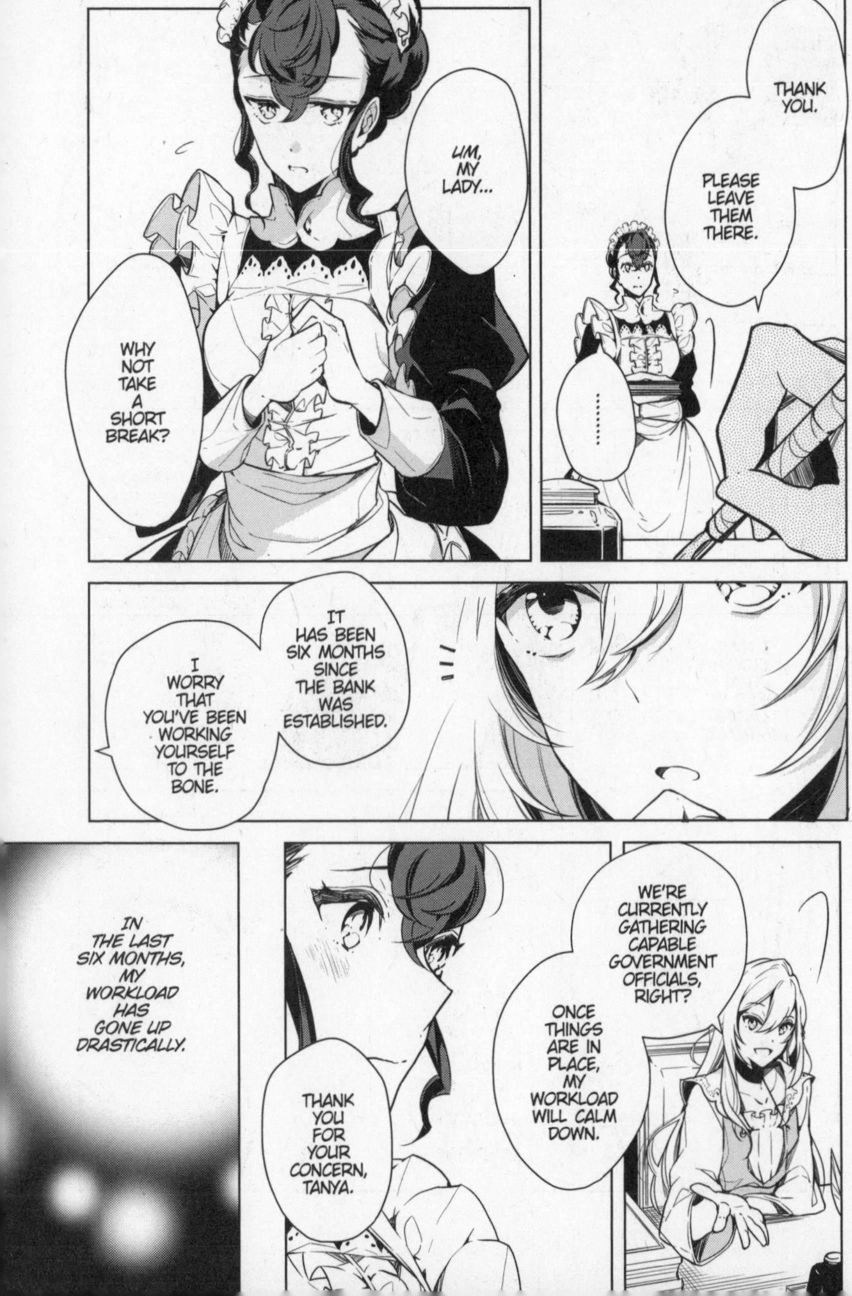
THANK YOU.
PLEASE LEAVE THEM THERE.
......
UM, MY LADY...
WHY NOT TAKE A SHORT BREAK?
IT HAS BEEN SIX MONTHS SINCE THE BANK WAS ESTABLISHED.
I WORRY THAT YOU'VE BEEN WORKING YOURSELF TO THE BONE.
WE'RE CURRENTLY GATHERING CAPABLE GOVERNMENT OFFICIALS, RIGHT?
ONCE THINGS ARE IN PLACE, MY WORKLOAD WILL CALM DOWN.
THANK YOU FOR YOUR CONCERN, TANYA.
IN THE LAST SIX MONTHS, MY WORKLOAD HAS GONE UP DRASTICALLY.

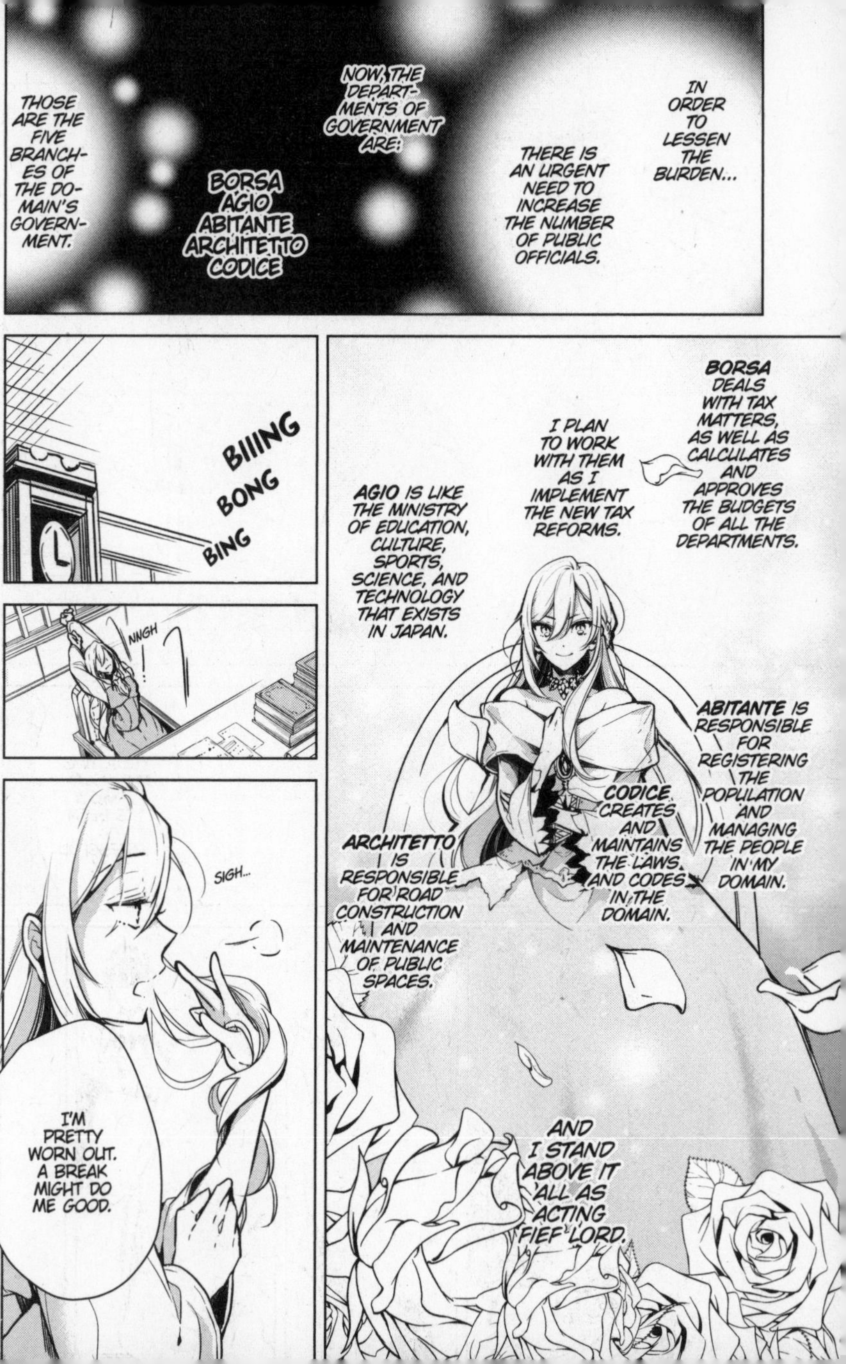
IN ORDER TO LESSEN THE BURDEN...
THERE IS AN URGENT NEED TO INCREASE THE NUMBER OF PUBLIC OFFICIALS.
NOW, THE DEPARTMENTS OF GOVERNMENT ARE:
BORSA
AGIO
ABITANTE
ARCHITETTO
CODICE
THOSE ARE THE FIVE BRANCHES OF THE DOMAIN'S GOVERNMENT.
BORSA DEALS WITH TAX MATTERS, AS WELL AS CALCULATES AND APPROVES THE BUDGETS OF ALL THE DEPARTMENTS.
I PLAN TO WORK WITH THEM AS I IMPLEMENT THE NEW TAX REFORMS.
AGIO IS LIKE THE MINISTRY OF EDUCATION, CULTURE, SPORTS, SCIENCE, AND TECHNOLOGY THAT EXISTS IN JAPAN.
ABITANTE IS RESPONSIBLE FOR REGISTERING THE POPULATION AND MANAGING THE PEOPLE IN MY DOMAIN.
CODICE CREATES AND MAINTAINS THE LAWS AND CODES IN THE DOMAIN.
ARCHITETTO IS RESPONSIBLE FOR ROAD CONSTRUCTION AND MAINTENANCE OF PUBLIC SPACES.
AND I STAND ABOVE IT ALL AS ACTING FIEF LORD.
BIIING
BONG
BING
NNGH
!
SIGH...
I'M PRETTY WORN OUT. A BREAK MIGHT DO ME GOOD.

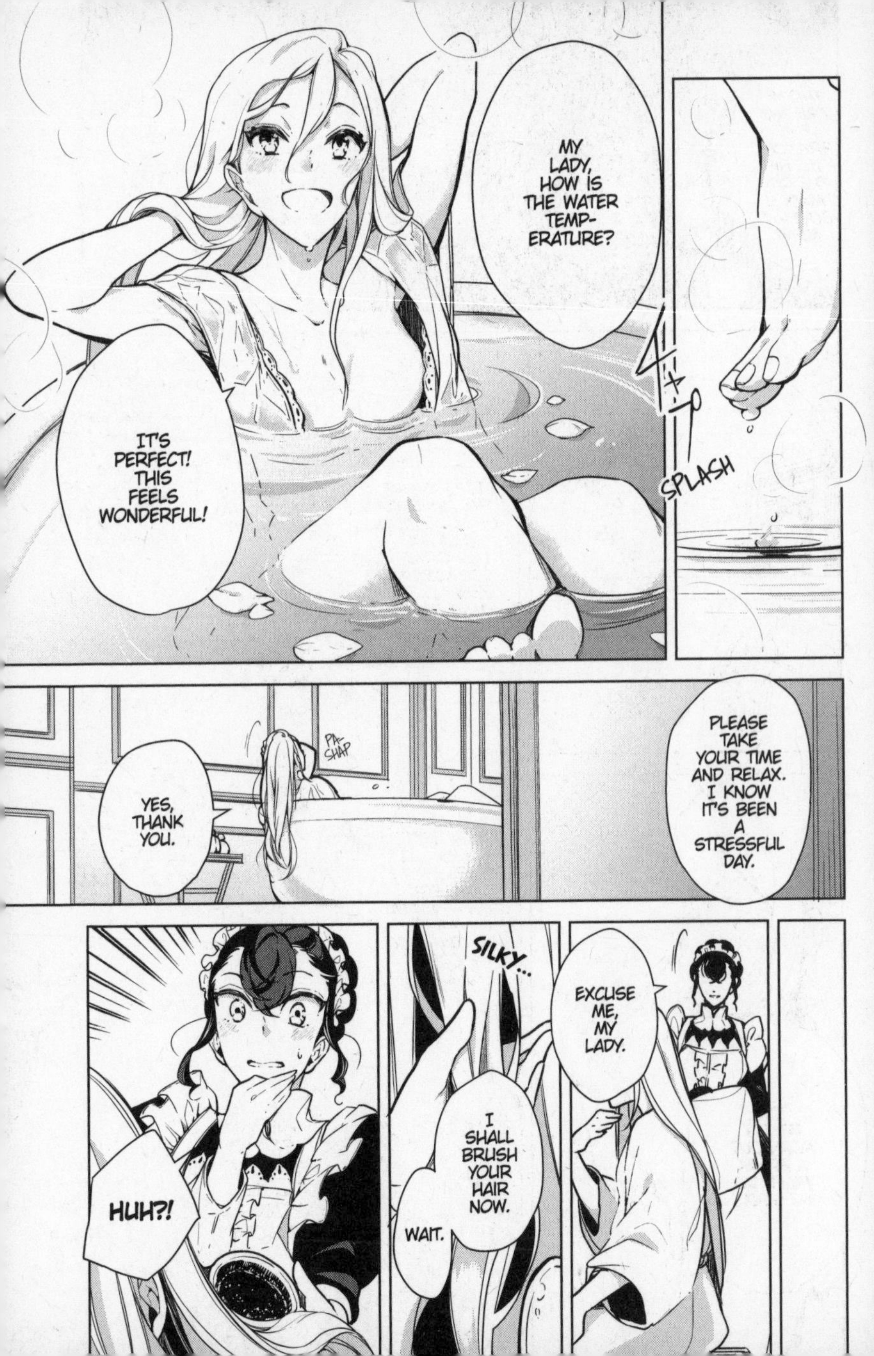
SPLASH
MY LADY, HOW IS THE WATER TEMP-ERATURE?
IT'S PERFECT! THIS FEELS WONDERFUL!
PLEASE TAKE YOUR TIME AND RELAX. I KNOW IT'S BEEN A STRESSFUL DAY.
PA-SHAP
YES, THANK YOU.
EXCUSE ME, MY LADY.
I SHALL BRUSH YOUR HAIR NOW.
SILKY...
WAIT.
HUH?!

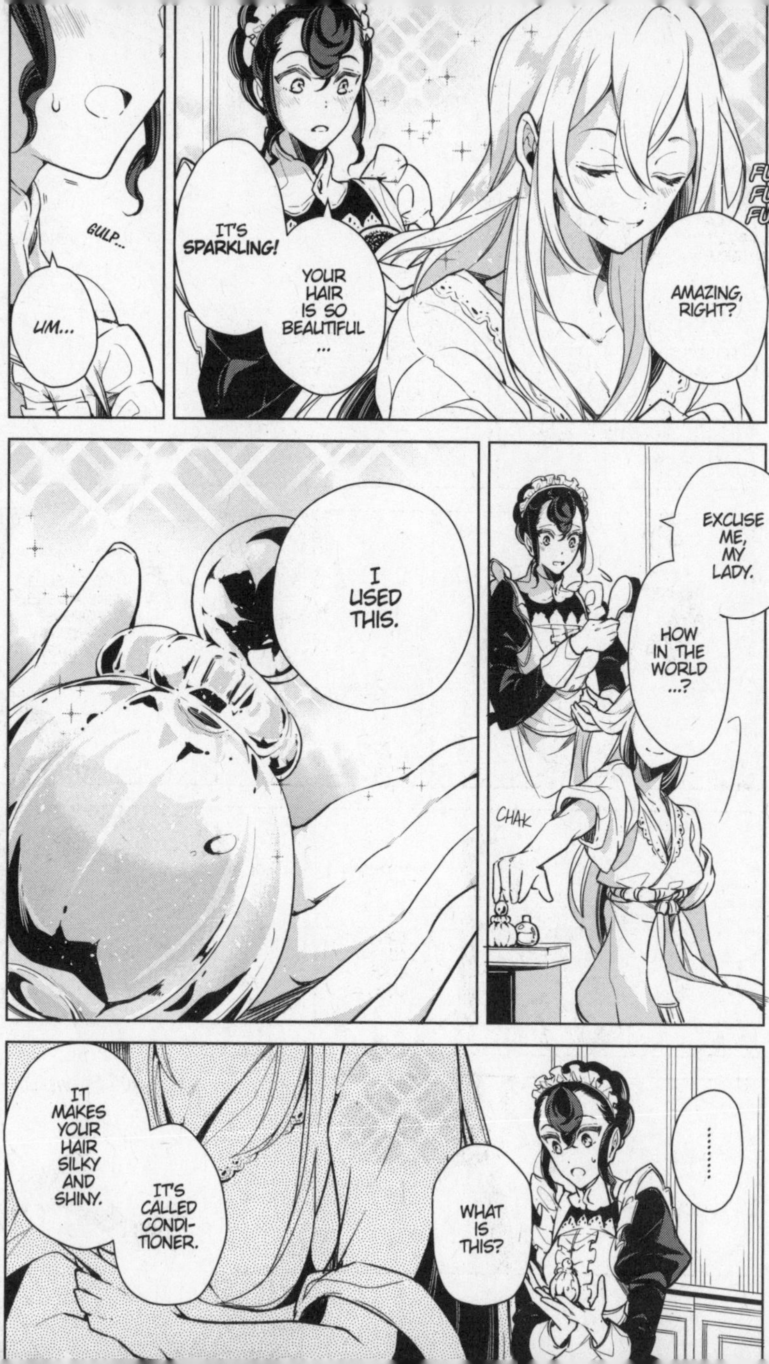
AMAZING, RIGHT?
FU FU FU!
IT'S SPARKLING!
YOUR HAIR IS SO BEAUTIFUL ...
GULP...
UM...
EXCUSE ME, MY LADY.
HOW IN THE WORLD ...?
CHAK
I USED THIS.
......
WHAT IS THIS?
IT'S CALLED CONDI-TIONER.
IT MAKES YOUR HAIR SILKY AND SHINY.

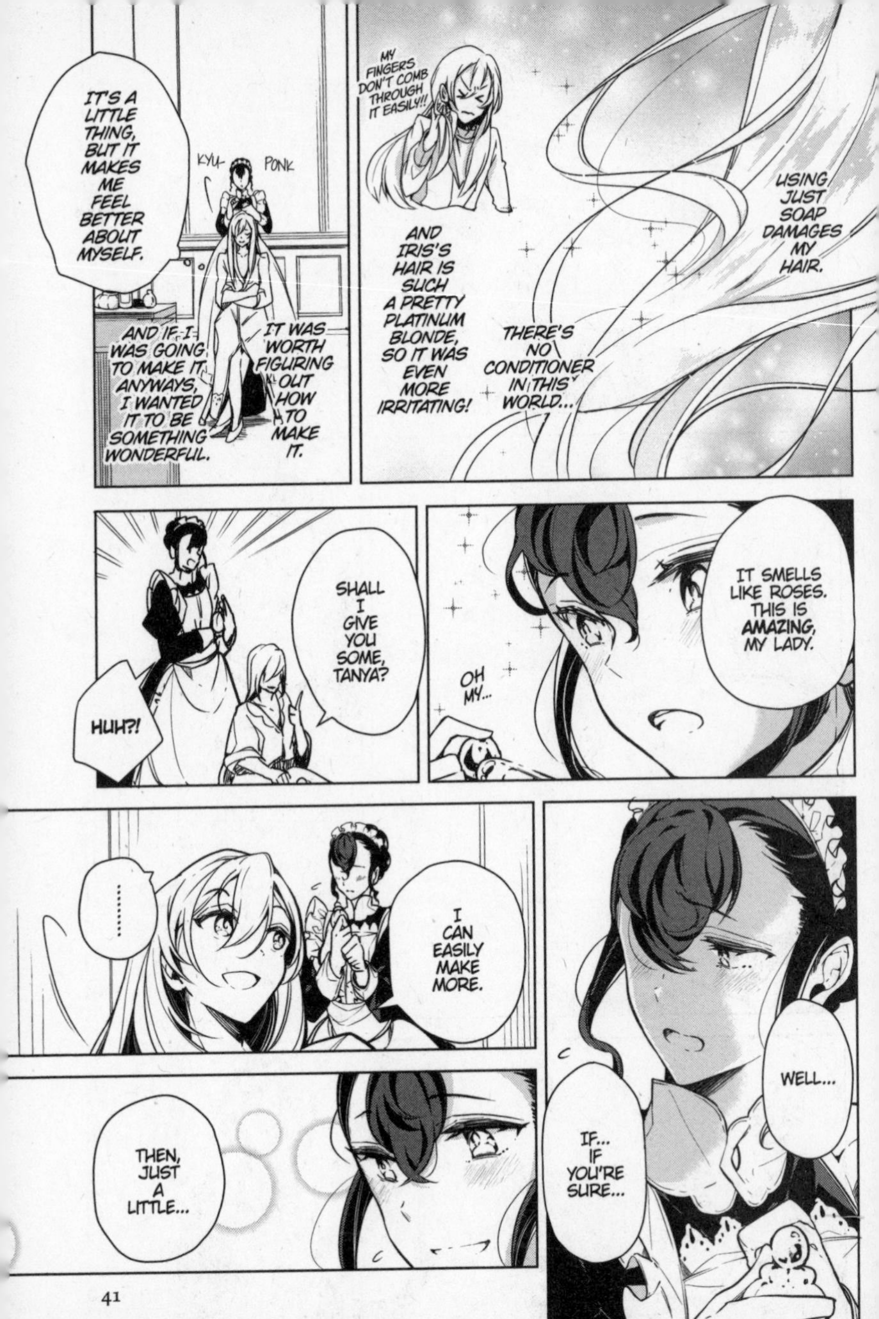
USING JUST SOAP DAMAGES MY HAIR.
THERE'S NO CONDITIONER IN THIS WORLD...
AND IRIS'S HAIR IS SUCH A PRETTY PLATINUM BLONDE, SO IT WAS EVEN MORE IRRITATING!
MY FINGERS DON'T COMB THROUGH IT EASILY!!
IT'S A LITTLE THING, BUT IT MAKES ME FEEL BETTER ABOUT MYSELF.
KYU-
PONK
IT WAS WORTH FIGURING OUT HOW TO MAKE IT.
AND IF I WAS GOING TO MAKE IT ANYWAYS, I WANTED IT TO BE SOMETHING WONDERFUL.
IT SMELLS LIKE ROSES. THIS IS AMAZING, MY LADY.
OH MY...
SHALL I GIVE YOU SOME, TANYA?
HUH?!
WELL...
IF... IF YOU'RE SURE...
I CAN EASILY MAKE MORE.
....
THEN, JUST A LITTLE...

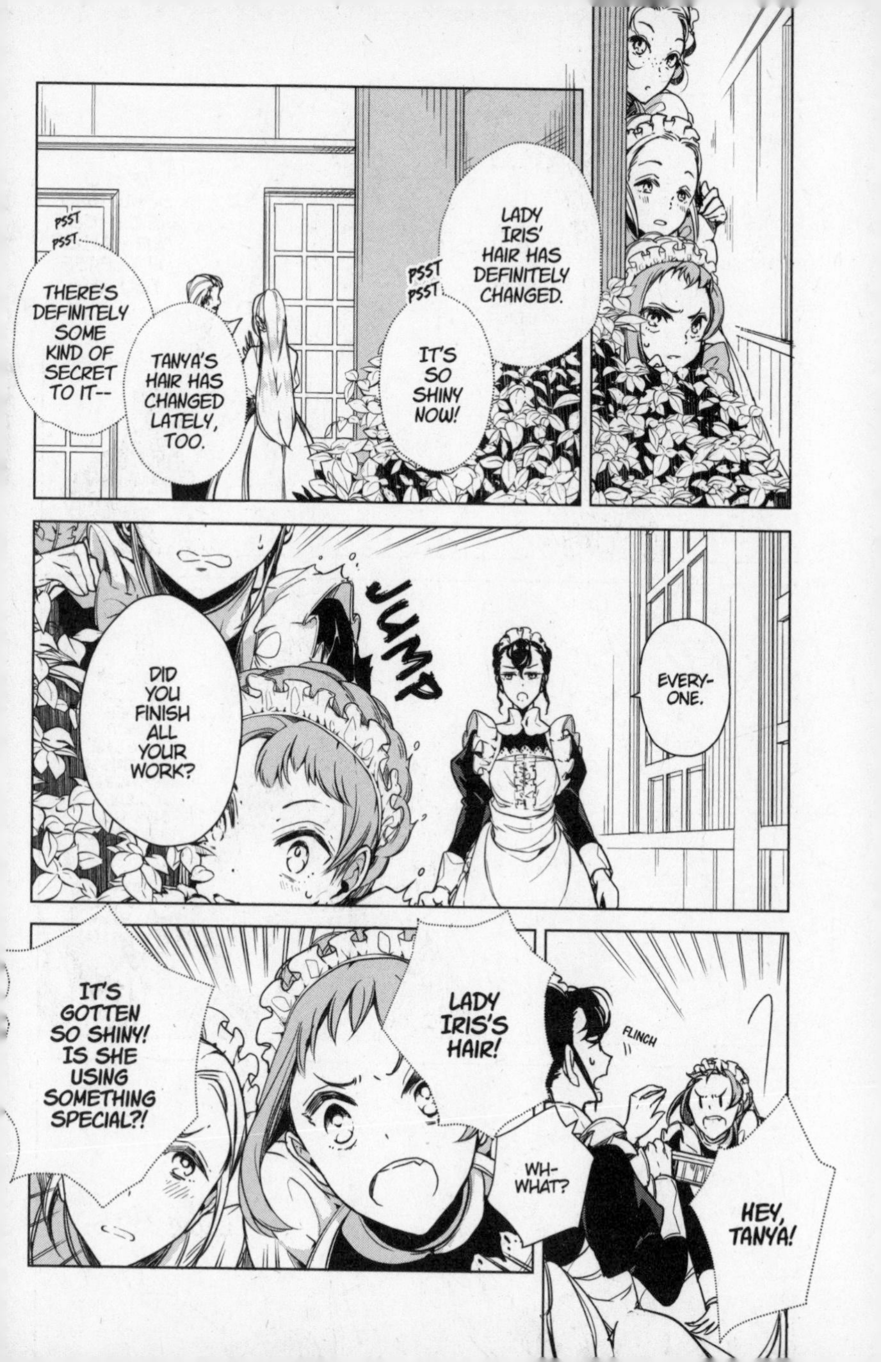
LADY IRIS' HAIR HAS DEFINITELY CHANGED.
PSST PSST
IT'S SO SHINY NOW!
TANYA'S HAIR HAS CHANGED LATELY, TOO.
PSST PSST
THERE'S DEFINITELY SOME KIND OF SECRET TO IT--
EVERY-ONE.
JUMP
DID YOU FINISH ALL YOUR WORK?
HEY, TANYA!
FLINCH
WH-WHAT?
LADY IRIS'S HAIR!
IT'S GOTTEN SO SHINY! IS SHE USING SOMETHING SPECIAL?!

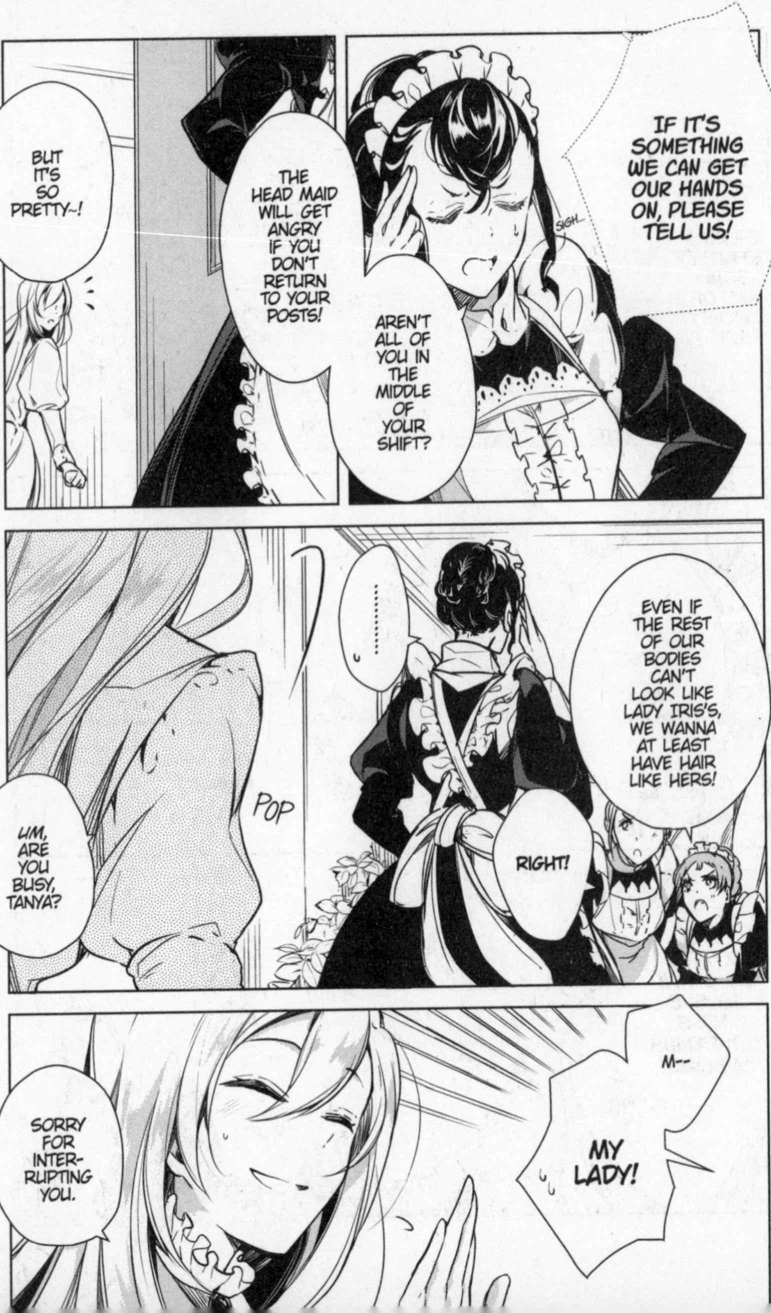
IF IT'S SOMETHING WE CAN GET OUR HANDS ON, PLEASE TELL US!
SIGH...
AREN'T ALL OF YOU IN THE MIDDLE OF YOUR SHIFT?
THE HEAD MAID WILL GET ANGRY IF YOU DON'T RETURN TO YOUR POSTS!
BUT IT'S SO PRETTY~!
EVEN IF THE REST OF OUR BODIES CAN'T LOOK LIKE LADY IRIS'S, WE WANNA AT LEAST HAVE HAIR LIKE HERS!
RIGHT!
......
POP
UM, ARE YOU BUSY, TANYA?
M--
MY LADY!
SORRY FOR INTER-RUPTING YOU.

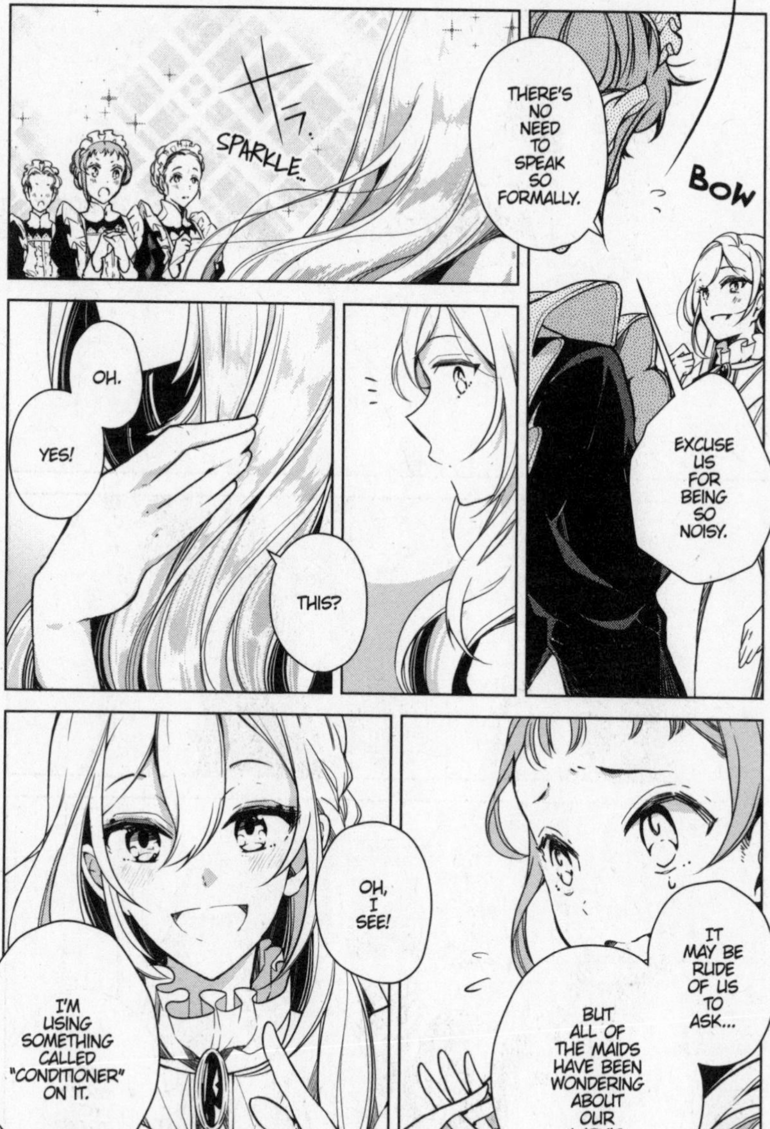
THERE'S NO NEED TO SPEAK SO FORMALLY.
BOW
EXCUSE US FOR BEING SO NOISY.
SPARKLE...
OH.
YES!
THIS?
IT MAY BE RUDE OF US TO ASK...
BUT ALL OF THE MAIDS HAVE BEEN WONDERING ABOUT OUR LADY'S HAIR...
OH, I SEE!
I'M USING SOMETHING CALLED "CONDITIONER" ON IT.

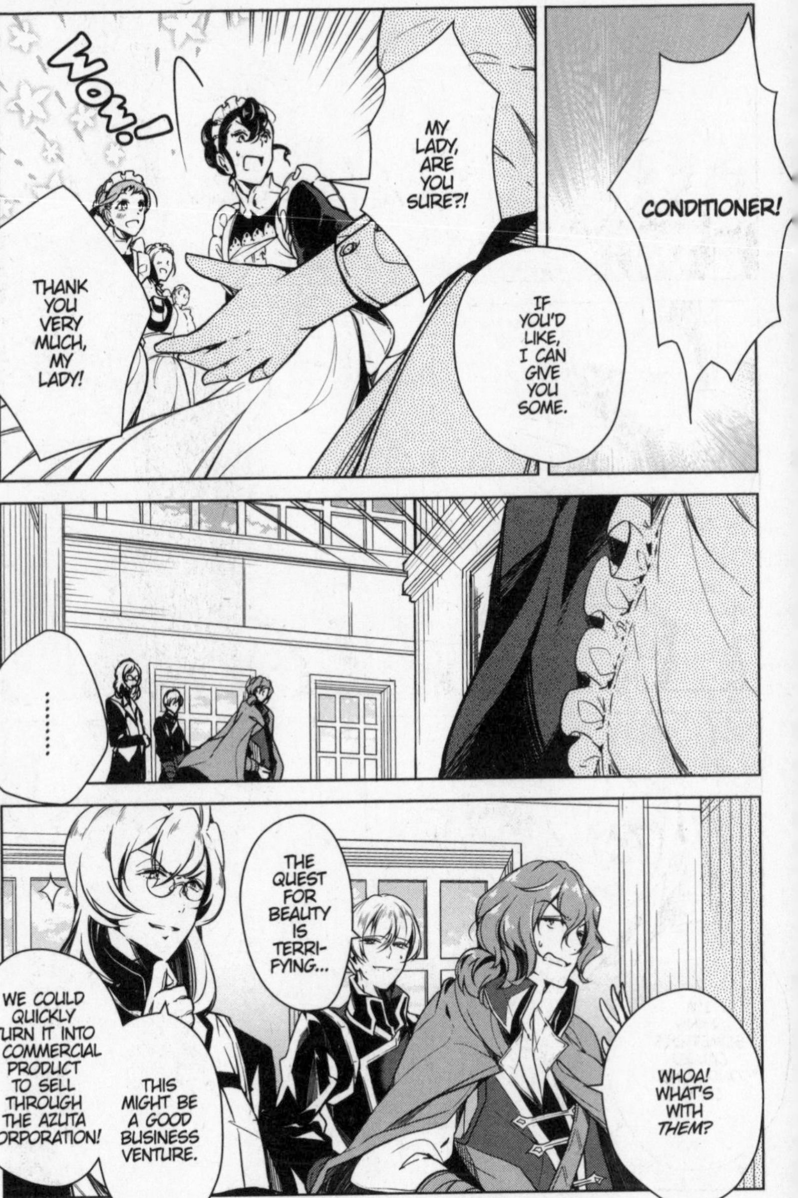
CONDITIONER!
IF YOU'D LIKE, I CAN GIVE YOU SOME.
MY LADY, ARE YOU SURE?!
WOW!
THANK YOU VERY MUCH, MY LADY!
......
WHOA! WHAT'S WITH THEM?
THE QUEST FOR BEAUTY IS TERRI-FYING...
THIS MIGHT BE A GOOD BUSINESS VENTURE.
WE COULD QUICKLY TURN IT INTO A COMMERCIAL PRODUCT TO SELL THROUGH THE AZUTA CORPORATION!

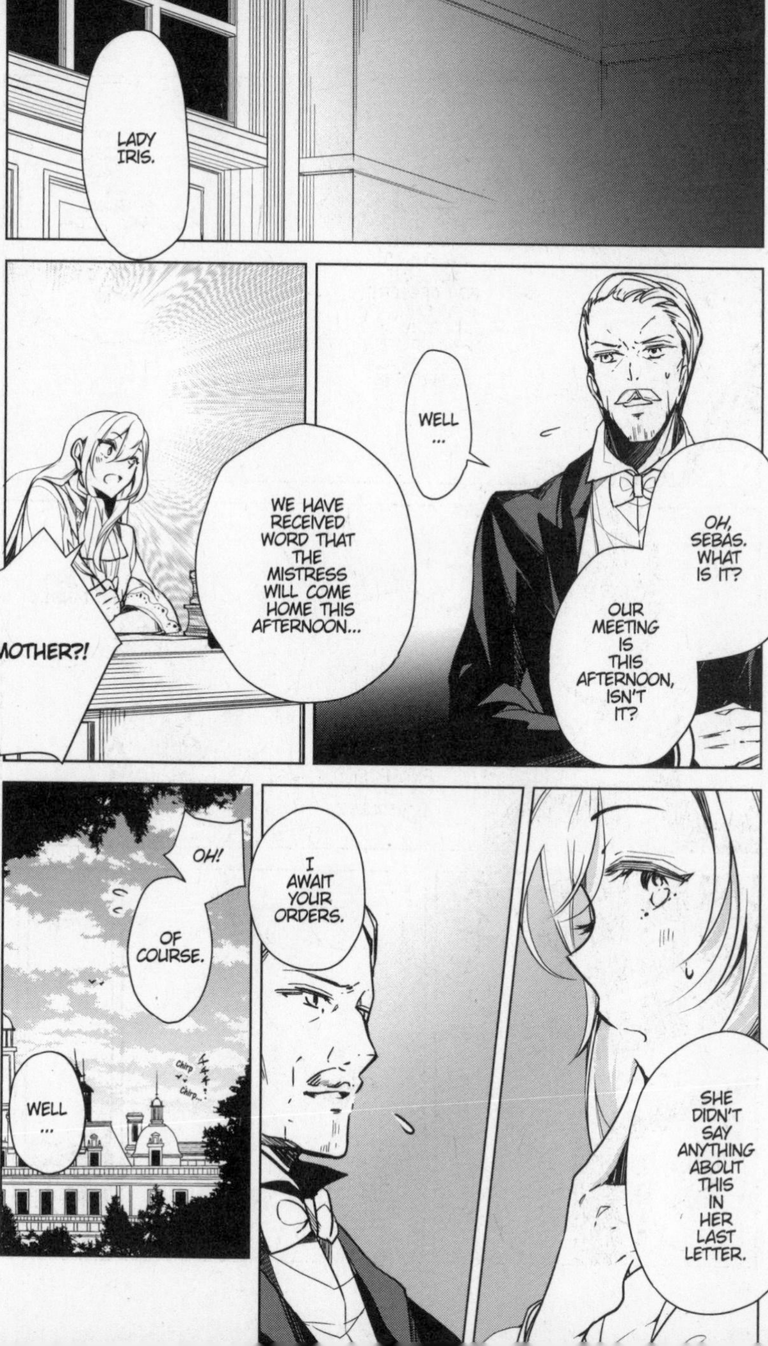
LADY IRIS.
OH, SEBAS. WHAT IS IT?
OUR MEETING IS THIS AFTERNOON, ISN'T IT?
WELL ...
WE HAVE RECEIVED WORD THAT THE MISTRESS WILL COME HOME THIS AFTERNOON...
MOTHER?!
SHE DIDN'T SAY ANYTHING ABOUT THIS IN HER LAST LETTER.
I AWAIT YOUR ORDERS.
OH!
OF COURSE.
Chirp Chirp...
WELL ...

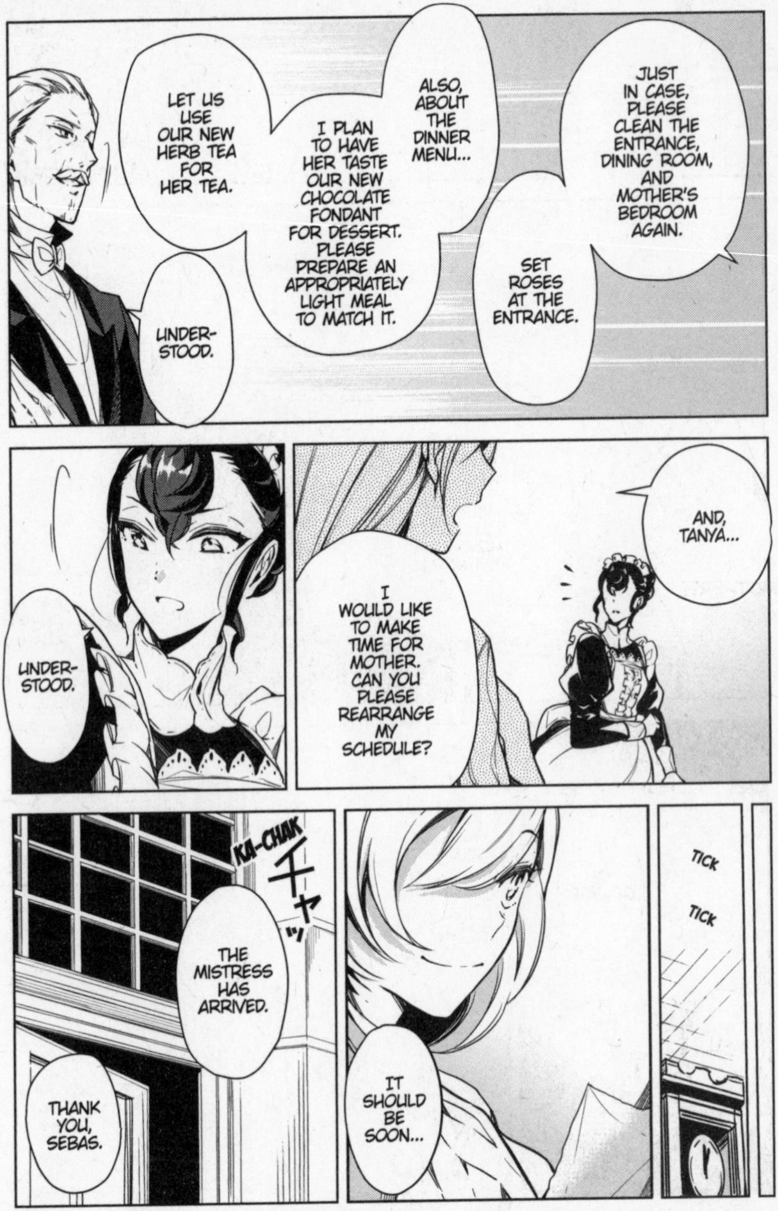
JUST IN CASE, PLEASE CLEAN THE ENTRANCE, DINING ROOM, AND MOTHER'S BEDROOM AGAIN.
SET ROSES AT THE ENTRANCE.
ALSO, ABOUT THE DINNER MENU...
I PLAN TO HAVE HER TASTE OUR NEW CHOCOLATE FONDANT FOR DESSERT. PLEASE PREPARE AN APPROPRIATELY LIGHT MEAL TO MATCH IT.
LET US USE OUR NEW HERB TEA FOR HER TEA.
UNDER-STOOD.
AND, TANYA...
I WOULD LIKE TO MAKE TIME FOR MOTHER. CAN YOU PLEASE REARRANGE MY SCHEDULE?
UNDER-STOOD.
TICK
TICK
IT SHOULD BE SOON...
KA-CHAK
チャッ
THE MISTRESS HAS ARRIVED.
THANK YOU, SEBAS.

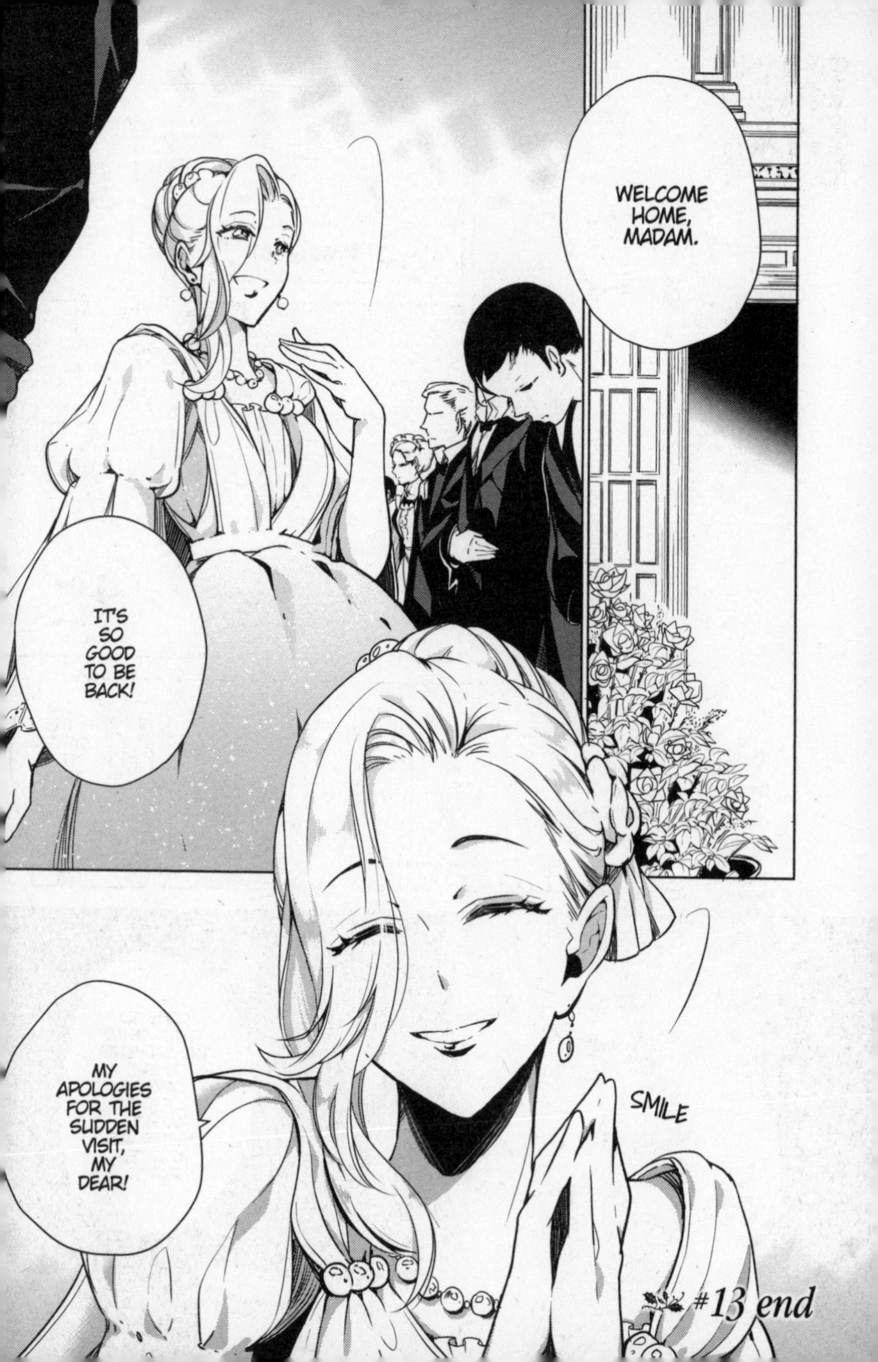
WELCOME HOME, MADAM.
IT'S SO GOOD TO BE BACK!
SMILE
MY APOLOGIES FOR THE SUDDEN VISIT, MY DEAR!
#13 end

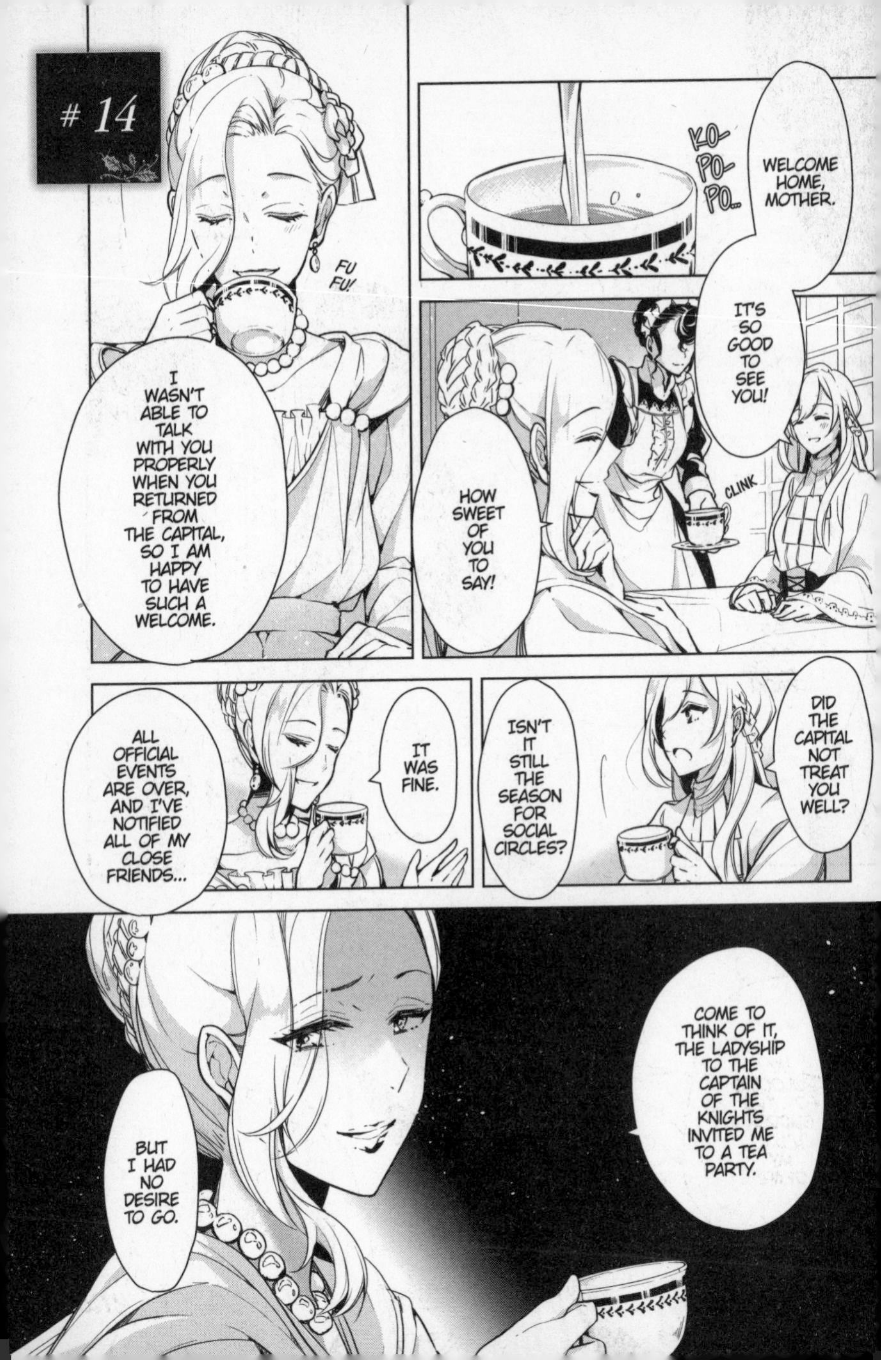
WELCOME HOME, MOTHER.
KO-PO-PO...
IT'S SO GOOD TO SEE YOU!
CLINK
HOW SWEET OF YOU TO SAY!
14
FU FU!
I WASN'T ABLE TO TALK WITH YOU PROPERLY WHEN YOU RETURNED FROM THE CAPITAL, SO I AM HAPPY TO HAVE SUCH A WELCOME.
DID THE CAPITAL NOT TREAT YOU WELL?
ISN'T IT STILL THE SEASON FOR SOCIAL CIRCLES?
IT WAS FINE.
ALL OFFICIAL EVENTS ARE OVER, AND I'VE NOTIFIED ALL OF MY CLOSE FRIENDS...
COME TO THINK OF IT, THE LADYSHIP TO THE CAPTAIN OF THE KNIGHTS INVITED ME TO A TEA PARTY.
BUT I HAD NO DESIRE TO GO.

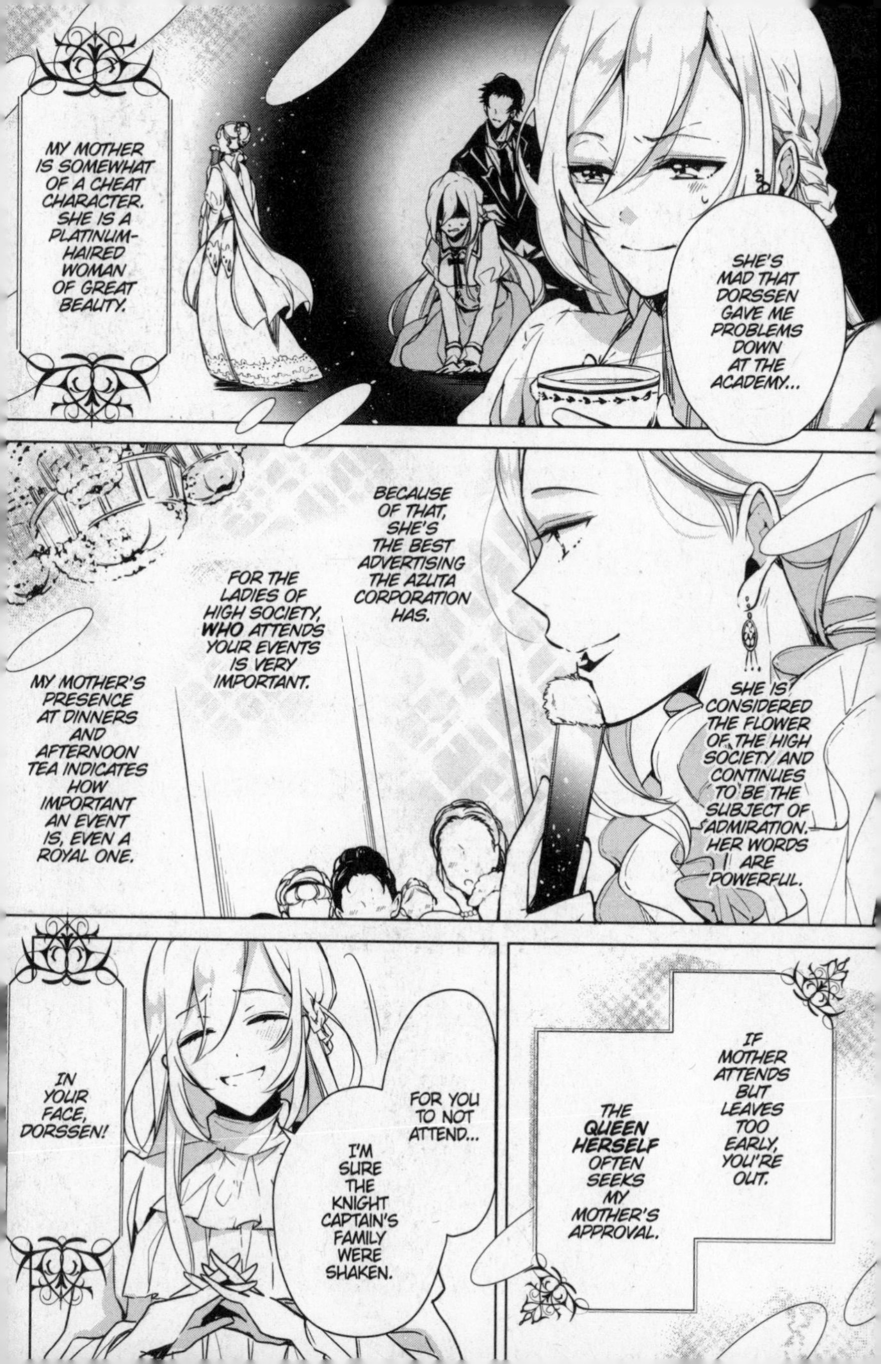
SHE'S MAD THAT DORSSEN GAVE ME PROBLEMS DOWN AT THE ACADEMY...
MY MOTHER IS SOMEWHAT OF A CHEAT CHARACTER. SHE IS A PLATINUM-HAIRED WOMAN OF GREAT BEAUTY.
SHE IS CONSIDERED THE FLOWER OF THE HIGH SOCIETY AND CONTINUES TO BE THE SUBJECT OF ADMIRATION. HER WORDS ARE POWERFUL.
BECAUSE OF THAT, SHE'S THE BEST ADVERTISING THE AZUTA CORPORATION HAS.
FOR THE LADIES OF HIGH SOCIETY, WHO ATTENDS YOUR EVENTS IS VERY IMPORTANT.
MY MOTHER'S PRESENCE AT DINNERS AND AFTERNOON TEA INDICATES HOW IMPORTANT AN EVENT IS, EVEN A ROYAL ONE.
IF MOTHER ATTENDS BUT LEAVES TOO EARLY, YOU'RE OUT.
THE QUEEN HERSELF OFTEN SEEKS MY MOTHER'S APPROVAL.
FOR YOU TO NOT ATTEND...
I'M SURE THE KNIGHT CAPTAIN'S FAMILY WERE SHAKEN.
IN YOUR FACE, DORSSEN!

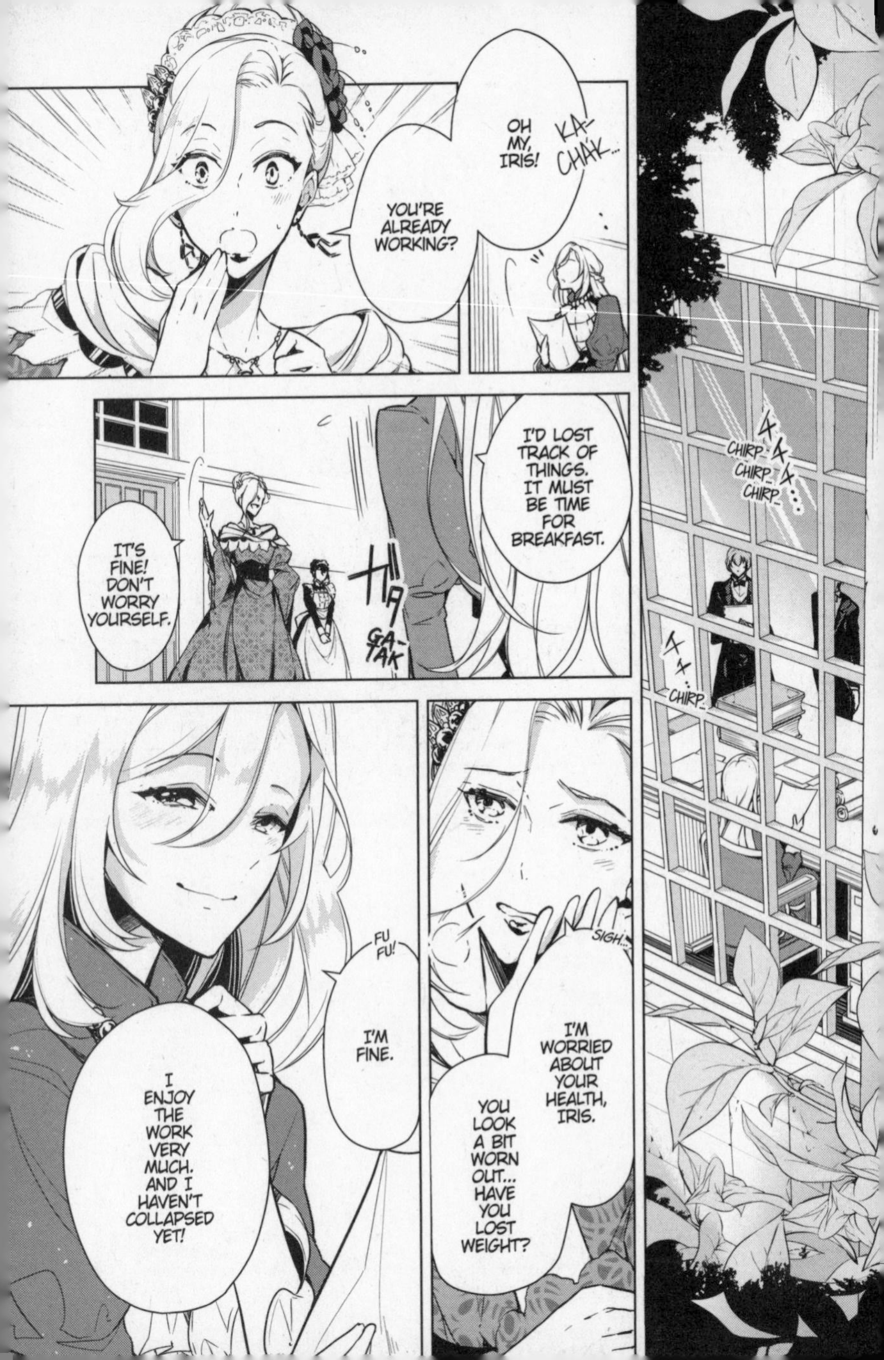

CHIRP... CHIRP... CHIRP...
CHIRP...
KA-CHAK...
OH MY, IRIS!
YOU'RE ALREADY WORKING?
I'D LOST TRACK OF THINGS. IT MUST BE TIME FOR BREAKFAST.
GA-TAK
IT'S FINE! DON'T WORRY YOURSELF.
SIGH...
I'M WORRIED ABOUT YOUR HEALTH, IRIS.
YOU LOOK A BIT WORN OUT... HAVE YOU LOST WEIGHT?
FU FU!
I'M FINE.
I ENJOY THE WORK VERY MUCH. AND I HAVEN'T COLLAPSED YET!

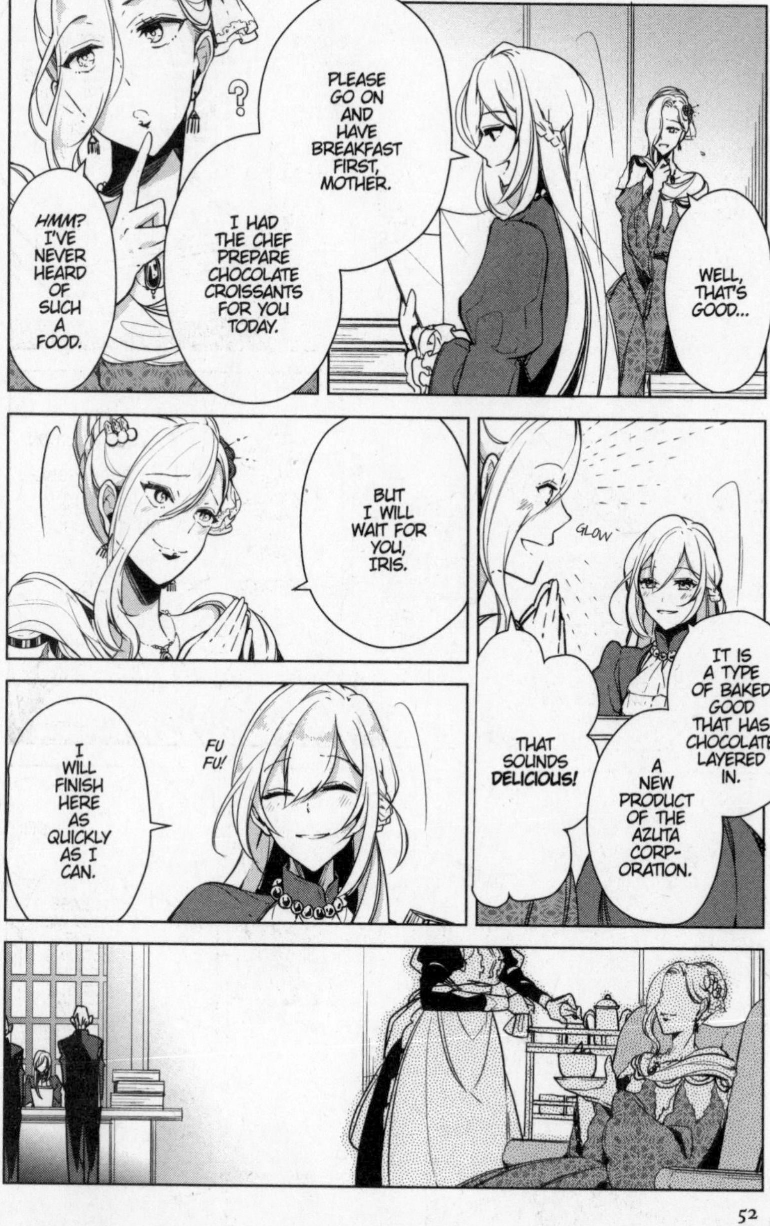
WELL, THAT'S GOOD...
PLEASE GO ON AND HAVE BREAKFAST FIRST, MOTHER.
I HAD THE CHEF PREPARE CHOCOLATE CROISSANTS FOR YOU TODAY.
?
HMM? I'VE NEVER HEARD OF SUCH A FOOD.
GLOW
IT IS A TYPE OF BAKED GOOD THAT HAS CHOCOLATE LAYERED IN.
THAT SOUNDS DELICIOUS!
A NEW PRODUCT OF THE AZUTA CORP-ORATION.
BUT I WILL WAIT FOR YOU, IRIS.
FU FU!
I WILL FINISH HERE AS QUICKLY AS I CAN.

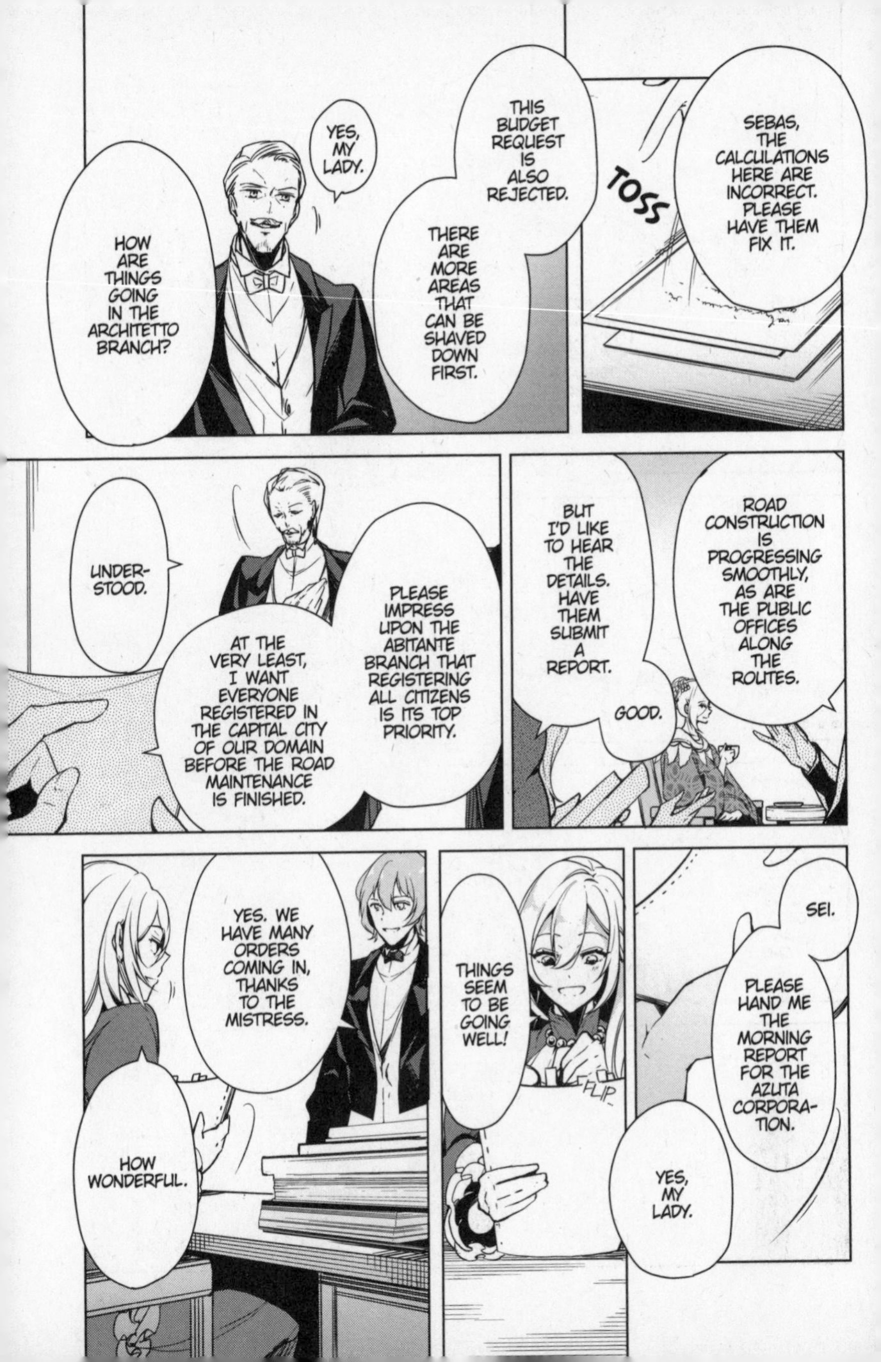
SEBAS, THE CALCULATIONS HERE ARE INCORRECT. PLEASE HAVE THEM FIX IT.
TOSS
THIS BUDGET REQUEST IS ALSO REJECTED.
THERE ARE MORE AREAS THAT CAN BE SHAVED DOWN FIRST.
YES, MY LADY.
HOW ARE THINGS GOING IN THE ARCHITETTO BRANCH?
ROAD CONSTRUCTION IS PROGRESSING SMOOTHLY, AS ARE THE PUBLIC OFFICES ALONG THE ROUTES.
BUT I'D LIKE TO HEAR THE DETAILS. HAVE THEM SUBMIT A REPORT.
GOOD.
PLEASE IMPRESS UPON THE ABITANTE BRANCH THAT REGISTERING ALL CITIZENS IS ITS TOP PRIORITY.
AT THE VERY LEAST, I WANT EVERYONE REGISTERED IN THE CAPITAL CITY OF OUR DOMAIN BEFORE THE ROAD MAINTENANCE IS FINISHED.
UNDER-STOOD.
SEI.
PLEASE HAND ME THE MORNING REPORT FOR THE AZUTA CORPORA-TION.
YES, MY LADY.
THINGS SEEM TO BE GOING WELL!
FLIP
YES. WE HAVE MANY ORDERS COMING IN, THANKS TO THE MISTRESS.
HOW WONDERFUL.

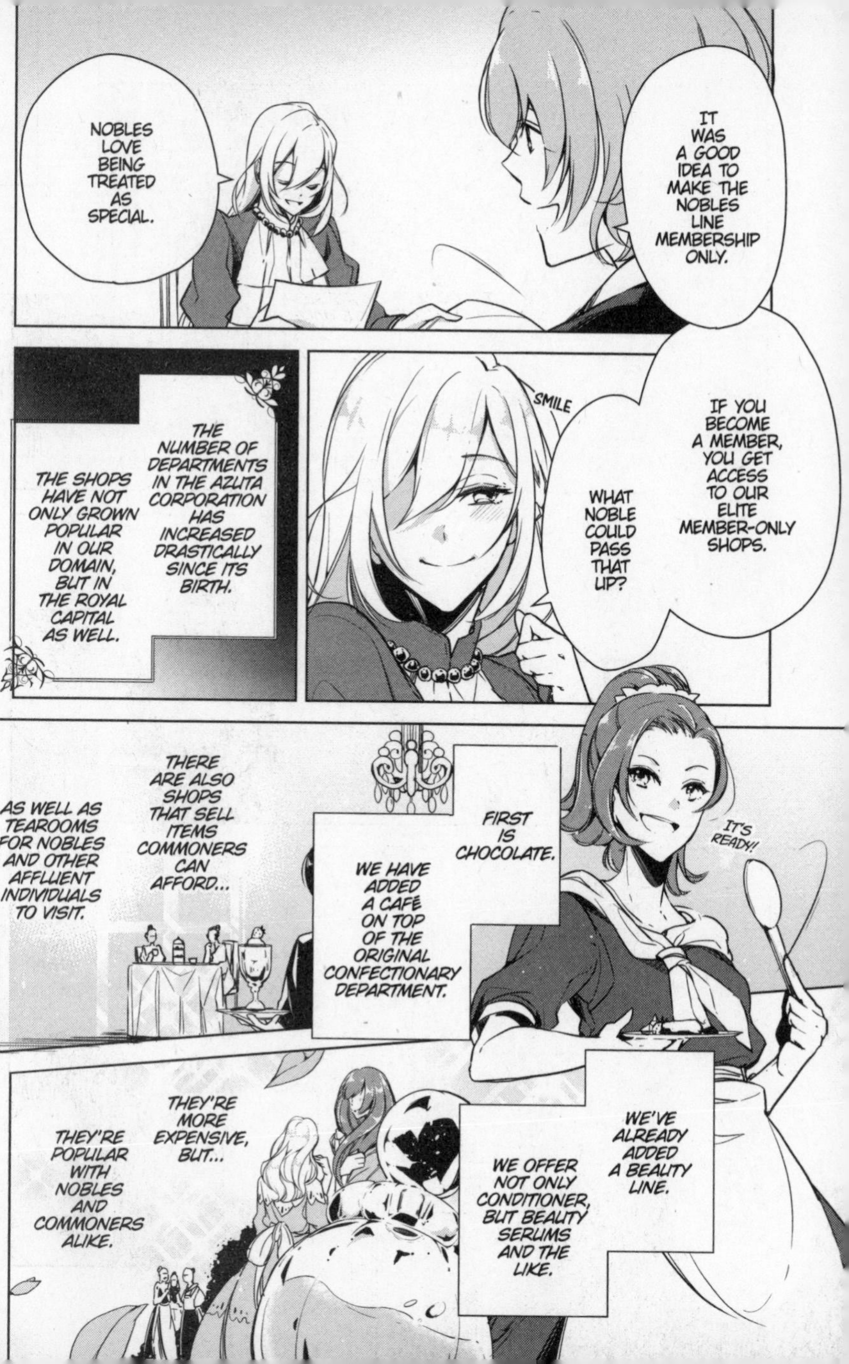
IT WAS A GOOD IDEA TO MAKE THE NOBLES LINE MEMBERSHIP ONLY.
NOBLES LOVE BEING TREATED AS SPECIAL.
IF YOU BECOME A MEMBER, YOU GET ACCESS TO OUR ELITE MEMBER-ONLY SHOPS.
WHAT NOBLE COULD PASS THAT UP?
SMILE
THE NUMBER OF DEPARTMENTS IN THE AZUTA CORPORATION HAS INCREASED DRASTICALLY SINCE ITS BIRTH.
THE SHOPS HAVE NOT ONLY GROWN POPULAR IN OUR DOMAIN, BUT IN THE ROYAL CAPITAL AS WELL.
IT'S READY!!
FIRST IS CHOCOLATE.
WE HAVE ADDED A CAFÉ ON TOP OF THE ORIGINAL CONFECTIONARY DEPARTMENT.
THERE ARE ALSO SHOPS THAT SELL ITEMS COMMONERS CAN AFFORD...
AS WELL AS TEAROOMS FOR NOBLES AND OTHER AFFLUENT INDIVIDUALS TO VISIT.
WE'VE ALREADY ADDED A BEAUTY LINE.
WE OFFER NOT ONLY CONDITIONER, BUT BEAUTY SERUMS AND THE LIKE.
THEY'RE MORE EXPENSIVE, BUT...
THEY'RE POPULAR WITH NOBLES AND COMMONERS ALIKE.

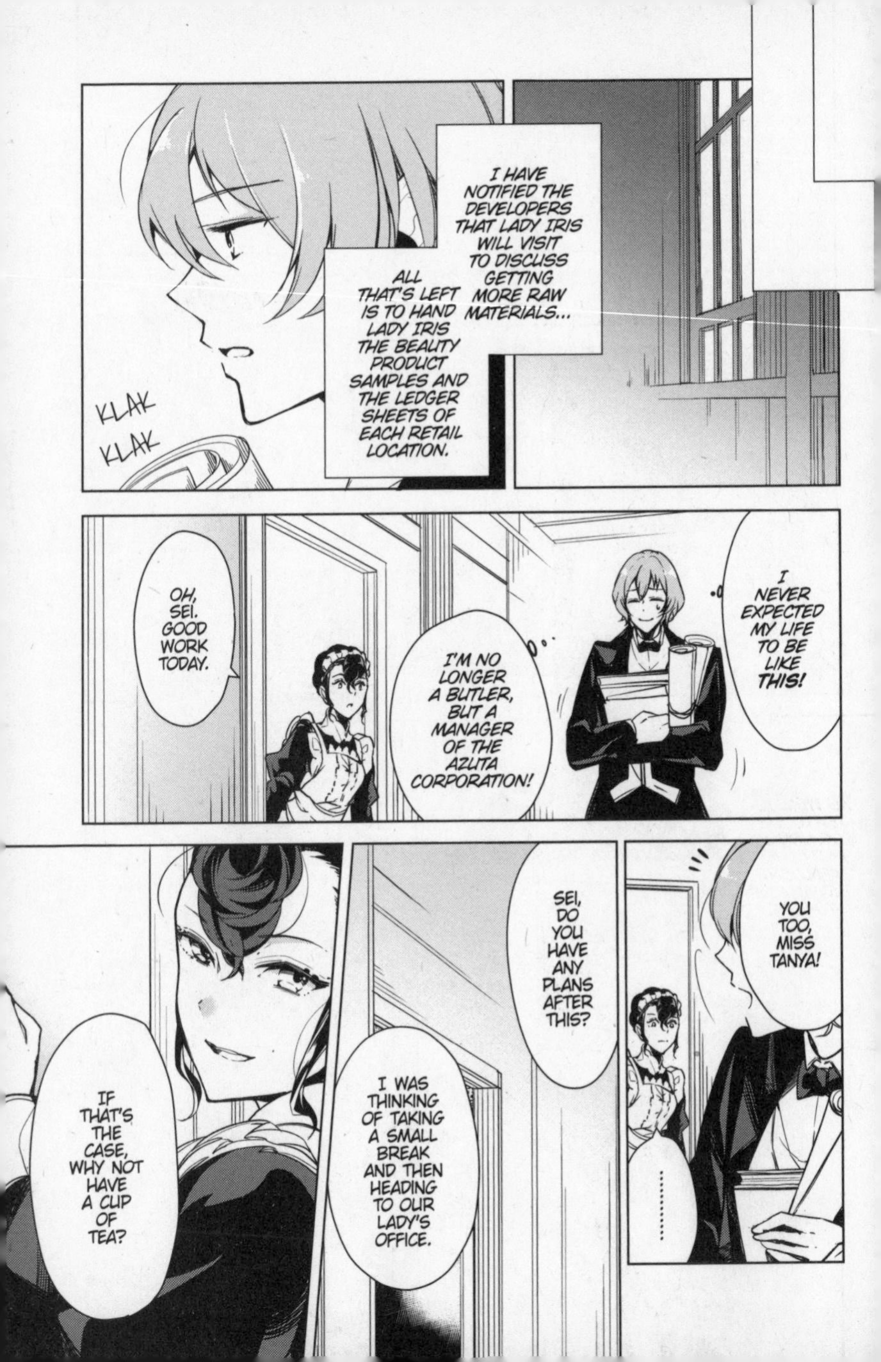
I HAVE NOTIFIED THE DEVELOPERS THAT LADY IRIS WILL VISIT TO DISCUSS GETTING MORE RAW MATERIALS...
ALL THAT'S LEFT IS TO HAND LADY IRIS THE BEAUTY PRODUCT SAMPLES AND THE LEDGER SHEETS OF EACH RETAIL LOCATION.
KLAK
KLAK
I NEVER EXPECTED MY LIFE TO BE LIKE THIS!
I'M NO LONGER A BUTLER, BUT A MANAGER OF THE AZUTA CORPORATION!
OH, SEI. GOOD WORK TODAY.
YOU TOO, MISS TANYA!
......
SEI, DO YOU HAVE ANY PLANS AFTER THIS?
I WAS THINKING OF TAKING A SMALL BREAK AND THEN HEADING TO OUR LADY'S OFFICE.
IF THAT'S THE CASE, WHY NOT HAVE A CUP OF TEA?

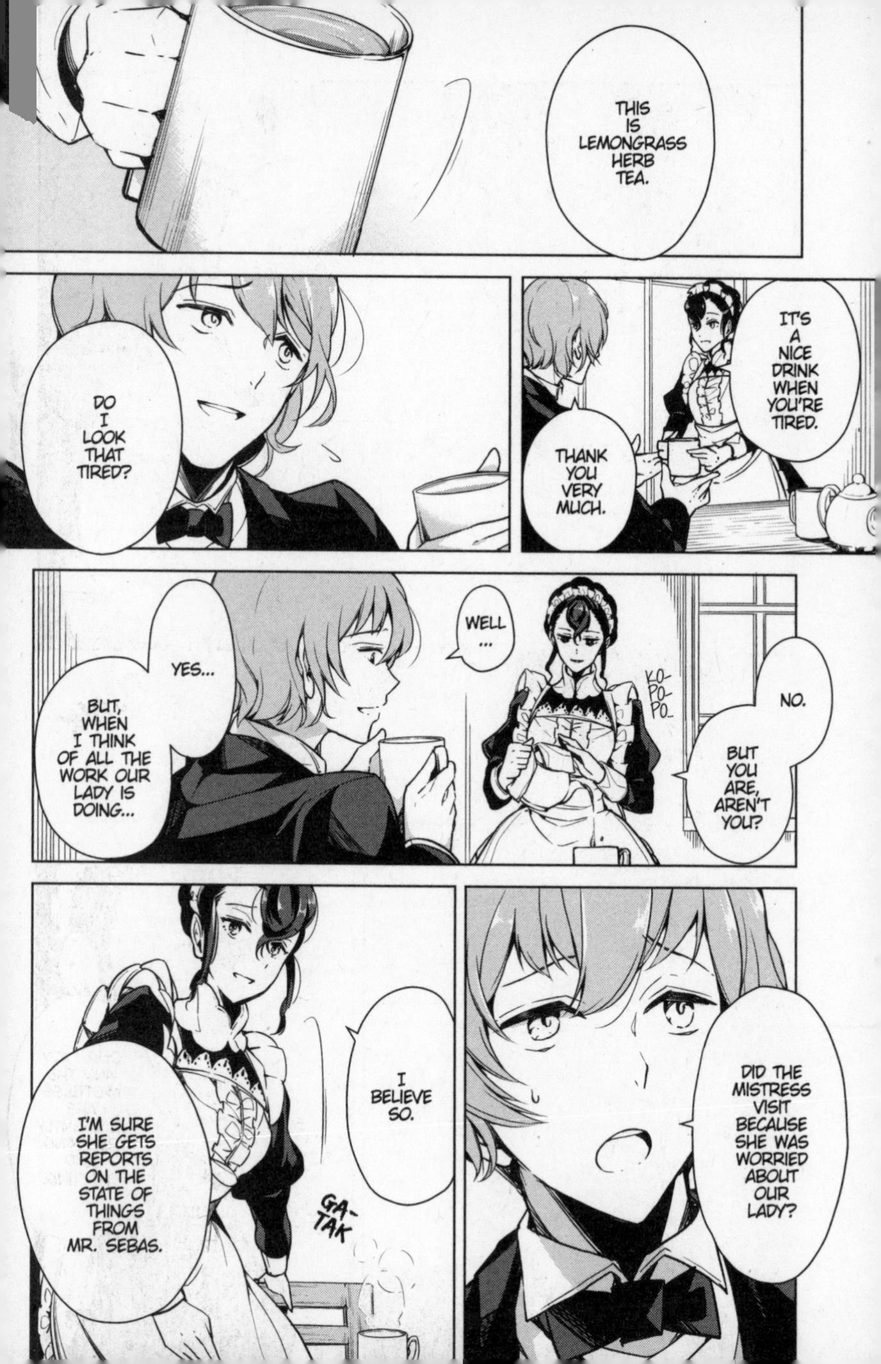
THIS IS LEMONGRASS HERB TEA.
IT'S A NICE DRINK WHEN YOU'RE TIRED.
THANK YOU VERY MUCH.
DO I LOOK THAT TIRED?
NO.
BUT YOU ARE, AREN'T YOU?
KO-PO-PO...
WELL ...
YES...
BUT, WHEN I THINK OF ALL THE WORK OUR LADY IS DOING...
DID THE MISTRESS VISIT BECAUSE SHE WAS WORRIED ABOUT OUR LADY?
I BELIEVE SO.
GA-TAK
I'M SURE SHE GETS REPORTS ON THE STATE OF THINGS FROM MR. SEBAS.

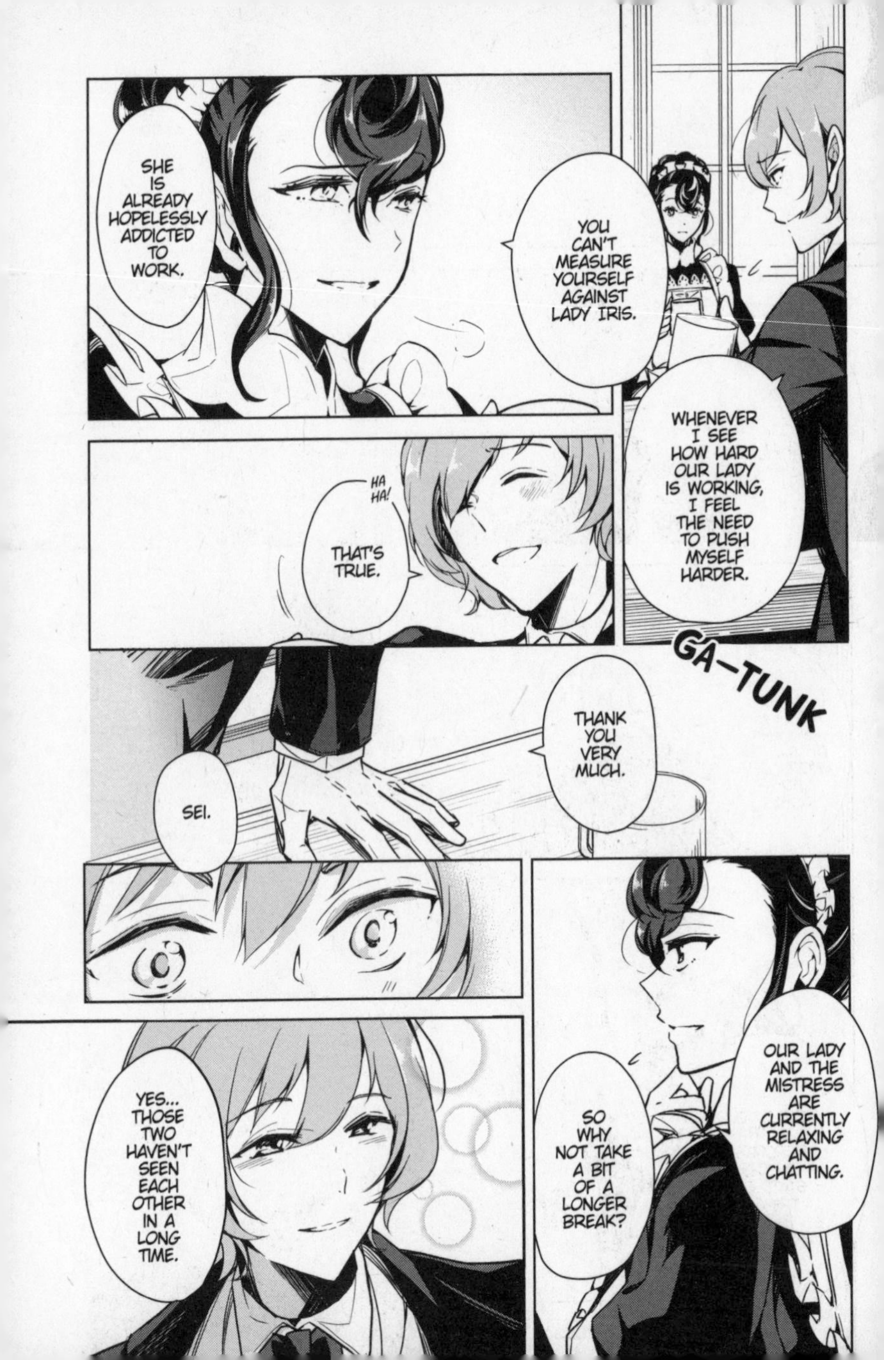
WHENEVER I SEE HOW HARD OUR LADY IS WORKING, I FEEL THE NEED TO PUSH MYSELF HARDER.
YOU CAN'T MEASURE YOURSELF AGAINST LADY IRIS.
SHE IS ALREADY HOPELESSLY ADDICTED TO WORK.
HA HA!
THAT'S TRUE.
GA-TUNK
THANK YOU VERY MUCH.
SEI.
OUR LADY AND THE MISTRESS ARE CURRENTLY RELAXING AND CHATTING.
SO WHY NOT TAKE A BIT OF A LONGER BREAK?
YES... THOSE TWO HAVEN'T SEEN EACH OTHER IN A LONG TIME.

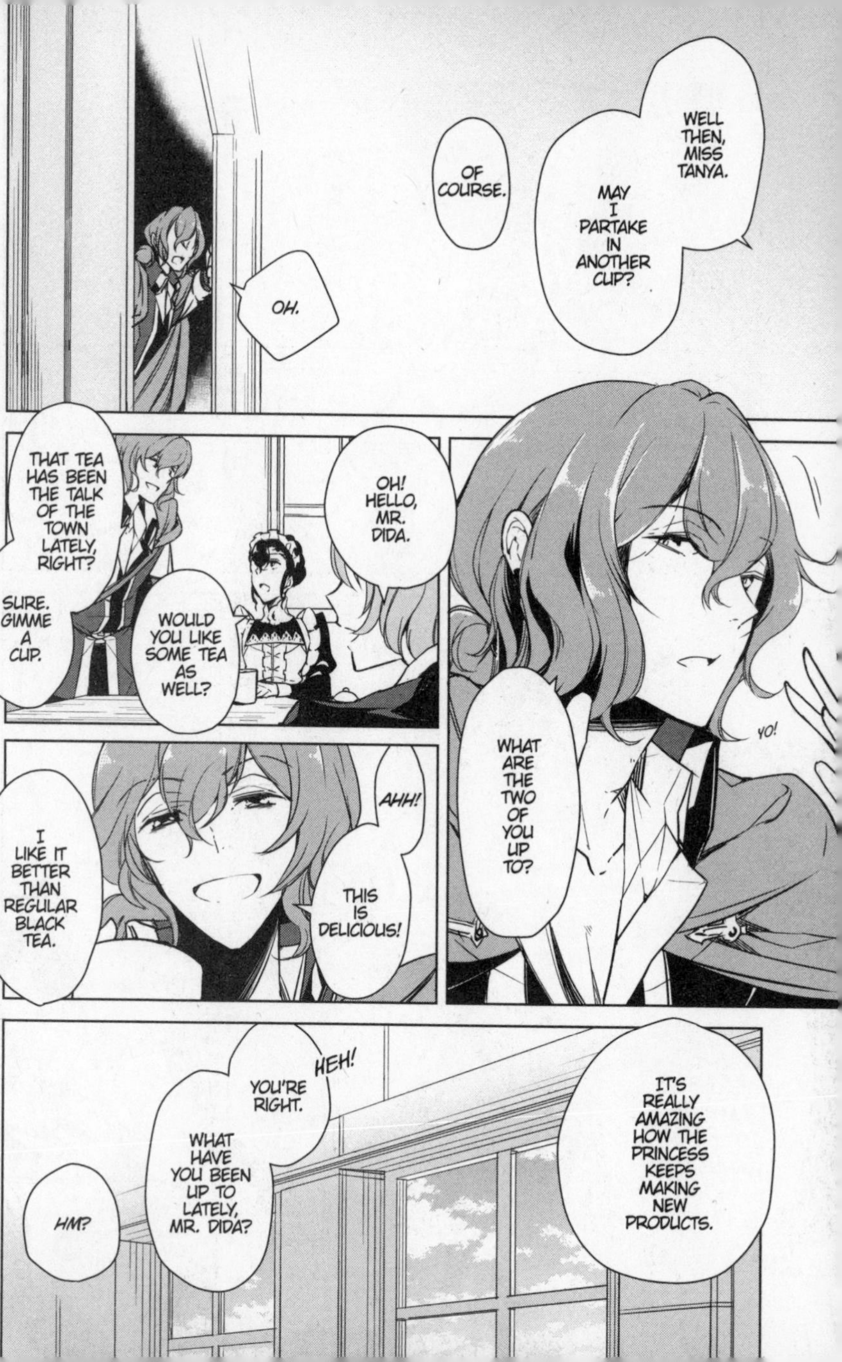
WELL THEN, MISS TANYA.
MAY I PARTAKE IN ANOTHER CUP?
OF COURSE.
OH.
YO!
WHAT ARE THE TWO OF YOU UP TO?
OH! HELLO, MR. DIDA.
THAT TEA HAS BEEN THE TALK OF THE TOWN LATELY, RIGHT?
WOULD YOU LIKE SOME TEA AS WELL?
SURE. GIMME A CUP.
AHH!
THIS IS DELICIOUS!
I LIKE IT BETTER THAN REGULAR BLACK TEA.
IT'S REALLY AMAZING HOW THE PRINCESS KEEPS MAKING NEW PRODUCTS.
HEH!
YOU'RE RIGHT.
WHAT HAVE YOU BEEN UP TO LATELY, MR. DIDA?
HM?

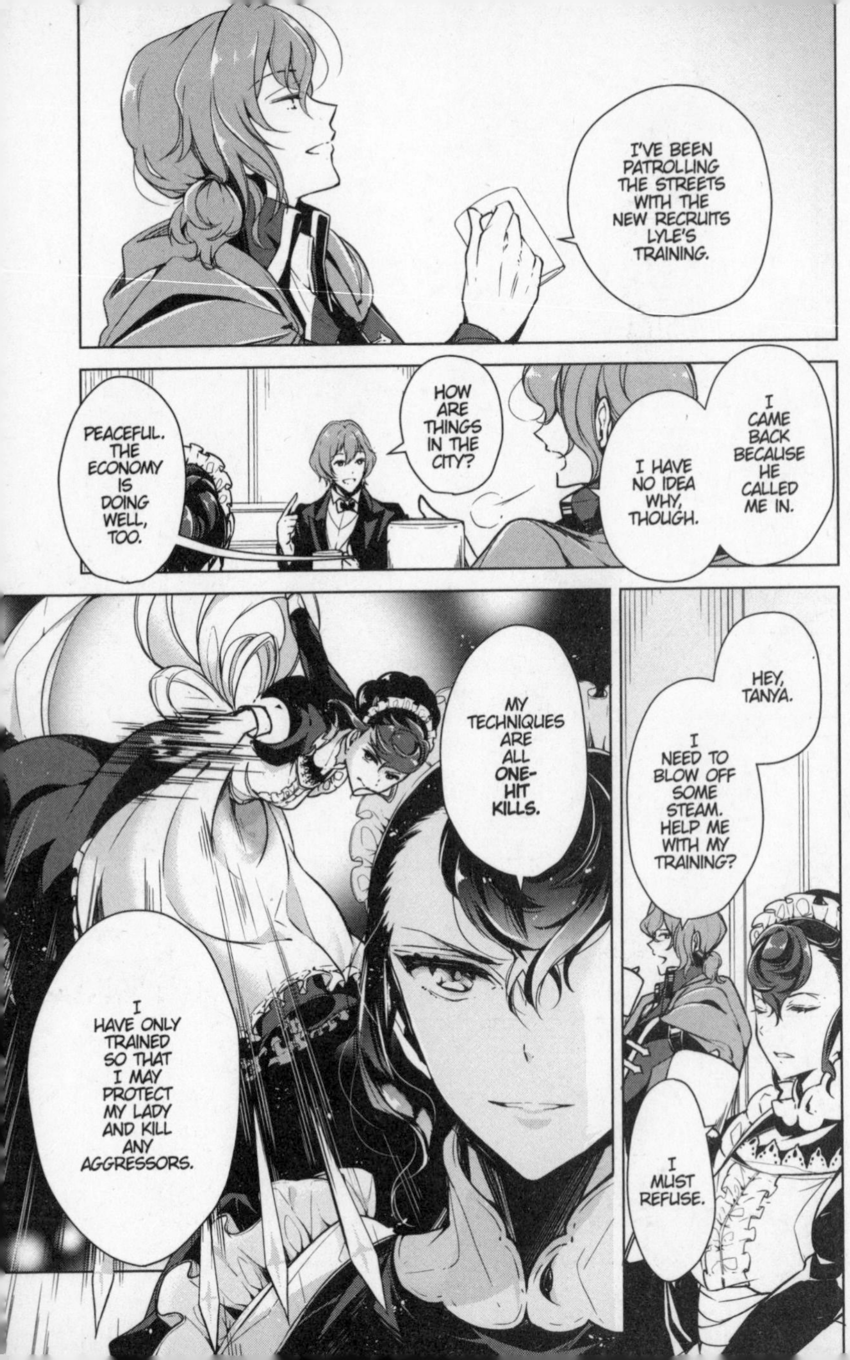
I'VE BEEN PATROLLING THE STREETS WITH THE NEW RECRUITS LYLE'S TRAINING.
I CAME BACK BECAUSE HE CALLED ME IN.
I HAVE NO IDEA WHY, THOUGH.
HOW ARE THINGS IN THE CITY?
PEACEFUL. THE ECONOMY IS DOING WELL, TOO.
HEY, TANYA.
I NEED TO BLOW OFF SOME STEAM. HELP ME WITH MY TRAINING?
I MUST REFUSE.
MY TECHNIQUES ARE ALL ONE-HIT KILLS.
I HAVE ONLY TRAINED SO THAT I MAY PROTECT MY LADY AND KILL ANY AGGRESSORS.

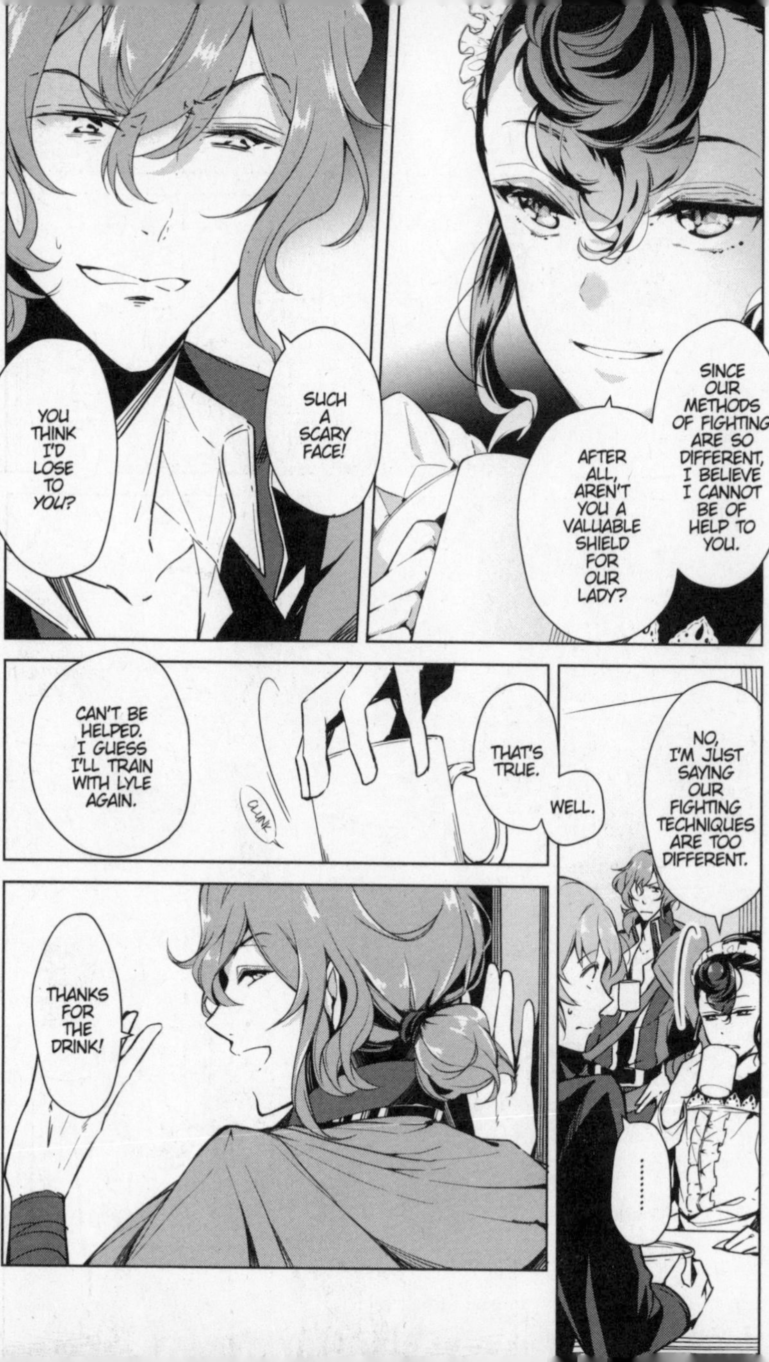
SINCE OUR METHODS OF FIGHTING ARE SO DIFFERENT, I BELIEVE I CANNOT BE OF HELP TO YOU.
AFTER ALL, AREN'T YOU A VALUABLE SHIELD FOR OUR LADY?
SUCH A SCARY FACE!
YOU THINK I'D LOSE TO YOU?
NO, I'M JUST SAYING OUR FIGHTING TECHNIQUES ARE TOO DIFFERENT.
......
WELL.
THAT'S TRUE.
CLUNK
CAN'T BE HELPED. I GUESS I'LL TRAIN WITH LYLE AGAIN.
THANKS FOR THE DRINK!

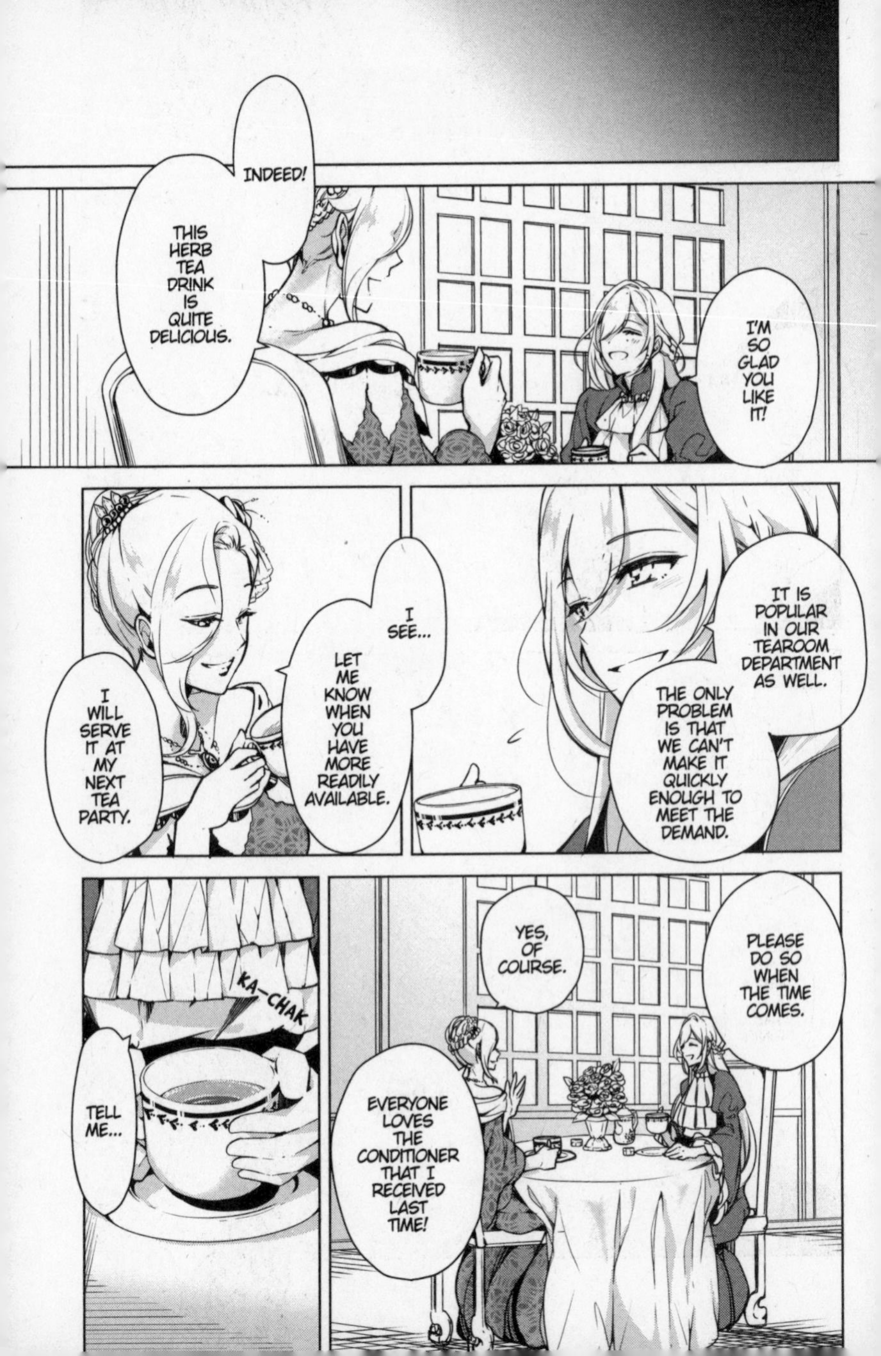
INDEED!
THIS HERB TEA DRINK IS QUITE DELICIOUS.
I'M SO GLAD YOU LIKE IT!
IT IS POPULAR IN OUR TEAROOM DEPARTMENT AS WELL.
THE ONLY PROBLEM IS THAT WE CAN'T MAKE IT QUICKLY ENOUGH TO MEET THE DEMAND.
I SEE...
LET ME KNOW WHEN YOU HAVE MORE READILY AVAILABLE.
I WILL SERVE IT AT MY NEXT TEA PARTY.
PLEASE DO SO WHEN THE TIME COMES.
YES, OF COURSE.
EVERYONE LOVES THE CONDITIONER THAT I RECEIVED LAST TIME!
KA-CHAK
TELL ME...

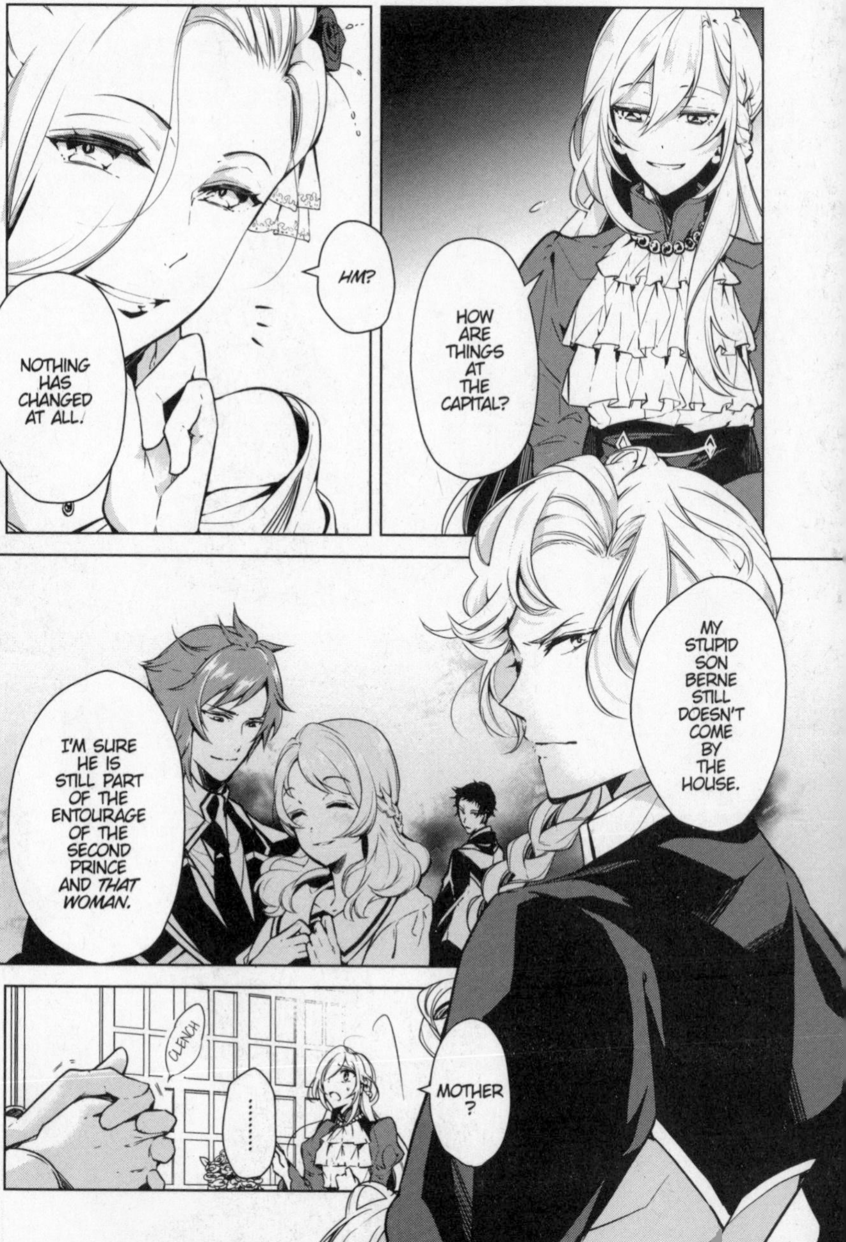
HOW ARE THINGS AT THE CAPITAL?
HM?
NOTHING HAS CHANGED AT ALL.
MY STUPID SON BERNE STILL DOESN'T COME BY THE HOUSE.
I'M SURE HE IS STILL PART OF THE ENTOURAGE OF THE SECOND PRINCE AND *THAT WOMAN*.
MOTHER?
......
CLENCH

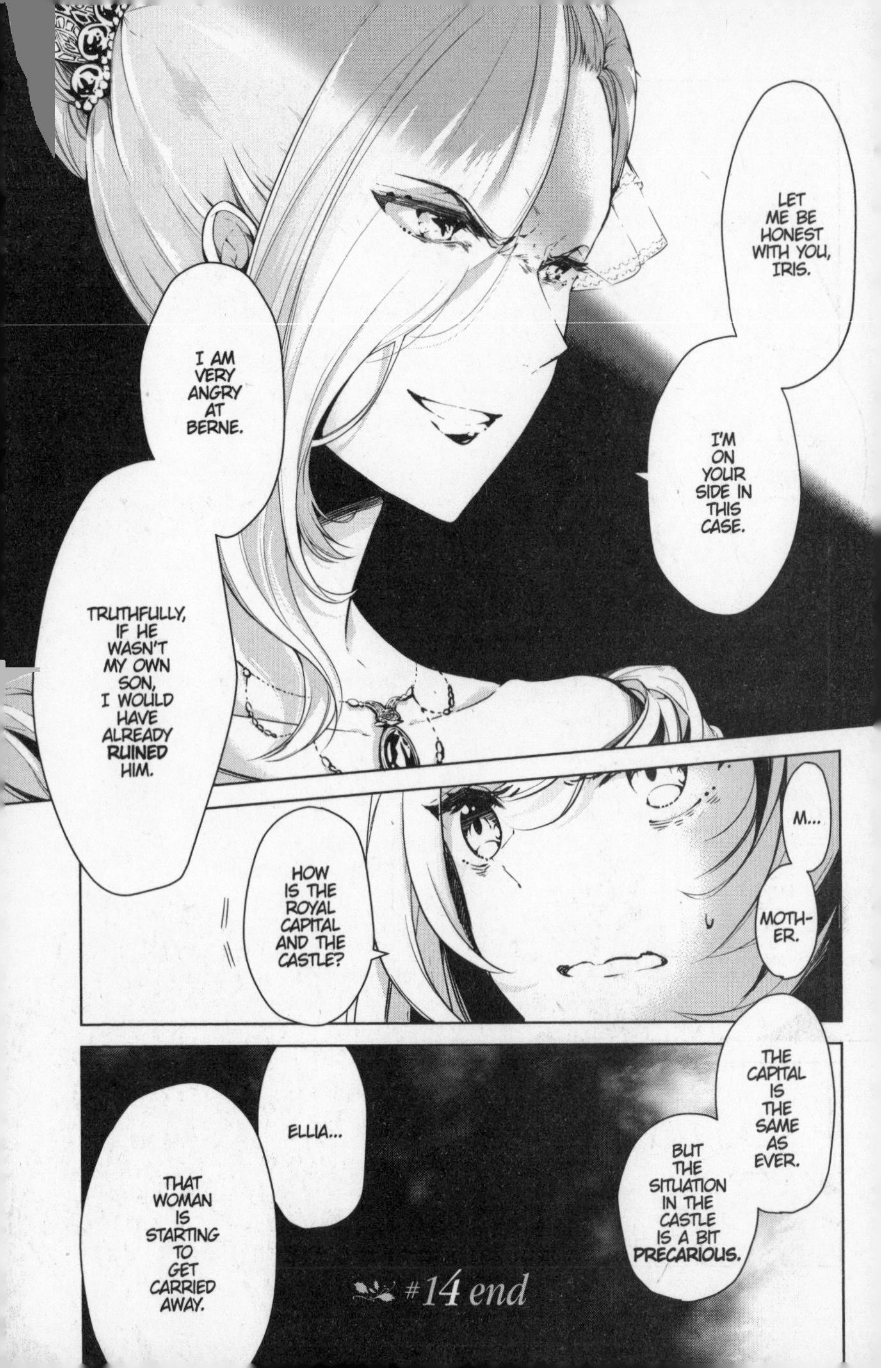
LET ME BE HONEST WITH YOU, IRIS.
I'M ON YOUR SIDE IN THIS CASE.
I AM VERY ANGRY AT BERNE.
TRUTHFULLY, IF HE WASN'T MY OWN SON, I WOULD HAVE ALREADY RUINED HIM.
M...
MOTH-ER.
HOW IS THE ROYAL CAPITAL AND THE CASTLE?
THE CAPITAL IS THE SAME AS EVER.
BUT THE SITUATION IN THE CASTLE IS A BIT PRECARIOUS.
ELLIA...
THAT WOMAN IS STARTING TO GET CARRIED AWAY.
#14 end

KO-PO-PO...

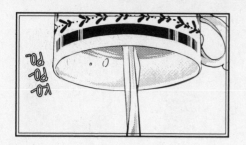

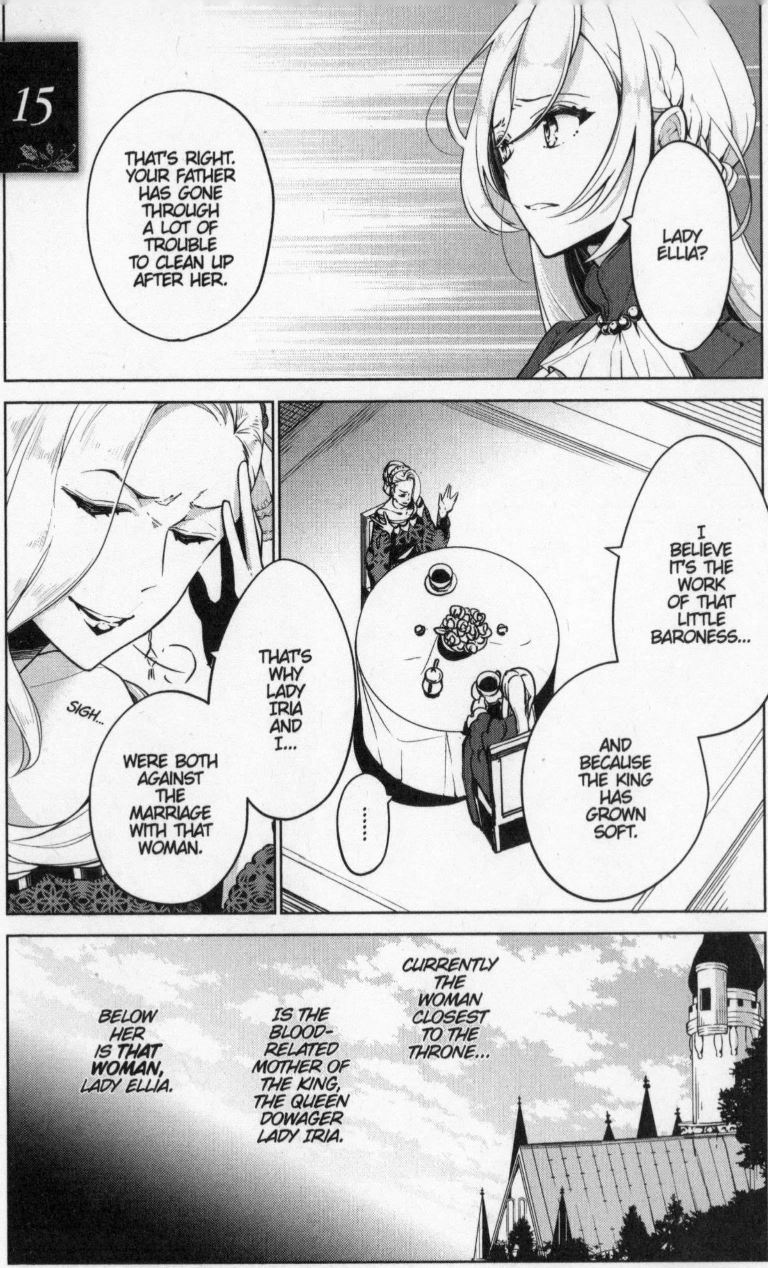

15
LADY ELLIA?
THAT'S RIGHT. YOUR FATHER HAS GONE THROUGH A LOT OF TROUBLE TO CLEAN UP AFTER HER.
I BELIEVE IT'S THE WORK OF THAT LITTLE BARONESS...
AND BECAUSE THE KING HAS GROWN SOFT.
......
THAT'S WHY LADY IRIA AND I...
SIGH...
WERE BOTH AGAINST THE MARRIAGE WITH THAT WOMAN.
CURRENTLY THE WOMAN CLOSEST TO THE THRONE...
IS THE BLOOD-RELATED MOTHER OF THE KING, THE QUEEN DOWAGER LADY IRIA.
BELOW HER IS THAT WOMAN, LADY ELLIA.

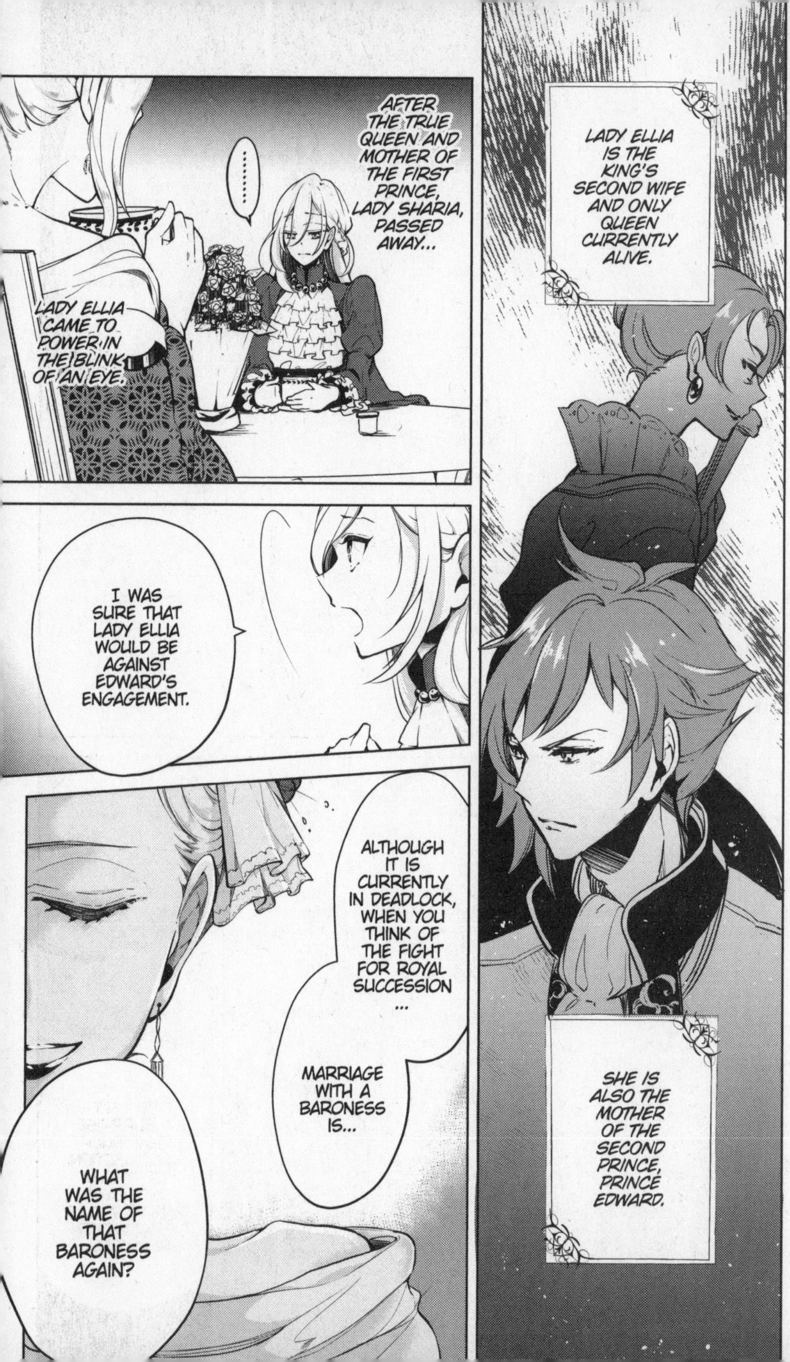
LADY ELLIA IS THE KING'S SECOND WIFE AND ONLY QUEEN CURRENTLY ALIVE.
SHE IS ALSO THE MOTHER OF THE SECOND PRINCE, PRINCE EDWARD.
AFTER THE TRUE QUEEN AND MOTHER OF THE FIRST PRINCE, LADY SHARIA, PASSED AWAY...
......
LADY ELLIA CAME TO POWER IN THE BLINK OF AN EYE.
I WAS SURE THAT LADY ELLIA WOULD BE AGAINST EDWARD'S ENGAGEMENT.
ALTHOUGH IT IS CURRENTLY IN DEADLOCK, WHEN YOU THINK OF THE FIGHT FOR ROYAL SUCCESSION ...
MARRIAGE WITH A BARONESS IS...
WHAT WAS THE NAME OF THAT BARONESS AGAIN?

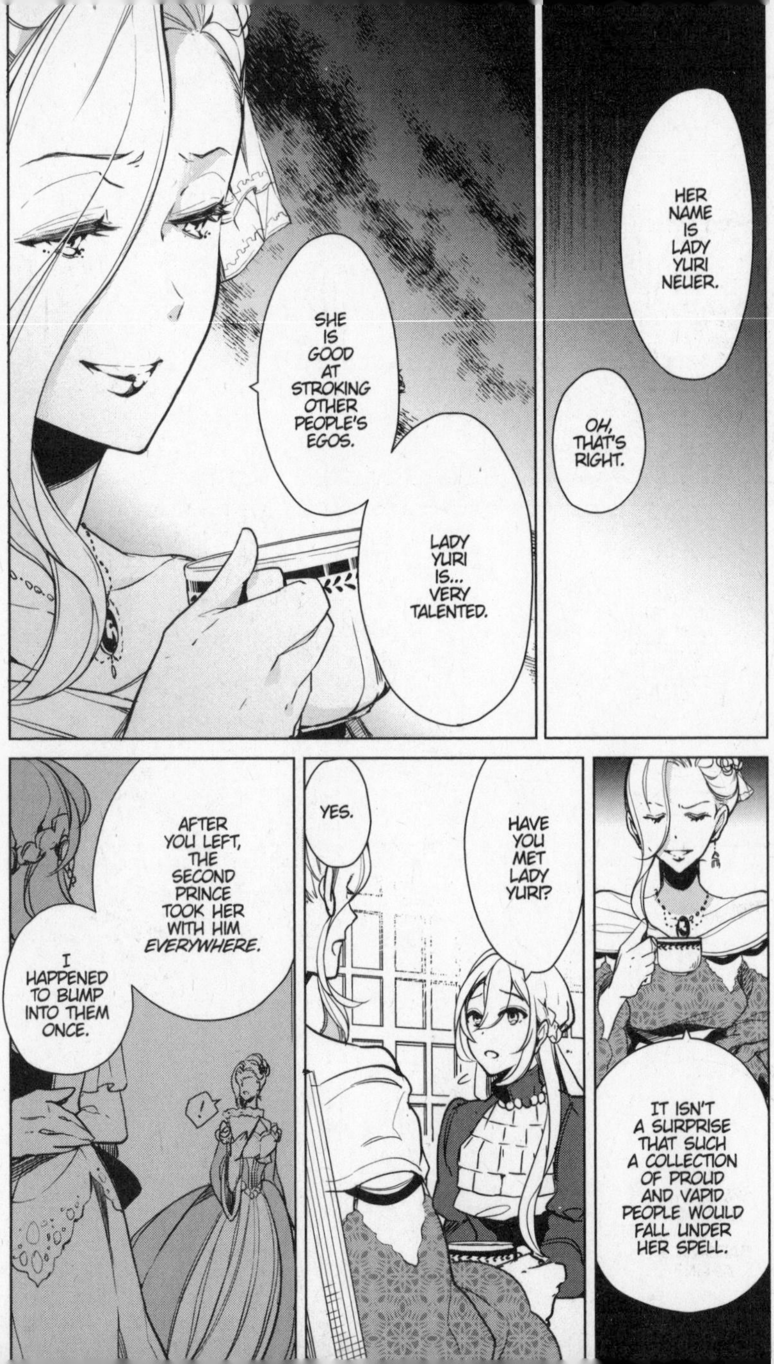
HER NAME IS LADY YURI NEUER.
OH, THAT'S RIGHT.
SHE IS GOOD AT STROKING OTHER PEOPLE'S EGOS.
LADY YURI IS... VERY TALENTED.
IT ISN'T A SURPRISE THAT SUCH A COLLECTION OF PROUD AND VAPID PEOPLE WOULD FALL UNDER HER SPELL.
HAVE YOU MET LADY YURI?
YES.
AFTER YOU LEFT, THE SECOND PRINCE TOOK HER WITH HIM *EVERYWHERE*.
I HAPPENED TO BUMP INTO THEM ONCE.
!

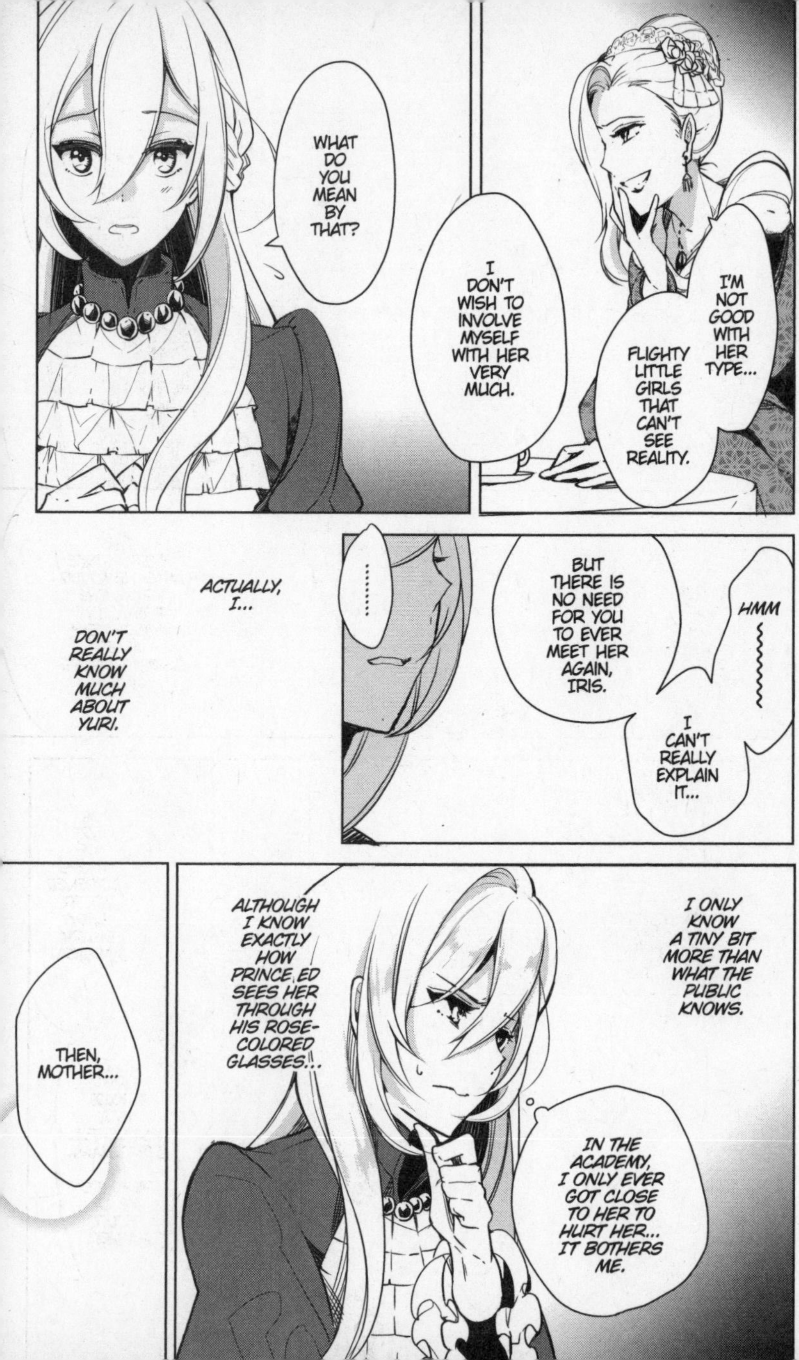
I'M NOT GOOD WITH HER TYPE...
FLIGHTY LITTLE GIRLS THAT CAN'T SEE REALITY.
I DON'T WISH TO INVOLVE MYSELF WITH HER VERY MUCH.
WHAT DO YOU MEAN BY THAT?
HMM~~~
I CAN'T REALLY EXPLAIN IT...
BUT THERE IS NO NEED FOR YOU TO EVER MEET HER AGAIN, IRIS.
......
ACTUALLY, I...
DON'T REALLY KNOW MUCH ABOUT YURI.
I ONLY KNOW A TINY BIT MORE THAN WHAT THE PUBLIC KNOWS.
ALTHOUGH I KNOW EXACTLY HOW PRINCE ED SEES HER THROUGH HIS ROSE-COLORED GLASSES...
IN THE ACADEMY, I ONLY EVER GOT CLOSE TO HER TO HURT HER... IT BOTHERS ME.
THEN, MOTHER...

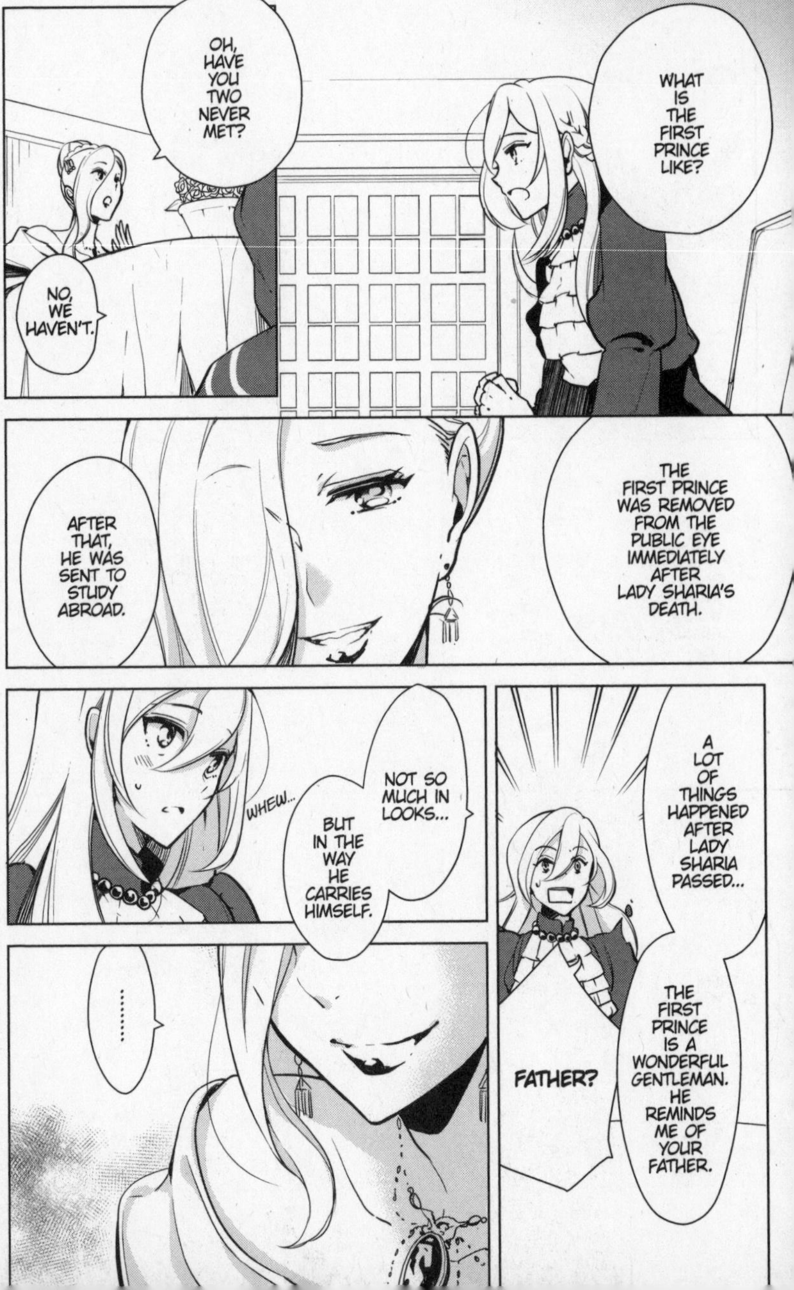
WHAT IS THE FIRST PRINCE LIKE?
OH, HAVE YOU TWO NEVER MET?
NO, WE HAVEN'T.
THE FIRST PRINCE WAS REMOVED FROM THE PUBLIC EYE IMMEDIATELY AFTER LADY SHARIA'S DEATH.
AFTER THAT, HE WAS SENT TO STUDY ABROAD.
A LOT OF THINGS HAPPENED AFTER LADY SHARIA PASSED...
THE FIRST PRINCE IS A WONDERFUL GENTLEMAN. HE REMINDS ME OF YOUR FATHER.
FATHER?
NOT SO MUCH IN LOOKS...
WHEW...
BUT IN THE WAY HE CARRIES HIMSELF.
......

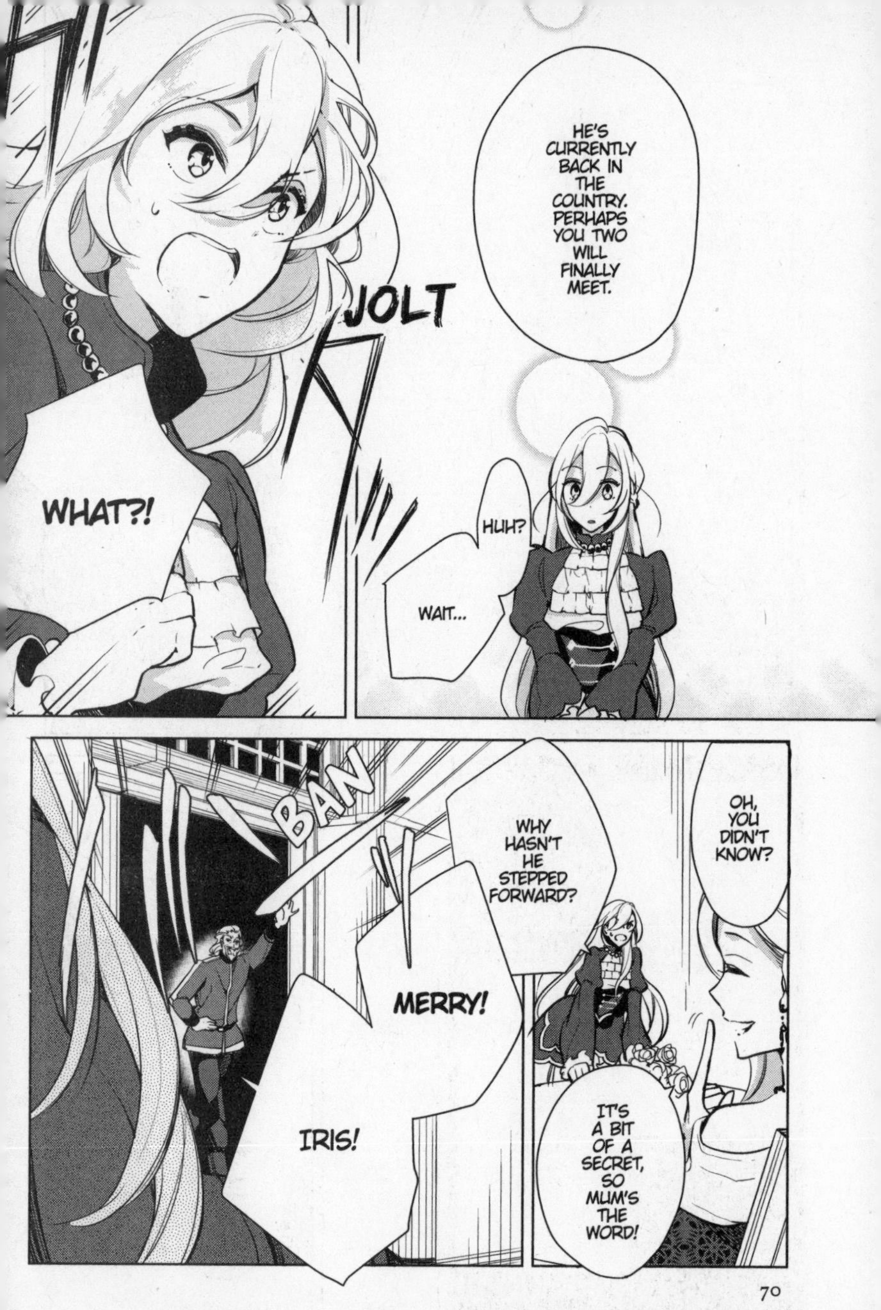
HE'S CURRENTLY BACK IN THE COUNTRY. PERHAPS YOU TWO WILL FINALLY MEET.
HUH?
WAIT...
JOLT
WHAT?!
OH, YOU DIDN'T KNOW?
IT'S A BIT OF A SECRET, SO MUM'S THE WORD!
WHY HASN'T HE STEPPED FORWARD?
BAN
MERRY!
IRIS!

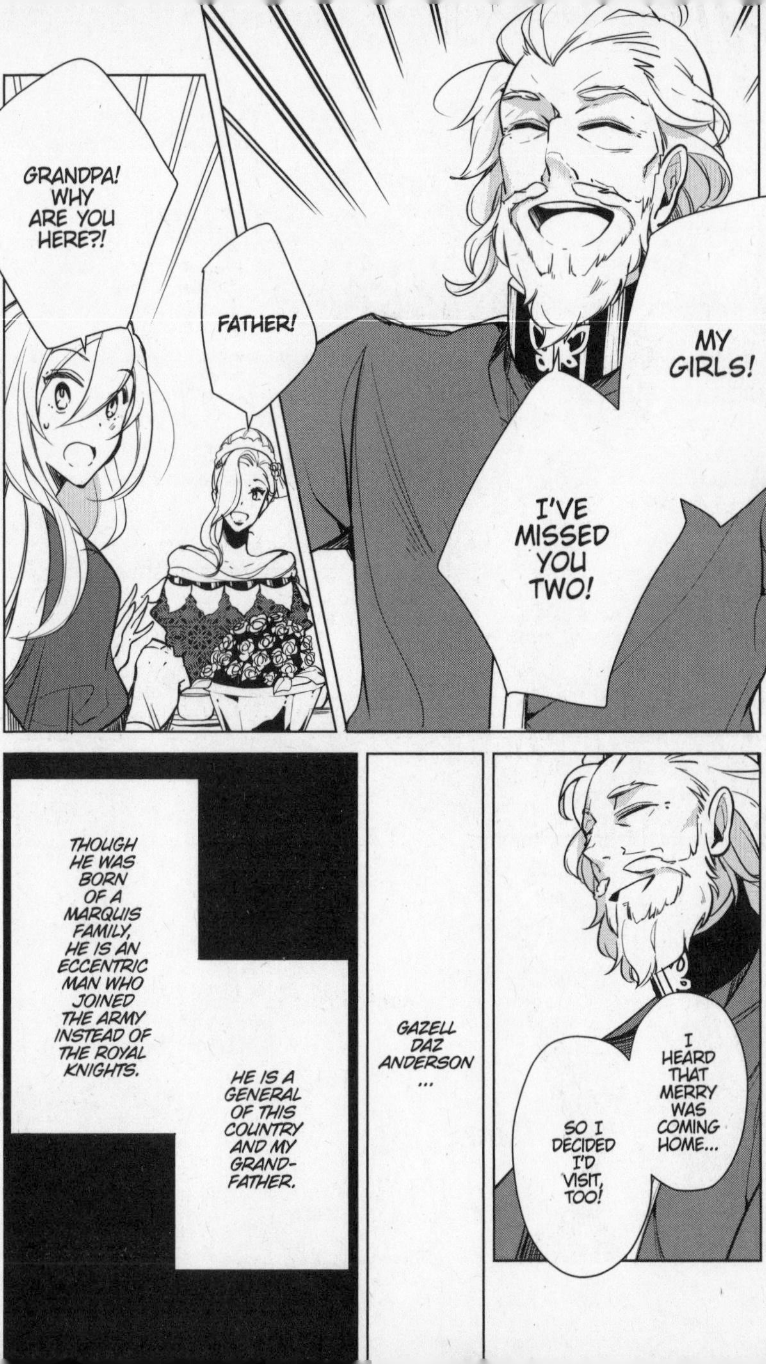
MY GIRLS!
I'VE MISSED YOU TWO!
GRANDPA! WHY ARE YOU HERE?!
FATHER!
I HEARD THAT MERRY WAS COMING HOME...
SO I DECIDED I'D VISIT, TOO!
GAZELL DAZ ANDERSON ...
THOUGH HE WAS BORN OF A MARQUIS FAMILY, HE IS AN ECCENTRIC MAN WHO JOINED THE ARMY INSTEAD OF THE ROYAL KNIGHTS.
HE IS A GENERAL OF THIS COUNTRY AND MY GRAND-FATHER.

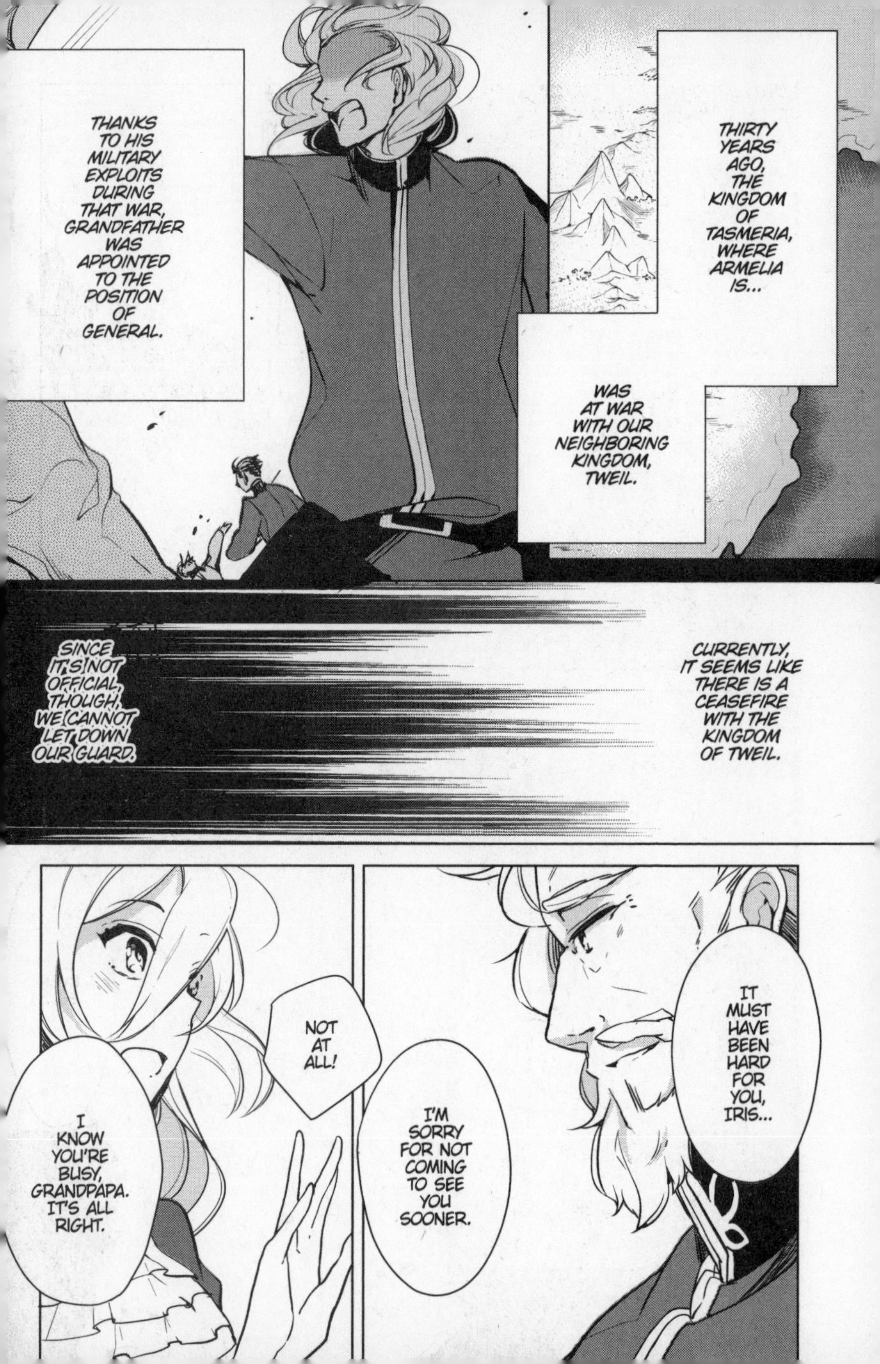
THIRTY YEARS AGO, THE KINGDOM OF TASMERIA, WHERE ARMELIA IS...
WAS AT WAR WITH OUR NEIGHBORING KINGDOM, TWEIL.
THANKS TO HIS MILITARY EXPLOITS DURING THAT WAR, GRANDFATHER WAS APPOINTED TO THE POSITION OF GENERAL.
CURRENTLY, IT SEEMS LIKE THERE IS A CEASEFIRE WITH THE KINGDOM OF TWEIL.
SINCE IT'S NOT OFFICIAL, THOUGH, WE CANNOT LET DOWN OUR GUARD.
IT MUST HAVE BEEN HARD FOR YOU, IRIS...
I'M SORRY FOR NOT COMING TO SEE YOU SOONER.
NOT AT ALL!
I KNOW YOU'RE BUSY, GRANDPAPA. IT'S ALL RIGHT.

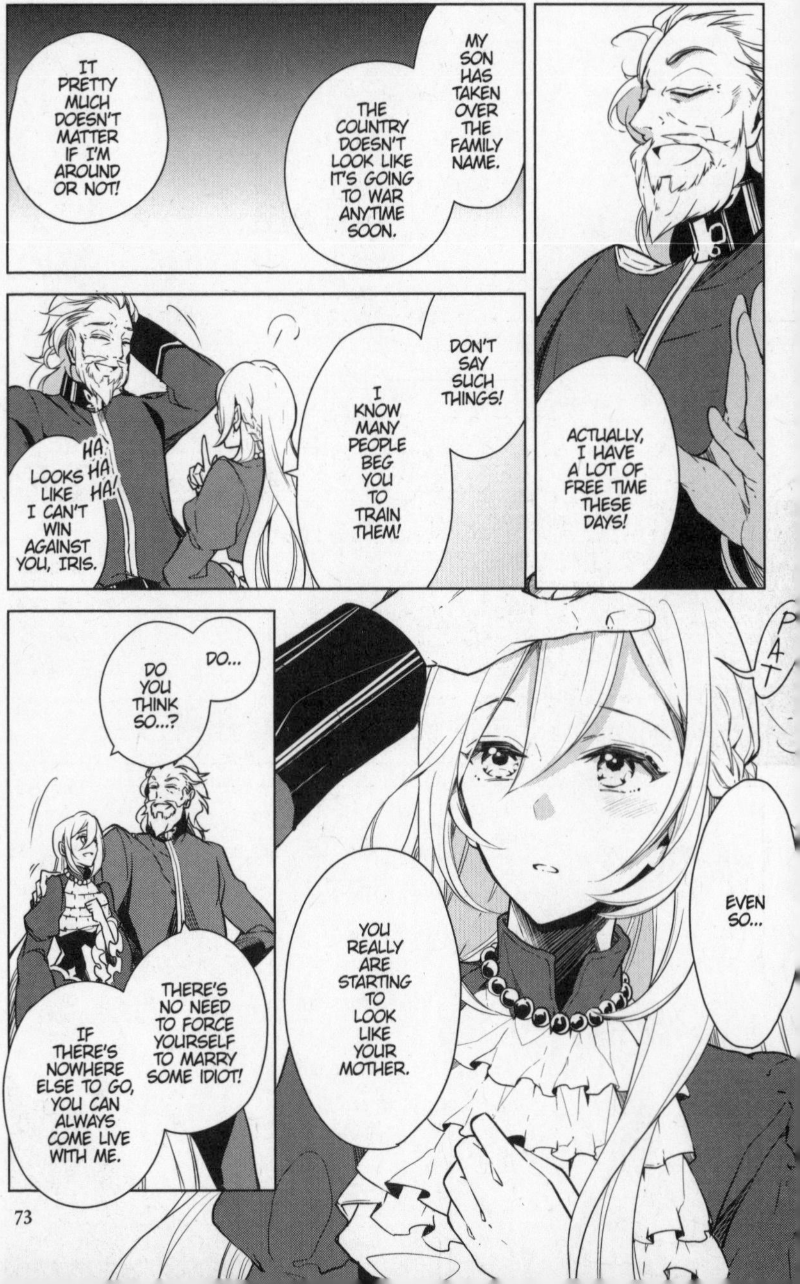

ACTUALLY, I HAVE A LOT OF FREE TIME THESE DAYS!
MY SON HAS TAKEN OVER THE FAMILY NAME.
THE COUNTRY DOESN'T LOOK LIKE IT'S GOING TO WAR ANYTIME SOON.
IT PRETTY MUCH DOESN'T MATTER IF I'M AROUND OR NOT!
DON'T SAY SUCH THINGS!
I KNOW MANY PEOPLE BEG YOU TO TRAIN THEM!
HA HA HA!
LOOKS LIKE I CAN'T WIN AGAINST YOU, IRIS.
PAT
EVEN SO...
YOU REALLY ARE STARTING TO LOOK LIKE YOUR MOTHER.
DO...
DO YOU THINK SO...?
THERE'S NO NEED TO FORCE YOURSELF TO MARRY SOME IDIOT!
IF THERE'S NOWHERE ELSE TO GO, YOU CAN ALWAYS COME LIVE WITH ME.

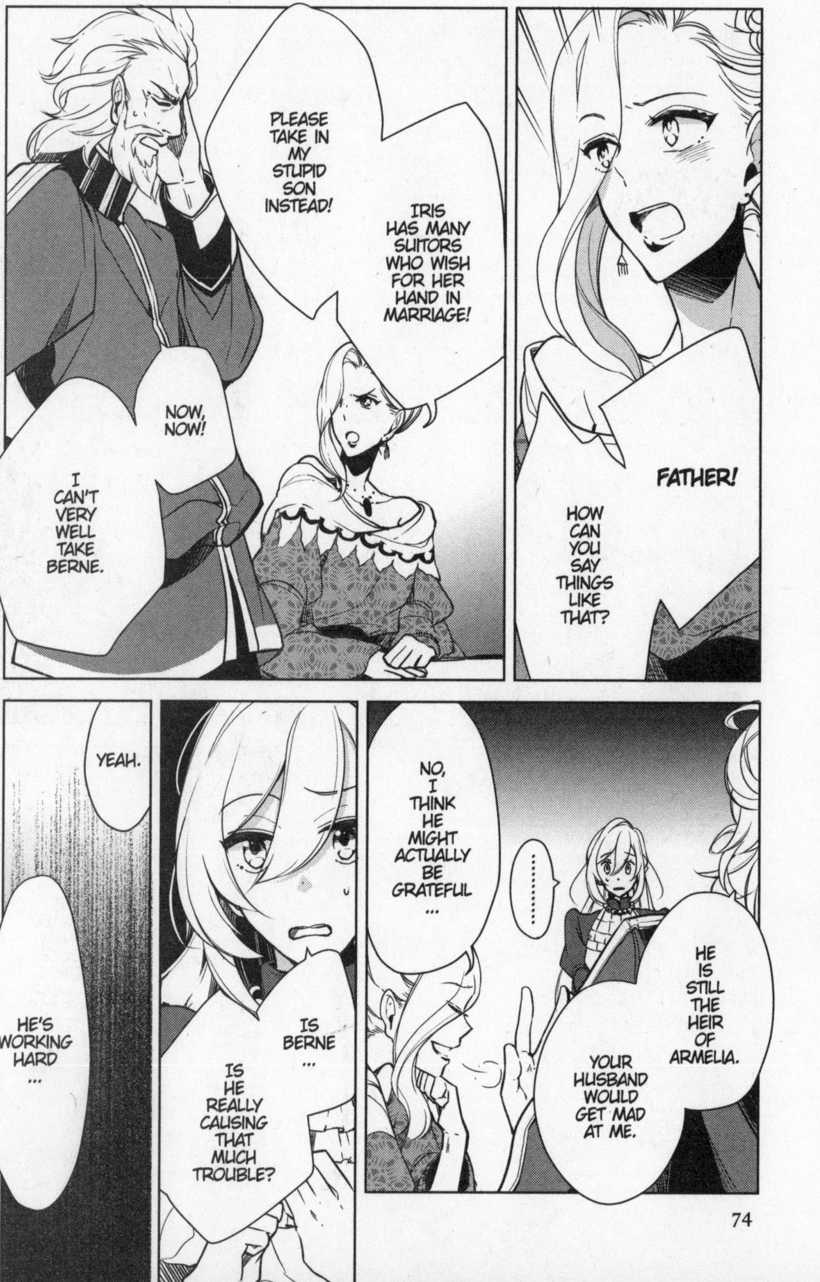
FATHER!
HOW CAN YOU SAY THINGS LIKE THAT?
IRIS HAS MANY SUITORS WHO WISH FOR HER HAND IN MARRIAGE!
PLEASE TAKE IN MY STUPID SON INSTEAD!
NOW, NOW!
I CAN'T VERY WELL TAKE BERNE.
HE IS STILL THE HEIR OF ARMELIA.
YOUR HUSBAND WOULD GET MAD AT ME.
....
NO, I THINK HE MIGHT ACTUALLY BE GRATEFUL...
IS BERNE...
IS HE REALLY CAUSING THAT MUCH TROUBLE?
YEAH.
HE'S WORKING HARD...

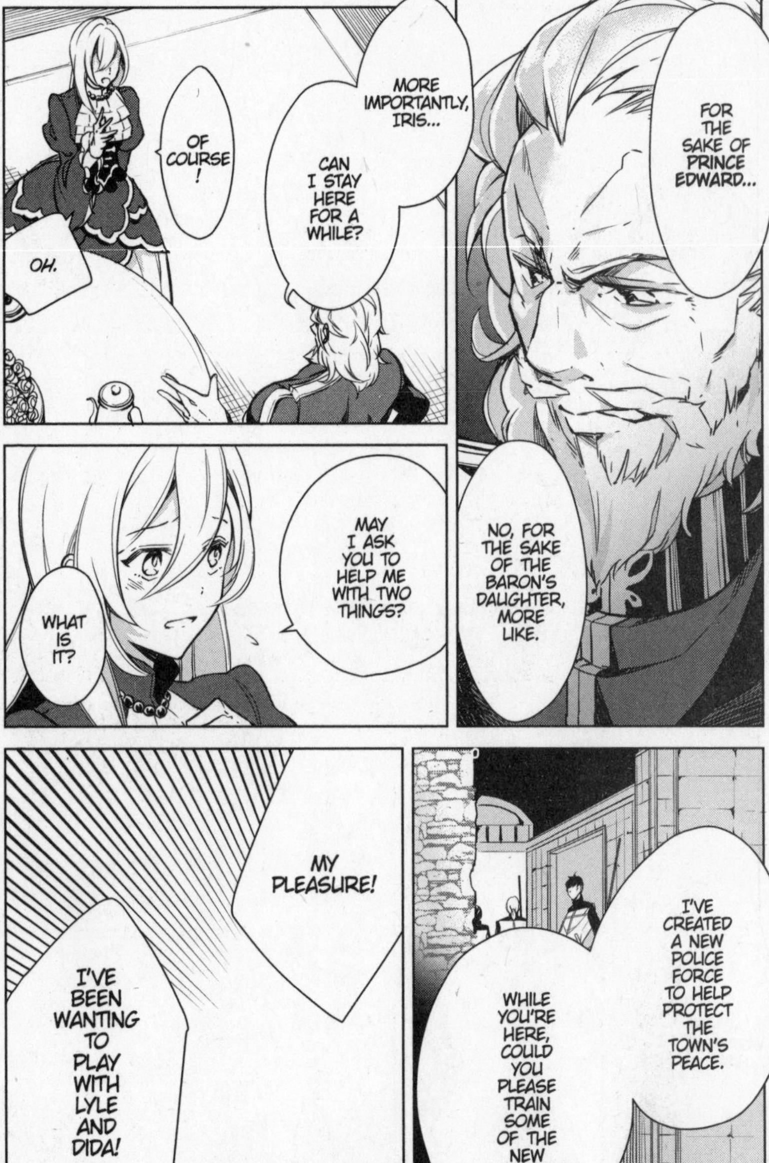
FOR THE SAKE OF PRINCE EDWARD...
NO, FOR THE SAKE OF THE BARON'S DAUGHTER, MORE LIKE.
MORE IMPORTANTLY, IRIS...
CAN I STAY HERE FOR A WHILE?
OF COURSE!
OH.
MAY I ASK YOU TO HELP ME WITH TWO THINGS?
WHAT IS IT?
I'VE CREATED A NEW POLICE FORCE TO HELP PROTECT THE TOWN'S PEACE.
WHILE YOU'RE HERE, COULD YOU PLEASE TRAIN SOME OF THE NEW RECRUITS?
MY PLEASURE!
I'VE BEEN WANTING TO PLAY WITH LYLE AND DIDA!

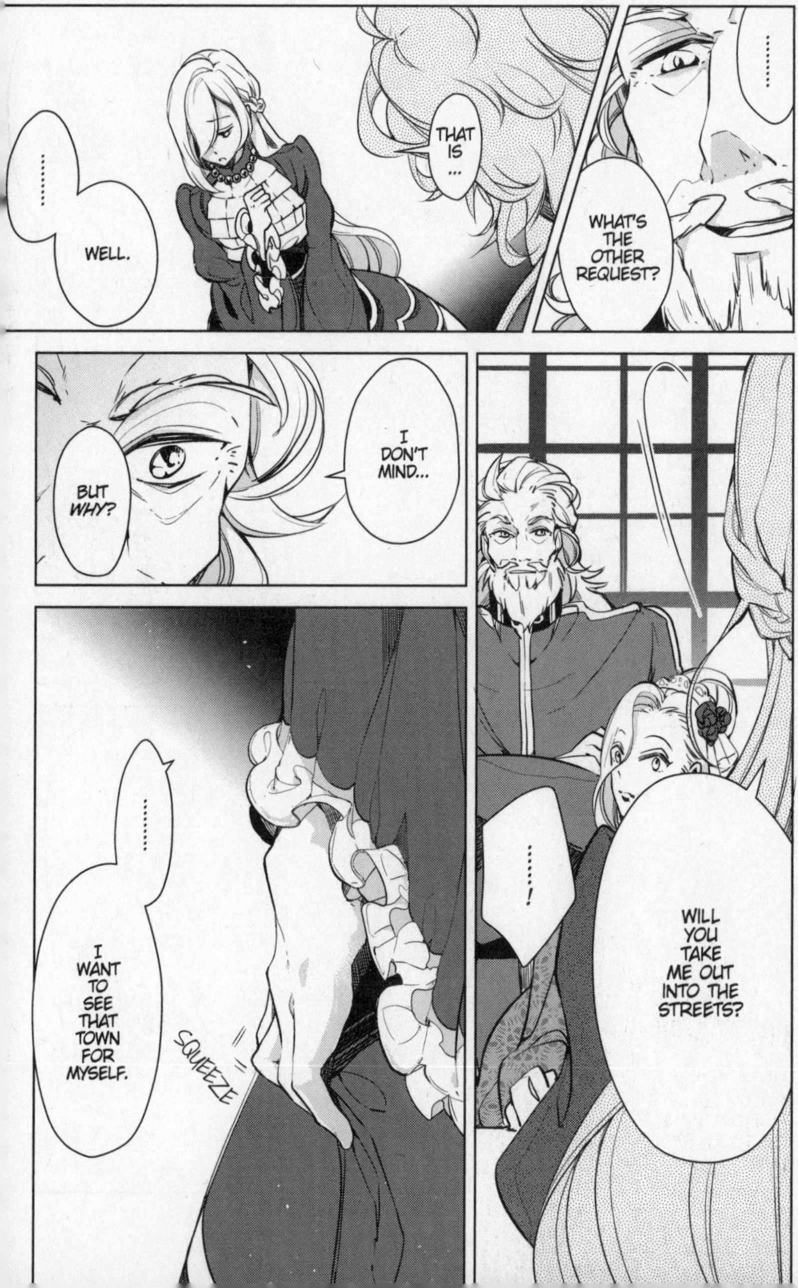
......
WHAT'S THE OTHER REQUEST?
THAT IS ...
......
WELL.
......!
WILL YOU TAKE ME OUT INTO THE STREETS?
I DON'T MIND...
BUT WHY?
......
I WANT TO SEE THAT TOWN FOR MYSELF.
SQUEEZE

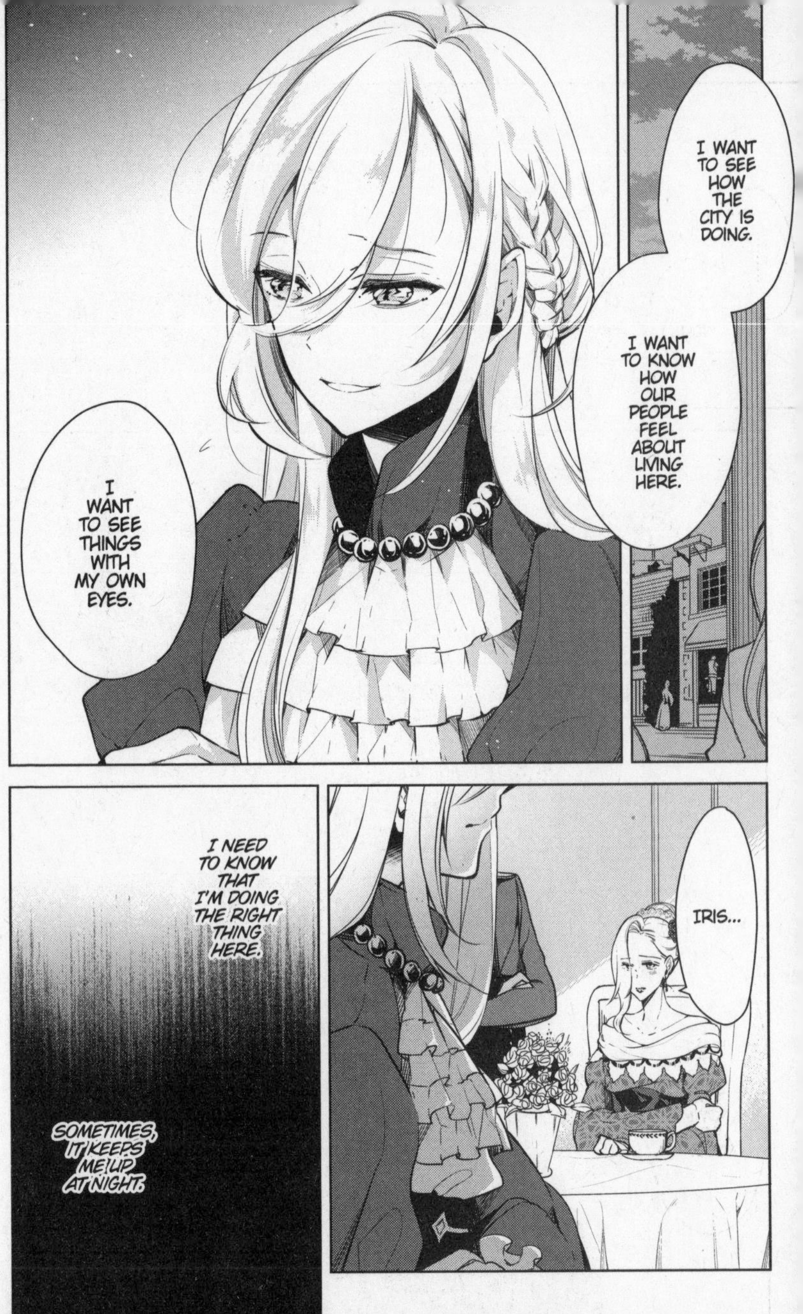
I WANT TO SEE HOW THE CITY IS DOING.
I WANT TO KNOW HOW OUR PEOPLE FEEL ABOUT LIVING HERE.
I WANT TO SEE THINGS WITH MY OWN EYES.
IRIS...
I NEED TO KNOW THAT I'M DOING THE RIGHT THING HERE.
SOMETIMES, IT KEEPS ME UP AT NIGHT.

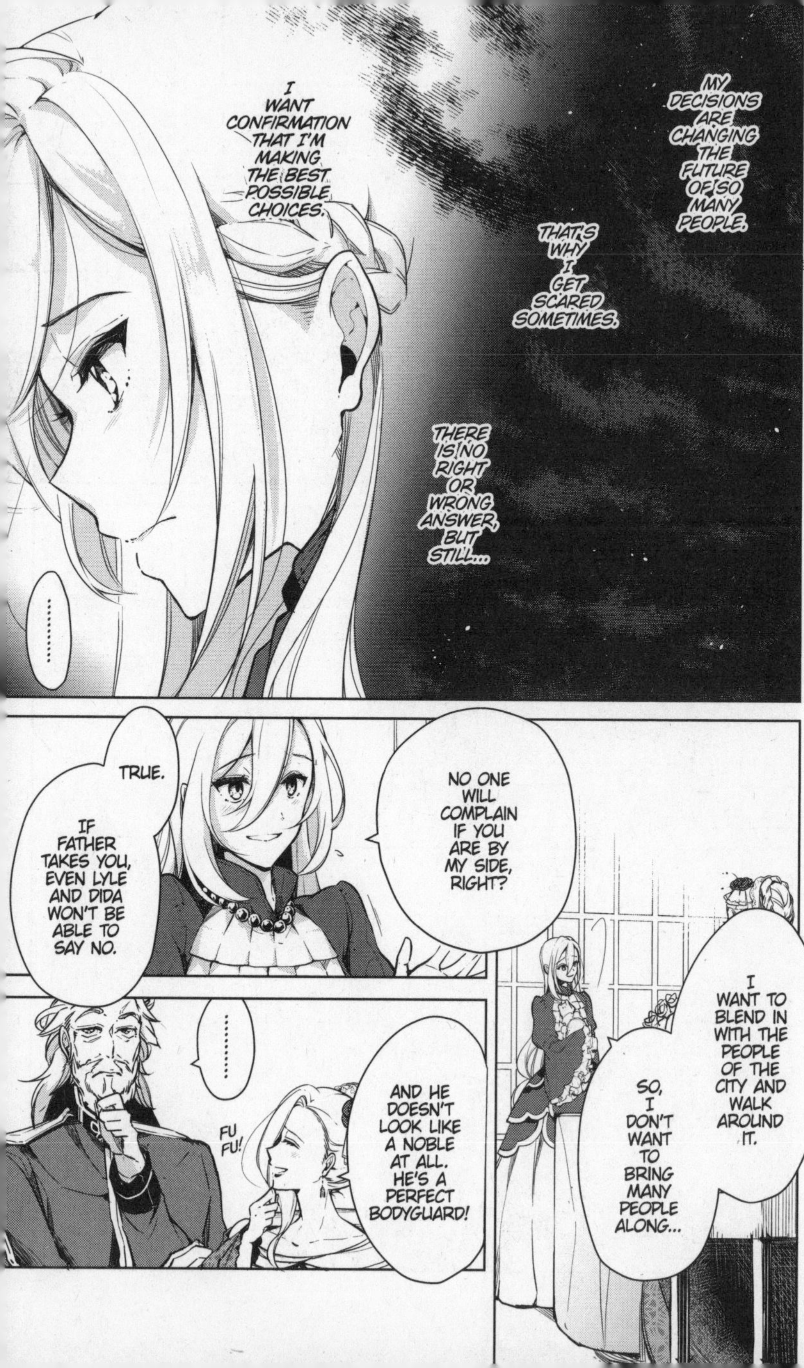
MY DECISIONS ARE CHANGING THE FUTURE OF SO MANY PEOPLE.
THAT'S WHY I GET SCARED SOMETIMES.
THERE IS NO RIGHT OR WRONG ANSWER, BUT STILL...
I WANT CONFIRMATION THAT I'M MAKING THE BEST POSSIBLE CHOICES.
......
I WANT TO BLEND IN WITH THE PEOPLE OF THE CITY AND WALK AROUND IT.
SO, I DON'T WANT TO BRING MANY PEOPLE ALONG...
NO ONE WILL COMPLAIN IF YOU ARE BY MY SIDE, RIGHT?
TRUE.
IF FATHER TAKES YOU, EVEN LYLE AND DIDA WON'T BE ABLE TO SAY NO.
AND HE DOESN'T LOOK LIKE A NOBLE AT ALL. HE'S A PERFECT BODYGUARD!
FU FU!
......

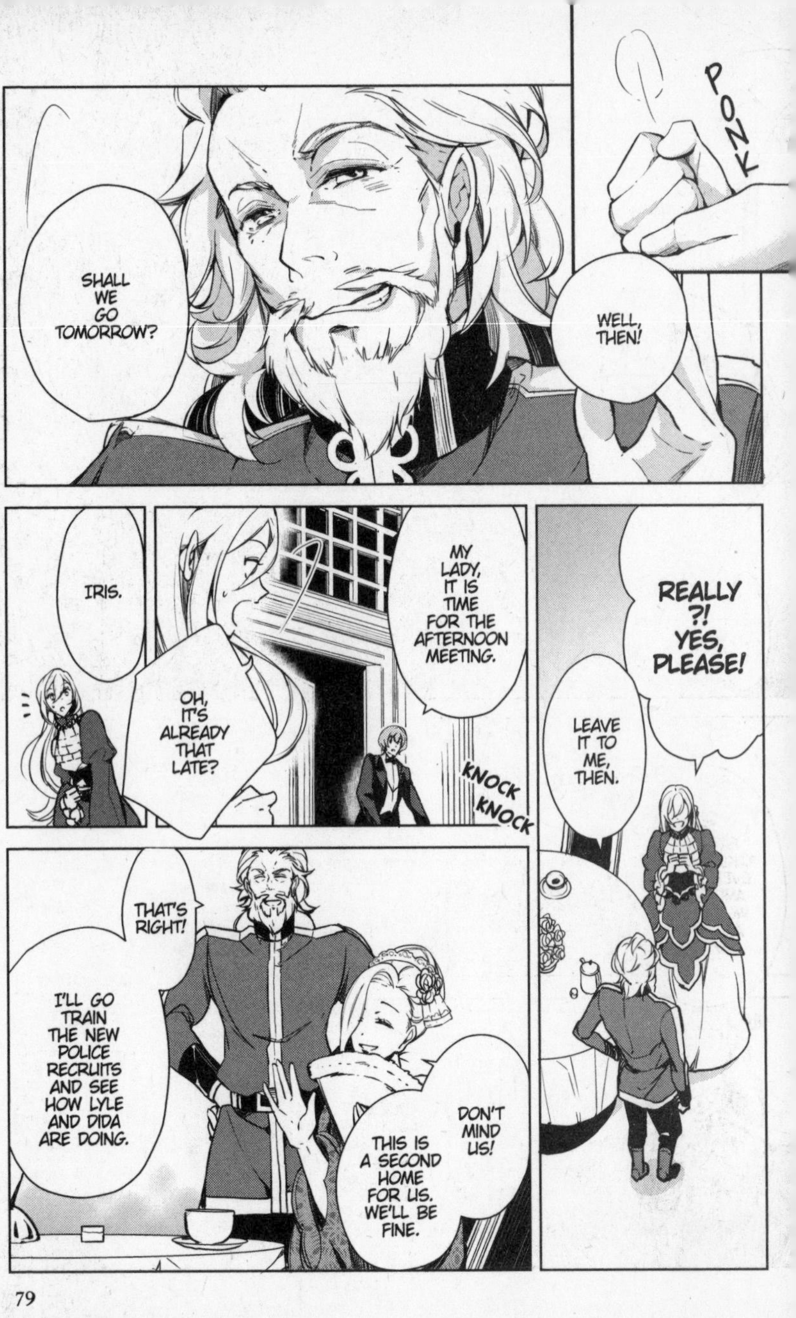
PONK
WELL, THEN!
SHALL WE GO TOMORROW?
REALLY ?! YES, PLEASE!
LEAVE IT TO ME, THEN.
MY LADY, IT IS TIME FOR THE AFTERNOON MEETING.
KNOCK KNOCK
OH, IT'S ALREADY THAT LATE?
IRIS.
THAT'S RIGHT!
I'LL GO TRAIN THE NEW POLICE RECRUITS AND SEE HOW LYLE AND DIDA ARE DOING.
DON'T MIND US!
THIS IS A SECOND HOME FOR US. WE'LL BE FINE.

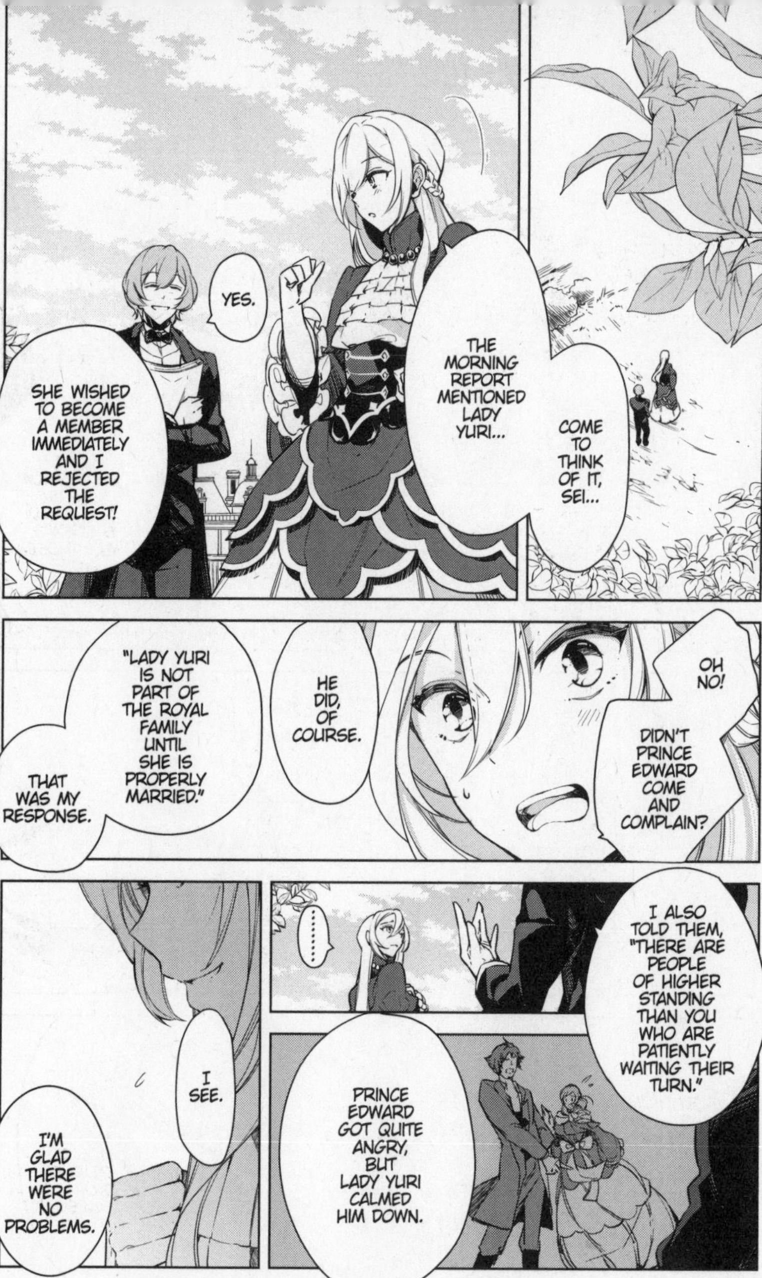
COME TO THINK OF IT, SEI...
THE MORNING REPORT MENTIONED LADY YURI...
YES.
SHE WISHED TO BECOME A MEMBER IMMEDIATELY AND I REJECTED THE REQUEST!
OH NO!
DIDN'T PRINCE EDWARD COME AND COMPLAIN?
HE DID, OF COURSE.
"LADY YURI IS NOT PART OF THE ROYAL FAMILY UNTIL SHE IS PROPERLY MARRIED."
THAT WAS MY RESPONSE.
I ALSO TOLD THEM, "THERE ARE PEOPLE OF HIGHER STANDING THAN YOU WHO ARE PATIENTLY WAITING THEIR TURN."
....
PRINCE EDWARD GOT QUITE ANGRY, BUT LADY YURI CALMED HIM DOWN.
I SEE.
I'M GLAD THERE WERE NO PROBLEMS.

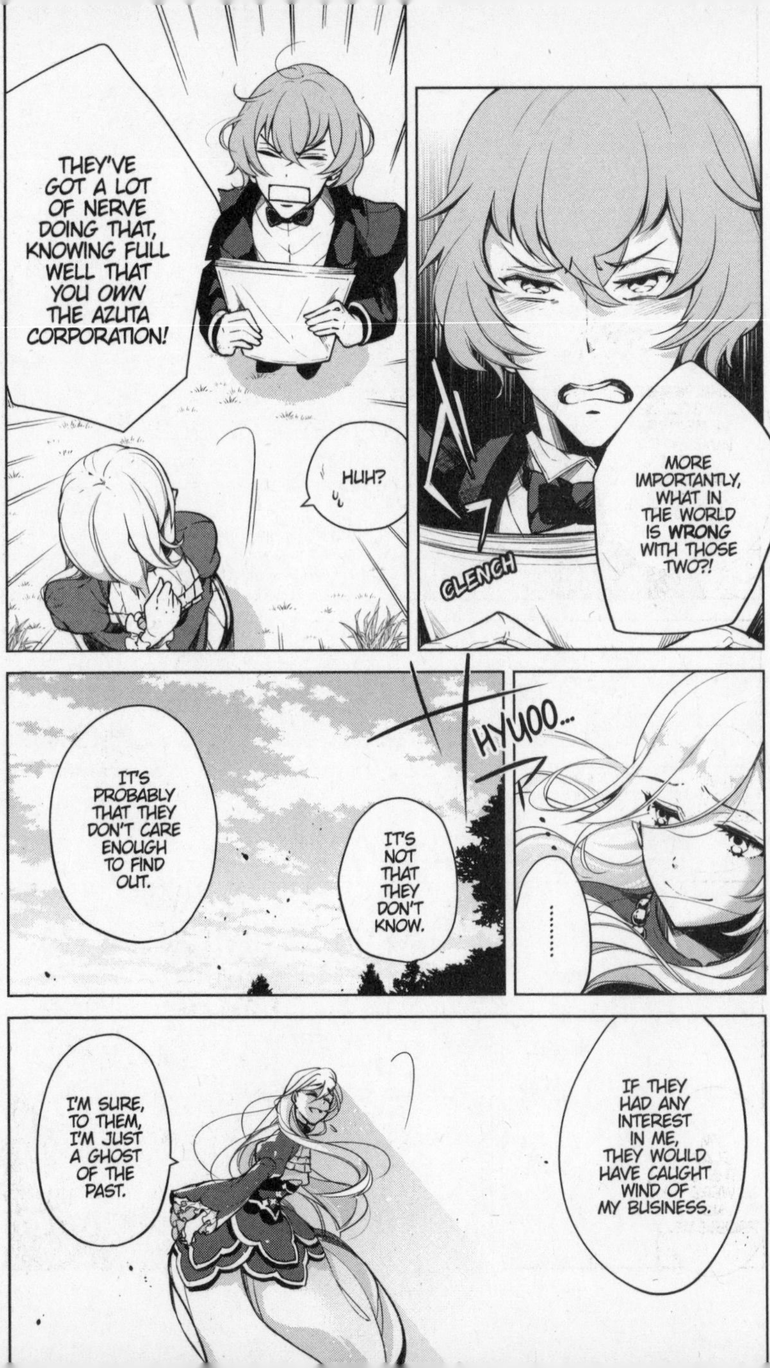
MORE IMPORTANTLY, WHAT IN THE WORLD IS WRONG WITH THOSE TWO?!
CLENCH
THEY'VE GOT A LOT OF NERVE DOING THAT, KNOWING FULL WELL THAT YOU OWN THE AZUTA CORPORATION!
HUH?
HYUOO...
......
IT'S NOT THAT THEY DON'T KNOW.
IT'S PROBABLY THAT THEY DON'T CARE ENOUGH TO FIND OUT.
IF THEY HAD ANY INTEREST IN ME, THEY WOULD HAVE CAUGHT WIND OF MY BUSINESS.
I'M SURE, TO THEM, I'M JUST A GHOST OF THE PAST.

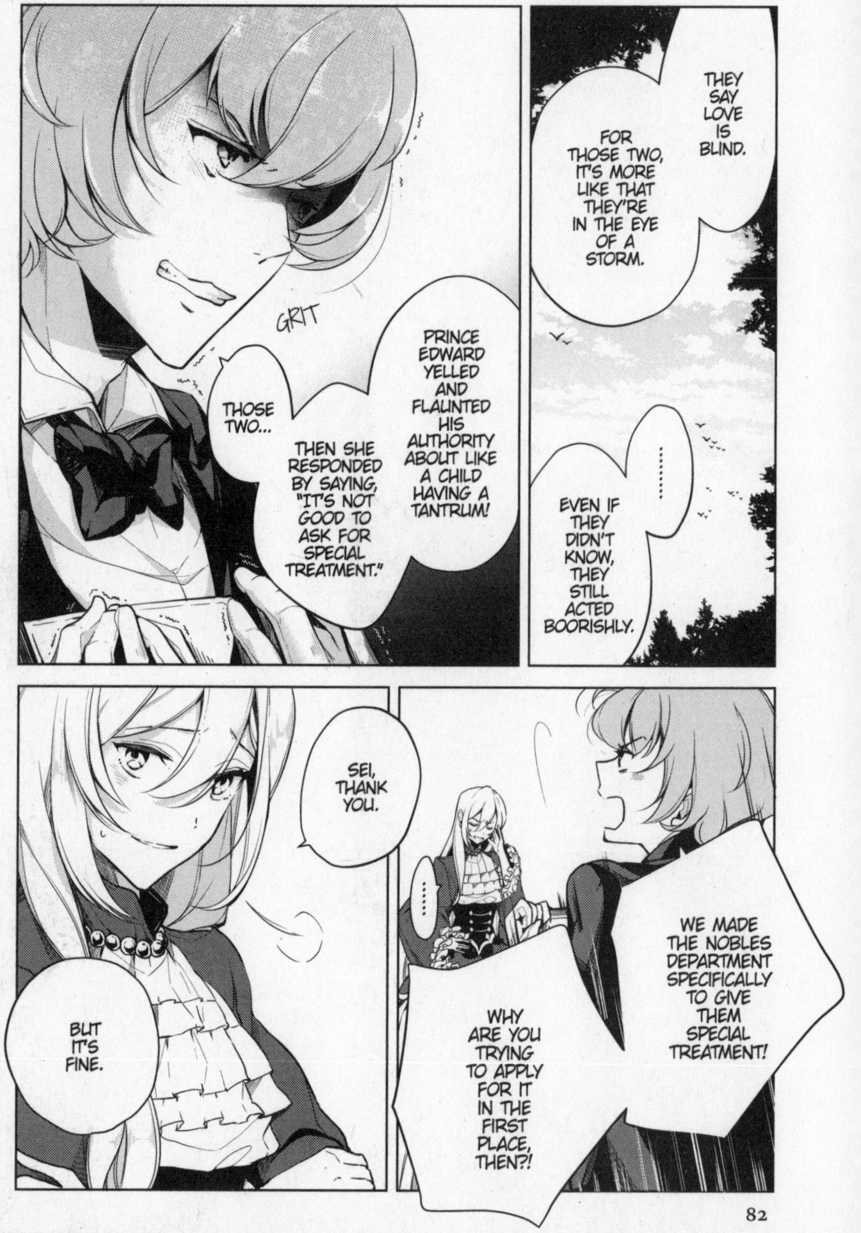
THEY SAY LOVE IS BLIND.
FOR THOSE TWO, IT'S MORE LIKE THAT THEY'RE IN THE EYE OF A STORM.
......
EVEN IF THEY DIDN'T KNOW, THEY STILL ACTED BOORISHLY.
GRIT
PRINCE EDWARD YELLED AND FLAUNTED HIS AUTHORITY ABOUT LIKE A CHILD HAVING A TANTRUM!
THEN SHE RESPONDED BY SAYING, "IT'S NOT GOOD TO ASK FOR SPECIAL TREATMENT."
THOSE TWO...
WE MADE THE NOBLES DEPARTMENT SPECIFICALLY TO GIVE THEM SPECIAL TREATMENT!
WHY ARE YOU TRYING TO APPLY FOR IT IN THE FIRST PLACE, THEN?!
......
SEI, THANK YOU.
BUT IT'S FINE.

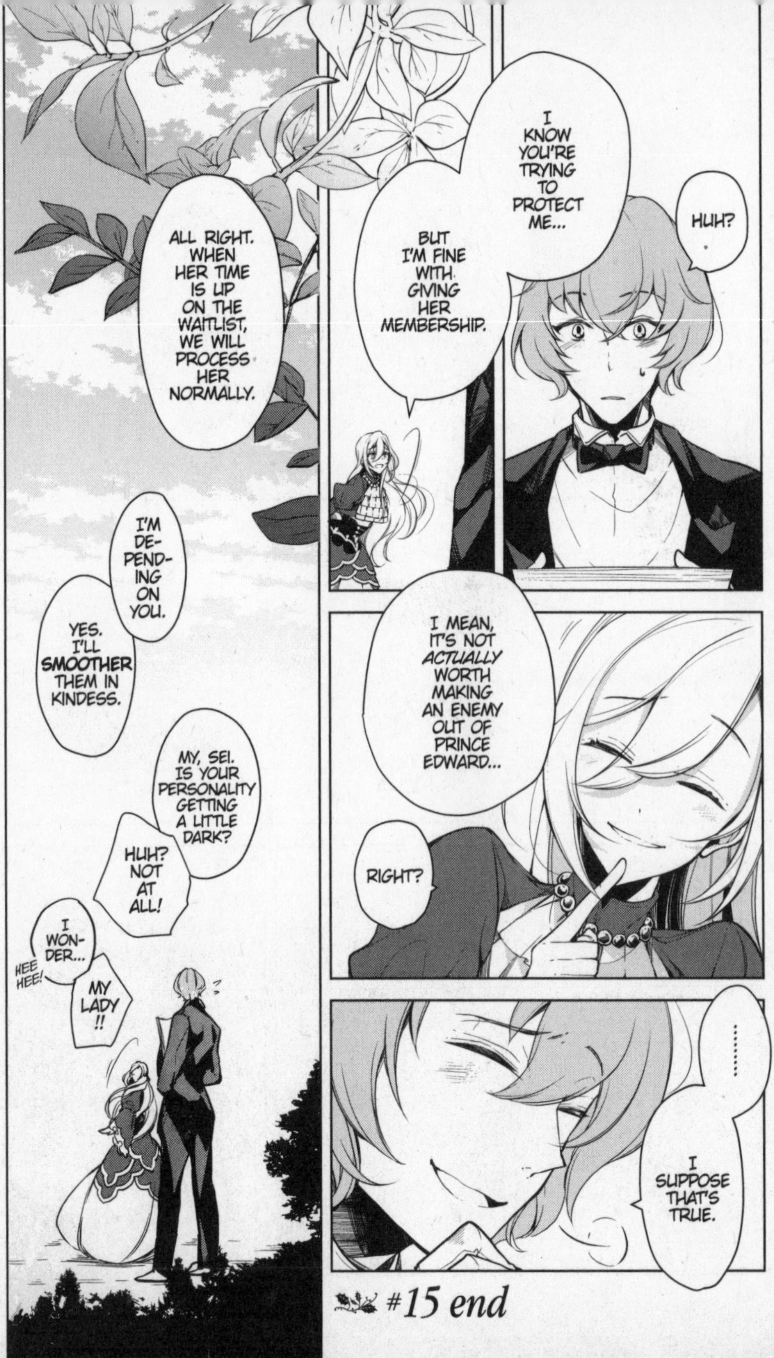
HUH?
I KNOW YOU'RE TRYING TO PROTECT ME...
BUT I'M FINE WITH GIVING HER MEMBERSHIP.
I MEAN, IT'S NOT ACTUALLY WORTH MAKING AN ENEMY OUT OF PRINCE EDWARD...
RIGHT?
......
I SUPPOSE THAT'S TRUE.
ALL RIGHT. WHEN HER TIME IS UP ON THE WAITLIST, WE WILL PROCESS HER NORMALLY.
I'M DE-PEND-ING ON YOU.
YES. I'LL SMOOTHER THEM IN KINDESS.
MY, SEI. IS YOUR PERSONALITY GETTING A LITTLE DARK?
HUH? NOT AT ALL!
I WON-DER...
HEE HEE!
MY LADY!!

#15 end

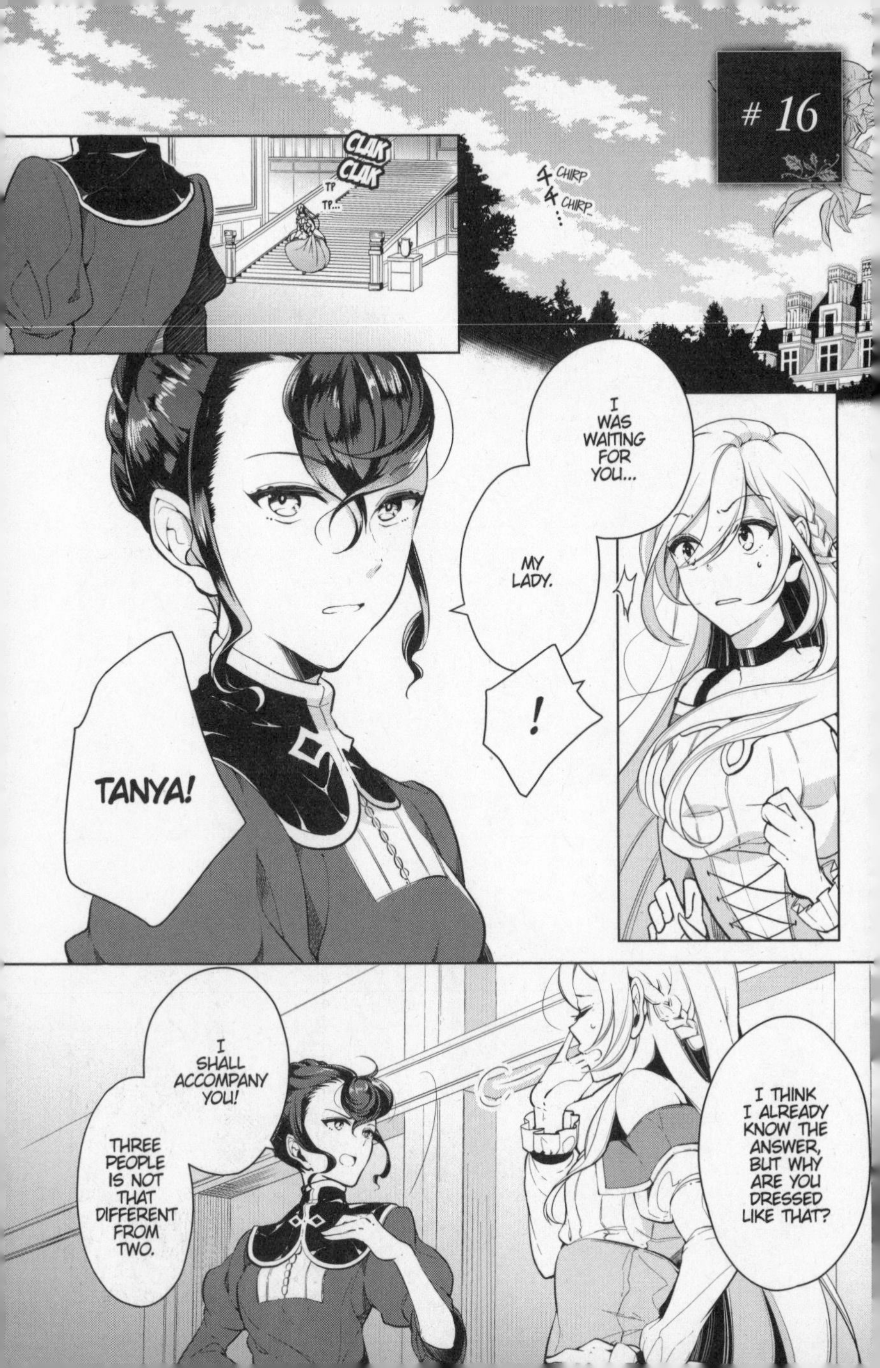

16
CHIRP
CHIRP...
CLAK
CLAK
TP
TP...
I WAS WAITING FOR YOU...
MY LADY.
!
TANYA!
I THINK I ALREADY KNOW THE ANSWER, BUT WHY ARE YOU DRESSED LIKE THAT?
I SHALL ACCOMPANY YOU!
THREE PEOPLE IS NOT THAT DIFFERENT FROM TWO.

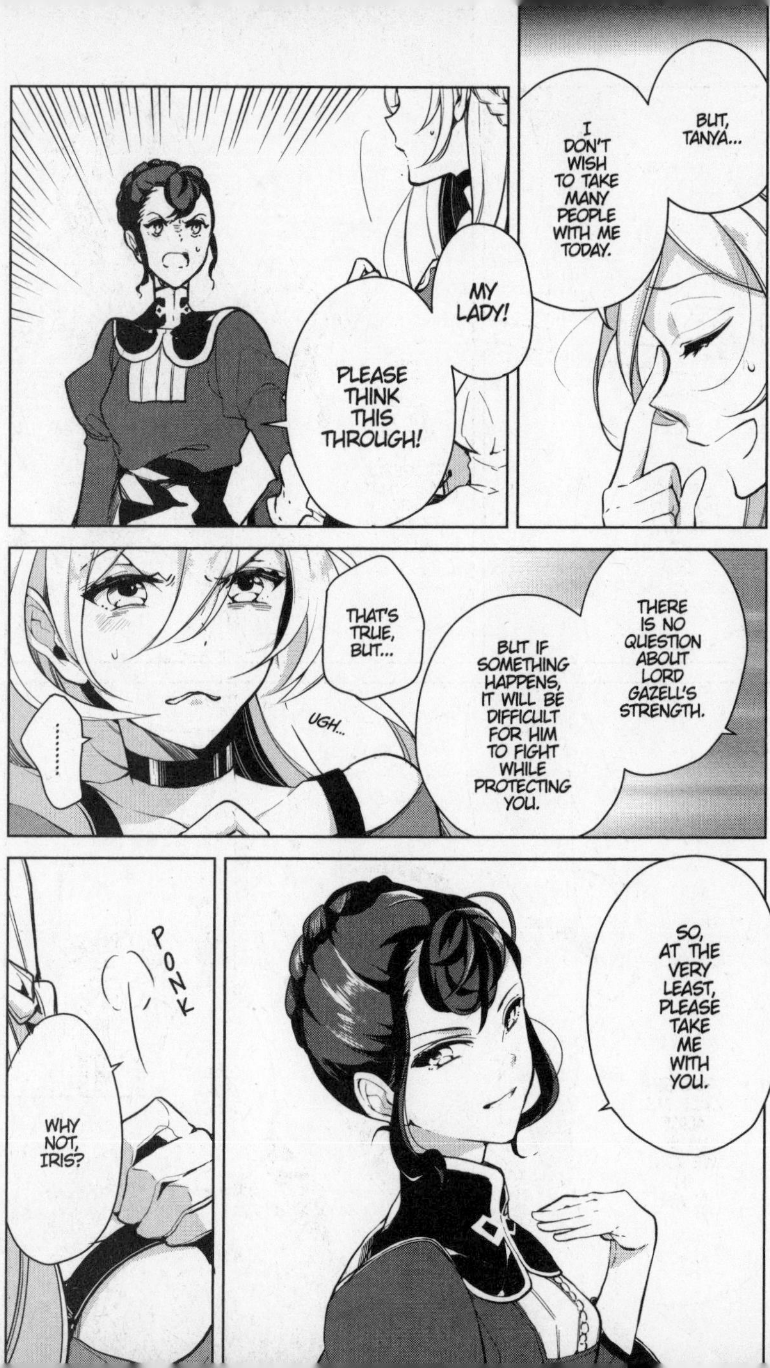
BUT, TANYA...
I DON'T WISH TO TAKE MANY PEOPLE WITH ME TODAY.
MY LADY!
PLEASE THINK THIS THROUGH!
THERE IS NO QUESTION ABOUT LORD GAZELL'S STRENGTH.
BUT IF SOMETHING HAPPENS, IT WILL BE DIFFICULT FOR HIM TO FIGHT WHILE PROTECTING YOU.
THAT'S TRUE, BUT...
UGH...
......
SO, AT THE VERY LEAST, PLEASE TAKE ME WITH YOU.
PONK
WHY NOT, IRIS?

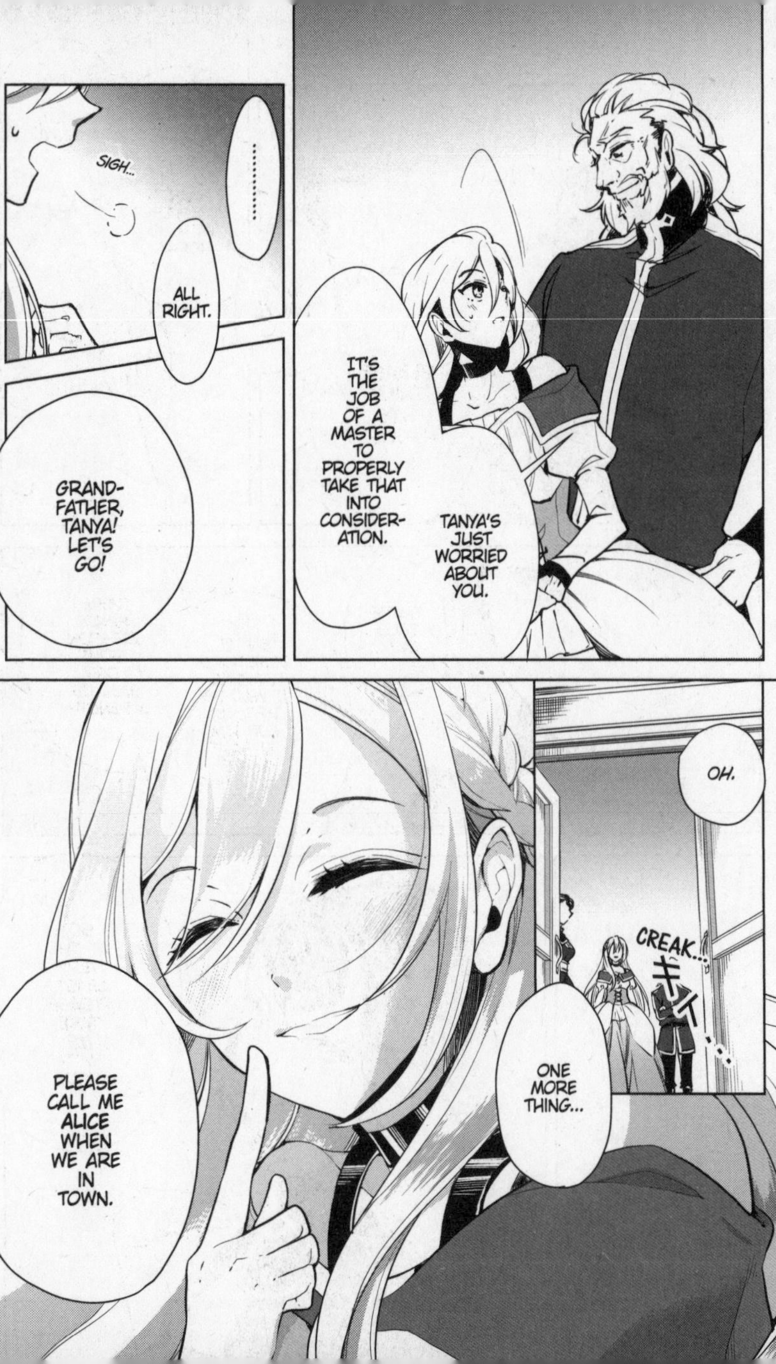
IT'S THE JOB OF A MASTER TO PROPERLY TAKE THAT INTO CONSIDER-ATION.
TANYA'S JUST WORRIED ABOUT YOU.
......
SIGH...
ALL RIGHT.
GRAND-FATHER, TANYA! LET'S GO!
OH.
CREAK...
キィ...
ONE MORE THING...
PLEASE CALL ME ALICE WHEN WE ARE IN TOWN.

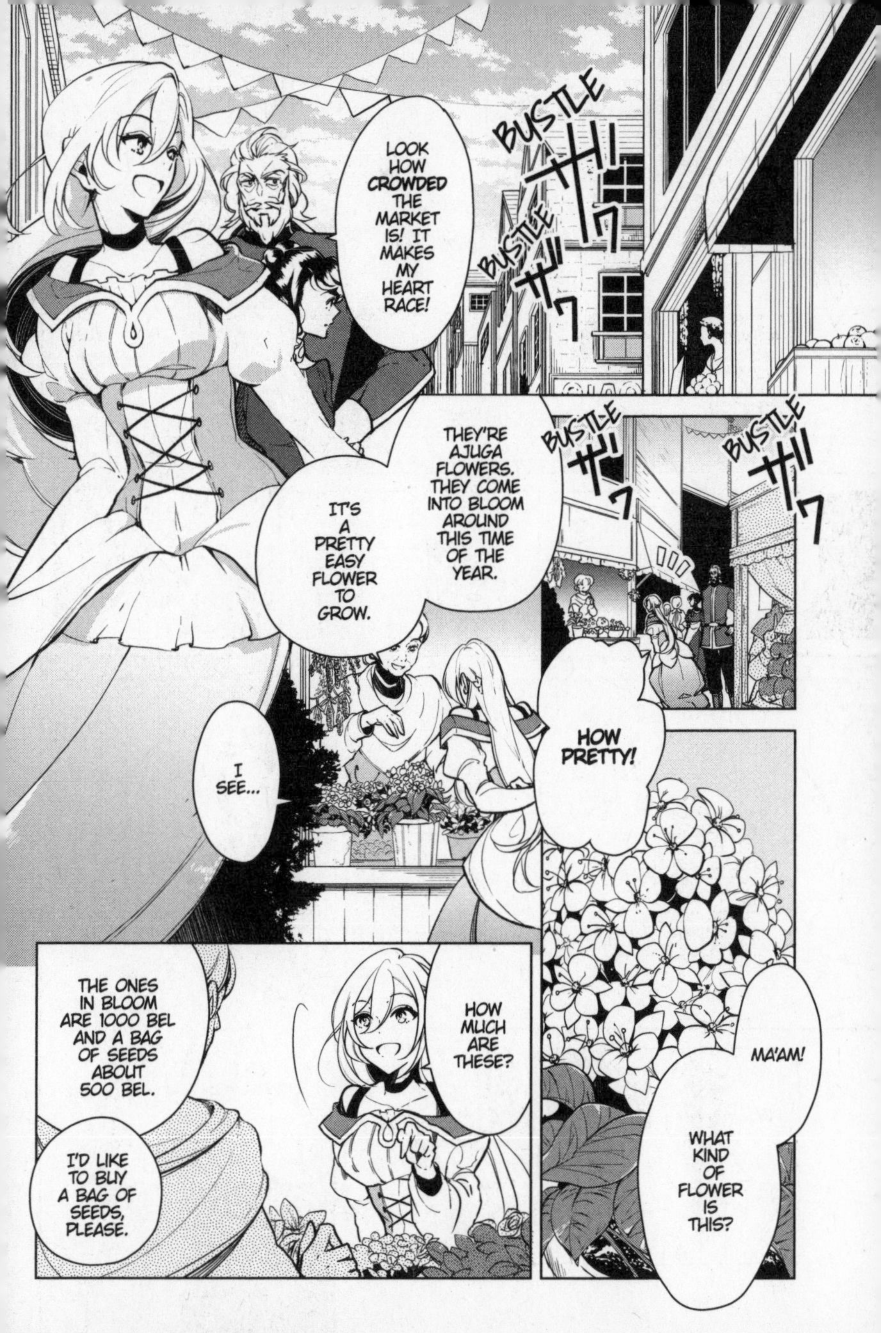
BUSTLE
BUSTLE
LOOK HOW CROWDED THE MARKET IS! IT MAKES MY HEART RACE!
BUSTLE
BUSTLE
HOW PRETTY!
MA'AM!
WHAT KIND OF FLOWER IS THIS?
THEY'RE AJUGA FLOWERS. THEY COME INTO BLOOM AROUND THIS TIME OF THE YEAR.
IT'S A PRETTY EASY FLOWER TO GROW.
I SEE...
HOW MUCH ARE THESE?
THE ONES IN BLOOM ARE 1000 BEL AND A BAG OF SEEDS ABOUT 500 BEL.
I'D LIKE TO BUY A BAG OF SEEDS, PLEASE.

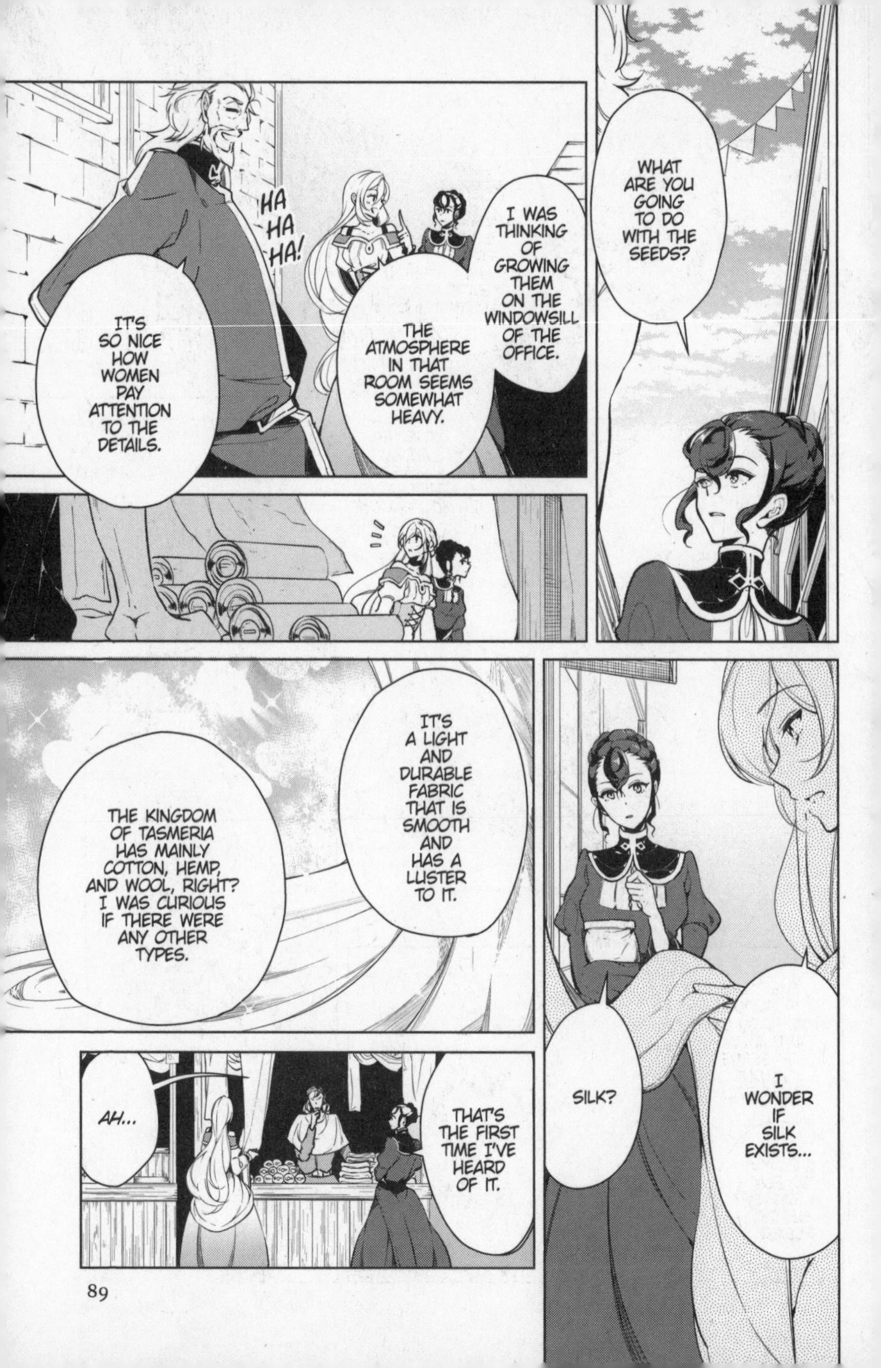
WHAT ARE YOU GOING TO DO WITH THE SEEDS?
I WAS THINKING OF GROWING THEM ON THE WINDOWSILL OF THE OFFICE.
THE ATMOSPHERE IN THAT ROOM SEEMS SOMEWHAT HEAVY.
HA HA HA!
IT'S SO NICE HOW WOMEN PAY ATTENTION TO THE DETAILS.
I WONDER IF SILK EXISTS...
SILK?
IT'S A LIGHT AND DURABLE FABRIC THAT IS SMOOTH AND HAS A LUSTER TO IT.
THE KINGDOM OF TASMERIA HAS MAINLY COTTON, HEMP, AND WOOL, RIGHT? I WAS CURIOUS IF THERE WERE ANY OTHER TYPES.
THAT'S THE FIRST TIME I'VE HEARD OF IT.
AH...

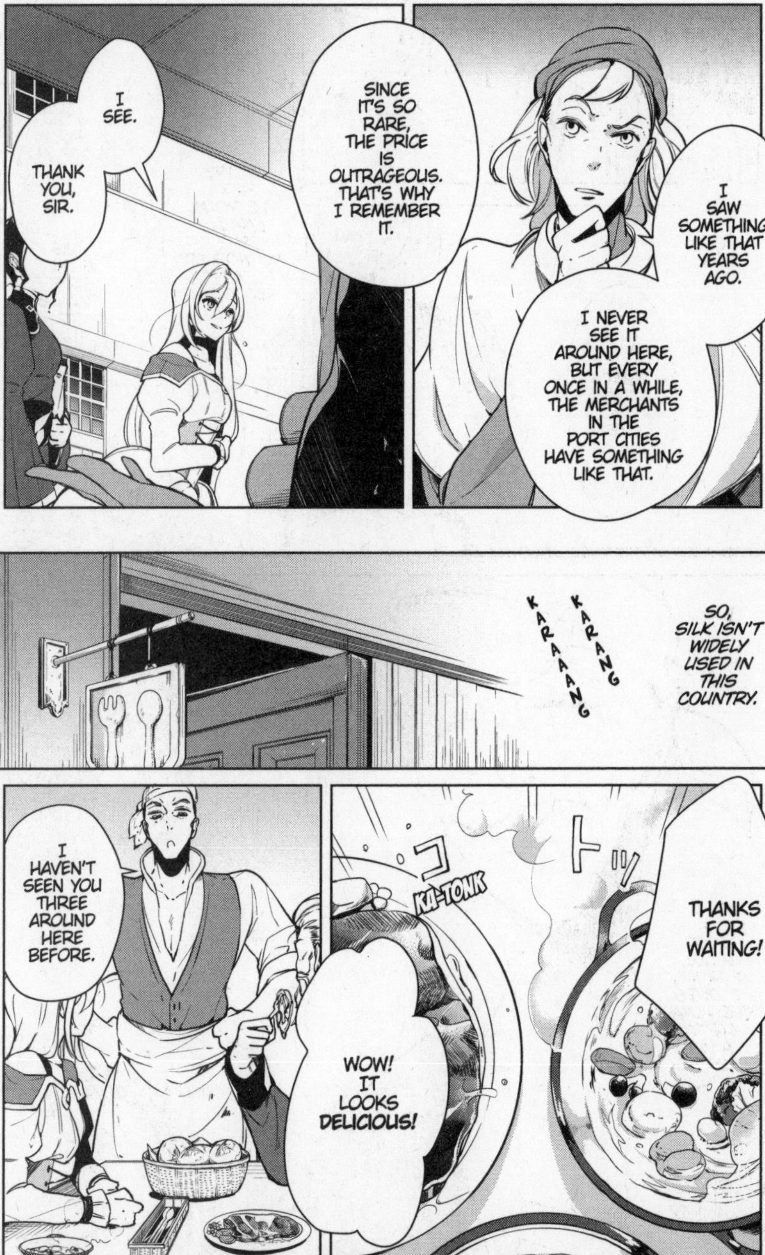
I SAW SOMETHING LIKE THAT YEARS AGO.
I NEVER SEE IT AROUND HERE, BUT EVERY ONCE IN A WHILE, THE MERCHANTS IN THE PORT CITIES HAVE SOMETHING LIKE THAT.
SINCE IT'S SO RARE, THE PRICE IS OUTRAGEOUS. THAT'S WHY I REMEMBER IT.
I SEE.
THANK YOU, SIR.
SO, SILK ISN'T WIDELY USED IN THIS COUNTRY.
KARANG
KARAAANG
THANKS FOR WAITING!
KA-TONK
WOW! IT LOOKS DELICIOUS!
I HAVEN'T SEEN YOU THREE AROUND HERE BEFORE.

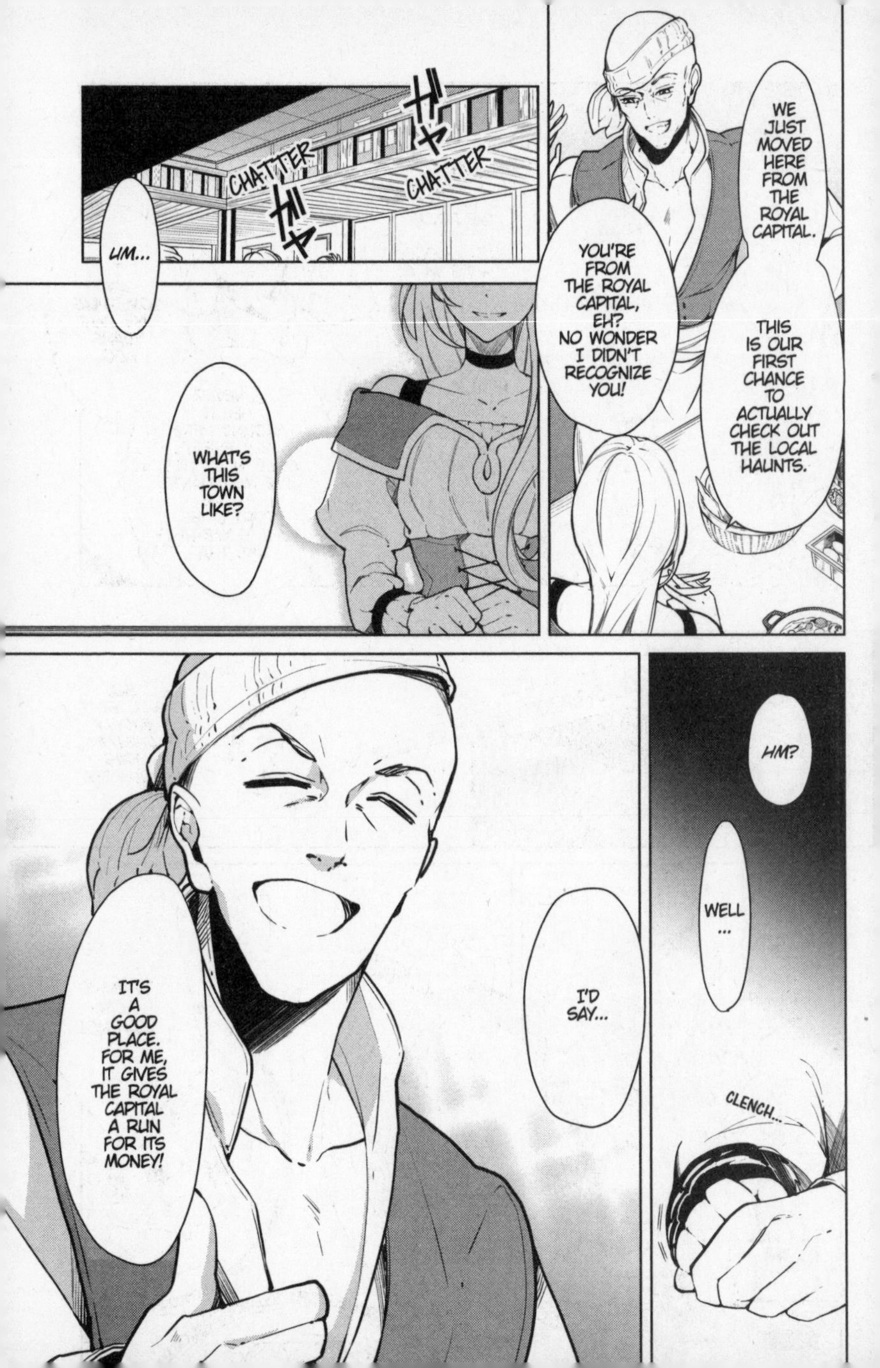
WE JUST MOVED HERE FROM THE ROYAL CAPITAL.
THIS IS OUR FIRST CHANCE TO ACTUALLY CHECK OUT THE LOCAL HAUNTS.
YOU'RE FROM THE ROYAL CAPITAL, EH? NO WONDER I DIDN'T RECOGNIZE YOU!
CHATTER
CHATTER
UM...
WHAT'S THIS TOWN LIKE?
HM?
WELL...
CLENCH...
I'D SAY...
IT'S A GOOD PLACE. FOR ME, IT GIVES THE ROYAL CAPITAL A RUN FOR ITS MONEY!

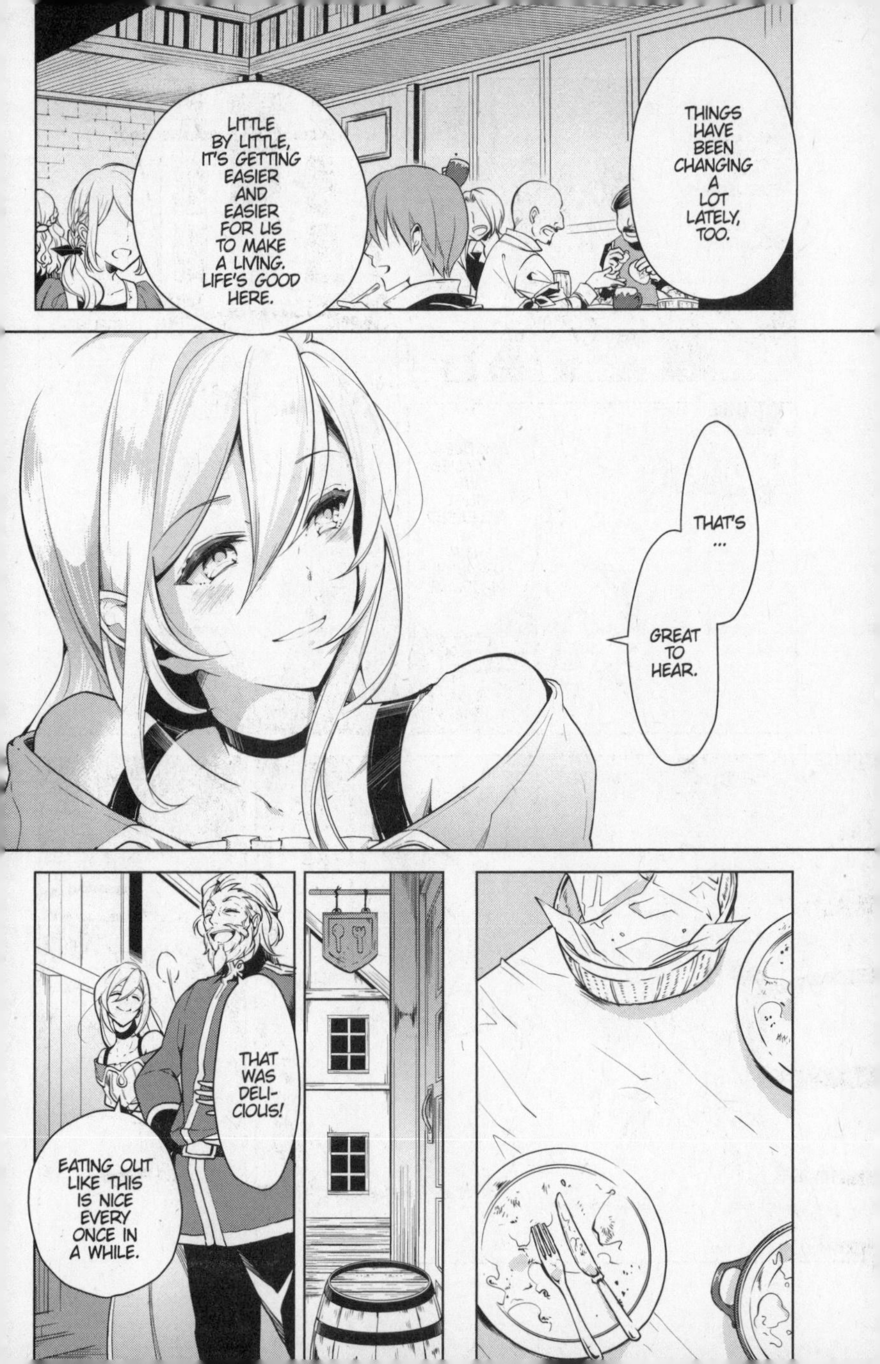
THINGS HAVE BEEN CHANGING A LOT LATELY, TOO.
LITTLE BY LITTLE, IT'S GETTING EASIER AND EASIER FOR US TO MAKE A LIVING. LIFE'S GOOD HERE.
THAT'S... GREAT TO HEAR.
THAT WAS DELI-CIOUS!
EATING OUT LIKE THIS IS NICE EVERY ONCE IN A WHILE.

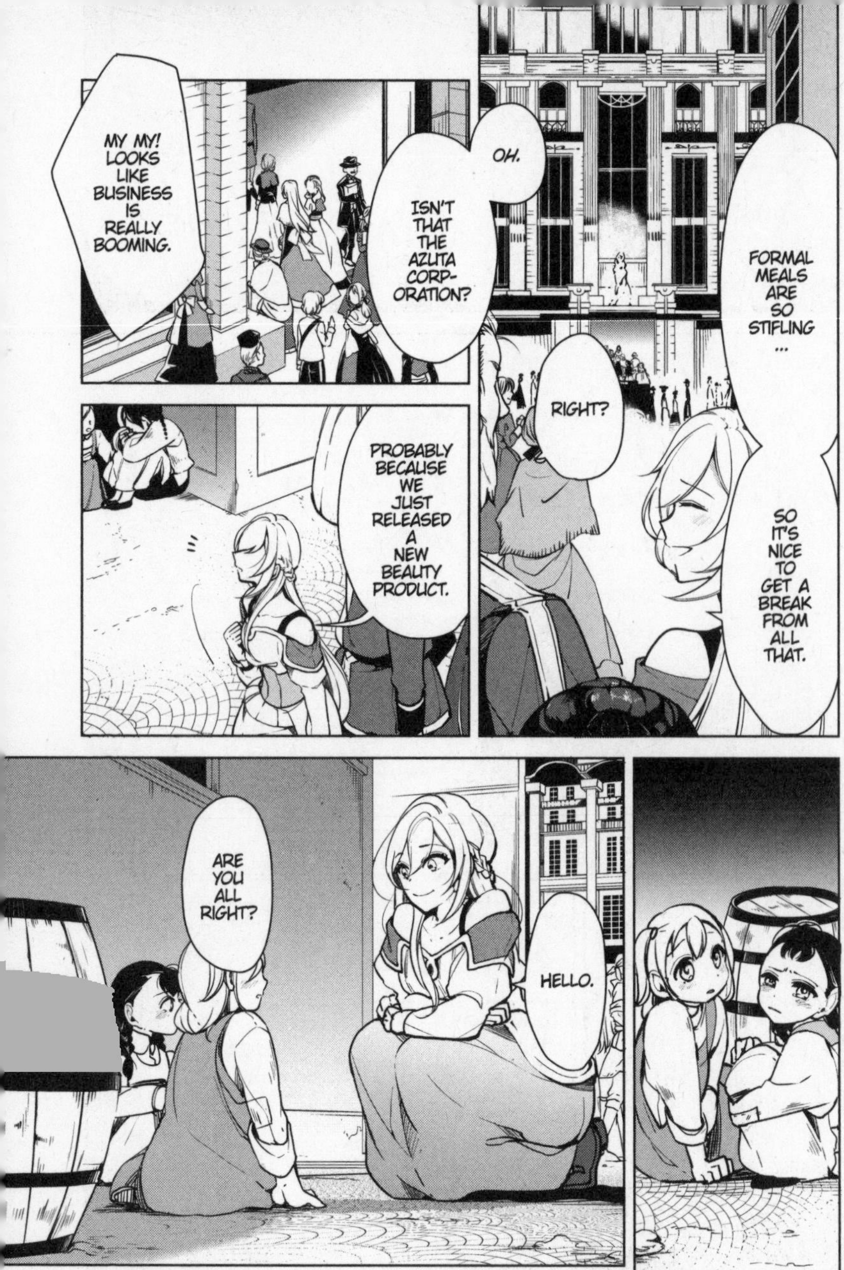
FORMAL MEALS ARE SO STIFLING ...
RIGHT?
SO IT'S NICE TO GET A BREAK FROM ALL THAT.
OH.
ISN'T THAT THE AZUTA CORP-ORATION?
MY MY! LOOKS LIKE BUSINESS IS REALLY BOOMING.
PROBABLY BECAUSE WE JUST RELEASED A NEW BEAUTY PRODUCT.
HELLO.
ARE YOU ALL RIGHT?

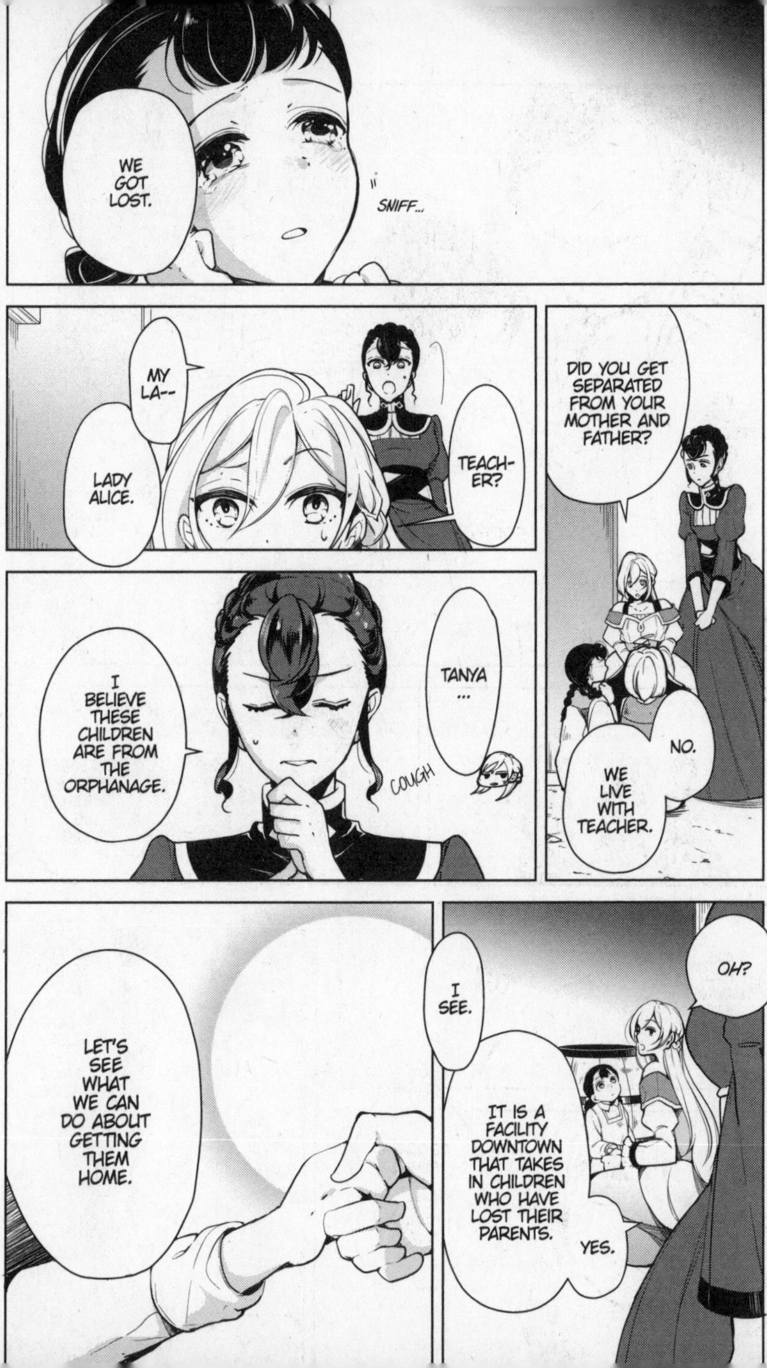
WE GOT LOST.
SNIFF...
DID YOU GET SEPARATED FROM YOUR MOTHER AND FATHER?
NO.
WE LIVE WITH TEACHER.
TEACHER?
MY LA--
LADY ALICE.
TANYA...
COUGH
I BELIEVE THESE CHILDREN ARE FROM THE ORPHANAGE.
OH?
YES.
IT IS A FACILITY DOWNTOWN THAT TAKES IN CHILDREN WHO HAVE LOST THEIR PARENTS.
I SEE.
LET'S SEE WHAT WE CAN DO ABOUT GETTING THEM HOME.

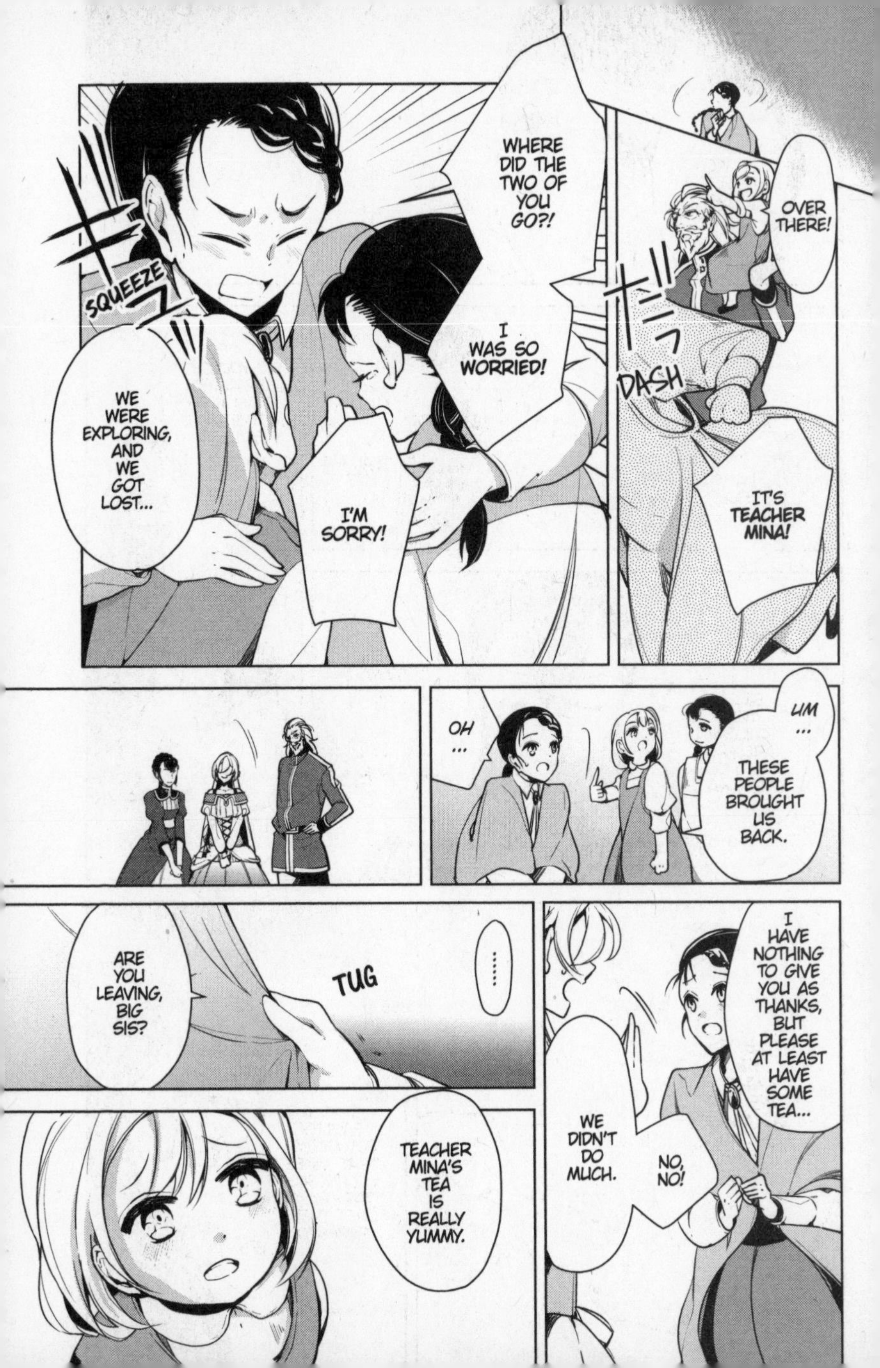
OVER THERE!
IT'S TEACHER MINA!
DASH
WHERE DID THE TWO OF YOU GO?!
I WAS SO WORRIED!
I'M SORRY!
SQUEEZE
WE WERE EXPLORING, AND WE GOT LOST...
UM ...
THESE PEOPLE BROUGHT US BACK.
OH ...
I HAVE NOTHING TO GIVE YOU AS THANKS, BUT PLEASE AT LEAST HAVE SOME TEA...
NO, NO!
WE DIDN'T DO MUCH.
TEACHER MINA'S TEA IS REALLY YUMMY.
......
TUG
ARE YOU LEAVING, BIG SIS?

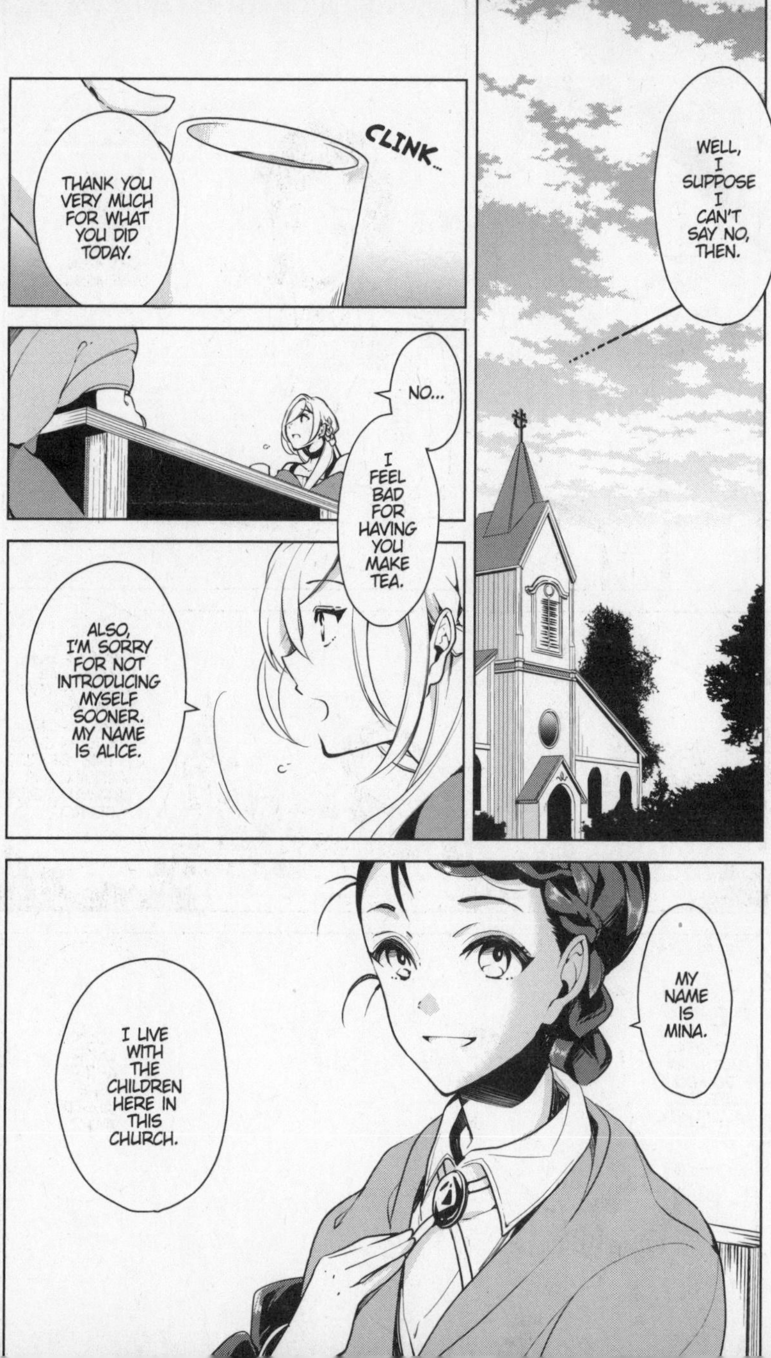
WELL, I SUPPOSE I CAN'T SAY NO, THEN.
CLINK...
THANK YOU VERY MUCH FOR WHAT YOU DID TODAY.
NO...
I FEEL BAD FOR HAVING YOU MAKE TEA.
ALSO, I'M SORRY FOR NOT INTRODUCING MYSELF SOONER. MY NAME IS ALICE.
MY NAME IS MINA.
I LIVE WITH THE CHILDREN HERE IN THIS CHURCH.

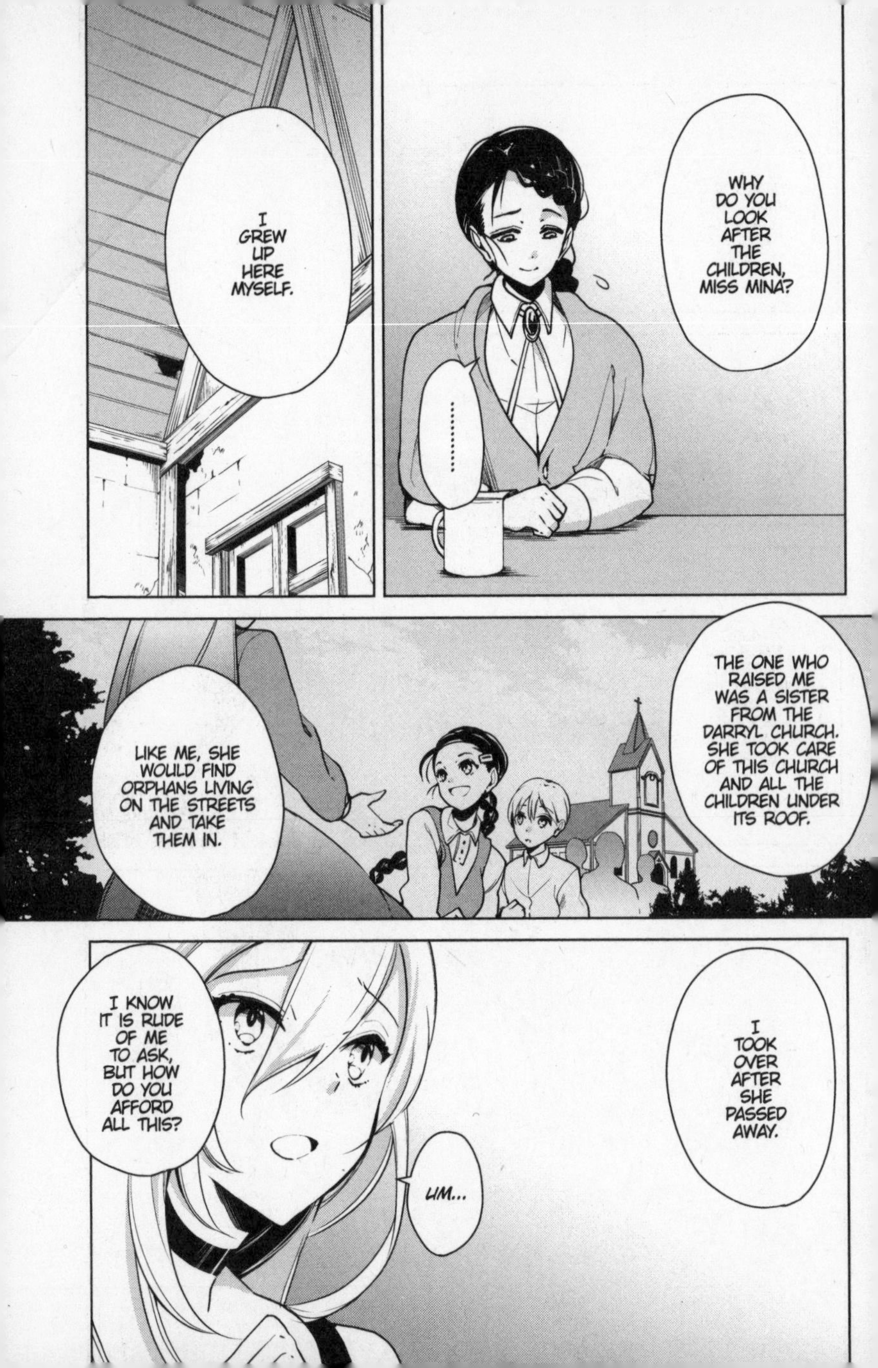
WHY DO YOU LOOK AFTER THE CHILDREN, MISS MINA?
......
I GREW UP HERE MYSELF.
THE ONE WHO RAISED ME WAS A SISTER FROM THE DARRYL CHURCH. SHE TOOK CARE OF THIS CHURCH AND ALL THE CHILDREN UNDER ITS ROOF.
LIKE ME, SHE WOULD FIND ORPHANS LIVING ON THE STREETS AND TAKE THEM IN.
I TOOK OVER AFTER SHE PASSED AWAY.
UM...
I KNOW IT IS RUDE OF ME TO ASK, BUT HOW DO YOU AFFORD ALL THIS?

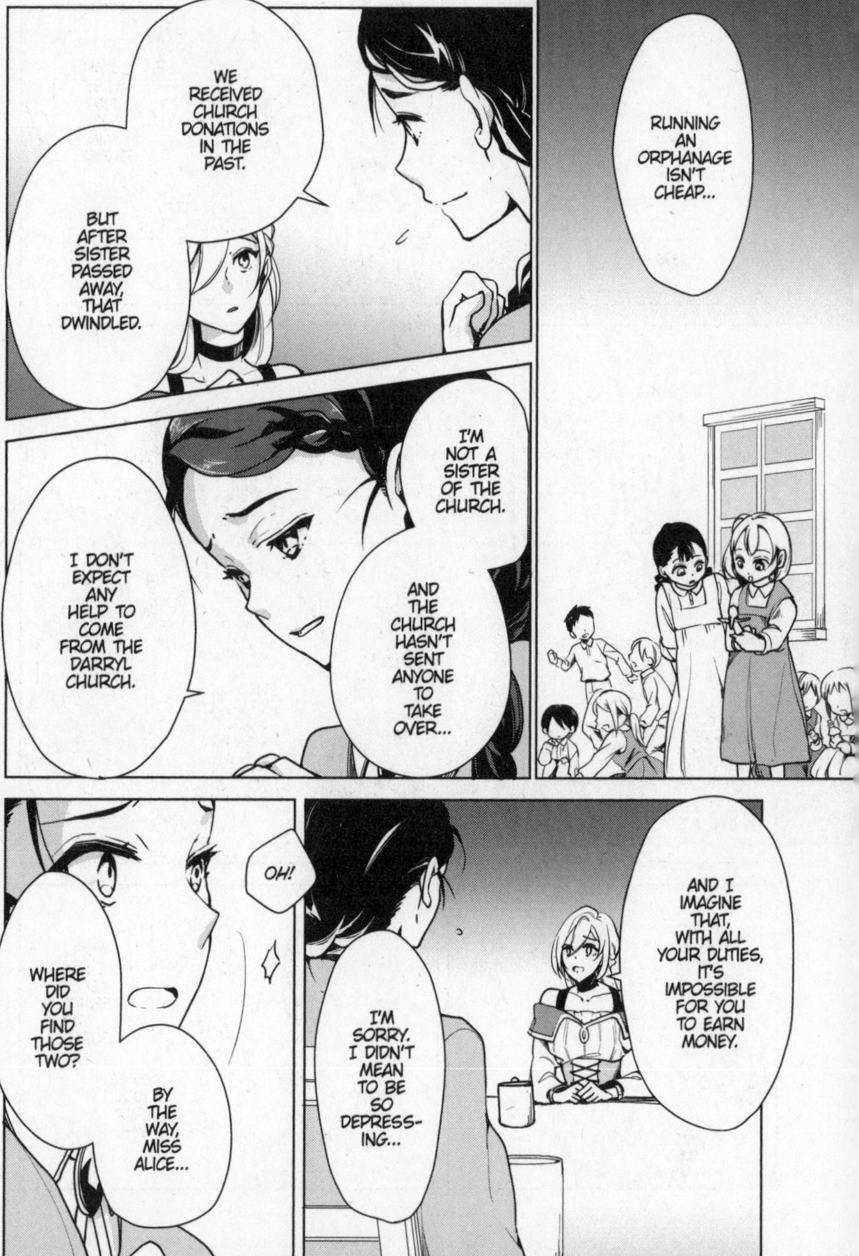
RUNNING AN ORPHANAGE ISN'T CHEAP...
WE RECEIVED CHURCH DONATIONS IN THE PAST.
BUT AFTER SISTER PASSED AWAY, THAT DWINDLED.
I'M NOT A SISTER OF THE CHURCH.
AND THE CHURCH HASN'T SENT ANYONE TO TAKE OVER...
I DON'T EXPECT ANY HELP TO COME FROM THE DARRYL CHURCH.
AND I IMAGINE THAT, WITH ALL YOUR DUTIES, IT'S IMPOSSIBLE FOR YOU TO EARN MONEY.
I'M SORRY. I DIDN'T MEAN TO BE SO DEPRESS-ING...
OH!
BY THE WAY, MISS ALICE...
WHERE DID YOU FIND THOSE TWO?

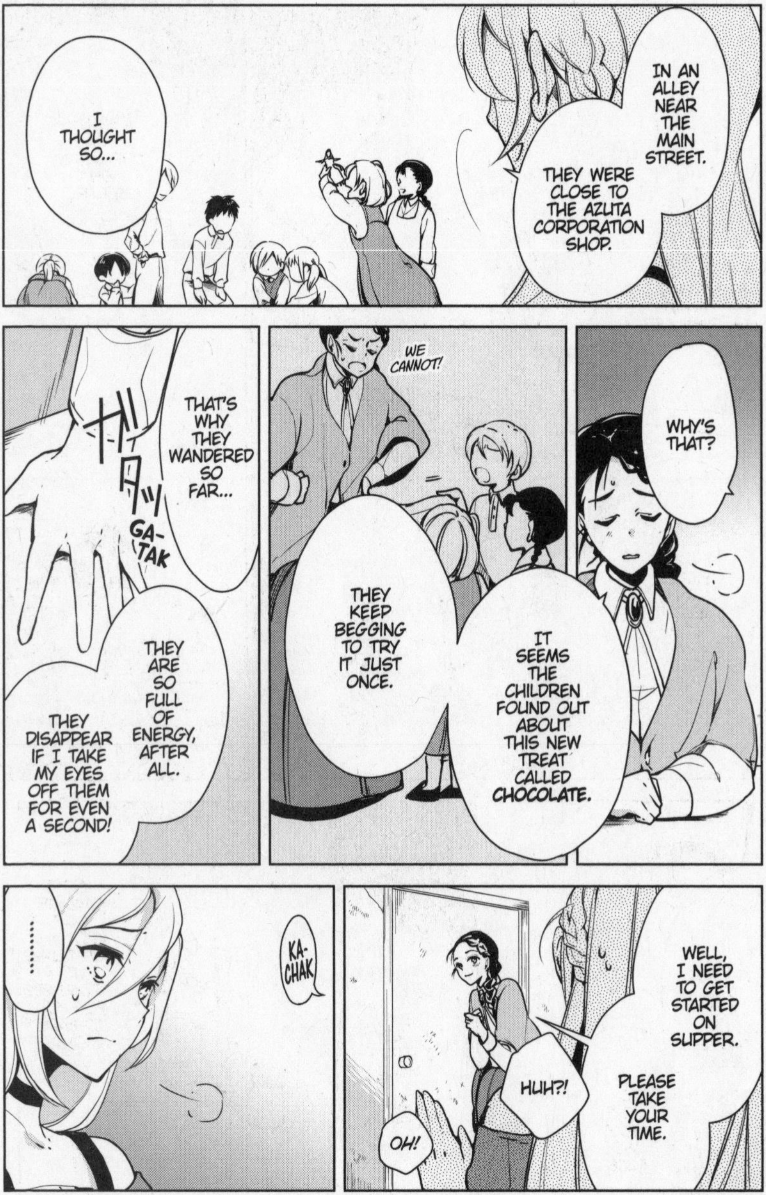
IN AN ALLEY NEAR THE MAIN STREET.
THEY WERE CLOSE TO THE AZUTA CORPORATION SHOP.
I THOUGHT SO...
WHY'S THAT?
IT SEEMS THE CHILDREN FOUND OUT ABOUT THIS NEW TREAT CALLED CHOCOLATE.
WE CANNOT!
THEY KEEP BEGGING TO TRY IT JUST ONCE.
THAT'S WHY THEY WANDERED SO FAR...
GA-TAK
THEY ARE SO FULL OF ENERGY, AFTER ALL.
THEY DISAPPEAR IF I TAKE MY EYES OFF THEM FOR EVEN A SECOND!
WELL, I NEED TO GET STARTED ON SUPPER.
PLEASE TAKE YOUR TIME.
HUH?!
OH!
KA-CHAK
....

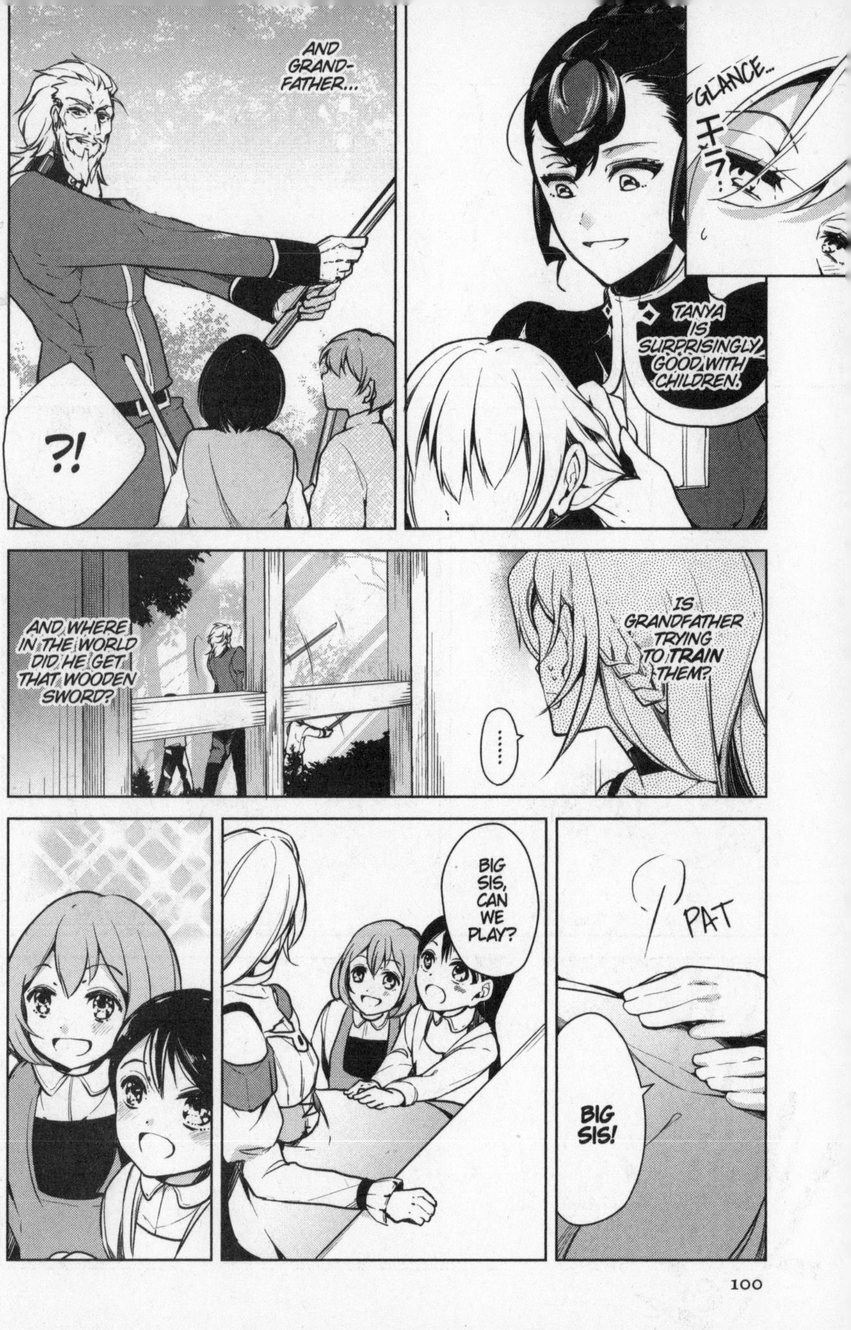
GLANCE...
チラ…
TANYA IS SURPRISINGLY GOOD WITH CHILDREN.
AND GRAND-FATHER...
?!
IS GRANDFATHER TRYING TO TRAIN THEM?
......
AND WHERE IN THE WORLD DID HE GET THAT WOODEN SWORD?
PAT
BIG SIS!
BIG SIS, CAN WE PLAY?

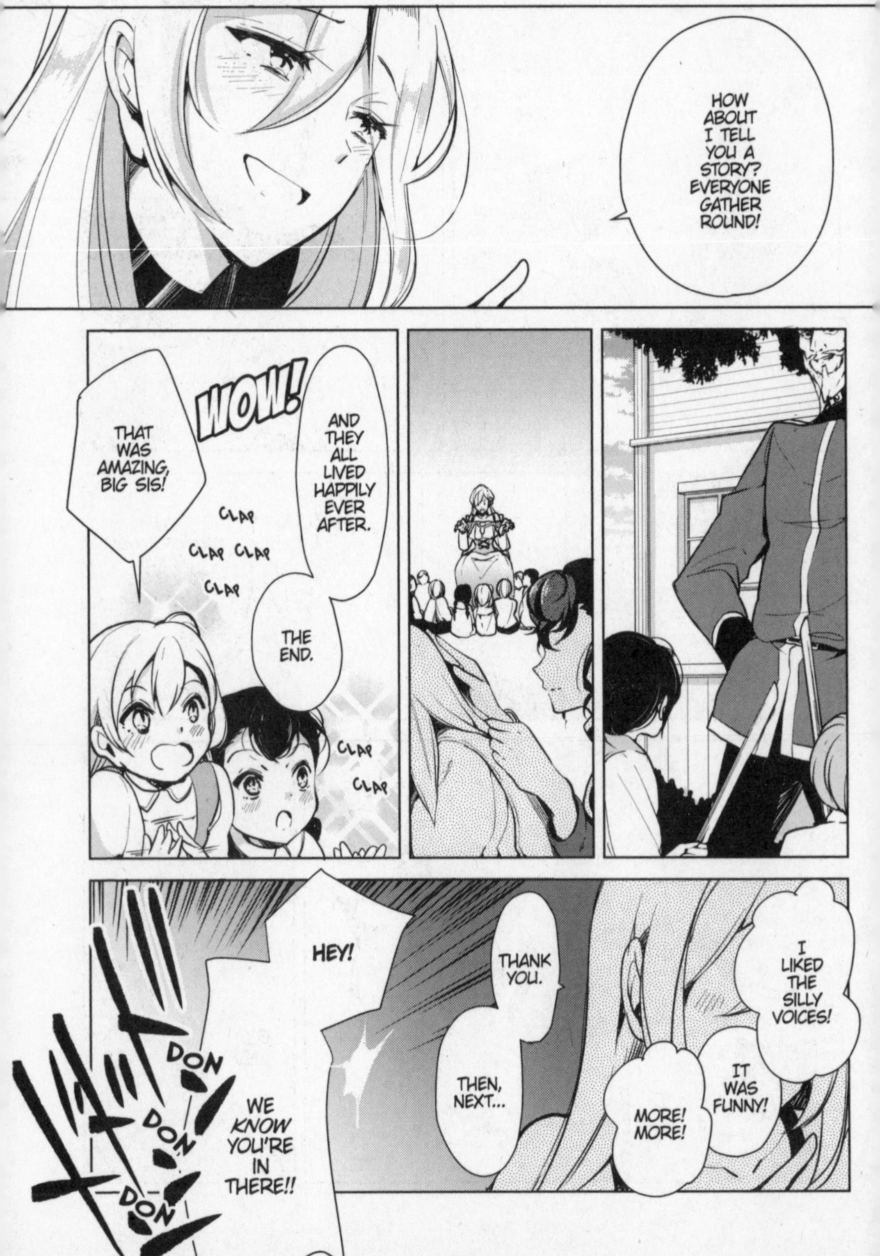
HOW ABOUT I TELL YOU A STORY? EVERYONE GATHER ROUND!
AND THEY ALL LIVED HAPPILY EVER AFTER.
THE END.
WOW!
THAT WAS AMAZING, BIG SIS!
CLAP
CLAP CLAP
CLAP
CLAP
CLAP
I LIKED THE SILLY VOICES!
IT WAS FUNNY!
MORE! MORE!
THANK YOU.
THEN, NEXT...
HEY!
WE KNOW YOU'RE IN THERE!!
DON
DON
DON

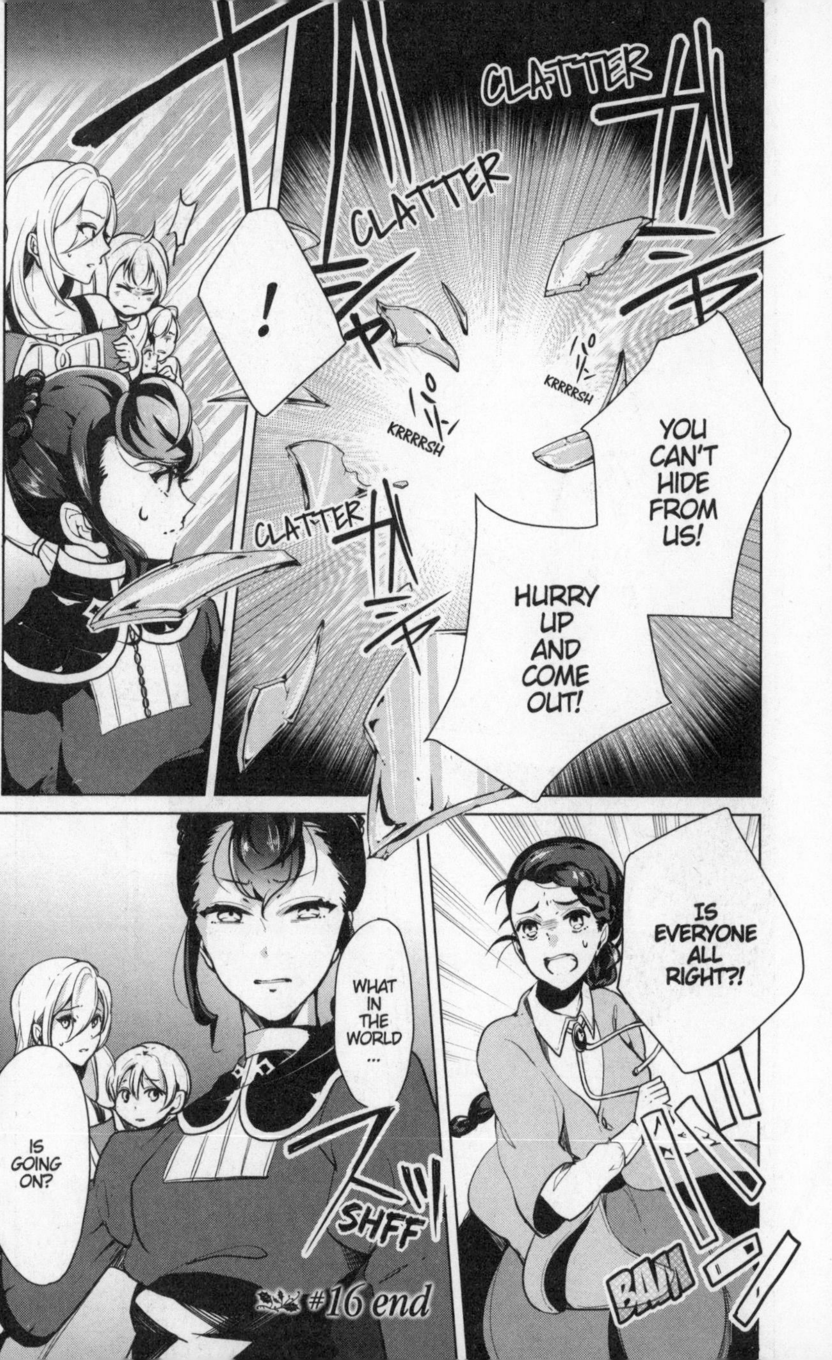
CLATTER
CLATTER
!
YOU CAN'T HIDE FROM US!
HURRY UP AND COME OUT!
KRRRRSH
KRRRRSH
CLATTER
IS EVERYONE ALL RIGHT?!
BAM
WHAT IN THE WORLD ...
IS GOING ON?
SHFF
#16 end

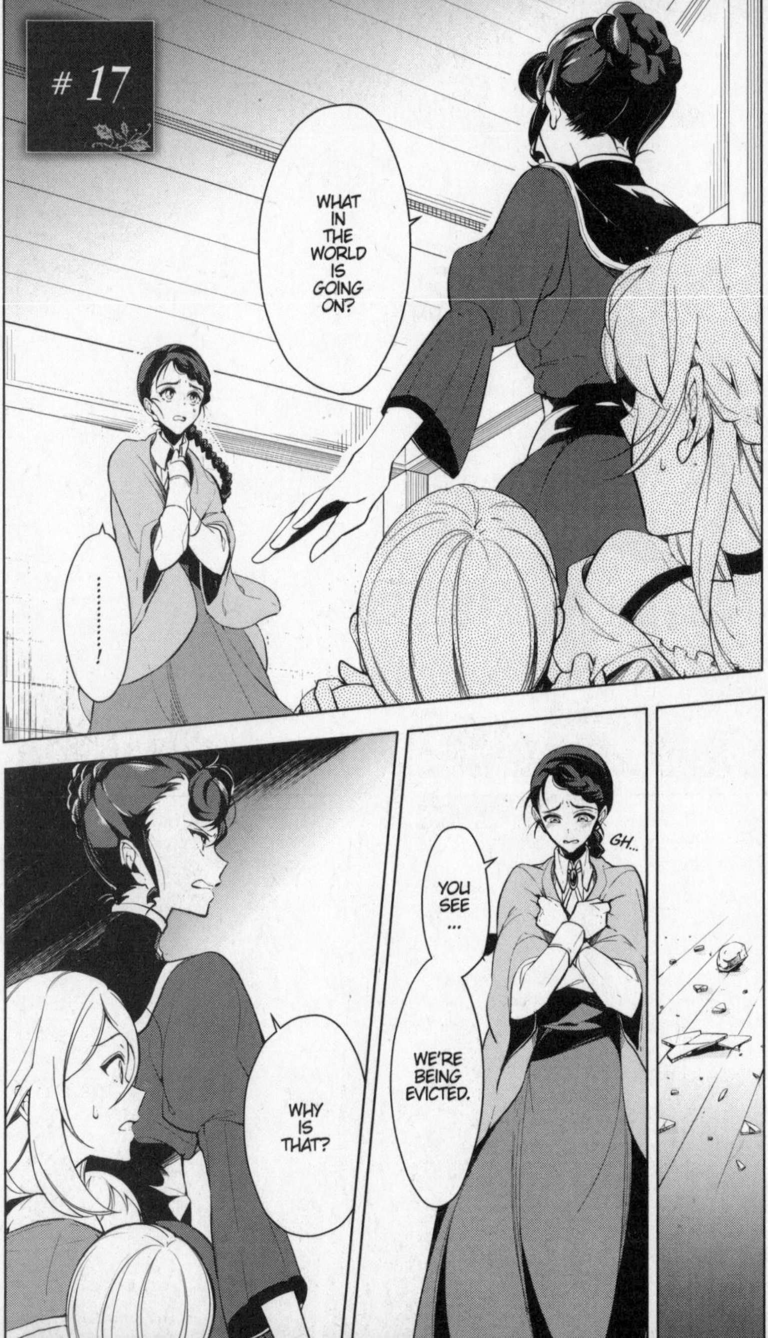

17
WHAT IN THE WORLD IS GOING ON?
.......!
GH...
YOU SEE...
WE'RE BEING EVICTED.
WHY IS THAT?

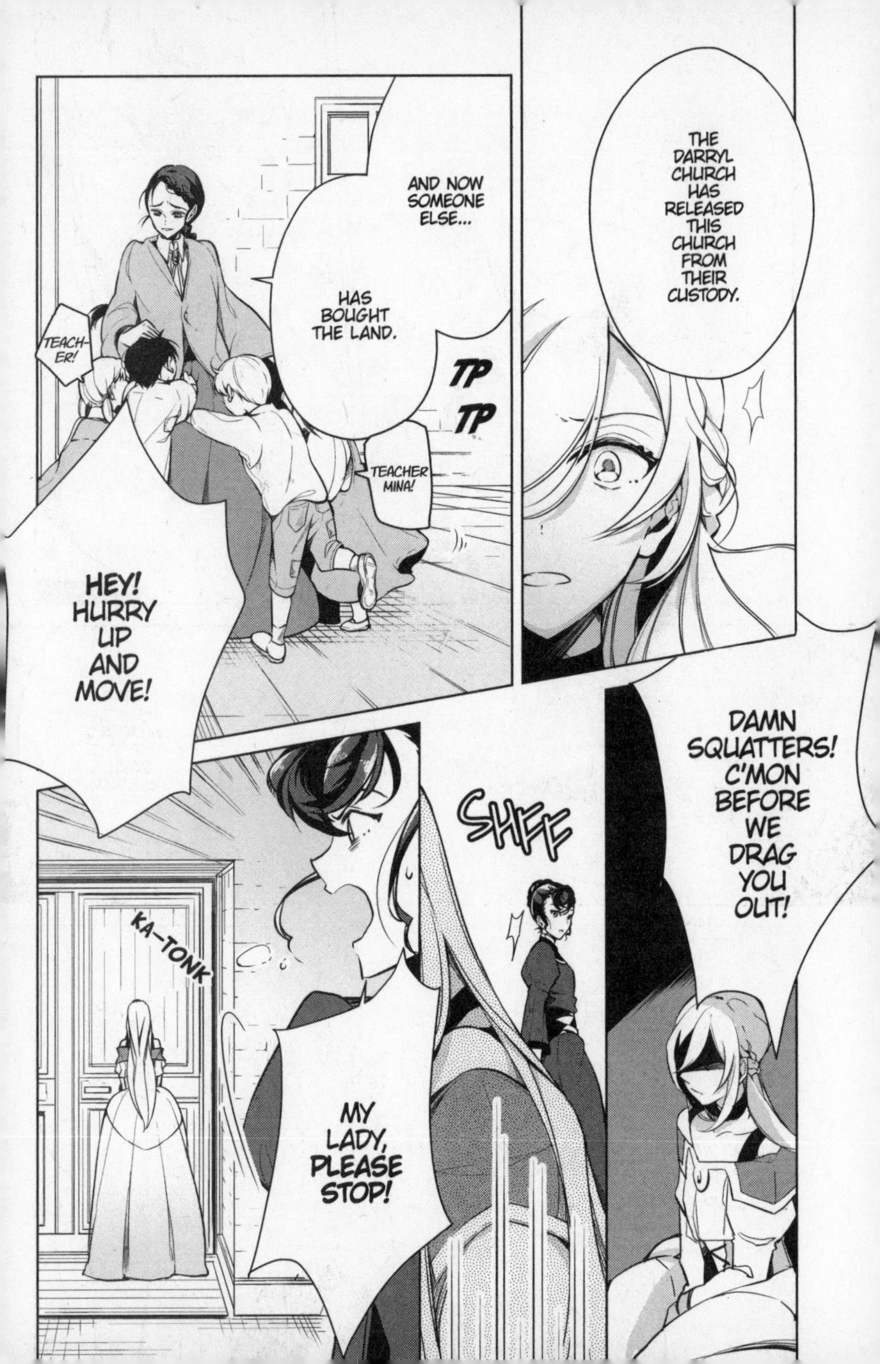
THE DARRYL CHURCH HAS RELEASED THIS CHURCH FROM THEIR CUSTODY.
AND NOW SOMEONE ELSE...
HAS BOUGHT THE LAND.
TP
TP
TEACHER MINA!
TEACHER!
HEY! HURRY UP AND MOVE!
DAMN SQUATTERS! C'MON BEFORE WE DRAG YOU OUT!
SHFF
MY LADY, PLEASE STOP!
KA-TONK

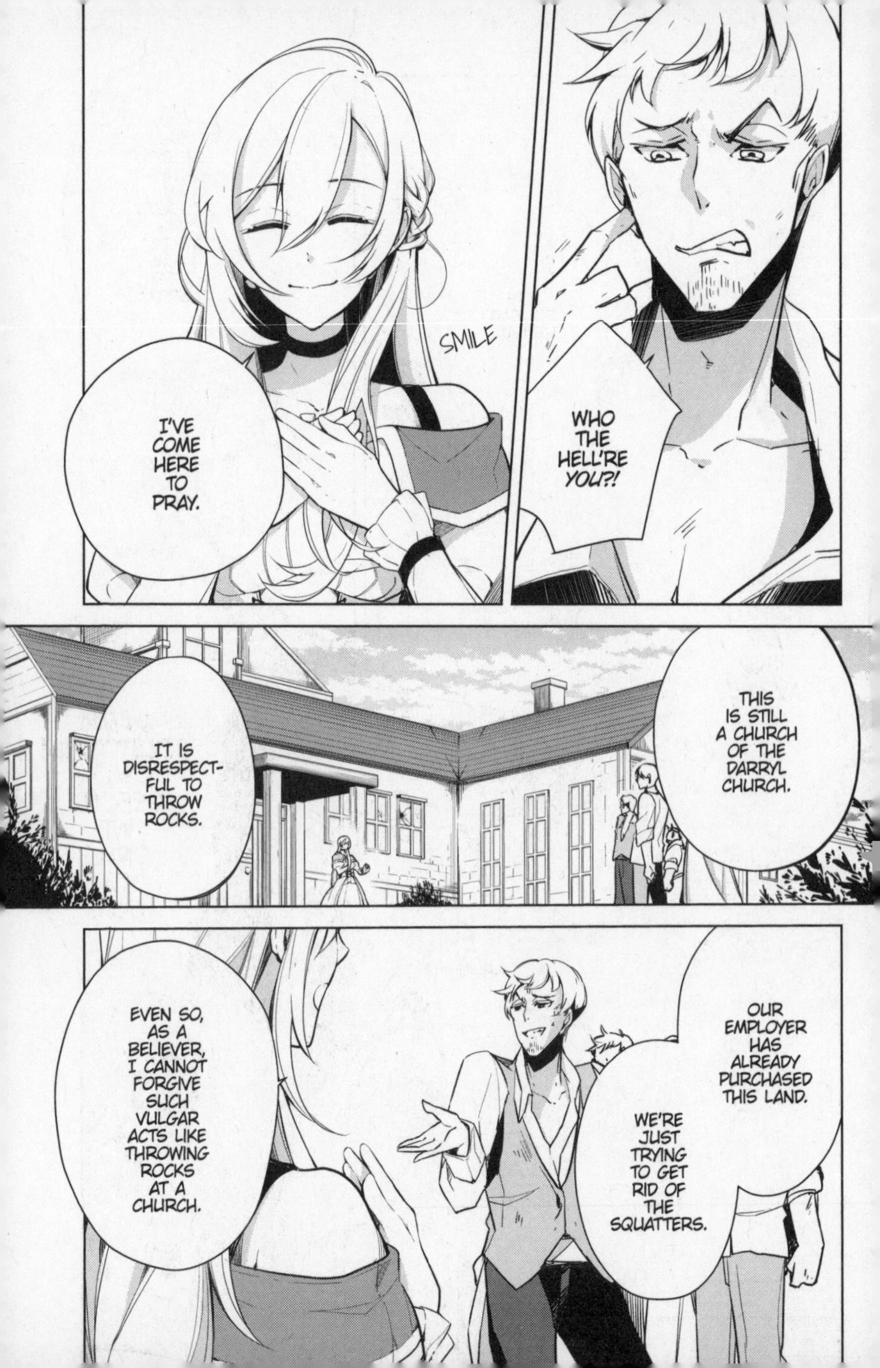
WHO THE HELL'RE YOU?!
SMILE
I'VE COME HERE TO PRAY.
THIS IS STILL A CHURCH OF THE DARRYL CHURCH.
IT IS DISRESPECTFUL TO THROW ROCKS.
OUR EMPLOYER HAS ALREADY PURCHASED THIS LAND.
WE'RE JUST TRYING TO GET RID OF THE SQUATTERS.
EVEN SO, AS A BELIEVER, I CANNOT FORGIVE SUCH VULGAR ACTS LIKE THROWING ROCKS AT A CHURCH.

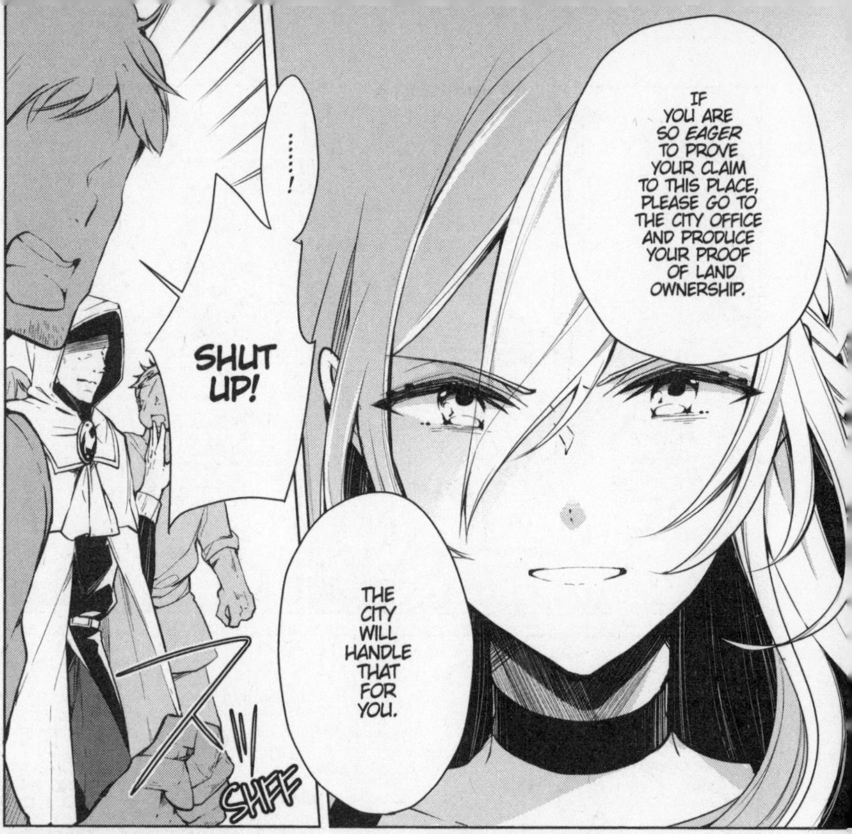
IF YOU ARE SO EAGER TO PROVE YOUR CLAIM TO THIS PLACE, PLEASE GO TO THE CITY OFFICE AND PRODUCE YOUR PROOF OF LAND OWNERSHIP.
......!
SHUT UP!
THE CITY WILL HANDLE THAT FOR YOU.
SHFF
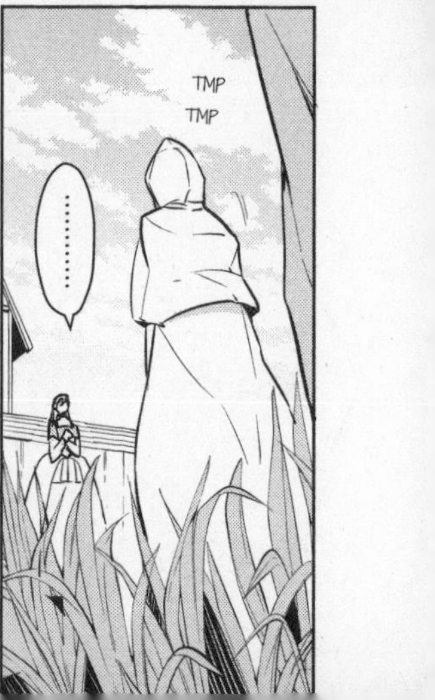
TMP
TMP
....
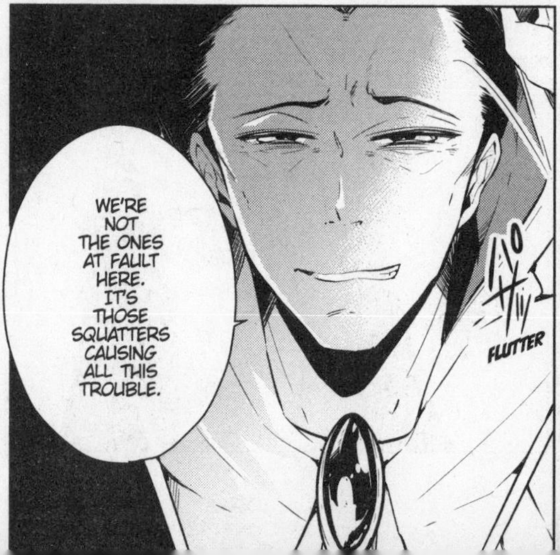
FLUTTER
WE'RE NOT THE ONES AT FAULT HERE. IT'S THOSE SQUATTERS CAUSING ALL THIS TROUBLE.

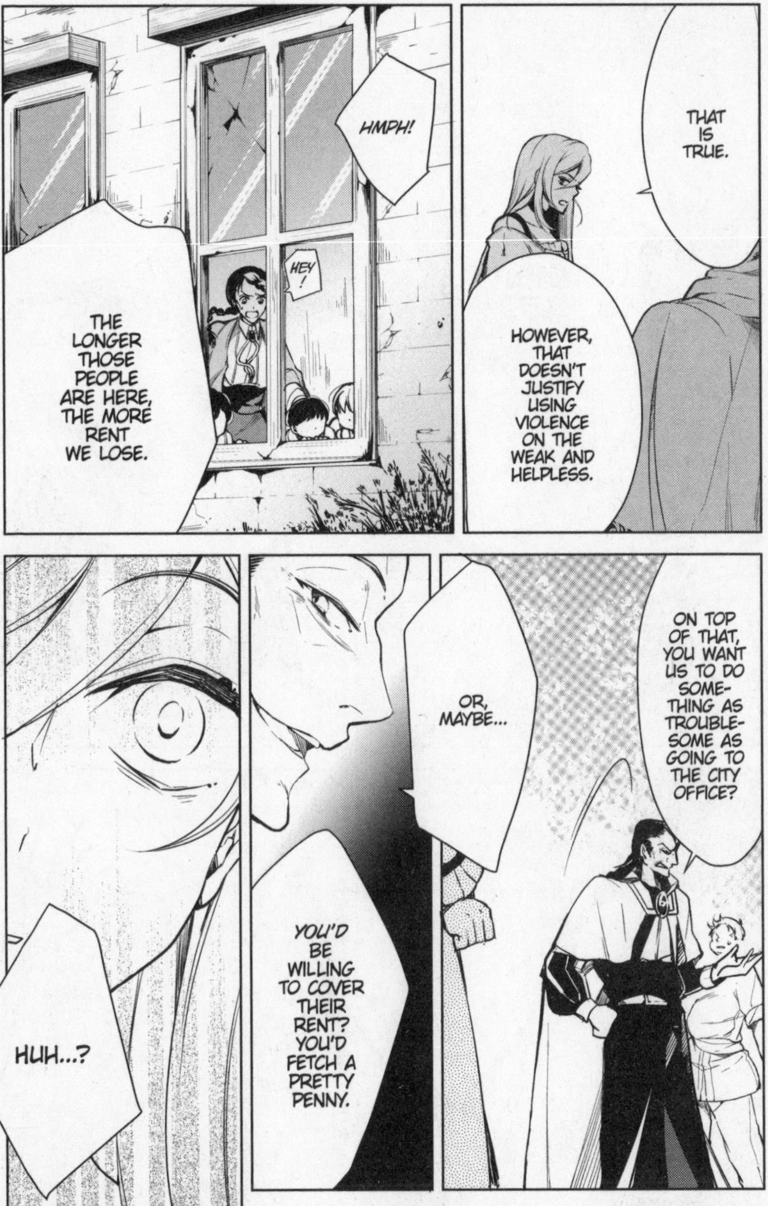
THAT IS TRUE.
HOWEVER, THAT DOESN'T JUSTIFY USING VIOLENCE ON THE WEAK AND HELPLESS.
HMPH!
HEY!
THE LONGER THOSE PEOPLE ARE HERE, THE MORE RENT WE LOSE.
ON TOP OF THAT, YOU WANT US TO DO SOME-THING AS TROUBLE-SOME AS GOING TO THE CITY OFFICE?
OR, MAYBE...
YOU'D BE WILLING TO COVER THEIR RENT? YOU'D FETCH A PRETTY PENNY.
HUH...?

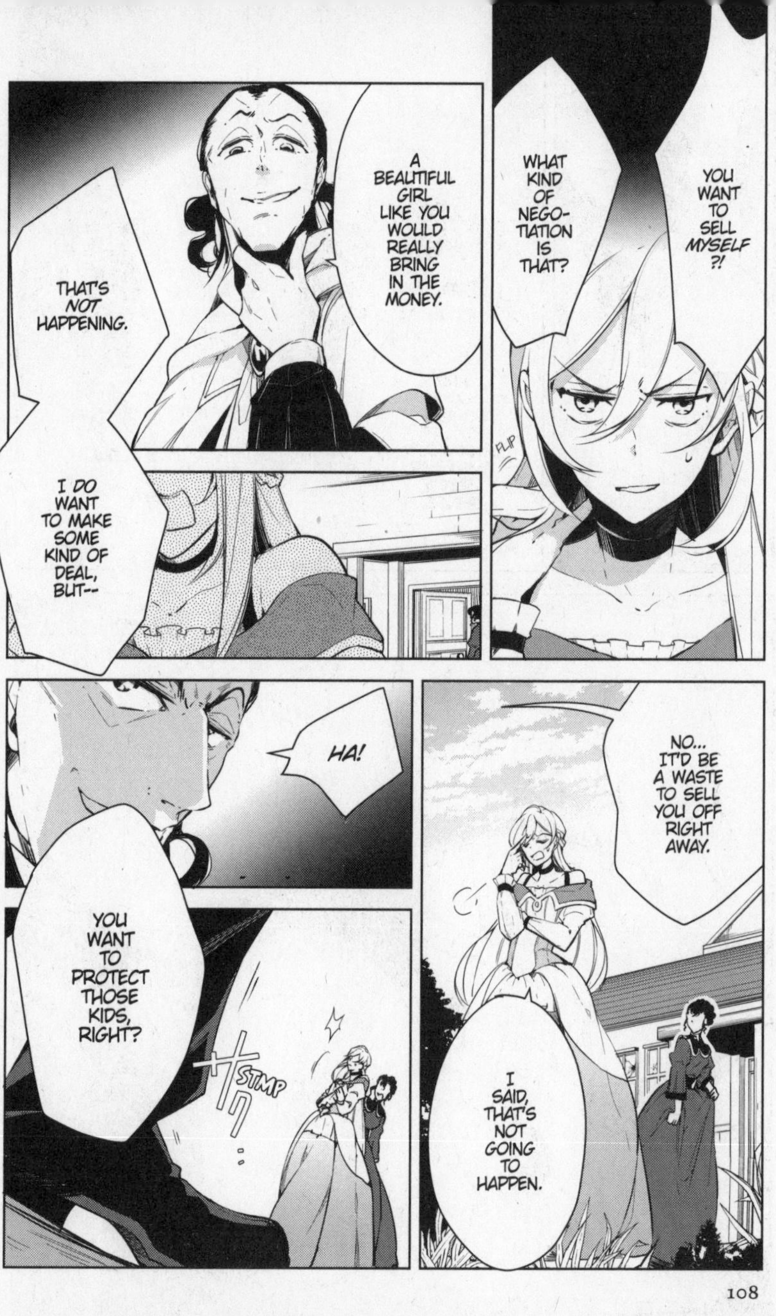
YOU WANT TO SELL *MYSELF* ?!
WHAT KIND OF NEGO-TIATION IS THAT?
A BEAUTIFUL GIRL LIKE YOU WOULD REALLY BRING IN THE MONEY.
THAT'S *NOT* HAPPENING.
FLIP
I *DO* WANT TO MAKE SOME KIND OF DEAL, BUT--
NO... IT'D BE A WASTE TO SELL YOU OFF RIGHT AWAY.
I SAID, THAT'S NOT GOING TO HAPPEN.
HA!
YOU WANT TO PROTECT THOSE KIDS, RIGHT?
STMP

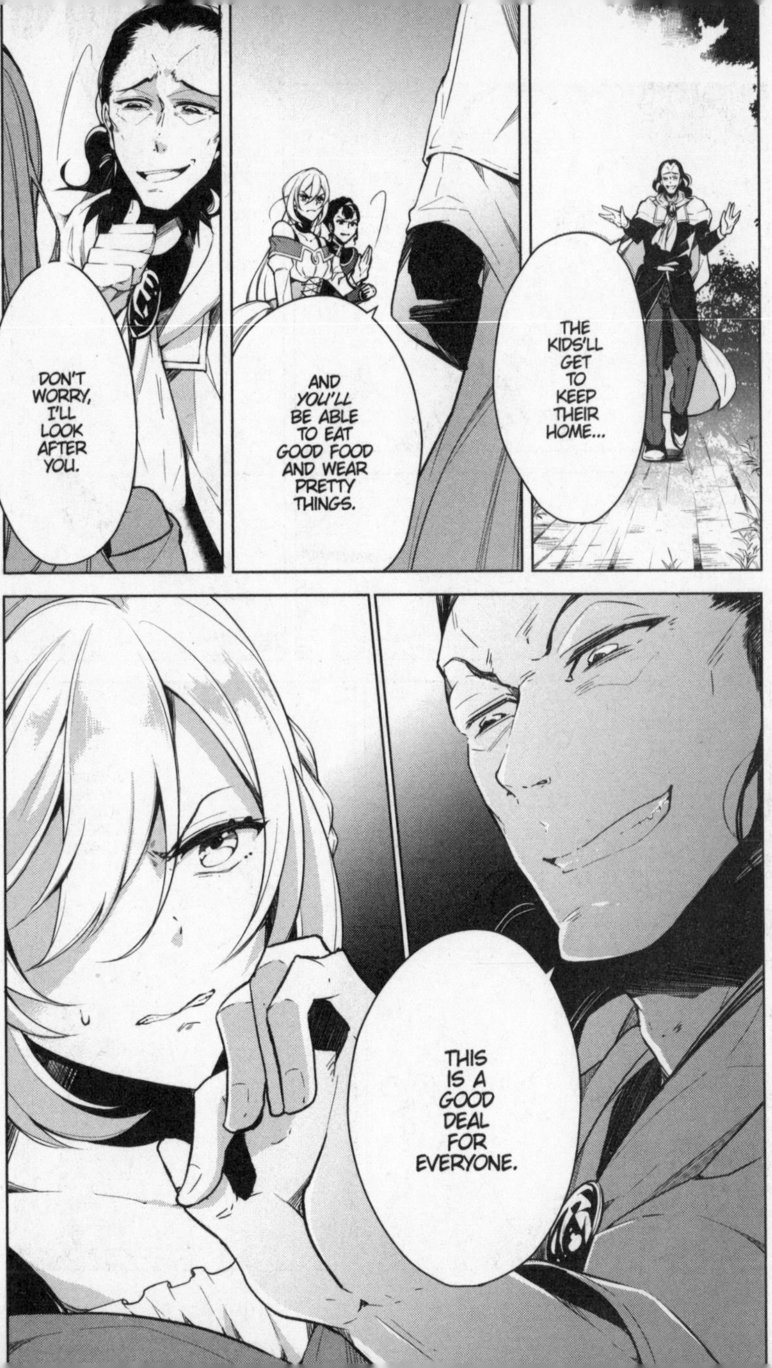
THE KIDS'LL GET TO KEEP THEIR HOME...
AND YOU'LL BE ABLE TO EAT GOOD FOOD AND WEAR PRETTY THINGS.
DON'T WORRY, I'LL LOOK AFTER YOU.
THIS IS A GOOD DEAL FOR EVERYONE.

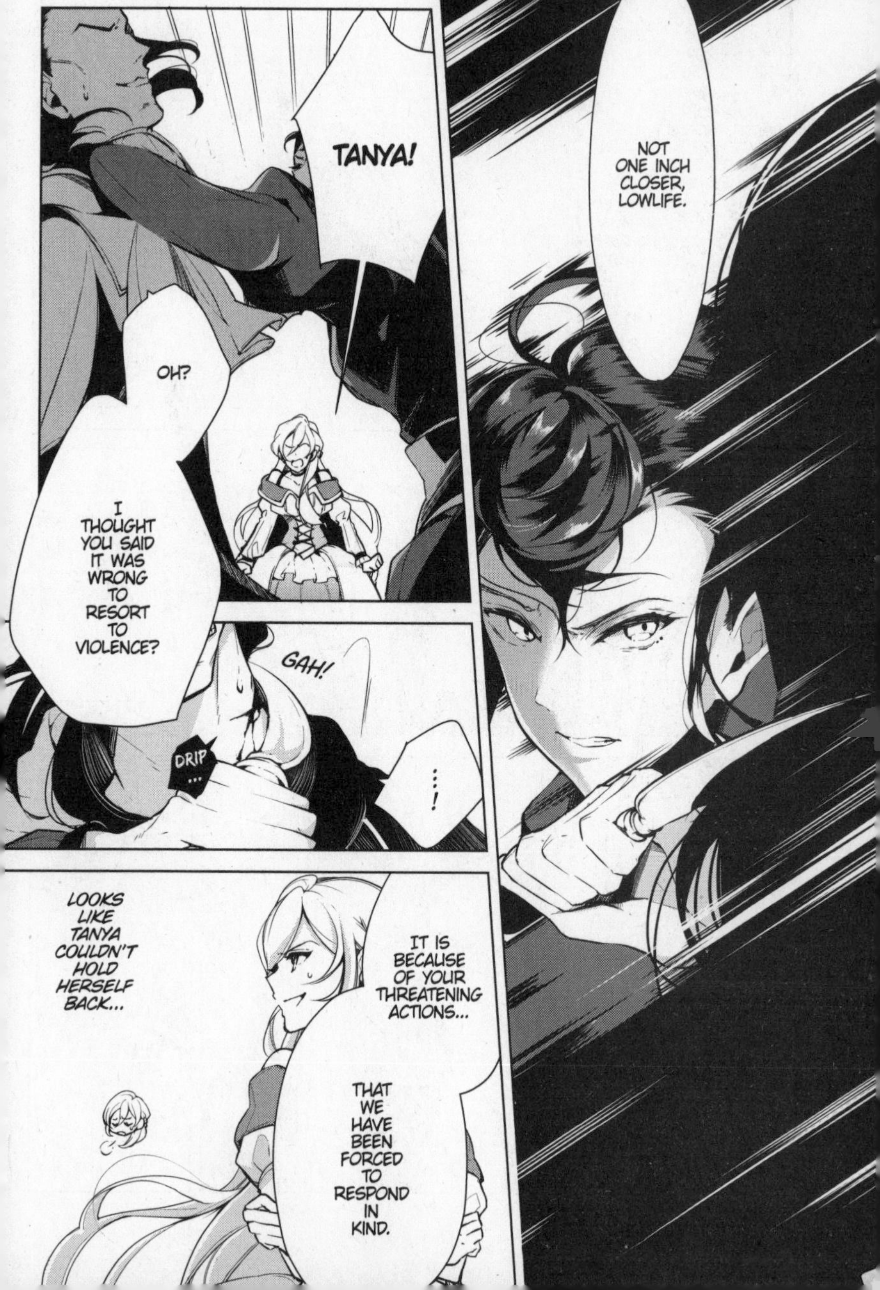
NOT ONE INCH CLOSER, LOWLIFE.
TANYA!
OH?
I THOUGHT YOU SAID IT WAS WRONG TO RESORT TO VIOLENCE?
GAH!
DRIP...
...!
IT IS BECAUSE OF YOUR THREATENING ACTIONS...
THAT WE HAVE BEEN FORCED TO RESPOND IN KIND.
LOOKS LIKE TANYA COULDN'T HOLD HERSELF BACK...

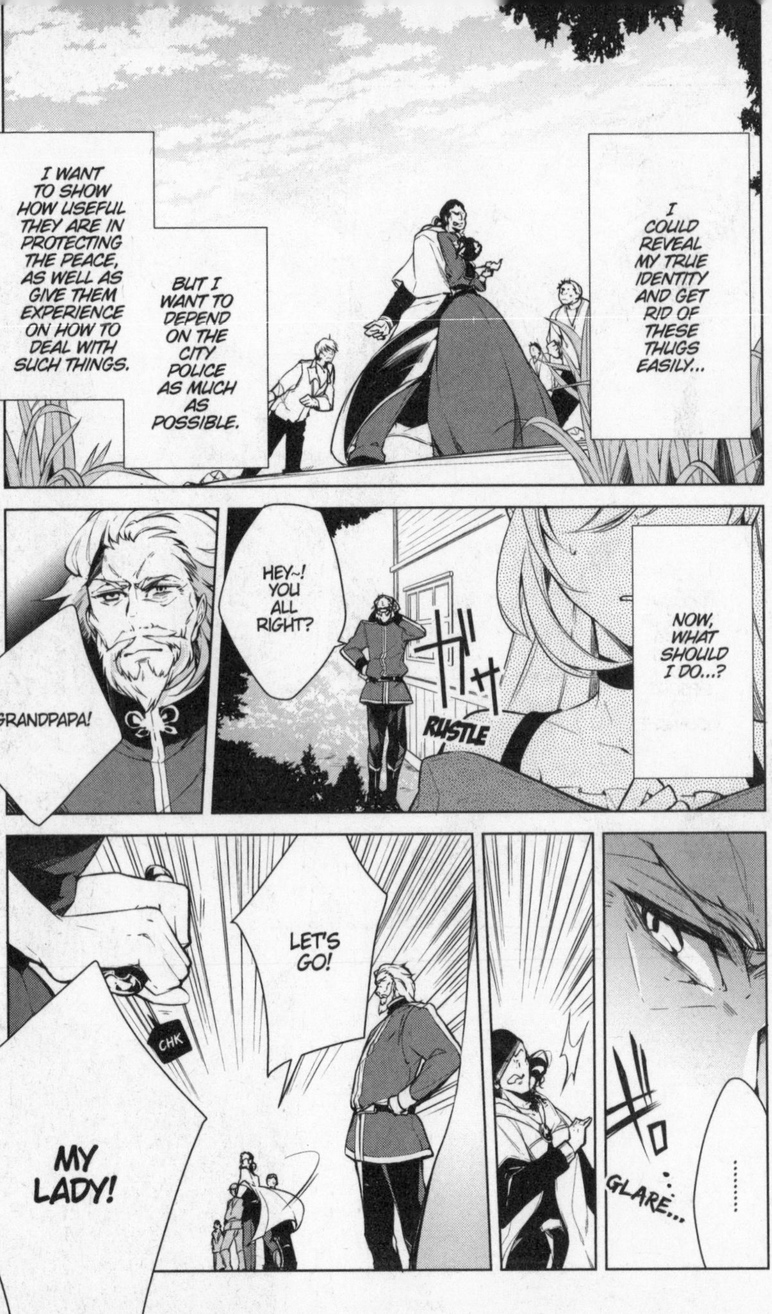
I COULD REVEAL MY TRUE IDENTITY AND GET RID OF THESE THUGS EASILY...
BUT I WANT TO DEPEND ON THE CITY POLICE AS MUCH AS POSSIBLE.
I WANT TO SHOW HOW USEFUL THEY ARE IN PROTECTING THE PEACE, AS WELL AS GIVE THEM EXPERIENCE ON HOW TO DEAL WITH SUCH THINGS.
NOW, WHAT SHOULD I DO...?
ザッ
RUSTLE
HEY~! YOU ALL RIGHT?
GRANDPAPA!
......
GLARE...
LET'S GO!
CHK
MY LADY!

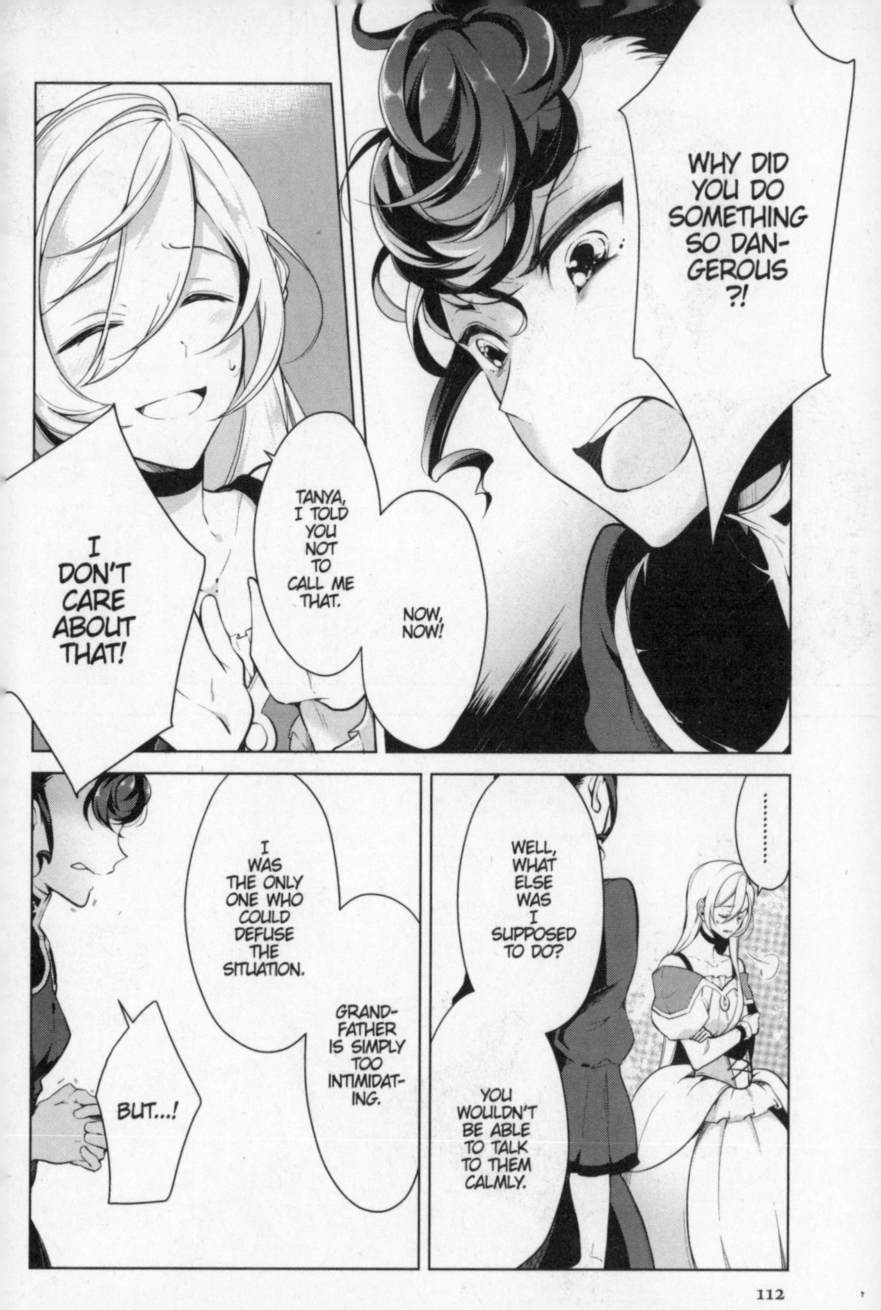
WHY DID YOU DO SOMETHING SO DANGEROUS?!
TANYA, I TOLD YOU NOT TO CALL ME THAT.
NOW, NOW!
I DON'T CARE ABOUT THAT!
......
WELL, WHAT ELSE WAS I SUPPOSED TO DO?
YOU WOULDN'T BE ABLE TO TALK TO THEM CALMLY.
I WAS THE ONLY ONE WHO COULD DEFUSE THE SITUATION.
GRANDFATHER IS SIMPLY TOO INTIMIDATING.
BUT...!

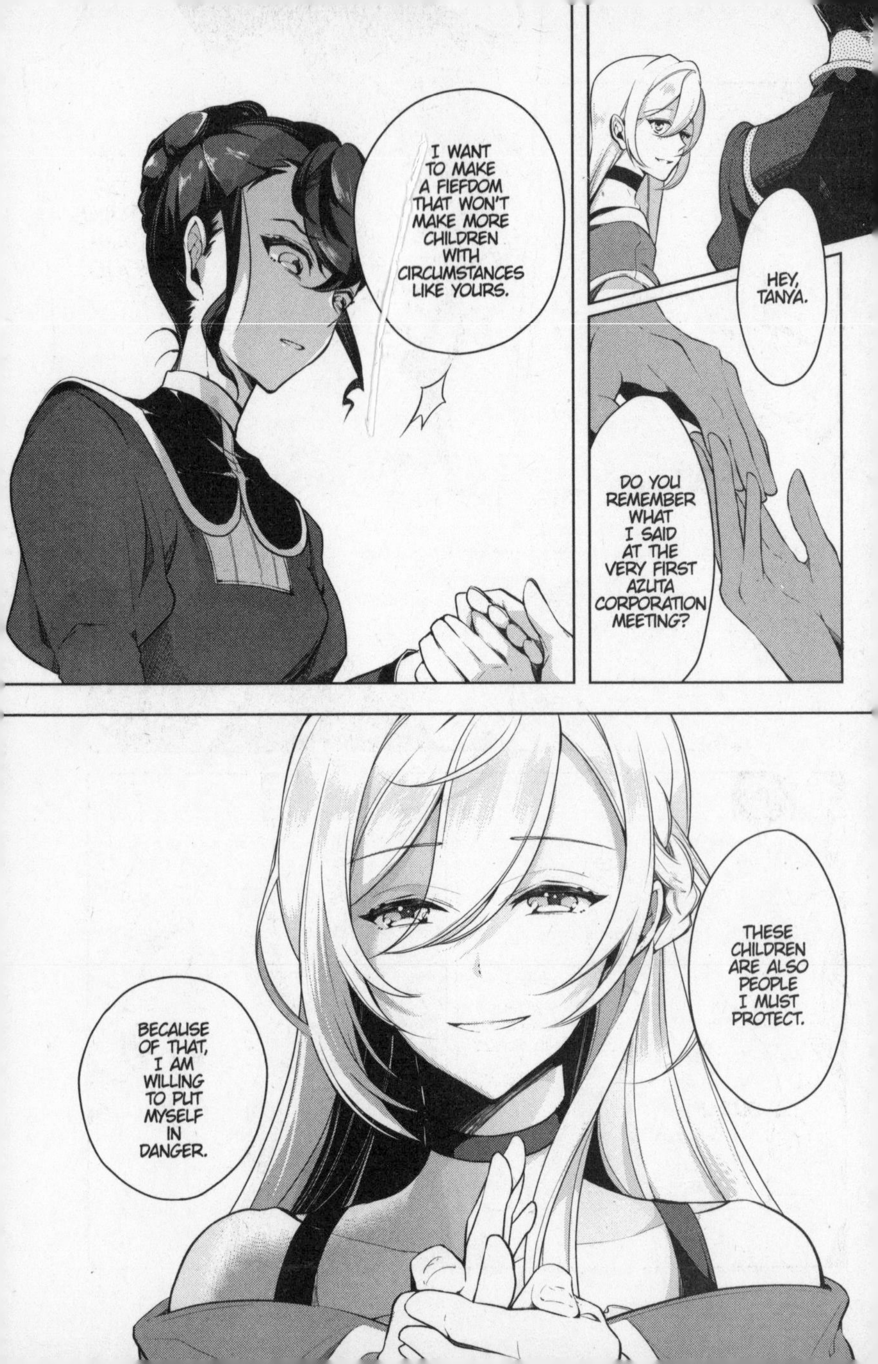
HEY, TANYA.
DO YOU REMEMBER WHAT I SAID AT THE VERY FIRST AZUTA CORPORATION MEETING?
I WANT TO MAKE A FIEFDOM THAT WON'T MAKE MORE CHILDREN WITH CIRCUMSTANCES LIKE YOURS.
THESE CHILDREN ARE ALSO PEOPLE I MUST PROTECT.
BECAUSE OF THAT, I AM WILLING TO PUT MYSELF IN DANGER.

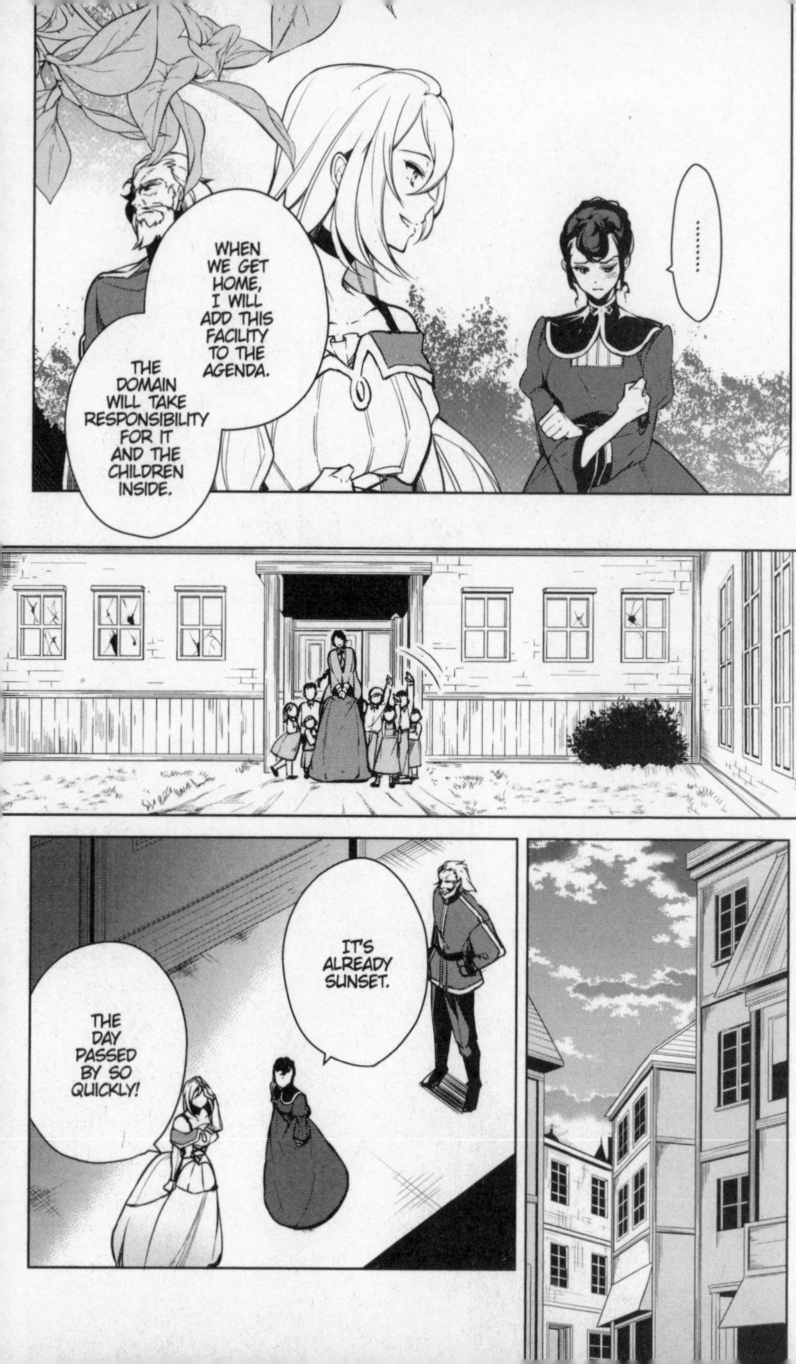
......
WHEN WE GET HOME, I WILL ADD THIS FACILITY TO THE AGENDA.
THE DOMAIN WILL TAKE RESPONSIBILITY FOR IT AND THE CHILDREN INSIDE.
IT'S ALREADY SUNSET.
THE DAY PASSED BY SO QUICKLY!

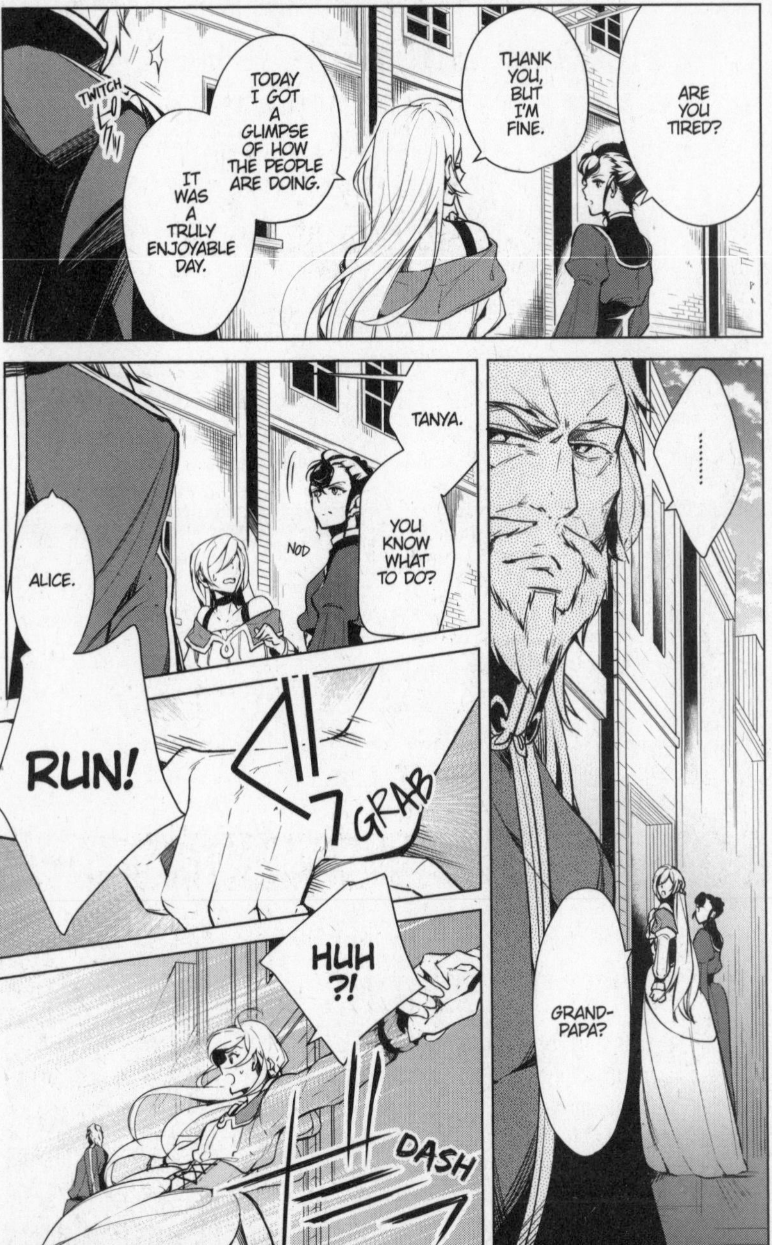
ARE YOU TIRED?
THANK YOU, BUT I'M FINE.
TODAY I GOT A GLIMPSE OF HOW THE PEOPLE ARE DOING.
IT WAS A TRULY ENJOYABLE DAY.
TWITCH
......
GRAND-PAPA?
TANYA.
YOU KNOW WHAT TO DO?
NOD
ALICE.
RUN!
GRAB
HUH ?!
DASH

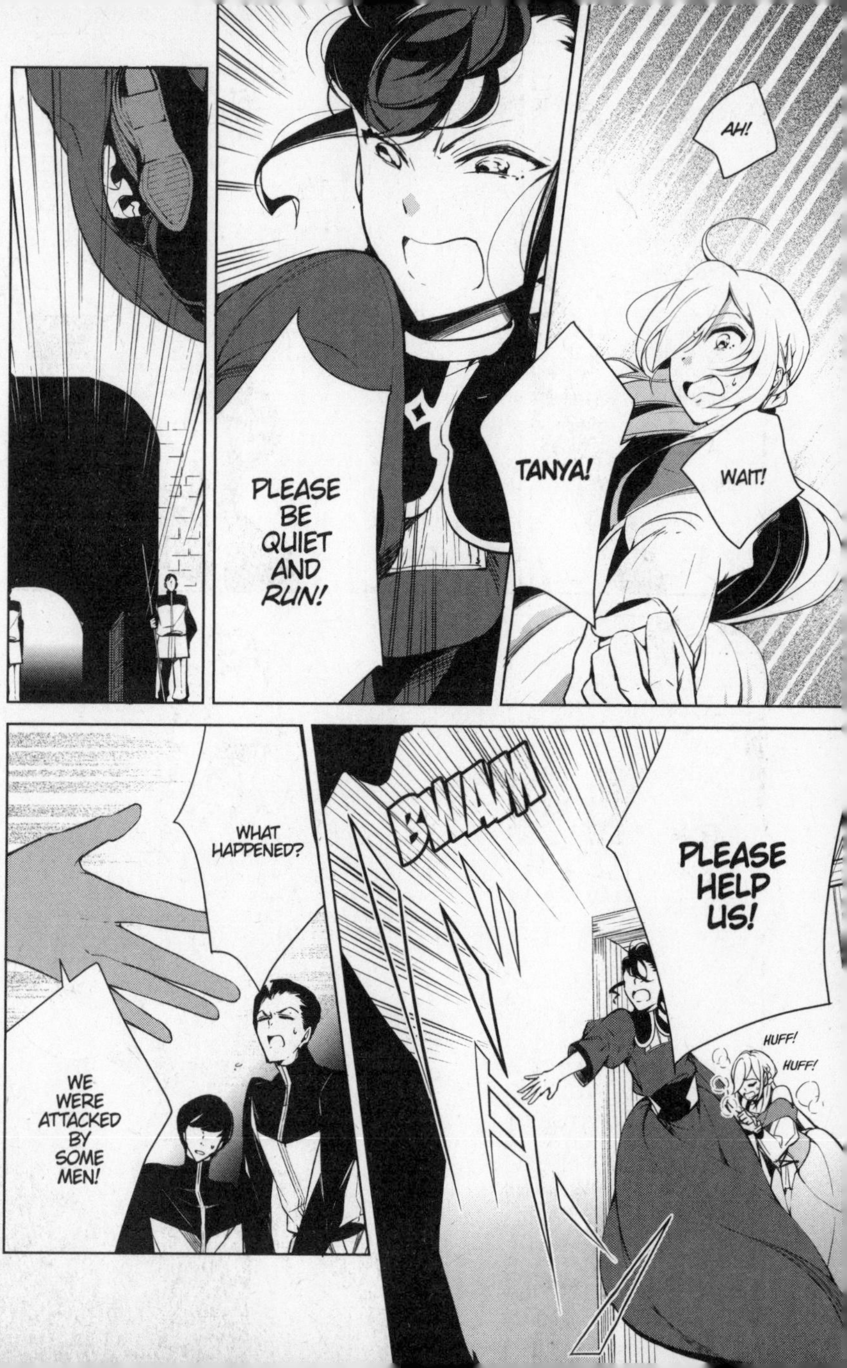
AH!
WAIT!
TANYA!
PLEASE BE QUIET AND RUN!
HUFF! HUFF!
PLEASE HELP US!
BWAM
WHAT HAPPENED?
WE WERE ATTACKED BY SOME MEN!

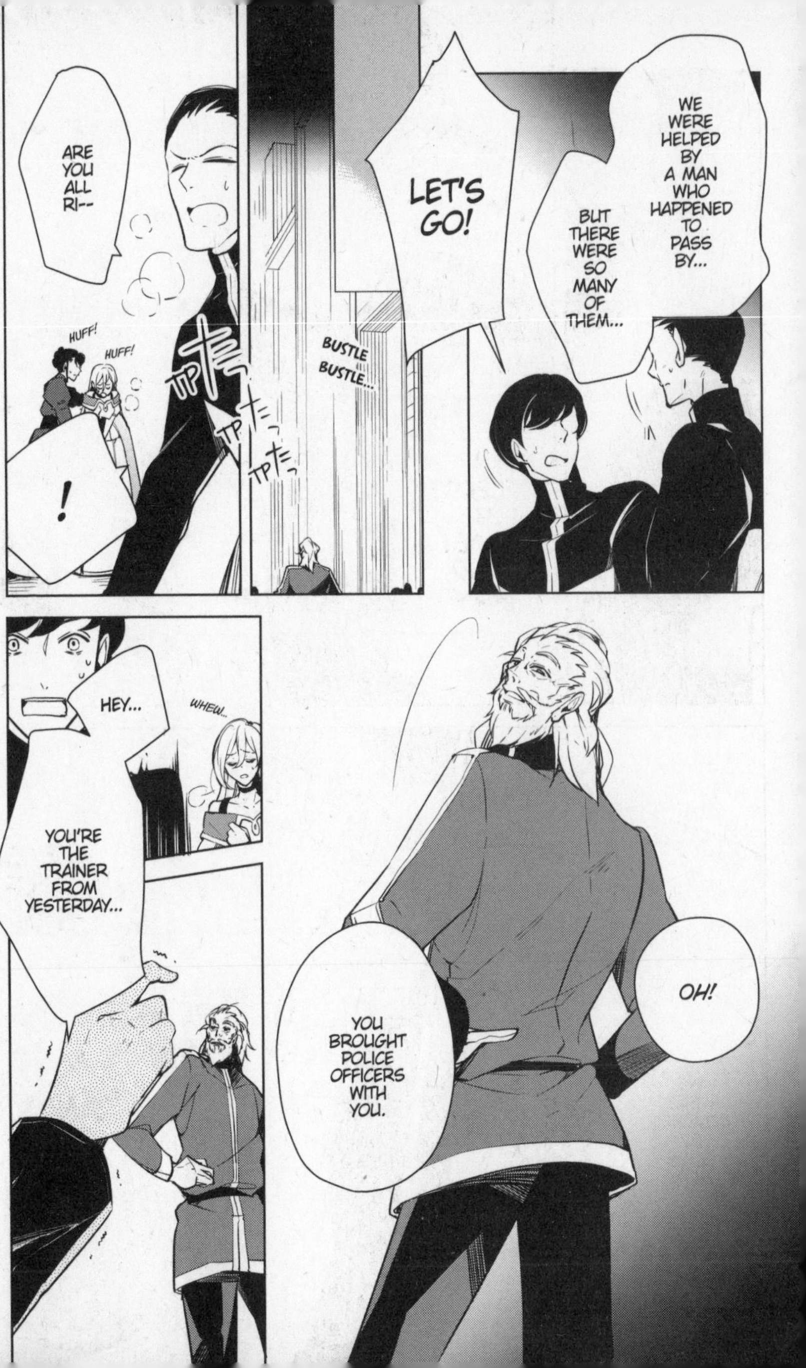
WE WERE HELPED BY A MAN WHO HAPPENED TO PASS BY...
BUT THERE WERE SO MANY OF THEM...
LET'S GO!
BUSTLE BUSTLE...
TP TP TP
ARE YOU ALL RI--
HUFF! HUFF!
!
OH!
YOU BROUGHT POLICE OFFICERS WITH YOU.
HEY...
WHEW...
YOU'RE THE TRAINER FROM YESTERDAY...

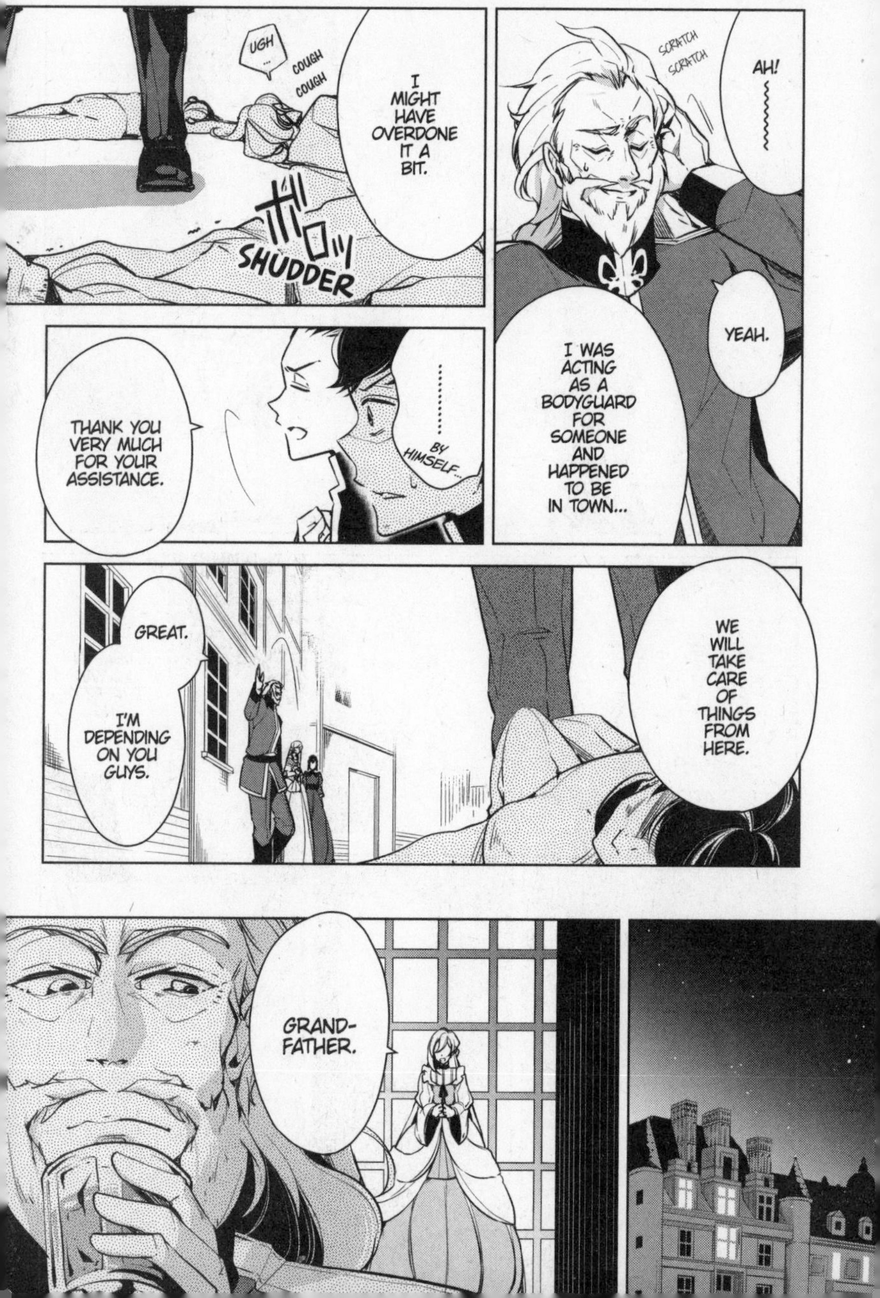
AH! ~~~~~
SCRATCH SCRATCH
YEAH.
I WAS ACTING AS A BODYGUARD FOR SOMEONE AND HAPPENED TO BE IN TOWN...
I MIGHT HAVE OVERDONE IT A BIT.
UGH ...
COUGH COUGH
SHUDDER
...... BY HIMSELF...
THANK YOU VERY MUCH FOR YOUR ASSISTANCE.
WE WILL TAKE CARE OF THINGS FROM HERE.
GREAT.
I'M DEPENDING ON YOU GUYS.
GRAND-FATHER.

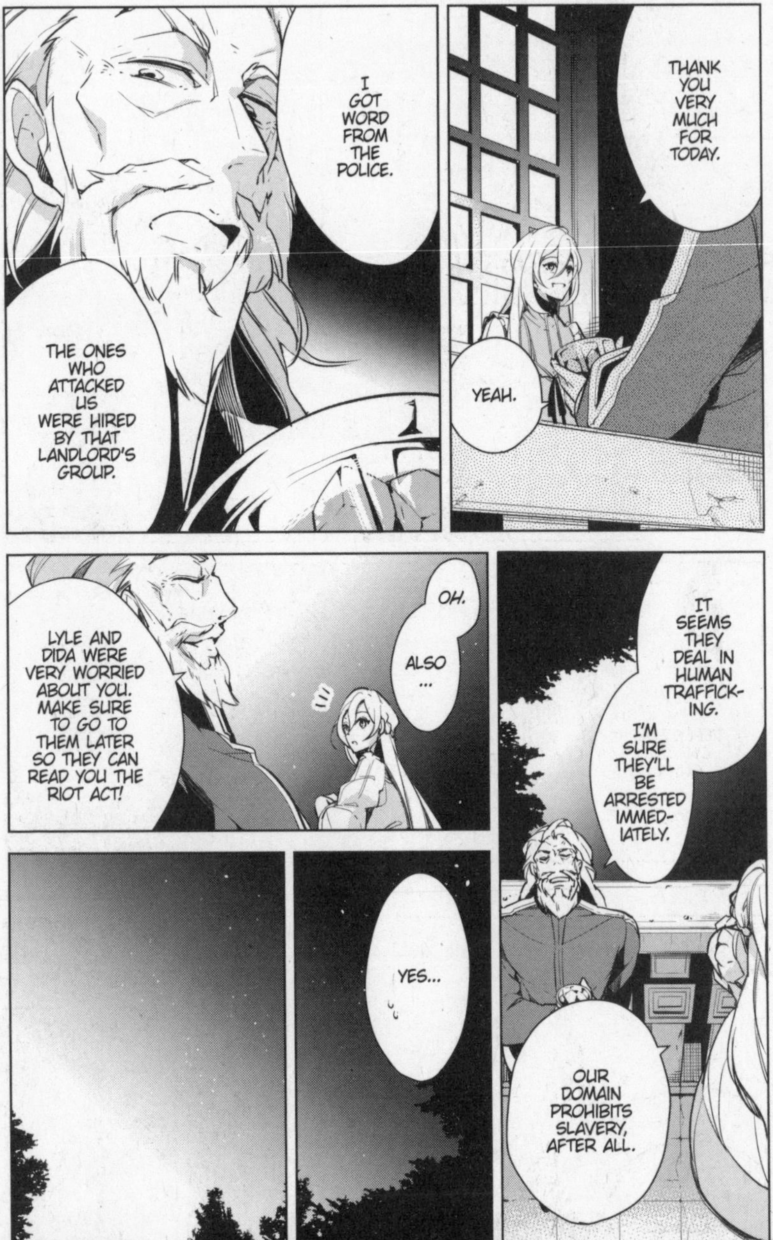
THANK YOU VERY MUCH FOR TODAY.
YEAH.
I GOT WORD FROM THE POLICE.
THE ONES WHO ATTACKED US WERE HIRED BY THAT LANDLORD'S GROUP.
IT SEEMS THEY DEAL IN HUMAN TRAFFICK-ING.
I'M SURE THEY'LL BE ARRESTED IMMED-IATELY.
OUR DOMAIN PROHIBITS SLAVERY, AFTER ALL.
OH.
ALSO ...
LYLE AND DIDA WERE VERY WORRIED ABOUT YOU. MAKE SURE TO GO TO THEM LATER SO THEY CAN READ YOU THE RIOT ACT!
YES...

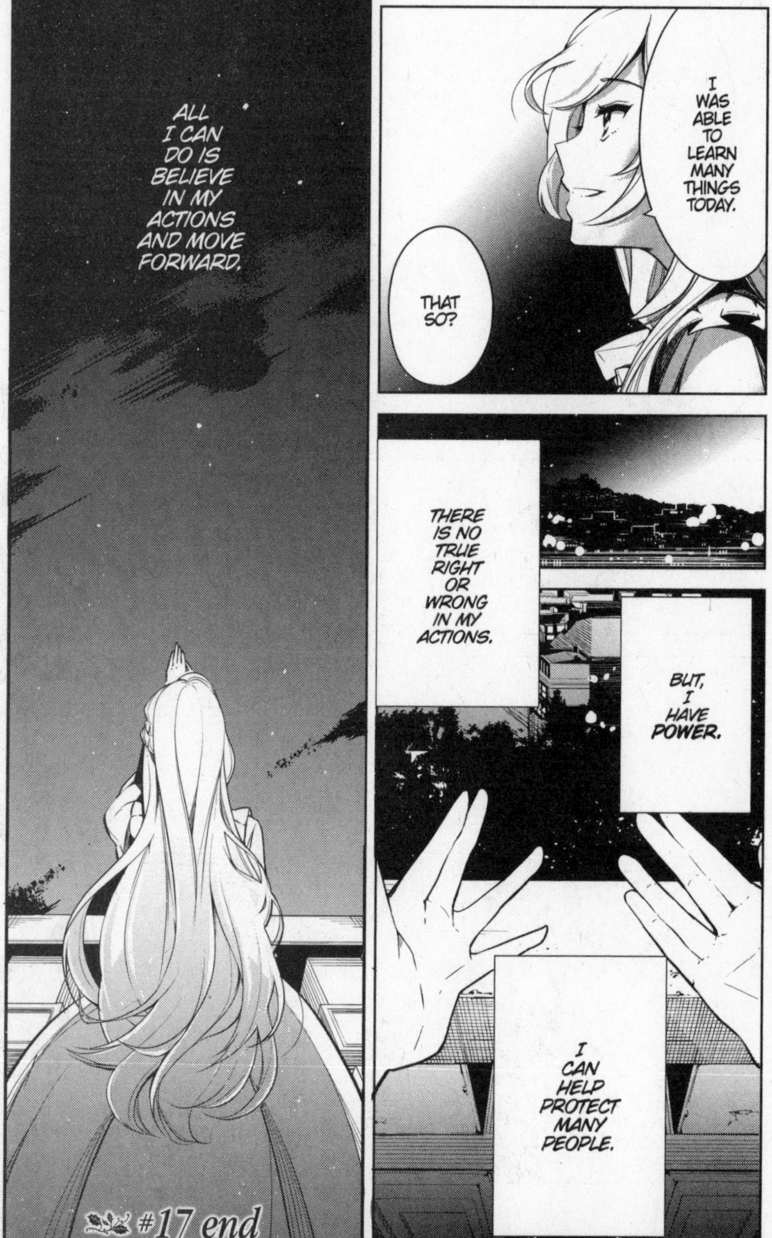
I WAS ABLE TO LEARN MANY THINGS TODAY.
THAT SO?
THERE IS NO TRUE RIGHT OR WRONG IN MY ACTIONS.
BUT, I HAVE POWER.
I CAN HELP PROTECT MANY PEOPLE.
ALL I CAN DO IS BELIEVE IN MY ACTIONS AND MOVE FORWARD.
#17 end

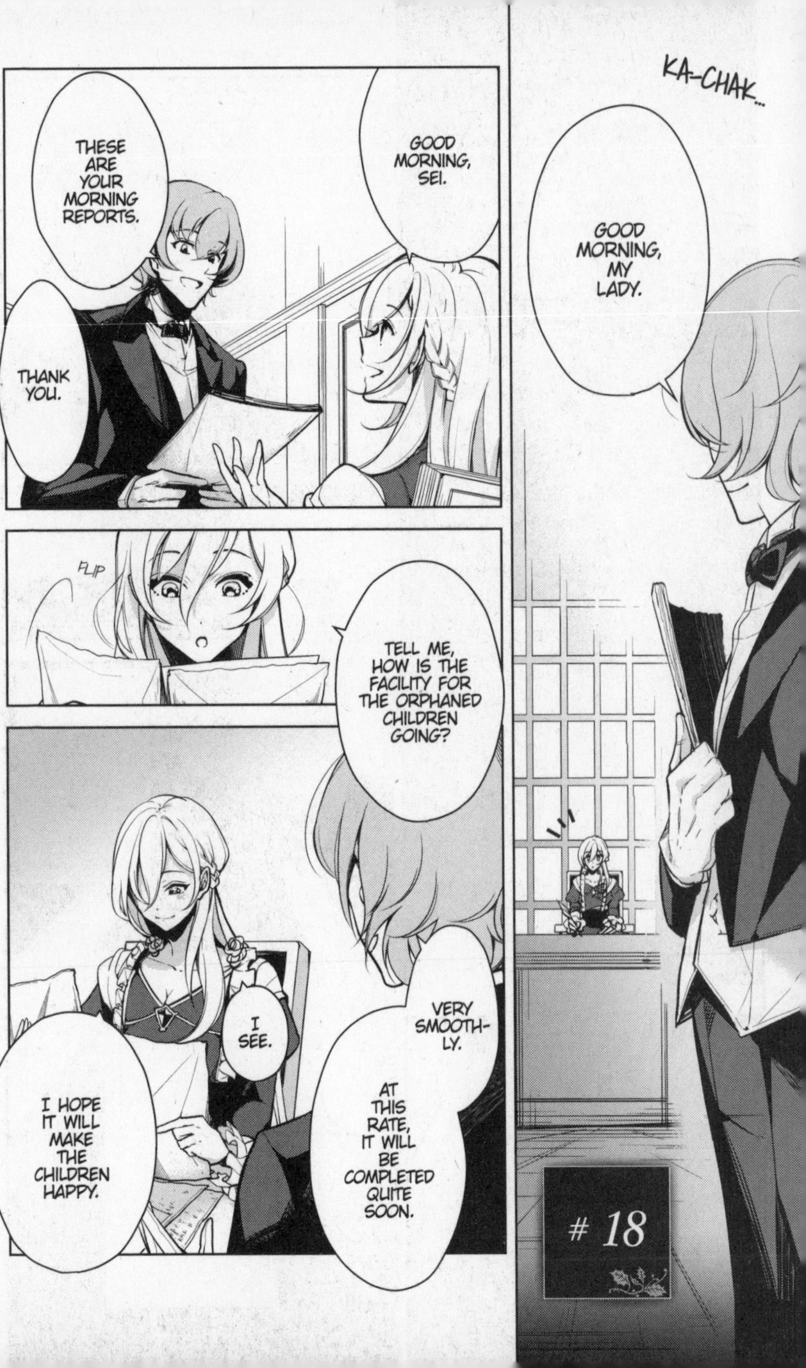
KA-CHAK...
GOOD MORNING, MY LADY.
18
GOOD MORNING, SEI.
THESE ARE YOUR MORNING REPORTS.
THANK YOU.
FLIP
TELL ME, HOW IS THE FACILITY FOR THE ORPHANED CHILDREN GOING?
VERY SMOOTH-LY.
AT THIS RATE, IT WILL BE COMPLETED QUITE SOON.
I SEE.
I HOPE IT WILL MAKE THE CHILDREN HAPPY.

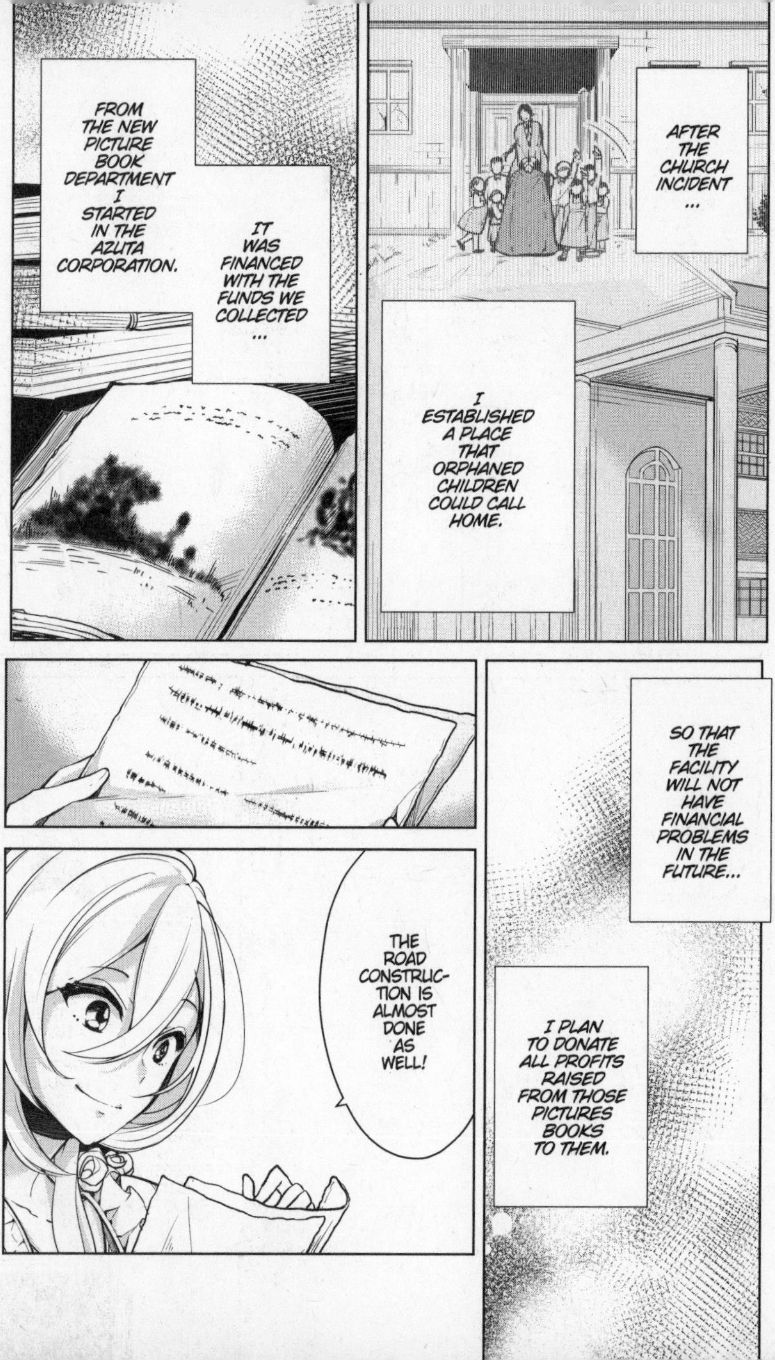
AFTER THE CHURCH INCIDENT ...
I ESTABLISHED A PLACE THAT ORPHANED CHILDREN COULD CALL HOME.
FROM THE NEW PICTURE BOOK DEPARTMENT I STARTED IN THE AZUTA CORPORATION.
IT WAS FINANCED WITH THE FUNDS WE COLLECTED ...
SO THAT THE FACILITY WILL NOT HAVE FINANCIAL PROBLEMS IN THE FUTURE...
I PLAN TO DONATE ALL PROFITS RAISED FROM THOSE PICTURES BOOKS TO THEM.
THE ROAD CONSTRUC-TION IS ALMOST DONE AS WELL!

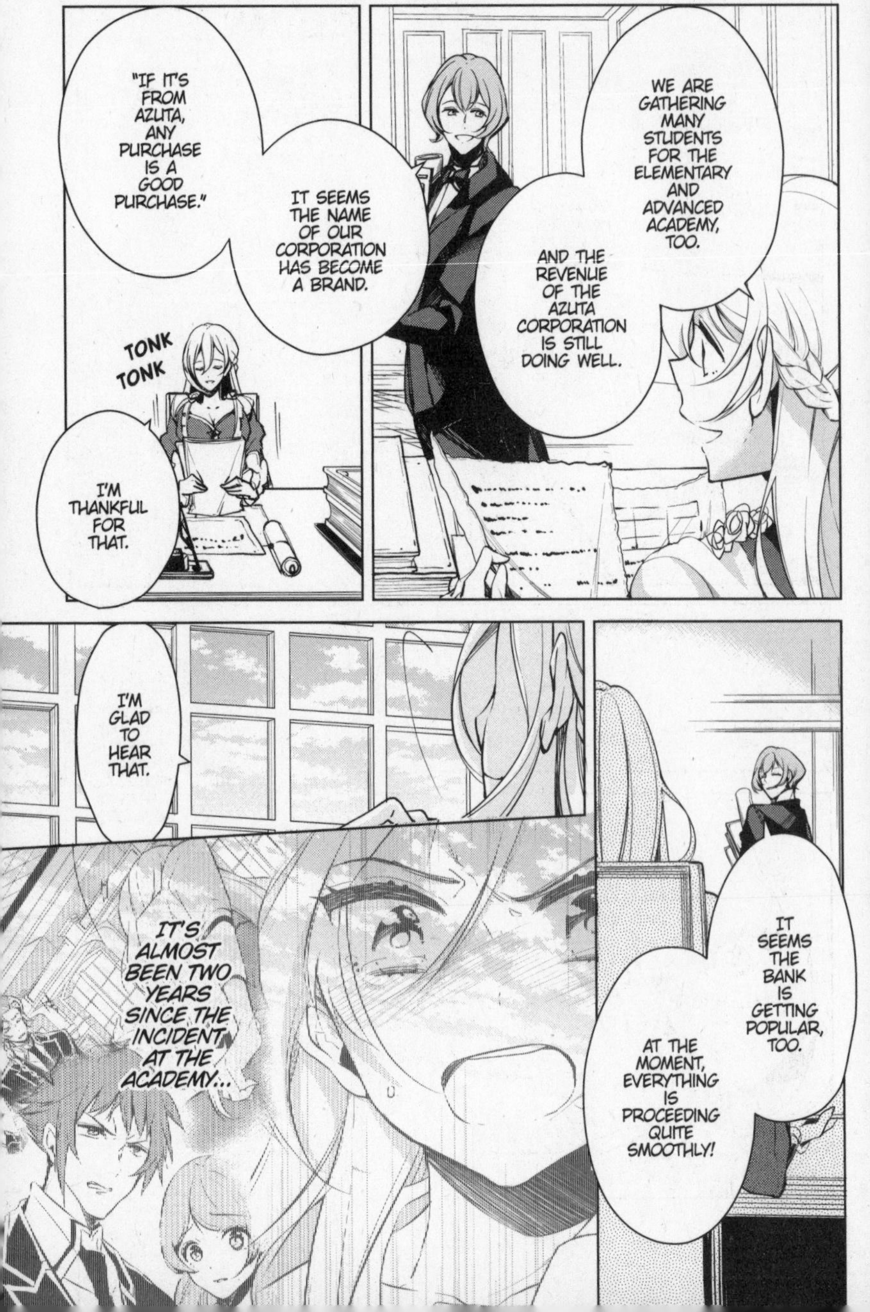
WE ARE GATHERING MANY STUDENTS FOR THE ELEMENTARY AND ADVANCED ACADEMY, TOO.
AND THE REVENUE OF THE AZUTA CORPORATION IS STILL DOING WELL.
"IF IT'S FROM AZUTA, ANY PURCHASE IS A GOOD PURCHASE."
IT SEEMS THE NAME OF OUR CORPORATION HAS BECOME A BRAND.
TONK TONK
I'M THANKFUL FOR THAT.
IT SEEMS THE BANK IS GETTING POPULAR, TOO.
AT THE MOMENT, EVERYTHING IS PROCEEDING QUITE SMOOTHLY!
I'M GLAD TO HEAR THAT.
IT'S ALMOST BEEN TWO YEARS SINCE THE INCIDENT AT THE ACADEMY...

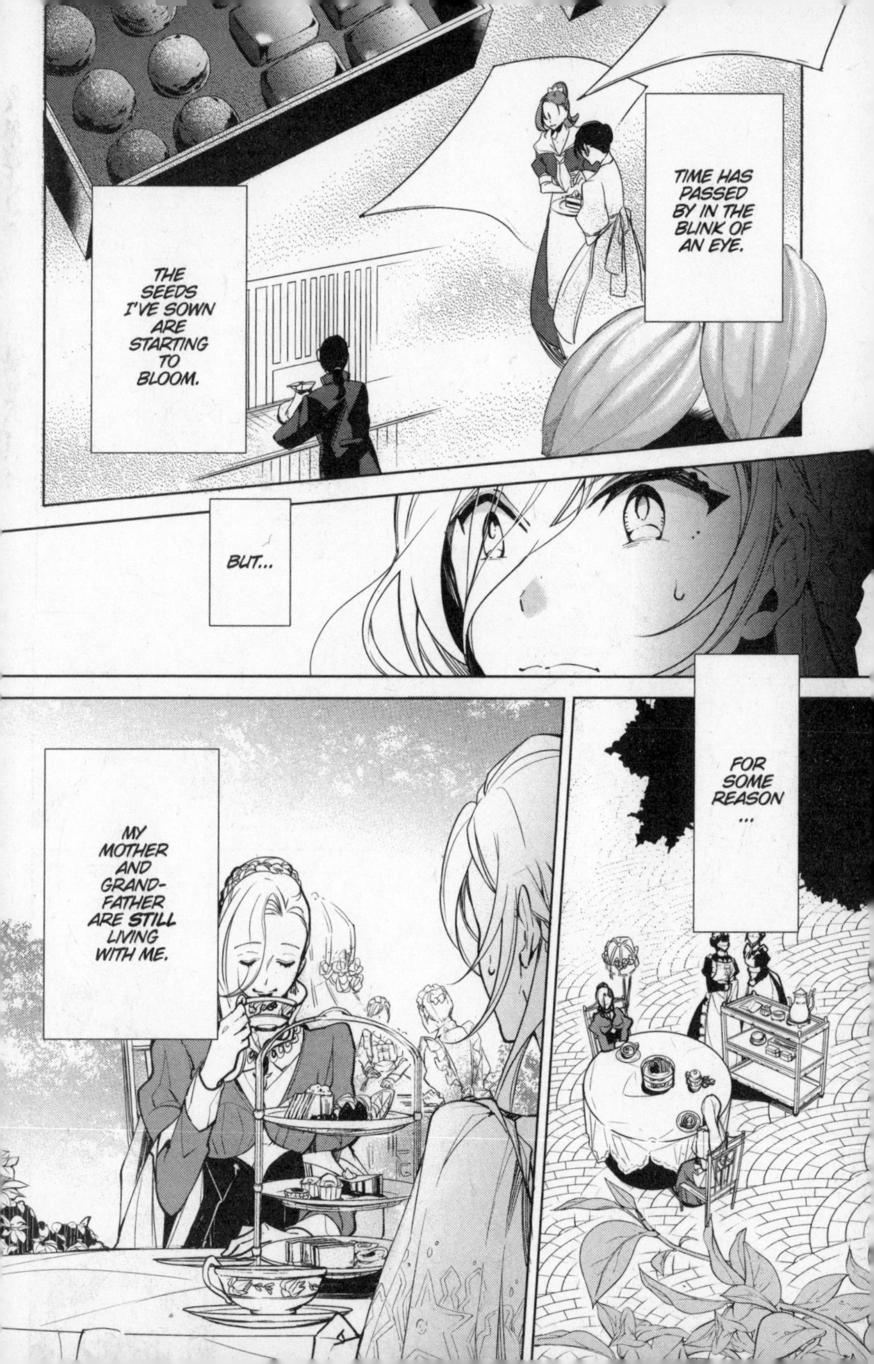
TIME HAS PASSED BY IN THE BLINK OF AN EYE.
THE SEEDS I'VE SOWN ARE STARTING TO BLOOM.
BUT...
FOR SOME REASON...
MY MOTHER AND GRAND-FATHER ARE STILL LIVING WITH ME.

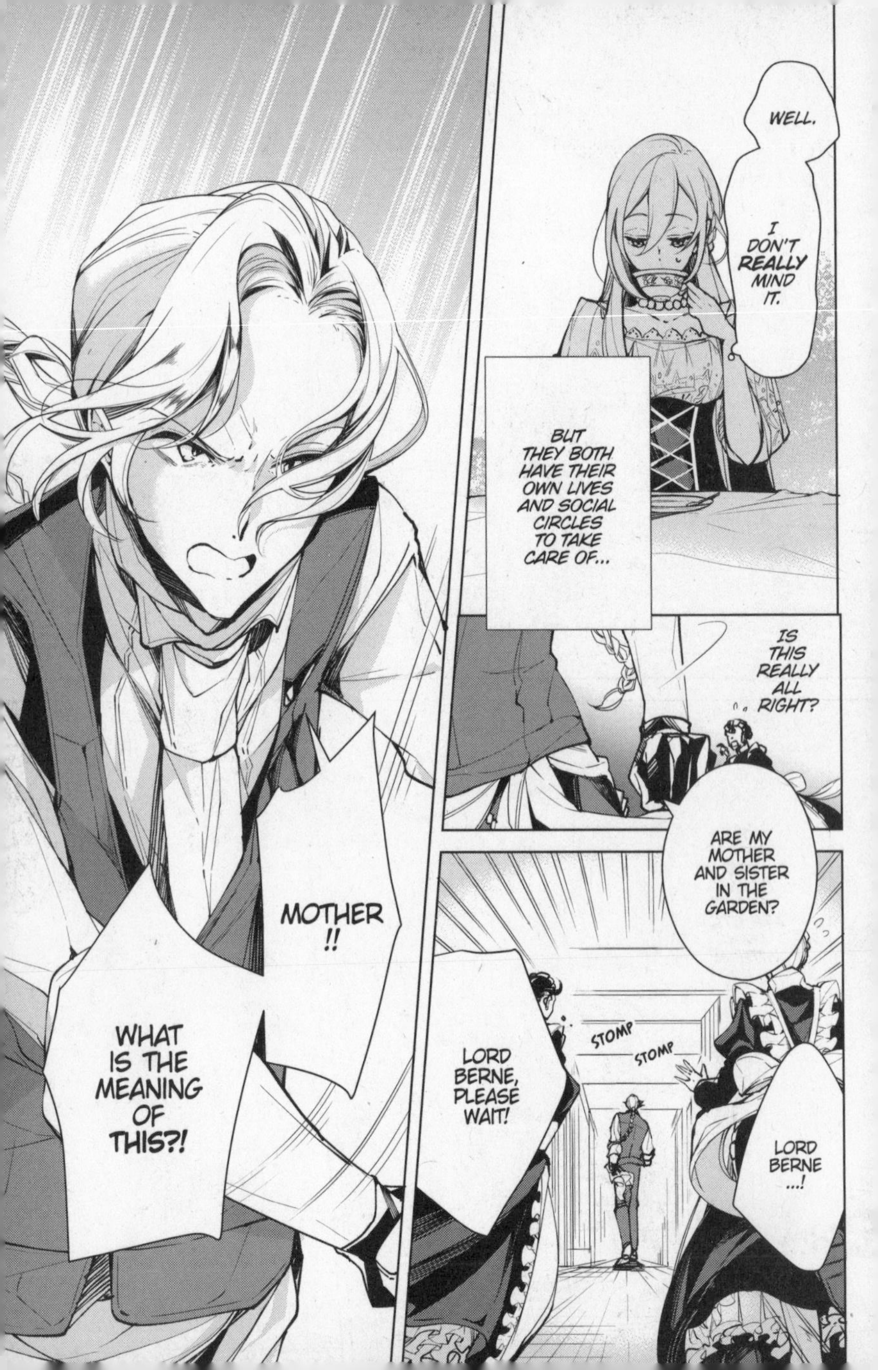
WELL.
I DON'T REALLY MIND IT.
BUT THEY BOTH HAVE THEIR OWN LIVES AND SOCIAL CIRCLES TO TAKE CARE OF...
IS THIS REALLY ALL RIGHT?
ARE MY MOTHER AND SISTER IN THE GARDEN?
STOMP
STOMP
LORD BERNE ...!
LORD BERNE, PLEASE WAIT!
MOTHER !!
WHAT IS THE MEANING OF THIS?!

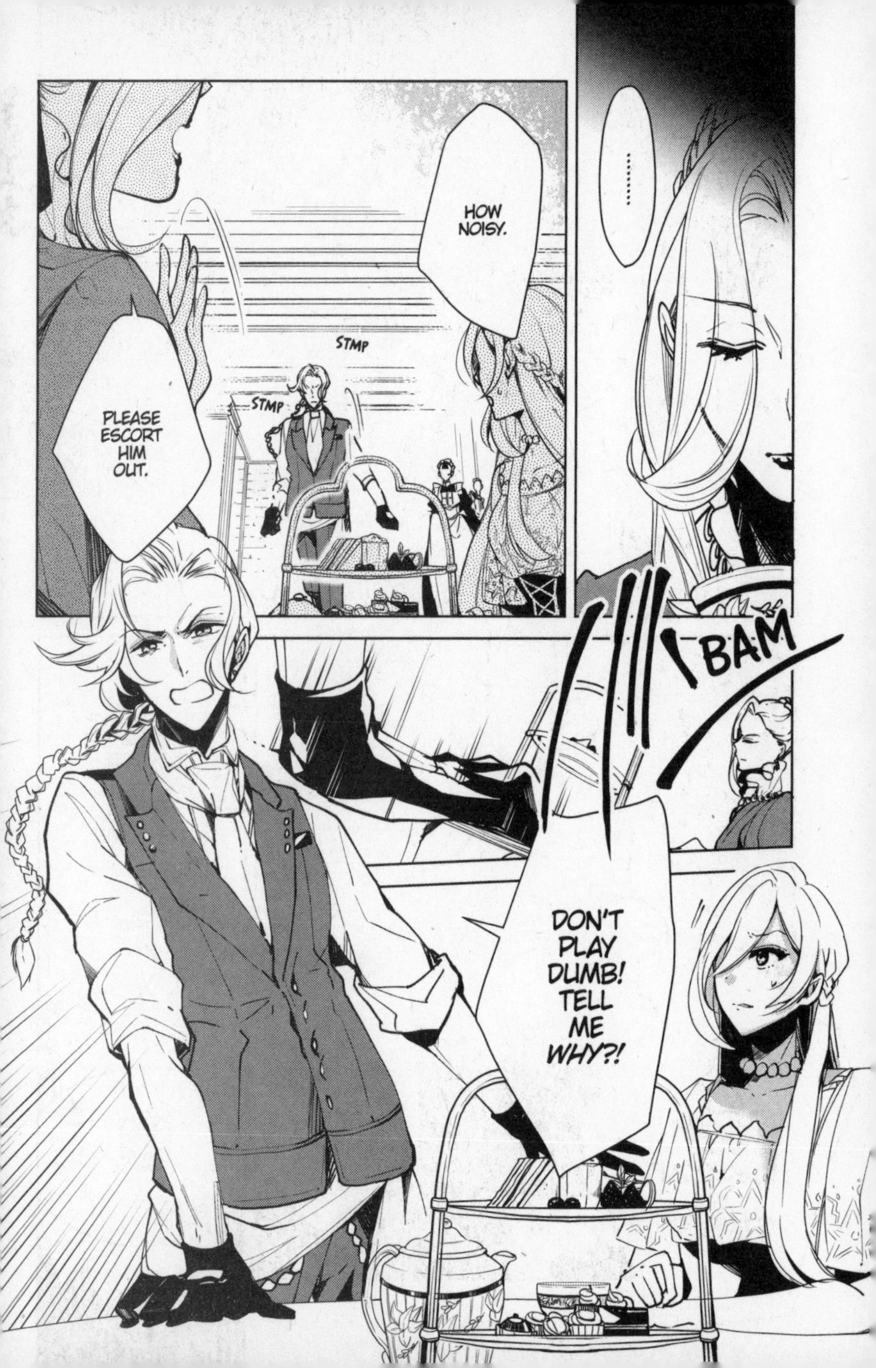
......
HOW NOISY.
STMP
STMP
PLEASE ESCORT HIM OUT.
BAM
DON'T PLAY DUMB! TELL ME WHY?!

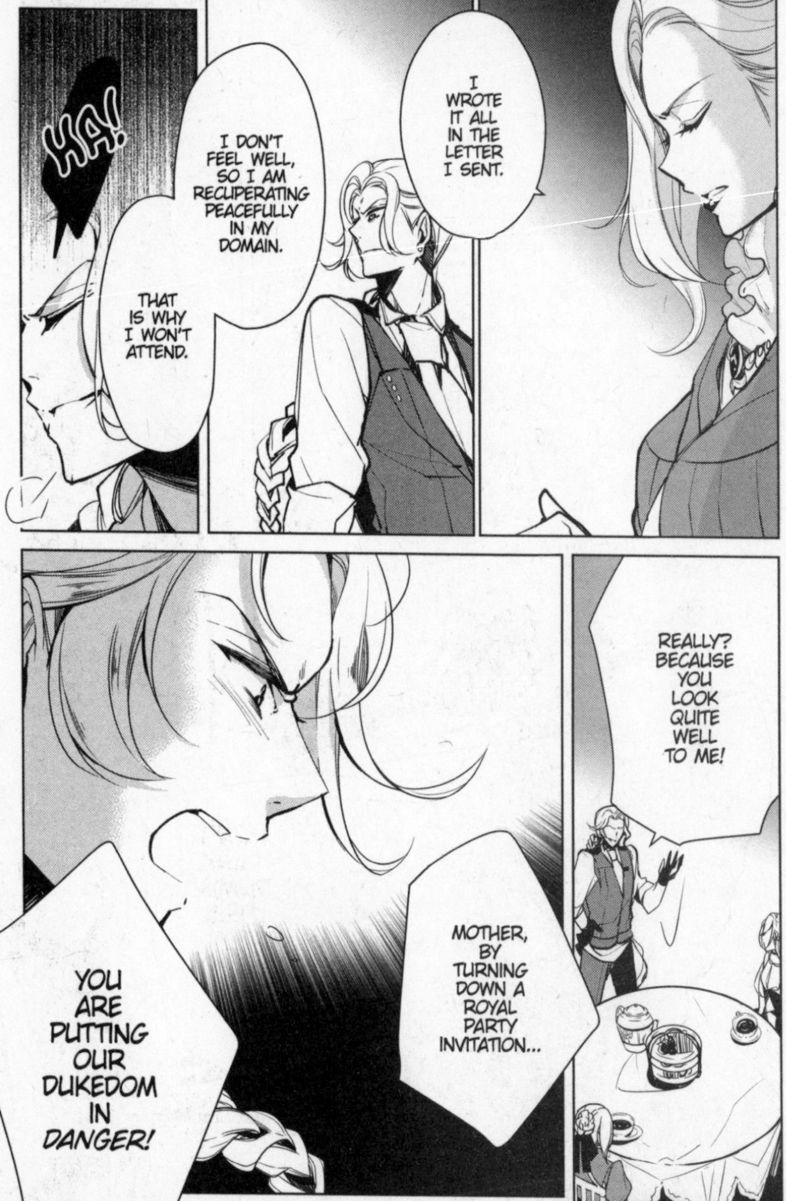
I WROTE IT ALL IN THE LETTER I SENT.
I DON'T FEEL WELL, SO I AM RECUPERATING PEACEFULLY IN MY DOMAIN.
THAT IS WHY I WON'T ATTEND.
HA!
REALLY? BECAUSE YOU LOOK QUITE WELL TO ME!
MOTHER, BY TURNING DOWN A ROYAL PARTY INVITATION...
YOU ARE PUTTING OUR DUKEDOM IN DANGER!

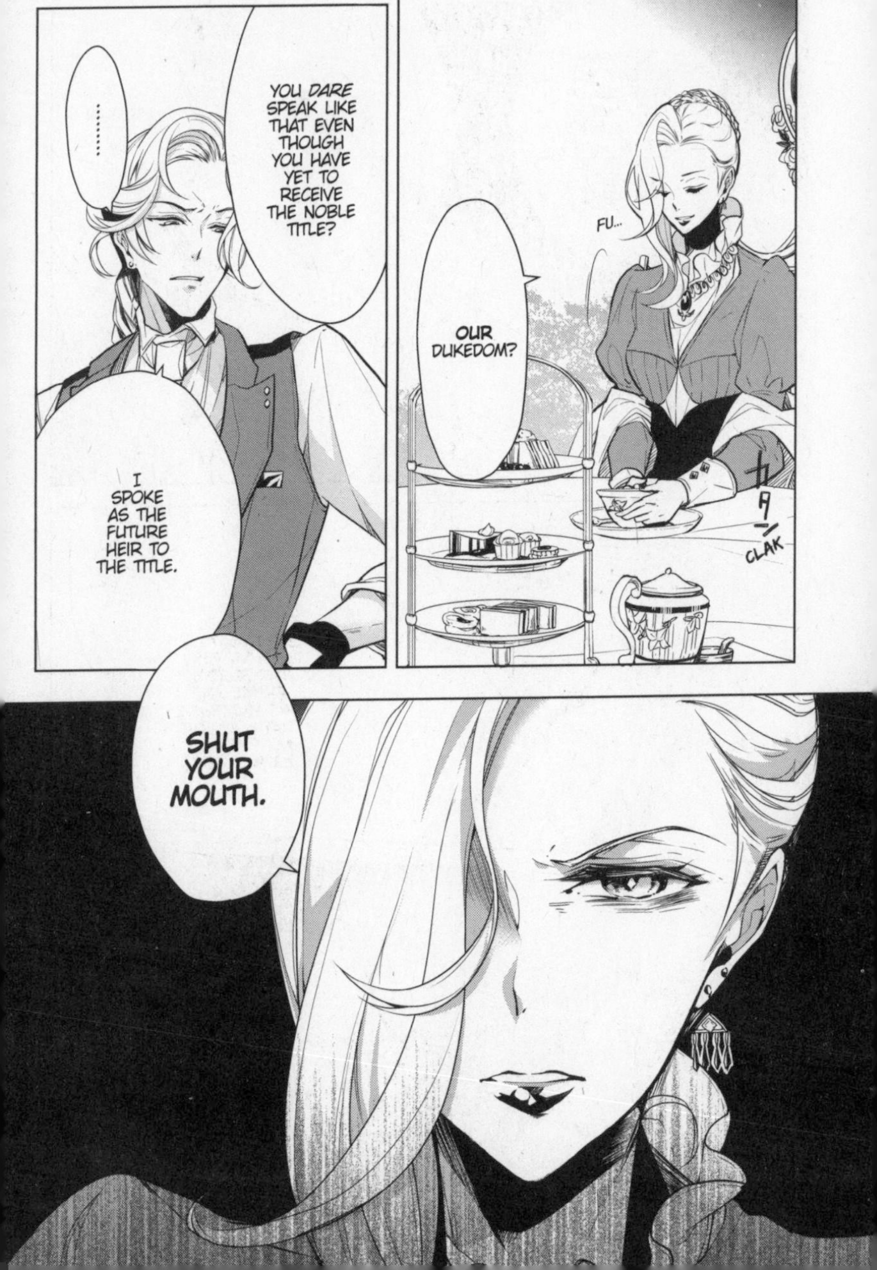
FU...
OUR DUKEDOM?
カタ
CLAK
YOU DARE SPEAK LIKE THAT EVEN THOUGH YOU HAVE YET TO RECEIVE THE NOBLE TITLE?
......
I SPOKE AS THE FUTURE HEIR TO THE TITLE.
SHUT YOUR MOUTH.

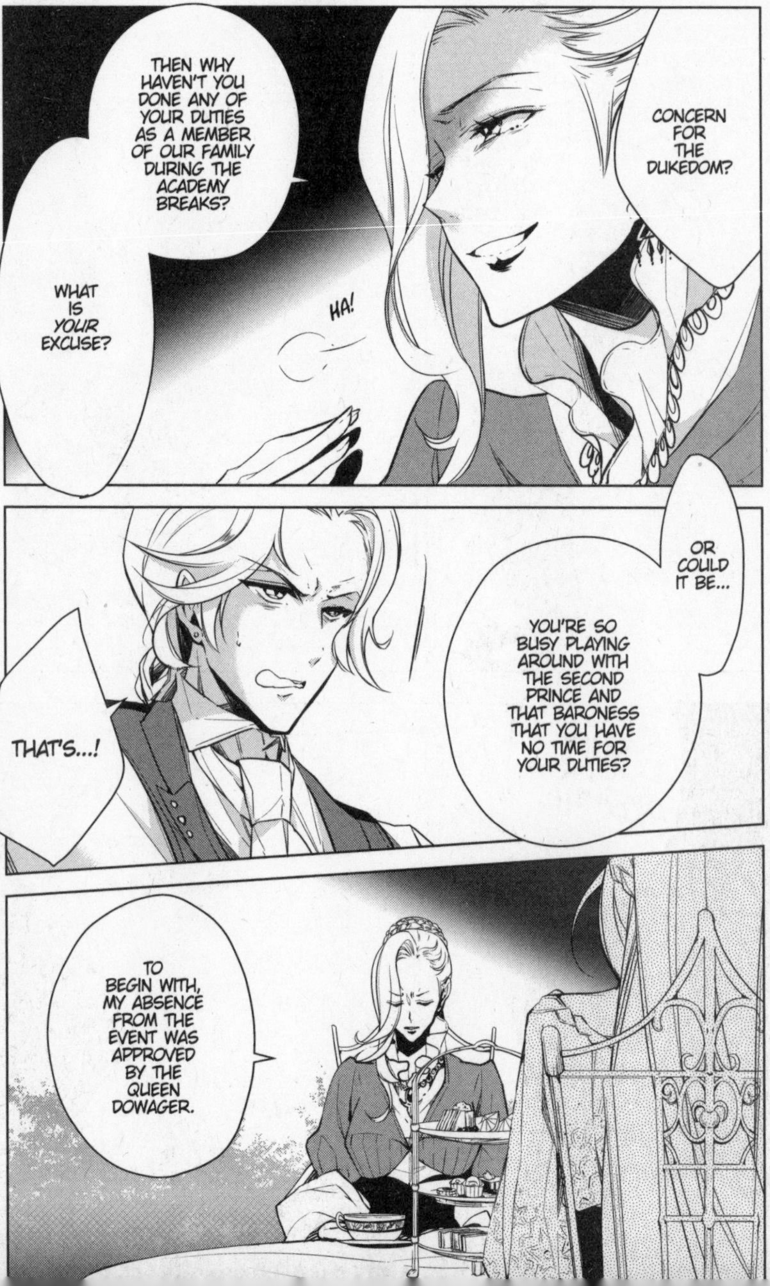
CONCERN FOR THE DUKEDOM?
THEN WHY HAVEN'T YOU DONE ANY OF YOUR DUTIES AS A MEMBER OF OUR FAMILY DURING THE ACADEMY BREAKS?
HA!
WHAT IS YOUR EXCUSE?
OR COULD IT BE...
YOU'RE SO BUSY PLAYING AROUND WITH THE SECOND PRINCE AND THAT BARONESS THAT YOU HAVE NO TIME FOR YOUR DUTIES?
THAT'S...!
TO BEGIN WITH, MY ABSENCE FROM THE EVENT WAS APPROVED BY THE QUEEN DOWAGER.

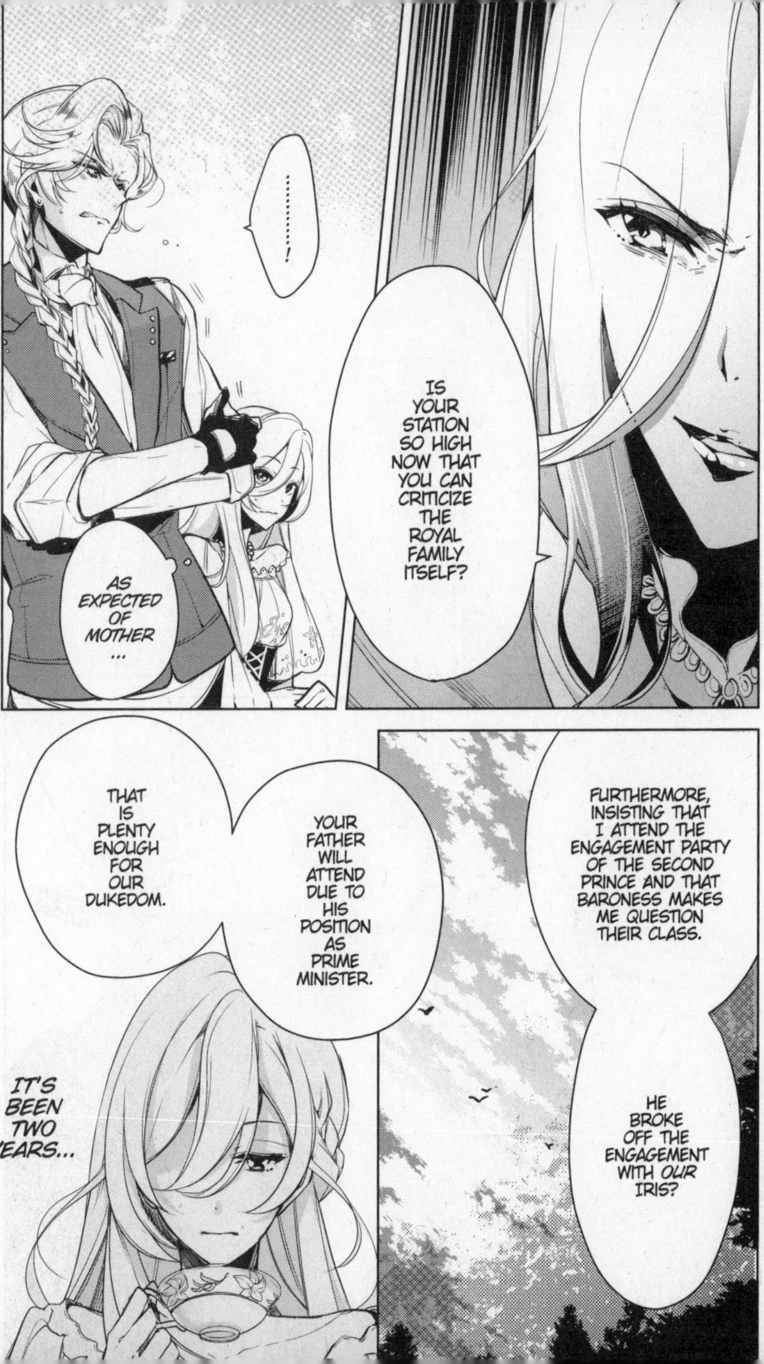
IS YOUR STATION SO HIGH NOW THAT YOU CAN CRITICIZE THE ROYAL FAMILY ITSELF?
......!
AS EXPECTED OF MOTHER ...
FURTHERMORE, INSISTING THAT I ATTEND THE ENGAGEMENT PARTY OF THE SECOND PRINCE AND THAT BARONESS MAKES ME QUESTION THEIR CLASS.
HE BROKE OFF THE ENGAGEMENT WITH OUR IRIS?
YOUR FATHER WILL ATTEND DUE TO HIS POSITION AS PRIME MINISTER.
THAT IS PLENTY ENOUGH FOR OUR DUKEDOM.
IT'S BEEN TWO YEARS...

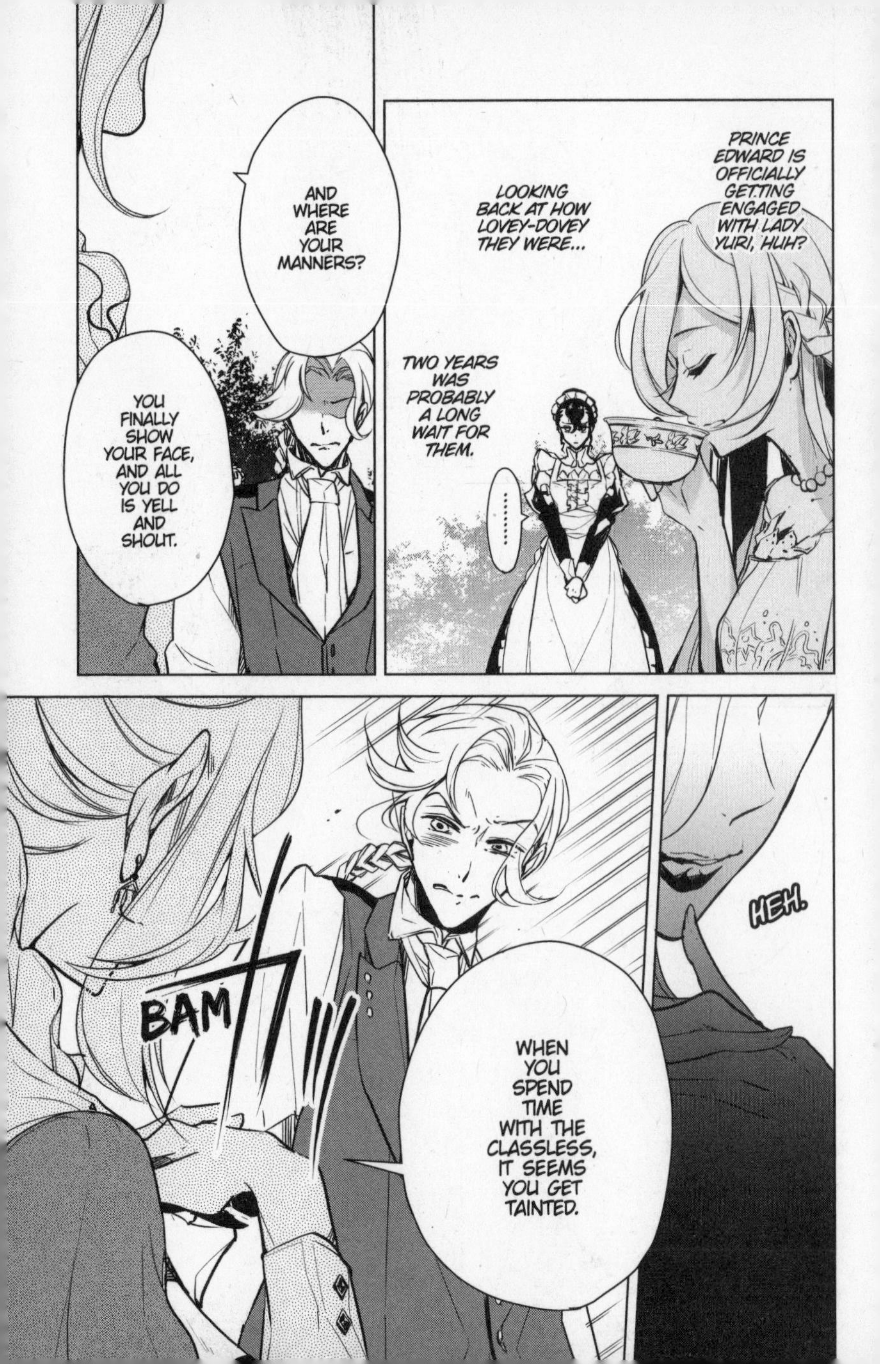
PRINCE EDWARD IS OFFICIALLY GETTING ENGAGED WITH LADY YURI, HUH?
LOOKING BACK AT HOW LOVEY-DOVEY THEY WERE...
TWO YEARS WAS PROBABLY A LONG WAIT FOR THEM.
......
YOU FINALLY SHOW YOUR FACE, AND ALL YOU DO IS YELL AND SHOUT.
AND WHERE ARE YOUR MANNERS?
HEH.
WHEN YOU SPEND TIME WITH THE CLASSLESS, IT SEEMS YOU GET TAINTED.
BAM

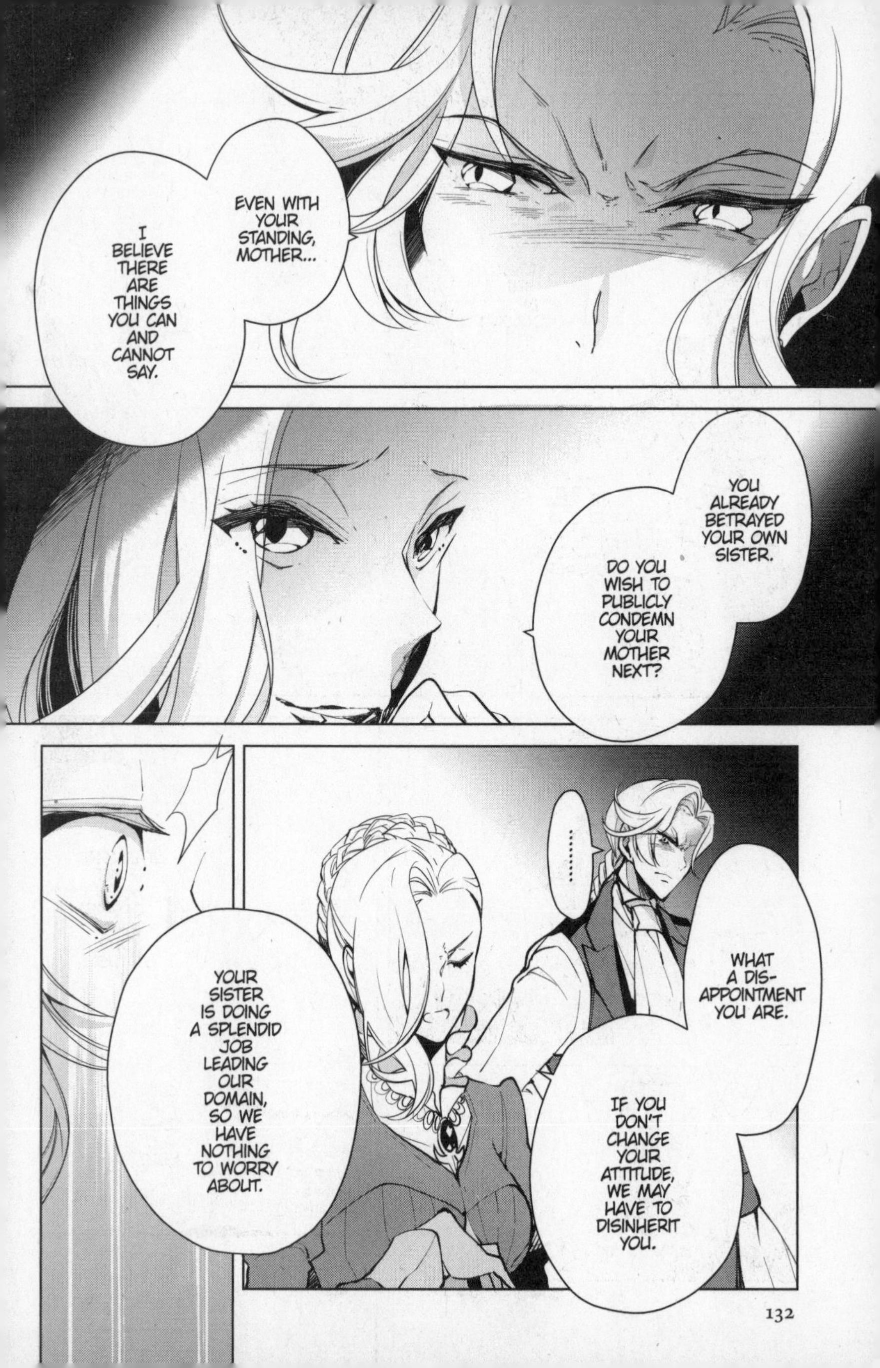
EVEN WITH YOUR STANDING, MOTHER...
I BELIEVE THERE ARE THINGS YOU CAN AND CANNOT SAY.
YOU ALREADY BETRAYED YOUR OWN SISTER.
DO YOU WISH TO PUBLICLY CONDEMN YOUR MOTHER NEXT?
......
WHAT A DIS-APPOINTMENT YOU ARE.
IF YOU DON'T CHANGE YOUR ATTITUDE, WE MAY HAVE TO DISINHERIT YOU.
YOUR SISTER IS DOING A SPLENDID JOB LEADING OUR DOMAIN, SO WE HAVE NOTHING TO WORRY ABOUT.

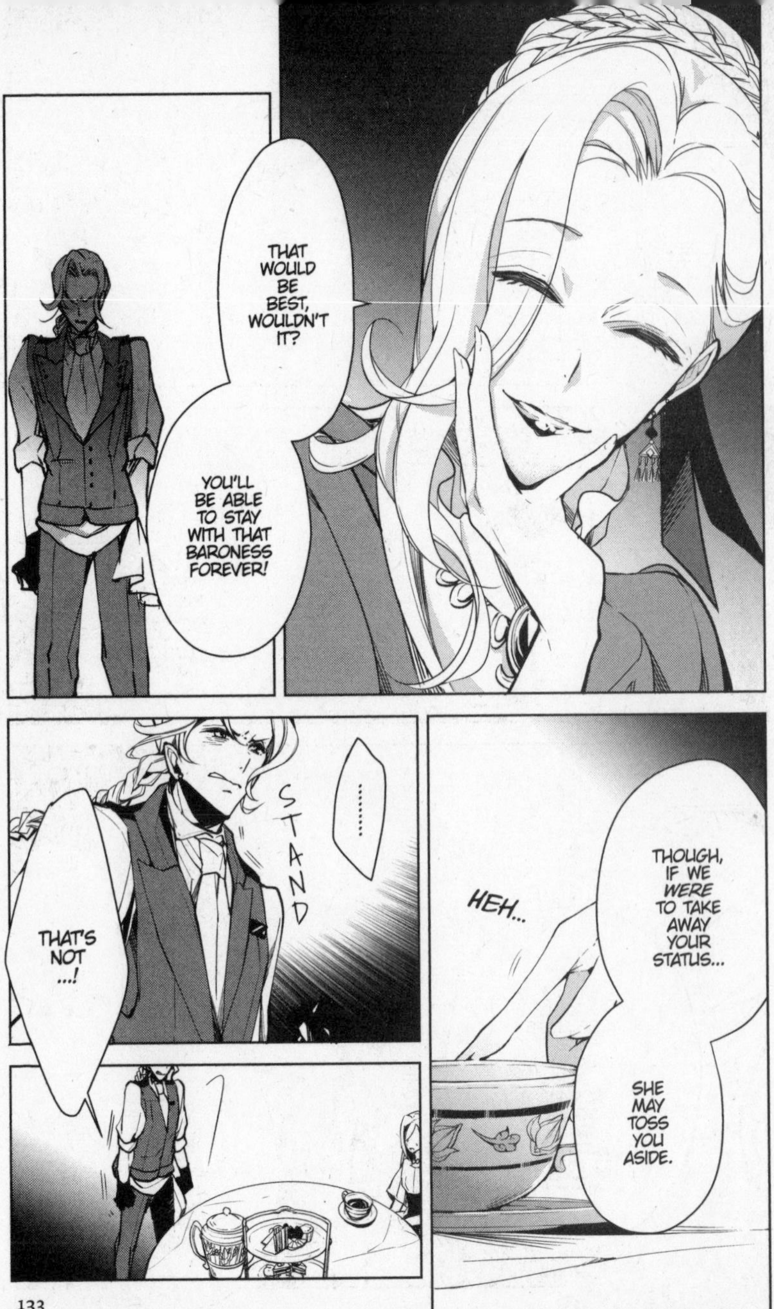
THAT WOULD BE BEST, WOULDN'T IT?
YOU'LL BE ABLE TO STAY WITH THAT BARONESS FOREVER!
THOUGH, IF WE *WERE* TO TAKE AWAY YOUR STATUS...
HEH...
SHE MAY TOSS YOU ASIDE.
......
STAND
THAT'S NOT ...!

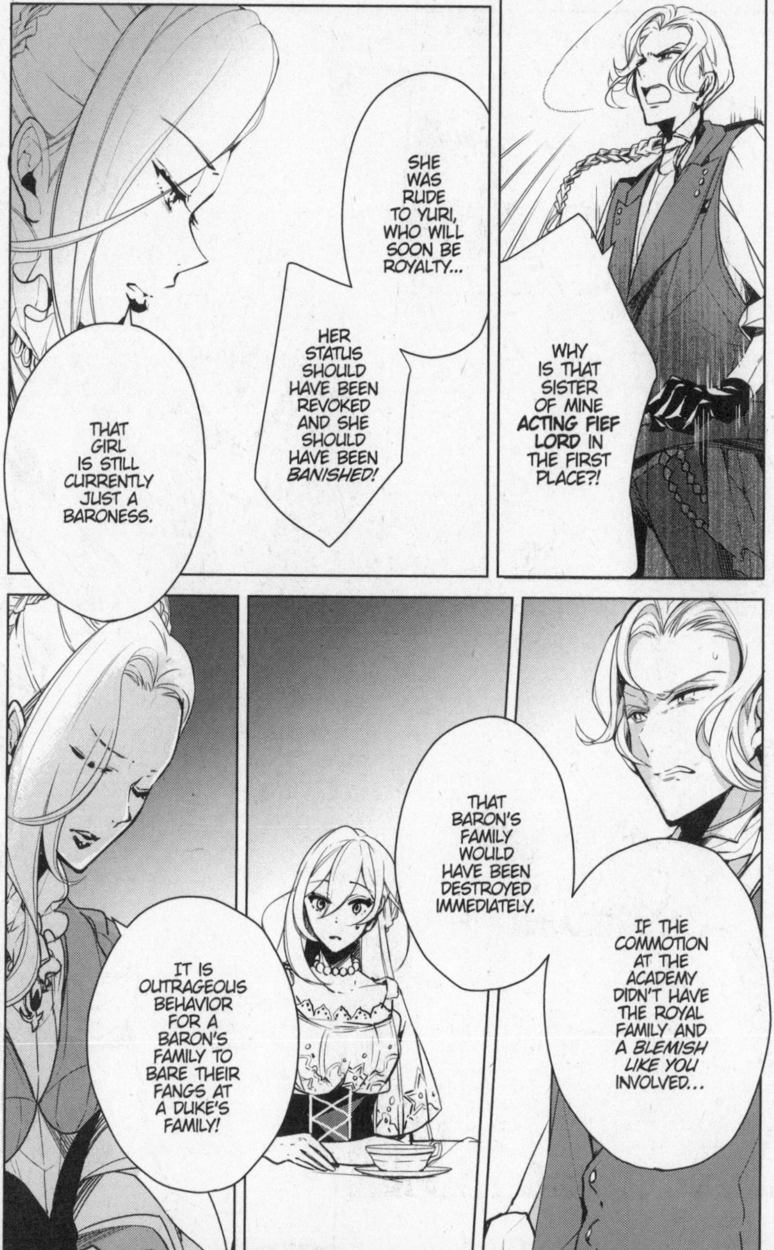
WHY IS THAT SISTER OF MINE ACTING FIEF LORD IN THE FIRST PLACE?!
SHE WAS RUDE TO YURI, WHO WILL SOON BE ROYALTY...
HER STATUS SHOULD HAVE BEEN REVOKED AND SHE SHOULD HAVE BEEN *BANISHED!*
THAT GIRL IS STILL CURRENTLY JUST A BARONESS.
IF THE COMMOTION AT THE ACADEMY DIDN'T HAVE THE ROYAL FAMILY AND A *BLEMISH LIKE YOU* INVOLVED...
THAT BARON'S FAMILY WOULD HAVE BEEN DESTROYED IMMEDIATELY.
IT IS OUTRAGEOUS BEHAVIOR FOR A BARON'S FAMILY TO BARE THEIR FANGS AT A DUKE'S FAMILY!

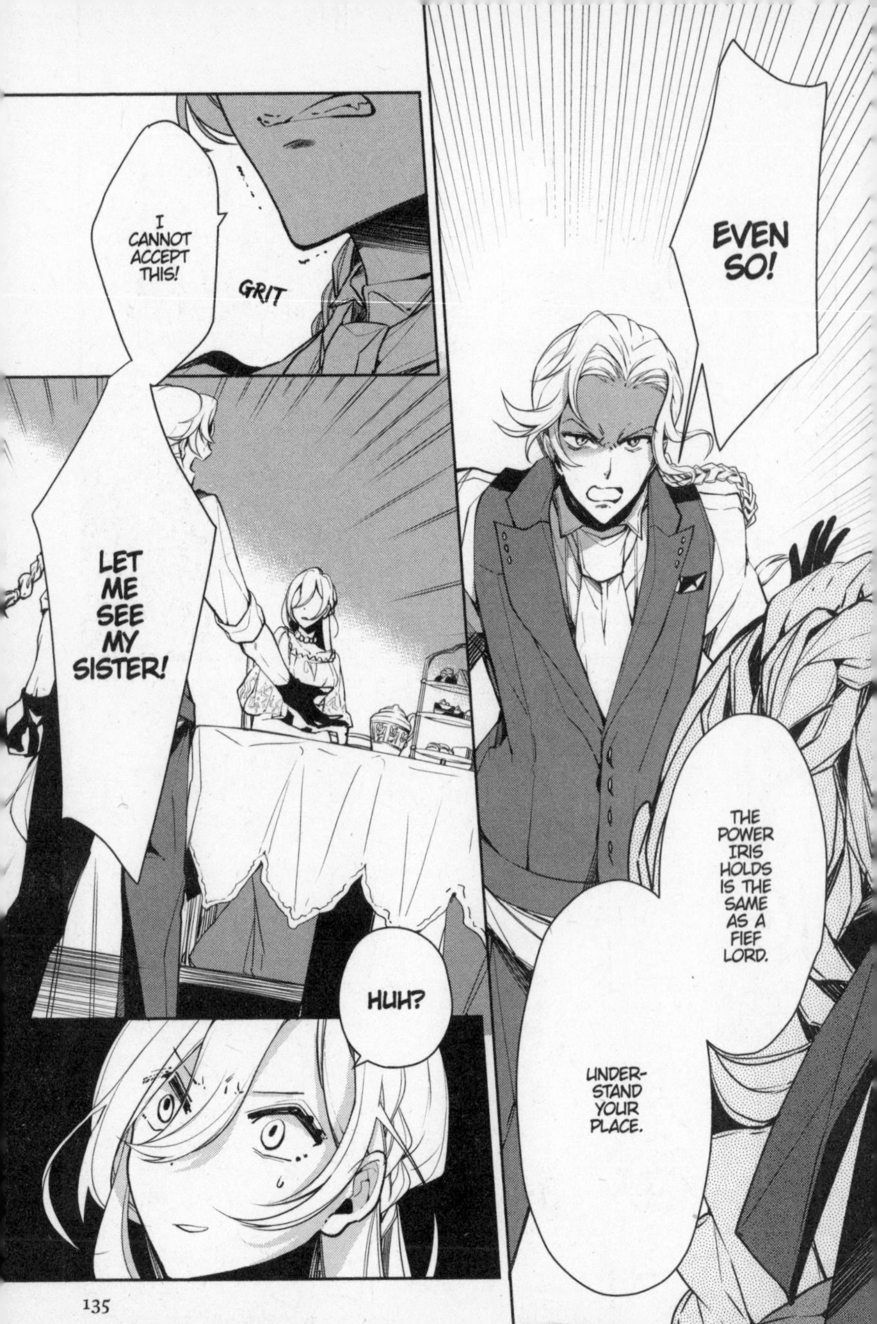
EVEN SO!
THE POWER IRIS HOLDS IS THE SAME AS A FIEF LORD.
UNDER-STAND YOUR PLACE.
I CANNOT ACCEPT THIS!
GRIT
LET ME SEE MY SISTER!
HUH?

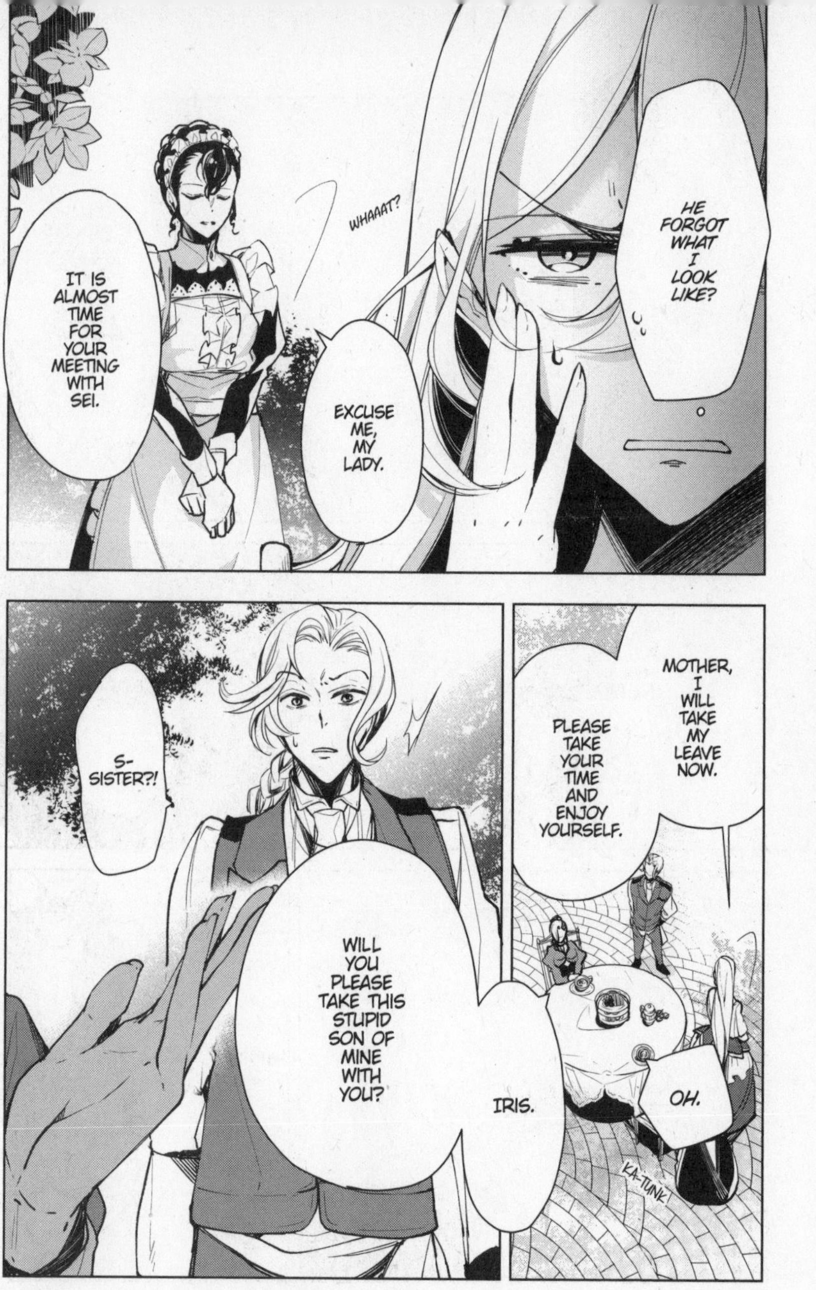
HE FORGOT WHAT I LOOK LIKE?
WHAAAT?
EXCUSE ME, MY LADY.
IT IS ALMOST TIME FOR YOUR MEETING WITH SEI.
MOTHER, I WILL TAKE MY LEAVE NOW.
PLEASE TAKE YOUR TIME AND ENJOY YOURSELF.
OH.
KA-TUNK!
S-SISTER?!
IRIS.
WILL YOU PLEASE TAKE THIS STUPID SON OF MINE WITH YOU?

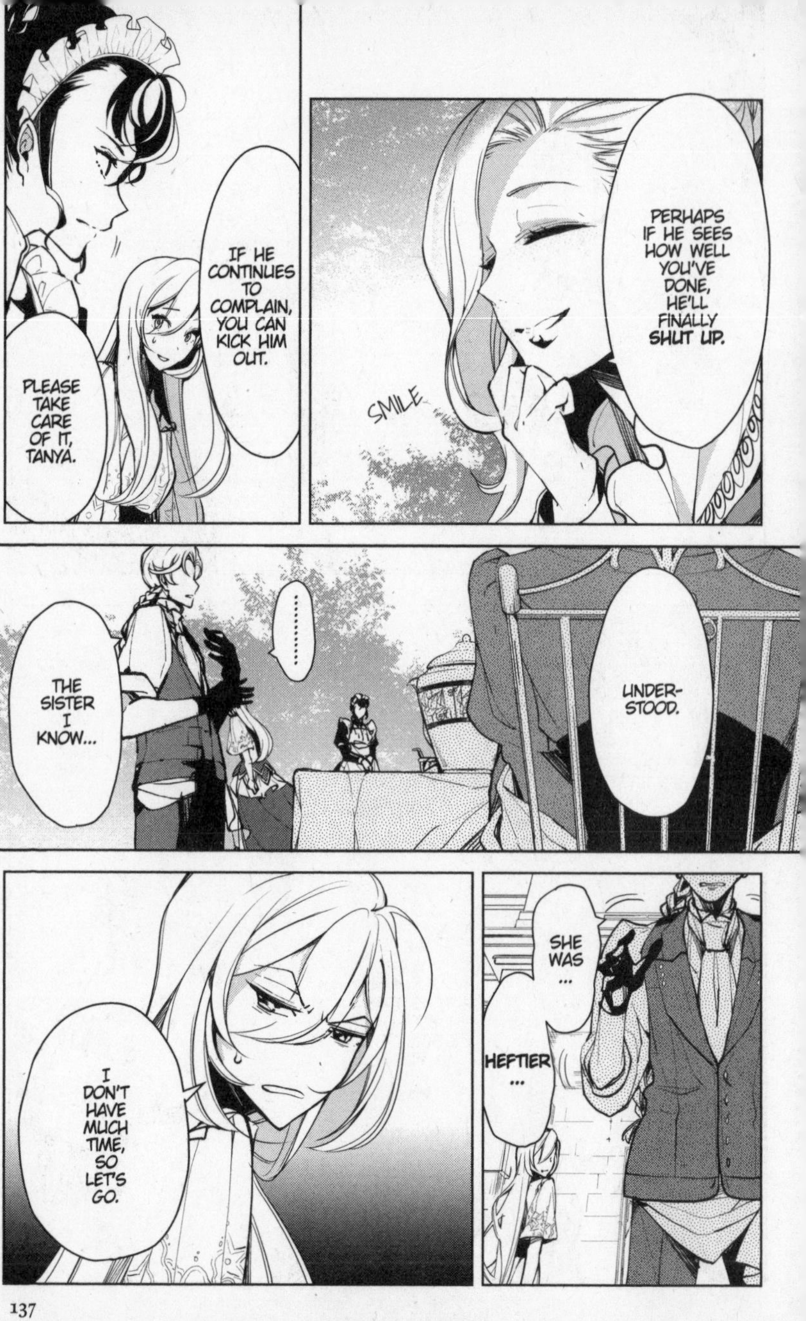
PERHAPS IF HE SEES HOW WELL YOU'VE DONE, HE'LL FINALLY SHUT UP.
SMILE
IF HE CONTINUES TO COMPLAIN, YOU CAN KICK HIM OUT.
PLEASE TAKE CARE OF IT, TANYA.
UNDER-STOOD.
....
THE SISTER I KNOW...
SHE WAS...
HEFTIER...
I DON'T HAVE MUCH TIME, SO LET'S GO.

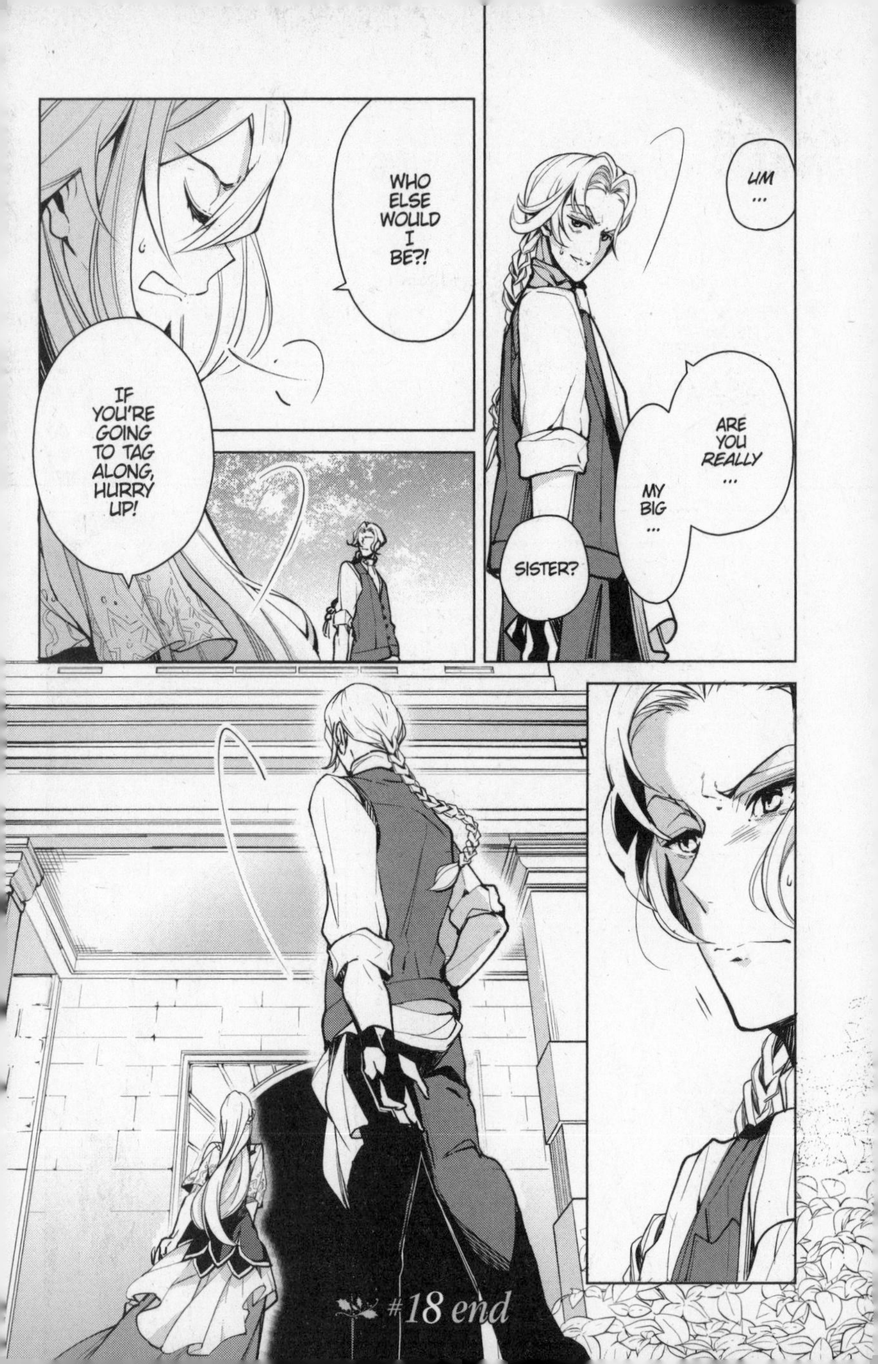
UM ...
ARE YOU REALLY ...
MY BIG ...
SISTER?
WHO ELSE WOULD I BE?!
IF YOU'RE GOING TO TAG ALONG, HURRY UP!
#18 end

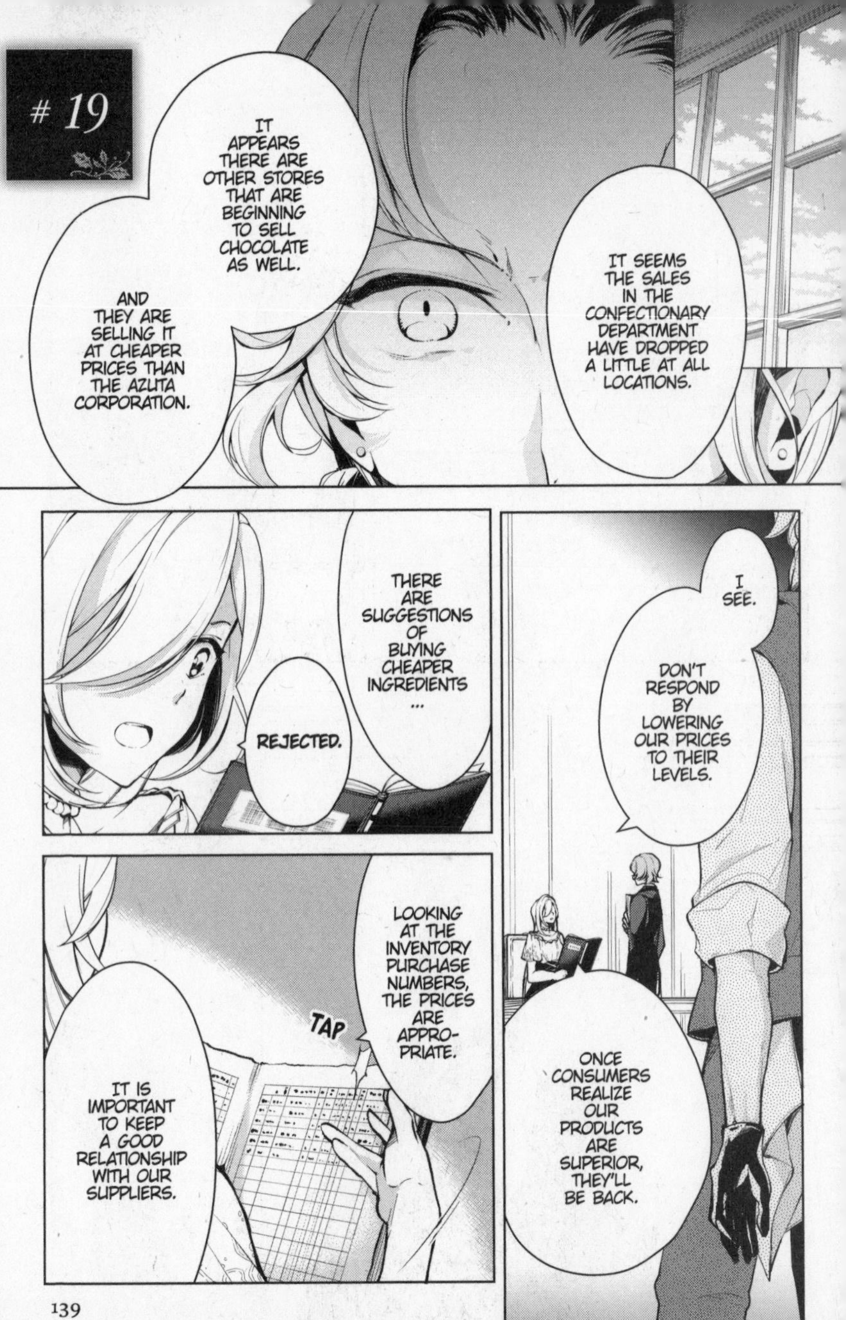

19
IT SEEMS THE SALES IN THE CONFECTIONARY DEPARTMENT HAVE DROPPED A LITTLE AT ALL LOCATIONS.
IT APPEARS THERE ARE OTHER STORES THAT ARE BEGINNING TO SELL CHOCOLATE AS WELL.
AND THEY ARE SELLING IT AT CHEAPER PRICES THAN THE AZUTA CORPORATION.
I SEE.
DON'T RESPOND BY LOWERING OUR PRICES TO THEIR LEVELS.
ONCE CONSUMERS REALIZE OUR PRODUCTS ARE SUPERIOR, THEY'LL BE BACK.
THERE ARE SUGGESTIONS OF BUYING CHEAPER INGREDIENTS ...
REJECTED.
LOOKING AT THE INVENTORY PURCHASE NUMBERS, THE PRICES ARE APPRO- PRIATE.
TAP
IT IS IMPORTANT TO KEEP A GOOD RELATIONSHIP WITH OUR SUPPLIERS.

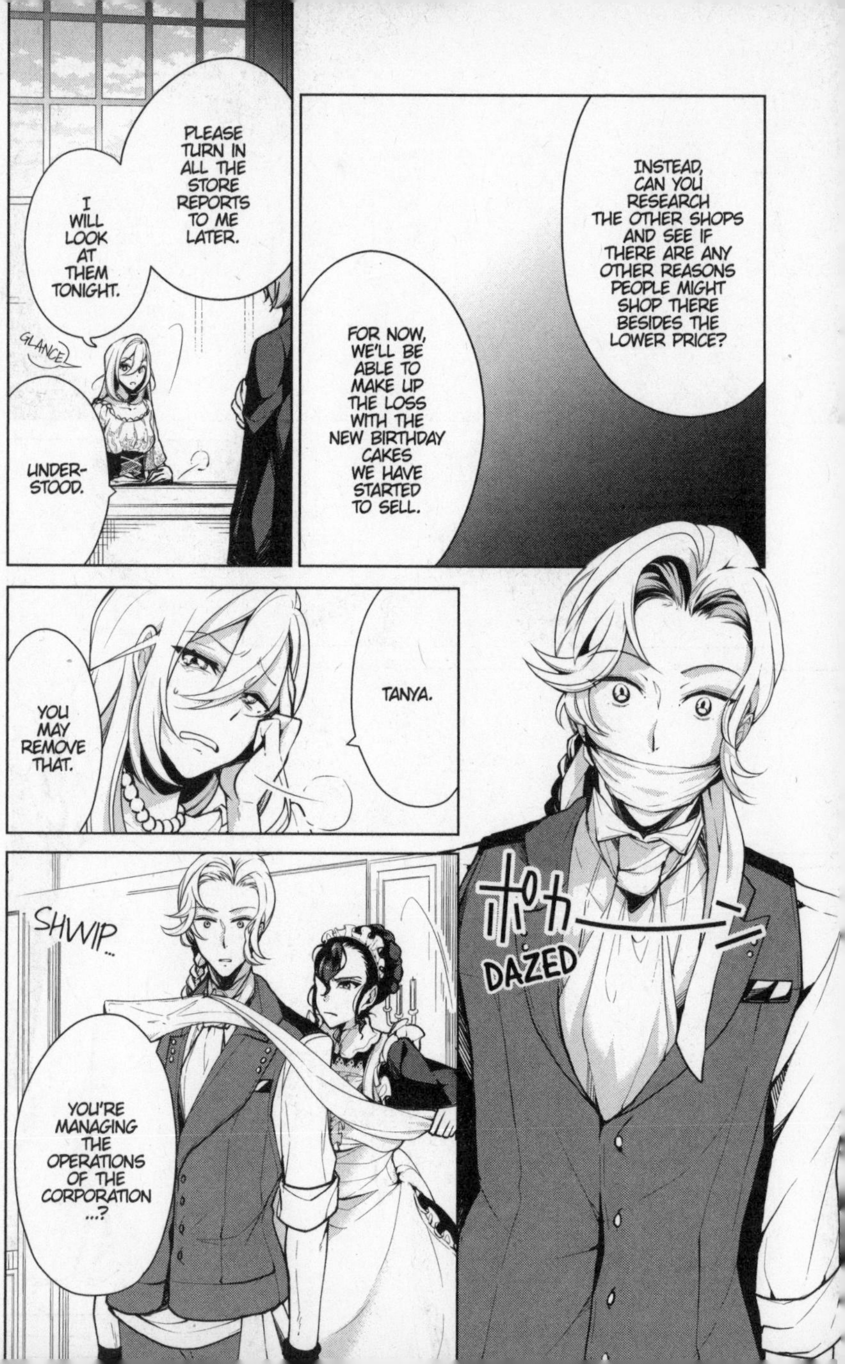
INSTEAD, CAN YOU RESEARCH THE OTHER SHOPS AND SEE IF THERE ARE ANY OTHER REASONS PEOPLE MIGHT SHOP THERE BESIDES THE LOWER PRICE?
FOR NOW, WE'LL BE ABLE TO MAKE UP THE LOSS WITH THE NEW BIRTHDAY CAKES WE HAVE STARTED TO SELL.
PLEASE TURN IN ALL THE STORE REPORTS TO ME LATER.
I WILL LOOK AT THEM TONIGHT.
GLANCE
UNDER-STOOD.
ポカー
DAZED
TANYA.
YOU MAY REMOVE THAT.
SHWIP...
YOU'RE MANAGING THE OPERATIONS OF THE CORPORATION ...?

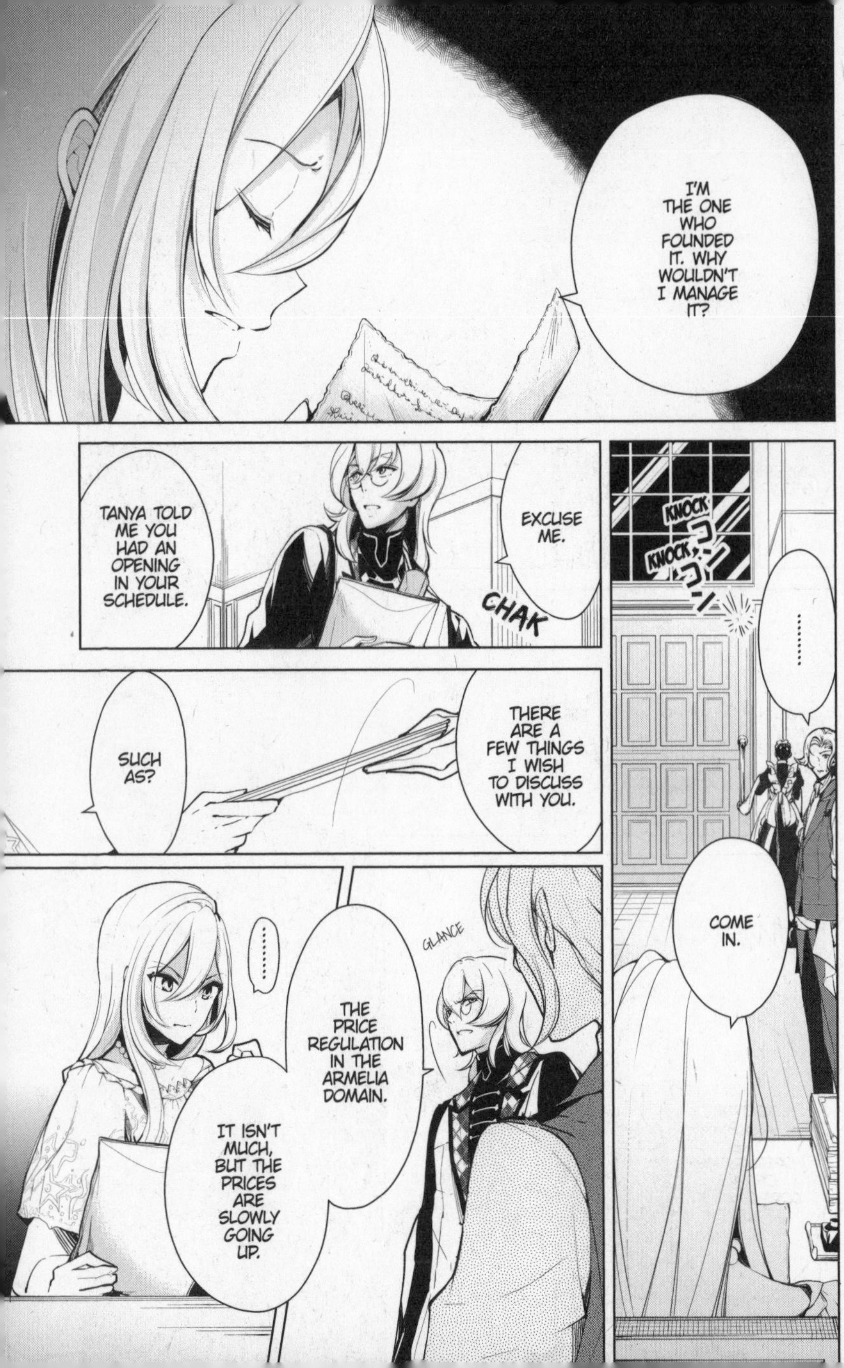
I'M THE ONE WHO FOUNDED IT. WHY WOULDN'T I MANAGE IT?
KNOCK, KNOCK
......
COME IN.
EXCUSE ME.
CHAK
TANYA TOLD ME YOU HAD AN OPENING IN YOUR SCHEDULE.
THERE ARE A FEW THINGS I WISH TO DISCUSS WITH YOU.
SUCH AS?
GLANCE
THE PRICE REGULATION IN THE ARMELIA DOMAIN.
......
IT ISN'T MUCH, BUT THE PRICES ARE SLOWLY GOING UP.

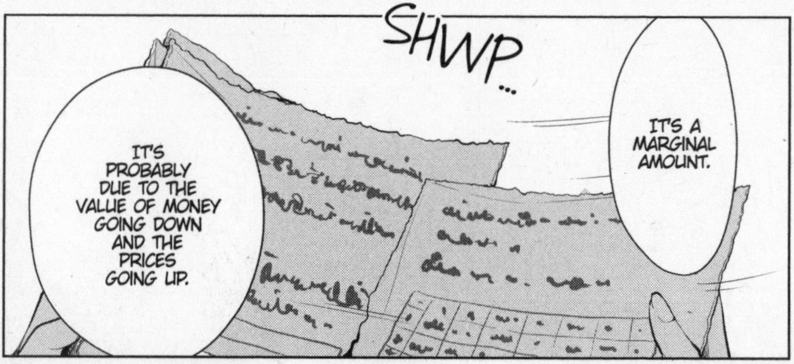
IT'S A MARGINAL AMOUNT.
SHWP...
IT'S PROBABLY DUE TO THE VALUE OF MONEY GOING DOWN AND THE PRICES GOING UP.
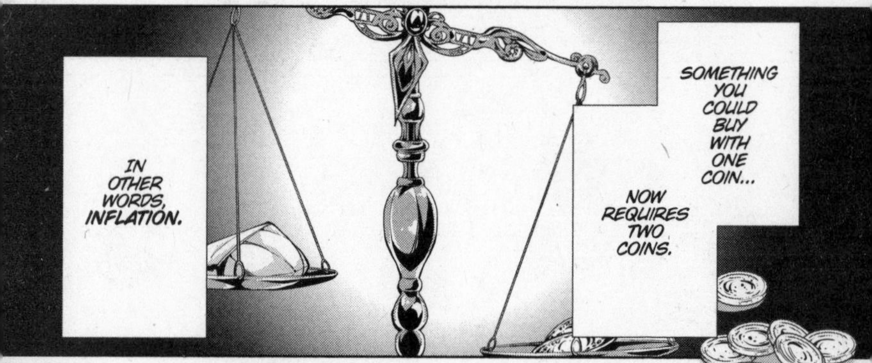
SOMETHING YOU COULD BUY WITH ONE COIN...
NOW REQUIRES TWO COINS.
IN OTHER WORDS, INFLATION.
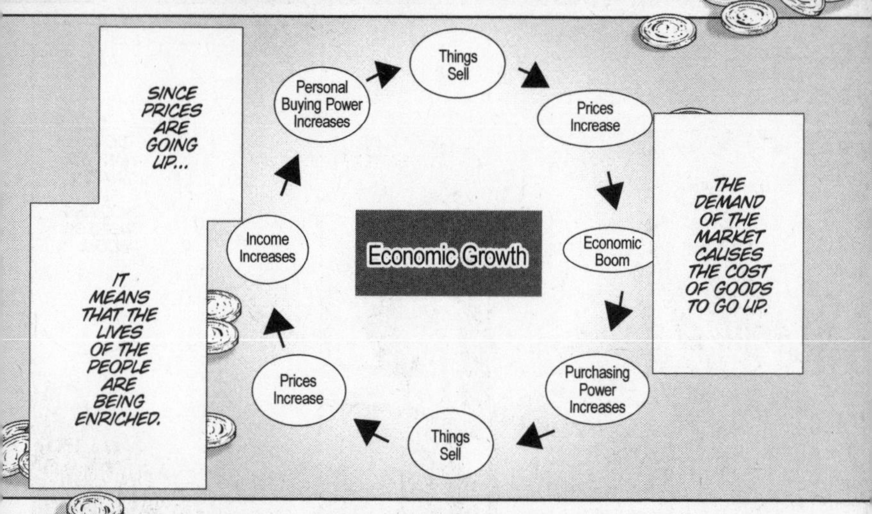
THE DEMAND OF THE MARKET CAUSES THE COST OF GOODS TO GO UP.
Economic Growth
Income Increases
Personal Buying Power Increases
Things Sell
Prices Increase
Economic Boom
Purchasing Power Increases
Things Sell
Prices Increase
SINCE PRICES ARE GOING UP...
IT MEANS THAT THE LIVES OF THE PEOPLE ARE BEING ENRICHED.

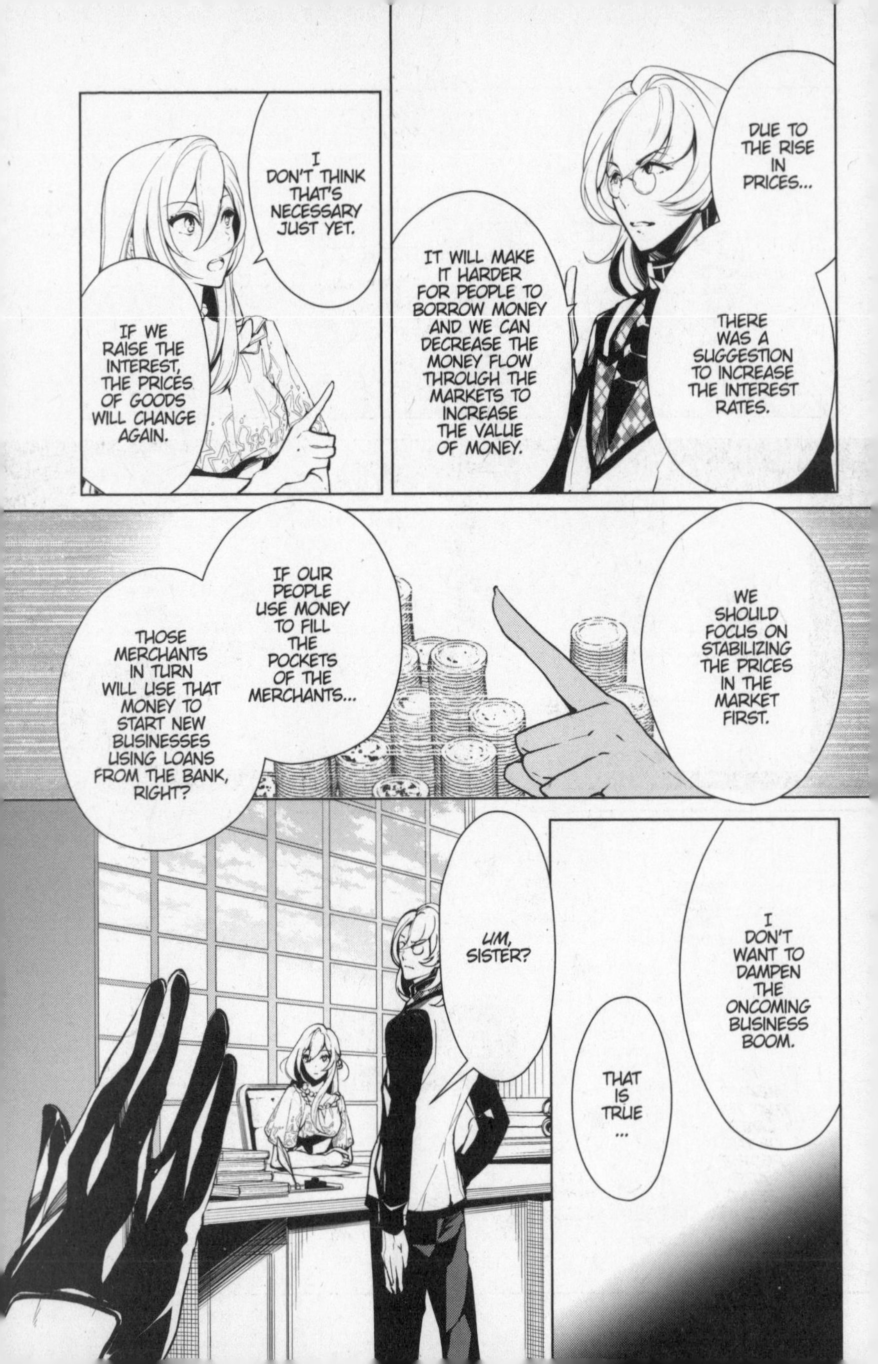
DUE TO THE RISE IN PRICES...
THERE WAS A SUGGESTION TO INCREASE THE INTEREST RATES.
IT WILL MAKE IT HARDER FOR PEOPLE TO BORROW MONEY AND WE CAN DECREASE THE MONEY FLOW THROUGH THE MARKETS TO INCREASE THE VALUE OF MONEY.
I DON'T THINK THAT'S NECESSARY JUST YET.
IF WE RAISE THE INTEREST, THE PRICES OF GOODS WILL CHANGE AGAIN.
WE SHOULD FOCUS ON STABILIZING THE PRICES IN THE MARKET FIRST.
IF OUR PEOPLE USE MONEY TO FILL THE POCKETS OF THE MERCHANTS...
THOSE MERCHANTS IN TURN WILL USE THAT MONEY TO START NEW BUSINESSES USING LOANS FROM THE BANK, RIGHT?
I DON'T WANT TO DAMPEN THE ONCOMING BUSINESS BOOM.
THAT IS TRUE ...
UM, SISTER?

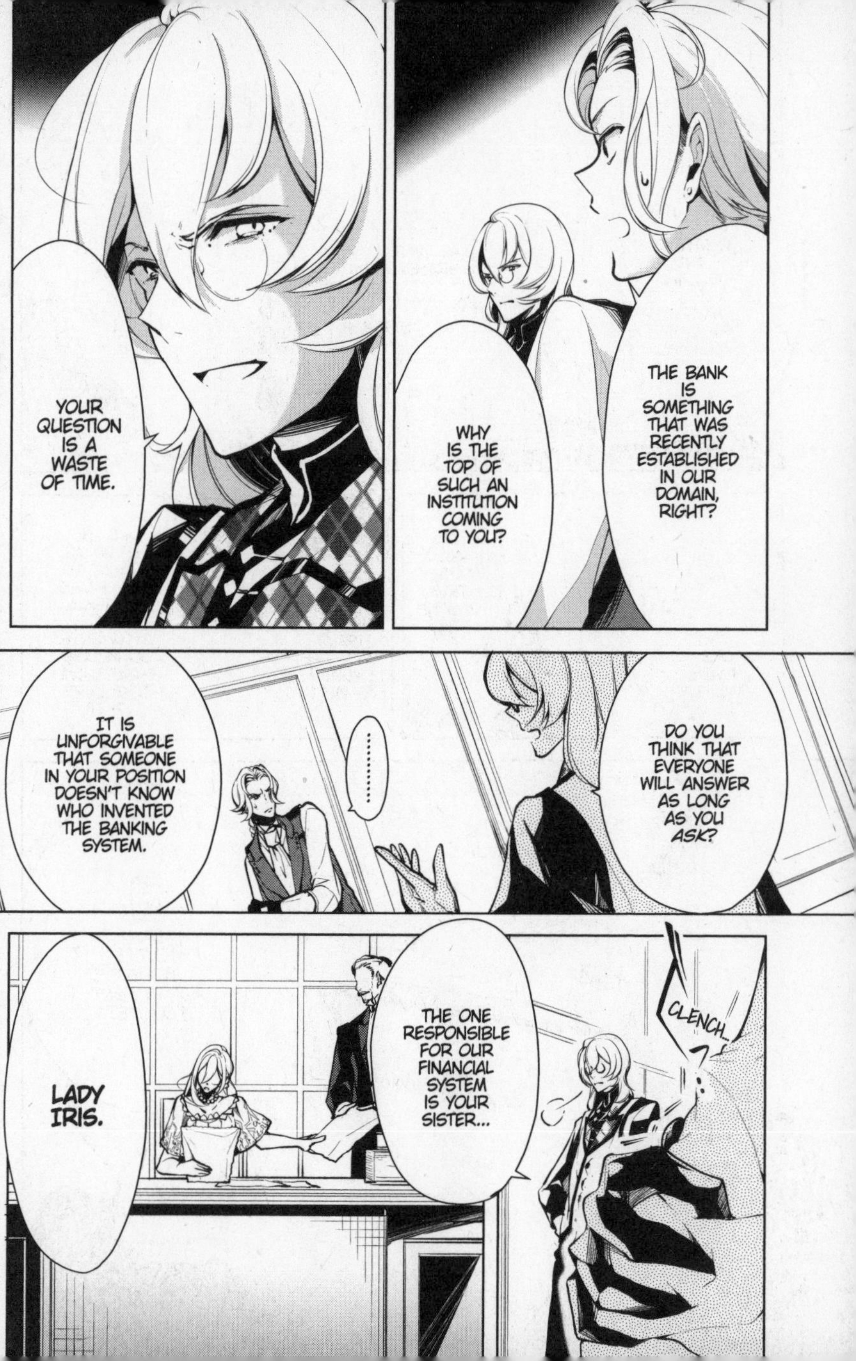
THE BANK IS SOMETHING THAT WAS RECENTLY ESTABLISHED IN OUR DOMAIN, RIGHT?
WHY IS THE TOP OF SUCH AN INSTITUTION COMING TO YOU?
YOUR QUESTION IS A WASTE OF TIME.
DO YOU THINK THAT EVERYONE WILL ANSWER AS LONG AS YOU ASK?
....
IT IS UNFORGIVABLE THAT SOMEONE IN YOUR POSITION DOESN'T KNOW WHO INVENTED THE BANKING SYSTEM.
CLENCH...
THE ONE RESPONSIBLE FOR OUR FINANCIAL SYSTEM IS YOUR SISTER...
LADY IRIS.

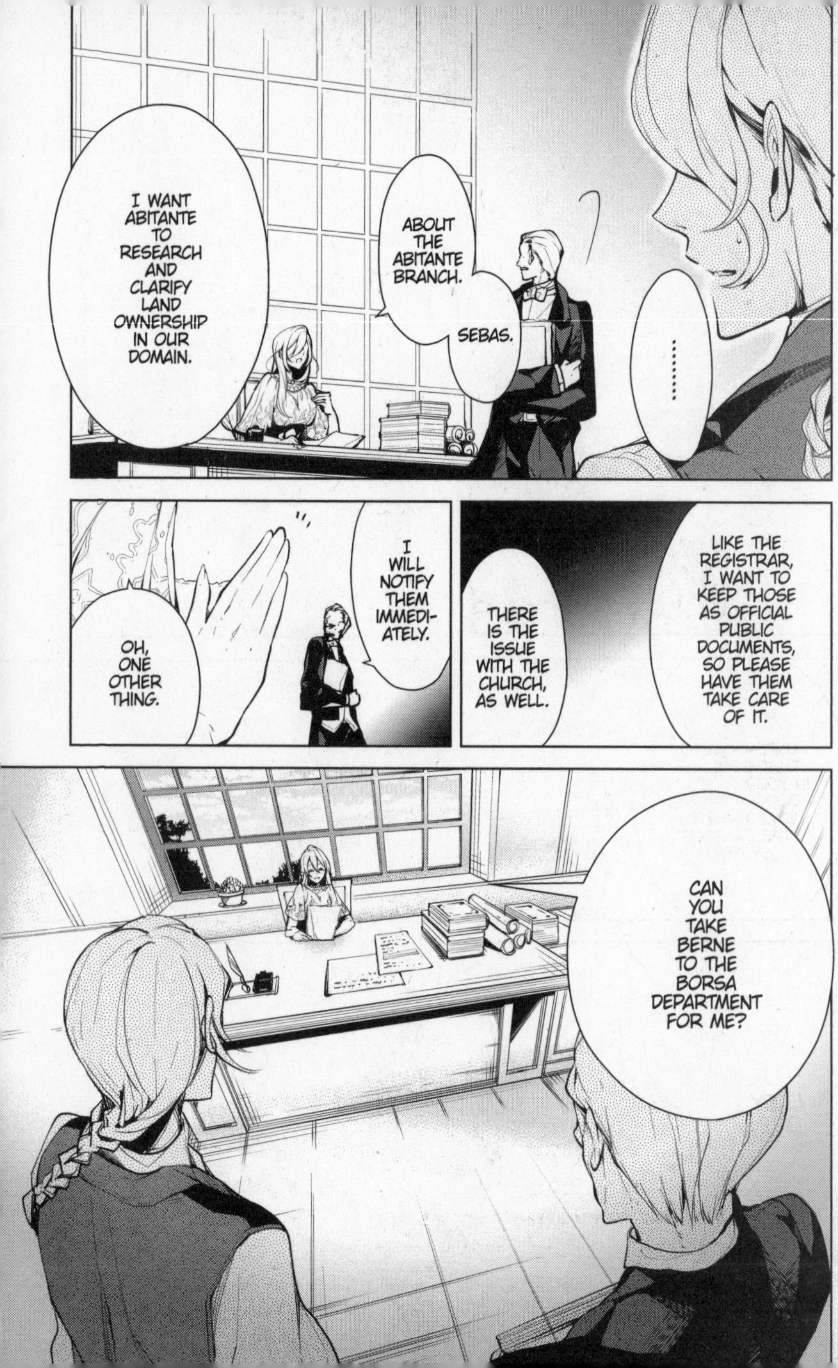
......
SEBAS.
ABOUT THE ABITANTE BRANCH.
I WANT ABITANTE TO RESEARCH AND CLARIFY LAND OWNERSHIP IN OUR DOMAIN.
LIKE THE REGISTRAR, I WANT TO KEEP THOSE AS OFFICIAL PUBLIC DOCUMENTS, SO PLEASE HAVE THEM TAKE CARE OF IT.
THERE IS THE ISSUE WITH THE CHURCH, AS WELL.
I WILL NOTIFY THEM IMMEDIATELY.
OH, ONE OTHER THING.
CAN YOU TAKE BERNE TO THE BORSA DEPARTMENT FOR ME?

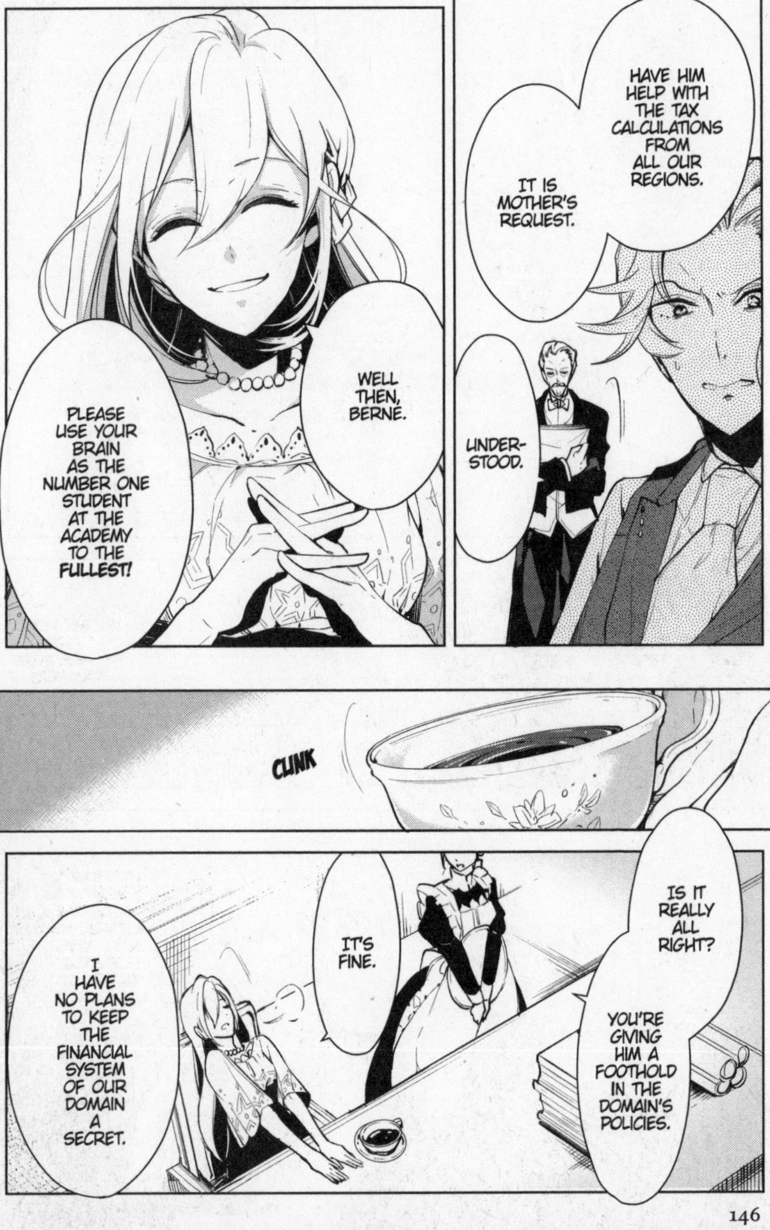
HAVE HIM HELP WITH THE TAX CALCULATIONS FROM ALL OUR REGIONS.
IT IS MOTHER'S REQUEST.
UNDER-STOOD.
WELL THEN, BERNE.
PLEASE USE YOUR BRAIN AS THE NUMBER ONE STUDENT AT THE ACADEMY TO THE FULLEST!
CLINK
IS IT REALLY ALL RIGHT?
YOU'RE GIVING HIM A FOOTHOLD IN THE DOMAIN'S POLICIES.
IT'S FINE.
I HAVE NO PLANS TO KEEP THE FINANCIAL SYSTEM OF OUR DOMAIN A SECRET.

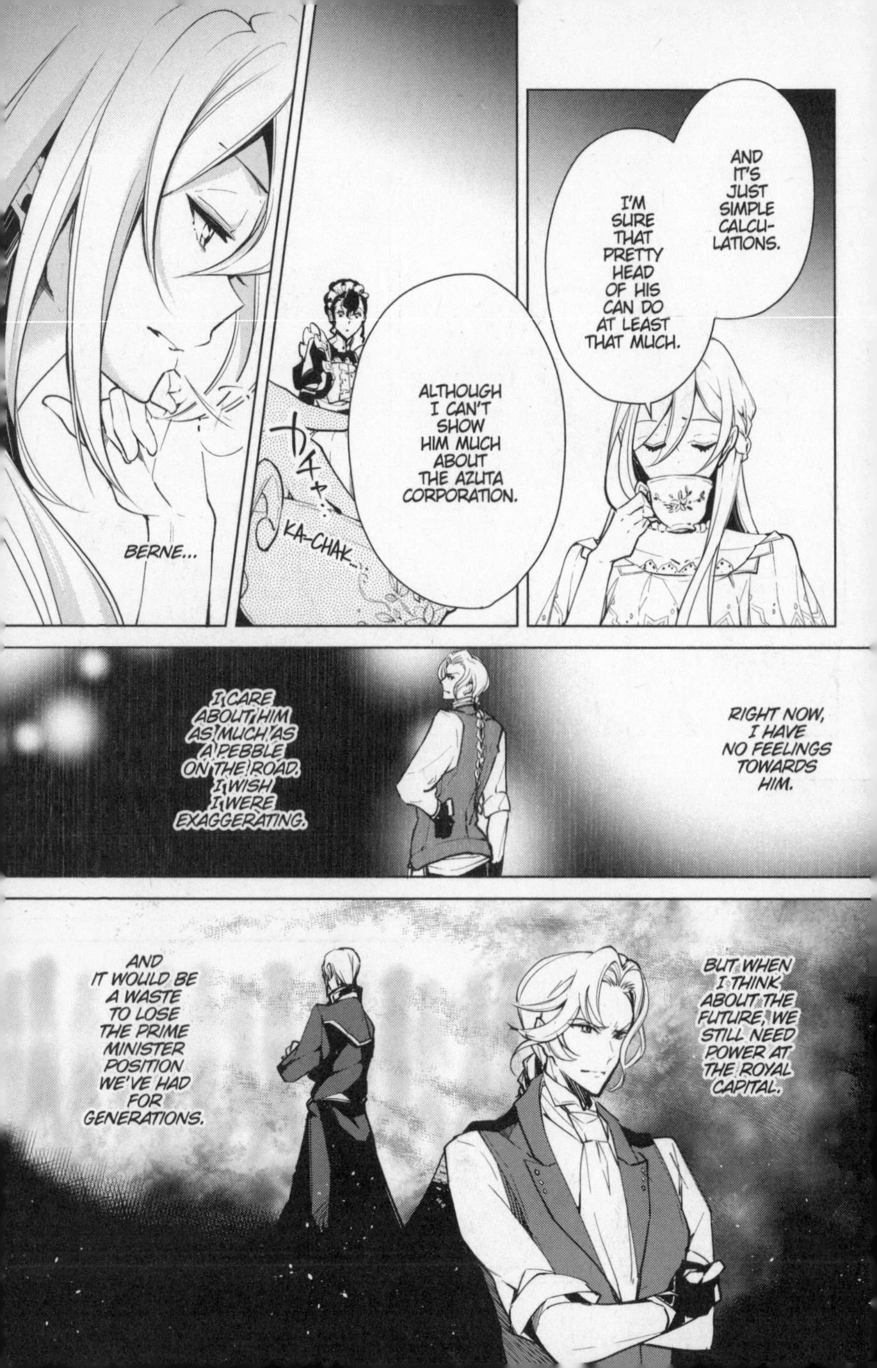
AND IT'S JUST SIMPLE CALCU-LATIONS.
I'M SURE THAT PRETTY HEAD OF HIS CAN DO AT LEAST THAT MUCH.
ALTHOUGH I CAN'T SHOW HIM MUCH ABOUT THE AZUTA CORPORATION.
KA-CHAK...
BERNE...
RIGHT NOW, I HAVE NO FEELINGS TOWARDS HIM.
I CARE ABOUT HIM AS MUCH AS A PEBBLE ON THE ROAD. I WISH I WERE EXAGGERATING.
BUT WHEN I THINK ABOUT THE FUTURE, WE STILL NEED POWER AT THE ROYAL CAPITAL.
AND IT WOULD BE A WASTE TO LOSE THE PRIME MINISTER POSITION WE'VE HAD FOR GENERATIONS.

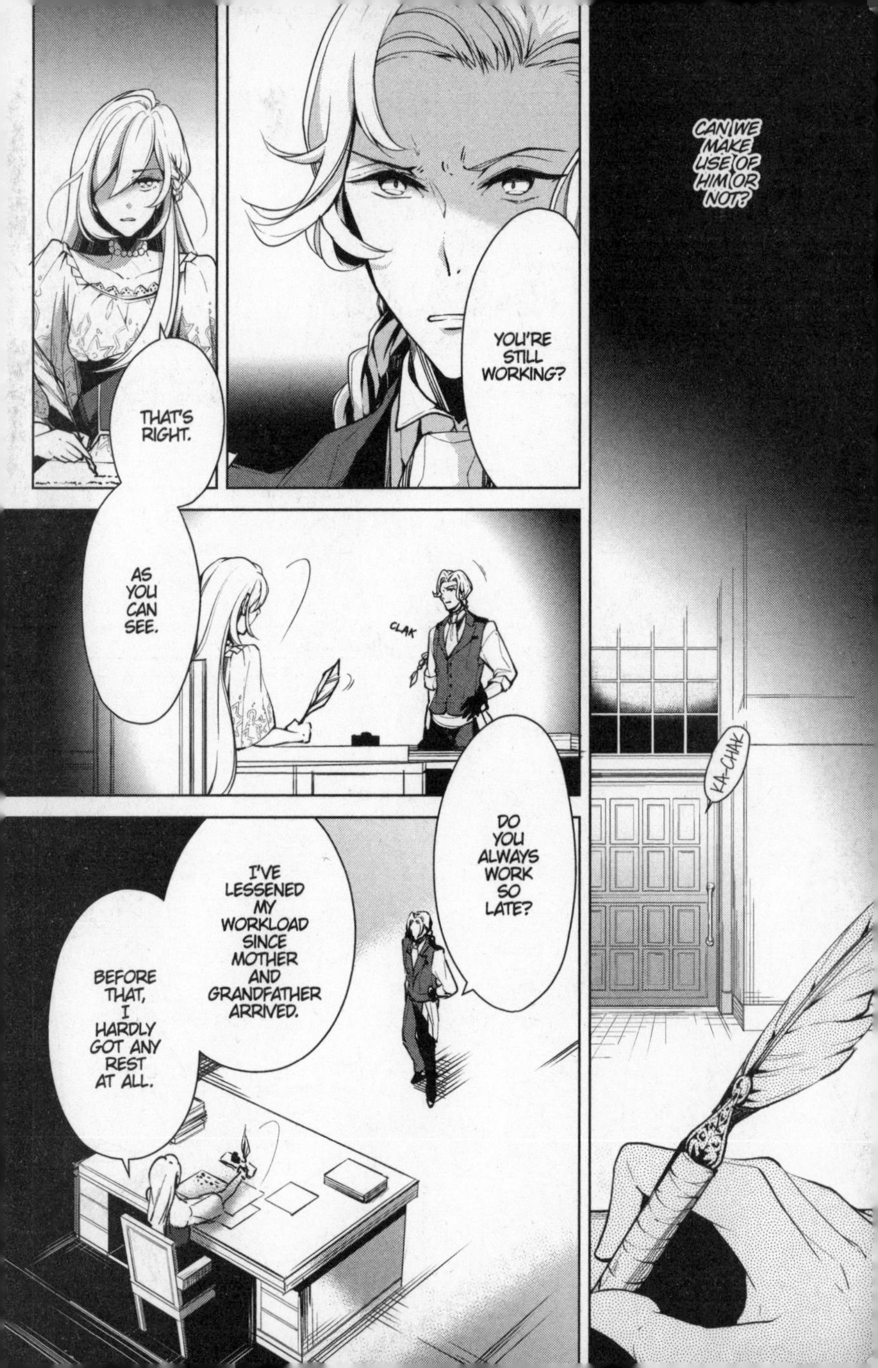
CAN WE MAKE USE OF HIM OR NOT?
KA-CHAK
YOU'RE STILL WORKING?
THAT'S RIGHT.
AS YOU CAN SEE.
CLAK
DO YOU ALWAYS WORK SO LATE?
I'VE LESSENED MY WORKLOAD SINCE MOTHER AND GRANDFATHER ARRIVED.
BEFORE THAT, I HARDLY GOT ANY REST AT ALL.

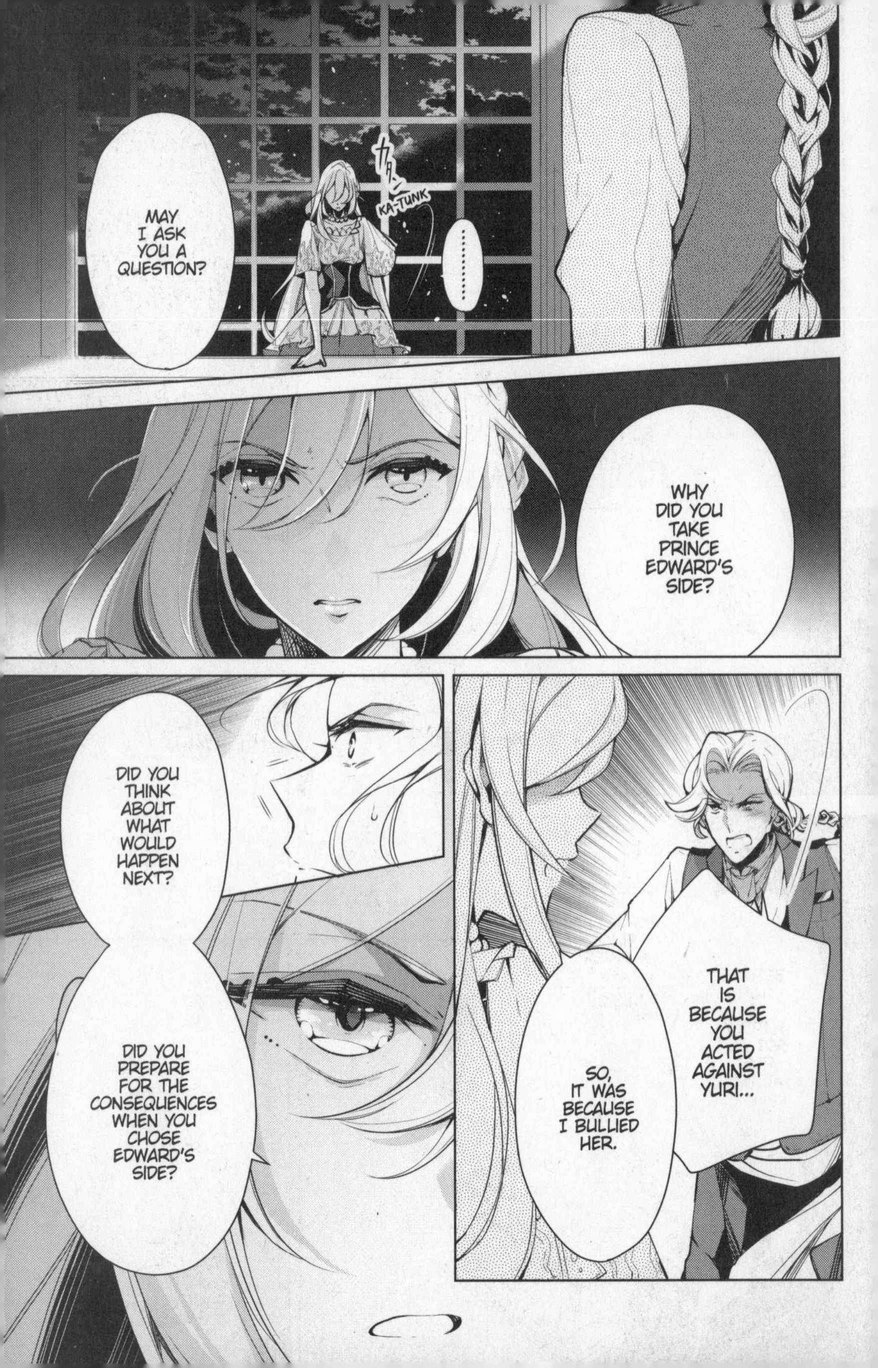

KA-TUNK
……
MAY I ASK YOU A QUESTION?
WHY DID YOU TAKE PRINCE EDWARD'S SIDE?
THAT IS BECAUSE YOU ACTED AGAINST YURI...
SO, IT WAS BECAUSE I BULLIED HER.
DID YOU THINK ABOUT WHAT WOULD HAPPEN NEXT?
DID YOU PREPARE FOR THE CONSEQUENCES WHEN YOU CHOSE EDWARD'S SIDE?

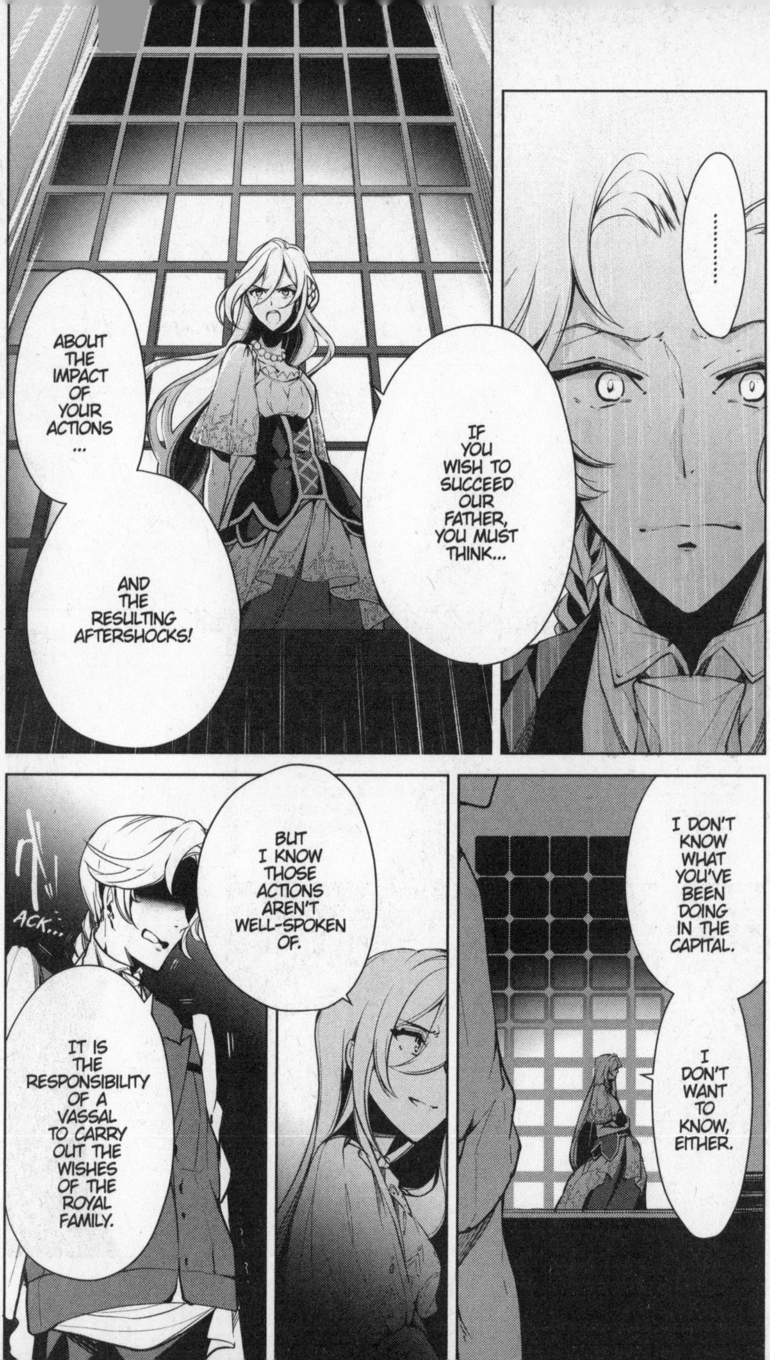
......
IF YOU WISH TO SUCCEED OUR FATHER, YOU MUST THINK...
ABOUT THE IMPACT OF YOUR ACTIONS ...
AND THE RESULTING AFTERSHOCKS!
I DON'T KNOW WHAT YOU'VE BEEN DOING IN THE CAPITAL.
I DON'T WANT TO KNOW, EITHER.
BUT I KNOW THOSE ACTIONS AREN'T WELL-SPOKEN OF.
ACK...
IT IS THE RESPONSIBILITY OF A VASSAL TO CARRY OUT THE WISHES OF THE ROYAL FAMILY.

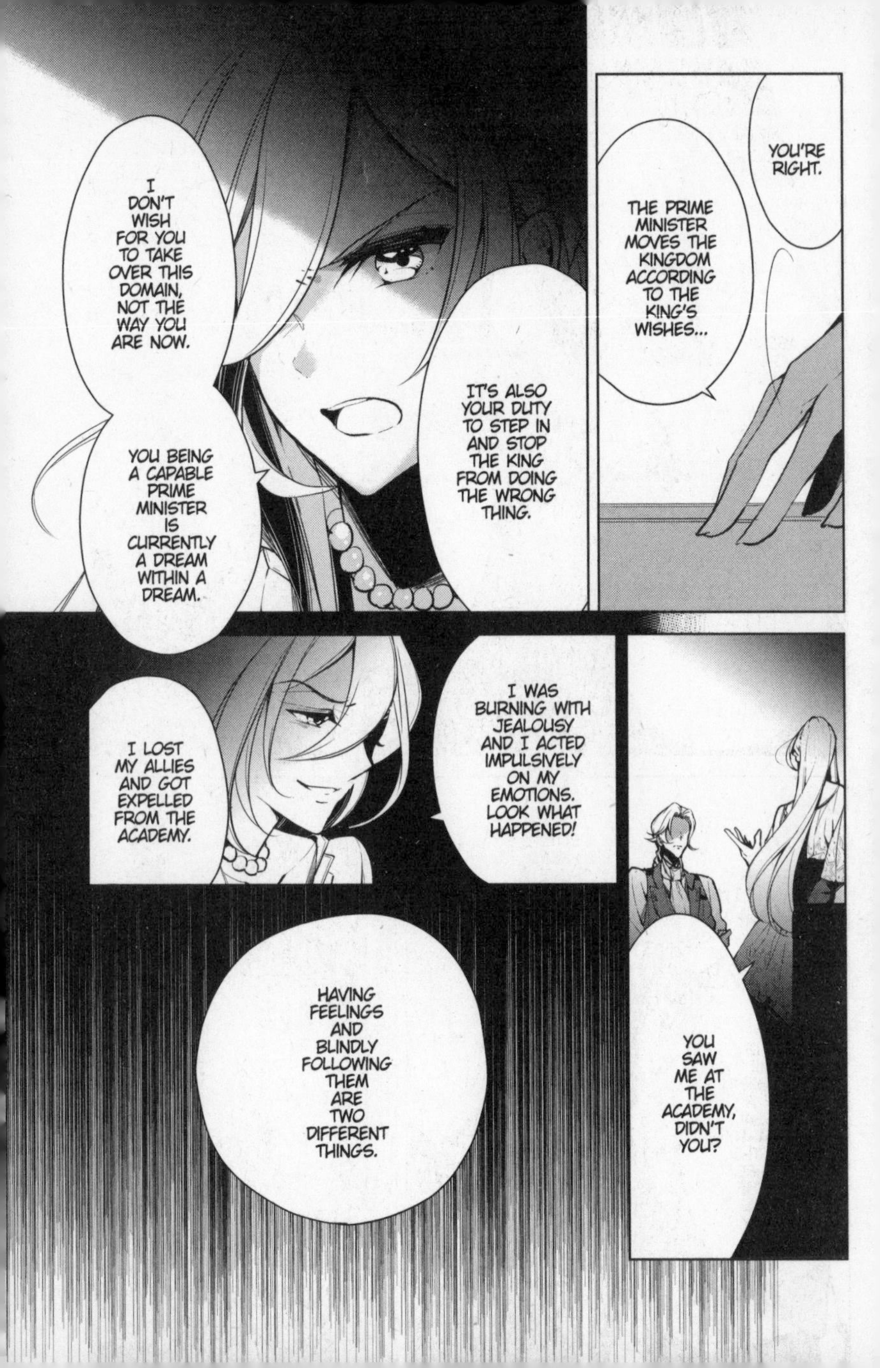
YOU'RE RIGHT.
THE PRIME MINISTER MOVES THE KINGDOM ACCORDING TO THE KING'S WISHES...
I DON'T WISH FOR YOU TO TAKE OVER THIS DOMAIN, NOT THE WAY YOU ARE NOW.
YOU BEING A CAPABLE PRIME MINISTER IS CURRENTLY A DREAM WITHIN A DREAM.
IT'S ALSO YOUR DUTY TO STEP IN AND STOP THE KING FROM DOING THE WRONG THING.
YOU SAW ME AT THE ACADEMY, DIDN'T YOU?
I WAS BURNING WITH JEALOUSY AND I ACTED IMPULSIVELY ON MY EMOTIONS. LOOK WHAT HAPPENED!
I LOST MY ALLIES AND GOT EXPELLED FROM THE ACADEMY.
HAVING FEELINGS AND BLINDLY FOLLOWING THEM ARE TWO DIFFERENT THINGS.

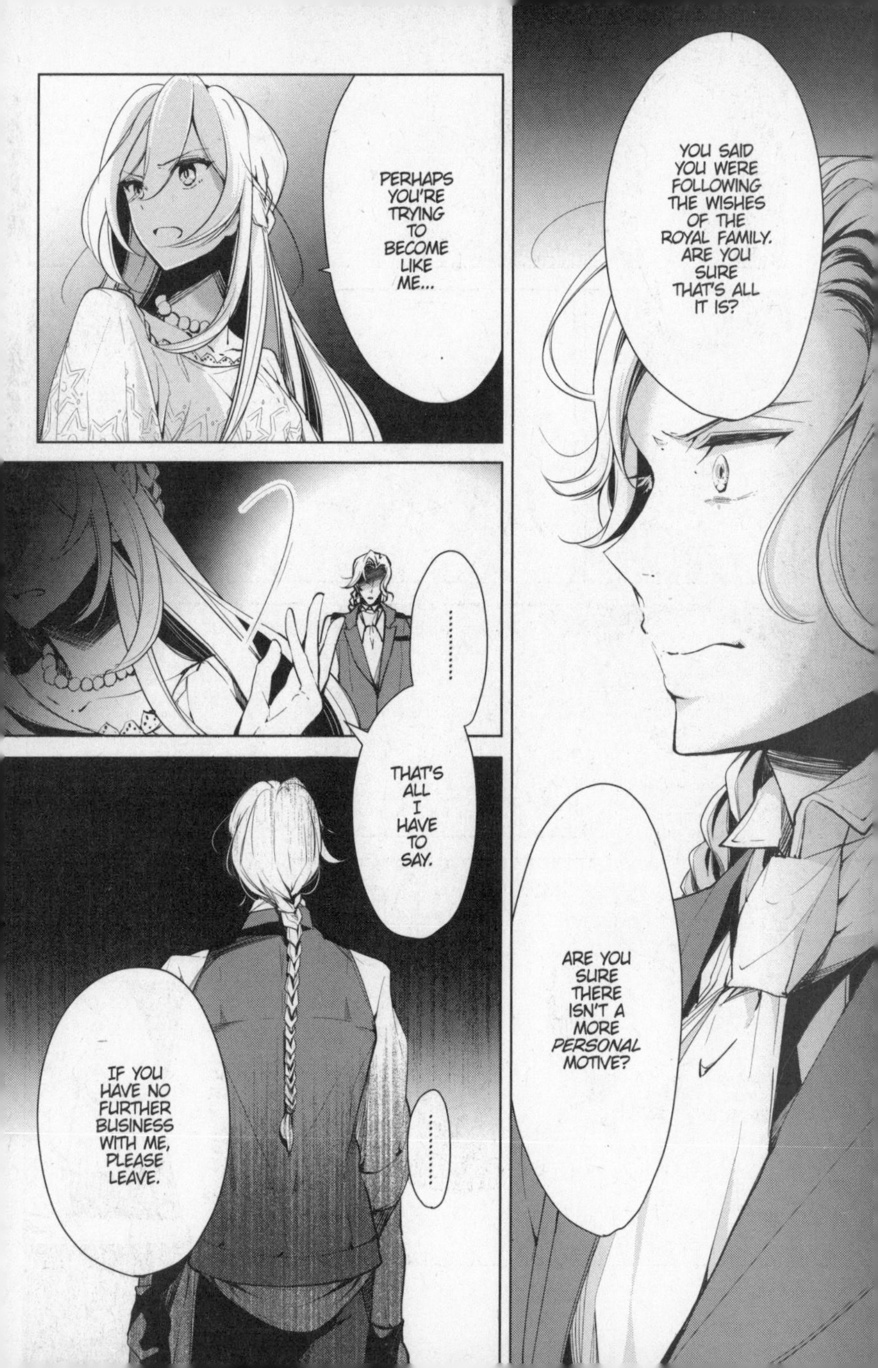
YOU SAID YOU WERE FOLLOWING THE WISHES OF THE ROYAL FAMILY. ARE YOU SURE THAT'S ALL IT IS?
ARE YOU SURE THERE ISN'T A MORE *PERSONAL* MOTIVE?
PERHAPS YOU'RE TRYING TO BECOME LIKE ME...
......
THAT'S ALL I HAVE TO SAY.
......
IF YOU HAVE NO FURTHER BUSINESS WITH ME, PLEASE LEAVE.

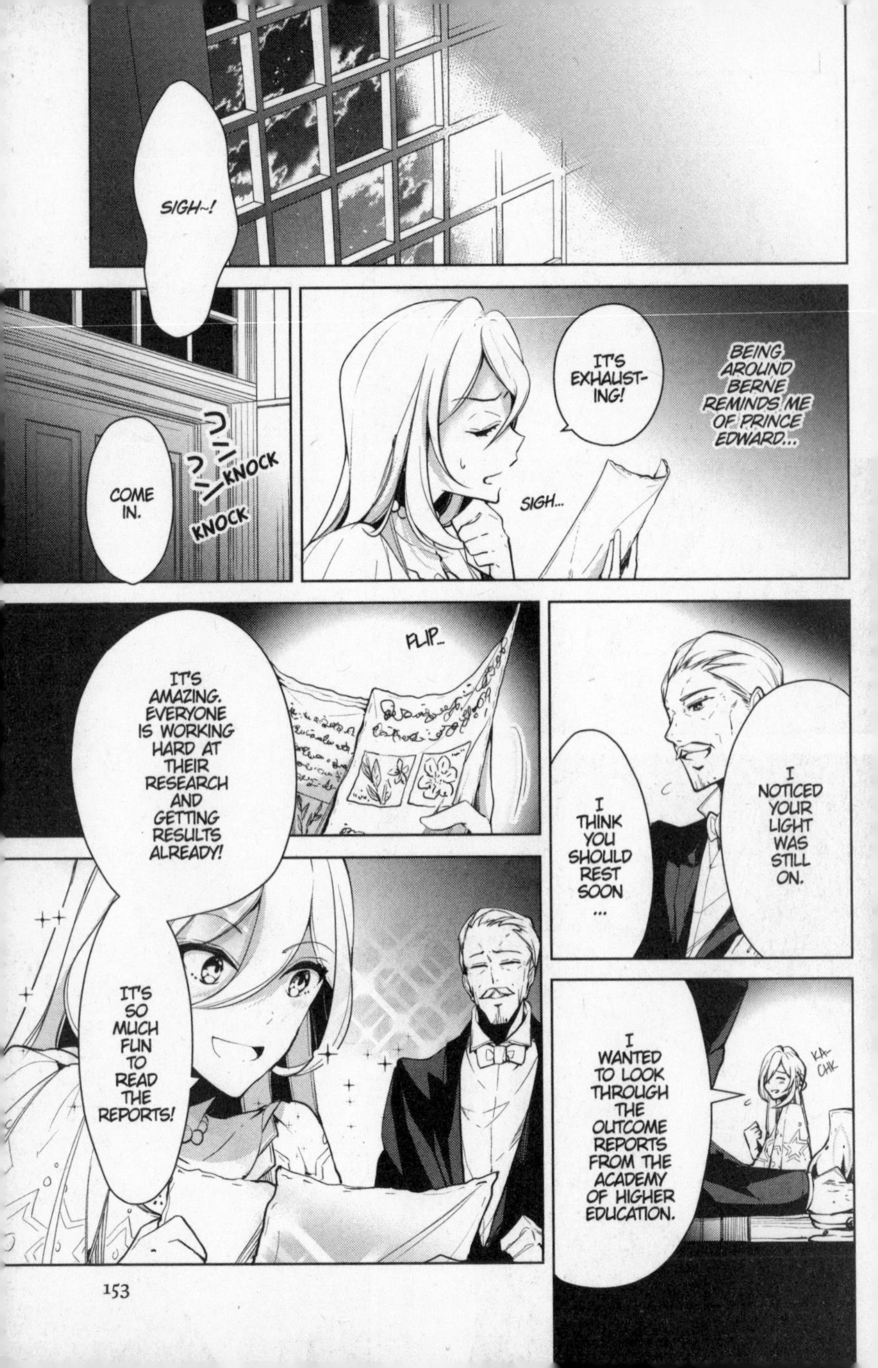
SIGH~!
IT'S EXHAUSTING!
BEING AROUND BERNE REMINDS ME OF PRINCE EDWARD...
SIGH...
KNOCK
KNOCK
COME IN.
I NOTICED YOUR LIGHT WAS STILL ON.
I THINK YOU SHOULD REST SOON ...
I WANTED TO LOOK THROUGH THE OUTCOME REPORTS FROM THE ACADEMY OF HIGHER EDUCATION.
KA-CHK
FLIP...
IT'S AMAZING. EVERYONE IS WORKING HARD AT THEIR RESEARCH AND GETTING RESULTS ALREADY!
IT'S SO MUCH FUN TO READ THE REPORTS!

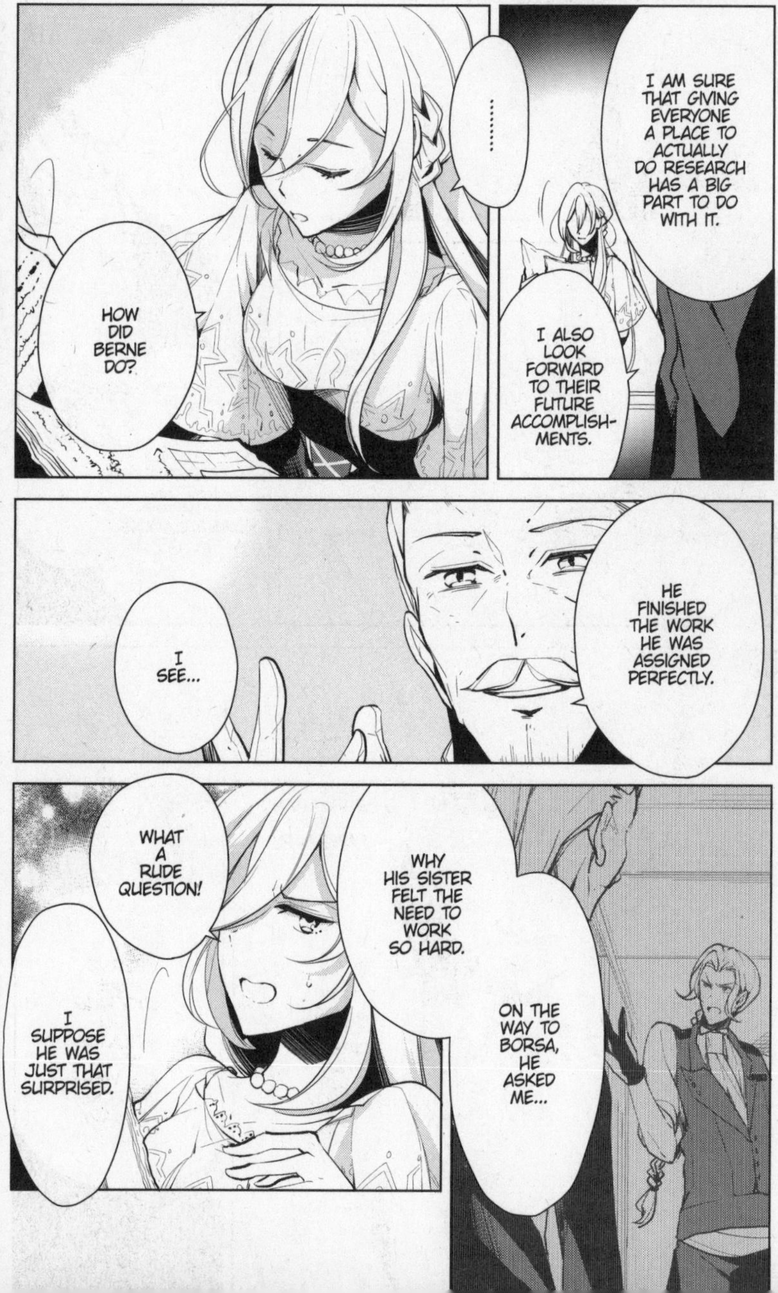
I AM SURE THAT GIVING EVERYONE A PLACE TO ACTUALLY DO RESEARCH HAS A BIG PART TO DO WITH IT.
I ALSO LOOK FORWARD TO THEIR FUTURE ACCOMPLISHMENTS.
......
HOW DID BERNE DO?
HE FINISHED THE WORK HE WAS ASSIGNED PERFECTLY.
I SEE...
ON THE WAY TO BORSA, HE ASKED ME...
WHY HIS SISTER FELT THE NEED TO WORK SO HARD.
WHAT A RUDE QUESTION!
I SUPPOSE HE WAS JUST THAT SURPRISED.

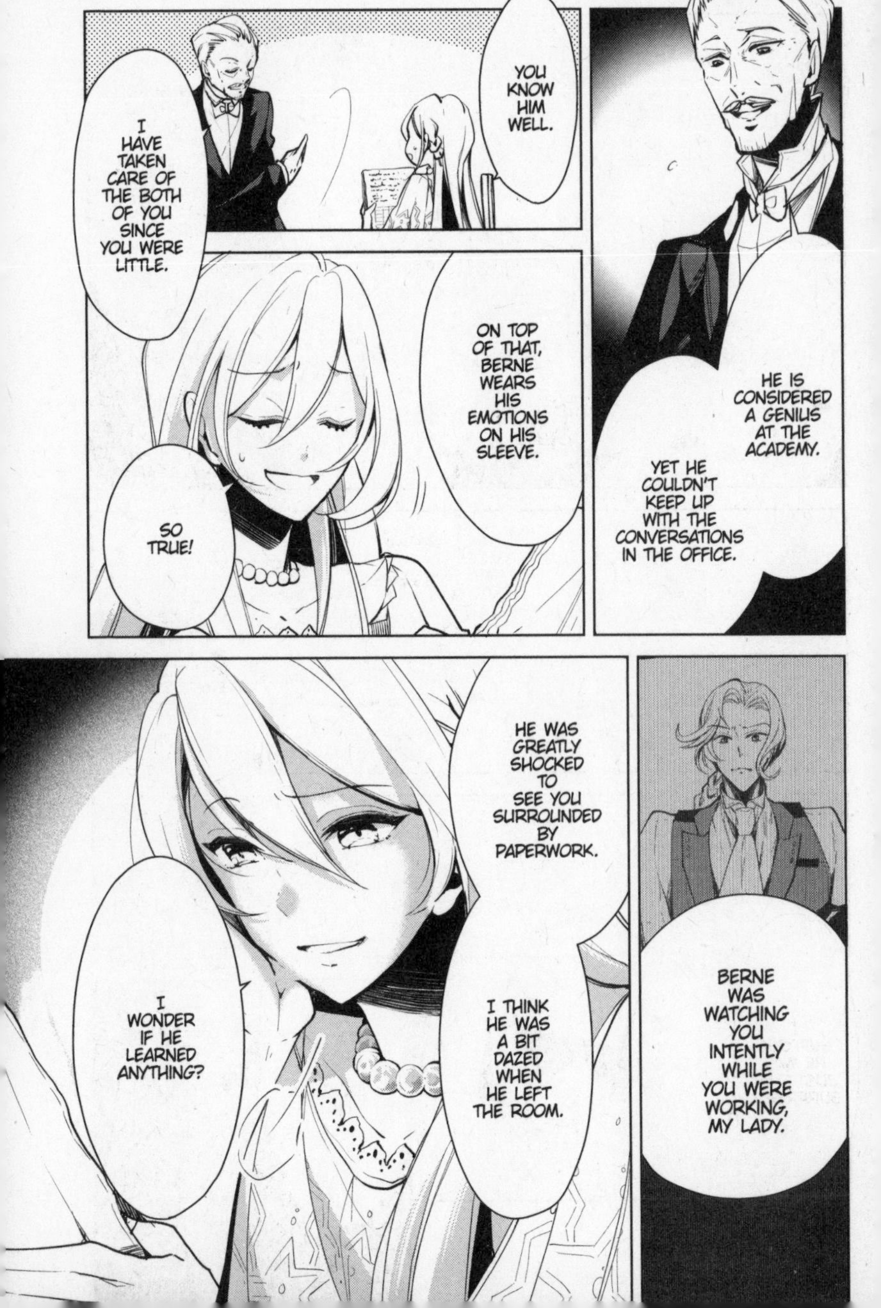
HE IS CONSIDERED A GENIUS AT THE ACADEMY.
YET HE COULDN'T KEEP UP WITH THE CONVERSATIONS IN THE OFFICE.
YOU KNOW HIM WELL.
I HAVE TAKEN CARE OF THE BOTH OF YOU SINCE YOU WERE LITTLE.
ON TOP OF THAT, BERNE WEARS HIS EMOTIONS ON HIS SLEEVE.
SO TRUE!
BERNE WAS WATCHING YOU INTENTLY WHILE YOU WERE WORKING, MY LADY.
HE WAS GREATLY SHOCKED TO SEE YOU SURROUNDED BY PAPERWORK.
I THINK HE WAS A BIT DAZED WHEN HE LEFT THE ROOM.
I WONDER IF HE LEARNED ANYTHING?

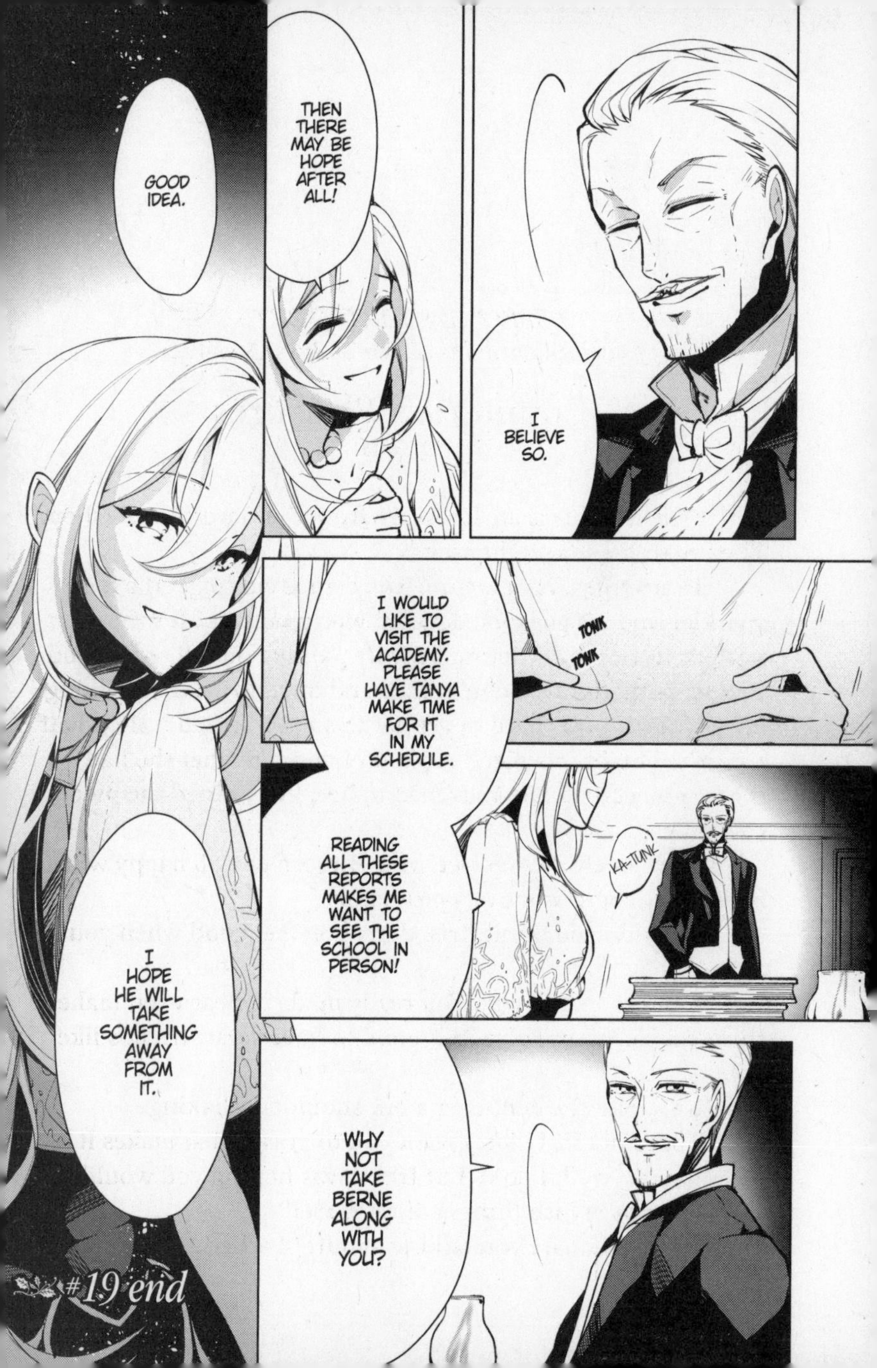
I BELIEVE SO.
THEN THERE MAY BE HOPE AFTER ALL!
TONK TONK
I WOULD LIKE TO VISIT THE ACADEMY. PLEASE HAVE TANYA MAKE TIME FOR IT IN MY SCHEDULE.
KA-TUNK
READING ALL THESE REPORTS MAKES ME WANT TO SEE THE SCHOOL IN PERSON!
WHY NOT TAKE BERNE ALONG WITH YOU?
GOOD IDEA.
I HOPE HE WILL TAKE SOMETHING AWAY FROM IT.
#19 end

SPECIAL SHORT STORY

Accomplishments of the Duke's Daughter

Counterfeit Pleasures

By Reia

"I see. So, this is an accessory from the Gardini workshop. They're so popular right now!"

"That's right! Isn't it cute? The gem is cut to get the most sparkle! And it's got such detailed workmanship! It's the perfect accessory." Mimosa happily pointed out all of its good points. Mimosa loved cute things and once she started talking about them, it was hard to get her to stop. She had waited half a year to obtain this piece of jewelry and now that she had it, she was ecstatic. As I listened to her, I examined the piece carefully.

It was lovely. I could see why Mimosa was so happy with it. It easily could make any girl happy.

"What do you think? Iris, don't you feel good when you look at it?"

"Mimosa, thank you. You really made it clear what makes this designer so popular. It is good to have smart friends like you."

As I spoke she bent over a bit, shoulders shaking.

"That's not it! I didn't want you to grasp what makes it popular...er, well, I do... But Iris! I was hoping you would start to enjoy stylish things a little more!"

"Huh? What are you talking about?" I asked.

"I understand that you are busy with work. But...when is the last time you dressed up and went out?"

I had no reply to Mimosa's words. The only times I've gone out lately was for visitations or meetings. I dressed in a way befitting a duke's daughter, but...well, I could tell it wasn't the kind of answer that Mimosa was looking for.

Mimosa leaned in toward me, as if to scrutinize my darting eyes.

"The life of a flower is short. I think that it's good that you enjoy your work, but you cannot forget that you are a woman. Beauty is not gained in a day. Daily care and mindfulness make a woman beautiful. Same for the other way around."

I could understand her point of view. It's true that I hadn't even thought of dressing up lately. No matter how precious work was to me, it was a bit of a waste to be born a woman and not enjoy it. To begin with, I had been lucky enough to be reincarnated into this world. In my previous life all I ever did was work. I realized I was in danger of making that same mistake all over again.

"Mimosa, I understand. I will try to dress up a little more!"

Since I made such a declaration to Mimosa, I decided to go shopping as soon as I returned to the fiefdom.

As the acting fief lord and head of the Azuta Corporation, I did get a salary. Yet I hardly ever touched it. Why would I? I hardly ever went shopping. I barely even went out.

This would be a great chance to see the town some more!

It wasn't that I planned to do inspections on the side. No, it's just I hadn't had a chance to go outside lately so I wanted to see how things were in town.

I managed to get an entire day off. I told myself I'd forget about work and have fun!

"I admire your determination, Lady Iris, but...why am *I* here?" Moneda stood next to me. He had happened to visit

the house for a private matter and I dragged him into town with me. He said he also had the day off, so he was free to accompany me.

"I thought your knowledge would be useful, Moneda." Before managing the bank, he was the Merchants Guild's vice-chief of accounting. A man like that would be knowledgeable about trends.

"Well, it's fine. If you're looking for the shopping district, I believe it's this way." Tanya and I followed behind Moneda as he guided us.

"*Kyaa!* I can't believe that there is a Gardini accessory in a place like this!" We couldn't help but overhear those words while passing in front of a shop. The shop wasn't a jewelry store, but a general fashion store. It carried a variety of fashionable items from clothes to accessories.

The woman who had raised her voice was engrossed in picking out the perfect accessory. I glanced at the one she was currently examining. The accessory in her hand bothered me and I couldn't help but stare at it.

"I'll take this!" Her excitement was palpable.

"Thank you very much," said the shopkeeper. "It will be ten gold coins--"

"Just a moment, please." The woman and the shopkeeper turned toward me. The woman looked at me suspiciously as she tightened her hold on the accessory. The shopkeeper looked as me in surprise.

"This is a counterfeit. The workmanship of a Gardini accessory isn't this shoddy. On top of that, the stone isn't even real." Now both of them were glaring at me.

"Shopkeeper, she's right." Moneda was nearby and he spoke up to support me. Moneda kindly explained all the reasons that the accessory was clearly counterfeit. With his history with the Merchants' Guild, the two of them accepted his reasoning.

"I can't believe it's a fake... I can see why my father never took me seriously. I opened up this store to show him that I could run my own business..." the shopkeeper said. I couldn't help but pity him.

"It cannot be helped that you didn't notice. It was made pretty well. If you weren't a specialist, you wouldn't realize it right away. Though I have to say, you really should study up in order to avoid this kind of situation in the future." Though his words were strict, it sounded like Moneda felt sorry for the shopkeeper as well. "Although, I am surprised you noticed, my Lady." Moneda looked at me with interest. I was surprised myself.

Truthfully, I wouldn't have been able to discern good gems from bad ones in my previous life, but such things were expected of the daughter of the Duke of Armelia.

"I saw the real thing at my friend's house once." Perhaps it was because, in this world, I grew up surrounded by beautiful things. It seems I could tell what was valuable or not pretty accurately.

"I see..."

"More importantly, Moneda. This is a serious problem. Someone is selling counterfeits not as replicas, but as the real thing. We have to look into it immediately." Until everything was cleared up, even this depressed shopkeeper was under suspicion.

"Understood," said Moneda firmly.

A few weeks later, we successfully captured the counterfeiters.

Using the network Moneda created during his work at the Merchants Guild and Tanya's investigating on her own, we were able to close the case surprisingly quickly. The shopkeeper that was tricked was found to be the son of the owner of the leading grocery shop in the Armelia domain. Though he was a specialist in produce, he had interest in

fashion and, after a clash with his father, had opened up his own store.

Documents found during the seizure of goods proved that the shopkeeper had been duped by the counterfeiters. He was cleared of all wrongdoing. He was quite depressed but recovered after I offered him a business contract with the Azuta Corporation.

Time, as always, passed in the blink of an eye.

"My Lady, you have an invitation from Lady Mimosa. You are scheduled to go to the royal capital soon for some business. How shall I reply?"

I responded happily to Tanya's question.

"Of course, I'll go!"

A few days later, I told Mimosa how we had caught the counterfeiters. It was already too late when I noticed she had bent over a bit, shoulders shaking. That day, I was thoroughly scolded by Mimosa.

"That's not it! You were talking about going *shopping*. How did it become a story about a busting a counterfeiting ring?! To begin with, you..." She continued talking, her words washing over me.

I had completely forgotten by this point what had been my original reason to go to town. I said I would take more care to actually indulge my girly side next time. All of that had completely slipped my mind.

Next time, I will definitely go shopping! I thought as I listened to Mimosa's lecture.

~END~

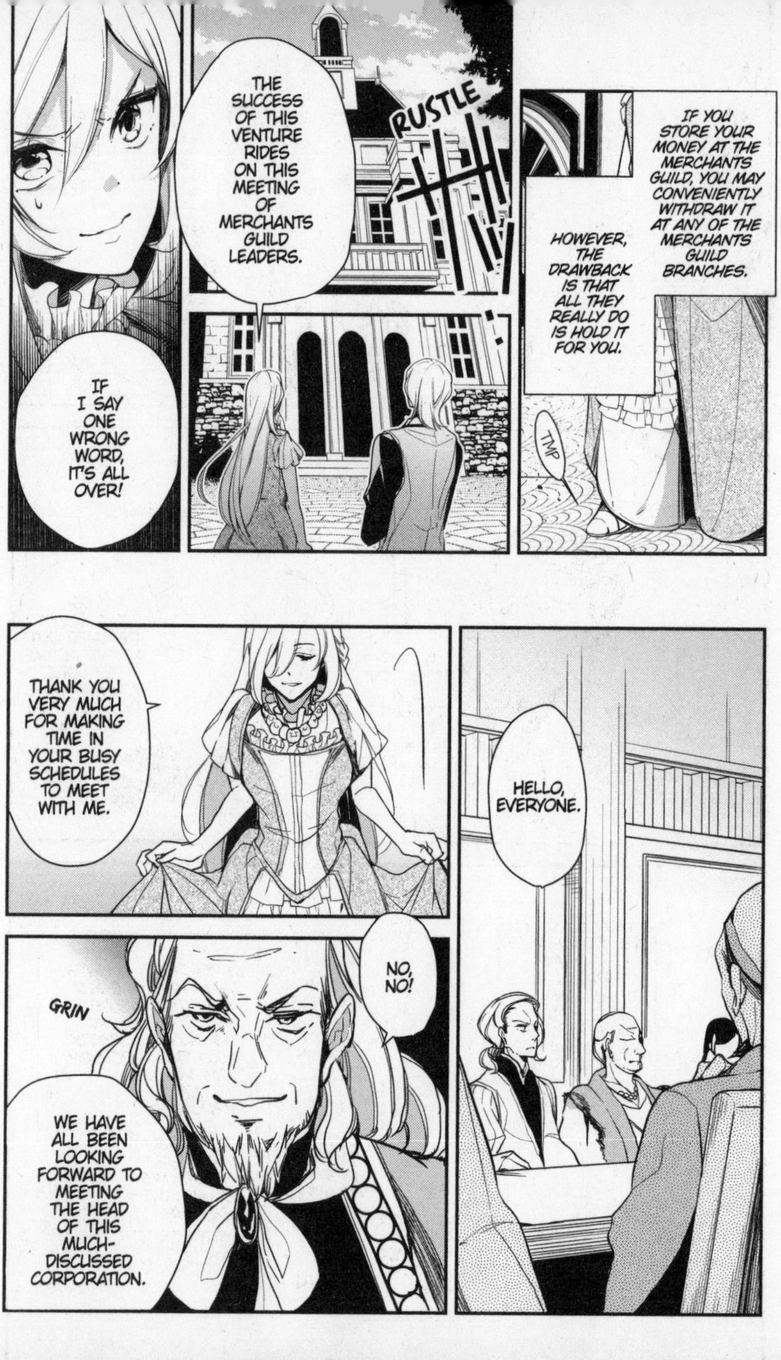
IF YOU STORE YOUR MONEY AT THE MERCHANTS GUILD, YOU MAY CONVENIENTLY WITHDRAW IT AT ANY OF THE MERCHANTS GUILD BRANCHES.
HOWEVER, THE DRAWBACK IS THAT ALL THEY REALLY DO IS HOLD IT FOR YOU.
TMP
RUSTLE
THE SUCCESS OF THIS VENTURE RIDES ON THIS MEETING OF MERCHANTS GUILD LEADERS.
IF I SAY ONE WRONG WORD, IT'S ALL OVER!
HELLO, EVERYONE.
THANK YOU VERY MUCH FOR MAKING TIME IN YOUR BUSY SCHEDULES TO MEET WITH ME.
NO, NO!
GRIN
WE HAVE ALL BEEN LOOKING FORWARD TO MEETING THE HEAD OF THIS MUCH-DISCUSSED CORPORATION.

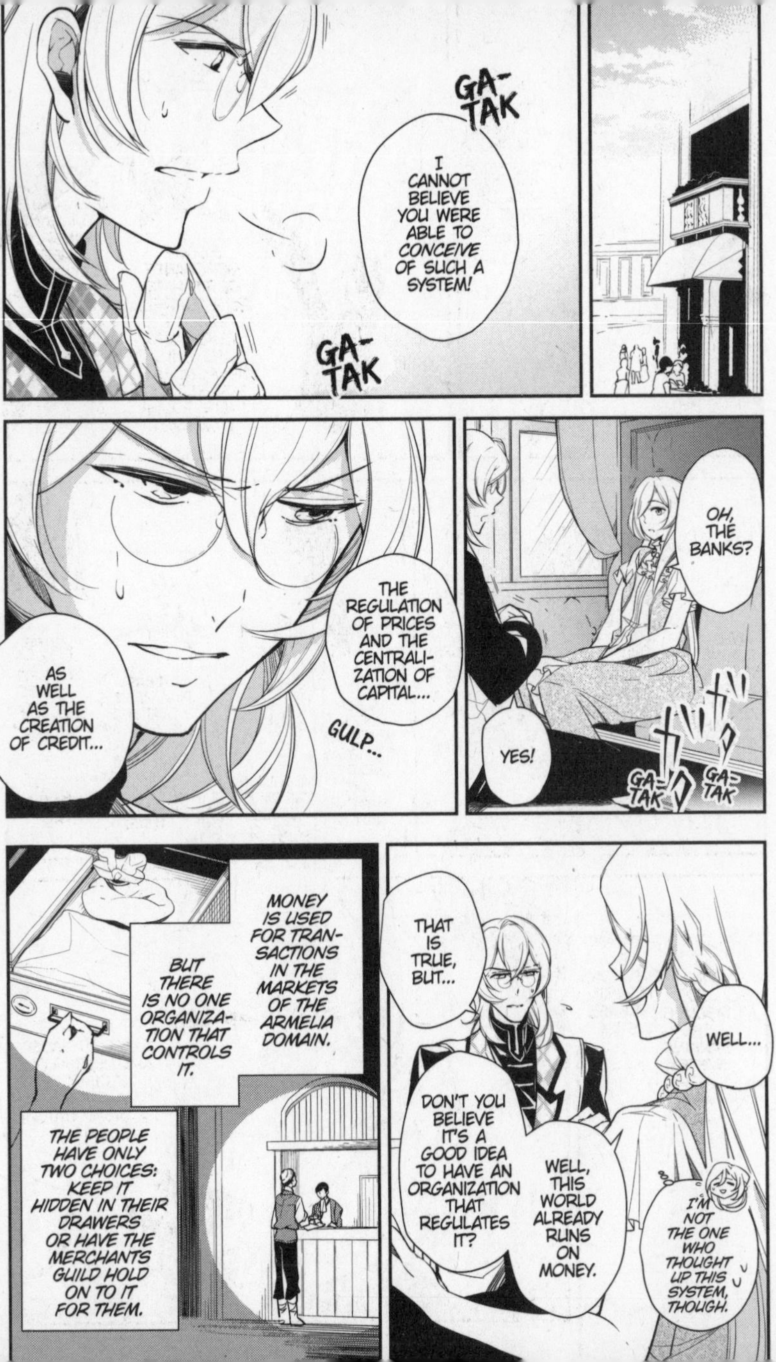
GA-TAK
I CANNOT BELIEVE YOU WERE ABLE TO CONCEIVE OF SUCH A SYSTEM!
GA-TAK
OH, THE BANKS?
YES!
GA-TAK
GA-TAK
THE REGULATION OF PRICES AND THE CENTRALIZATION OF CAPITAL...
AS WELL AS THE CREATION OF CREDIT...
GULP...
WELL...
THAT IS TRUE, BUT...
I'M NOT THE ONE WHO THOUGHT UP THIS SYSTEM, THOUGH.
WELL, THIS WORLD ALREADY RUNS ON MONEY.
DON'T YOU BELIEVE IT'S A GOOD IDEA TO HAVE AN ORGANIZATION THAT REGULATES IT?
MONEY IS USED FOR TRANSACTIONS IN THE MARKETS OF THE ARMELIA DOMAIN.
BUT THERE IS NO ONE ORGANIZATION THAT CONTROLS IT.
THE PEOPLE HAVE ONLY TWO CHOICES: KEEP IT HIDDEN IN THEIR DRAWERS OR HAVE THE MERCHANTS GUILD HOLD ON TO IT FOR THEM.

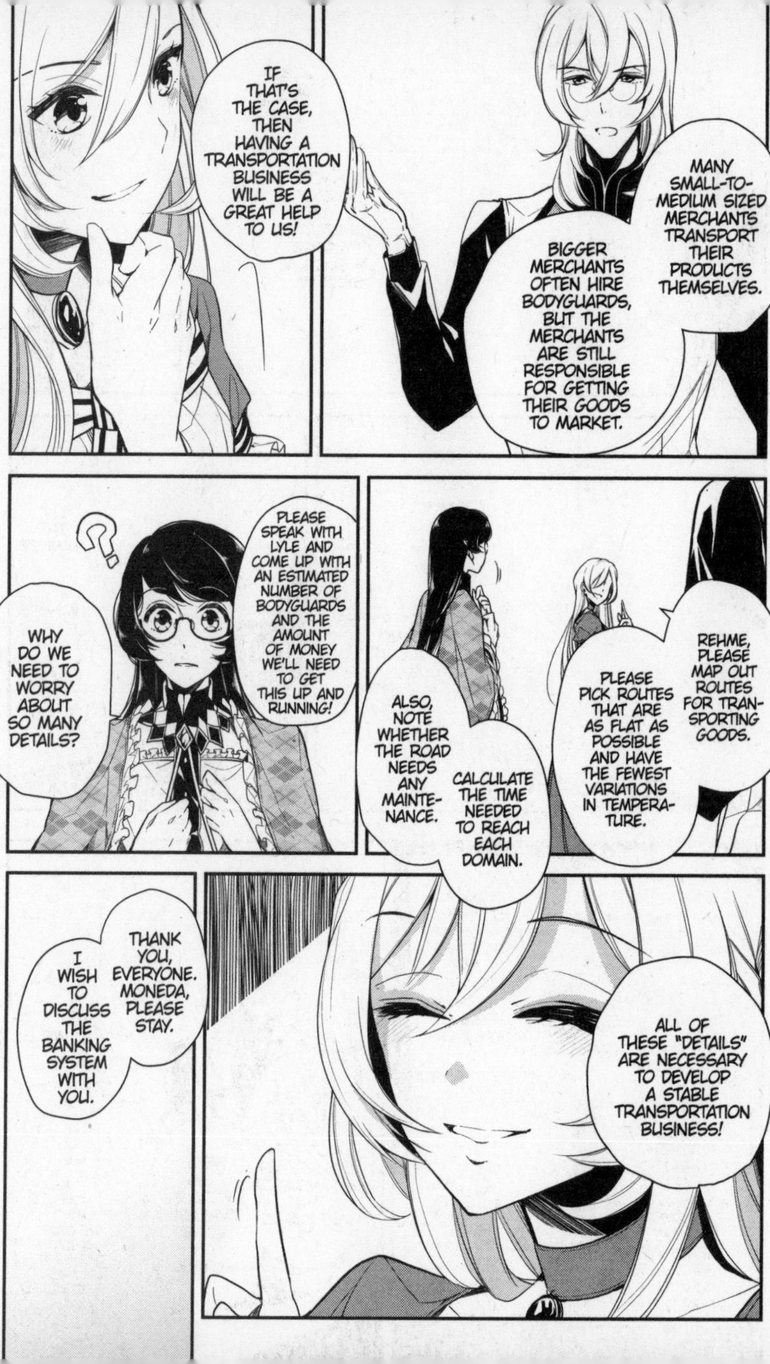
MANY SMALL-TO-MEDIUM SIZED MERCHANTS TRANSPORT THEIR PRODUCTS THEMSELVES.
BIGGER MERCHANTS OFTEN HIRE BODYGUARDS, BUT THE MERCHANTS ARE STILL RESPONSIBLE FOR GETTING THEIR GOODS TO MARKET.
IF THAT'S THE CASE, THEN HAVING A TRANSPORTATION BUSINESS WILL BE A GREAT HELP TO US!
REHME, PLEASE MAP OUT ROUTES FOR TRANSPORTING GOODS.
PLEASE PICK ROUTES THAT ARE AS FLAT AS POSSIBLE AND HAVE THE FEWEST VARIATIONS IN TEMPERATURE.
CALCULATE THE TIME NEEDED TO REACH EACH DOMAIN.
ALSO, NOTE WHETHER THE ROAD NEEDS ANY MAINTENANCE.
PLEASE SPEAK WITH LYLE AND COME UP WITH AN ESTIMATED NUMBER OF BODYGUARDS AND THE AMOUNT OF MONEY WE'LL NEED TO GET THIS UP AND RUNNING!
?
WHY DO WE NEED TO WORRY ABOUT SO MANY DETAILS?
ALL OF THESE "DETAILS" ARE NECESSARY TO DEVELOP A STABLE TRANSPORTATION BUSINESS!
THANK YOU, EVERYONE. MONEDA, PLEASE STAY.
I WISH TO DISCUSS THE BANKING SYSTEM WITH YOU.

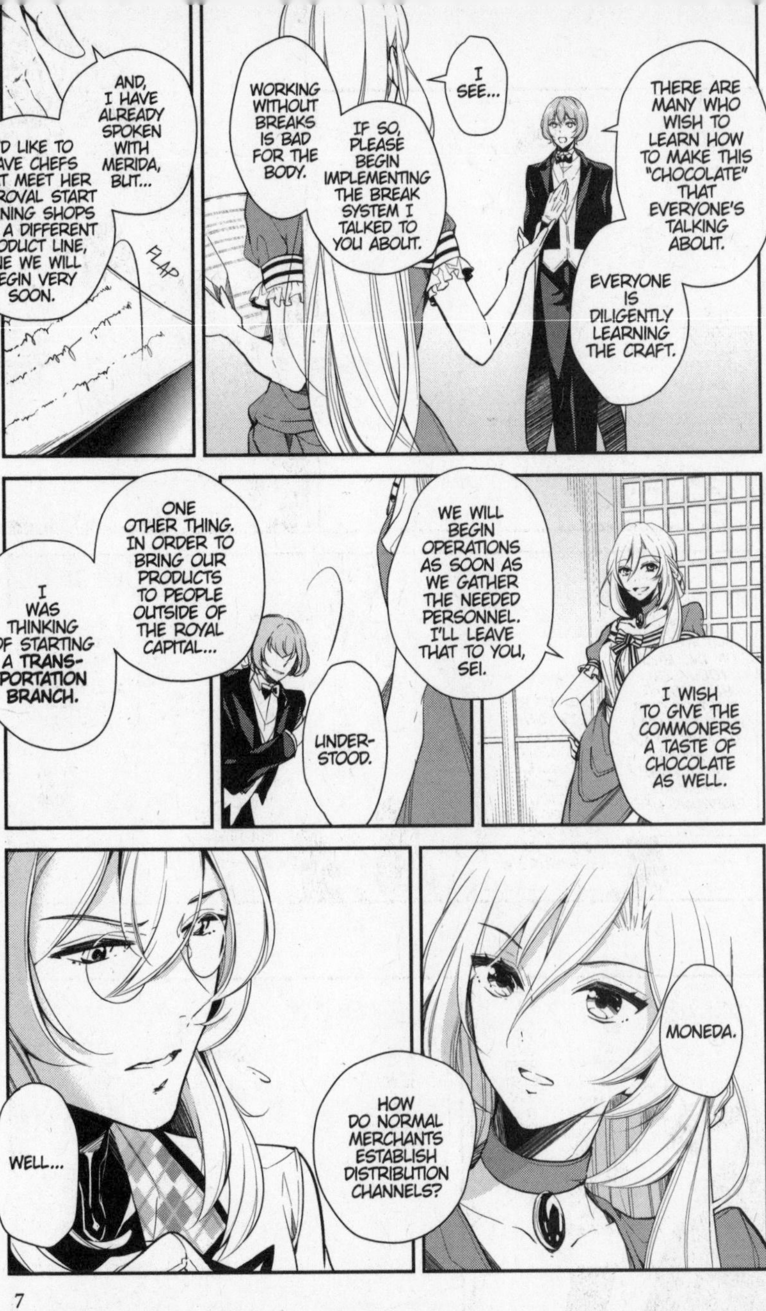
THERE ARE MANY WHO WISH TO LEARN HOW TO MAKE THIS "CHOCOLATE" THAT EVERYONE'S TALKING ABOUT.
EVERYONE IS DILIGENTLY LEARNING THE CRAFT.
I SEE...
IF SO, PLEASE BEGIN IMPLEMENTING THE BREAK SYSTEM I TALKED TO YOU ABOUT.
WORKING WITHOUT BREAKS IS BAD FOR THE BODY.
AND, I HAVE ALREADY SPOKEN WITH MERIDA, BUT...
I'D LIKE TO HAVE CHEFS THAT MEET HER APPROVAL START RUNNING SHOPS FOR A DIFFERENT PRODUCT LINE, ONE WE WILL BEGIN VERY SOON.
FLAP
I WISH TO GIVE THE COMMONERS A TASTE OF CHOCOLATE AS WELL.
WE WILL BEGIN OPERATIONS AS SOON AS WE GATHER THE NEEDED PERSONNEL. I'LL LEAVE THAT TO YOU, SEI.
UNDER-STOOD.
ONE OTHER THING. IN ORDER TO BRING OUR PRODUCTS TO PEOPLE OUTSIDE OF THE ROYAL CAPITAL...
I WAS THINKING OF STARTING A TRANS-PORTATION BRANCH.
MONEDA.
HOW DO NORMAL MERCHANTS ESTABLISH DISTRIBUTION CHANNELS?
WELL...

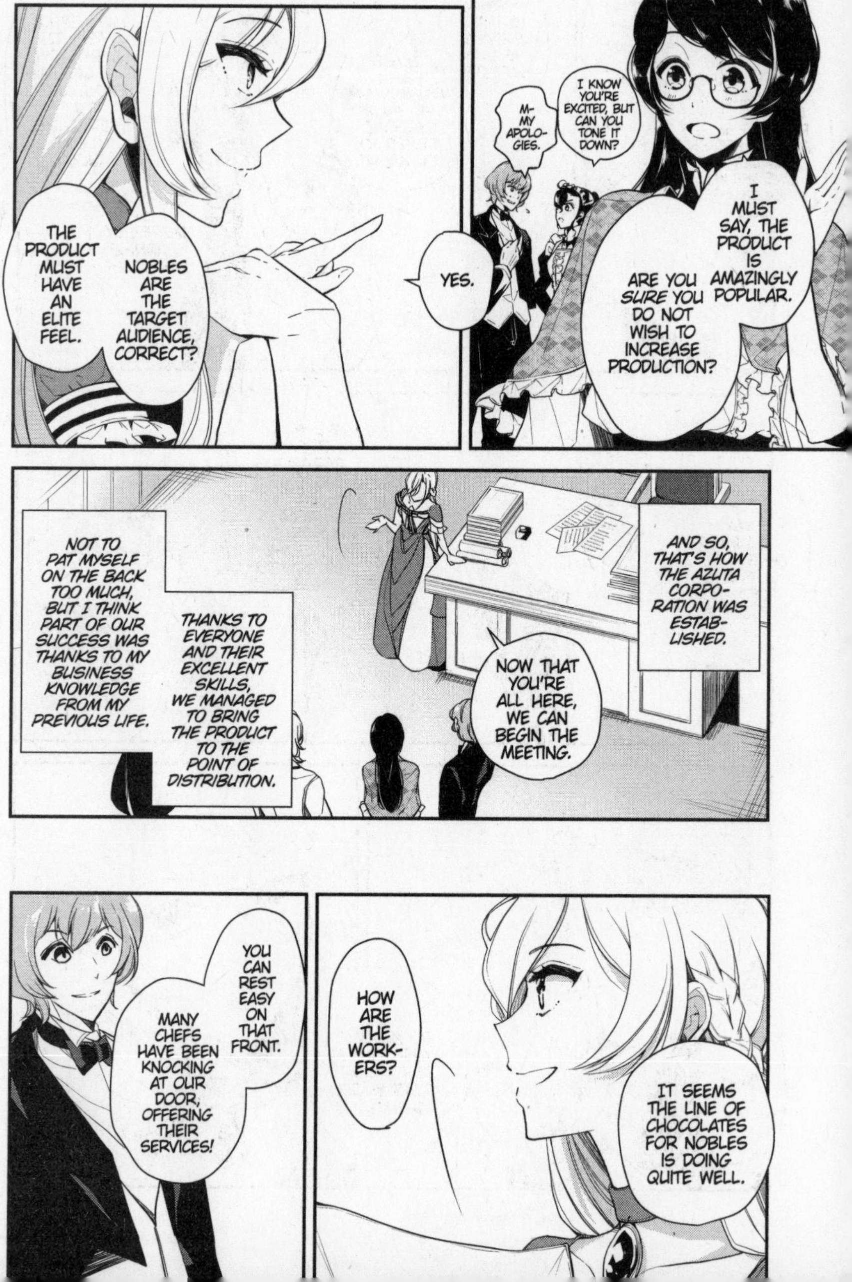
I MUST SAY, THE PRODUCT IS AMAZINGLY POPULAR.
ARE YOU SURE YOU DO NOT WISH TO INCREASE PRODUCTION?
I KNOW YOU'RE EXCITED, BUT CAN YOU TONE IT DOWN?
M-MY APOLOGIES.
YES.
NOBLES ARE THE TARGET AUDIENCE, CORRECT?
THE PRODUCT MUST HAVE AN ELITE FEEL.
AND SO, THAT'S HOW THE AZUTA CORPORATION WAS ESTABLISHED.
NOW THAT YOU'RE ALL HERE, WE CAN BEGIN THE MEETING.
THANKS TO EVERYONE AND THEIR EXCELLENT SKILLS, WE MANAGED TO BRING THE PRODUCT TO THE POINT OF DISTRIBUTION.
NOT TO PAT MYSELF ON THE BACK TOO MUCH, BUT I THINK PART OF OUR SUCCESS WAS THANKS TO MY BUSINESS KNOWLEDGE FROM MY PREVIOUS LIFE.
IT SEEMS THE LINE OF CHOCOLATES FOR NOBLES IS DOING QUITE WELL.
HOW ARE THE WORKERS?
YOU CAN REST EASY ON THAT FRONT.
MANY CHEFS HAVE BEEN KNOCKING AT OUR DOOR, OFFERING THEIR SERVICES!

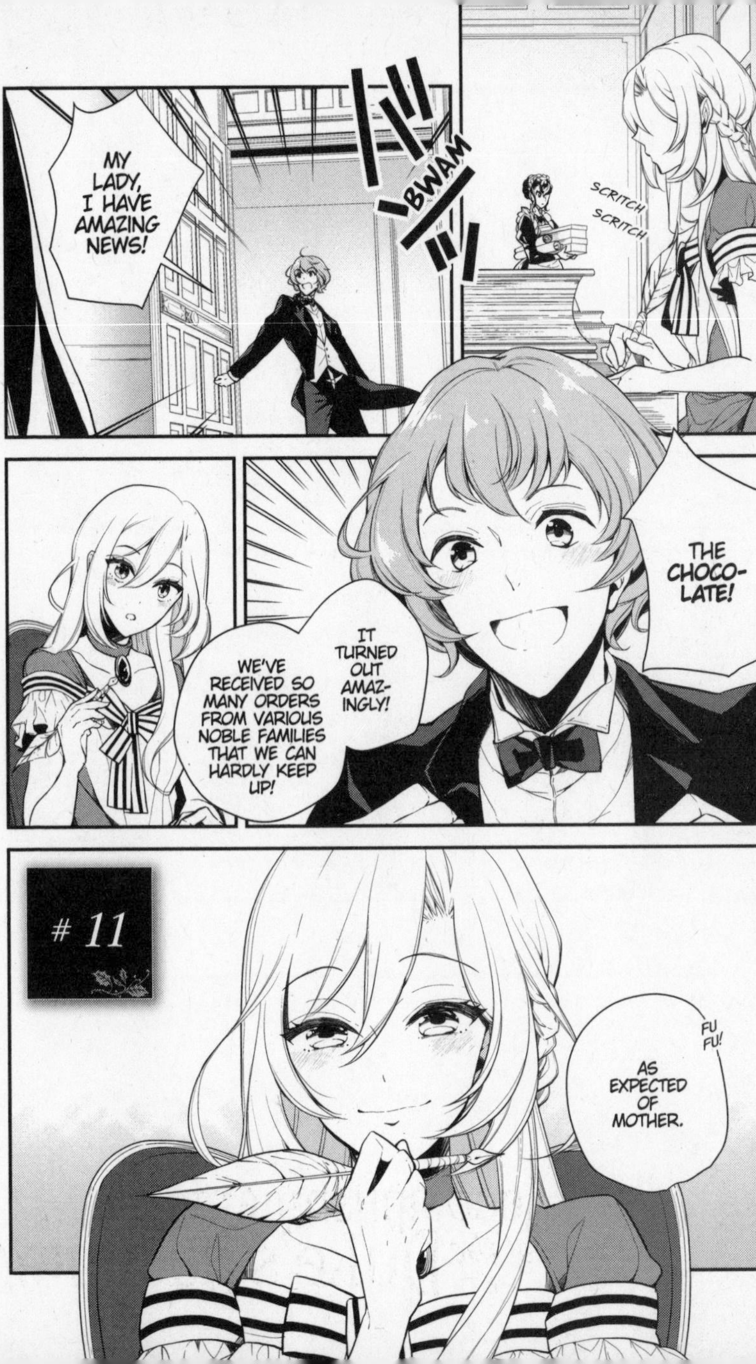
SCRITCH SCRITCH
BWAM
MY LADY, I HAVE AMAZING NEWS!
THE CHOCO-LATE!
IT TURNED OUT AMAZ-INGLY!
WE'VE RECEIVED SO MANY ORDERS FROM VARIOUS NOBLE FAMILIES THAT WE CAN HARDLY KEEP UP!
FU FU!
AS EXPECTED OF MOTHER.
11

Accomplishments
of the Duke's Daughter

CONTENTS

OXFORD WORLD'S CLASSICS

ELECTIVE AFFINITIES

JOHANN WOLFGANG VON GOETHE was born in 1749, the son of a well-to-do citizen of Frankfurt. As a young man he studied law and briefly practised as a lawyer, but creative writing was his chief concern. In the early 1770s he was the dominating figure of the German literary revival, his tragic novel *Werther* bringing him international fame.

In 1775 he settled permanently in the small duchy of Weimar where he became a minister of state and director of the court theatre; in 1782 he was ennobled as 'von Goethe'. His journey to Italy in 1786–8 influenced the development of his mature classical style; in the 1790s, he and his younger contemporary Schiller (1759–1805) were the joint architects of Weimar Classicism, the central phase of German literary culture.

Goethe wrote in all the literary *genres* but his interests extended far beyond literature and included a number of scientific subjects. His creative energies never ceased to take new forms and he was still writing original poetry at the age of more than 80. In 1806 he married Christiane Vulpius (1765–1816), having lived with her for eighteen years; they had one surviving son, August (1789–1830). Goethe died in 1832.

DAVID CONSTANTINE is a poet and translator. He has published volumes of poetry, short stories, and a novel, and has translated Hölderlin, Goethe, Kleist, and Brecht. From 2002 to 2012 he was co-editor (with Helen Constantine) of the journal *Modern Poetry in Translation*. His translations of Goethe's *Faust, Parts I and II* are published by Penguin; for Oxford World's Classics he has translated Goethe's *The Sorrows of Young Werther*. In 2010 he won the BBC National Short Story Award for 'Tea at the Midland', and in 2013 the Frank O'Connor International Short Story Award for *Tea at the Midland and Other Stories*.

OXFORD WORLD'S CLASSICS

*For over 100 years Oxford World's Classics have brought
readers closer to the world's great literature. Now with over 700
titles—from the 4,000-year-old myths of Mesopotamia to the
twentieth century's greatest novels—the series makes available
lesser-known as well as celebrated writing.*

*The pocket-sized hardbacks of the early years contained
introductions by Virginia Woolf, T. S. Eliot, Graham Greene,
and other literary figures which enriched the experience of reading.
Today the series is recognized for its fine scholarship and
reliability in texts that span world literature, drama and poetry,
religion, philosophy and politics. Each edition includes perceptive
commentary and essential background information to meet the
changing needs of readers.*

OXFORD WORLD'S CLASSICS

JOHANN WOLFGANG VON GOETHE

Elective Affinities
A Novel

Translated with an Introduction and Notes by
DAVID CONSTANTINE

OXFORD
UNIVERSITY PRESS

OXFORD
UNIVERSITY PRESS

Great Clarendon Street, Oxford OX2 6DP

Oxford University Press is a department of the University of Oxford.
It furthers the University's objective of excellence in research, scholarship,
and education by publishing worldwide in

Oxford New York

Athens Auckland Bangkok Bogotá Buenos Aires Calcutta
Cape Town Chennai Dar es Salaam Delhi Florence Hong Kong Istanbul
Karachi Kuala Lumpur Madrid Melbourne Mexico City Mumbai
Nairobi Paris São Paulo Singapore Taipei Tokyo Toronto Warsaw

with associated companies in Berlin Ibadan

Oxford is a registered trade mark of Oxford University Press
in the UK and in certain other countries

Published in the United States
by Oxford University Press Inc., New York

First published as a World's Classics paperback 1994
Reissued as an Oxford World's Classics paperback 1999
Reissued 2008

British Library Cataloguing in Publication Data

Data available

Library of Congress Cataloging in Publication Data

Goethe, Johann Wolfgang von, 1749–1832. (Wahlverwandtschaften. English]
Elective affinities: a novel / Johann Wolfgang von Goethe;
translated with an introduction and notes by David Constantine.
p. cm.—(Oxford world's classics)
Includes bibliographical references (p.).
I. Constantine, David, 1944– . II. Title. III. Series.
833'.6—dc20 PT2027.W213 1994 93–5741

ISBN 978-0-19-955536-9

12

Printed and bound in Great Britain
by Clays Ltd, Elcograf S.p.A.

CONTENTS

INTRODUCTION

Goethe's *Elective Affinities* began life as a Novelle, and was to have been inserted into *Wilhelm Meister's Years of Travel*. Goethe first mentioned it in April 1808, declared it finished on 30 July (already speaking of it as a *novel* suitable for publication in two small volumes), but took it up again the following spring and began the expansion into the novel we have now. He put himself under pressure by allowing printing to begin before the last chapters were written, and brought the whole thing out in October 1809. For years he had been in the habit of dictating his works (and not just his literary works—his letters and diaries too), and *Elective Affinities* was composed aloud and taken down by Goethe's secretary Riemer. Indeed, on a coach journey between Jena and Weimar in May 1808, before dictation began, Goethe recounted a large part of the (then) Novelle to his friend Heinrich Meyer, and did so almost as though it were already complete in his mind. The novel is told in a narrating voice and contains a Novelle told as an evening's entertainment but it does not read in the least like the spoken word. The discrepancy is an intriguing one, one of many.

Goethe was 60 when he published *Elective Affinities*. He had been in Weimar, employed at the Court, since 1775. Behind him already were enormous literary achievements: the novels *Werther* and *Wilhelm Meister's Apprentice Years*; dramas of his *Sturm und Drang* (*Götz, Egmont*), of his classicism (*Iphigenie, Tasso*), as well as *Faust* (the first part published after half a lifetime's preoccupation with the story in 1806), and a corpus of poetry of an abundance, variety, and revolutionary innovativeness without equal in German literature. Besides that he had done serious work in most branches of the contemporary sciences, notably in optics, geology, botany, and physiology, always in such a spirit as to affirm not only the wholeness and holiness of all creation but also the wholeness of all his own creative effort in art, in science, and in living. He was famous in Europe. Napoleon received him in 1808, and decorated him with the Cross of the Legion of Honour. In the pay of the Duke of Weimar, ennobled by him in 1788, given the title 'Excellency' in 1804, he became the alternative eminence of the place and at his house in the centre of the little town he received and entertained on a large scale. Weimar would have been very little without Goethe and the many talented men and women drawn there by him. He was not only part of the Establishment, in large measure he constituted it; and was for all that a difficult and scandalous person to have around.

In 1786, having served ten years at the Court and ten years also in a relationship with a rather severe married lady called Charlotte von Stein, Goethe broke away and, travelling incognito and telling nobody at home until he could present them with a *fait accompli*, he went to Italy—to Rome, Naples, and Sicily—for nearly two years. That interlude was decisive in more ways than can be discussed here. Put briefly, it confirmed or re-confirmed him in his vocation as a poet, and he resolved to live thenceforth in such a way as to serve that vocation best, which caused many contemporaries to think him inconsiderate and selfish. Italy itself put him at odds with Weimar society when he came home; he had shifted, they had not. Then he affronted them more definitely by taking a girl from the local artificial-flower factory, Christiane Vulpius, to live with him in his *Gartenhaus*, his house in the park, as his mistress. For her, but with Rome in mind, he composed the *Roman Elegies*, circulating them first among friends and publishing them in 1795 as the manifesto of a classicism whose central tenet was enjoyment, happiness, the life of the senses.

Christiane, as Goethe's mistress and because of her class, was not presentable. She withdrew when guests came. But in Goethe's published correspondence with her the tone on both sides is warmly and ordinarily human—domestic, tender, chatty, amusing. She lived with him until her death in 1816, and bore him five children, only one of whom survived. In 1806, when French troops passing through Weimar after their victory at Jena disrupted Goethe's household and threatened his life, Christiane behaved with great bravery and presence of mind, and in acknowledgement of that and to give her more protection in dangerous times, Goethe married her on 19 October, their son August being present as a witness. Goethe did not think this official sanction itself important—'She always was my wife', he used to say—but after it Christiane could at least be taken out and introduced. No more a lady married than unmarried, however, she was gossiped about hatefully by the real ladies.

It is worth mentioning Christiane Vulpius in this context since *Elective Affinities*, obviously, has to do with marriage. Goethe lived with her for eighteen years before they married, and though his relationship with her was not only the longest-lasting but also the fullest in his life, still he never felt obliged to forsake all others on her account, and between 1788 and 1816 was in love elsewhere, more or less passionately, more or less intimately, half-a-dozen times at least. Goethe loved women, the love of women is the chief inspiration of his poetry, really he was almost always in love. In 1824, then 74 and in love with an 18-year-old, he wrote a poem for the jubilee reissue of *Werther* lamenting the condition he was in as being no better than it had been when he wrote that novel of unhappy passion half-a-century before. Though bound and then also married to Christiane, he was frequently away from home—three months in 1797, four in 1808, five in 1815, six in 1810, seven in 1790, for example—and in her letters to him, and more in the published gossip of contemporaries, there are allusions to his infidelities. Goethe himself edited their correspondence before his death, and none of the letters written by Christiane in the years 1804–9 survived. Perhaps they contained too many recriminations. And there is other contemporary testimony that in that period, at the end of which *Elective Affinities* was written, Goethe's life with Christiane was more than usually troubled. Little more than a year after marrying her Goethe, withdrawing as he often did to Jena, met Minna Herzlieb there and soon began to feel for her more than he ought to have (as he put it). She was only 18. Goethe wrote a sequence of sonnets for her; and it has very often been said that she moved him to write *Elective Affinities* much as Charlotte Buff had moved him to write *Werther*, and that she appears in it as Ottilie. But it has also been said that if you are looking for the woman the one most likely is Sylvie von Ziegesar, whom Goethe was seeing frequently during his usual summer stay in Karlsbad in 1808. Goethe in Rome, whenever his incognito failed to protect him, was pestered by people wanting to know whether *Werther* were *true* or not, true in the sense of having really happened. He found this very tiresome. There was similar speculation as soon as *Elective Affinities* came out. And his own later remarks on the novel seemed to confirm the supposition that his own passionate life had gone into the writing of it. He said: 'There is in this novel, as every reader will recognize, a deeply passionate wound which even in healing is reluctant to close, a heart afraid of being made whole again.' In conversation with Eckermann, at the end of his life, he reiterated this emphasis: 'I lived every word of my *Elective Affinities*', he said. He was in no way distinguishing the novel by saying that. He had said the same about *Wilhelm Meister*, the felt truth of *Werther* and of his lyric poetry was manifest to everyone; indeed, all his works were, as he said himself, 'fragments of a great confession'. Still, the nearness and the livingness of the inspiration of *Elective Affinities* needs to be borne in mind, the more so as its tone is often remote and cold and its subject is the denial of life and a sort of freezing to death.

Elective Affinities is a lived book, then—in its different mode and tone as lived as *Werther*. But a further remark of Goethe's should deter us from reading it as autobiography and from seeking real-life models for its characters. Eckermann reports: 'He said there was nothing in his *Elective Affinities* which had not been really lived, but nothing was there in the form *in which* it had been lived.' Goethe has given us a novel, not an autobiography; which is to say that his life-experience occurs in it always and only as the novel itself requires. The novelist is released from matter-of-fact, from what was biographically or autobiographically so, and produces the kind of truth which it is peculiarly his business to produce. Had he not had the real experiences he would not have been equipped to produce that truth; but the truth he produces is other and more than those experiences. He conducts a sort of experiment with the material of his real experience, to see what is in it, what outcome it *might* have. In *Werther* he pushed the experiment consequentially through to destruction; and in doing so he believed he saved himself from his hero's end. A cooler, crueler experiment seems to be under way in *Elective Affinities*.

When *Elective Affinities* appeared it was felt by some to be a very immoral and by others to be a very moral book. The division was according to whether readers thought Goethe upheld the institution of marriage or undermined it. But that is not, in itself, a question anyone need bother to try to decide. *Elective Affinities* is no more a tract for or against marriage than it is an autobiography; it is a novel and is moral in the way that all great literature is moral: it quickens, through its art, an awareness of issues which we may call moral if by that we mean having to do with better and worse ways of living. There is never any easy passage from a literary work—not even from a novel in which moral issues, issues of human life, are depicted and rendered palpable—into practical life itself; and opinions as to what the 'message' of *Elective Affinities* is, what it teaches, have been and always will be wildly divergent. Goethe was aware and proud of the complexity of this work ('there are a lot of things hidden away in it', he said, and 'it needs reading three times'), and in any attempt to understand it and have it affect our lives as novels can and should, we must avoid being monolithic and reductive.

Just before the novel came out Goethe put an advertisement for it in a literary periodical. Writing in the third person he surmises that the author (himself) must have been led to his strange title by his continuing work in the physical sciences where, he says, we often make use of comparisons drawn from the world of human behaviour so that things which are essentially remote from us may be brought a little nearer; and in the novel, he continues, in a case concerning morality, doubtless the author was seeking to trace an expression used as an analogy in chemistry back to its origin in the life of the human spirit. 'Elective affinities' then, belonging properly in the world of chemistry but deriving from a human world of choice and inclination, is returned to that world as a note on or as a means of understanding the novel's human events. The advertisement concludes with a general remark, the essence of which is this: that there is after all only one Nature, and that

even in our human zone of it, the cheerful zone of reason and
freedom of choice, still there are traces, in the passions, of bleak
and irresistible Necessity. That question whether we—or the
characters in Goethe's novel—have any choice or not, is
central, of course. Charlotte, when the Captain and Eduard
explain the technical term to her, insists, very characteristically,
that we cannot properly speak of choice (election) in the case
of helplessly parting and combining chemical substances, and
that choice, the ability to choose a better course over a worse,
is what uniquely characterizes human beings. That discussion
takes place before the arrival of Ottilie. Some fifteen months
later, on the brink of the final catastrophe, both women believe
they are being hounded by a fate which quite overrides their
volition and their own codes of right and wrong. Charlotte
says: 'There are certain things which Fate determines on very
obstinately. Reason and virtue, duty and everything holy stand
in its way in vain. Something is set to happen as Fate sees fit
but which to us does not seem fit; and at length it will
accomplish its own end however we behave.' Ottilie writes (by
then she has ceased speaking): 'I have left my proper course
and am not to be allowed to resume it. Even if I were at one
with myself again, still in the world outside a malevolent spirit
has me in its power and seems to be thwarting me.' And in a
passage of great pathos as the account nears its end we are
shown the physical inability of Ottilie and Eduard to stay away
from one another when they are living in the same house. They
are drawn into proximity irresistibly.

But that is only one demonstration, perhaps the most poignant, of a compulsion all the characters have been under, to a
greater or lesser extent, throughout; to put it more precisely,
they suffer a continual restriction, contradiction, or reversal
(often cruelly ironic) of individual volition. This thwarting is the
negative revelation of the characters' own compulsive drive to
determine, control, order, and choose. And how often (it is part
of the same compulsion) they utter prophecies and hopes that
come to nothing! All the characters are driven in this way, not
just the four of the equation. Mittler, the Assistant, Luciane,
and the Architect all more or less significantly in their subordin-
ated roles are impelled to impose and shape things, at the very

least by wishing and most often by an active intervention; and almost always they are thwarted or achieve an unhappy opposite. The Assistant prophesies that Ottilie will be a source of happiness to herself and to others! His confident bid to marry her founders irrelevantly. Luciane bosses and interferes wherever she can—catastrophically in the case of the girl whose mind has been disturbed by a domestic accident. Renovating the chapel, and at the same time falling in love with Ottilie, the Architect is in fact preparing her tomb. And Mittler, most notoriously, belies his name ('mediator') and wreaks nothing but havoc whenever he intervenes. Intentions, hopes, and predictions proliferate, and scarcely one of them is happily fulfilled.

Events correctly predicted would be easier to manage. That is the commonest impulse: to forestall, control, and sanitize. The Captain subjugates the estate, on a map (which Eduard, falling in love, disfigures). The Captain is a lover of card-indexes and system; rigorously he separates business from what he calls 'life'. At his instigation the stream and the road through the village are tidied up, as are the villagers; begging is restricted and regulated. The people are either kept at a distance (neither Eduard nor the Captain wants any relationship with them other than that of command) or so arranged, in 'informal' family groups, that they do not offend the eye. Charlotte, having prettified the churchyard (which Eduard dislikes crossing and Mittler categorically refuses to enter), seeks to render her own household safe, learns about verdigris and lead glazes, and in alliance with the Captain appoints (all in vain as far as her own child, Ottilie, and Eduard are concerned) a surgeon to minister in the case of accidents. Again and again, in little things and in large, the characters struggle to shape life to their liking, and are all the while drifting towards catastrophe as inexorably as leaves on a mill-race. In a place the Revolution has not touched ('nothing gets done for the general good except through the exercise of unrestricted sovereign power', says the Captain), where all they do is footle and converse, they rehearse the old forms of their class to shape a manageable life, and are overwhelmed.

Of the four it is Charlotte who most, and most pathetically, embodies the continually thwarted drive to make life safe. She is renowned for her aplomb in 'difficult' social situations; she defuses conflict, smooths over unpleasantnesses. She shows most openly what characterizes them all (even Eduard, though he frees himself somewhat), and that is fearfulness in the face of life. She is, like Mittler, a great fixer, and has no more success than he does. She plans or has planned marriage for Ottilie with Eduard, the Captain, the Assistant. She speaks readily in aphorisms, as if (in the vain hope that) life could be reduced to them. In one extraordinary passage, climbing the hill to the new house, Ottilie accompanying her with the unlucky child, she rattles off truisms and wise old sayings like a desperate mantra. (Ottilie in her diary is just as bad.) Charlotte's caution when Eduard first suggests having the Captain to stay exceeds the real situation; she expresses instead something of the large reservoir of fearfulness which is in her, just below the surface, all the time. Again and again, long after the drift towards catastrophe has begun, she seeks pathetically to reverse the process, to return, to get back out of boundlessness into a safer enclosure. Her motive is always the same—fear; and as her aphorisms fail her she resorts to wishful thinking. She aims at prevention, she lives off *not*-wanting. Her realization at the end—that by resisting she has caused the death of her child—is a poignant moment, but still not an acknowledgement of her fundamental state, which is rather the absolute fear and denial of life.

As their lives slip out of control the characters refer repeatedly to Fate or to a fate which they feel to be directing or compelling them, and the narrator uses such language too. Eduard, obeying an instinct which at the very outset Charlotte had criticized in him, wagers his life in a war, and when he survives thinks Fate has saved him for happiness with Ottilie; he views the inscribed glass which did not shatter when expected to as a corroborating sign. But Charlotte and Ottilie, after the drowning of the child, view this determination, as it seems by an outside force, in a blacker aspect. To them it is something 'monstrous', the word (*ungeheuer*) becomes a leitmotif (one of several). They feel they are being overridden by something quite inhuman, by something to which their little human categories of right and wrong and all their efforts at personal volition are entirely irrelevant. But we need a nearer definition of this monstrous Fate, and rather than believe (or suppose Goethe to have believed) in the existence of exterior malignant forces let us say instead that what threatens the characters in *Elective Affinities* is life itself: they are being threatened by the demands of a real life, and their own denial of life, their attempts to repress, reduce, and prevent it, cause its demands to appear monstrous. In the end, indeed, by denying and resisting life they conjure up death, and succumb to it.

Goethe's novel is steeped in death. The second book is fixated on it, but in the first too—in the fear of the graveyard, the fear of poisoning, the fear of drowning—death nudges into prominence. Occasions which should be joyous—the laying of the foundation stone, the fireworks on Ottilie's birthday—are shadowed by death, and the christening in the second book meets death full on, when Mittler's intervention gives the aged parson the *coup de grâce*. The Architect, who will stand and watch one night over Ottilie's corpse, spends his time robbing tombs and showing his finds in society as though they were little fashionable commodities. This socializing, trivializing, aestheticizing of death no more reduces its real power than does Charlotte's prettification of the graveyard. And in his work—dilettante work—as a painter all the Architect does is decorate a tomb and encourage in Ottilie, when she sits and dreams under the finished ceiling, a willingness to side with death and duck the demands of life.

Art altogether, if landscape-gardening, *poses plastiques*, and *tableaux vivants* are to be called art, not only does not increase the sense of life, which true art does, but rather reduces it and joins in the drift towards death. The gardening, though with the arrival of the Captain it becomes less cramped, is still only a pastime, as, with the arrival of the Count, he realizes himself. And though the style aimed at is English and so, by comparison with the French, informal, this is still only the studied informality achieved also in the village when the villagers, spruced up for Sundays, gather before their cottages in 'natural' family groups. The principal impulse in the garden is still to control, arrange, and tame. They take a walk to the mill, it is a walk into unexplored territory and during it a profound advance is made in the new relationships, especially in that between Eduard and Ottilie. Their impulse immediately afterwards is to tame that walk, lay it out comfortably, so that it may be done and done again without fatigue or risk. The view from the new house, whose situation was chosen by Ottilie in the first upsurge of her love for Eduard, promises a good deal, since the Hall is excluded from it, but like the house itself, which is never properly lived in (but receives instead the corpse of the drowned child), that promise of novelty, openness, extension of life, is not fulfilled. The greatest scheme, the merging of the three ponds, threatens catastrophe at its inception when the boy is nearly drowned, and provides the scene of it when Charlotte's child is drowned. Ironically, by merging the ponds they were returning them to their former and in that sense more natural state; for they were once, as the Captain has found out, a mountain lake. Nature, especially water, 'the unsteady element', constitutes a threat throughout the novel; or, we might say, it is present as an alternative to the rigidity of the estate. That alternative, the way of greater naturalness, appears as a threat, and in the end as a deadly threat, to people afraid to embrace it. So life itself, the fate which is hounding them, must appear monstrous; indeed, must appear at last in the form of death.

The Architect is an adjutant of death. He turns the little boys, already marshalled in uniform in a corps, into a frieze for a summer-house. He assists Luciane by drawing her a pedantically detailed mausoleum. She herself displays a vitality which is merely social. Her tongue is so sharp that, as the narrator says, it is a wonder anything was left alive for fifteen miles around. In her party pieces, in her *poses plastiques*, her roles as a living statue, she prefigures the final freezing of Ottilie. The Count, assisted by the Architect, entertains the company with *tableaux vivants*, in which living people strike and hold an unnatural immobility. At Christmas then, in the nativity he induces Ottilie to star in, the Architect fixes a picture full of chilling ironies: her virginity, the borrowed baby, the child she will never bear. Ottilie freezes, stiffens, and that will be her fate. Already the narrator has said of her that with the departure of Eduard 'the life of her soul had been killed'. When she presses the drowned child to her uncovered breasts it freezes her to the heart. Frozen herself, Ottilie kills the life in Eduard. At the inn, when she will not speak, they confront one another, as Eduard says, like shades. Far from becoming a saint she becomes a vampire: she leaches the life from him and, having done so, and having resolutely sided with death in herself, she speaks at last and says—it is one of this chilling book's most chilling and sadistic utterances: 'Promise me you will live.' In her abstention from food she perfects the life of denial. She is its priestess. Her most characteristic gesture, which none who loves her has the heart to contradict, is a gesture of refusal and denial.

The form and tone of the novel itself—its symmetry and careful fixing of the scenes; the formality, often the stiltedness, of the dialogue, especially between husband and wife; its often difficult syntax; its narrator's remoteness, irony, and sententiousness—all these contribute to the oppressive rigidity and unnaturalness which is the world itself on that bizarre estate. And the strange child born of a double adultery, who resembles the Captain and Ottilie, by its very unnaturalness, even by its manifest artificiality as a literary device, puts a seal on the whole. Life wears that mark when it is perverted and repressed. Learning of its conception Eduard was 'turned to stone'. Viewing it dead, the Captain saw 'his frozen image'.

I began this reading of *Elective Affinities* by mentioning morality. Clearly, the moral issue of the novel is not whether the institution of marriage should be upheld or not. Mittler, unmarried himself and fatally ham-fisted, cannot be listened to (though he has been) as if he were the unassailable spokesman (Goethe's mouthpiece!) on the subject of marriage. He is far too frequently ironized, criticized, and countered. But nor does his opponent the Count deserve any more unqualified respect. The issue is elsewhere. The issue is whether life should be lived or not.

Then are the characters *wrong* to live the way they do? Charlotte, at the end, acknowledges that it was wrong to marry Eduard when, not having fought to do so the first time, a second chance was given them years later. He likewise realizes that was a mistake (though he pushed most to commit it). The question is, should they abide by their mistake? In love with Ottilie he thinks they should not, and Charlotte herself comes to that conclusion. Not that his marriage with Charlotte is worthless, but his love for Ottilie is better, in the sense that more of the person is engaged, and more deeply. There is ample demonstration of this, and Eduard himself is certain that having been an amateur and a dilettante all his life he has finally, in loving Ottilie, found something in which his personality is wholly taken up. There is much that is dislikeable about Eduard (as about all the characters in this, as it seems designedly, unsympathetic book) but he has this in his favour, as Goethe himself pointed out: that meeting Ottilie he loves unconditionally. His going to war, at least as he views it once he is there, is more a deliberate ordeal in the name of love than capitulation to a death-wish. He makes a trial of himself and his life. Having come through he feels he has a right to claim what his life, a real life now, most needs: Ottilie. He is the only one who breaks out (the Captain, though he comes and goes, gets ever more shadowy). He seeks by force of a lover's persuasion to animate the frozen Ottilie, and when he fails and she is dead he finds, to his credit, that he cannot follow after her by starving himself, because that way is *false* (as he says) and against his nature. He has at least the makings of salvation in him.

Marriage is not the issue, but by abiding in a marriage which is false Eduard and Charlotte extend at best a shallowness and at worst a fundamental falsity over all they undertake. Thus, although in real life there may be nothing particularly wrong (at least, nothing deserving of death) in landscape gardening, speaking in aphorisms, nor even in teaching children the way the Assistant does, in the novel, cumulatively, these things and many more like them typify a society which is set against any change or expansion of their lives. The Assistant's exercise of tight control over his pupils' wayward imaginations and his uneasiness at even the thought of life among 'monkeys, parrots, and blackamoors' in foreign parts, are akin to Charlotte's anxiety at any opportunity or threat of opening up. The novel has a social interest in that it depicts a class whose forms, already anachronistic in 1809, seem to be signalling their own desperate need for renewal. Incapable of that, they excite a sort of vengefulness instead. Love in that context, as so often in Goethe's work, arrives as an animating and revolutionary force; it turns destructive, indeed deadly, when the characters, stuck in dead forms, prove unable to accommodate it. Charlotte and Eduard are husband and wife but both are in love elsewhere. Eduard reanimates his marital passion by lasciviously remembering the past; and sustains it, and Charlotte responds, by thinking of somebody else. Having slept together they feel they have done wrong. As the narrator says: 'The present will not be denied its monstrous due.' The present, in this case, is the love each feels for a person outside their marriage, a love which has in it, at least potentially, the beginnings of a real life. That life demands its rights, and denied them it brings forth a monstrous recrimination.

The Novelle told by the English lord's companion to entertain the ladies offers a radical alternative to the novel's fatal trend. There the girl, drifting into a marriage which would be only nominal, liberates herself violently, throws herself upon the mercy of the river, and in so doing makes a provocative trial of herself to the man she loves. He responds instinctively, they are carried away out of the sphere of the merely social, and land in a place apart where, naked and nearly drowned, she is recovered, reanimated by her lover. That scene is remarkable for its drastic confrontation of death and sexual passion, and for the triumph of the latter: 'Now the intense desire to save overrode every other consideration. Nothing was left undone that might bring the beautiful, stiffening, naked body back to life. It worked. She opened her eyes, she saw her friend . . .' Sure of themselves, reborn into certainty, they face their families in bridal clothes, and force the issue in favour of love and life.

Eduard tries, and fails. Ottilie, allying herself with death, triumphs. 'Morality celebrates its victory', as Goethe said—a bitter victory.

The endings of most of Goethe's major works—of *Iphigenie*, *Tasso*, *Wilhelm Meister*, *Faust*—are notoriously problematic, not to say evasive. Perhaps only in *Werther* was he truly consequential to the end. The ending of *Elective Affinities* is Goethe at his shiftiest. Ottilie's saintliness is no such thing. She starves herself and kills the will to live in Eduard. Or was she still wavering when Mittler settled the issue with his usual aplomb? Eduard had hopes, and the others too thought she might begin speaking again on his birthday. She looked, the narrator says, like a person carrying a happy intention towards her friends. Were the clothes she laid out really her bridal wear? Were the asters for a wedding? At least we can say that any impulse in her towards love and life was being countered all the while by her refusing food. She was as ready for death—perversely, being young—as was the old parson when Mittler dispatched him at the christening. Shifting then through apparent miracles emphatically towards an after-life, Goethe offers us nothing we can believe in. The lovers may be buried together, now dead being permitted to lie side by side, but in there with them is the monstrous child, as a devilish irony in their unbelievable heaven. Transcendence of that kind is a poor compensation, and no redemption either from a life unlived. 'And they call me a heathen!' Goethe once expostulated: 'I had Gretchen executed and Ottilie starve herself to death. Isn't that Christian enough for them?'

Goethe was not an easy member of Weimar society, and he is no easier now. Nothing in the least bit cosy can be deduced out of *Elective Affinities*. The indictment of wrong living is quite merciless. It is a chilling, in some ways a repellent book, and would be nihilistic (the characters drifting helplessly to ruin) did it not, through the passion of Eduard and Ottilie and through their braver equivalents in the Novelle, call for its own wholehearted contradiction.

NOTE ON THE TRANSLATION

Goethe's *Die Wahlverwandtschaften* was translated into French (twice) and into Danish in 1810, only a year after its publication in Germany, but there was no English version until 1854. The translator then was Carlyle's disciple and biographer J. A. Froude, and *Elective Affinities* appeared among other 'Novels and Tales by Goethe' in a volume of Bohn's Standard Library. Mr Bohn himself introduced it with a warning that 'exceptions may be taken to some of the statements contained in this production of Goethe', but, quoting Carlyle ('Fidelity is all the merit a translator need aim at') he absolved Mr Froude at least of any blame. That version, several times reprinted, was the standard one until 1960. I know of four since then: by H. M. Waidson (1960, *Kindred by Choice*); by Elizabeth Mayer and Louise Bogan (1963); by R. J. Hollingdale for Penguin Classics in 1971; and by Judith Ryan in Volume XI of the American Suhrkamp edition of Goethe's works, in 1988.

There is no finality in translation. A good original can always be done differently, if not better, and may even need to be for every generation. Not that a new translation *updates* an original foreign work; it seeks another language, refreshes the element in which the original may live and be carried forward.

Translating Goethe's novel the tone is the hardest thing to get anywhere near right. Lexical sense is, often, hard enough, but tone of voice, aura and feel, are harder, impossibly hard. I was sure at least that I should not attempt to modernize the diction nor make the conversation seem more natural. The way the characters converse is expressive of their predicament. And the narrator's voice is not at all a homely or a sympathetic one. The world his characters inhabit is strange and oppressive. It would have been wrong, I think, to induce readers in modern English to feel at home there. On the other hand, translating a text from the beginning of the nineteenth century as the twentieth ends, it would be just as wrong to aim at a language of the past. Good writing is a living currency. Bringing it across—across the centuries and across the languages—a translator will be *very* unfaithful if the house he offers it is a museum.

But translators will talk for ever about the difficulty of the job. They have bad consciences. They know the original too well and live with a constant measure of their failure.

SELECT BIBLIOGRAPHY

Most things in English on Goethe's *Elective Affinities*—essays by
Hatfield, Stahl, Stopp, and the full-length study by Barnes
(1967)—quote from the text in German and may not be of
much help to a general reader. Introductions to previous
translations, especially Hollingdale's, will give easier access,
and there are individual chapters on the work in Hans Reiss's
Goethe's Novels (London, 1969) and Tony Tanner's *Adultery in the
Novel* (Baltimore, 1979). Goethe's life and works, the whole
phenomenon, may be approached via T. J. Reed's essay in the
Past Masters series (Oxford, 1984) and Nicholas Boyle's bio-
graphy, the first volume of which, to 1790, came out in 1991
(Oxford). Walter Benjamin's essay 'Goethes *Wahlverwandtschaf-
ten*', written in 1924 and many times reprinted, is the best thing
I know on the subject in German. Hans Härtl put together an
extraordinarily·interesting case-history of the book in his '*Die
Wahlverwandschaften': Eine Dokumentation der Wirkung von Goethes
Roman 1808–1832* (Berlin, 1983). The Hamburg edition of
Goethe's works is neat, reliable, and informative. *Die Wahlver-
wandtschaften*, with notes and a commentary by Benno von
Wiese, is contained in Volume VI. That is the text I used for
my translation.

A CHRONOLOGY OF
JOHANN WOLFGANG VON GOETHE

1749   28 August, Goethe born into a well-to-do family in Frank-
        furt am Main.

1755   Lisbon Earthquake.

1756–63 Seven Years War.

1752–65 Goethe privately educated. He has tutors in French, He-
        brew, Italian, English. His early reading: Klopstock, Homer
        in translation, the Bible, French classical dramatists.

1765–8 At the University of Leipzig reading Law and a good deal
        else. Friendships and love affairs (Käthchen Schönkopf),
        many poems in Rococo style, first comedies. First readings
        of Shakespeare.

1768   8 June, Winckelmann murdered in Trieste. August 1768–
        March 1770, Goethe mostly at home in Frankfurt, often ill.
        Interest in alchemy, association with Pietists.

1770–1 Student in Strasburg, in love with Friederike Brion, friend-
        ship with Herder, reading Shakespeare, Ossian, Homer.
        The breakthrough into his own poetic voice.

1771–4 In Frankfurt and Wetzlar. The first version of *Götz* in six
        weeks. Some legal, more literary activity. He writes many
        of the great poems of his *Sturm und Drang*. First version of
        Werther in the spring of 1774. *Götz* staged in Berlin. Vast
        success of *Werther*.

1775   In love with Lili Schönemann, engagement to her. Journey
        to Switzerland. *Egmont* begun. Invited to Weimar. *Urfaust*.
        Breaks off his engagement. November, arrives in Weimar
        and meets Charlotte von Stein.

1776   Herder moves to Weimar. Goethe becomes a servant of the
        State. Interest in the silver mines in Ilmenau, beginnings of
        his geological studies.

1776–86 Increasingly engaged in duties of the State (ennobled 1782);
        journeys on business and for pleasure to the Harz, Berlin,
        Switzerland; involvement with Charlotte von Stein; work
        for the Weimar theatre; scientific studies. Many poems,
        work on *Wilhelm Meister*, *Iphigenie*, *Tasso*. Things unfinished,
        frustration, and a feeling of confinement.

1786   September, flight to Italy. Arrives in Rome, 29 October.

1786–8 In Italy: Rome, Naples, Sicily, Rome. Lives among artists, studies to become one. The making of his classicism. *Iphigenie* recast in verse. *Egmont* finished. Further work on *Tasso* and *Faust*.

1788   18 June, back in Weimar. Released from most of his state duties. 12 July, begins living with Christiane Vulpius. September, the first of the *Roman Elegies*, work on *Tasso*.

1789   French Revolution. *Tasso* completed. 25 December, birth of a son, August, their only surviving child.

1790   March–June, second Italian journey (Venice)—a disappointment.

1792   Goethe in France, at the Battle of Valmy, with the Prussian forces.

1793   21 January, execution of Louis XVI. May–July, Goethe at the Siege of Mainz.

1794   Begins a correspondence with Schiller.

1795   *Roman Elegies* published. They give offence.

1796   *Hermann und Dorothea, Wilhelm Meister*.

1797   Ballads, with Schiller. In Switzerland again.

1798–9 Poems in classical metres (including *Achilleis*), renewed work on *Faust*.

1799   Schiller moves to Weimar.

1800–5 Poems, work on *Faust*, a great deal of scientific work.

1805   Death of Schiller. Goethe ill, withdrawn, depressed.

1806   *Faust, Part I* completed, Goethe marries Christiane Vulpius.

1807–9 Relationship with Minna Herzlieb. *Elective Affinities*, work on *Wilhelm Meister's Years of Travel*. Beginning work on the autobiography *Poetry and Truth*. Received by Napoleon, awarded the Cross of the Legion of Honour.

1812   Goethe meets Beethoven. The French retreat from Moscow.

1815   Waterloo.

1814–18 Relationship with Marianne von Willemer, poems of the *West-Östlicher Divan*.

1816   6 June, death of Christiane.

1816–17 Publication of the *Italian Journey*.

1821   *Wilhelm Meister's Years of Travel*.

1823–4 In love with Ulrike von Levetzow, writes the three poems of the *Trilogie der Leidenschaft*. From 1823, conversations with Eckermann.

1825–31 Continuing work on *Faust, Part II*.

1832   Death of Goethe, 22 March.

Elective Affinities

PART ONE

CHAPTER ONE

Eduard—let that be the name we give to a wealthy baron in the best years of his life—Eduard had spent the loveliest hours of an April afternoon in his nursery grafting young trees with shoots newly arrived for him. The job was just finished; he was putting the tools away in their case and contemplating his handiwork with some satisfaction when the Gardener approached and stood smiling at his master's willingness and industry.

'Have you seen my wife?' Eduard asked, making ready to leave.

'Over in the new grounds,' the Gardener replied. 'It is today she finishes the little summer-house she has been building by the rocks facing the Hall. Everything has turned out beautifully. Your Lordship will be sure to like it. The views are excellent: the village down below, the church a little to the right—you look out almost directly over the steeple—the Hall and the gardens opposite.'

'Indeed,' said Eduard, 'a few steps from here and I could see the people working.'

'And to the right', the Gardener continued, 'the valley opens and you can see into the distance over the fields with all their trees. Such a pleasant prospect. The path up the rocks is very prettily done. Her Ladyship knows what she is about. It is a pleasure to work for her.'

'Go now,' said Eduard, 'and ask will she be so kind as to wait for me. Say I look forward to the pleasure of seeing her new creation.'

The Gardener hurried away, and Eduard soon followed.

He descended the terraces, surveying, as he passed, the greenhouses and the forcing-beds; and reaching the water crossed it by a bridge, to where the path into the new grounds forked. One way, which led across the graveyard pretty directly to the rocks, he avoided, and took the other which bore left on a rather longer route through pleasant greenery, climbing gently. Where the two paths came together again he sat down for a moment on a convenient seat; then began the climb itself, and was brought by all manner of steps and terraces along the narrow path, rising more or less steeply, finally to the summer-house.

Charlotte was at the door to welcome her husband. He sat where she placed him so that through windows and door he could oversee at a glance the different views, in which the landscape appeared like a sequence of framed pictures. He was pleased, and expressed the hope that spring would soon bring to everything a yet more abundant life. 'My only critic-ism', he added, 'would be that one is perhaps a little cramped here.'

'Room enough for the two of us,' Charlotte replied.

'There is indeed,' said Eduard, 'and for a third, no doubt.'

'Why not?' Charlotte replied, 'and even for a fourth. For a larger company we shall make arrangements elsewhere.'

'Since we are here by ourselves,' said Eduard, 'and won't be disturbed and our mood is so cheerful and tranquil, let me admit that for some time now I have had something to say to you and have not been able to, although it is necessary that I should.'

'I rather thought so,' Charlotte replied, 'from your manner lately.'

'And to be frank,' Eduard continued, 'were it not that I am anxious to catch tomorrow morning's post and that we must make up our minds today, I should perhaps have kept silent a while longer.'

'What is it then?' Charlotte asked in a manner that was amicable and encouraging.

'It concerns our friend, the Captain.' Eduard answered. 'You know how unhappily he, like many others, is placed now through no fault of his own. How painful it must be for a man of his knowledge, talents, and abilities to find himself without proper employment and—I will say at once what I should like for him: I should like us to have him here for a time.'

'That will need careful consideration,' Charlotte replied. 'It will need to be looked at from more than one point of view.'

'Let me tell you what *I* think,' said Eduard in reply. 'There was in his last letter a sense of very deep discontent. Not that he is in any material need. He is quite capable of living frugally when he must, and I have myself seen to all the essentials. Nor does it trouble him to accept things from me. Throughout our lives we have got so much into one another's debt that it would be impossible now to calculate how our credit and debit with one another stands. His real misery is that he has no employment. It was always his pleasure, indeed his passion in life, to use the many different talents he has developed in himself daily and hourly for the benefit of others. And now to be idle, or to engage in further study and acquire new skills, being unable to use what he already possesses in such abundance—all in all, my darling, his situation is an unhappy one and he feels it worse and worse, being so isolated.'

'But I thought he had had offers from various quarters,' said Charlotte. 'I myself wrote on his behalf to several very active men and women among my friends, and not without good results, as I believed.'

'That is true,' Eduard replied, 'but these various opportunities, these offers themselves, further torment and upset him. None of the situations is suitable. He is not being asked to perform any real work, but to sacrifice himself—his time, his convictions, his whole way of being—and that he cannot do. The more I think about his predicament, the more I *feel* it, all the more keenly do I wish to have him here with us.'

'It does you great credit', said Charlotte in reply, 'that you think of your friend's circumstances with such sympathy, but you must let me urge you to think also of yourself, and of us.'

'I have,' Eduard replied. 'We can be sure that his presence here would bring us nothing but advantage and pleasure. We need not dwell on what he will cost me—certainly, it will be very little if he moves in with us. And nor will having him here cause us the least inconvenience. He can live in the east wing, and the rest will take care of itself. We should be doing him a great service, and there would be pleasure for us in his company, and profit too. For a long time now I have wanted the property and the district surveying. He will take charge of that, and supervise the work. It was your intention that we should manage the farms ourselves as soon as the present tenancies expire. But what a risky business that may be! He will be able to advise us in so many ways before we begin. I feel the need of a man like him. The local people have the necessary knowledge, but their way of presenting it is confused and not honest. The trained men from the town and the academies are clear and systematic, it is true, but they lack the insight that comes from being on the spot. I can count on our friend for both. And a hundred other opportunities will come of it too, all of them agreeable to contemplate, involving you also, things I am certain we shall be glad of. Enough: I am grateful to you for listening so sympathetically. Now it is your turn to be just as frank and circumstantial. Say whatever you have to say. I promise not to interrupt.'

'Very well then,' Charlotte replied, 'and I will begin by making a general observation. Men attend more to particular things and to the present, and rightly, since they are called upon to act and to influence events. Women, on the other hand, with an equal rightness attend more to the things that hang together in life, since a woman's fate and the fate of her family depend on such things hanging together and it is up to her to see to it that they do. Accordingly, let us look for a moment at our present and our past lives, and you will have to admit that inviting the Captain here does not *wholly* fit in with our intentions, our arrangements, and our plans.

'It always gives me pleasure to think of us as we were in the first years. We were young, we loved one another dearly, but were parted: you from me when your father, in his insatiable greed, bound you to a woman much your senior but rich; I from you when, my prospects being none of the best, I was obliged to say yes to a wealthy man whom I did not love but could respect. We were set free: you first, your good lady leaving you a sizeable fortune; and my turn came just as your travels ended and you were home. So we were reunited. What a pleasure it was then to recall the past! How we cherished our memories! We could enjoy one another's company undisturbed. You were eager for a closer union, I did not consent at once: our ages being roughly the same, I, as a woman, had doubtless grown older than you had as a man. But at length I had no wish to deny you what you seemed to think your only hope of happiness. You wanted to recover, by being with me, from all the unquiet times you had suffered at Court, in the army, and on your travels, to compose yourself and enjoy life; but by being with me alone. I sent my only daughter away to boarding-school, where, admittedly, there has been more variety in her development than would have been possible had she stayed in the country; but not just my daughter—I sent my niece Ottilie there too, though I am fond of her and she might have done better under my guidance here, helping me in the house. All that was done with your consent, solely in order that we should live for ourselves and enjoy undisturbed the happiness we had longed for early on and had now at last achieved. Thus we began our residence here in the country. I was to see to our internal affairs, and you to the external and to whatever concerned our projects as a whole. I have arranged my life so as to accommodate you in everything, so as to live for you alone. Do let us try it for a while at least, and see how well we can manage together as we are.'

'Since, as you say, it is how things hang together that concerns a woman most,' said Eduard in reply, 'any man who listens to your arguments step by step will be bound to acknowledge that you are right. And indeed you *are* right, or have been until today. The grounds on which we have based our lives so far are of a good sort. But shall we build nothing further on them and shall nothing further develop out of them? Is what I am doing in the gardens and you in the park to be only for hermits?'

'All well and good,' said Charlotte. 'But let us not fetch in anything which gets in our way or is foreign to us. Remember that our plans even concerning our recreation to some extent also depended on our being alone together. First you were going to put your travel-diaries in proper shape for me, and sort out the papers that belong with them, and with my help and counting on my interest turn all those notebooks and loose pages, priceless as they are and at present in such disorder, into a whole work that would give pleasure to us and to others. I promised to help you with the writing out, and how nice we thought it would be, so cosy and so very companionable, to travel in recollection through the lands we were not able to see together. And we have already made a start. Then in the evenings you have been getting out your flute again and accompanying me on the piano; and neighbours visit us and we visit them. All this, for me at least, looked like making the summer the happiest I ever thought to have.'

'And still,' said Eduard, rubbing his forehead, 'I cannot help thinking that nothing in what you are so sweetly and sensibly reminding me of would be at all disturbed by the presence of the Captain. On the contrary, it would be moved along more rapidly and with a new life. Some of the journeys he did with me; he made observations of his own, from his own different point of view. Using both sources we really would produce something handsome and complete.'

'Then let me admit quite openly,' said Charlotte, with some impatience, in reply, 'that my feelings are against the idea. I have a presentiment that nothing good will come of it.'

'That would make women quite invincible,' Eduard replied. 'First you are reasonable, so that it is not *possible* to contradict you; then charming, so that giving in to you is a pleasure; then full of feeling, so that a man wishes to avoid causing you any pain; then full of foreboding, which alarms him.'

'I am not superstitious,' Charlotte replied, 'and attach no importance to these vague promptings—if they were only that. But they are most often unconscious memories of fortunate and unfortunate consequences which, in our experience, have resulted from our own or other people's actions. And in any situation nothing is more significant than the intervention of a third party. I have seen friends, brothers and sisters, married couples, and couples in love whose relationships have been wholly altered and their circumstances entirely reshaped by the fortuitous or chosen advent of somebody new.'

'That might happen', said Eduard in reply, 'when people go blindly about their lives, but not if experience has already brought them some enlightenment and they are more conscious of what they are doing.'

'Consciousness, my dear,' said Charlotte to this, 'is an inadequate weapon, and may indeed be a dangerous one for whoever wields it. At the very least what results from our discussion is that we should not be in any hurry. Give me another day or two. Do not decide yet.'

'Things being as they are,' Eduard replied, 'we shall still be acting precipitately even if we leave it for several days. We have advanced the reasons for and against in turn. Now we have to decide, and really the best would be to toss a coin.'

'That or the dice,' said Charlotte in reply. 'I know your way when you cannot make up your mind. But in a matter as serious as this I should think it criminal.'

'But what shall I write to the Captain?' Eduard cried. 'For I must write at once.'

'A calm, sensible, and sympathetic letter,' said Charlotte.

'Then I might as well not write at all,' said Eduard.

'But there are times', said Charlotte, 'when it is necessary and an act of friendship to write nothing rather than not to write.'

CHAPTER TWO

Eduard was alone in his room. Charlotte's retelling the events of his past life and her calling to mind the circumstances and the projects they now shared had thrown him, excitable as he was, into a pleasant agitation. Whilst still in her company he had felt contented; and had, accordingly, thought out a letter to the Captain which should be friendly and sympathetic but also restrained and non-committal. When he went to his desk, however, and took up the Captain's letter and read it again, all the unhappiness of his excellent friend's situation came back to him; and the feelings by which he had lately been tormented were all renewed and it seemed to him impossible that he should abandon his friend in such a worrying state.

Eduard was not in the habit of denying himself anything. Being the only child of wealthy parents, spoiled by them, induced by them into an odd but highly advantageous marriage with a much older woman and further spoiled by her then in all manner of ways (for she was grateful that he behaved himself and sought to make it up to him with an abundant generosity) and soon becoming his own master when she died, and travelling as he pleased then, making any diversion or alteration as it suited him, wanting nothing excessive but wanting a good deal nevertheless and a good deal of variety; open, charitable, honest, brave when need be—what hindering of his wishes was he ever likely to encounter?

Every outcome had been as he had wished, even Charlotte he had got possession of, by his stubborn, indeed legendary fidelity finally winning her; and now for the first time he felt himself opposed, for the first time thwarted, and just when by having the friend of his youth to join him he might, so to speak, have rounded off his whole existence. He was put out, impatient, several times took up his pen and laid it down again, being unable to satisfy himself as to what he ought to write. He was unwilling to go against his wife's wishes, and unable to act as she had asked him to; feeling so unsettled, how should he write calmly, as he must? The most natural thing was to seek a postponement of the issue. In a few words he asked his friend's pardon that he had not written, and that the present letter would say nothing much, promising something more significant, something reassuring before long.

Next day, on a walk to the same place, Charlotte took the opportunity to resume the conversation, believing perhaps that the best way to blunt a purpose is continually to discuss it.

Eduard welcomed this return to the subject. He spoke after his usual manner, amicably and agreeably; for though, being highly susceptible, he easily took fire and pressed his desires very passionately and could make a person impatient by his persistence, his speech was nevertheless so modified by perfect consideration for whoever he was speaking to that it was impossible to dislike him even though he pestered.

It was thus, on the morning in question, that he first put Charlotte into the best of moods and then, turning the conversation in the nicest way, quite discomposed her, so that at last she exclaimed: 'Clearly you want me to grant my lover what I refused my husband.

'In any event,' she continued, 'I am not averse to your knowing that your wishes and your lively and considerate way of expressing them have not left me untouched and unmoved. They oblige me to make a confession. I have been concealing something too. I find myself in a situation similar to yours, and have already imposed upon myself just such a discipline as I expect you to impose upon yourself.'

'I am glad to hear it,' said Eduard. 'I see that in marriage it is necessary to quarrel from time to time, for that way we learn something about one another.'

'Let me admit then,' said Charlotte, 'that what you feel about the Captain I feel about Ottilie. It makes me unhappy to think of the poor child in her boarding-school. She is very much oppressed by her circumstances there. Whereas my daughter Luciane, born to be in the world and in that school preparing herself for the world, performs in languages and history and whatever else her teachers put to her with as much facility as she does in her exercises in music; and, naturally lively and blessed with a good memory, can forget everything, as it seems, and instantly remember it when she pleases; and excels all others in freedom of bearing, grace in dancing, ease and civility of conversation and, being by nature inclined to lead, has made herself the queen of her small circle; and whereas the Principal of that establishment views her as a minor divinity who, in her care, is blossoming as she ought, so doing her credit, promoting the school, and bringing it a further influx of young ladies; and whereas the first pages of the Principal's letters and monthly reports are nothing but hymns in praise of the virtues of this wonderful child, which I am well able to translate into my own prose—what she finally has to say about Ottilie is only apology upon apology that a girl becoming otherwise so very attractive will yet not develop, or show any abilities or accomplishments. What little she says besides is likewise perfectly intelligible to me, since I recognize in the child the whole character of her mother, my dearest friend, who grew up beside me and whose daughter, if I could be her teacher or had charge of her, I would bring up to be a quite exceptional person.

'But since it does not fit into our plans and since one should not be forever rearranging one's circumstances and forever fetching in new things, I let it rest, and when my daughter, who knows full well that poor Ottilie is wholly dependent on us, employs her own advantages against her, thereby undoing, to a certain extent, all our kindness, I keep even the distress this causes me under control.

'But who is so well bred that he will never, in a hurtful way, assert his superiority over others? And who stands so high that he will never have to suffer an oppression of that sort? These trials only increase Ottilie's worth; but since fully realizing how painful her situation is I have been doing my best to place her somewhere else. I expect an answer at any time now, and once I have it I shall not delay. That is how things are with me, my dear. So both of us, in the name of true friendship, have been harbouring similar worries. Let us bear them together, since they do not cancel one another out.'

'What strange creatures we are,' said Eduard with a smile. 'As though by removing the thing that worries us out of our sight we could thereby be rid of it. In a general way we are capable of all kinds of sacrifices, but much less so when it comes to something in particular. My mother was like that. So long as I was living at home, as a child and a young man, she was never able to rid herself of the anxieties of the moment. If I was back late from a ride, I was bound to have had an accident; if I ever got soaked, she was sure I should fall ill of a fever. But then I went away, I put some distance between us, and seemed scarcely to belong to her anymore.

'Looking at it more closely,' he went on, 'we are both behaving foolishly and irresponsibly in leaving two exceptionally worthy people, for whom we feel such affection and concern, in unhappy and oppressive circumstances only in order not to expose ourselves to any danger. If this is not selfishness I do not know what is. You take Ottilie, give me the Captain, and in God's name let us make a trial of it.'

'We *might* risk it,' said Charlotte thoughtfully, 'if the danger were only to ourselves. But do you think it advisable to have Ottilie in the same house as the Captain, a man of about your age, of an age, that is—let me say it to your face, although it flatters you—when a man becomes really capable of love at last, and really worthy of it, and have him here with a girl of such qualities as Ottilie's?'

'It puzzles me', said Eduard in reply, 'how you can rate Ottilie so highly. I can only suppose that she has inherited the affection you felt for her mother. It's true, she is pretty, and I do remember that the Captain drew my attention to her when we came back a year ago and met her and you together at your aunt's. She is pretty, her eyes especially are beautiful; but I am not aware that she made the least impression on me.'

'That is to your credit,' said Charlotte, 'for of course I was there too; and although she is a good deal younger than I am you were so taken with the charms of your older friend that you overlooked the beauty coming into being and promising so much. That too is a part of how you are, and it makes me very glad to share my life with you.'

For all her apparent candour, Charlotte was in fact concealing something. When Eduard returned from his travels she had introduced Ottilie to him in the deliberate intention of giving her foster-daughter the chance of an excellent match; for she had ceased to think of herself in relation to Eduard. And the

Captain, as an accomplice, was to bring Ottilie further into Eduard's notice; but Eduard had his earlier love for Charlotte obstinately in mind, and looked neither right nor left but was happy in the feeling that the good he had so passionately desired and which a series of events had denied him, as it seemed for ever, might finally now be his.

The couple were about to go down through the new grounds towards the Hall when a servant came climbing in haste to meet them. Laughing, he shouted up to them whilst still some distance below: 'Your Lordship! Your Ladyship! Come quickly! Mr Mittler is here. He arrived all of a sudden. He has been shouting at us to go and look for you and ask if he's wanted. "Am I wanted?" he shouted after us. "Do you hear? But be quick, be quick!" '

'Our comical friend!' Eduard exclaimed. 'He could not have come at a better moment. What do you say, Charlotte? Hurry back,' he said to the servant, 'and tell him he is indeed wanted. He must break his journey. See to his horse. Bring him indoors and give him something to eat. We'll be there directly.

'Let us go the quickest way,' he said to his wife, and took the path through the churchyard which he usually avoided. But how astonished he was when he saw that Charlotte's considerateness had been at work here too. Whilst taking all possible care of the old monuments she had brought such harmony and order into everything that the place seemed a pleasant one, on which the eyes and the imagination were glad to dwell.

She had treated the tombstones, even the oldest, with a proper respect. In order of age they had been set upright against the wall, or built into it, or in some other way fitted there; the high plinth of the church itself had been adorned and lent variety with them. Eduard was strangely moved and surprised as he came in at the little gate; he pressed Charlotte's hand, and there were tears in his eyes.

But the comical visitor soon chased these tears away. He would not be detained at the Hall but had ridden at a gallop through the village to the churchyard gate, and there he halted and called out to his friends: 'I hope this is not a joke. If I really am wanted I will stay to lunch. But don't hold me up, I still have a great deal to do.'

'Since you have taken the trouble to come this far,' Eduard
called out to him, 'ride in. We meet in a solemn place. But see
what a pretty appearance sorrow wears, thanks to Charlotte.'

'At this gate', the rider cried, 'I shall enter neither on horseback, nor in a carriage, nor on foot. These here are all at
peace, and no concern of mine. When I'm dragged in here feet
first, that will be time enough. Come now: are you in earnest?'

'We are indeed,' said Charlotte. 'We newly-weds are for the
first time in more difficulty and perplexity than we can extricate
ourselves from alone.'

'You don't look it,' he replied, 'but I'll take your word. And
if you are fooling, don't turn to me in future. Come quickly
now, I expect my horse would be glad of a rest.'

Soon the three of them were in the dining-room together; the
meal was served and Mittler told them what he had done that
day and what he intended doing. He was a peculiar man. He
had previously been a cleric, and in all his restless busyness in
office had most distinguished himself by his ability to cool and
resolve the quarrels, both domestic and between neighbours,
first of particular individuals, then of entire parishes and of
several great families. There were no divorces whilst he was in
the job, and the local courts were never bothered by disputes
and litigation from his district. He soon saw how necessary it
was for him to have a knowledge of the law. He devoted himself entirely to legal studies, and before long felt able to hold
his own against the cleverest in the profession. His sphere of
influence grew astonishingly, and he was about to be called to
Court, so that what he had begun from below could be completed from above, when he won a considerable sum of money
in a lottery, bought himself a modest estate, let it out, and made
it the centre of his activities; and kept firmly to the principle,
or rather obeyed his old habit and inclination, never to stay
long in any house where nothing wanted resolving and where
there was no need of any help. Those with a superstitious
conviction that names are meaningful assert that it was his
being called Mittler* which obliged him to follow this strangest
of vocations.

When dessert had been served the visitor earnestly enjoined
his hosts not to delay their revelations any longer, since he must

leave immediately after coffee. Husband and wife began their confessions then in every detail; but no sooner had he grasped what the matter was than he leapt up from the table in exasperation, rushed to the window, and gave orders to saddle his horse.

'Either you don't know me,' he exclaimed, 'or you don't understand me, or you are making mischief. I see no quarrel. I see no need of help. Do you think I exist to give advice? Giving advice is quite the most foolish job there is. Let everyone advise himself, and do what he can't help doing. If it turns out well, he can congratulate himself on his perspicacity and good luck; if it turns out badly, I'll be there. Any man who wants to be rid of an evil always knows what he wants; and anyone who wants something better than he's got is always as blind as a bat. You may laugh! I tell you, he's playing blindman's buff, he *may* catch it; but what? Do as you like: it's all the same. Have your friends here, or leave them where they are: all one. I've seen the most sensible things come to grief, and the most ridiculous succeed. Don't torment yourselves, and if one way or the other it ends badly don't torment yourselves then either. Just send for me, and you will have my help. Till then: good day.'

And he bestrode his horse, without waiting for coffee.

'See,' said Charlotte, 'how little help a third person is in the end when two who are close have got a little out of balance. We are more confused now, if that is possible, and less sure of ourselves than we were, wouldn't you say?'

And doubtless they would have wavered a while longer if a letter from the Captain had not arrived, in reply to Eduard's. He had decided to accept one of the positions offered him, even though it was not at all suitable. He was to share in the boredom of certain high and wealthy persons, and be expected to dispel it.

Eduard saw very clearly what the whole arrangement would be like, and put it to Charlotte in very graphic terms. 'Can we bear to think of our friend in such a situation?' he cried. 'You cannot be so cruel, Charlotte.'

'Our strange friend Mittler is right after all,' Charlotte replied. 'All such undertakings are a risk. What might come of it no one can anticipate. Such new circumstances may be product-ive of happiness and unhappiness without our being able to claim any particular credit or needing to feel ourselves particularly to blame. I do not have the strength to resist you any longer. Let us make a trial of it.* All I ask is that it should not be for too long. Let me exert myself even more energetically on his behalf and use my influence and contacts all I can, to get him a place which will suit him and give him some contentment.'

Eduard's gratitude to his wife was very keen, and he thanked her in the nicest way. Light-hearted then, he hurried to convey to his friend some proposals in a letter. Charlotte was required to second him in a postscript in her own hand, and to join her friendly invitation with his. She wrote in a fluent script, agreeably and obligingly, but also in a sort of haste, which was not usual with her; and finished by spoiling the look of the page with a blot, a thing she *never* did and which made her cross, and the more she tried to wipe it away the worse it looked.

Eduard made a joke of it, and since there was still room added another postscript: their friend should see by these signs with what impatience he was awaited, and match the speediness of his journey to the speed with which the letter had been written.

The messenger departed, and Eduard, wishing to show Charlotte his gratitude, sought to do so by insisting again and again that she must fetch Ottilie out of the boarding-school at once.

Charlotte begged for more time, and that evening managed to arouse in Eduard the desire for a musical entertainment. Charlotte was a very good pianist, Eduard not quite so good on the flute; for although from time to time he had worked hard at it he lacked the patience and the staying power necessary for the full development of such a talent. So he performed his part very unevenly—some passages well, though perhaps too quickly; but at others he slowed down, since he was not familiar with them, and it would have been very difficult for anyone else to get to the end of a duet with him. But Charlotte managed; she slowed down where necessary and elsewhere allowed herself to be carried away by him, and accomplished thus the dual responsibility of a good conductor and a shrewd housewife, who manage to keep a measure in the whole, even if the particular passages are not always in time.

CHAPTER THREE

The Captain came. He preceded his arrival with a letter so full of good sense that Charlotte's mind was entirely set at rest. Such frankness about himself, such clear-sightedness about his own situation and the situation of his friends, augured nothing but good.

Their first hours of talk were, as is usual among friends who have not seen each other for some time, lively, indeed almost exhausting. Towards evening Charlotte suggested a walk to the new grounds. The Captain was delighted by them and took note of all the beauties which the new paths had now made visible and able to be enjoyed. He had a practised eye, but was modest in what he looked for; and although he saw clearly what was desirable he did not, as many do, annoy the people who were showing him around their property by asking for more than the circumstances allowed or, worse still, by mentioning more perfect achievements seen elsewhere.

When they reached the summer-house they found it all decked out; admittedly only with artificial flowers and evergreens, but beautiful sheaves of real corn and other fruits of the field and orchard had been arranged there too, so that the whole made a very gay appearance and did credit to its author's artistic sense. 'I know my husband does not like his birthday or his name-day* to be celebrated', Charlotte said, 'but I am sure that today he will not mind my dedicating these few garlands to a triple occasion.'

'A triple one?' Eduard exclaimed.

'Yes indeed,' Charlotte replied. 'We can surely regard the arrival of our friend as an occasion, and have you both forgotten that today is your name-day? For are you not both called Otto?'*

The two friends shook hands across the little table. 'I had forgotten,' said Eduard, 'what we did when we were boys, in the name of friendship. We *were* both called Otto, but when we were at school together and it kept causing confusion I voluntarily renounced the name—neat and attractive though it is—in his favour.'

'Which was not so *very* generous of you,' said the Captain. 'For I perfectly well remember that you liked the name Eduard better, and indeed when spoken by pretty lips it does have a most agreeable sound.'

Now they were sitting, the three of them, around the same little table at which Charlotte had spoken so vehemently against the coming of their guest. Eduard, in his contentment, had no wish to remind his wife of that time; but he could not refrain from saying: 'There would be plenty of room for a fourth person besides.'

At that moment the sound of hunting-horns reached them from the direction of the Hall, and seemed to affirm and reinforce the hopes and sympathies of that company of friends. They listened in silence, withdrawing into their separate selves and feeling their happiness doubled by its being so beautifully shared.

It was Eduard who put an end to the interlude. He stood up and went outside the summer-house. He said to Charlotte: 'Let us take our friend to the top at once, or he will suppose this narrow valley to be all our inheritance and abode. Up there you can breathe, and the vision is enlarged.'

'We shall have to go the old way still,' Charlotte replied, 'which is quite an arduous climb. But I hope before long my steps and paths will make the going easier, right to the top.'

Over rocks and through bushes and undergrowth they climbed the last rise. There they were not on level ground but on a continuing and fertile ridge. Behind them the Hall and village had gone out of sight. Down below they could see a line of ponds; and beyond, bordering these, were wooded hills, and finally steep cliffs which vertically and very definitely ended the final reach of the water, their imposing shapes being reflected on its surface. In a cleft there, through which a stream, with some force, fell into the ponds, lay a mill, half hidden, which looked, in that setting, a place it would be delightful to repose in. In the whole arc as it lay under their gaze there was an abundant variation of height and depth, of shrub and woodland whose first green already indicated the richness and fullness that was to come. In one place or another the eye was drawn to particular groups of trees, and first, immediately below the friends as they stood looking, to a group of poplars and plane trees on the bank of the middle pond. These appeared to particular advantage, being in the best years of their growth, fresh, healthy, and striving for height and breadth.

To these trees especially Eduard drew his friend's attention. 'I planted them myself,' he cried, 'when I was young. They were little saplings, my father had them dug up when the big garden was being extended at the Hall, and I rescued them. It was in the summer. I do not doubt that they will be magnificent this year too, and grow a little more, in gratitude.'

In a cheerful contentment they returned to the house. The guest was given spacious and agreeable quarters in the east wing and had very soon arranged his books and papers and set up his instruments so as to continue with his usual activities. But during the first days Eduard would not leave him in peace; he conducted him everywhere, on horse or on foot, and made him acquainted with the district and with the estate; at the same time making known to him the desire he had long felt for a better knowledge and a more profitable use of it all.

'The first thing', said the Captain, 'would be for me to do a survey of the area with the compass. It is an easy job and a pleasant one, and although it will not give us perfect accuracy, still it will be useful and we shall have made an encouraging start. It is also something which can be done without much assistance, and which we can be sure of finishing. If you ever want more accurate measurements no doubt we shall find a way.'

The Captain was an expert at this sort of survey work. He had brought the necessary instruments with him, and began at once. He gave some instruction to Eduard and to a few servants and labourers who were to be his assistants in the business. The days were favourable; the evenings and the early mornings he spent transferring heights and features to the map. Soon everything was washed or shaded or coloured in, and Eduard saw his property coming forth from the paper in all clarity like a new creation. It was as though he were only now becoming acquainted with what he owned, and as though his ownership were only now confirmed.

This was a chance to discuss the estate and the things one might now, having had an overview, do with it more easily than when one's experiments with Nature were isolated, haphazard, and on the basis of only casual impressions.

'We must make that clear to my wife,' said Eduard.

'Do no such thing,' said the Captain, who never liked to put his own opinions in the way of anyone else's, having learned from experience that the views people hold are far too various ever to be collected in a common point, however reasonable the arguments for such agreement might be. 'Do no such thing!' he cried. 'She would surely be upset. Like everyone else who pursues these things in an amateur sort of way, what matters to her is that she is doing something and not whether anything is being done. In their dealings with Nature such people have a hesitant touch; they have a fondness for this little spot or that; they don't dare remove any obstacle, they are not bold enough to make sacrifices; they cannot visualize in advance the desired result, they try things out, which work or don't work, they make alterations, alter what should be left alone perhaps, and leave alone what should be altered, so that in the end it remains a piecemeal sort of job which may prompt and please but which will not satisfy.'

'Admit it,' said Eduard—'You are not happy with the work she has done.'

'If the idea itself, which is a very good one, had been fully carried out, there would be nothing to object to. She has toiled her way up the rocks and now, as you might say, makes everyone she takes there suffer likewise. Neither side by side nor in single file is it possible to walk with any freedom. One's pace is continually interrupted. And there are all sorts of other things wrong that might be pointed out.'

'Could it easily have been done in any other way?' Eduard asked.

'Very easily,' the Captain replied. 'All she needed to do was break away that one corner, nothing much anyway since the rock there is in small pieces, and she would have gained a fine sweeping curve for the climb and some spare stones besides to build up those places where otherwise the path would have been narrow and unshapely. But let this be in strictest confidence between you and me, or she will be upset and aggrieved. And what is already done we must let stand. If you do want to expend more money and effort there, then various very pleasing things could still be achieved from the summer-house upwards and on to the ridge.'

Thus the two friends found much to occupy them in the present, but they had besides a lively pleasure in remembering the past, and in this Charlotte readily joined them. It was also decided that, as soon as the first work outdoors was completed, a start should be made on the travel-diaries and the past be recalled in that way too.

There was, it must be said, less for Charlotte and Eduard to discuss together alone, especially now that he had on his mind the criticisms—which he thought justified—made of her work in the grounds. For a long time he kept to himself the views that the Captain had confided in him; but at last, when he saw his wife beginning again the labour of her little steps and paths, now from the summer-house towards the ridge, he restrained himself no longer, and after some hesitation came to the point and disclosed his new insights to her.

Charlotte was halted in her tracks. She was intelligent enough to see that the men were right; but what was done, having turned out the way it had, contradicted them; she had thought it right and what was wanted, and even where it had now been criticized she was fond of it, in every part; she fought against being convinced, she defended her little creation, railed against men for immediately thinking on a grand scale, for making a great work out of what had been an amusement and an entertainment, and for not considering the costs which an enlarged plan would be bound to entail. She was upset, hurt, aggrieved; she could not let go of the old, nor quite reject the new; but, decisive as she was, she at once called a halt to the work and gave herself time to think the matter over and come to her own conclusions.

Being now without this activity and amusement, and since the men meanwhile were pursuing their affairs ever more companionably—seeing to the ornamental gardens and the glasshouses with especial eagerness, and in between times keeping up with the usual gentlemanly occupations such as hunting and the buying, swapping, breaking in, and training of horses—Charlotte felt herself daily more alone. Still more of her energies went into letter-writing, also on the Captain's behalf; but there were lonely hours nevertheless. All the more welcome and entertaining, then, were the reports she had from the boarding-school.

To a lengthy letter of the Principal's, expatiating as usual on Luciane's progress, was added a brief postscript, together with an enclosure in the hand of a male assistant in the establishment, both of which are here communicated.

The Principal's Postscript

'On the subject of Ottilie, your Ladyship, I can really only repeat what is contained in my earlier reports. Though I have no reason to chide her, I cannot be content with her either. She is, as she always was, modest and agreeable towards others; but her very self-effacingness and her readiness to be of service are not, in my view, wholly to be approved. Your Ladyship recently sent her some money and various materials. The first she has made no use of; and the latter also are still lying there untouched. It is true she keeps her things very clean and in good order, and seems only for that reason to change her clothes. Nor do I think it meritorious in her that she eats and drinks so little. Our meals are never excessive, but there is nothing I like better than to see children eating their fill of tasty and wholesome food. We give considerable thought to what we set before them, and it should be eaten up. But I can never bring Ottilie to do so. Indeed, if there is ever a pause in a meal because the serving girls are slow, she will invent some task or other, simply in order to pass over one of the dishes or the dessert. In all this it needs, however, to be borne in mind that she does sometimes, as I have only recently found out, suffer from headaches on the left side, which pass, it is true, but which may well be painful and of some significance. So much for Ottilie. She is of course a lovely child and we are very fond of her.'

The Assistant's Enclosure

'Our excellent Principal usually allows me to read the letters in which she communicates her observations on her charges to their parents and guardians. Those which she addresses to your Ladyship I always read with a double attention and a double pleasure; for whilst we must congratulate you on having a daughter who unites in herself all the brilliant qualities through which one rises in the world, I at least must deem you to be no less happy for having, in your foster-daughter, a child born to be a kindness and a contentment to others and surely also to be happy herself. Ottilie is almost the only child in our care over whom I am unable to be of one mind with our much-esteemed Principal. I do not at all hold it against that always active lady that she should ask to see the fruits of her care both outwardly and clearly; but there are fruits of a hidden kind too, and they are the true and the richest ones and will develop sooner or later into a life of beauty. Such a one is your foster-daughter without a doubt. All the time I have taught her I have seen her going forwards, always at the same pace, slowly forwards, never back. Perhaps children always need to begin at the beginning: she certainly does. If a thing does not derive from what has gone before she cannot grasp it. Confront her with anything, however easily intelligible, and she will appear nonplussed and even recalcitrant if for her it is without connection. But if the connecting links can be discovered and made clear to her she can grasp even the most difficult matters.

'Advancing slowly in this way she falls behind the other girls who, being quite differently gifted, are forever racing ahead and grasp everything, even unconnected things, very easily and easily retain them and put them to use then without trouble. Accordingly, if the pace of instruction is quickened she learns nothing at all and can manage nothing; and that is the case in certain of the courses given by excellent but speedy and impatient teachers. There have been complaints about her handwriting, and about her inability to grasp the rules of grammar. I went into these complaints: it is true, she writes slowly and without fluency if you like, but not timidly and nor does she misshape her letters. What I taught her of the French language, which is admittedly not my subject, she grasped without difficulty since I proceeded step by step. I agree it is very odd: she knows many things and she knows them well; but when she is asked she seems to know nothing.

'If I might finish with a general observation, I should say that she does not learn like one who is being taught but like one who intends to teach; not like a pupil, but like a future teacher. Your Ladyship may think it strange that, being myself a teacher and an educator, I can find no better way of praising a person than to declare her to be one of my own kind. Your Ladyship's finer insight and deeper knowledge of people and of the world will extract the best from my limited but well-meant opinions. You will be persuaded that in this child too there lies the promise of much happiness. I remain your obedient servant and conclude with the hope that I might be permitted to write to you again as soon as I think I have something pleasing and significant to say.'

Charlotte was delighted by this letter. Its contents approximated very closely to her own views of Ottilie; at the same time she could not refrain from smiling, since the teacher's interest seemed to her warmer than simple insight into the virtues of a pupil would usually arouse. In her calm and unprejudiced way she contemplated this relationship, as she had so many others; she valued the sympathy shown to Ottilie by a man of good sense, for her life had sufficiently confirmed her in the view that every true attachment is a very valuable thing in a world where indifference and antipathy are all-too-well established.

CHAPTER FOUR

The topographical chart, on which the features of the estate and its surroundings were clearly depicted, on quite a large scale, in pen and in different colours, and to which the Captain had given a firm basis by taking trigonometrical measurements, was soon finished; for he was ever active, he needed less sleep than almost anyone, his days were given always to the immediate purpose, and as a consequence by evening something had always been achieved.

'Let us now', he said to his friend, 'move to the rest, to an inventory of the property, for which enough preparatory work has surely already been done. From it our assessments of rents and other matters will follow naturally. And let one thing above all be agreed and instituted: keep everything which is really business separate from life. Business wants seriousness and a strict rule, but life capriciousness; in business we must be thoroughly consequential, but in our lives a certain inconsequentiality is often called for, is indeed delightful and heartening. If you are secure in the first you can move all the more freely in the second; whereas if you mix the two your freedom will carry your security away and end it.'

Eduard felt a gentle reproach in these proposals. Though not by nature untidy he could never manage to order his papers into different categories. Things he had to settle with other people and things which depended upon nobody but himself were not kept separate; and in the same way he did not sufficiently separate business and serious employment from amusement and diversion. Now it was made easy for him by a friend's exertions, by a second self creating the two halves into which the one self is not always willing to divide.

In the wing of the house occupied by the Captain they set up a repository for present matters and an archive for the past; brought together all the documents, papers, and reports from their various containers, closets, cupboards, and chests, and so in no time at all a pleasing tidiness had been imposed upon the chaos and everything was properly classified and sorted under

headings. They found what they wanted in a greater completeness than they had hoped. They were much helped in their
work by an elderly clerk, who all day long and even into the
night never left his desk. He was a man with whom Eduard had
always been dissatisfied in the past.

'I scarcely recognize him,' said Eduard to his friend. 'How
busy and useful the man is!' The Captain replied: 'That is
because we do not give him anything new to do until he has
finished the first job in his own good time. In that way, as you
see, he accomplishes a great deal. But if we pester him he can
do nothing whatsoever.'

The two friends, spending their days together thus, did not
fail to pay Charlotte regular visits in the evenings. If no company were present from the neighbouring places and estates,
which was often the case, then their conversation and their
reading mostly concerned those things by which the well-being,
the advantage, and the comfort of civil society are enhanced.

Charlotte, always one to use the present time, seeing her
husband contented, felt a fresh motivation in her own life too.
Various domestic provisions which she had long wished to
make but had not quite known how to were now accomplished
through the industry of the Captain. The household medicine
chest, which had been poorly stocked, was improved and
Charlotte herself made able, through some simple reading and
instruction, to put her natural energy and helpfulness to more
frequent and more effective use.

Whilst they were giving thought to those emergencies which,
though commonplace, all too often come without any warning,
they assembled everything which might be necessary for the
prevention of drowning, and with good reason, since there were
so many ponds, waterways, weirs, and sluices in the vicinity
and accidents of that kind did quite often occur. The Captain
saw to this item with very great thoroughness, and Eduard let
slip the remark that a case of that sort had made a very strange
and momentous intervention* into his friend's life. But when
the Captain said nothing in reply and seemed to be evading
some unhappy memory, Eduard likewise went no further, and
Charlotte too, being herself in a general way *au courant*, passed
over the remark.

'These precautionary measures', said the Captain one evening, 'are all well and good. But we still lack what matters most:
a reliable man who knows how to use all the things we have
provided. There is a field-surgeon of my acquaintance whom I
might suggest as being very suitable and who may be had for
a modest remuneration, an excellent man in his job and one
by whom, in the treatment of certain violent internal disorders,
I have often been better served than by famous doctors; and it
is after all immediate assistance that we have most need of in
the country.'

He was sent for at once; and husband and wife were delighted to be able to spend on such necessary things sums of
money that might otherwise have gone on nothing in particular.

Thus Charlotte made use of the Captain's knowledge and
energy in her own fashion and began to be entirely happy at
his presence and to feel easy in her mind at whatever might
ensue from it. She usually had questions to put to him, and
since she was a person who valued life she sought to remove
everything harmful and everything lethal. The lead glaze on
earthenware and the verdigris on copper vessels had caused
her anxiety. She asked for instruction in the matter, which
naturally meant going back to basic concepts in physics and
chemistry.

Occasional but always welcome stimulus to such conversations was given by Eduard's love of reading aloud. He had a
deep and very melodious voice and had once been famous and
appreciated for his lively and heartfelt renderings of poetical
and rhetorical works. Now other subjects occupied him and he
read aloud from other writings, and latterly such as had to do
with physics, chemistry, and things of a technical nature.

One of his peculiarities, but one which other people may
perhaps share, was that he found it unbearable to have anybody looking over his shoulder as he read. In earlier times,
when reading poems, plays, and stories aloud, this was doubtless due to the intense desire that any reader has, like the
poet, actor, or story-teller himself, to surprise, to make pauses,
to arouse expectations; which intended effect is of course very
much impaired if another person's eyes are hurrying ahead

to know what is coming. And for that reason, when he was reading he would always seat himself in such a position as to have nobody behind him. There being only the three of them this precaution was unnecessary; and since it was now not a matter of exciting the feelings or surprising the imagination, Eduard himself paid no especial heed.

But then one evening, having seated himself carelessly, he became aware that Charlotte was reading over his shoulder. His old irritation revived, and he rebuked her in terms that were somewhat ungentle: 'Once and for all I do wish people would refrain from habits that are an annoyance in society. If I am reading aloud to someone is it not as though I were telling him something? What is written or printed stands in place of my own opinions and my own feelings; and would I go to the trouble of speaking if there were a little window in my forehead or in my breast so that the man to whom I was communicating my thoughts one by one and offering him my emotions one by one could always know far in advance what my direction was? Somebody reading over my shoulder always makes me feel I'm being torn in two.'

Charlotte, whose aplomb in larger and smaller gatherings showed especially in her way of neutralizing any unpleasant, vehement, or even merely animated utterance, of interrupting any conversation that was dragging on, and of enlivening any that was faltering, on this occasion too was well served by her gift. 'I am sure you will forgive me,' she said, 'if I confess what happened. I heard you reading about relations between things and at once began thinking about *my* relations,* of one or two of my cousins who are rather a worry to me at present. When I began listening again I realized that it was entirely inanimate things you were reading about and I looked over your shoulder to get my bearings.'

'It was an analogy which misled and confused you,' said Eduard. 'All we are concerned with here is earths and minerals, but human beings are very narcissistic, they like to see themselves everywhere and be the foil for the rest of creation.'

'They do indeed!' said the Captain, and he continued: 'That is man's way with everything he encounters outside himself. He credits the minerals and the plants, the elements and the gods with his own wisdom and his own folly and with his will and whims.'

'I wonder,' Charlotte asked, 'though I do not wish to lead you too far from the present topic, whether you would mind telling me in a few words what the nature of these relationships is.'

'I shall be very glad to,' the Captain replied, since it was to him that Charlotte had turned with her question, 'as well as I can, at least, from what I read about it some ten years ago. Whether people in the scientific world still think the same on the subject, whether it accords with the newer doctrines, I could not say.'

'It is a bad business', Eduard cried, 'that we cannot nowadays learn anything that will last a lifetime. Our forefathers stuck to the teaching they were given when they were young, but we have to unlearn everything every five years if we are not to go completely out of fashion.'

'We women', said Charlotte, 'are not quite so particular. And to be honest, all that really concerns me is what the word means. For nothing makes one more ridiculous in society than using a new coinage or a technical term wrongly. I should simply like to know what sense the expression has when it is used with reference to these particular things. The science behind it we can leave to the experts, who in my experience will be unlikely ever to agree.'

'But where shall we begin, so as to get most quickly to the heart of the matter?' said Eduard, after a silence, to the Captain. He, having thought for a moment, replied: 'If I may be permitted to begin, as it might seem, at the very beginning, we shall soon be there.'

'Be assured of my complete attention,' said Charlotte, laying her work aside.

So the Captain began: 'The first thing we notice about all the substances we encounter in Nature is that each is always drawn to itself. It may sound strange to say something so self-evident, but only once we have fully understood the things we are familiar with can we proceed together towards the things with which we are not familiar.'

Eduard interrupted him: 'We might make it easy for her and for ourselves by giving examples. Think of water, oil, or mercury and you will see a unity, a coherence in their composition. From this united state they will never depart, unless by force or some other intervention. Remove that force and they at once restore themselves to wholeness.'

'Quite so,' said Charlotte in agreement. 'Raindrops quickly unite to form streams. And quicksilver amazed us as children when we played with it and split it into little beads and let it run together again.'

'And I may be permitted', the Captain added, 'to mention one significant detail in passing: that what decisively and always characterizes that very pure self-attraction of substances in liquid form is spherical shape. The falling raindrop is round; you yourself have already mentioned the little beads of mercury; and falling drops of molten lead, if they have time to solidify completely, are spherical when they land.'

'Let me run ahead,' said Charlotte, 'and see if I can guess what you are aiming at. Just as everything has an attraction to itself so too there must be a relationship with other things.'

'And that will vary according to the different natures of the things concerned,' said Eduard in haste. 'Sometimes they will meet as friends and old acquaintances and come together quickly and be united without either altering the other at all, as wine for example mixes with water. But others will remain strangers side by side and will never unite even if mechanically ground and mixed. Thus oil and water shaken together will immediately separate again.'

'It would not take much', said Charlotte, 'to see people of one's own acquaintance in these simple forms; and I am particularly reminded of the social circles people move in. But what these inanimate substances most resemble are the large social groups which confront one another in the world: the classes and the different occupations, the nobility and the third estate, the soldier and the civilian.'

'And yet,' Eduard replied, 'just as these may be joined by custom and the law, so in our world of chemistry there are agents which will bind together the things that are holding one another off.'

'Thus,' the Captain interjected, 'we join oil and water by the agency of an alkaline salt.'

'Not so fast with your lecture,' said Charlotte. 'Let me prove I am keeping up. Have we not already come to relationships and affinities?'

'We have indeed,' the Captain replied, 'and let us at once now get to know them in what they are and in what they do. We say of those natures which on meeting speedily connect and inter-react that they have an affinity for one another. This affinity may be very remarkable. Alkalis and acids, although opposed to one another and perhaps precisely because they are so opposed, will in a most decisive way seek out, take hold of, and modify one another and form, in so doing, a new substance together. We have only to think of lime, which manifests towards all acids a strong inclination, a decided wish for union. As soon as our chemistry cabinet arrives we shall show you various experiments which are very entertaining and which will give you a clearer idea than words, names, and technical terms may do.'

'I must confess', said Charlotte, 'that when you speak of these wondrous entities as related they seem to me not so much blood relations as related in spirit and in the soul. In precisely this way true and important friendships may come about between people: opposing qualities make an intenser union possible. I look forward to witnessing what mysterious effects you will produce for me. And now—', she said, turning to Eduard—'I shan't spoil your reading any more and, being so much better informed, will listen attentively to what you have to say.'

'Since you have asked us for explanations,' Eduard replied, 'we cannot let you off so lightly, for the complicated cases are in fact the most interesting. Only through them do we realize the degree of affinity and how near, strong, remote, or slight the relations are. Affinities are only really interesting when they bring about separations.'

'Does that unhappy word', cried Charlotte, 'which we hear all too often in the world today, occur in the sciences too?'

'Indeed it does,' Eduard replied. 'Significantly, it used to be high praise to say of the chemists that they were skilled in the art of separation.'*

'But not any more?' said Charlotte in reply, 'and that is only right and proper. Bringing things together is a harder task, and a worthier one. A man skilled in the art of bringing things together would be welcome in every walk of life. But now since you are launched into your subject do give me a few examples.'

'Then let us return forthwith', said the Captain, 'to things we have already mentioned and discussed. For example, what we call limestone is a more or less pure oxide of calcium tightly combined with a weak acid known to us in gaseous form. If a piece of that rock is placed in dilute sulphuric acid this combines with the calcium to form gypsum; the gaseous weak acid, on the other hand, escapes. A separation and a new combination have come about and one even feels justified in using the term "elective affinity", because it really does seem as though one relationship were preferred to another and a choice made for one over the other.'

'Forgive me,' said Charlotte, 'just as I forgive the scientist, but I would never call that a choice, rather a necessity in Nature, and scarcely even that since in the end it is perhaps only a matter of opportunity. Opportunity makes thieves, they say, and also relationships; and as for the natural substances you were speaking of, it seems to me that the only choice lies in the hands of the chemist himself, who brings them together. Once they *have* been brought together, heaven help them! In the case in point my sympathy is with the gaseous acid obliged to drift around in space once again.'

'All it need do', the Captain replied, 'is combine with water, to bring refreshment to the sick and the healthy then as a mineral spring.'

'All very well for the gypsum,' said Charlotte. 'He is a finished thing, a body, he is taken care of, whereas that poor creature driven out may have a great deal to put up with before finding a home.'

'Unless I am very much mistaken,' said Eduard with a smile, 'your remarks are not entirely innocent. Admit it! I suppose in your view I am the lime—seized by sulphuric acid in the person of the Captain, torn from your agreeable company and transformed into an unco-operative gypsum.'

'If your conscience', said Charlotte in reply, 'prompts you to such reflections then I need not worry. These comparisons are very entertaining, everyone likes playing with analogies. But a human being is after all superior by several degrees to those natural substances, and having been rather lax in our use of the fine words "choice" and "elective affinity" we might do well to return to our inner selves and ask in all seriousness what the validity of such expressions in this context is. Alas, I know of enough cases in which a close and, as it seemed, indissoluble relationship was annulled by the casual arrival of a third party, and one of the pair, previously joined so beautifully, driven out into empty space.'

'But in that respect', said Eduard, 'chemists are much more gallant. They add a fourth party, so that nobody goes without.'

'Indeed,' said the Captain, 'and those cases are the most significant and the most remarkable in which the attraction and the affinity, the desertion and the uniting, can be seen, so to speak, crosswise: when four substances, united until that moment two by two, are brought into contact, desert their previous union, and unite afresh. In this letting go and seizing hold, this fleeing one thing and seeking another, one is really inclined to discern some higher prescription; one ascribes to such substances a sort of volition and power to choose and the technical term "elective affinities" seems perfectly justified.'

'Describe such a case to me,' said Charlotte.

But the Captain replied: 'One cannot do these things justice in words and one ought not to try. As I said, as soon as I can show you the experiments themselves everything will be clearer and more agreeable. At present you would have to make do with frightful technical terms which would give you no real idea. These entities, which seem lifeless and are yet in themselves always disposed to be active, need to be seen at work. They need an observer who will watch with some engagement of his sympathy how they seek one another out, how they attract and seize, destroy, devour, and consume one another and at once emerge from the closest possible union in a renewed and novel and unexpected form: it is then one credits them with eternal life, indeed with sense and understanding, since our own senses seem scarcely adequate to the task of observing them properly and our reason scarcely competent to grasp them.'

'I do not deny', said Eduard, 'that the strange technical terms will be bound to seem cumbersome and even ridiculous to anyone not reconciled to them by physical observation and by having grasped the concepts they represent. But for the time being we could easily express the relationships we are speaking of here with letters.'

'If you don't think it will seem pedantic,' said the Captain in reply, 'I can doubtless summarize what I was saying by using such symbols. Imagine an A closely bound to a B and by a variety of means and even by force not able to be separated from it; imagine a C in a similar relationship with a D; now bring the two pairs into contact; A will go over to D, C to B, without our being able to say who first left the other, who first with another was united again.'

'Well then,' said Eduard interrupting, 'until we have seen all this with our own eyes we shall think of these formulae as a sort of parable, out of which we can abstract a lesson for our own immediate use. You are the A, Charlotte, and I am your B: for do I not depend on you and come after you as the B does the A? The C is quite obviously the Captain, who for the time being has to some extent taken me away from you. Now it would be right and proper, to prevent you from departing into the void, to provide you with a D, and quite without question that must be the amiable young lady Ottilie, and you must not now make any further objection to her joining us.'

'Very well,' said Charlotte in reply, 'even though the illustration does not seem to me to fit our case exactly. I think it a lucky chance that today we are in complete agreement for once and that these natural and elective affinities have made it easier for me to disclose something to you. Let me then admit that this afternoon I decided to have Ottilie here. My housekeeper, who has served me so faithfully, is leaving to be married. So much for what concerns my side of the matter and my advantage. The reasons which concern Ottilie herself you will read out to us. I shan't look over your shoulder, and of course do not need to, knowing what they are. But read to us.' So saying she took out a letter and handed it to Eduard.

CHAPTER FIVE

The Principal's Letter

'Your Ladyship will forgive me if I say very little today. After
the public examination, now completed, of our achievements
with our pupils in the last year, I must write to all the parents
and guardians of the outcome. Besides, I can afford to be brief,
since in a very few words I can tell you a great deal. Your
daughter has proved herself the first in every sense. The
enclosed testimonials and her own letter describing the prizes
she has received and expressing the satisfaction she feels at so
pleasing a success, will set your mind at rest, and more than
that will be a delight to you. My own delight is somewhat
tempered since I foresee that we shall not much longer have
any cause to hold back among us a young lady who has already
advanced so far. I respectfully take my leave and at some date
in the near future shall be so bold as to communicate to you
what, in my view, her best course would be. My good friend
the Assistant will write to you about Ottilie.'

The Assistant's Letter

Our respected Principal permits me to write about Ottilie in
part because, thinking as she does, it would pain her to
communicate what has to be communicated, and in part also
because she herself has to make an apology and would rather
do it through me.

'Since I know only too well how little our dear Ottilie is able
to express what she has in her and what her strengths are, I
was somewhat anxious about the public examination, and all
the more so since absolutely no preparation for it is possible
and if it were to take the usual form we should not be able to
prepare Ottilie even to make a good appearance. By the
outcome my anxieties were all-too-fully justified: she did not
receive any prizes and is also among those not given a
testimonial. Need I dwell on it? In the handwriting others did

not shape their letters quite so well as she did, but had much greater fluency; at reckoning everyone was quicker, and the difficult problems, at which she does better, were not set in this examination. Many outdid her at chattering and holding forth in French; in history she was not ready with her names and dates; in geography she needed to attend more to political classifications. In music she found neither the time nor the necessary calm for the presentation of her few modest pieces. In drawing she would certainly have won the prize: her outlines were clear and the execution both painstaking and intelligent. But unfortunately she had begun something too large, and did not finish.

'When the pupils had been dismissed and the examiners were making up their minds and allowing us, the teachers, to say a word at least, I soon saw that Ottilie was either not being mentioned at all or, if she were, then with indifference if not disapproval. I thought I might win some favour for her by describing frankly what she was like, and this I attempted with a double eagerness, first because I could speak with conviction and secondly because in earlier years I had found myself in the same unhappy predicament. I was listened to attentively; however, when I had finished the principal examiner made the following courteous but very definite reply: "We take it for granted that a person has talents. They must be developed into real abilities. This is the purpose of all education, this is the express and unmistakable intention of parents and guardians and, unspokenly, only half-consciously, of the children themselves. And this is the object of the examination, which judges teachers and pupils together. From what you have told us we may be very hopeful on the child's account, and you are certainly to be praised for your close attention to your pupils' talents. Convert these by this time next year into real abilities and neither you nor your favoured pupil will want for applause."

'I had already resigned myself to what followed, but I had not anticipated a worse thing, which occurred immediately after it. Our excellent Principal who, like a good shepherd, does not like to see even one of her sheep lost or, as was the case here, unadorned, when the gentlemen had taken their leave could not conceal her impatience and said to Ottilie who, whilst the others were enjoying their prizes, stood quite calmly at the window: "But for heaven's sake tell me how it is possible to seem so stupid without being it!" Ottilie replied with perfect composure: "Forgive me, Ma'am, I happen to have my head-ache again today, and quite badly." "No one would know!" said the Principal, usually such a sympathetic lady, and turned away crossly.

'Now, it is true: no one would know. For Ottilie's features do not alter nor have I ever seen her put her hand to her temple.

'And that was still not everything. Miss Luciane, your Lady-ship, always lively and outspoken, was on that day, in her triumph, very boisterous and overweening. She danced round the room with her prizes and testimonials and even waved them in Ottilie's face. "You came off badly, didn't you?" she cried. Ottilie answered her with perfect composure: "There will be other examination days." "But you will always be last," your young lady cried, and danced away.

'Ottilie seemed composed to everyone else, but not to me. If she is combating some inner, unpleasant and powerful emotion this shows itself in the different colouring of her face. Her left cheek becomes red for a moment, whilst the right turns pale. I observed this sign, and my sympathy for her would not be restrained. I took the Principal aside, spoke earnestly with her about the matter. The excellent woman saw her mistake. We conferred, we had a long discussion, and without on that account becoming long-winded let me present to your Lady-ship our decision and our request: that you have Ottilie home for a while. You will yourself be the best person to understand our reasons. If you agree to this course, I shall say more about how the dear child might be handled. If your daughter leaves us then, as seems likely, we shall be delighted to have Ottilie back.

'One more thing, which I might perhaps later omit to men-tion: I have never seen Ottilie demand anything, nor even ask for anything with any urgency. On the other hand there have been occasions, though not many, when she has sought to refuse something which was being asked of her. She does this with a gesture which, for anyone who has understood its meaning, is irresistible. She presses the palms of her raised hands together and brings them towards her breast, bowing very slightly as she does so and giving whoever is making a demand on her such a look that he gladly renounces everything he might be demanding or desiring. If your Ladyship should ever witness this gesture, which is not very likely, treating her as you do, then think of me and be indulgent with Ottilie.'

Eduard had read out these letters, smiling as he did so and shaking his head. Nor was there any lack of comment upon the persons involved and upon the situation.

'Enough!' Eduard cried at last. 'It is decided: let her come! Then you will be taken care of, my dear, and we can now bring forward a proposition of our own. It is becoming very necessary that I join the Captain in the east wing. Evenings and mornings are quite the best times to work together. In exchange you will have the nicest rooms on your side of the house for yourself and Ottilie.'

Charlotte made no objection, and Eduard elaborated upon the lives they would lead henceforth. He said, among other things: 'It is very considerate of our niece to have headaches on the left side; I sometimes have them on the right. If we get them together and are sitting opposite and I am leaning on my right elbow and she on her left, each head on a hand inclined in a different way, we shall make a fine pair of corresponding images.'

The Captain thought this perilous; but Eduard cried: 'Beware of the D, my dear chap. For what would B do if C were taken from him?'

'I should have thought', said Charlotte in reply, 'that that was obvious.'

'Of course it is!' Eduard cried. 'He would go back to his A, to his Alpha and Omega!' And he leapt to his feet and took Charlotte in his arms.

CHAPTER SIX

A carriage, bringing Ottilie, drew up. Charlotte went to meet her; the child hurried forward, threw herself at her feet, and embraced her knees.

'Why such abasement?' Charlotte asked in some confusion, and sought to raise her.

'I don't really mean it as an abasement', Ottilie replied, and remained where she was. 'Only I am so happy to remember the time when I was no higher than your knee and was already so sure of your love.'

She stood up, and Charlotte embraced her warmly. She was introduced to the men and at once, as a guest, treated with especial respect. Beauty is everywhere a welcome guest. She seemed to listen closely to the conversation, without herself taking part.

Next morning Eduard said to Charlotte: 'She is an agreeable and entertaining girl.'

'Entertaining?' Charlotte replied with a smile. 'She never opened her mouth.'

'Really?' said Eduard in reply, and seemed to be thinking about it. 'How very strange!'

Charlotte gave the new arrival only a few indications how the house was to be managed. Ottilie had quickly seen—or rather, and better, had quickly *felt*—the whole order of things. She grasped without difficulty what she had to do for everyone and for each person in particular. Everything happened punctually. She could arrange things without seeming to give orders, and if there was any delay she at once did the job herself.

As soon as she saw how many hours she had at her disposal she asked Charlotte to let her make a timetable, which she kept to strictly. She did the work set before her in a manner Charlotte had been informed about by the Assistant. She was left to do things as she liked. Only occasionally Charlotte sought to prompt her. For example, she would sometimes surreptitiously give her worn quills to use, to induce a greater fluency in her handwriting; but before long they were sharpened again.

The ladies had decided to speak French together whenever they were alone, and Charlotte kept this up all the more keenly seeing that Ottilie was more forthcoming in the foreign language and once practising it had been made into a duty. In French she often seemed to say more than she intended. Charlotte was particularly amused by her occasional, very pointed, and yet affectionate description of everything in her boarding-school. Ottilie became a welcome companion, and Charlotte hoped one day to have in her a reliable friend.

Meanwhile she took out those papers again which had to do with Ottilie, to remind herself what, in the past, the Principal and the Assistant had said about the child, and to compare their judgements with the present person. For Charlotte was of the opinion that it was never too soon to acquaint oneself with the character of the people one had to live with, so as to know what was to be expected of them, what might be improved in them, and what once and for all must be allowed and forgiven them.

Though she found in this examination nothing new, certain things she was already familiar with became more significant and more striking. Ottilie's moderation in eating and drinking, for example, did really cause her concern.

The women next gave their attention to the question of dress. Charlotte asked of Ottilie that she should dress so as to make a finer and more elegant appearance. At once the child, ever willing and assiduous, went to work on the materials she had already had as a present, and with very little help from anyone else soon managed to make clothes of them which were extremely becoming. The new fashions in dress enhanced her appearance; for since that which is attractive in a woman extends also over all she wears, it is as though we see her continually afresh and with new pleasure when she lends her qualities to a new apparel.

She thus became to the men, at once and more and more, what we can properly call a solace to the eye.* For if the emerald by its splendid colour is kind to the sight—indeed, may even work healingly on that noble faculty—human beauty works with a far greater power on the outer and the inner senses. Whoever looks on beauty is immune against the advent of any evil; he feels in accord with himself and with the world.

Thus, in many ways their society had gained by Ottilie's arrival. The two men kept more regularly to the hour, indeed to the minute of their appointments. They were always as prompt as should be for meals, or to take tea or a walk. And especially in the evenings they were not in such a hurry to leave the table. Charlotte noticed as much, and observed them both. She wished to establish whether one was more decisive in this than the other; but she could not discern any difference. Both were altogether more sociable. In their conversation they seemed to be mindful of what would be likely to arouse Ottilie's interest, and of what she would be likely to understand or know something about. If they were reading or recounting something, they would break off and wait for her to return. They became gentler and generally more communicative.

In response to this Ottilie's willingness to be of service increased daily. The better she got to know the house, its people, their circumstances, the more eagerly she made her contribution, ever-more quickly understanding every glance, every movement, an unfinished word, a sound. Her quiet attentiveness remained constant, as did also her calm busyness. And so her sitting and standing, coming and going, fetching and carrying, and sitting down again were one eternal change without a hint of agitation, an eternal movement giving pleasure. Furthermore, she trod so softly that they never heard her come or go.

Ottilie's properly obliging ways were a great joy to Charlotte. There was only one thing which seemed to her not quite appropriate, and she let it be known. 'It is a commendable act of kindness', she said to Ottilie one day, 'to bend down quickly if somebody drops something and to pick it up forthwith. We show ourselves, in a manner of speaking, willing to serve that person. But in society one must consider whom one is showing such submissiveness to. Towards other women I shall not prescribe you any rules. You are young. Towards women who are older than you and who are your superiors in society it is a duty; towards your equals it is an attractive courtesy, and to women younger than you or below you it shows you to be human and good-natured. But it is not quite proper for a woman to show herself submissive and willing to be of service towards men in this way.'

'I shall try to get out of the habit,' said Ottilie in reply. 'Meanwhile you will forgive me this little impropriety if I tell you how I got into it. We were taught history. I have not retained as much as I doubtless ought to have, for I never knew what I should need it for. Only isolated scenes made an impression on me. This one for instance:

'When Charles I of England stood before his so-called judges the gold knob of the little staff he carried fell to the floor. Accustomed, if ever such a thing happened, to having everyone bustling to help he seemed to look around him and to expect that on this occasion too someone would do him this small service. Nobody moved; he bent down himself and picked up the knob. Rightly or wrongly, I thought this such a painful thing—I don't know whether I should have done—that since then I have never been able to see anyone drop anything without bending down for it. But since of course that may not always be a proper thing to do and since—' she continued with a smile—'I cannot on every occasion tell my story, I shall in future be a little more restrained.'

Meanwhile continuous progress was being made on the schemes the men felt themselves called upon to pursue. Indeed, every day there was something new to be thought about and undertaken.

One day, when they were walking through the village together, they noticed with displeasure how much less clean and tidy it was than those villages whose inhabitants are so for very want of space.

'You will remember', said the Captain, 'that when we were travelling through Switzerland we remarked how pleasingly and effectively one might improve the so-called parkland of a country house by obliging a village situated as this one is to adopt not the Swiss style of building but those very advantageous virtues, Swiss neatness and cleanliness.'

'Here, for example,' said Eduard in reply, 'that would be quite feasible. The hill where the Hall is falls away to a point; the village is built in a fairly regular semicircle facing it; between them runs the stream, and to stop it flooding one man has used stones, another stakes, another old rafters, and his neighbour planks, nobody doing any good to anybody else, but each on the contrary causing himself and everyone else only damage and disadvantage. And the road likewise goes up and down and through the water and over the stones in a very unintelligent way. If the people would only co-operate it would not take much to put up a wall all along here in an arc and raise the road behind it to the level of the houses, create a pleasing open space, encourage some tidiness and, by thinking on a larger scale, be rid of all these trivial annoyances and short-comings at a stroke.'

'Let us try it,' said the Captain, running his eye over the scene and assessing it rapidly.

'I dislike having to do with peasants and tradespeople,' said Eduard, 'unless I can actually give them orders.'

'I can hardly blame you,' the Captain replied. 'In my own life I have had more than enough trouble from such dealings. How hard people find it to set the sacrifice that must be made against the benefits that would result. Or to want the end and not reject the means. And many even confuse the means and the end, are pleased by the former and lose sight of the latter. They want every evil curing at the point of its appearance, and pay no attention to where it actually has its origins and cause. That is why any consultation is so difficult, especially with the lower classes who in day-to-day matters are perfectly sensible but who seldom see further ahead than tomorrow. And if it happens that in any communal undertaking one party stands to lose and another to gain, then seeking to proceed by agree-ment will be futile. Anything which is really for the common good will be done by the unrestricted exercise of sovereign power, or not at all.'

Whilst they were standing there in conversation a beggar approached them. His effrontery seemed greater than his need. Eduard, cross at the interruption and unsettled, told him off, having first several times in a more measured fashion but vainly motioned him away; but when the fellow retreated only gradu-ally, muttering and even answering back and defiantly claiming a beggar's rights and that, though he might be refused alms, he should not be insulted since he was as much under the protection of God and the Law as anyone else, Eduard lost all control.

The Captain said then, to soothe him: 'Let us see to it, having had this encounter, that our supervision of local matters extends to cover mendicancy too. Of course, one must give alms, but it is better not to give them oneself, and certainly not on one's home ground. Moderation and consistency in all things, including charity. Too great a generosity will attract beggars, not keep them away; whereas when a man is travelling he might well choose to appear to some pauper by the roadside like Good Luck itself and throw him a gift beyond all expectation as he hurries by. The village and the Hall being situated as they are, we should easily be able to make a suitable arrangement. It is a thing I have already given some thought to.

'At one end of the village is the inn, and an elderly and respectable married couple live at the other. You need to leave a small sum of money in both places. Nothing will be given to a person entering the village, only to a person leaving it, and since both places are also on the roads leading up to the Hall anyone heading that way will be referred to one or other of them instead.'

'Come along,' said Eduard, 'let us arrange it at once. We can always see to the details later.'

They went to the innkeeper and to the elderly couple, and the thing was done.

'I know very well', said Eduard as they climbed the hill back to the Hall together, 'that insight and resolution are what matter in life. You were, for example, entirely right in your judgement of the work my wife was doing in the grounds, and you gave me at the same time an indication as to how it might be improved which, I readily admit, I at once passed on to her.'

'I guessed as much,' said the Captain, 'and wished you hadn't. You made her unsure, she has left everything lying and on this one account is at odds with us, avoids all mention of it and has not invited us to the summer-house again though she does go up there with Ottilie between times.'

'We must not let ourselves be put off by that,' Eduard replied. 'If I am once persuaded that some good thing could and ought to happen I cannot rest until I have seen it done. We have found ways and means in the past, have we not? Let us make it our entertainment one evening that we get out the volumes on English country houses, with the engravings, and then your map of the estate. We treat it first as though it were problematical and not a serious proposition. That we are in earnest will be obvious soon enough.'

It was done as Eduard suggested. When the volumes were opened they saw for each case an outline of the terrain and drawings of the landscape in its first rough and natural state, then on other pages depictions of the changes wrought on it by art in such a way as to utilize and enhance all the good already present there. The transition to their own property, to their own surroundings and to what might be made of them, was an easy one.

Though it was a pleasure now to base their deliberations on the map drawn by the Captain, still they could not entirely get away from that first conception which had been Charlotte's starting point. But they devised an easier ascent to the ridge; and they would put up a sort of pavilion high on the slopes against a pleasant little copse; it would bear on the Hall, it would be visible from the Hall windows, and from it the Hall and the gardens would be overlooked.

The Captain had considered everything carefully and made his calculations; and he returned to the subject of the road through the village, the wall along the stream and the filling in that would be needed there. 'Building an easy way up to the ridge,' he said, 'I shall gain just the quantity of stone I need for that wall. When one thing fits into another like that both can be achieved with less expense and more expeditiously.'

'But now this is my concern,' said Charlotte. 'A definite sum will have to be set aside. If we know how much is needed for a project of this kind then we can divide it up, if not week by week at least month by month. The purse is in my hands, I pay the bills and keep the accounts.'

'You don't seem to trust us very far,' said Eduard.

'No,' Charlotte replied, 'not very far in matters of whim. There we have more control than you do.'

The arrangement was agreed, the work soon begun, the Captain always present and Charlotte now almost daily a witness of his earnest and resolute mind. He for his part learned to know her better and both began to find it easy to work together and get results.

It is in any such undertaking as it is in dancing: two people in step are bound to become dependent on one another, and a mutual goodwill inevitably develops. That Charlotte was indeed well disposed towards the Captain since getting to know him more closely was proved for certain when in all serenity and with no disagreeable feelings whatsoever she allowed him to destroy a very pretty resting place which in her first endeavours she had picked out and beautified particularly but which stood now in the way of his plan.

CHAPTER SEVEN

Since now Charlotte and the Captain were occupied together it followed that Eduard was more in the company of Ottilie. Feelings of a quietly affectionate nature had in any case for some time already inclined him towards her. She was helpful and considerate to everyone, but most of all to him, or so he flattered himself. And without question: she had already noticed exactly what things he liked to eat, how he liked them served, how much sugar he took in his tea—nothing of that sort escaped her. She was most careful to shield him from draughts, since he was inordinately sensitive to them and on that account was sometimes at odds with his wife who liked as much air as possible. She likewise always knew what needed to be done in the orchard and the garden. She sought to further the things he desired and prevent those by which he might be irritated; to such an extent that before long she had become his guardian angel, he could not manage without her, and began to find it painful when she was not there. Added to that, she seemed more talkative and more open when they were alone together.

There was still something childlike about Eduard even as he grew older, and Ottilie, young herself, liked this in him especially. They took pleasure in remembering earlier occasions when they had seen one another; these memories went back into the very first period of Eduard's affection for Charlotte. Ottilie claimed to be able to remember them as the handsomest pair at Court; and when Eduard refused to believe that she could remember anything so early in her childhood, she insisted that one occasion in particular was still perfectly fresh in her mind: how once when he came in she had hidden her face in Charlotte's skirts, and not out of fear but out of a childish astonishment. She might have added: because he had made such a lively impression on her, because she had liked him so much.

Things being thus, a good deal of business which the two men had earlier taken up together now to some extent faltered, so that it became necessary for them to get a clear view again, draft a few memoranda, write letters. Accordingly, they agreed to meet in their office room, where they found their old copyist sitting idle. They set to work, and soon gave him things to do, without noticing that they were putting on to him several matters which formerly they had been accustomed to dealing with themselves. The Captain had difficulties with the very first memorandum, and Eduard with the very first letter. They struggled for a while among rough drafts and rewritings until Eduard, who was making the least headway, asked what the time was.

Then it turned out that the Captain, for the first time in many years, had forgotten to wind his watch; and they began to suspect, if not already actually to feel, that time was becoming unimportant to them.

Whilst the men thus to some extent pursued their affairs less energetically, the industry of the women only increased. In general a family's usual mode of life, engendered by the given persons and by necessary circumstances, will take even an extraordinary new affection, a developing passion, into itself as into a vessel, and quite some time may elapse before this new ingredient causes any noticeable fermentation and rises foaming over the brim.

The affections arising mutually among our friends had the happiest effect. Their souls were opened and a general goodwill came forth out of the particular. Each was contented, and did not begrudge the others a like contentment.

Such a condition elevates the spirit by enlarging the feelings, so that everything one does and projects tends towards boundlessness. The friends no longer kept within the house. Their walks extended, and whilst Eduard and Ottilie hurried ahead to decide the paths and clear a way, the Captain and Charlotte followed behind at a sedater pace, conversing seriously and taking pleasure in many a newly discovered spot and in many an unexpected view.

Their walk led them one day from the eastern gate down to the inn, over the bridge and towards the ponds, which they kept to then, near the water, as far as it was usual to go, until the banks became impeded by a bushy hillside and later by cliffs and ceased to be passable.

But Eduard, who was familiar with the locality from the days of his going out hunting there, pushed ahead with Ottilie on an overgrown path, knowing that the old mill, which was hidden in the gully, could not be far off. The little-used path soon gave out, however, and they became lost among mossy rocks in a dense undergrowth. But not for long: they soon heard the mill-wheels and knew they were close.

Stepping out on to a spur they saw the strange wooden building, black and ancient, below them in the little ravine, under the shadow of tall trees and the high rock faces. They decided without more ado to climb down over the moss and broken rock, Eduard leading; and when he looked up and Ottilie, stepping lightly without fear or apprehension, was following him and keeping her balance beautifully from stone to stone, he seemed to see a being from heaven hovering above him. And when at times, coming to a difficult place, she seized his outstretched hand or even leaned on his shoulder for support, then there was no denying that it was a woman, with all her delicacy and lightness, who was touching him. He could almost have wished that she might stumble and slip so that he could catch her up in his arms and press her to his heart. But he never would have done this, and for more than one reason: he was afraid of offending her, and also of harming her.

Our meaning here will be plain in a moment. For when he was down and sitting opposite her under the tall trees at the rustic table, and the miller's friendly wife had been sent for milk and the miller himself, full of welcome, had been sent to find Charlotte and the Captain, Eduard after some hesitation began to speak:

'My dear Ottilie, there is something I want you to do. Forgive me for asking, even if you refuse. You make no secret of the fact—and why should you?—that under your dress, on your bosom, you wear a miniature. It is the portrait of your father, of that excellent man whom you scarcely knew and who in every sense deserves a place near your heart. But forgive me: the picture is unsuitably large, and the metal and the glass alarm me unspeakably whenever you lift up a child or carry something or if the carriage sways or when we are pushing through the undergrowth, or just now coming down the rocks.

I am terrified by the possibility that some unforeseen knock or fall or contact might be harmful or even fatal to you. To please me then: remove the picture, not from your thoughts, not from your room—indeed, give it the finest and holiest place in your apartment—but remove from your bosom a thing whose presence seems to me in my perhaps exaggerated nervousness so very dangerous.'

Ottilie said nothing and had looked straight ahead of her as he spoke; then, neither hurrying nor hesitating, looking more towards heaven than at Eduard, she undid the chain, drew out the portrait, pressed it against her forehead, and handed it to her friend with the words: 'Keep it for me until we are home. I have no better way of showing you how much I appreciate your friendly concern.'

Her friend did not dare press the picture to his lips, but he took her hand and pressed it against his eyes. They were perhaps the loveliest hands that had ever been clasped together. It was as if a weight had been lifted from his heart, as if a dividing wall between himself and Ottilie had been removed.

Led by the miller, Charlotte and the Captain came down on an easier path. There was a welcoming, and joyfulness and refreshment. They were unwilling to take the same way home, and Eduard suggested a rocky path on the other side of the stream which brought them, with some exertion on their part, back into a view of the ponds. Now they were traversing a mixed woodland and, looking away, they had sight of frequent villages, little open towns, and dairy farms in green and fertile surroundings; and, nearest, one remote holding that lay very snugly in the woodland high up. The region was revealed most beautifully and in its greatest richness before and behind them once they had climbed the gradual slope, and there they entered a cheerful copse of trees and, emerging from it, found themselves on the rocky eminence facing the Hall.

How delighted they were by their more or less unexpected arrival at that place. They had done the tour of a little world; they were standing where the new building was to be, and looking across again at the windows of their home.

They climbed down to the summer-house and sat there all four together for the first time. It was, very naturally, the unanimous wish that the day's walk, which they had done slowly and not without difficulty, should be so devised and accommodated that it could be done more companionably, at a stroll and in comfort. Everyone made suggestions, and they calculated that the route for which they had needed several hours, if it were well laid out, must lead back to the Hall in an hour. Below the mill, where the stream flowed into the ponds, they were already erecting a bridge which would shorten the way and adorn the landscape when Charlotte reined in their inventive imaginations a little by reminding them of the costs which such an undertaking would entail.

'There too we have a solution,' Eduard replied. 'All we need do is sell the holding in the woods that looks so well situated but brings in so little, and spend the revenue on this project, and in that way, having the pleasure of a priceless walk, we enjoy the profits of a good investment, whereas at present, according to our last accounts at the end of the year, we draw, to our annoyance, only a pitiable income from it.'

Charlotte herself, as a good housekeeper, could make no real objection. The matter had come under discussion before now. The Captain proposed dividing up the parcels of land among the farmers who had their living in the woodlands; but in Eduard's view there was a quicker and easier way of proceeding. The present tenant, who had already made offers, should have it and pay in instalments, and in like instalments their own project would be undertaken stage by stage according to a plan.

So reasonable and measured an arrangement was bound to meet with approval, and the whole company was already imagining the leisurely new paths and along them and near them, waiting to be discovered, the pleasantest places for rest and for a view.

At home that evening, in order to have a picture of everything in greater detail, they at once took out the new map of the estate. They followed the way they had gone and saw how in one or two places it might be improved. All their earlier proposals were discussed again in the light of their most recent thinking; the situation of the new house, opposite the Hall, was given renewed approval, and the whole circular route to it and from it decided on.

Ottilie had not offered any opinion when Eduard finally turned the map, which until then had lain before Charlotte, towards her and invited her to speak her mind and, when she hesitated a moment, urged her in the friendliest way not to be silent, nothing was ruled out, everything was open still.

Ottilie laid her finger on the highest flat surface of the ridge. 'I would build the house here,' she said. 'True, you would not see the Hall, the trees would hide it; but what you would gain would be the feeling of being in a new and different world, since the village and all the dwelling places would be hidden too. The view over the ponds, towards the mill, towards the high ground, the mountains, out into the country, is extraordinarily beautiful, as I noticed when we passed.'

'She is right!' Eduard cried. 'How could it have escaped us? This is what you mean, Ottilie, is it not?' And taking a pencil he drew in a crude and emphatic oblong on the ridge.

The Captain winced; it pained him to see his careful and neatly drawn map disfigured in this way; but, after gently expressing his unhappiness, he controlled himself and considered the proposal. 'Ottilie is right,' he said. 'Would we not after all go quite some distance to drink coffee or eat a fish we should not have enjoyed so much at home? We want novelty, variety. Building the Hall where they did, an older generation showed good sense, for it has shelter from the winds and is near the things we need every day; but a house intended more for social gatherings than for living in will be very well placed up there, and many pleasant hours may be spent in it during the summer months.'

The more they discussed the matter the more persuaded they became; and Eduard could not conceal his delight that it was Ottilie's idea. He was as proud as if he had thought of it himself.

CHAPTER EIGHT

The very next morning the Captain made an examination of the site, drew first a rough sketch and then, when all four had conferred again at the place itself, did an exact plan along with an estimate of the costs and everything else that might be required. The necessary preparations were begun. The business of selling the farmstead was at once resumed. Again the two men had plenty to do together.

The Captain observed to Eduard that it would be a nice thing, indeed that it was almost their obligation, to celebrate Charlotte's birthday by laying the foundation stone. Eduard's old antipathy towards such occasions was soon overcome, since it quickly occurred to him to celebrate Ottilie's birthday, which fell later, in a similarly ceremonious fashion.

Charlotte, who thought the new projects and what they entailed a significant, serious, even almost a worrying matter, spent her time going over again, for herself, the estimates and the schedule of work and disbursements. They saw less of one another during the day, and were all the more desirous of one another's company in the evening.

Ottilie meanwhile had become entirely the mistress of the household, and how could it be otherwise, given her quiet and steady conduct? Besides, her whole disposition was towards the house and domestic matters, rather than towards the world and a life in the open air. Eduard soon noticed that really she only went with them on their walks to be obliging, and in the evenings stayed longer out of doors only to be sociable, and indeed would sometimes find something that needed doing in the house as an excuse to go indoors again. Very soon, then, he managed to arrange their walks together so as to be home before sunset, and began reading poetry aloud again, which he had not done for a long time, and particularly poems into whose reading he could put the expression of a pure but passionate love.

In the evenings they usually sat around a low table on seats which they fetched to it: Charlotte on the sofa, Ottilie on a chair opposite her, and the men taking the two sides. Ottilie sat on Eduard's right, which was where he pushed the light when he was reading. Thereupon Ottilie moved closer, to see the book itself, for she was another who trusted her own eyes more than somebody else's lips; and Eduard likewise moved nearer, to make it in every way easier for her; indeed, he often made longer pauses than was necessary, so that he would on no account turn the page before she had come to the end of it.

Charlotte and the Captain noticed this, of course, and now and then smiled across at one another; but both were surprised by another occasion when Ottilie's silent affection was made manifest.

Once, when tiresome visitors had deprived the little company of a part of an evening, Eduard proposed that they should remain a while together. He felt in the mood to take up his flute again, which for a long time had not been usual. Charlotte began looking for the sonatas which they were accustomed to perform together, and since they were not to be found Ottilie, after some hesitation, admitted that she had taken them to her room.

'And you could accompany me on the piano?' Eduard cried, his eyes shining with delight. 'And will you?'

'Yes,' said Ottilie. 'We shall manage, I daresay.' She fetched the music and sat down at the piano. Those listening noticed and were amazed how completely Ottilie had learned the piece for herself, but what amazed them even more was how she managed to accommodate it to Eduard's manner of playing. 'Managed to accommodate' is not the right expression; for whereas Charlotte skilfully and of her own free will held back to suit her husband when he hesitated and kept up with him when he raced ahead, it seemed that Ottilie, who had heard them play the sonatas on a number of occasions, had only learned them in the way that belonged to the man she was accompanying. She had made his faults so much her own that in the end something whole and alive came out of them that did not keep proper time, it is true, but was extremely agreeable and pleasing to listen to nevertheless. The composer himself would have been delighted to see his work distorted in such a loving way.

The Captain and Charlotte watched this strange and unexpected encounter in silence, and with such feelings as one often has when witnessing childish acts which, because of their worrying consequences one cannot entirely approve of but cannot disapprove of either, which one indeed may even be bound to envy. For in fact their own affection was developing no less than that between Eduard and Ottilie, and perhaps even more dangerously since both were more serious, surer of themselves, and more capable of self-restraint.

The Captain was already beginning to feel that a process of irresistible habituation was threatening to bind him to Charlotte. He forced himself to avoid those times when Charlotte usually came out into the grounds; rose very early, saw to everything necessary, and withdrew then to his own wing of the house, to work. For the first few days Charlotte thought it accidental and went looking for him in all the likely places; then she believed she understood his intention, and respected him all the more.

If now the Captain avoided being alone with Charlotte, he was all the more active in furthering and hastening the preparations for the splendid celebration of her approaching birthday; for whilst he was laying the easy path from below, beginning behind the village, he had at the same time, in order to extract stone, as he said, ordered the work to start from the top, and had arranged and calculated everything so that only in the night before the event should the two halves of the path be joined. For the new house up above, the cellar had been not so much dug as hewn out of the rock, and a fine foundation-stone had been sculpted, with little compartments and a coping.

This combination of outward activity, of small, affectionate, and secret purposes, with feelings within which were being more or less repressed, rather dampened the company's enjoyment when they were together; so much so that Eduard, who felt that something was lacking, one evening urged the Captain to get out his violin and accompany Charlotte on the piano. The Captain gave way to the general wish and together they performed one of the hardest pieces with feeling, ease, and freedom, which gave them and their two listeners the greatest satisfaction. They promised one another frequent repeat performances and practices together.

'They do better than we do, Ottilie,' said Eduard. 'Let us admire them, but enjoy our own partnership none the less.'

CHAPTER NINE

The birthday had arrived and everything was ready. The village street had been raised and bordered by a wall, against the stream. The path which passed the church, continuing for a while on the course laid down for it by Charlotte, now wound its way up among the rocks, having the summer-house first on the left above it, then, after doubling back entirely, on the left below it, and so gradually reached the top.

There were many guests that day. They went to church where, dressed for a great occasion, the whole parish was assembled. After the service the boys, the young men, and the grown men, as it had been arranged, left first; then came the Hall with all their party and their retinue; girls, young women, and married women brought up the rear.

On the bend a raised-up place had been set into the rock; here, at the Captain's suggestion, Charlotte and the guests paused for breath. They had a view over the whole route, the company of men, already come up, and the women following them, now going past. On a day of splendid weather it was an exceptionally beautiful scene. Charlotte was surprised, moved, and she pressed the Captain's hand affectionately.

They followed the crowd which, at a leisurely pace, had climbed ahead and had by now formed a ring around the site of the new building. The owner himself then and those closest to him, as well as the highest-ranking guests, were invited to descend into the depths where the foundation stone, supported under one side, was ready to be laid down. A mason, resplendently dressed, trowel in one hand and hammer in the other, gave a fine speech in rhyme which we must do less than justice to and reproduce here in prose.

'Three things,' he began, 'are needful in a building: that it is in the right place, that it has good foundations, and that it is perfectly executed. The first is really the business of the man whose house it will be. For just as in town only the prince and the municipality can decide where any building should be allowed, so in the country it is the privilege of the man who

owns the land to say: my dwelling place shall be here and nowhere else.'

Eduard and Ottilie did not dare to look at one another when
they heard these words, although they were close and face to
face.

'In the third, the execution, men of very many trades are
involved; indeed, few trades are *not* involved. But the second,
the foundation, is the responsibility of the mason and, to speak
the truth, it is the most important in the whole undertaking. It
is a serious business, and our invitation is a serious one: for this
occasion is celebrated in the depths. Here within the confines
of this excavated space you do us the honour of appearing as
witnesses of our secret proceedings. In a moment this sculpted
stone will be laid down and these walls of earth, for the present
still decorated with beautiful and dignified living figures, will
soon no longer be accessible, they will be underground.

'This foundation stone, whose corner will mark the right-
hand corner of the building, whose squareness will signify its
regularity, and whose horizontal and vertical setting will ensure
the plumb and level trueness of all the outside and inside
walls, might now be laid in place without more ado, for it would
surely rest on its own weight. But there shall be lime* here too,
in a mortar, to bind; for just as people who are naturally inclined to one another hold together better still when cemented
by the Law, so likewise stones, suited in shape, are joined even
better by these powers that bind; and since it is not proper that
you should be idle while others are active, you will, I am sure,
be willing to take a part in the work.'

So saying, he gave Charlotte his trowel and with it she threw
mortar under the stone. Several others were encouraged to do
the same, then the stone was lowered; whereupon Charlotte
and the rest were handed the hammer and expressly blessed the
union of the stone with the ground, by tapping three times.

The speaker continued: 'The mason's work, now open to the
sky, though it is not always performed in concealment will
finish in concealment nevertheless. The foundations, properly
laid, will be filled in; and even with the walls, which we raise
in the daylight, it is rare that we are remembered in the end.
The stone-cutter's work and the sculptor's are more visible, and

when the decorator extinguishes all trace of our hands and claims our work for his own because he covers it and colours it and smooths it over, that too we must accept.

'Who then more than the mason will be concerned to make what he does right for himself, by doing it right? Who has more reason than he has to nourish his own self-respect? When the house has been built, the floors levelled and tiled, the outside ornamented, he will still see in through all the layers and still discern those regular and careful joints to which the whole owes its existence and its stay.

'But just as anyone who has done something wrong is bound to be afraid that despite all his efforts it will come to light one day, so too a man who has done the right thing in secret must always expect it to surface against his will. For that reason we make this foundation stone into a memorial stone as well. In the various cavities carved here various things are to be laid, as evidence, for a distant posterity. These sealed metal containers hold written memorials; all manner of curious things have been engraved into these metal plates; the best old wines will be buried in these beautiful glass bottles, with a note of their vintage; and there are besides different coins minted in the present year—all this we have received through the generosity of the man for whom we build. And there is still room, should any guest or spectator feel inclined to make over something to posterity.'

There was a short pause, and the mason looked around him; but as is usually the case on such occasions nobody was prepared, everyone was taken by surprise, until finally a young and cheerful army officer began, and said: 'If I am to contribute something which has not yet been laid down in this treasure house I must cut a couple of buttons off my uniform, for surely they also deserve to be passed on to posterity.' No sooner said than done! Now others had similar ideas. The ladies hurried to put in little combs from their hair; bottles of smelling salts and other fine articles were likewise sacrificed. Only Ottilie hesitated, until Eduard with a friendly word broke in upon her contemplation of all the things which had been contributed and placed in the receptacles. Thereupon she undid from her neck the golden chain on which the picture of her father had hung and laid it down gently over the other jewellery. Eduard then, in some haste, at once had the cover fitted on and sealed.

The young mason, having been the busiest in these proceedings, now resumed his manner of a public speaker, and continued: 'We lay down this stone for ever, to secure the longest enjoyment of the house by its present and future owners. However, whilst here, as it were, burying a treasure we are mindful also, in this most fundamental of all matters, of the fleetingness of human things. We entertain the possibility that the lid here so securely sealed might one day be raised again, which could only happen if all that we have not yet even built were then to be destroyed.

'But precisely in order that it shall be built let us bring our thoughts back from the future and into the present. Let us, as soon as today's festivities are over, at once go on with our work so that none who follow at their own tasks upon our foundations need ever be idle but the building will rise up speedily and be finished and at the windows, which are not yet there, the master of the house with his nearest and dearest and his guests may look around him cheerfully, and their good health and the health of all present we hereby drink to now.'

So saying he emptied, at a draught, a beautifully cut glass and threw it into the air; for we mark the superabundance of our joy by destroying the vessel we made use of when we were joyful. But on this occasion it happened differently: the glass did not fall to the ground again, and not because of a miracle.

In order to get on with the building the ground in the far corner had already been completely dug out and a start made on the walls, and for this purpose scaffolding had been erected to the full height that would be required.

For this occasion, for the benefit of the workers themselves, it had been planked and a crowd of spectators permitted up. The glass rose to their height and was caught by one of them, who thought this a very happy occurrence and omen for himself. He was showing the glass around, without letting it out of his hand, and on it could be seen the letters E and O engraved together in a very decorative intertwining. It was one of the glasses which had been made for Eduard when he was young.

The scaffold was empty again, the most agile among the guests climbed up to look around, and there was no end to their praise of the prospects on all sides; for anyone standing on a high place, and even only one storey higher, discovers all manner of things. Looking out into the open country several new villages became visible; the silver line of the river could be seen clearly; indeed, one viewer claimed to be able to see the towers of the capital. In the other direction, behind the wooded hills, rose the blue peaks of a distant range of mountains; and the immediate vicinity could be seen entire. 'All it needs,' somebody cried, 'is for the three ponds to be made into one lake; then the view would lack nothing grand or desirable.'

'That could be done,' said the Captain. 'They used to be a mountain lake in earlier times.'

'But spare my copse of plane trees and poplars,' said Eduard, 'that stand so handsomely by the middle pond. Look—' he turned to Ottilie, led her a few steps forward and pointed down—'I planted those trees myself.'

'How long have they been there?' Ottilie asked.

'About as long,' Eduard replied, 'as you have been on earth. Yes, I was already planting trees when you were still in your cradle, my dear child.'

The company returned to the Hall. After dinner they were invited to take a walk through the village, to inspect the improvements there too. Instructed by the Captain the villagers had assembled in front of their houses; they were not standing in rows but were grouped naturally in their families, some, as the evening demanded, busy with tasks, others resting on newly provided benches. And they had been given the pleasant duty of repeating this cleanliness and orderliness at least every Sunday and every holiday.

When the true sociability of the heart, such as had arisen among our friends, is interrupted by any larger company, that will always be unwelcome. All four were pleased to find themselves alone again in the spacious drawing-room; but this homely feeling was somewhat spoiled when Eduard was handed a letter announcing the arrival of new guests on the following day.

'As we expected,' Eduard exclaimed to Charlotte, 'the Count will not let us down: he arrives tomorrow.'

'Then the Baroness will not be far away,' Charlotte replied.

'Indeed not!' said Eduard. 'She will make her own way here tomorrow too. They ask to be accommodated overnight and will leave next day together.'

'Then we must prepare things at once, Ottilie,' said Charlotte.

'What orders do you have?' Ottilie asked.

Charlotte gave some general indications, and Ottilie withdrew.

The Captain enquired after the relationship of these two persons, since he knew about it only in the most general way. Some time ago, both already married, they had fallen passionately in love with one another. Two marriages were shaken, and not without scandal; there was talk of divorce. In the case of the Baroness it became possible, but not in the Count's. They were obliged to pretend to separate, but their relationship continued; and though during the winter in the capital they could not be together, they made up for it in summer when they could travel and visit the spas. Both were a little older than Eduard and Charlotte and all four had been close friends since their earliest years at Court together. Good relations had been maintained, without that implying complete mutual approval. But on this occasion Charlotte did feel their arrival to be in a certain sense wholly inopportune, and if she were entirely honest as to the reason, it was on account of Ottilie. The child was too young, too good and innocent, to be exposed to such an example.

'They might have waited a day or two,' said Eduard, just as Ottilie came back into the room, 'until the farm was quite sold. The contract is ready, I have one copy here, we need the second, and our old clerk is not at all well.' The Captain offered his services, Charlotte also; but there were reasons why they should not. 'Give it to me,' said Ottilie, rather in haste.

'You won't manage it,' said Charlotte.

'I should have to have it by the day after tomorrow,' said Eduard, 'first thing. And it is long.'

'It will be ready,' Ottilie cried, and the document was already in her hands.

Next morning when they were looking out from an upper window for their guests, whom they wanted to be sure to go and meet, Eduard said: 'Who is that riding so slowly down the road towards us?' The Captain described the rider's appearance more closely. 'It's him,' said Eduard. 'The details which you see better than I do exactly fit the whole which I see very well. It's Mittler. But why is he riding slowly, and so very slowly at that?'

The figure drew nearer, and it was indeed Mittler. They welcomed him with affection as he came slowly up the steps. 'Why did you not come yesterday?' Eduard shouted.

'I dislike noisy occasions,' he replied. 'But I am here today to celebrate my friend's birthday with you quietly after the event.'

'How can you afford the time?' Eduard asked in jest.

'You owe my visit, which you may or may not be glad of, to a thought which occurred to me yesterday. I had spent half the day very agreeably in a household in which I had acted as a peacemaker, and then I heard that a birthday was being celebrated over here. "Really, one might call it selfishness," I said to myself, "that you are only willing to enjoy yourself with people you have reconciled. Why do you not enjoy yourself for once with friends who are never at odds?" With the result that here I am. I have done as I said I should.'

'Yesterday you would have had a lot of company,' said Charlotte, 'but not much today. There will be the Count and the Baroness, who have given you trouble in the past.'

That strange and welcome man sprang then in lively exasperation out from among the four companions and looked about him at once for his hat and riding-crop. 'Something will always come and spoil it if ever I allow myself a moment's peace and quiet. But why do I not keep to what I am? I should not have come, and now I am driven away. For I will not be under one roof with them; and beware: they bring nothing but ill. They are like leaven, they propagate their own infection.'

They tried to placate him, but in vain. 'Anyone who assaults the estate of matrimony,' he cried, 'anyone who in word and worse in deed undermines that foundation of all moral order has me to deal with; and if I cannot better him I keep out of his way. Marriage is the basis and the pinnacle of culture. It makes the uncultured gentle and in it the most cultured can best demonstrate their gentleness. It must never be dissolved, for it brings so much happiness that in comparison any individual unhappiness is of no significance. And what do people mean when they speak of unhappiness? It is impatience, which comes over them from time to time and then they are pleased to call themselves unhappy. Only let the moment pass and you will think yourselves fortunate that something which has stood so long still stands. There is never a sufficient reason for separation. The human condition is so rich in joy and sorrow that it cannot be calculated what a man and wife owe one another. The debt is infinite, and can only be paid through eternity. It may not always be easy, that I do not doubt, and why should it be? Are we not also married to our consciences, which we should also be glad to be rid of often enough, since they are more difficult than ever a man or woman might be to us?'

Thus he held forth, vehemently, and would doubtless have continued for quite some time if coach-horns had not announced the arrival of the two parties who, as though according to a programme, drove up before the house from their separate directions simultaneously. As the household hurried to meet them Mittler hid himself, had his horse brought down to the inn, and rode away in a bad temper.

CHAPTER TEN

The guests were welcomed and led inside. They were delighted to be back in the house and in the rooms in which they had once spent many happy days, and which for some considerable time they had not revisited. Our friends were just as glad to see them there. The Count, and the Baroness too, might be numbered among those tall and handsome figures who are almost more pleasing to look at in middle age than in their youth; for though perhaps their first bloom may have passed, now they incline one not only to like them but also to feel towards them a decided confidence. This couple too were very easy to be with. They confronted the circumstances of life in a free and open-minded way, and this and their cheerfulness and their obvious lack of embarrassment were felt at once, and a rare courtesy gave limits to everything yet no one was aware of any constraint.

Their effect upon the company was immediate. The new arrivals, coming straight from society, as was apparent even in their clothes, their belongings, and in everything about them, were something of a contrast to our friends in their rural and secretly passionate state, but this very soon passed as old memories and a present interest mixed and rapid and lively talk quickly drew everyone together.

But before long there was a separation. The women withdrew to their own wing of the house, and in exchanging confidences and at the same time beginning to appraise the newest fashions in morning wear, hats, and suchlike, they found plenty to amuse them, whilst the men gave their attention to the new carriages and had horses brought out and at once began to deal and swap.

Not until dinner did everyone come together again. They had dressed, and in this too the visitors appeared to advantage. Everything they wore was new and as if never seen before and yet through use already accustomed and comfortable.

The conversation was lively and went to and fro, for in such company everything and nothing seems of interest. They conversed in French, to exclude the servants, and ranged with complacent boldness over worldly matters of a high and of a middling importance. On one topic the talk remained longer than perhaps it should have done, when Charlotte asked after an old friend and was dismayed to hear that she was about to be divorced.

'It is very disagreeable', said Charlotte. 'We imagine our absent friends to be safe and well, we suppose a particular dear person to be quite catered for, and the next we hear her fate is precarious and she has been obliged to set off again on paths that may again be less than safe.'

The Count replied: 'Really, my dear, we have only ourselves to blame if such vicissitudes surprise us. We do so like to think that earthly things will last, and especially marriages, and concerning these we are beguiled by what we see again and again in the theatre into notions which do not accord with the way of the world. In comedy marriage is depicted as the final goal of desires whose fulfilment is postponed and hindered for the duration of several acts, and the instant it is achieved the curtain falls and that moment of satisfaction reverberates in us. In the real world things are different. The play continues behind the curtain, and if the curtain rises again we do not like to watch or listen any further.'

'It cannot be quite so bad,' said Charlotte with a smile, 'since we see people who have already quitted the stage very willing to act a part on it again.'

'There can be no objection to that', said the Count. 'One might well wish to take on another role, and anyone who knows how the world is must see that in marriage too it is only this settled everlastingness in a world of such mutability which is somewhat out of place. I had a friend whose speciality in humour was suggesting new laws. He used to assert that all marriages should only be contracted for a period of five years. Five, he would say, is a nice, uneven, and holy number and that period is just sufficient to get to know one another, bring a few children into the world, fall out and—the nicest thing of all—make it up again. "How happy the early part would be!" he used to exclaim. Two or three years at least would go by quite pleasantly. Then very likely one of the partners would be anxious to see the relationship last longer, the desire to please would increase the closer they got to the ending of the contract. The indifferent—indeed, even a discontented—partner would be appeased and won over by such behaviour. They would be no more aware of the passage of time than one ever is in pleasant company, and would be very agreeably surprised when at last they noticed that their term had passed and had been tacitly extended.'

Clever and amusing though this was, and although, as Charlotte appreciated, the frivolous suggestion could be given a deep moral sense, talk of that kind was unpalatable to her, and particularly on account of Ottilie. She was well aware that there is nothing more dangerous than a conversation which takes liberties and treats as usual, commonplace, or even praiseworthy a situation which is reprehensible or half reprehensible; and surely it must be deemed dangerous whenever the marriage bond is belittled in that way. She sought, therefore, adroitly as ever, to change the subject; but failing to, she was sorry that Ottilie had managed things so well that there was no cause for her to leave the table. The girl, watchful, never flustered, had a perfect understanding with the major-domo; a glance from her sufficed, and everything ran smoothly, even though two or three of the servants were new and inexpert.

And so the Count, insensitive to Charlotte's efforts to change the subject, continued with it. He was never usually one to be the least tiresome in conversation, but this matter was too close to his heart and his difficulties in getting a divorce from his wife had embittered him against everything that concerned the marriage bond, which he himself none the less passionately desired to enter into with the Baroness.

'That friend of mine', he continued, 'made another legislative proposal. A marriage should only be held to be indissoluble when both partners, or at least one of them, had been married for the third time. For, incontrovertibly, any such person would have demonstrated that marriage for him or her was something he or she could not do without. And it would also have become known how such persons had behaved in their previous relationships, whether they had any peculiarities, which often give more cause for separation than real faults do. It would thus be up to both parties to find out about one another; and attention should be paid to the married and the unmarried alike, since one never knew what the future might bring.'

'That would at least greatly increase society's interest in these matters', said Eduard. 'For really, as things are, once you marry nobody enquires any further after your virtues or your vices.'

'If that *were* the system,' the Baroness interjected with a smile, 'our good friends here would have already successfully completed two of the stages and could now be preparing themselves for the third.'

'They were lucky', said the Count. 'In their case Death did willingly what the courts, when it is left to them, do very unwillingly.'

'Let us leave the dead in peace', Charlotte answered with some seriousness in her look.

'Why should we,' the Count replied, 'if we can remember them with respect? They were not too demanding, they made do with quite a moderate number of years, and when they left they did a great deal of good.'

'If only such situations did not waste the best years of one's life', said the Baroness, suppressing a sigh.

'Indeed,' said the Count, 'it might drive one to despair, if it were not the case that very few things in the world turn out as one had hoped. Children do not do what they promise; young people very rarely, and if they keep faith the world itself will not keep faith with them.'

Charlotte, glad to see the conversation changing tack, replied in cheerful tones: 'Well, we must in any case accustom ourselves soon enough to only a partial and fragmentary enjoyment of the good things of life.'

'Certainly,' the Count replied, 'you have both enjoyed very happy times. If I think of the years when you and Eduard were the handsomest pair at Court, nothing now approaches the brilliance of those times, nor are there people now as resplendent as you were. When you danced together all eyes were upon you, and how sought after you were whilst having eyes only for one another!'

'Since so much has changed,' said Charlotte, 'we may perhaps, in all modesty, permit ourselves to listen to such flatteries.'

'In my own mind', said the Count, 'I have often blamed Eduard for not being more persistent. His peculiar parents would surely have relented in the end, and an extra ten years, youthful ones at that, are not to be sniffed at.'

'I must put in a word in his defence', said the Baroness. 'Charlotte was not entirely blameless. She did look elsewhere a little, it must be said. And although she loved Eduard dearly and in secret had decided upon him for her husband, I can vouch for how much she tormented him on occasions, so that he was easily persuaded that he should travel, take himself off, and get used to doing without her, which was a fateful decision.'

Eduard bowed to the Baroness and seemed grateful for her intercession.

'But then', she continued, 'there is one thing I must add to excuse Charlotte. The man who was courting her at that time had long been outstanding in his devotion and was, when one got to know him better, certainly more sympathetic than you are all willing to admit.'

'My dear lady,' the Count replied in somewhat heated tones, 'let us say quite frankly that you were yourself not entirely indifferent to him and that Charlotte had more to fear from you than from anyone else. I think it a very pretty trait in women that they retain their affection for a particular man so long—indeed, that no sort of separation causes them to waver in it or abandon it.'

'This is a quality which men may possess in even higher degree', the Baroness replied. 'In your own case at least, my dear Count, I have observed that nobody has more sway over you than a woman you were once fond of. I have seen you do more when asked a favour by such a one than you might on behalf of the woman currently in your affections.'

'There may be no answer to a reproach of that kind,' said the Count, 'but as for Charlotte's first husband, I disliked the man for this reason: that he broke up a handsome couple, two people intended by Providence for one another who, once joined, need never have worried about the five-year term nor have looked ahead to any second or third contract.'

'We shall do our best', said Charlotte, 'to catch up on what we have missed.'

'Keep to that,' said the Count. 'For your first marriages', he continued with some vehemence, 'were after all marriages of the detestable kind. But then unfortunately marriage altogether has something—forgive me if I put this strongly—rather vulgar about it. It spoils the tenderest relationships, and really all it has to offer is a crass sort of security which perhaps one of the parties at least is pleased enough to have. But it is all a formality, and they seem to have come together only so that both thenceforth may go their separate ways.'

At that moment Charlotte, wishing to get away from this subject once and for all, tried a bold shift of direction and was successful. The talk became more general, husband and wife, and the Captain, were able to take part; even Ottilie was induced to say something, and dessert was taken in the happiest mood, a wealth of fruit piled up in pretty baskets and a bright abundance of flowers beautifully arranged in gorgeous vases doing most to foster it.

There was mention too of what had been done in the grounds, and an inspection took place immediately after dinner. Ottilie withdrew, saying she had things in the house to see to; but in reality she went on with her work of copying. The Count was engaged in conversation by the Captain; Charlotte joined them later. When they had climbed on to the ridge and the Captain had obligingly hurried down again to fetch the map, the Count said to Charlotte: 'I like the man exceedingly. He has both a wide and a coherent knowledge. And what he does seems very serious and consequential too. What he is achieving here would, in a higher sphere, be of great importance.'

To hear the Captain praised like this gave Charlotte intense satisfaction. But she composed herself and reinforced what the Count had said in a clear and level manner. Then how he astonished her when he continued: 'I have made his acquaintance at exactly the right time. I know a position which would suit the man perfectly, and by recommending him, and securing his happiness, I shall oblige a highly placed friend of mine in the best possible way.'

It was as though a thunderbolt had struck Charlotte. The Count noticed nothing; for women, accustomed to controlling themselves at all times, retain even in the most extraordinary situations an apparent composure. But she was no longer listening to what the Count was saying as he went on: 'It is not in my nature to dally once I am convinced of a thing. Mentally I have already written my letter, and now I am in a hurry to set it down. Will you get me a messenger I can despatch this evening?'

Inwardly Charlotte was distraught. Surprised both by these propositions and by herself, she could not utter a word. Fortunately the Count continued to speak of his plans for the Captain, and it was all-too obvious to Charlotte how advantageous they were. Then, not before time, the Captain appeared and unrolled his map for the Count to see. But what new eyes she saw her friend with now, now that she was to lose him! Bowing hastily she turned away and hurried down to the summer-house. Long before she got there the tears had started from her eyes, and she flung herself into the narrow confines of that little hermitage and gave herself over entirely to a grief, a passion, a despair of whose possibility only a moment since she had had not the slightest apprehension.

Eduard had gone with the Baroness in the other direction, as far as the ponds. She was a shrewd woman, and liked to know everything that was going on. Feeling her way in the conversation, she soon noticed how expansive Eduard was apt to become in praise of Ottilie; and she led him on, always in the most natural way, until it seemed to her certain that here was a passion, and not one at its outset either, but one already established.

Married women, though they may not be fond of one another, are nevertheless in tacit allegiance, especially against young girls. The consequences of such an attachment were immediately obvious to her, knowing the world as she did. Moreover, earlier that morning she had been speaking about Ottilie to Charlotte, had disapproved of the child's residing in the country, especially given the quietness of her temperament, and had proposed taking Ottilie into town, to live with a friend of hers who was much concerned with the education of her only daughter and was, precisely, on the look-out for an agreeable companion who should be instated as a second child and share in all the daughter's advantages. Charlotte had said she would think about it.

Now the insight into Eduard's feelings had confirmed the Baroness in her plan, but the more certain she became the more she feigned still to be indulging Eduard. For no one was more mistress of herself than she, and such self-control in extraordinary situations accustoms us to dissemble even in ordinary ones and inclines us, since we have so much power over ourselves, to extend it over others too and thus to compensate somewhat by an external triumph for an inner loss.

Most often this attitude is accompanied by a sort of secret delight at other people's blindness, at how unwittingly they go into the trap. We take pleasure not only in our own present triumph but also in the thought of the shameful realization awaiting them. Thus the Baroness was malicious enough to invite Eduard and Charlotte for the vintage on her estates and to answer the question whether they might bring Ottilie with them in terms he could interpret after his own desires.

Eduard began at once to speak rhapsodically of the splendid country, the great river, the hills, rocks, vineyards, ancient castles, outings on the water, all the festivities accompanying the picking and the pressing of the grapes, and so forth, and was already, in the innocence of his heart, openly looking forward to the effect such scenes would have on Ottilie's unspoilt mind. At that moment they saw Ottilie approaching, and the Baroness was quick to ask Eduard not to say anything about their autumn journey since things looked forward to so long usually did not happen. Eduard promised, but hurried her forward to meet Ottilie and in the end ran several paces ahead of her, to meet the girl himself. His whole being was expressive of a heartfelt joy. He kissed her hands, and pressed into them a bunch of wild flowers which he had picked along the way. Watching, the Baroness felt something close to bitterness. For though she might not approve of what was perhaps blameworthy in this passion, she could not bear to see what was sweet and delightful in it bestowed on that intruding nobody of a girl.

By the time they sat down to supper an entirely different mood had come over the company. The Count, who had written his letter and dispatched the messenger with it even before supper, was in conversation with the Captain and in a sensible and modest fashion was drawing him out more and more, having seated him at his side for the evening. This meant that the Baroness, to the right of the Count, could have very little talk with him; and she had just as little with Eduard who, thirsty at the start and then excited, did not stint himself with the wine and was conversing very animatedly with Ottilie, whom he had placed by him, whilst Charlotte, sitting on the Captain's left, found it hard, indeed almost impossible, to conceal the trouble she felt.

The Baroness had time enough to observe things. She saw Charlotte's discomfort, and since all she knew of was Eduard's relationship with Ottilie she soon persuaded herself that Charlotte too was concerned and upset by her husband's behaviour, and she gave more thought to how she might now best achieve her ends.

Even when they rose from table there was a division in the company. The Count, wishing really to fathom the Captain, was obliged to try several approaches before he could find out what he wished to know; for the Captain was a quiet, not at all conceited, and altogether laconic man. They walked up and down along one side of the room, whilst Eduard, excited by the wine and by his hopes, was laughing with Ottilie at the window, Charlotte and the Baroness meanwhile walking together in silence to and fro on the other side of the room. Their silence and their standing idly by at length caused a faltering in the rest of the company. The women withdrew to their wing, the men to theirs, and the day seemed to have been concluded.

CHAPTER ELEVEN

Eduard accompanied the Count to his room and was easily led by their talk to stay with him for a while. The Count was losing himself in the past, animatedly remembering Charlotte's beauty, expatiating upon it, as an amateur of these things, with a good deal of passion: 'A beautiful foot is one of Nature's greatest gifts. The grace of it never fades. I was watching her today as she walked. One would still like to kiss her shoe and do as the Sarmatians* did whose highest tribute to a revered and beautiful woman—barbaric no doubt but heartfelt never-theless—was to drink a health to her out of her shoe.'

Their praises did not rest there, at the tip of the foot; they were, after all, old friends. They passed from the person herself to old stories and adventures, and recalled the obstacles which at the time had been placed in the way of the two lovers to prevent their meeting, and what trouble they had gone to, what strategies they had devised, simply in order to be able to speak their love.

'Do you remember', the Count continued, 'what a friend in need I was to you and how very unselfish, when their Majesties were visiting an uncle in that immense and labyrinthine house? The day had been spent in ceremonies and formal dress; a part of the night at least was to be for the lovers and their freer discourse.'

'You had taken good note of how to get to where the ladies-in-waiting had their rooms,' said Eduard. 'We made our way successfully to my own beloved lady.'

'Who,' said the Count, 'giving more thought to propriety than to my contentment, had kept a very ill-favoured chaper-one by her; so that whilst you, with looks and words, were getting on splendidly, my own lot was most unenviable.'

'Only yesterday,' said Eduard, 'when we knew you were coming, my wife and I were remembering the story, and espe-cially how you and I got back. We missed our way and found ourselves at the guardroom. Since we knew how to proceed from there we saw no reason not to go through, as we had already elsewhere along our route. But what a surprise we had when we opened the doors! The way was blocked with mattresses on which the guards were lying out like giants in several rows asleep. The only man awake looked at us in astonishment. But being full of a youthful courage and impertinence we stepped quite coolly over the stretched-out boots, without even one of those snoring sons of Anak* waking up.'

'I was very tempted to stumble and make a noise,' said the Count. 'For what a strange resurrection we should have witnessed then!'

At that moment the great clock struck twelve.

'Midnight,' said the Count with a smile. 'The time has come. My dear Baron, I must ask a favour of you. Guide me tonight as I guided you then. I promised the Baroness I would call on her. We have not had a word alone together all day. It is so long since we saw one another and only natural that we should want a little time in private. Show me how to get there, I shall find my own way back. Certainly I shan't have to stumble over guardsmen's boots.'

'I shall be very glad to do you that favour,' Eduard replied. 'Any host would. But the three ladies are all together in that wing. Who knows whether we might not find them still talking or what else we might do that would look very odd?'

'Have no fear,' said the Count, 'the Baroness is expecting me. She will certainly be in her room by now, and alone.'

'It is a simple matter,' said Eduard, and taking a light he went ahead of the Count down a secret stairway which led to a long corridor. At the end of this he opened a small door. They climbed a spiral staircase; at the top, on a narrow landing, Eduard gave the Count the light and showed him a concealed door on the right which opened at the first touch, admitted the Count, and left Eduard alone in the dark.

Another door on the left led into Charlotte's bedroom. He heard voices and listened. Charlotte was speaking to her maid. 'Is Ottilie already in bed?' 'No,' said the girl, 'she is still downstairs writing.' 'Then light the night-light,' said Charlotte, 'and you can go. It is late. I'll put the candle out and see myself to bed.'

It filled Eduard with joy to hear that Ottilie was still writing. 'She is busy for me!' he said to himself in triumph. Enclosed by the darkness entirely within himself, he could see her sitting there, writing; he seemed to approach her, to see her as she turned to him; he felt an irresistible longing to be near her again. But from where he stood there was no way down to the entresol where she lived. He stood now at the door of his wife's room, a strange confusion took place in his heart; he tried to open the door, he found it locked, he knocked softly, Charlotte did not hear him.

She was walking agitatedly up and down in the larger adjoining room. Again and again she returned to what, since the Count's unexpected proposal, her mind had already wrestled with more than enough. It was as though the Captain were there before her eyes. He filled the house still, the walks were still enlivened by his presence, and he was to go away from her and everything be empty! She said all the things to herself that can be said, indeed she even anticipated, as people do, the poor consolation that even such sorrows will be lessened by the passage of time. She cursed the time it would take to lessen them; she cursed the time when they would have been lessened. How dead that time would be!

Finally, then, having recourse to tears was all the more welcome, since she rarely did. She threw herself down on the sofa and let her sorrow overwhelm her utterly. Eduard, for his part, could not leave the door; he knocked again, and a third time somewhat louder, so that Charlotte heard it quite clearly through the night-time stillness and sprang up in alarm. Her first thought was that it might, that it must be the Captain; her second that that was impossible. She supposed she must have been mistaken; but she had heard it, she wanted to have heard it, and was afraid she had. She went into the bedroom and quietly approached the secret door, which was locked. Now she upbraided herself for being afraid. 'Very likely the Countess needs something', she said, and called out then in a steady and sober voice: 'Is anyone there?' A low voice answered: '*I* am.' 'Who?' Charlotte replied, not being able to tell. To her it seemed the Captain was at the door. Then the voice came again, rather louder: 'Eduard!' She opened, and her husband stood before her. He greeted her flippantly. She was able to take up the tone. He enveloped his mysterious visit in mysterious explanations. 'But let me confess my real reason for coming,' he said at last. 'I have vowed I shall kiss your shoe before the morning.'

'It is a long time since you thought of doing that,' said Charlotte.

'So much the worse,' Eduard replied, 'and so much the better.'

She had seated herself in an armchair so that the slightness of her nightwear would not be so exposed to his eyes. He went down on his knees before her, and she could not prevent him from kissing her shoe nor, when the shoe came off in his hand, from taking hold of her foot and pressing it tenderly against his breast.

Charlotte was one of those women who, moderate by nature, in their marriages continue without effort or ulterior motive to behave as they did during the courtship. She never sought to arouse her husband, scarcely did she even respond to his desire; but without coldness or any off-putting severity she always resembled a loving bride-to-be who in her innermost self still shies away even from what is permissible. And that night Eduard found her so in a double sense. How passionately she wished her husband gone; for the phantom of her friend seemed to be reproaching her. But the things that should have caused Eduard to leave only attracted him the more. A certain agitation was apparent in her. She had been weeping, and if weaker people are mostly less attractive when they weep, those whom we know to be usually strong and composed gain by it immeasurably. Eduard was so lovable, so gentle, so pressing; he begged to be allowed to stay with her, he never demanded it, but now in earnest and now amusingly he sought to persuade and never bethought himself that he had rights, and boldly in the end extinguished the candle.

By lamplight then, in a twilight, the heart's desires and the imagination at once asserted their rights over reality. Eduard held Ottilie in his arms; now closer, now receding, the Captain hovered before Charlotte's soul; and thus absent and present in the queerest fashion were intermingled, in excitement and delight.

But the present will not be denied its monstrous due. They spent a part of the night in all manner of talk and pleasantry which was the freer because, alas, the heart had no part in it. But when Eduard woke next morning in the arms of his wife the day seemed to look in upon him ominously, the sun, so it seemed to him, was illuminating a crime; he crept from her side, and she found herself alone, in the strangest way, when she awoke.

CHAPTER TWELVE

When the company reassembled for breakfast an attentive observer would have been able to deduce from each person's bearing how differently they were thinking and feeling. The Count and the Baroness met one another with the cheerfulness and contentment that lovers feel when, having suffered a period of separation, they have again reassured themselves of their mutual affection; whereas Charlotte and Eduard felt something like shame and remorse at the sight of the Captain and Ottilie. For love by its very nature claims all rightness for itself, all other rights vanish in the face of love. Ottilie was like a child in her good humour; she might be said to be open, after her fashion. The Captain looked grave; it had become all too clear to him in his conversations with the Count, who had wakened in him everything that for some time had been lying dormant, that he was not in any real sense doing what he was meant to do, but was only drifting along in a state of semi-idleness. No sooner had the two guests departed than yet more visitors arrived, which suited Charlotte who was anxious to forget herself and be distracted; but did not suit Eduard who felt doubly inclined to concern himself with Ottilie; and they were just as unwelcome to Ottilie herself, since she had not yet finished the copying which had absolutely to be ready early next day. When finally the visitors took their leave she hurried to her room at once.

It was evening. Eduard, Charlotte, and the Captain, who had strolled a little way with the visitors until they got into their carriage, decided to take a further walk as far as the ponds. At considerable expense Eduard had sent away for a rowing-boat, and it had arrived. They wanted to see whether it handled easily.

It was moored on the shore of the middle pond not far from a few ancient oak trees which had already been included in a future project. There was to be a landing-stage here, and under the trees a place to sit and rest, in a structure which would serve as a landmark for anyone coming across the water.

'Where will be the best place to land on the other side?'
Eduard asked. 'Near my plane trees, I should think.'

'They are a little too far to the right,' said the Captain. 'Landing lower down, one would be nearer the Hall. But we must
think about it.'

The Captain was already standing in the stern of the boat
and had taken one of the oars. Charlotte climbed in, then
Eduard, who took the other oar; but whilst he was already
pushing off he thought of Ottilie, thought that this boating trip
would detain him, that he would get back from it who knew
when. He made up his mind at once, jumped ashore again,
handed the Captain his oar, and, with a hasty excuse, hurried
home.

There he learned that Ottilie had shut herself in her room
and was writing. Though he was pleased that she was doing
something for him it distressed him keenly that he was not able
to see her at once. His impatience increased by the minute.
He paced up and down in the big drawing-room, tried all
manner of things but could concentrate on nothing. What
he wanted was to see her, and see her alone, before Charlotte came back with the Captain. It grew dark, the candles
were lit.

At last she came in, radiantly lovable. The feeling that she
had done something for her friend had enhanced her whole
being beyond itself. She laid down the original and the copy
on the table in front of Eduard. 'Shall we compare?' she said
with a smile. Eduard did not know what to reply. He looked at
her, he looked at the copy. The first pages were written with
the greatest care, in a delicate female hand; then the writing
seemed to change, to become easier and freer; but how great
was his astonishment when he ran his eyes over the final
pages. 'In heaven's name!' he cried. 'What is this? That is my
handwriting.' He looked at Ottilie, and again at the pages.
Especially the ending was exactly as if he had written it himself.
Ottilie said nothing, but she was looking into his eyes with the
greatest satisfaction. Eduard raised his arms. 'You love me!' he
cried. 'Ottilie, you love me!' And they held one another in a
tight embrace. It would not have been possible to say who first
seized hold of the other.

Thereupon Eduard's world was turned around: he was no longer what he had been, the world no longer what it had been. They stood before one another, he held her hands, they looked into one another's eyes, they were about to embrace again.

Charlotte came in with the Captain. When they apologized for staying out so long Eduard gave a secret smile. 'You are back far too soon,' he said to himself.

They sat down to supper. The day's visitors were discussed. Eduard, excited and full of love, spoke well of everyone, always considerately, often approvingly. Charlotte, not quite of his opinion, noticed this mood and teased him for being so mild and indulgent, since usually when company left his comments on them were very harsh.

Passionately and with heartfelt conviction Eduard cried: 'Only love one person utterly and all the others will seem lovable too.' Ottilie cast down her eyes and Charlotte stared into the distance.

The Captain spoke. 'It is somewhat the same with feelings of respect and reverence,' he said. 'You learn to recognize what is of value in the world only by finding one fit object for such sentiments.'

Charlotte withdrew to her bedroom as soon as she could, and gave herself up to the memory of what had happened that evening between her and the Captain.

When Eduard, springing ashore and pushing off the boat, had thus himself given over his wife and his friend to the unsteady element, Charlotte saw the man on whose account she had already suffered so much in secret now sitting before her in the twilight and with two oars propelling the craft anywhere he liked. She felt a deep melancholy, such as she had rarely felt before. The circuiting boat, the splashing of the oars, a chill breath of wind over the surface, the sighing of the reeds, the last flights of birds, the glimpses and the glimpsed reflections of the first stars: there was something ghostly about it all in the general stillness. It seemed to her that her friend was taking her far away, to expose her, to leave her alone. In her heart she was strangely agitated, and she could not weep.

The Captain meanwhile was explaining to her what form the new projects ought to take, in his view. He was full of praise for the boat, which could be rowed and steered easily by one person with the two oars. She would learn herself, it was a pleasure sometimes to be moving on the water all alone and to be one's own ferryman and helmsman.

At these words his friend was afflicted by the thought of their coming separation. 'Is he saying that on purpose?' she asked herself. 'Does he know? Does he suspect? Or did he mean nothing by it and was he foretelling my fate unawares?' She was seized by a great sadness, an impatience; she asked him to land just as soon as he could and go back to the Hall with her.

It was the first time the Captain had rowed over the ponds, and although he had made a general survey of the depths there were still particular places he was not familiar with. Darkness was coming on, he directed his course towards where he supposed there might be an easy place to disembark and where he knew it was not far to the path which led to the Hall. But from this course he was somewhat distracted when Charlotte, in a sort of fearfulness, again expressed the wish to be ashore. He redoubled his exertions and was approaching the bank, but unfortunately found himself halted whilst still at a little distance from it; he had run aground, and his efforts to get free again were in vain. What was to be done? He had no choice but to climb into the water, which was shallow enough, and carry his friend to the shore. Glad of his burden he crossed safely, being strong enough not to stagger or give her any cause for alarm, but still she had wound her arms fearfully round his neck. He held her tight and pressed her against him. Not until they had reached a grassy slope did he put her down, and not without agitation and confusion. She still hung on his neck; he took her into his arms again and kissed her, with intensity, on the mouth—but lay a second later at her feet, pressed her hands to his lips, and cried: 'Charlotte, will you forgive me?'

The kiss which her friend had dared to give her and which she had almost given him in return brought Charlotte to her senses. She pressed his hand but did not raise him. Bending down to him and laying a hand on his shoulder she cried: 'We cannot prevent this moment from marking an epoch in our lives; but whether it be one worthy of us, that we can still decide. You must leave, my dear friend, and you will leave. The

Count is making arrangements to advance you, which is a cause of joy to me and also of grief. I wanted to say nothing about it, until it was certain; but now the moment obliges me to reveal my secret. I can forgive you and forgive myself only if we have the courage to alter our situation, since it is not within our power to alter our feelings.' She raised him up, took his arm to support herself, and they returned to the Hall in silence.

But now she stood in her bedroom where she was bound to feel and think of herself as Eduard's wife. Help in this contradictory state came to her from her character which, already much tested, was sound. Accustomed always to being self-aware and to having control over herself, now too she did not find it difficult, by force of earnest consideration, to approach the desired equilibrium; indeed, she could not help smiling at herself when she thought of the strange visit Eduard had paid her in the night. But at once she was seized by a curious apprehension, a joyous and anxious trembling, which resolved itself into a woman's most sacred hopes and longings. She was moved to kneel and repeat the vows she had made to Eduard at the altar. Friendship, affection, and renunciation passed before her in serene images. She felt herself inwardly restored. Soon a sweet tiredness came over her, and peacefully she slept.

CHAPTER THIRTEEN

Eduard, for his part, was in a quite different mood. He was so little disposed to sleep that it did not even occur to him to undress. A thousand times he kissed the copy of the document, the beginning in Ottilie's childish and diffident hand; he hardly dared kiss the ending since the writing looked so much like his own. 'If only it were a different document!' he said to himself; but even so it was the loveliest assurance that what he most desired was fulfilled. And would it not remain in his hands and for ever and ever be pressed to his heart, even after a stranger's signature had defaced it?

The waning moon came up over the woods. The warm air drew him out of doors; he went here and there, he was the most restless and the happiest of mortal men. He walked through the gardens, they were too confining; he ran into the fields, there the space was too great. He was drawn back to the Hall; he found himself under Ottilie's windows. He sat down on the terrace, on a flight of steps. 'Now walls and locks and bolts keep us apart,' he said to himself, 'but our hearts are not kept apart. If she were here she would fall into my arms and I into hers, and what do I need beyond that certainty?' There was quietness all about him, not a breath of wind; so quiet he could hear the burrowing of busy creatures under the earth where night and day are alike. He gave himself up entirely to his dreams of happiness, fell asleep at last, and when he woke the sun was already rising with a splendid aspect and getting the better of the early mists.

He found he was the first awake on his property. His workers seemed to him late arriving. When they came they seemed to him too few and the work planned for the day was too little for his wishes. He wanted more workers, they were promised and taken on in the course of the day. But even then he thought the numbers insufficient to get his intentions carried out quickly. The work gave him no pleasure any more; he wanted everything finished, and for whom? He wanted the paths laid so that Ottilie could walk on them in comfort, and seats already in place so that Ottilie could sit and rest. And at the new house too he did what he could to hasten things along: he wanted the roof on by Ottilie's birthday. Neither in his feelings nor in his actions was there any measure. Knowing that he loved and was loved drove Eduard into boundlessness. How changed in their appearance were all the rooms and all his surroundings! He no longer knew where he was in his own home. Ottilie's presence consumed everything; he was entirely absorbed in her, no other consideration occurred to him, his conscience uttered not a word; everything in his nature which had been restrained broke loose, his whole being streamed towards Ottilie.

The Captain observed this passionate activity and wished he might prevent its unhappy consequences. The works being thus one-sidedly and excessively hastened along were based, as he had intended them, on a model of tranquil and amicable co-existence. He had effected the sale of the farmstead, the first payment had been received, Charlotte, as agreed, had added it to her funds. But in the very first week she was obliged to practise and encourage sobriety, patience, and orderliness even more than usual; for in all the haste the money set aside would not go far.

Much had been begun and much remained to be done. How could he leave Charlotte in that situation? They conferred, and agreed they would rather speed up the schedule of work themselves, borrow money for that purpose, and pay it back as the instalments still due on the sale of the farm came in. By ceding the franchise this could be done almost without loss; their hands would be untied, and since everything was now under way and there were enough workmen, they would get more done at one time and so bring matters to a successful conclusion quickly. Eduard was happy with the arrangement since it accorded with his own intentions.

In her innermost heart, meanwhile, Charlotte was abiding by what she had thought and decided for herself, and her friend, in a manly fashion, gave her his support, being of one mind with her. But this only increased their intimacy. They exchanged their views on the subject of Eduard's passion; they exchanged advice. Charlotte drew Ottilie closer, kept a stricter watch over her, and the more she got to know her own heart the deeper she was able to see into the girl's. It seemed to her there was no help but to send the child away.

She now thought it a happy chance that Luciane had received such outstandingly good reports at school; for her great aunt, having been informed, now wished her to move into her house once and for all, to have her company and to take her into society. Ottilie could go back to the boarding-school; the Captain would leave, his future assured; and everything would be as it was a few months previously—indeed, even better than it was. Charlotte hoped she would quickly restore her own relationship with Eduard, and in her thinking she arrived at such a rational settlement of everything that she became more and more confirmed in the illusion that a return to an earlier and more restricted condition would be possible, that a thing now violently released could be brought back into confinement.

Eduard meanwhile was acutely aware of the obstacles being placed in his way. He soon noticed that he and Ottilie were being kept apart, that it was being made difficult for him to speak to her alone or even to be near her except in company; and feeling exasperated by this he began to feel the same about other things too. When he did manage to snatch a word with her it was not only to assure her of his love but also to complain about his wife and about the Captain. He had no sense that by his haste in the business he was himself on the way to exhausting their funds; he was bitterly critical of Charlotte and the Captain, saying they were acting against the original agreement; but he had himself accepted the second agreement and had indeed occasioned it and made it necessary.

Hatred is partisan, but love even more so. Ottilie too began to be somewhat estranged from Charlotte and the Captain. When on one occasion Eduard was complaining about the latter, saying that as a friend, and their circumstances being what they were, he was not acting entirely honestly, Ottilie made a thoughtless reply: 'He has displeased me before now by not being entirely honest with you. I once heard him say to Charlotte: "I do wish Eduard would not subject us to his flute-playing. He will never get any better at it, and it is tiresome to have to listen to it." You can imagine how much that hurt me, since I love accompanying you.'

She had no sooner said this than her spirit whispered to her that she ought to have kept silent; but too late. Eduard's expression changed. He had never been so angered; he was assailed in his dearest ambitions; without in the least overestimating himself he did have an innocent desire to do well. And what amused him and gave him pleasure should surely be treated considerately by his friends. He did not think how frightful it is for others to have their ears tormented by a mediocre talent. He was insulted, furious, beyond ever forgiving. He felt himself absolved from all responsibilities.

The need to be with Ottilie, to see her, to whisper something to her, to confide in her, grew daily. He decided to write to her and to ask her to begin a secret correspondence with him. The scrap of paper on which, not wasting any words, he had done this was lying on his desk and blew off in a draught as his valet entered to curl his hair. To test the heat of the tongs the man was used to picking up scraps of paper from the floor; on this occasion he picked up the note, twisted it swiftly, and it was scorched. Seeing what had happened Eduard snatched the paper out of his hand. Soon afterwards he sat down to write it again; the words did not come quite so easily the second time. He had doubts, anxieties, which he overcame, however. He pressed the note into Ottilie's hand when next he was able to approach her.

Ottilie's reply came without delay. Eduard put the note, unread, into his waistcoat which, fashionably short, did not retain it very well. It slipped out and fell to the floor without his noticing. Charlotte saw it and picked it up, glanced at it, and handed it to him. 'Here is something you have written,' she said, 'which you would perhaps be sorry to lose.'

He was shaken. 'Is she acting?' he wondered. 'Does she know what is in the note or is she misled by the similarity of the handwriting?' He hoped and believed it was the latter. He was warned, doubly warned, but these strange accidental signs by means of which a higher power seems to be speaking to us were unintelligible to his passion; indeed, as his passion led him on it irked him more and more to be held, as he thought deliberately, under constraint. Their companionableness was vanishing. His heart had closed, and when he was obliged to be together with his friend or with his wife he could not discover and reanimate the old affection for them in his bosom. In silence reproaching himself for this, as he was bound to, only made him uncomfortable, and he had recourse to a sort of gaiety which, being without love, was also without any of his usual grace.

Her own deep feeling helped Charlotte through these trials. She harboured the earnest intention to renounce her affections, beautiful and noble though they were.

It was her heartfelt wish to be able to help Eduard and Ottilie too. She saw very well that separation alone would not be sufficient to cure such an ill. She resolved to discuss the matter openly with the child; but could not, the memory of her own moment of weakness stood in her way. She tried to express herself generally on the subject; but generalities fitted her own state too, which she was shy of uttering. Every hint she might give Ottilie pointed back into her own heart. She wanted to warn, and felt that she herself might still be in need of warning.

So she continued to keep the lovers apart and to say nothing, but by that the situation was not improved. Gentle insinuations, which escaped her occasionally, had no effect on Ottilie since Eduard had persuaded her of Charlotte's affection for the Captain and that Charlotte herself desired a divorce which he was now intending to bring about, in a decent fashion.

Ottilie, borne along by the feeling of her own innocence, heading towards the happiness she most desired, lived only for Eduard. Strengthened in everything good by her love for him, more joyful, on his account, in everything she did, more open to others, she found herself in a heaven on earth.

So all in their different fashions pursued their daily lives, thoughtfully or not; everything seemed to be following its usual course, as is the way in monstrously strange circumstances when everything is at stake: we go on with our lives as though nothing were the matter.

CHAPTER FOURTEEN

In the meantime a letter had arrived for the Captain from the Count. Two letters really: one to make public, which opened up very fine prospects but for some time in the future; and another which contained a definite offer for the present, an important position at Court and as an administrator, the rank of major, a handsome salary, and other advantages, but which because of various contingent circumstances was to be kept secret still. Accordingly, the Captain told his friends about his future prospects and concealed from them what was so imminent.

He went on with his present business very actively, and in secret made arrangements so that everything should proceed unhindered once he was gone. It suited him too, now that a date should be fixed for things to be finished, that Ottilie's birthday was hastening things along. Without there being any express understanding between them the two friends were once again glad to be working together. Eduard was delighted that by raising money in advance their resources had been strengthened; the whole undertaking was advancing rapidly.

In the Captain's view they ought not now to have gone ahead with making the three ponds into a lake. The lowest dam would need fortifying, the two middle ones removing; it was a considerable and somewhat dubious undertaking, in more ways than one. But both tasks, which could of course be connected, had already been begun, and in them they were glad of a certain young architect, a former pupil of the Captain's, who, by hiring competent artisans and by whenever possible allocating the different jobs himself, was making good progress in a work that looked solid and likely to last; which secretly delighted the Captain, for his own withdrawal would thus not be felt. On principle he would never quit any business he had taken on and had not finished until he was sure he had been adequately replaced. Indeed, he despised men who make their own departures felt by first creating confusion where they are employed and who, in their gross self-importance, seek to undo whatever they themselves will no longer be engaged in.

Thus there was constant hard work towards the celebration of Ottilie's birthday, without anyone saying so, or even to themselves fully admitting it. As Charlotte saw things—which was not with any jealousy—the celebration should not be of too emphatic a kind. Given her youth, her fortune, her relationship to the family, it would not be right for Ottilie to seem too much the queen of the day. And Eduard would not have it discussed, since everything was to arise as if of itself, and give surprise and be delightful in a natural way.

Tacitly then, they all came to agree upon a pretext: the day should be for the roofing of the new house, without mention of anything else, and for that occasion it could be announced to friends and to the local people that there would be a celebration.

But Eduard's affections were boundless. Desiring to possess Ottilie, he was just as immoderate in the giving of himself and of presents and promises. For some of the gifts with which he wanted to honour Ottilie on the day Charlotte made proposals that were far too poor. He spoke with his valet who saw to his wardrobe and was constantly in dealings with tradespeople and people from the fashion houses. The valet, knowledgeable not only about the nicest things to give but also about how best to give them, at once placed an order in town for an extremely attractive box: covered in red morocco, studded with steel nails, and filled with presents that were worthy of such a vessel.

And he suggested something else to Eduard. There were a few fireworks, which no one had ever bothered to let off. These could be added to and improved. Eduard seized on the idea, and the valet undertook to see it carried out. It was to remain a secret.

The Captain, meanwhile, as the day approached, had made his arrangements for proper order, arrangements which he deemed very necessary when large numbers of people were invited or attracted to one location. And he had gone to some trouble to prevent begging and other things which are a nuisance and detract from the charm of a festive occasion.

But Eduard, together with his accomplice in the matter, busied himself principally with the fireworks. They were to be let off at the middle pond, in front of the great oak trees; on the opposite bank, under the plane trees, the spectators would foregather and at a proper distance, in comfort and safety, would see the show reflected in the water and floating and burning on the surface itself.

Accordingly, under another pretext, Eduard had the undergrowth, grass, and moss removed from the space beneath the plane trees, and when this was done and the ground was clear it became apparent just how splendidly the trees had grown, how tall they were and how broad. Eduard was overjoyed. 'It was about this time of year when I planted them,' he said to himself. 'How long ago would that be?' As soon as he got home he looked through the old diaries which his father, especially when in the country, had kept very conscientiously. There could be no mention of Eduard's having planted the trees, but another important domestic event on the same day which he still remembered was bound to have been noted. He leafed through a few volumes, found the particular circumstance, then to his amazement, to his delight, he noticed a most marvellous coincidence. The day and the year when the trees were planted was also the day and the year when Ottilie was born.

CHAPTER FIFTEEN

At last the day Eduard had longed for dawned, and guests began
to arrive, a great number, for invitations had been sent out far
and wide and some who had not been at the laying of the
foundation stone and had heard so many delightful things about
it were all the more eager not to miss this second occasion.

Before lunch the carpenters appeared in the courtyard, making music and bearing numerous hoops of greenery and flowers
all piled unsteadily in one abundant crown. They recited a
greeting and requested, as was the custom, silk scarves and
ribbons from the ladies, for decoration. Whilst lunch was in
progress they went on their way in a jovial procession, and
having halted in the village for a while, there too relieving the
women and girls of a good number of ribbons, they came at last,
accompanied and expected by a large crowd, on to the ridge
where the new house stood, roofed.

After lunch Charlotte held the company back somewhat. She
did not want there to be any ceremonious and formal procession, and so people made their way to the site in a leisurely
fashion, in their different groups, without attention to rank and
order. Charlotte lingered with Ottilie, which rather made
matters worse; for since Ottilie was actually the last to arrive it
seemed as if the fanfare and the drums had only waited for her,
as if the commencement of the celebrations were signalled by
her arrival.

To soften the appearance of the house it had been decorated,
according to the Captain's tasteful directions, with greenery
and flowers; but unknown to him Eduard had got the Architect
to inscribe the date, in flowers, on the cornice. To that there
could perhaps be no objection; but the Captain arrived just in
time to prevent Ottilie's name appearing in floral splendour on
the space below. He found a tactful way of putting a stop to
this and of removing from view those letters which had already
been made up.

The pole of flowers had been set in place and was visible for
miles around. Its scarves and ribbons fluttered gaily, and a

short speech went away with the wind, largely unheard. The ceremony was at an end, and now the dancing was to begin on the space before the house which had been levelled and set around with greenery. A smart young carpenter came forward with a girl to be Eduard's partner, and himself invited Ottilie, who was at Eduard's side. The two pairs at once had others following them, and before long Eduard swapped his nimble peasant girl for Ottilie and danced the round with her. The younger among Eduard's and Charlotte's guests joined cheerfully with the local people in the dancing whilst the older ones watched.

Then, before the company dispersed along different walks, it was agreed they would reassemble at sunset under the plane trees. Eduard was there first, made all the arrangements, and conferred with his valet who, across the water, together with the firework-maker, was to have charge of the spectacle.

When the Captain saw what provision had been made he was not best pleased; he wished to speak with Eduard about the crush of spectators that must be expected, but Eduard begged him, somewhat abruptly, to leave this part of the festivities in his sole care.

The people had already pressed forward on to the dams whose upper surfaces, which had been scoured clean of their grass, were uneven and unsafe. The sun went down, it was twilight, and whilst they were waiting for it to be darker the guests under the plane trees were served with refreshments. They thought the place incomparably fine and took pleasure in imagining the view from there across a wide lake with such variety around it.

A quiet evening, not a breath of wind, for the nocturnal festivity conditions promised to be ideal; but suddenly there was a terrible uproar. Large clods of earth had come loose from the dam, several people were seen falling into the water. The ground had given way under the pressing and stamping of an ever-increasing crowd. Everyone wanted the best place, and now nobody could advance or retreat.

The company leapt up and ran to the spot, but more to see what was happening than to do anything about it. And what *could* they do when no one could get through? Together with a few others equally determined, the Captain hurried over and at once drove the crowd down off the dam on to the banks so that the rescuers hauling the people out of the water should not be hindered. Soon all, by their own or others' exertions, were on dry land again, all but one, a boy whose panic-stricken efforts, instead of bringing him nearer the dam, had carried him further away. He seemed at the end of his strength, only now and then a hand or a foot lifted above the surface. Unhappily, the rowing boat was on the far side, laden with fireworks, it could only be unloaded slowly, help was a long time coming. Then the Captain made up his mind, he threw off his outer garments, all eyes were upon him, and his solid and powerful form filled everyone with confidence; but a cry of amazement rose out of the crowd when he dived into the water. He was watched all the way, and soon, being a strong swimmer, he had reached the boy and brought him, but dead as it seemed, to the dam.

Meanwhile the boat had been rowed across, the Captain climbed in and enquired very closely among all those present whether indeed everyone was saved. The Surgeon arrived and took charge of the boy believed dead; Charlotte approached, she begged the Captain to look after himself, to go back to the Hall and change his clothes. But he lingered, until people whose judgement could be trusted, who had been close witnesses of events and had themselves been among the rescuers, gave him the most solemn assurances that everyone was safe.

Charlotte watched him set off for the Hall; it occurred to her that the wine and the tea and whatever else might be needed were locked away, and that in such situations people often do not manage things properly; she hurried through the guests who, after the distraction, were still under the plane trees. Eduard was busy persuading them all to stay; he was about to give the signal, the fireworks would begin. Charlotte approached and begged him to postpone an entertainment that was no longer appropriate, that in the present moment could not be enjoyed. They must consider the child, she said, and the man who rescued him. 'The Surgeon will do his duty', Eduard replied. 'He has everything he needs, if we press around him we shall only be in his way.'

Charlotte insisted, and motioned to Ottilie who at once made ready to leave. Eduard seized her hand and cried: 'We will not end our day in a hospital. She is wasted as a nurse. The seeming dead will revive without our help and the living will dry off.'

Charlotte said nothing, and left. Some followed her, others followed Eduard and Ottilie; in the end nobody wanted to be last and they all followed Charlotte. Eduard and Ottilie found themselves alone under the plane trees. He insisted on staying, though she begged him urgently and fearfully to return to the Hall with her. 'No, Ottilie', he cried. 'Extraordinary things do not come to pass in smooth and usual ways. This evening's extraordinary event brings us together sooner. You are mine. I have said it and sworn it so often already, and that is enough of saying it and swearing it. Now let it happen.'

The boat had come over from the other side. It was the valet, who asked in some embarrassment what was to happen now about the fireworks. 'Let them off', Eduard shouted across to him. 'You were the one they were intended for, Ottilie, you alone, and now you will be the only one to watch them. Let me sit at your side and enjoy them with you.' He was gentle, diffident, and sat down by her without touching her.

Rockets lifted off in a rush, crackers banged, Roman candles ascended, fiery serpents twisted and burst, sprays of sparks came off the Catherine wheels, and all were single first, then paired, then all together and ever more violently coming after and together. Eduard, inflamed, watched the fiery spectacle in a lively contentment. But to Ottilie's gentle and agitated spirit this constant creation and disappearance in noise and flashing light was more alarming than pleasant. She leaned timidly against Eduard, and this greater closeness, this trust, filled him with the feeling that now she was completely his.

Darkness had scarcely resumed its proper sovereignty when the moon rose and lit up the paths for the pair as they returned. A figure, hat in hand, barred their way and begged them for alms, since on that festive day he had not had his due. The moon shone into his face, and Eduard recognized the beggar who had importuned him previously. But in his great happiness now he could not be indignant, and he forgot that

on that day more than ever begging was especially frowned
upon. He did not search his pockets long, and gave a gold coin.
He would have liked to make everyone happy, his own happiness seemed so boundless.

At the Hall meanwhile everything had ended well. The
Surgeon's ministrations, the fact that all they needed was to
hand, Charlotte's assistance, everything worked together and
the boy was returned to life. The guests dispersed, either to see
something of the fireworks from a distance, or, after such mixed
events, to return to the peace and quiet of their own homes.

The Captain too, quickly changing his clothes, had taken an
active part in all the work of welfare; now there was peace of
mind and he found himself alone with Charlotte. Gently he let
her know that he would soon be leaving. She had experienced
so much in the course of the evening that this revelation had
little effect upon her; she had seen how her friend had offered
the sacrifice of himself, how he had saved a life, and that his
own life was safe. These wondrous events seemed to her to
presage a significant future, but not an unhappy one.

Eduard, entering with Ottilie, was likewise informed of the
Captain's imminent departure. He suspected that Charlotte
must have known for some time, but was far too preoccupied
with himself and his own plans to have any sense of grievance.

On the contrary, he listened attentively and contentedly
to the account of the advantageous and prestigious position
which the Captain would occupy. His own secret wishes hurried, without restraint, ahead of events. Already he saw Charlotte united with the Captain and himself with Ottilie. On that
festive day he could not have been given a better present.

But Ottilie's astonishment was great when she went to her
room and found the marvellous box on the table. She opened
it at once. The things inside were all so beautifully packed and
arranged that she shrank from taking any out, and scarcely
lifted them. Muslins, cambrics, silks, shawls, and lace-work outdid one another in their delicacy, prettiness, and costliness. And
there was jewellery too. She understood the thought behind it
all: to dress her from head to foot, and more than once; but
everything was so costly and exotic that she could not bring
herself to think of it as hers.

CHAPTER SIXTEEN

Next morning the Captain was gone. He left behind him a heartfelt and grateful letter to his friends. He and Charlotte had said their poor, tongue-tied farewells the night before. She felt the separation to be final, and accepted it; for in the Count's second letter, which finally the Captain had shown her, there was mention of the prospect of an advantageous marriage as well; and although he himself paid no attention to this point, she thought it a certainty and renounced him utterly.

But now she felt justified in demanding of others what she had demanded of herself. Since she had not found it impossible others ought to find it possible too. In this belief she broached the subject with her husband, and did so openly and confidently, feeling that the matter must now be settled once and for all.

'Our friend has left us,' she said, 'you and I are as we were, and might return now completely to our former condition, if we wished.'

Eduard, who heard nothing except what favoured his passion, thought Charlotte must be referring to the time before their marriage and, in a rather indirect manner, be raising hopes of a divorce. Therefore he answered, with a smile: 'Why not? All it needs is that we come to an agreement.'

He was then grievously disappointed when Charlotte replied: 'And it also rests with us to change Ottilie's circumstances. We have a double opportunity of providing for her in a way which will be desirable. She can go back to the boarding-school, since my daughter has now moved to her great aunt's; or she can have a place in a very respectable household and share with an only daughter there all the advantages of an appropriate upbringing.'

'But by now', Eduard replied with some composure, 'Ottilie has been so spoilt among friends here that any other company will hardly be welcome to her.'

'We have all been spoilt,' said Charlotte, 'and you not least. But now the time has come for us to be sensible and to give serious thought to what will be best for all the members of our little circle, and not to refuse to make sacrifices.'

'I certainly do not think it right', said Eduard, 'that Ottilie should be sacrificed, which would be the case if at the present moment we thrust her down among strangers. The Captain was visited by good fortune whilst he was here; we can say goodbye to him with quiet minds and even with some satisfaction. But who knows what lies in store for Ottilie? Why the hurry?'

'What lies in store for us is obvious', Charlotte replied in some agitation, and since she was determined to speak her mind once and for all she continued: 'You love Ottilie, you are growing accustomed to her. Affection and passion have been engendered and are thriving on her side too. Why not say outright what every hour of the day admits and confesses to us? Shall we not at least have the foresight to ask ourselves how it will end?'

'Though one cannot make any immediate reply to that,' said Eduard, taking a hold on himself, 'this much can be said: that we should first of all decide to wait and see what the future will teach us if we cannot at the moment already tell how a thing may turn out.'

'But in our case', Charlotte replied, 'no great prescience is needed to see how things will turn out, and this much, at the very least, can be said here and now: that we are both too old to go wandering blindly where we either do not want to or ought not to go. We are our own responsibility, nobody else's; we must ourselves be friends and mentors to ourselves. Nobody is asking us to ruin our lives, nor to expose ourselves to censure and, very likely, ridicule.'

'But can you blame me,' said Eduard, unable to match the clear, pure language of his wife, 'can you reproach me for having Ottilie's happiness at heart? And I do not mean some future happiness—that can never be counted on—but her happiness now. Imagine it honestly and allow yourself no illusions: Ottilie wrenched from our company and answerable to strangers—to ask her to suffer such an alteration would take more cruelty than I, at least, feel myself capable of.'

Charlotte could see very well that behind his pretence her husband was resolute. Only now did she feel how far he had moved away from her. In some agitation she exclaimed: 'Can Ottilie be happy if she causes our separation? If she robs me of a husband and his children of their father?'

'I should have thought our children were provided for', said Eduard smiling coldly; but he added then in rather friendlier tones: 'Besides, it is surely premature to think of going to such extremes.'

'Passion goes to extremes immediately', Charlotte remarked. 'Do not refuse the good advice and the help I am offering us both. Soon it will be too late. In a dark time the one who sees clearest must be the one to act and help. I am that one on this occasion. My dear, my dearest Eduard, do as I ask. Surely you cannot expect me to give up my hard-won happiness, the rights I treasure most, and you—and all without demur?'

'Who said any such thing?' Eduard replied in some embarrassment.

'You did,' said Charlotte. 'By wanting to keep Ottilie with us are you not agreeing to everything that will surely come of it? I have no wish to insist, but if you are not able to overcome your inclinations at least you will have to stop deceiving yourself.'

Eduard felt the truth of what she said. Words uttered are a terrible thing when they suddenly express what the heart has already long since permitted itself; and only in order to gain a moment's respite Eduard replied: 'I am still not quite clear what it is you intend.'

'My intention was', said Charlotte, 'to discuss the two proposals with you. There is much good in each. The school would suit Ottilie best, if I consider how the child is at present. But the larger and wider situation promises more if I consider what she must become.' Thereupon she gave her husband a detailed account of the two situations, and concluded with the words: 'I would myself prefer the lady's house to the boarding-school, and for several reasons, but especially because I do not wish to increase the affection, indeed the passion, of the young man whose heart Ottilie won when she was there.'

Eduard let it seem that he agreed with her, but only to buy time. Charlotte, determined to do something that would be decisive, at once seized the opportunity, since Eduard made no immediate objection, to settle it that Ottilie's departure, for which in secret she had already made all the preparations, should take place in a day or so.

Eduard shuddered, he thought himself betrayed and his wife's affectionate language calculated, contrived, and shaped to separate him from his happiness for ever. It seemed he was leaving the matter all to her; but inwardly his own decision had already been taken. To win at least a breathing-space, to prevent the imminent and incalculable disaster of Ottilie's removal, he decided to leave home himself, and not without Charlotte's knowledge either; but in the way he put it to her she was led to think that he did not wish to be present at Ottilie's departure, indeed that thenceforth he did not wish to see her again. Charlotte, believing herself victorious, did everything to help. He ordered the horses, gave his valet the necessary instructions, what he should pack and how he should follow on, and then, at the very last moment, he sat down and wrote.

Eduard to Charlotte

'The misfortune which has befallen us, my dear, may be able to be remedied or not, but I know this much: that if I am not here and now to succumb to despair I must find a respite for me and for us all. Since I am sacrificing myself I can make demands. I am leaving my house and will only come back when the prospects are more favourable and more peaceable. Be the owner of it meanwhile, but with Ottilie. I want to live in the knowledge that she is with you and not among strangers. Look after her, treat her as you used to, as you always have, and more lovingly still, be kinder and gentler. I promise I shall not seek to have any secret dealings with Ottilie. Let me be rather for a while in complete ignorance of your lives; I shall think the best. Think of me likewise, you and she. There is only one thing: I beg and beseech you not to make any attempt to send Ottilie to live anywhere else or to change her situation. Outside the sphere of your house and grounds, in the care of strangers, she belongs to me and I will have possession of her. But if you honour my affections, my wishes, my grief, if you flatter my illusions and my hopes, I will not resist the remedy should it be offered me.'

These last phrases came from his pen, not from his heart. Indeed, seeing the words on the page he began to weep bitterly. Was he then in some way to give up the happiness, or misery, of loving Ottilie? Now he began to realize what he was doing. He was going away, without knowing what would result. For the time being at least he was not to see her; could he feel at all certain of ever seeing her again? But the letter was written, the horses were waiting; at any moment he risked catching sight of Ottilie and having his resolution instantly destroyed. He took hold of himself, thought that after all he could come back whenever he liked and that from a distance he might actually approach more closely to the satisfaction of his wishes. And he contemplated the alternative: that if he stayed Ottilie would be driven from the house. He sealed the letter, ran down the steps, and mounted his horse.

Riding by the inn he saw the beggar to whom he had given so generously the night before. The man was sitting in the garden, at ease, eating a midday meal. He got to his feet and bowed respectfully, indeed reverentially to Eduard. This figure had stood in Eduard's way when he was walking with Ottilie on his arm only the night before, and grieved him now by reminding him of the happiest hour of his life. His suffering grew, the sense of what he was leaving behind became unbearable; he looked again in the direction of the beggar. 'Oh, I envy you!' he cried. 'You are still nourished by yesterday's alms, but yesterday's happiness no longer nourishes me.'

CHAPTER SEVENTEEN

Ottilie went to the window, having heard somebody ride away, and caught a last glimpse of Eduard. She thought it strange that he should leave the house without seeing her and without wishing her good-day. She grew anxious and ever-more puzzled when Charlotte took her for a long walk and spoke of many things but never—and it seemed deliberate—mentioned her husband. She was doubly surprised then on their return to find the table only set for two.

Things we are used to, small in themselves perhaps, are never easy to do without, but we suffer real pain at their absence only when the occasion itself is significant. Eduard and the Captain were missing, for the first time in months Charlotte had arranged the table herself, and it seemed to Ottilie that she had been deposed. The two women sat opposite one another; Charlotte spoke quite openly of the Captain's new appointment and of the small hope they had of seeing him again in the near future. Ottilie's only comfort in her situation was to be able to suppose that Eduard had ridden after his friend to go with him a part of the way.

But when they rose from table they saw Eduard's travelling carriage under the window, and when Charlotte asked rather crossly who had ordered it there she was told it was the valet who still had things to collect. It took all of Ottilie's self-control to conceal her astonishment and her pain.

The valet entered with further requests. He wanted his master's tankard, a few silver spoons, and some other items, which seemed to Ottilie to indicate a long journey and a lengthy absence. Charlotte rebuked him for asking: she did not understand what he meant, surely all his master's things were in his, the valet's, keeping. The valet, whose sole interest was of course to speak with Ottilie and for that reason under whatever pretext to lure her from the room, excused himself adroitly and repeated his requests, which Ottilie wished to grant him; but Charlotte refused, he was obliged to withdraw, and the carriage rattled away.

It was a terrible moment for Ottilie. She did not understand or comprehend, but that Eduard had been taken away from her for a lengthy period, that much she could feel. Charlotte sensed what her condition was, and left her alone. We dare not describe her pain, her tears. She suffered boundlessly. All she asked was that God would help her through the day; she survived that day and the night, and when she found herself again it seemed to her a meeting with a different person.

She was neither composed nor resigned, but after so great a loss she still had her being, and now there were other things to be afraid of. Her first anxiety, as soon as she began to think again, was that she might be sent away herself, now that the men were gone. She never guessed that Eduard by his threats had seen to it that she would remain at Charlotte's side; but Charlotte's own behaviour reassured her somewhat. She kept the child busy and only rarely and unwillingly let her out of sight; and although she was well aware that words can do very little against a determined passion, still she knew the power of calm reflection and so made a point of discussing things with Ottilie.

Thus it was a great comfort for Ottilie when one day Charlotte, very conscious of the import of her words, made the following judicious observation: 'People whose passions have got them into difficulties will always be grateful if we, by our calmness, can help them free again. Let us engage ourselves joyfully and cheerfully in the things the men have left unfinished; that way we can best look forward to their return, by preserving and furthering through our moderation those things which their tempestuous and impatient natures threatened to destroy.'

'Since you are speaking of moderation, my dear aunt,' said Ottilie in reply, 'I will admit that what at once occurs to me is how immoderate men are, and especially in relation to wine. It has often saddened and distressed me to watch good sense, intelligence, consideration for others, charming and amiable manners being lost for hours at a time, and instead of all the good that a talented man can do or permit, to see catastrophe and confusion threatening. And how often it results in rash decisions!'

Charlotte agreed with her, but did not continue the conversation since she was well aware that once again Ottilie was only thinking of Eduard, who if not habitually at least more often than might be wished would raise the degree of his pleasure, his talkativeness, and his practical energies by drinking wine.

When Charlotte made her remarks the men, and especially Eduard, were able to approach again in Ottilie's thoughts, and so it was all the more remarkable to her when Charlotte spoke of a marriage the Captain was about to enter into as of something well known and definite, for this made everything look very different from how she had envisaged it on the basis of Eduard's earlier assurances. These things caused Ottilie to pay ever-more attention to Charlotte's every utterance, every hint, every act, every step. Ottilie had grown astute, sharp, suspicious, without knowing it.

Charlotte meanwhile, having looked hard at all the details of her circumstances, addressed herself to them in her usual decisive and orderly manner, and insisted on Ottilie's constant participation too. Though she did not stint, she drew her household tightly in again; and now, all things considered, she viewed the passionate events as a sort of happy chance. For as things were going they might easily have got beyond all limits; and their agreeably fortunate and comfortable situation, had they not come to their senses in time, might, by living life at too rapid a rate, have been if not destroyed at least severely shaken.

She did not interrupt the work already begun in the grounds. On the contrary, she pushed ahead with whatever had to be ready as a basis for future development, but that was all. Her husband, when he came home, must find enough that would keep him pleasantly occupied.

In these works and projects the Architect's way of proceeding seemed to her beyond praise. Soon the lake stretched out before her eyes and the newly created shores were grassed over or beautified by all manner of planting. All the rough work on the new house was finished off and everything necessary for its preservation seen to; then she made a halt at a point where it would be a pleasure to begin again. In so doing she was cheerful and tranquil. Ottilie only seemed it, for she saw in all things only signs as to whether Eduard was expected soon or not. In all things nothing interested her except this consideration.

Thus she welcomed an arrangement by which the local boys were enrolled to keep the gardens tidy, for these had become extensive. It was an idea Eduard himself had entertained. The boys were fitted out with a sort of cheerful livery which they put on in the evenings after a thorough cleansing of their persons. This wardrobe was kept at the Hall; the most sensible and meticulous boy had been given charge of it; the whole exercise was directed by the Architect, and very soon all the boys had acquired a certain dexterity. Their training showed off well, they performed their duties in something of a military manner. Certainly, when they arrived with their scrapers, billhooks, rakes, little spades, mattocks, and fan-shaped brooms, others coming after with baskets to carry away the weeds and stones, or dragging the enormous iron roller, they made a pretty and heart-warming procession in which the Architect noted a charming sequence of poses and activities for the frieze of a summer-house, whereas Ottilie saw only a sort of parade in it which would soon be welcoming home the returning lord.

This gave her the heart and the desire to welcome him with something similar. Efforts had been made already to encourage the village girls in sewing, knitting, spinning, and other female tasks. These virtues too had increased with the promotion of cleanliness and a pretty appearance in the village. Ottilie was always involved, but in a rather casual fashion, as the occasion arose and as her mood dictated. Now she resolved to pursue it more thoroughly and consequentially. But girls cannot be marshalled into a company as boys can. She followed her instincts, and without being quite explicit about it she sought to do nothing more than inculcate upon every girl an attachment to home, to parents and brothers and sisters.

She was successful with many. But about one lively little girl there were constant complaints that she lacked all address and would do nothing whatsoever in the house. Ottilie could not be unsympathetic to the child since she was especially friendly towards Ottilie herself. She came up and walked with her and ran alongside whenever Ottilie allowed it. On those occasions she was busy, cheerful, and tireless. The child seemed to need to be attached to a beautiful mistress. At first Ottilie tolerated her company; then grew fond of her; finally they became inseparable, and Nanni went with her mistress everywhere.

Often Ottilie made her way to the garden; it gladdened her heart to see everything coming on so beautifully. The soft fruits and the cherries were finishing, though on the last of them Nanni feasted with particular relish. As he looked to the fruit that would be ready in such abundance in the autumn the Gardener was constantly put in mind of his master, and never without wishing him home. Ottilie loved listening to the old man. He was perfect in his job, and never ceased speaking of Eduard when she was there.

When Ottilie said how pleased she was that the grafting done in the spring had taken so well, the Gardener expressed some concern: 'I sincerely hope that his Lordship will not be disappointed. If he were here this autumn he would see what delicious kinds there are still in the old garden from his father's day. Fruit-growers nowadays are not so reliable as the Carthusians* used to be. The names in the catalogues sound honest enough, of course. But you graft and bring them on, and finally when they fruit it is not worth having such trees in the garden.'

But again and again, almost as often as he saw her, the faithful old servant asked Ottilie about his master's return and when it would be. And when Ottilie could not tell him, though he said nothing Ottilie could see it distressed him and that he believed she would not confide in him, and it pained her to have her ignorance thus forcibly brought home. But still she could not keep away from these beds and borders. Seeds they had in part and plants they had entirely put in the ground together were now in full bloom and scarcely needed any more tending except by Nanni, always ready with her watering-can. How feelingly Ottilie contemplated the later flowers now just showing! Their brightness and abundance were to have been the glory of Eduard's birthday and the expression of her affection and her gratitude; and though sometimes she still promised herself that she would see the day celebrated, her hope was not always equally vigorous. Doubts and anxieties were forever whispering around the poor girl's soul.

Nor was it likely that any real and frank understanding would again be established with Charlotte. For of course the situations of the two women were very different. If everything remained as it had been, if they returned again into the way of lawful life, then Charlotte's present happiness increased and the prospect of a happy future opened before her; Ottilie, on the other hand, lost everything. And it is right to say everything: for it was in Eduard that she had first found life and joy, and in her present condition she felt an infinite emptiness such as she had scarcely had any inkling of before. For a heart that is searching will of course feel a lack; but a heart that has suffered a loss feels deprived. Longing is transformed into discontent and impatience, and a woman's spirit, used to waiting upon an outcome, inclines her now to step outside her normal sphere, to be active and enterprising and to do something for her happiness herself.

Ottilie had not given Eduard up. And how could she, even though Charlotte, shrewdly enough, despite her own conviction to the contrary, pretended she had and that it was understood and had been decided that between her husband and Ottilie a friendly and tranquil relationship was possible. But how often at nights, having locked herself in, Ottilie knelt before the open box and looked at her birthday presents, not one of which she had used or cut or made up. And how often the poor girl hurried at sunrise from the house in which previously she had found all her happiness into the open air, into places she had used not to like. She was not even content remaining on dry land. She jumped into the boat and rowed herself out into the middle of the lake, then took up a travel book, let the waves of the agitated surface rock her, read, dreamed herself into foreign lands, and always found her friend there. All along she had remained close to his heart, and he to hers.

CHAPTER EIGHTEEN

We have already made the acquaintance of Mittler. It was only to be expected that he, always so curiously busy, hearing of the misfortune which had befallen his friends (though none of them had as yet sent to him for help), should be disposed to prove and practise his friendship and his skill in their case too. But it seemed to him advisable that first he should wait a while; for he knew only too well that in confusions of a moral kind educated people are harder to assist than uneducated. Accordingly, he left them to themselves for a time; but in the end could not bear it any longer, and hastened to visit Eduard, having already discovered his whereabouts.

The way led him to a pleasant valley over whose sweet green floor, through meadows and many trees, the abundant waters of an ever-lively stream meandered or rushed. Fertile fields and plentiful orchards stretched away over the gentle slopes. There was space between the villages, the whole scene had a peaceful character, and the particular parts, if not especially suitable for painting, seemed so for life itself.

His eyes lit finally on a well-kept farmstead with a clean and simple dwelling-house surrounded by gardens. He supposed this to be Eduard's present home, and he was not mistaken.

We can say this much about our solitary friend: that in his privacy he had abandoned himself wholly to his passion and was making many plans and nourishing many hopes. He could not deny that he wished to see Ottilie here, that he wished to bring her, to lure her here, and there were other things besides, permissible and impermissible, that he let his thoughts entertain. Then his imagination reeled among the possibilities. If he was not to possess her here, rightfully possess her, then he would make over to her the possession of the property. Here she should live quietly for herself and be independent; she should be happy and, whenever he let his imagination torment him further, then perhaps be happy with another man.

So his days passed in a perpetual veering between hope and pain, between tears and cheerfulness, between plans, preparations, and despair. He was not surprised to see Mittler. He had been expecting his arrival for quite some time, and was thus even half glad of it. Against him, if he came as Charlotte's emissary, he had already devised a variety of prevarications, excuses, and, to follow them, some more-decisive proposals; but if he brought news of Ottilie Mittler was as welcome as a messenger from heaven.

He was cross, therefore, and aggrieved when he learned that Mittler had not come from home but of his own accord. Eduard's heart closed against him and the conversation could not get under way. But Mittler knew very well that a mind preoccupied with love has an urgent need to speak and be disburdened before a friend of what is happening within, and he was for that reason willing, after a few exchanges, to relinquish his usual role on this occasion and play the confidant instead of the go-between.

Having then censured Eduard, in a friendly fashion, for the solitariness of his life, he was given this reply: 'Oh, I do not know how I might spend my time more agreeably! I am always preoccupied with her, always close to her. I have the inestimable advantage of being able to imagine where Ottilie is, where she walks, where she stands, where she takes her rest. I see her before me doing what she usually does, always busying herself and always, it is true, with things that please me best. But I go further than this, for how can I be happy away from her? I fall to imagining how Ottilie might come to me. I write tender loving letters in her name to myself; I answer her, and keep the pages in one place together. I have promised not to make a move in her direction, and I will keep my promise. But what binds her, that she should not turn to me? Has Charlotte perhaps been so cruel as to require her to promise and swear that she will not write to me and will not give me any news of herself? That would be natural and likely, yet I find it outrageous and unbearable. If she loves me, as I believe she does, as I know she does, why will she not resolve, why does she not dare to flee and throw herself into my arms? She ought to, I sometimes think, she could do. When there is some movement in the hall I look towards the door. I think and hope it might be her about to enter. Oh, and since what is possible is impossible I imagine the impossible must be possible. At night when I wake and the lamp casts an unsteady light over the room I think her shape, her ghost, a sense of her must come flitting by and approach and take hold of me if only for a moment, so that I should have a sort of assurance that she is thinking of me and is mine.

'One joy remains. When I was near her I never dreamed of her; but now at a distance we are together in dreams, and, strangely enough, since I have made the acquaintance of other attractive women in the neighbourhood it is now that her image appears to me in dreams, as if to say: "Look where you like. You will not find anyone more beautiful or fitter to be loved than I am." And thus her image enters all my dreams. Everything that happens to me with her gets confused and transposed. We might be signing a contract: her hand is there and so is mine, her name and mine, they erase one another, they intertwine. Nor are these blissful tricks of the imagination without pain. Sometimes she does something which offends against the pure idea I have of her; and then indeed I feel how much I love her for I become distressed beyond all expression. Sometimes she teases me quite against her nature and torments me; but then at once her image changes, her beautiful, round, heavenly little face is elongated—she is someone else. But still I am tormented, unsatisfied, and broken into pieces.

'Don't smile, my dear Mittler. Or smile if you like. Oh, I am not ashamed of this devotion, or call it a foolish and raging passion if you will. No, I have never been in love, only now am I discovering what it means. Everything in my life to date has been only a prelude, a postponement, only passing the time, wasting time, until I got to know her, until I loved her and wholly and really loved her. It has been said against me—if not to my face then certainly behind my back—that I am an amateur, that I have no particular talent for anything. That may be so, but only because I had not found the thing I can excel at. Now show me the man whose talent for loving exceeds mine.

'Admittedly, it is a talent full of misery, and rich in pain and tears; but I find it so natural to me, so peculiarly mine, that I am not likely ever to give it up.'

Doubtless this vivid and heartfelt utterance had afforded Eduard some relief; but now also and all at once every single detail of his strange situation had become clear to him, the painful contradictions overwhelmed him, and he began to weep and did so unrestrainedly, for he had been made weak by his confidences.

Mittler, not able to go against his own hasty temperament and implacable good sense and less than ever likely to since he saw himself deflected from the purpose of his journey by Eduard's painful and passionate outpourings, now frankly and emphatically expressed his disapproval. Eduard, he said, should pull himself together, should consider what his standing as a man required of him, should bear in mind that what does most honour to a human being is that he keep a grip on himself in misfortune and suffer pain with equanimity and decorum, so as to be highly esteemed, honoured, and set up as a model.

Upset as he was and riven by feelings of the most painful kind, these words were bound to seem hollow and worthless to Eduard. 'Easy for a comfortable and contented man to talk like that,' he cried, 'but he would be ashamed if he knew how he grates on a man who is suffering. We are supposed to be infinite in our patience, but people set in their comfortable ways will not acknowledge that there might be such a thing as infinite torment too. There are cases, indeed there are, in which solace is despicable and the only honourable course is to despair. The noble poets of Greece, who knew how to depict heroes, did not at all mind letting them weep when they were in the grip of pain. "Tears are a sign of goodness in a man,"* they used to say. I will not live with people whose hearts are stony and whose eyes are dry! I curse those who are happy and who want the unhappy man for a spectacle or not at all. To have their approval he must conduct himself nobly even in the cruellest physical and mental tribulation; and for their applause at his death he must die before their eyes with a proper decency, like a gladiator. My dear Mittler, I am grateful for your visit; but you would do me a great favour now if you would take a stroll in the garden and round about. Come back later. Meanwhile I shall seek to compose myself and to be more like you.'

But Mittler softened, preferring not to break off a conversation which it might be hard to start up again. Nor was Eduard averse to going on, since their talk was in any case heading towards its natural end.

'All this thinking about it and discussing it will do no good,' said Eduard, 'but at least in speaking I have for the first time realized and for the first time definitely felt what I ought to do and what I am now determined to do. I see my present and my future life before me. My only options are misery or delight. Bring about a divorce, my dear fellow. That is what is needed, and it has already happened. Get me Charlotte's consent. I shan't go into why I believe it to be obtainable. Go and see her, there's a good fellow, ease all our minds, make us happy.'

Mittler was taken aback. Eduard continued: 'My fate cannot be separated from Ottilie's, and we are not destined to perish. See this glass. Our initials are cut in it. A man full of joy in an act of celebration flung it into the air so that no one else should ever drink out of it. It was to have shattered on the stony ground, but it was caught before it fell. Now I have bought it back at a high price and I drink from it daily and daily confirm myself in the belief that relationships fate has decided are indestructible.'

'Woe is me!' cried Mittler. 'What a deal of patience one has to have with one's friends! Now of all things I am up against superstition—which I have always detested as the most pernicious interferer in human affairs. We play around with prophecies, presentiments, and dreams, to lend some significance to our everyday lives. But when life itself becomes significant and when everything about us is in commotion those phantoms only make the tempests all the more terrible.'

'But in the uncertainty of life,' Eduard cried, 'leave a heart struggling between hope and fear at least some sort of guiding star that it can look to, even if not steer by.'

'I should be glad to,' Mittler replied, 'if there were any hope of consistency in it; but I have always found that nobody takes any notice of warning signs; only the flattering and promising ones receive attention, and only in them do people have any faith.'

Since Mittler saw himself being led now even into the regions of darkness, where he felt more and more uncomfortable the longer he stayed, he agreed with a rather greater readiness to do as Eduard was urging him to do, and visit Charlotte. For what further arguments could he bring against Eduard at present? What he could still do, as he saw it, was gain time and find out how things stood with the women.

He hurried to Charlotte, and found her, as ever, composed and cheerful. She gladly informed him of all that had happened, for Eduard's words had only enabled him to grasp the effects. He advanced from his own side cautiously, but could not bring himself to utter the word 'divorce' even in passing. How great then were his surprise, astonishment, and—in accordance with his views—delight when Charlotte, after so much that was disagreeable, went on to say: 'I cannot but believe, cannot but hope that all will be well, that Eduard will come back again. How can it be otherwise, since I am expecting a child?'

'Do I hear aright?' Mittler exclaimed.

'Indeed you do,' Charlotte replied.

'A thousand blessings on this piece of news!' he cried, clapping his hands. 'I know the power of this argument on a man's mind. How many marriages have I not seen it hasten, strengthen, restore! Hope such as you now have is worth any number of words. Truly, it is the best hope in the world. But,' he went on, 'for my own part I should have every reason to feel aggrieved. I see very well that this particular case does nothing for my self-esteem. My efforts will not earn me any thanks from you. I am rather like that doctor, a friend of mine, who was always successful in curing the poor, for wages in heaven, but rarely cured a rich man who would have paid him well. It is fortunate that this present matter will resolve itself, for my exertions and my speeches would have done no good.'

Charlotte now asked him to convey the news to Eduard, take a letter from her, and see what was to be done and set in train. But Mittler declined. 'There is nothing more to do!' he cried. 'Write your letter. Any messenger will serve as well as I. For I must be off now to where I am needed more. I shan't come again, except to congratulate you. I shall come to the christening.'

On this occasion, as often before, Charlotte was displeased with Mittler. Being quick, he did some good, but his hastiness caused some failures too. Nobody was more dependent on opinions arrived at very rapidly in advance.

Charlotte's messenger came to Eduard, and was received by him half in fright. The decision in the letter could just as well be no as yes. For a long time he did not dare open it. He was dumbfounded when he read it. By the following passage, with which the letter ended, he was as if turned to stone:

'Think of that night when you came like an adventurous lover to visit your wife and drew her irresistibly and took her as a mistress, as a bride, into your arms. Let us honour in this strange chance a disposition of Heaven by which there will be a new bond in our relationship just as our life's happiness threatens to come asunder and disappear.'

It would be hard to describe what happened in Eduard's soul after that moment. In such a press of feelings old habits and old inclinations finally come to the fore again, to kill time and to fill life up with something. Hunting and war are one such recourse a nobleman always has at his disposal. Eduard longed for some external danger to balance the inner one. He longed to go under, for his existence was threatening to become unbearable; indeed, he found solace in the thought that he would no longer exist and might thereby make his friends and loved ones happy. Nobody put any obstacle in the way of his desire, since he kept his decision secret. In all proper form he drew up his will. It was a sweet feeling being able to leave his present dwelling-place to Ottilie. Charlotte, the unborn child, the Captain, the servants, were all provided for. His plans were helped by a renewal of the war. His youthful soldiering, being of a trivial kind, had irritated him greatly, and he had left the service for that reason. Now it was a splendid feeling to follow a general of whom he could say to himself: under his leadership death is probable and victory certain.

Ottilie, once Charlotte's secret was known to her too, being shocked as Eduard had been, and even more so, withdrew into herself. She had nothing more to say. She could not hope, nor was wishing allowed her. But her diary gives us an insight into her inner life, and we have in mind to disclose some items from it.

PART TWO

CHAPTER ONE

It often happens in ordinary life as in an epic poem (where we admire it as poetic artifice) that when the principal characters withdraw, remove themselves from view, become inactive, at once some second or third and until then scarcely noticed person takes their place and, by the entire engagement of himself, like them seems worthy of our attention, sympathetic interest, and even our approval and our praise.

Thus day by day after the departure of the Captain and of Eduard, the Architect became more important. So many matters depended on him entirely for their organization and execution. He was exact, sensible, and energetic in carrying out his duties; assisted the ladies in a variety of ways and kept them entertained when their quiet lives grew tedious. His very appearance was of a kind to inspire trust and kindle affection. He was a youth in the full sense of the word, a fine figure, slim, if anything a little too tall, modest without being timid, eager to confide but never importunate. He would gladly take on any responsibility and go to any trouble, and having a very good head for figures he had soon understood all the management of the household and his helpful influence extended everywhere. It was usually left to him to receive visitors, and if they arrived unexpectedly he either succeeded in putting them off or, at the very least, so prepared the women that no inconvenience resulted.

Among those giving him a good deal of trouble was a young lawyer sent one day by a gentleman of the neighbourhood to discuss a matter which, though of no very great significance, nevertheless touched Charlotte closely. We are obliged to consider this incident because it gave an impetus to various things which might otherwise have lain dormant for a long time.

The reader will remember the changes Charlotte had made in the churchyard. All the memorial stones had been removed from their places and set along the wall and along the plinth of the church. The space thus vacated had been levelled. Apart from one broad path which led to the church and past it to a little gate on the far side, everywhere else had been sown with different kinds of clover, now beautifully verdant and flowering. New graves were to be dug in a certain order starting from the far corner, but the site afterwards was always to be levelled and sown in the same manner. Nobody could deny that by this arrangement churchgoers on Sundays and holy days were afforded a prospect that was both cheerful and in keeping. Even the parson, though advanced in years and attached to the old ways and at first not especially happy with what had been done, was now delighted to sit like Philemon with his Baucis* under the old lime trees at his back door and see before him not the bumpy graves but a fine colourful carpet, which moreover would be of benefit to his household since Charlotte had granted the parsonage sole use of the piece of land.

But notwithstanding all this several parishioners had earlier expressed their disapproval of the fact that the place where their ancestors lay buried was now no longer marked and that the memory of them was thereby, as it were, extinguished; for though the well-preserved headstones showed who was buried they did not show where, and where was what really mattered in the view of many.

Precisely that view was taken by a local family who, several years before, had reserved a portion of this general resting-place for their own members and had made a small endowment to the church in exchange. Now the young lawyer had been sent to cancel the endowment and to announce that the payments would be discontinued because the conditions under which they had so far been made had been unilaterally set aside and all representations and objections ignored. Charlotte, the author of the change, wished to speak to the young man herself. Forcefully, yet without undue vehemence, he set out his own and his client's arguments, and in doing so gave those present much to think about.

'We see', he said after a short preamble in which he explained to their satisfaction why he had intruded upon them, 'we see the meanest and the highest much concerned to mark the place where their dear ones lie. The poorest farm labourer, burying his child, finds some kind of comfort in setting a frail wooden cross on the grave and adorning it with a wreath to keep the memory alive at least as long as his sorrow lasts, even though such a mark, like grief itself, is annulled by time. The better-off turn such crosses into iron ones, strengthen and protect them in a variety of ways, and several years might be the length of their survival. But since these too sink down in time and become unnoticeable the landed families think it supremely important to raise a stone that may be counted on to last for several generations and can be renewed and refurbished by their descendants. But it is not the stone itself we are drawn to, but what is contained beneath it, what nearby has been committed to the earth. It is not just a matter of remembrance, but of the person too, and not of memory so much as of presence. I can more easily and intimately approach a departed loved one in a grave than in a memorial stone, for the stone itself is of little importance. But around it, as around a milestone, husbands and wives, relatives and friends should still foregather, even after death, and the living must have the right to turn away strangers and ill-wishers and keep them at a distance from their own loved ones who are at rest.

'Thus I think it entirely just that my client should revoke the endowment; and it is moreover a very moderate response, for his family has been offended in a way for which no compensation is imaginable. They must forego the bitter-sweet satisfaction of paying their respects to their beloved dead and also the hope and comfort of one day resting with them side by side.'

'The matter is not so important', Charlotte replied, 'that we need upset ourselves by going to law over it. I so little regret what I have done that I will gladly compensate the church for its losses. But I must tell you frankly that your arguments have not convinced me. The pure sense of a final and general equality, at least after death, seems to me of more solace than this selfish and stubborn continuation of our personalities, allegiances, and material circumstances. And what is your view?' she asked, turning to the Architect.

'In such a dispute', he replied, 'I should prefer neither to take part nor to have the casting vote. But let me in all modesty say what touches me most, in my way of seeing things, as an artist. Since we are no longer so fortunate as to be able to hold in our arms the remains of our loved ones in a funerary vase; since we are neither rich enough nor serene enough to preserve them unspoilt in large and ornate sarcophagi; since even in the churches there is no longer room for us and our kith and kin, but we are turned out of doors—we all have reason to approve of the procedure your Ladyship has introduced. If the members of a parish lie side by side in rows then they are indeed lying next to and among their own; and if the earth is one day to receive us all I can think of nothing more natural and cleanly than that the mounds accidentally created and gradually subsiding should be levelled at once so that the coverlet, borne by all, shall be made to rest lightly on all.'

'And must it all pass without any sign of remembrance?' Ottilie asked. 'With nothing that will aid our memory?'

'By no means!' the Architect continued. 'We are not being asked to give up remembrance, only the particular place. It is the dearest wish of every architect and sculptor that people should turn to him, to his art, to work of his hands, for some perpetuation of their lives; which is why I should like to see well-thought-out and well-executed monuments, and not strewn around singly and casually but set up in one place where they can expect to last. Since nowadays even the saintly and the mighty no longer insist on lying in person in the churches, let us at least, either there or in beautiful buildings near the places of burial, set up monuments and memorial inscriptions. There are a thousand forms they might be given and a thousand ways of ornamenting them.'

'If artists are as well off as you say,' Charlotte replied, 'why is it all we ever get from them are urns and petty obelisks and broken columns? Instead of the thousand good ideas you were boasting of I have only ever seen a thousand repetitions.'

'That may be so in these parts,' the Architect answered, 'but not everywhere. And then good ideas and their proper application are altogether a difficult matter. Especially in this case it is hard to counter the seriousness of the subject, and in treating what is distressing to avoid merely causing distress. As far as sketches for all kinds of monument are concerned, I have a large collection and will show you them when you like; but the finest memorial is always the person's own image. Better than anything else this gives an idea of what he was; it provides the best text to his life's greater or lesser quantity of music; but it needs to be done when he is at his best, and normally it isn't. Nobody thinks of preserving living forms, or when they do it happens in an unsatisfactory way. They take a quick cast of the dead man's face, set the resulting mask on a block of stone, and call it a bust of him. Only very rarely is the artist able to bring such a thing wholly back to life again.'

'Perhaps without knowing it or intending it', said Charlotte, 'you have turned this conversation entirely to my advantage. The likeness of a person is surely an independent thing; wherever it stands, it stands for itself and we shall not require it to designate the actual place of burial. But, to be honest, I have a strange sort of antipathy even towards such images, for they seem always to be silently reproaching me; they point towards something distant and departed, and remind me how difficult it is properly to honour the present. If we think how many people we have seen and known, and admit how little we have been to them and how little they to us, what a strange feeling that is! We meet a witty man and have no conversation with him, a learned man and learn nothing from him, a well-travelled man and find nothing out, and one full of love and do nothing that would have pleased him.

'And this happens, unfortunately, not just with those who are passing through. Societies and families behave in this way towards their dearest members, cities towards their worthiest citizens, peoples towards their finest princes, nations towards their most outstanding men and women.

'I have heard it asked why we speak so unreservedly well of the dead but of the living always with a certain caution. And the answer was: because from the dead we have nothing to fear, whereas the living may still cross us. Of such impurity is our concern for the memory of others; it is mostly only selfish and unserious. But nothing is more serious than that we keep our dealings with the living always active and alive.'

CHAPTER TWO

Stirred by this encounter and by the ensuing conversations, they went next day to the burial-ground and the Architect made several happy suggestions as to how it might be beautified and rendered more cheerful. Thereafter his concern extended to the church itself, a building which from the start had attracted his attention.

The church had stood for several centuries; it was a thoroughly German work, well proportioned and pleasingly ornamented. There was good reason to believe that the man who had built a nearby monastery had proved his worth here too, with insight and affection, on this smaller building. Its effect was earnest and agreeable still, even though the conversion of the interior to suit the Protestant form of worship had deprived it of some of its quiet and majesty.

The Architect easily begged a little money from Charlotte, to restore both the outside and the interior of the church in the early style and bring the whole into harmony with the field of resurrection in which it stood. He was very skilled himself, and some of the workers still building the new house could of course be kept on until this pious work too was completed.

They were now exploring the building itself with all its surroundings and outbuildings when, to the great astonishment and delight of the Architect, they came upon a small and hitherto almost unnoticed side chapel whose proportions were even more subtle, even lighter, and whose ornamentation was even more pleasing and conscientious. It also contained several carved and painted remnants of the older form of worship, when the different festivals had been marked by different images and implements and celebrated each in its special way.

The Architect could not resist at once including the chapel in his plans. This small space should be restored particularly as a memorial of earlier times and of their taste. He saw how he would like the empty surfaces decorated, and looked forward

to using his talents as a painter; but for the time being he kept
this a secret from the others.

First of all he did as he had promised and showed the women
the various copies and sketches he had made of ancient
funerary monuments, urns, and related things, and when the
conversation turned to the simpler burial mounds of the
northern peoples he produced his collection of weapons and
implements which had been found in them. He had everything
together very neatly and portably in drawers and compartments on trays fitted into these and lined with cloth, so that the
ancient and solemn objects seemed in his handling of them
almost modish, it was a pleasure to look at them, like looking
into little trinket boxes at a milliner's. And once he had got into
the way of showing things, since their solitude required some
entertainment, he appeared before them every evening with a
part of his treasures. They were mostly of German origin: tiny
one-sided and weightier coins, seals, and other things of that
kind. These all directed the imagination to earlier times, and
when he illustrated his discourses with the beginnings of
printing, with woodcuts and the first engravings, and since one
might say that the church too, day by day, in the same spirit,
in its colours and other decoration, was growing towards the
past, they almost began to wonder whether they were living in
the modern age at all, and whether their dwelling now among
quite different customs, habits, modes of life, and convictions
were not merely a dream.

After such preparation, a larger portfolio which he produced
last had the best effect of all. True, it contained for the most
part only line drawings of figures which, however, having been
traced from the pictures themselves, had retained their ancient
character entirely, and how this charmed the company when
they saw! A perfect purity of existence gazed out from all the
figures; there was an undeniable goodness, if not nobility, in
them all. Joyous composure, willing acknowledgement of something above us worthy of reverence, a quiet giving of the self in
love and expectation were expressed in every face and every
gesture. The old man with the bald crown, the curly-headed
boy, the cheerful youth, the earnest adult, the transfigured
saint, the hovering angel, all seem blessed in a state of innocent

sufficiency, in a pious waiting. The most commonplace occurrence had in it a trace of heavenly life, and every character there seemed meant for an act of worship.

Most no doubt gaze at such a region as at a vanished golden age, a lost paradise. Perhaps only Ottilie could feel herself to be among her own kind there.

Who then could have refused the Architect when he offered to decorate the panels of the chapel ceiling after the prompting of these archetypal images, and in so doing to make a definite memorial of himself in a place where he had been so happy? He expounded on this with some wistfulness. He could see that as things stood he would not be able to stay for ever in such perfect company; indeed, that he might have to depart before very long.

These days, though not rich in events, did offer many occasions for serious conversation. We shall therefore take this opportunity to communicate something of what Ottilie noted down from them, and can think of no better transition than a comparison forcefully suggested to us by a reading of her charming pages.

We have heard of a peculiar custom in the English navy. All the ropes, however strong or weak, on all of His Majesty's ships, are woven in such a way that a red thread goes through the whole length and cannot be extracted from it without undoing it all, and by this thread even the smallest pieces are recognizable as belonging to the Crown.

In the same way there runs through Ottilie's diary a thread of love and devotion which unites everything and characterizes the whole. Thus the remarks, observations, the quoted maxims and whatever else may appear all become quite peculiarly the writer's own and significant for her. Every single item here selected and communicated constitutes a most decided proof of that.

From Ottilie's Diary

'To be at rest one day with those we love is the sweetest thing we can imagine if ever we let our thoughts go beyond this life. "To be gathered to one's people" is such a warm expression.

'By various kinds of reminder and memorial our distant and departed ones may be brought a little nearer. None is so important as a portrait. There is something oddly pleasurable in talking with a beloved portrait, even if it is not a good likeness, just as there is sometimes in quarrelling with a friend. In an enjoyable way we feel our separateness and yet we cannot part.

'We sometimes converse with a person who is present as though with a portrait. He does not need to speak, or look at us, or concern himself with us; we see him, we feel our relationship with him, indeed our relations with him may even develop, without his doing anything about it, without his feeling anything of it, but relating to us merely as a portrait would.

'We are never content with portraits of people we know. For that reason I have always felt sorry for portrait painters. We rarely ask the impossible of anyone, but of them we do. They are required to get everybody's relationship with the subject, everybody's affection or dislike, into the picture; and not merely represent their own view of a person but what everybody else's might be too. I do not wonder if such artists gradually close up and become indifferent and wilful. This would be of no consequence except that it costs us the likenesses of many well-loved people.

'It must be agreed that the Architect's collection of weapons and ancient utensils, which were buried along with the body under great mounds of earth and slabs of stone, is proof of how futile is the provision human beings make for the preservation of their personalities after death. And how paradoxical we are! The Architect admits that he has himself opened such ancestral tombs and continues nevertheless to concern himself with memorials for posterity.

'But why take it so strictly? Is everything we do done for eternity? Do we not dress in the morning only to undress in the evening? Do we not leave on journeys only to return? And why should we not wish to be beside our loved ones even if only for a century?

'When we see the many gravestones sinking down or being worn away by the feet of churchgoers, and even churches themselves fallen in on their memorial stones, still life after death may seem a sort of second life into which we enter as a picture with its caption and dwell there longer than in our real and living lives. But then that picture too, that second existence, fades sooner or later. As over people, so over their monuments, Time maintains its rights.'

CHAPTER THREE

It is such an agreeable feeling to be busy with something one is only half-competent to do that nobody should criticize the dilettante for taking up an art he will never learn, or blame the artist who leaves the territory of his own art for the pleasure of trying himself in a neighbouring one.

This seems an appropriate way of viewing how the Architect proceeded to paint the chapel. The colours were ready, measurements taken, cartoons done; he had given up any claim to originality; he stuck to his tracings; his sole endeavour was to dispose the seated and the hovering figures in the best manner and tastefully decorate the space with them.

The scaffolding was in place, the work advanced, and once something the eyes could appreciate had already been achieved he was content that Charlotte should visit him with Ottilie. The living faces of the angels, the lively drapery on the background of a blue heaven delighted the eye, their tranquil and pious natures called on the soul to collect itself, and a very tender effect was brought about.

The women had climbed up to join him on the scaffolding, and no sooner had Ottilie seen how measuredly and easily the work was going forward than all she had earlier received through teaching at once seemed to grow in her and she took a brush and paint and, being directed what to do, put in the numerous folds of a robe with as much neatness as skill.

Charlotte, who was always glad to see Ottilie in any way occupied and distracted, left the pair to it, and went off to follow her own thoughts and work through for herself all the reflections and concerns which she could not communicate to anyone else.

When ordinary people are agitated and made anxious by everyday inconveniences they may extract a smile of sympathy from us; but we look with reverence at a personality in which the seed of a large fate has been sown and which must wait upon the future growth of this conception and is not permitted and is not able to hasten the good or the ill, the happiness or the unhappiness, destined to come forth from it.

Through Charlotte's messenger, sent to him in his solitude, Eduard had replied in a friendly and sympathetic manner, but with more composure and seriousness than intimacy and love. Shortly afterwards he had vanished, and his wife could get no news of him until at last she came across his name in the newspapers, where he was mentioned with honour among those who had distinguished themselves in an important military engagement. Now she knew which way he had taken, she learned he had escaped from grave dangers; but she realized at once that he would seek out even graver ones, and it was all too clear to her that, in every sense, he would be hard to hold back from a final extreme. In her solitary thinking she dwelled constantly upon these cares, and might turn them any way she liked but no perspective gave her any comfort.

Ottilie, suspecting nothing of all this, had meanwhile taken a very great liking to her new work and easily obtained Charlotte's permission to continue with it regularly. Now they made rapid progress and the azure heavens were soon populated with fit inhabitants. Through sustained practice Ottilie and the Architect attained to a greater freedom in the last pictures; they grew markedly better. The faces too, which were left to the Architect to paint, gradually began to manifest a quite peculiar quality: they all began to look like Ottilie. The presence of the beautiful child must doubtless have made such a lively impression upon the soul of the young man, who had no preconceptions as to faces, either from art or life, that gradually in passing from the eye to the hand nothing was lost, indeed by the finish both worked wholly in harmony. Enough, one of the last faces succeeded perfectly so that it seemed as if Ottilie herself were looking down out of the heavenly regions.

The ceiling was finished; it had been intended simply to leave the walls and only go over them with a lighter brownish colour and pick out the delicate columns and the ornamental carvings in something darker. But, as always happens, one thing led to another and it was decided to have festoons of fruit and flowers as well which would, so to speak, join heaven and earth together. Here Ottilie was wholly in her element. The gardens provided her with the loveliest patterns, and although the garlands were very richly done, the work was completed earlier than expected.

Still everything looked untidy and unfinished. The scaffolding lay in confusion, the planks thrown down anyhow, and the uneven floor was further disfigured by splashes of paint. The Architect begged a week's grace, during which time the ladies were not to enter the chapel. At length then, on a beautiful evening, he asked them both to make their way there; but wished to be excused from accompanying them, and at once took his leave.

'Whatever surprise he may have prepared for us', said Charlotte when he had gone, 'I am really not in the mood for it at present. Go by yourself, will you, and tell me about it. He is certain to have done something we shall be pleased with. I shall enjoy it first in your account, then gladly in reality afterwards.'

Ottilie, who knew that in many respects Charlotte was protecting herself, avoiding any emotional excitement and above all any surprises, at once set off alone, and could not help looking out for the Architect, who was, however, nowhere to be seen and had perhaps concealed himself. She went into the church, which she found open. The work here had been finished some time before, and the place cleaned and opened for services again. She approached the door of the chapel. It was heavy, set with bronze, but it opened easily on a sight which, being unexpected in a familiar place, astonished her.

Through the single high window a solemn radiance entered, a beautiful fusion of different colours of glass. This lent the whole an unfamiliar air and produced a quite peculiar mood. The beauty of the vaulted ceiling and the walls was enhanced by an attractive floor of specially shaped tiles laid in a pleasing pattern on a screed of plaster. The Architect had ordered these in secret, as well as the little panes of coloured glass, and was able to put everything together very quickly. Places to sit had been provided too. Several beautifully carved choir-stalls had been found among the antiquities of the church and set around the walls in a tasteful manner.

Ottilie was delighted by the familiar parts now appearing before her as an unfamiliar whole. She stood, walked to and fro, looked and looked again; finally she sat down in one of the stalls, and it seemed to her, as she looked up and around, as though she existed and did not exist, as though she had feelings and had none, as though everything might vanish before her eyes or she herself might vanish even as she looked; and only when the sun went from the window, which until then it had illuminated very brilliantly, did Ottilie wake and come back to herself, and hurry away to the Hall.

She felt how strangely this event had fallen. It was the evening before Eduard's birthday. Needless to say, she had hoped to celebrate the day in quite another fashion. Was not everything to have been decorated for the occasion? But the whole abundance of autumn flowers was still unplucked. There were the sunflowers still, turning towards heaven, and the asters looking ahead with quiet and modest faces; and what had at all been made into garlands had served as patterns to decorate a place which, if it were not to remain an artist's whim, if it were ever to have a proper use, only seemed fit to be their common burial place.

Then she could not help thinking of the noise and bustle with which Eduard had celebrated her birthday, and of the newly roofed house and the great amity they had looked forward to in it. And she seemed to see with her very eyes, hear with her very ears, the fireworks going off again, and imagined them more and more the lonelier she became; but only felt herself to be yet more alone. She could no longer take his arm and had no hope of ever finding support in him again.

From Ottilie's Diary

'I must note down something the young artist said: "Artists and artisans both demonstrate with perfect clarity that a person is least able to appropriate for himself those things which are most peculiarly his. His works leave him as birds do the nest in which they were hatched."

'In this respect an architect's fate is the strangest of all. How often he employs his whole intellect and warmth of feeling in the creation of rooms from which he must exclude himself. Royal halls owe their splendour to him, and he may not share in the enjoyment of their finest effects. In temples he draws a line between himself and the holy of holies; the steps he built to ceremonies that lift up the heart, he may no longer climb; just as the goldsmith worships only from afar the monstrance he wrought in the fire and set with jewels. With the keys of the palace the architect hands over all its comforts to the wealthy man, and has not the least part in them. Surely in this way art must little by little grow away from the artist, if the work, like a child provided for, no longer reaches back to touch its father. And how much better off art was in the days when it had to do almost only with what was public, with what belonged to everyone and thus to the artist too.

'One idea the ancient peoples had is very solemn and may seem terrifying. They imagined their ancestors sitting on thrones, in a circle, in a vast cave, conversing without words. For a new arrival, if he merited it, they rose, and welcomed him with a bow. Yesterday when I was sitting in the chapel, and opposite my carved seat there were several others set around, that idea seemed to me very sympathetic and pleasing. "Why can you not remain seated," I said to myself, "seated in silence in an inward contemplation, for a long long time, until the friends arrived for whom you would rise and show them to their places with a friendly bow?" The stained-glass window turns the daylight to a solemn twilight, and someone ought to donate a sanctuary lamp so that the night would not be entirely dark either.

'Whatever we do, we always conceive of ourselves as seeing. I think we only dream so as not to cease seeing. It might well be that one day the inner light will break forth from us so that we shall no longer have need of any other.

'The year is dying away. The wind passes over the stubble and there is nothing for it to seize and shake; only the red berries on those slender trees seem to wish to remind us of something more cheerful, just as the beat of the thresher wakes in us the thought that in the corn that has fallen to the sickle much life and nourishment lies hidden.'

CHAPTER FOUR

After such events, after such a bringing-home to her of the transience and rapid passing of things, how strangely must Ottilie have been affected by the news, which could no longer be kept from her, that Eduard had put his life under the fickle sway of war. She thought then, alas, all the things that in her situation she had reason to think. Fortunately a human being can comprehend only a certain degree of unhappiness; anything beyond it destroys him or leaves him cold. There are situations in which fear and hope become one and the same, cancel one another out, and lose themselves in a dark insensateness. How else could we know the people we love best to be in continual danger and yet go on with our daily lives as usual?

Thus it looked like an intervention of Ottilie's guardian angel when, suddenly into the quiet in which, being lonely and unoccupied, she seemed about to founder, a tumultuous host was fetched, which by engaging her outwardly as much as could be and by bringing her out of herself, at the same time awoke in her a feeling of her own strength.

Charlotte's daughter Luciane had scarcely left her school and made her entry into society and surrounded herself in her aunt's house with a numerous company, than her wish to please was gratified and a very wealthy young man soon felt a passionate desire to possess her. His considerable fortune gave him a right to call the best of everything his own and he seemed to want nothing but a perfect wife whom the world could envy him as they envied him everything else.

This family matter had already caused Charlotte a good deal of work, all her thoughts and her correspondence were given over to it, except when they were directed towards seeking more news of Eduard; with the result that latterly Ottilie had been left more to herself than usual. She was aware that Luciane was expected and had accordingly made what domestic provision was most necessary; but the visit was not thought to be so very imminent. They were still thinking they would write, make arrangements, be more particular, when suddenly the storm broke over the Hall and over Ottilie.

Servants and ladies' maids arrived, and horse-litters bearing trunks and boxes; it was already like a double or triple contingent of visitors; but only then did the guests themselves appear; the great aunt with Luciane and some lady friends, the intended himself, likewise not unaccompanied. The vestibule was full of valises, portmanteaus, and other leather containers. The numerous little boxes and cases were only with difficulty sorted out. The baggage and the carrying of it were endless. Between times it rained in torrents, which caused much discomfort. In the face of this frenzy Ottilie remained efficient and unperturbed; indeed, her cheerful competence was shown at its very best, for she had soon found a proper place for everyone and everything. Every guest was accommodated, all were made comfortable in the ways that suited them, and all felt well looked after because they were not prevented from looking after themselves.

After their very arduous journey they would all have been glad of a little peace and quiet; the young man would have liked to get to know his future mother-in-law and assure her of his love and goodwill; but Luciane could not rest. She had been allowed to take up riding, and now it was her joy. Her husband-to-be owned some fine horses, and forthwith the company was obliged to mount. The wind and the weather made no difference; it was as though the whole purpose of life was to get wet and dry off again. If it occurred to her to go out on foot she never considered what clothes she was wearing or how she was shod. She had to see the park she had heard so much about. What could not be done on horseback was hurried through on foot. She had soon seen everything and given her opinion on everything. Being so quick in her manner she was hard to contradict. The company had to put up with a good deal, her maids especially, who never got to the end of washing and ironing, undoing and sewing things on.

No sooner had she exhausted the house and the grounds than she felt herself called upon to pay visits in the neighbourhood. Since they rode and drove at a pace, this neighbourhood extended pretty far. The Hall was swamped with return visits and before long, so as not to miss one another, particular days were set.

Whilst Charlotte was settling the details of the business with the aunt and the young man's agent, and Ottilie, and those under her, were mobilizing huntsmen and gardeners, fishermen and tradespeople so that with such a crowd in the house there should not be any shortages, Luciane appeared still like a fiery comet towing a long train behind. She soon found the usual entertainments quite insipid. It was as much as she would do to leave the most elderly visitors in peace at the card table; whoever was at all mobile—and she might charm or bully almost anybody into mobility—was commandeered, if not for dancing then for animated guessing games and forfeits. And although all this, including the paying of the forfeits, centred on herself, it was also true that nobody, and especially none of the men, whatever he might be like, went quite without some recompense; indeed, a few elderly persons of consequence were won over entirely when she found out that it happened to be their birthdays or name-days and celebrated them specially. She was helped by her very characteristic talent for making everyone feel favoured but each privately the most favoured of all, the man most conspicuously guilty of this weakness being in fact the oldest present.

Though she seemed bent on winning over men who counted for something—who had rank, consequence, reputation, or some other important quality in their favour—on being the ruination of wisdom and good sense, and on gaining approval for her wild and fantastical nature even among the sober-minded, she nevertheless did not neglect the young; each had his part, his day, an hour when she chose to charm and captivate him. She had quickly set her sights on the Architect who, however, looked forth so untroubledly from among his long dark locks, stood at a distance with such upright serenity, answered all questions briefly and sensibly, but seemed so disinclined to enter further into anything, that finally she decided, half crossly and half schemingly, to make him the star of the day and win him for her court with all the rest.

It was not for nothing that she had brought so much luggage with her, and more had followed. She had made provision for endless changes of clothes. Three or four times in the course of the day she would change for the fun of it into and out of the clothes that society is used to seeing, but now and again would appear in thorough fancy dress, as a peasant girl or a fisher-wife, a fairy, a flower-girl. She would even dress up as an old woman, all the better to show off her fresh young face from under the cap; and really she so confused the actual and the imaginary it was as if there were a sort of nixie* in the family.

But what these costumes chiefly served for were *poses plastiques** and mime dances, in which she was adept at repres-enting different characters. One cavalier in her entourage had made himself capable of accompanying her gestures at the piano with what little music was necessary; conferring briefly beforehand, they were at once in accord.

One day, when they had paused for a while during a very lively ball, being urged as it seemed on the spur of the moment (though in fact at her own secret instigation) to give one of her performances, she appeared confused and surprised, and con-trary to her usual habit had to be asked several times. She seemed undecided, would not choose, asked for a subject as the *improvisatori** do, until at last her piano-playing assistant, very likely by prior arrangement, sat himself down, began to play a funeral march, and said she should give them her Artemisia,* a role she had learned to excel in. She yielded, and appeared after a brief absence, to the tender and melancholy notes of the funeral march, as the royal widow, with measured steps, bearing an urn. Behind her a large blackboard was carried in, and a golden drawing-pen into which was fitted a sharp piece of chalk.

One of her admirers and adjutants, to whom she whispered something, at once went and invited, obliged, and more or less dragged forth the Architect, to do a drawing of the tomb of Mausolus, and play alongside her in the performance, not as an extra, but importantly, in his professional capacity. Though outwardly appearing most embarrassed—for in his modern, tight-fitting, entirely black plain clothing he contrasted very strangely with the gauzes, crapes, fringes, spangles, tassels, and crowns—inwardly he at once took hold of himself; but that only increased the strangeness of the spectacle. With the greatest seriousness he stepped up to the large blackboard, which was held by a couple of page-boys, and carefully and exactly drew a mausoleum, which it is true would have been more appropriate for a Lombard* king than for a Carian, but so beautifully proportioned, so solemn in its parts, so inventive in its ornamentation, that the audience watched with pleasure whilst it was being created and admired it finished.

Throughout he had scarcely turned to the queen, but had given all his attention to what he was doing. Finally, when he bowed to her and indicated that he believed her orders had been carried out, she held out the urn to him and showed that she wished to see it depicted on the summit of the monument. He obliged, though unwillingly, for the urn was not in character with the rest of the sketch. As for Luciane, she was now at long last delivered from her state of impatience, for it had not been at all her wish to have a scrupulous drawing from him. Had he sketched in very roughly something looking vaguely like a monument and spent the rest of the time attending to her, that would have been more in accordance with her real purpose and her wishes. As it was, his behaviour put her into the greatest embarrassment. Grieving, giving instructions, making suggestions, expressing approval at what was gradually being created, she did her best to ring the changes, and once or twice she almost forcibly turned him round so as to be in some sort of relationship with him, but his manner was far too stiff and all too often she had to have recourse to the urn, pressing it against her heart, gazing at heaven, and in the end, since such situations must always intensify, she looked more like a widow of Ephesus* than a queen of Caria. Thus the performance went on and on; the pianist, patient enough on other occasions, was at a loss to know where his playing should go next. He sent up a prayer of thanks when he saw the urn in place on the pyramid, and involuntarily, as the queen was about to express her gratitude, he struck up a jolly tune, which was quite out of keeping with the character of the performance but entirely restored the good spirits of the audience, who hurried then in two halves to offer to the lady, for her expressiveness, and to the Architect, for his skilful and attractive drawing, their warm congratulations.

Chief among those who talked to the Architect was Luciane's fiancé. 'I am sorry', he said, 'that the drawing is so impermanent. You must at least allow me to have it brought up to my room, and to discuss it with you.' 'If you would like me to,' said the Architect, 'I can show you careful drawings of such buildings and monuments. This one is only a casual and rapid sketch.'

Ottilie was near, she approached the two men. 'Be sure', she said to the Architect, 'that you find an occasion to show the Baron your collection. He is a friend of the arts and of antiquity. I should be glad if you got to know one another better.'

Luciane came by and asked what they were speaking about.

'About a collection of works of art,' the Baron replied, 'which this gentleman owns and which he would be willing to show us on some occasion.'

'But he must fetch them at once,' Luciane cried. 'Will you not bring them at once?' she added caressingly, and took his hands in hers with affection.

'This might not be the right moment,' the Architect replied.

'What!' Luciane cried in an imperious voice. 'Will you disobey your queen's command?' Then she began to beg him, teasingly.

'Don't be stubborn,' said Ottilie, half under her breath.

The Architect withdrew with a bow that was neither acquiescence nor refusal.

He had no sooner gone than Luciane began rushing around the room with a pet greyhound. 'Oh dear,' she cried, happening to bump into her mother, 'how very unhappy I am! I didn't bring my monkey with me. I was advised against it, but it was only the servants not wanting to be bothered. And now I have to do without him. But I shall have him sent for, somebody must go and fetch him for me. If I could only see a picture of him, that would make me happy. I shall certainly have him painted and he shan't leave my side ever again.'

'Perhaps I can console you,' said Charlotte in reply. 'We have a whole volume of pictures of monkeys in the library, the strangest things. Shall I have it fetched?' Luciane screamed with delight, and the folio was brought. The sight of these abominable creatures, already human enough in their appearance and made still more so by the artist, filled Luciane with the greatest delight. But what pleased her best was to find in every one of the animals some resemblance to people she knew. There she was merciless.

One looked like an uncle of hers, another like M. who dealt in women's trinkets, another like the Reverend S., and another was the spitting image of a certain somebody else whose name escaped her. 'Oh, monkeys are wonderful!' she cried. 'Really, they quite outdo the *Incroyables*,* and I cannot think why they are barred from polite society.'

She said this in polite society, but nobody took it amiss. First charming enough to get away with many things, in the end she was ill-behaved enough to get away with anything.

Ottilie meanwhile was in conversation with Luciane's fiancé. She was hoping the Architect would return, and with his more serious and more tasteful exhibits liberate the company from the world of monkeys. It was in this expectation that she had been speaking with the Baron and had mentioned certain items to him particularly. But the Architect failed to appear, and when at last he did return he mingled with the company, bringing nothing with him and giving no indication that anything had been asked of him. Ottilie was for a moment—how shall we describe it?—aggrieved, indignant, taken aback. She had spoken kindly to him, she wanted the Baron to have some enjoyment more in his own style since, though he loved Luciane infinitely, her behaviour did seem to be paining him.

The monkeys had to make way for some refreshments. Then party games, and even dancing again, and finally a joyless sitting around, joyless but feverish efforts to revive an already defunct pleasure, lasted on this occasion, as on others, well beyond midnight. For Luciane was already accustomed to not being able to get out of her bed in the morning nor into it at night.

Fewer events are recorded in Ottilie's diary around this time, but maxims and aphorisms having to do with life and abstracted from life are more abundant. But since most of them cannot have come from her own thinking it is likely that somebody must have given her a book from which she copied out what was congenial. Some things of her own and of a more intimate relevance will no doubt be recognizable by the red thread.

From Ottilie's Diary

'We like looking into the future because we should like, by wishing, to draw what is still fluid and shapeless in it towards us here to our advantage.

'It is difficult to be at any large gathering without thinking that chance which has brought so many together ought to have brought our friends there too.

'However retiringly you live, before you know it you become a borrower or a lender.

'If we ever meet anyone who owes us thanks we think of it at once. How often do we meet someone we owe thanks to and do not think of it?

'To speak of ourselves to others comes naturally; to take in what others say about themselves, in the spirit in which they say it, is a matter of culture.

'No one would speak much in company if he were aware how often he misunderstands other people.

'The reason we garble things when we pass them on is doubtless that we did not understand them in the first place.

'A person who holds forth without ever flattering his listeners, excites disgust.

'Every word spoken excites its contradiction.

'Contradiction and flattery both make for poor conversation.

'The pleasantest society is one in which a genial respect is observed among all its members.

'Nothing so characterizes a man as what he finds ridiculous.

'We laugh when the elements of a moral discrepancy are brought home to our senses in a harmless way.

'A sensual man often laughs when there is nothing to laugh at. Whatever provokes him, he expresses his inner well-being.

'A commonsensical man finds almost everything ridiculous, a wise man almost nothing.

'An elderly man was reproved for still bothering with young women. He replied: "It is the only way to rejuvenate oneself, and everyone wants that."

'We do not mind having our faults pointed out to us, we do not mind being punished for them, patiently we suffer a good deal on their account; but we become impatient should we have to cure ourselves of them.

'Certain failings are necessary for an individual's existence. We should be sorry if old friends were ever cured of certain of their peculiarities.

'We say "He is not long for this world" if a man does something out of character.

'What sort of failings may we keep and even cultivate in ourselves? Those which are more congenial than harmful to other people.

'Passions are failings or virtues, only intensified.

'Passions are real phoenixes. As the old one burns out the new one rises immediately out of the ashes.

'Great passions are a hopeless sickness. What might cure them is what really makes them dangerous.

'Passion is both intensified and moderated by being confessed. Perhaps nowhere else is a middle course more desirable than in what we say and what we do not say to those we love.'

CHAPTER FIVE

Thus Luciane made them drunk on life and drove them on and on through a social whirl. Her court increased daily, in part because her doings excited and attracted people, in part because others were attached to her by courtesies and acts of kindness. She was in the highest degree generous; for since, through the goodwill of her aunt and her fiancé, so much that was beautiful and expensive had suddenly come to her she seemed to possess nothing that was really her own, nor to know the value of the things heaped upon her. So without a moment's hesitation she might take off an expensive shawl and put it around the shoulders of a young woman who seemed to her, in comparison with others, to be poorly dressed, and she did this in such an adroit and teasing manner that nobody could refuse the gift. One of her entourage always carried a purse and was commanded wherever they went to find out the oldest and the sickest and relieve them, at least for the moment. In this way she acquired an excellent reputation throughout the neighbourhood, which became inconvenient at times since it attracted too many people in need, who importuned her.

But what most enhanced her reputation was her conspicuous, kind, and persistent behaviour towards an unfortunate young man who would not come into society because he had lost his right hand, even though this had happened honourably in battle and he was good-looking and well-proportioned otherwise. His injury caused him such unhappiness, it was so distasteful to him always, on being introduced, to have to tell the story of his misfortune, that he preferred to hide himself away, give himself up to reading and other studies, and once and for all have nothing to do with society.

This young man's existence became known to her. He was made to appear, first in a small party, then in a larger, then in the largest. She behaved more charmingly towards him than towards anyone else; indeed, by her very pressing willingness to be of service, by her acts of compensation, she succeeded in making him value his loss. He had to sit by her at table, she cut up his food so that he only needed to use his fork. If persons of greater age or higher rank replaced him next to her she extended her attentiveness right across the table and sent the servants hurrying to supply what her being at a distance threatened to deprive him of. Finally she encouraged him to write with his left hand; all his attempts had to be sent to her, so that near and far she was always in a relationship with him. The young man scarcely recognized himself, and really from that time on he began a new life.

It might be supposed that behaviour of this sort would be displeasing to the man she was to marry; but quite the opposite was the case. He thought it a great virtue in her that she went to such trouble, and was all the more unperturbed by it for knowing her almost exaggerated tendency to rebuff anything in the least little bit compromising. She would come at anyone just as she pleased, everyone was in danger of being pushed, jostled, or in some other way tormented by her; but nobody was permitted to do the same in return, nobody might take hold of her if he felt like it, nobody respond in kind, not even remotely, to the liberties she took herself; and thus she held other people within the strictest bounds of decency towards herself, whilst seeming at every moment to transgress those bounds in her dealings with them.

Altogether it was as though she had decided as a matter of principle to expose herself equally to praise and blame, affection and dislike. For whilst in many ways seeking to make people fond of her, she most often undid it again by speaking maliciously of everyone. So always after visiting in the neighbourhood, when she and her company had been welcomed in apartments and great houses, returning home she would demonstrate in the most unrestrained fashion how inclined she was to view all human relations only from their ridiculous side. Here were three brothers overtaken by old age whilst still courteously disputing who should marry first; here a young woman small in stature married to a very large old man; elsewhere, contrariwise, a cheerful little man and a clumsy giant of a wife. In one house children were forever getting in the way; in another a most numerous party seemed to her lacking because no children were present. Childless old couples should be off to their graves as quickly as possible, so that there might be some laughter in the house again at long last. Young couples should travel, keeping house was not the thing for them. And as she was with people so she was also with their possessions, with their houses, their furnishings, their tableware. She was especially inclined to make jokes about what people put on their walls. From the oldest high-warp tapestries to the most modern papers, from the most dignified family portraits to the most frivolous modern engravings, they all suffered, they were all so to speak annihilated by her mocking remarks, so that it was a wonder anything was left alive for fifteen miles around.

There was perhaps no real malice in this perpetual negation; it was mostly a sort of self-centred mischievousness; but a real bitterness had developed in her relationship with Ottilie. She looked down contemptuously on the sweet child's tranquil and ceaseless activity, which everyone noticed and commended; and when Ottilie's care of the gardens and greenhouses was mentioned she not only made fun of it by appearing to wonder—though they were in the depths of winter—that neither flowers nor fruit were to be seen, but thenceforth ordered in so much greenery, so many sprays of anything with buds on, to waste every day on decorating the room and the table, that it grieved Ottilie and the Gardener who saw their hopes for the coming year and perhaps for some time longer thus destroyed.

Nor would she leave Ottilie in peace in the domestic routine where she was content to be. Ottilie must come with them on their drives and sleigh-rides; to the balls given in the neighbourhood; and why should she fear the snow and the cold and the violent storms at night-time since numerous other people were able to survive them? The delicate child suffered a good deal from all this, and Luciane gained nothing; for although Ottilie dressed very simply she was always the most beautiful, or seemed it at least to the men. Her gentle attractiveness drew all the men around her, whether her place in the great rooms was first or last; indeed, Luciane's fiancé himself often conversed with her, and all the more so because he wanted her advice and collaboration in a matter that was concerning him.

He had got to know the Architect better, had spoken at some length with him about historical matters whilst looking at his collection of works of art, and on other occasions too, especially when viewing the chapel, had begun to appreciate his talents. The Baron was young, rich; he was a collector, he had in mind to build; his passion was lively, his knowledge slight; it seemed to him that in the Architect he had found a man who would serve his purposes in more ways than one. He had spoken to his future wife of this intention; she commended him on it and was delighted with the proposal, but perhaps more in order to take the young man away from Ottilie, for whom she suspected him of having a fondness, than because she supposed she might make any use of his talents herself. For although he had been very active in her impromptu performances and for this or that occasion had often come forward with the necessary materials, she still always thought that she knew best; and since her ideas were mostly commonplace, a nimble servant was as competent to carry them out as the finest artist. When she thought of staging a celebration for a person's birthday or for some other day of honour in his life she never rose beyond an altar, to sacrifice at, or the placing of a wreath upon a head that might be a living one or might be a plaster cast.

When the Baron asked about the Architect's position in the house Ottilie was able to answer him precisely. She knew that Charlotte had already made efforts to get him a new situation; for if Luciane's party had not arrived the young man would have departed as soon as the chapel was completed, since all building work was to be suspended throughout the winter, necessarily; and thus it would be a very good thing if this skilful artist could be employed again and advanced by a new patron.

Ottilie's personal relationship with the Architect was entirely pure and straightforward. His agreeable and energetic presence had entertained and delighted her as would that of an older brother. Her feelings for him remained on the placid, passionless surface of a blood relationship; for there was no more room in her heart; it was packed full with her love for Eduard, and only God, who permeates all things, could share in its possession.

Meanwhile, as winter deepened, as the weather grew wilder, the roads more impassable, it seemed all the more attractive to spend the diminishing days in such good company. There were brief ebbs, but again and again a flood-tide of visitors came over the house. Officers arrived from distant garrisons, the cultured ones bringing great benefit, the coarser ones annoyance to the company; there were civilians too, in any number, and one day, quite unexpectedly, the Count and the Baroness drove up together.

Now truly by their presence a real court seemed to be constituted. The men of rank and good reputation surrounded the Count, and the women gave the Baroness her due. They were not long wondering why the pair were together and so cheerful; for they learned that the Count's wife had died and that a new union would be concluded just as soon as was decent. Ottilie remembered their first visit and every word that had been spoken on the subject of marriage and divorce, union and separation, hope, expectation, loss, and renunciation. Both parties, then quite without prospects, now stood before her so close to the happiness they had hoped for, and she could not help sighing.

As soon as Luciane heard that the Count was a lover of music she organized a concert; she wanted them to hear her sing and play the guitar. The concert took place. She did not play badly, her voice was agreeable; but as for the words, they were as unintelligible as they always are whenever a beautiful German girl sings and accompanies herself on the guitar. But everyone assured her that her singing had been most expressive, and the applause was as loud as she could have wished. One strange upset occurred, however. There was a poet in the party whom she particularly wished to attach to herself in the hope that he would address some of his poems to her, and for that reason she had sung during the evening almost only things by him. He was, as everyone was, altogether polite to her, but she had expected more. She several times prompted him; but he said nothing further until at last, at the end of her patience, she sent one of her courtiers to him, to ascertain whether he had not been charmed to hear his superb poems so superbly rendered. 'My poems?' he replied in astonishment.

'Forgive me, my dear sir,' he went on, 'I heard nothing but vowel sounds, and not all of those. But it is certainly my duty to show myself grateful for so charming an intention.' The courtier was silent, and kept what he had heard to himself. The poet tried to extricate himself from the affair with a few mellifluous compliments. She let it be understood that it was her wish to have something written especially for her. He would not have been so uncivil, of course, but really he might as well have handed her the alphabet to make up whatever eulogy she liked out of it for whatever melody she happened to have available. In the end her pride *was* hurt, as things turned out. Soon afterwards she discovered that on the very same evening he had taken one of Ottilie's favourite melodies and set some exceptionally lovely and more-than-obliging verses to it.

Luciane, who like all her sort was forever mixing up things that were right for her and things that were not, decided now to try her hand at recitations. She had a good memory but, if we are to be honest, her delivery was unintelligent, and vehement without being passionate. She recited ballads, stories, and other things usually thought suitable for such performance. But she had acquired the unfortunate habit of accompanying the words with gestures, which in a disagreeable fashion confuses rather than connects what is really epic and lyrical with the dramatic.

The Count, a man of some insight who had soon appraised the party, their likings, passions, and forms of amusement, happily or unhappily directed Luciane towards a new form of presentation which suited her personality very well indeed. 'I see around me,' he said, 'several fine-looking people who ought certainly to be able to imitate the movements and poses one sees in pictures. Have you never tried representing actual well-known paintings? Reproductions of that sort, though they require a good deal of preparation, are unbelievably charming in their effects.'

It was soon clear to Luciane that she would be quite in her element here. Her height, her full figure, her regular but interesting face, her light-brown plaited hair, her slim neck, everything seemed intended for a painting; and had she realized that she looked more beautiful when she stood still than when she moved (for then she did not always manage to be graceful, which spoiled things) she would have given herself up with even more eagerness to this art of living pictures.

Now followed a search for engravings of famous paintings. The first choice was *Belisarius* by van Dyck.* An elderly man, tall and well-built, was to represent the blind general, seated, and the Architect the grieving warrior who stands before him, which character he indeed rather resembled. Luciane, half in modesty, had chosen for herself the young girl in the background who is counting money from a purse into the palm of her hand, whilst an old woman seems to be trying to dissuade her from giving so much. Another female figure, actually offering him alms, was represented too.

With this and other paintings they occupied themselves most earnestly. The Count gave the Architect some indications as to what would be necessary, and he at once set up a theatre for it and took charge of the lighting. They were already deep in the preparations before realizing that an enterprise of this sort involves considerable expense, and that in the country in the middle of winter they were lacking many things they needed. Accordingly, so that the proceedings should not be halted, Luciane had almost her entire wardrobe cut up to supply the various costumes as the painters, whimsically enough, had decided them.

The evening came, the tableaux were presented before a large audience to general applause. There was music first, of a kind to raise expectations. They opened with *Belisarius*. The figures were so matching, the colours distributed so felicitously, the lighting so well contrived that the audience did indeed think themselves in another world; except that the presence of the real instead of the illusory produced a sort of unease.

The curtain fell, and on request was raised again more than once. The company was then diverted by a musical interlude, prior to being astonished by a picture of a loftier kind. It was Poussin's well-known depiction of Ahasuerus and Esther.* This time Luciane had bethought herself better. In the figure of the queen fallen down in a faint she had scope for the display of all her charms, and for the girls surrounding and supporting her she had cleverly selected only such as were pretty and shapely, among them, however, none being in the least able to compare with her. Ottilie was excluded from this tableau, as from all the others. To be seated on the golden throne, to represent the Zeus-like king, they had chosen the strongest and handsomest man of the party, so that in this tableau a truly incomparable perfection was achieved.

For the third they had chosen the so-called *Paternal Admonition* by Ter Borch.* Our own Wille's splendid engraving of it must surely be known to all. A noble and chivalrous-looking father, seated, one leg thrown over the other, is addressing his daughter, who is standing before him, with what seems to be the utmost seriousness. She herself, a splendid figure in a wonderfully pleated white satin gown, is only seen from behind, but her whole being seems to indicate that she is taking his words to heart. At the same time it is obvious from the father's bearing and gestures that the admonition is neither vehement nor humiliating. As for the mother, she seems to be hiding a slight embarrassment by gazing into a wine glass which she is about to empty.

On this occasion Luciane was to appear in her full glory. Her plaits, the shape of her head, neck, and nape were beautiful beyond belief, and her waist, which is a part scarcely able to be seen in the classical dresses women wear nowadays, was shown off to its best advantage, in all its neatness and grace, by the older costume; and the Architect had been at pains to arrange the abundant folds of white satin with the utmost naturalness, so that unquestionably this living reproduction by far exceeded the original and threw the whole audience into raptures. There was no end to the encores, and the quite natural desire that so beautiful a creature, having been seen sufficiently from the back, should also be looked at face to face grew so pressing that one impatient and comical fellow shouted out the words sometimes written at the foot of a page: 'Tournez s'il vous plaît', and his cry was taken up. But the actors were too well aware of their own advantage and had understood the sense of these productions far too well to give in to the general clamour. The contrite-looking daughter stood as she was without letting the audience see the expression on her face; the father remained seated in the pose of admonition, and the mother never lifted her nose and eyes from the transparent glass in which, though she seemed to be drinking, the wine was never less.—We need do no more than mention the little pieces that came after. They were Dutch tavern and fairground scenes.

The Count and the Baroness departed, promising to return in the first happy weeks of their imminent union; and Charlotte hoped that after two strenuous months she might now be rid of the rest of the company too. She was sure of her daughter's happiness, once the first tumult of her youthful and bridal days was done, for her husband-to-be thought himself the luckiest man in the world. Abundantly wealthy and moderate in his temperament he seemed curiously flattered by the privilege of possessing a woman all the world was bound to admire. He had got so much into the way of relating everything to her, and to himself only through her, that it made him uncomfortable if a newcomer did not immediately and wholly address himself to her but instead sought a closer connection with him, paying her no particular attention, which often happened, especially with older people, because of his own good qualities. It was soon settled that the Architect should join them in the New Year and spend Shrovetide in town with them, where, in further perform-ances of the magnificent tableaux and in a hundred other things, Luciane counted on being blissfully happy, the more so since her aunt and her fiancé seemed to think any expense insignificant if it were necessary for her pleasure.

It was time to leave, but they were incapable of doing so in a normal way. They were saying in jest, but loud enough to be heard, that Charlotte's winter supplies would soon be ex-hausted when the gentleman who had stood as Belisarius and who was certainly not without funds, being carried away by Luciane's qualities, which for a long time now he had been an admirer of, grew reckless and cried: 'Then let us do as the Poles do! Come to me next and exhaust my supplies, and so on, each in turn.' What he offered was at once accepted. Luciane gave him her hand on it. Next day they had packed, and the swarm fell upon another property. There they had room enough, but less comfort and convenience. Much ensued that was not quite right, which delighted Luciane at least. Their lives became wilder and ever-more riotous. There were shooting parties in the deep snow, and other such discomforts. The women were not excused any more than the men, and so they proceeded, hunting, horse-riding, sleigh-riding and making a noise, from one estate to the next, until they approached the capital. There news and tales of pleasure at Court and in town turned their imaginations in another direction, and drew Luciane and all her company, her aunt having gone on ahead, irresistibly into other circles of life.

From Ottilie's Diary

'The world will always take a man as he presents himself; but it is up to him to present himself as something. Difficult people are more bearable than insignificant ones.

'There is nothing that cannot be imposed upon society, except what matters.

'We do not get to know people when they come to us; we have to go to them to find out what they are like.

'I almost find it natural that we object to things in visitors and that as soon as they have gone our comments on them are not of the kindest; for in a sense we have a right to judge them by our own standards. Even sensible and fair-minded people are inclined to be harsh on such occasions.

'On the other hand when we have been visiting and have seen others in their own surroundings, in their familiar ways, in their necessary and unavoidable circumstances, and how they busy themselves and how they have adapted, it shows only ignorance and ill will if we find ridiculous things which in more than one sense ought to seem to us worthy of respect.

'We should achieve through what we call politeness and good manners the things which may otherwise only be achieved by force or not even by force.

'The natural element of good manners is the company of women.

'How may a person be well-mannered and yet preserve his character and his peculiarity?

'It would be nice if what is peculiar about him were brought out precisely by his manners. Everyone appreciates exceptional qualities, so long as they give no trouble.

'The greatest advantages in life, as in society, are enjoyed by the soldier who is also a man of culture.

'Coarse military men at least do not betray their characters, and since underneath their brute strength there is most often affability it is possible to get on with them too, should that be necessary.

'Nobody is more tiresome than an awkward civilian. We have a right to expect some polish in his case since he never has to concern himself with anything coarse.

'If we live with people who have a keen sense of what is proper we become anxious on their account whenever anything improper occurs. Thus I always feel for and with Charlotte if anyone rocks in his chair, because that pains her unbearably.

'Nobody would intrude upon us with his spectacles on his nose if he knew that we women at once lose all desire to look at him or speak to him.

'Being intimate where one should be respectful is always ridiculous. Nobody would lay aside his hat having scarcely said good-day if he knew how comical it looks.

'There is no outward sign of politeness that does not have a basis deep in morality. A proper education would convey both the sign and that basis together.

'Good manners are a mirror in which everyone is reflected.

'There is a politeness of the heart, akin to love. From it derives the easiest politeness of outward behaviour.

'Voluntary dependence is the finest condition, and how would that be possible without love?

'We are never further from our wishes than when we imagine ourselves in possession of what we wished for.

'No one is more enslaved than the man who believes himself to be free and is not.

'So soon as a man declares himself to be free he at once feels bound by circumstances. If he dares to declare himself bound, he feels himself free.

'Against the great advantages of another person there is no remedy but love.

'It is a frightful thing to see stupid people proud of an outstanding man.

'A servant is said not to have any heroes. But that is only because it takes a hero to recognize a hero. The servant will doubtless know how to value people of his own kind.

'There is no greater comfort for mediocrity than that genius is not immortal.

'Even the greatest men are connected to the times they live in by some weakness.

'We usually think people more dangerous than they are.

'Fools and the wise are equally harmless. But half-fools and the half-wise, these are the most dangerous.

'There is no surer way of evading the world than art, and no surer way of attaching oneself to it.

'Even in moments of the greatest happiness and the greatest tribulation we need the artist.

'Art concerns itself with that which is weighty and good.

'To see what is difficult handled with ease gives us a sight of the impossible.

'Difficulties increase the nearer we get to our goal.

'To sow is not so onerous as to reap.'

CHAPTER SIX

A compensation for the upheaval caused to Charlotte by the visit was that she came to understand her daughter perfectly. She was much helped in this by her own experience of the world. It was not the first time she had encountered such a strange character, though never before one so extreme. And yet she knew from experience that people of that kind, when life and different events and parental circumstances have worked on them, may mature to become very congenial and lovable, as their selfishness moderates and their wild enthusiasms and energies take some definite course. Charlotte, as Luciane's mother, was understandably more tolerant of what was perhaps for other people a disagreeable spectacle; for strangers will ask that a child be agreeable or at least not tiresome now, but a parent may rightly and properly look to the future.

In an odd and unexpected way, however, Charlotte was to be affected by her daughter after she had gone. For Luciane had left a bad name behind her, and not just because of things she had done that were blameworthy but also because of other things too that might have been thought commendable. Luciane seemed to have made it a rule not only to rejoice with them that rejoiced but also to weep with them that wept and, fully to indulge her spirit of contradiction, on occasion to turn rejoicing into glumness and tears to laughter. Wherever she visited she asked after those too sick and weak to appear. She went to them in their rooms, played the doctor, and out of a medical chest which she always had with her in her carriage forced some drastic remedy on each; such treatment then, as might be expected, succeeded or failed as chance decided.

She was quite pitiless in these good works and would brook no opposition, being entirely convinced of the merit of what she was doing. But she was unsuccessful also in an attempt on the moral front, and it was this that made work for Charlotte, since it had repercussions that were being talked about. She only got to hear of it after Luciane had gone. Ottilie, who had been present at that very party, was required to give her a detailed account.

One of the daughters of a well-respected house had had the misfortune to cause the death of a younger sibling and could not get over it or be herself again. She kept to her room, in a silent preoccupation, and could only bear the sight even of her own family if they came to her singly; for if there were several people together she at once suspected they were talking about her and her condition among themselves. With any person alone her conversation was perfectly rational and she would talk then for hours.

Luciane had got to hear of her and had at once secretly determined, when she visited the house, to work a sort of miracle and restore the young woman to society. She behaved more circumspectly than usual, got herself admitted alone into the troubled girl's presence, and won her trust, apparently through music. Only at the end she spoiled things. Since what she wanted was to make a stir she brought the beautiful pale child, whom she thought sufficiently prepared, one evening suddenly into a lively and brilliant company; and perhaps even that might have come off but the people themselves were clumsy, out of curiosity and apprehension, first crowding around the invalid, then avoiding her, and by their whispering and their furtive stares making her confused and agitated. It was more than the girl's delicate sensibility could bear. With fearful screams of horror at the approach of something monstrous, as it seemed, she fled. The party dispersed in all directions, and Ottilie was one of those who brought the girl, by now completely unconscious, back to her room.

Luciane meanwhile, in a manner characteristic of her, had given the remaining members of the party a severe dressing down, without in the least considering that all the blame was hers, and without allowing this or any other failure to deter her from continuing to busy herself.

The girl's condition had worsened since then; indeed, the malady in her soul had so intensified that the parents could no longer keep the poor child at home but had been obliged to put her into the care of a public institution. There was nothing Charlotte could do except seek, by being especially kind towards the family, to alleviate in some measure at least the suffering caused by her daughter. The affair had made a deep impression on Ottilie; she pitied the poor girl all the more since she was convinced, and told Charlotte as much, that the illness would have been curable had it been treated in a consequential manner.

And since we usually speak more about past chagrins than about past pleasures, Ottilie brought up the little misunderstanding she had had with the Architect that evening when he had been unwilling to show the company his collection, despite her having asked him to in the friendliest manner. His uncooperative behaviour, perplexing at the time, had continued to trouble her, she did not know why. Her feelings were entirely right; for what a girl like Ottilie might ask, a young man like the Architect ought not to refuse. But when at last she gently reproached him with it his excuses had some validity.

'If you knew,' he said, 'how roughly even cultured people handle the most precious works of art, you would forgive me for not wishing to have mine passed around. They seem not to know that a medal should be held along the edge. Instead they touch the face, however beautifully and cleanly stamped it is, they rub the loveliest pieces between finger and thumb as if that were the way to appreciate artistic forms! They never think that you need both hands for a large sheet of paper and they reach for a priceless engraving, an irreplaceable drawing, with one, just as an insolent politician seizes hold of a newspaper and shows you in advance what he thinks about world events by crumpling its pages. It never occurs to them that if twenty people in succession treat a work of art like that there will be very little left for the twenty-first to see.'

'Have I not sometimes upset you in that way?' Ottilie asked. 'Have I not perhaps occasionally damaged your treasures without suspecting it?'

'Never!' the Architect replied. 'Never! How could you? You were born with a sense of what is right and proper.'

'Be that as it may,' Ottilie replied, 'it would be no bad thing if in future a very full chapter were included in the books of good manners, after the chapters on how to behave at table, on how to behave in museums and with collections of works of art.'

'Certainly,' said the Architect, 'curators and private collec-
tors would then be much more willing to show people their
rarities.'

Ottilie had long since forgiven him; but when he seemed to
take her reproach very much to heart and again and again
assured her that he liked people to see his collection, that he
would gladly put himself out for friends, then she felt that his
delicate feelings had been hurt by her and that she must make
it up to him. She was thus not well placed to refuse absolutely
a request he made to her in the aftermath of this conversation,
even though, quickly consulting her heart, she did not see how
she could do as he wished.

The matter was as follows. It had pained him greatly that
Luciane's jealousy had kept Ottilie out of the tableaux; and he
had also noticed, with regret, that Charlotte, not feeling well,
had been present only intermittently at this brilliant item in
their entertainments. Now before he left he wished to give
further proof of his gratitude by staging, for the honour of the
former and the amusement of the latter, a far more beautiful
production than all the others had been. And there was perhaps another secret motive, one he was not aware of himself:
that he was finding it so hard to leave this house, this family,
indeed it seemed to him impossible that he should go away
from the sight of Ottilie's eyes, whose calm and friendly looks
had lately been almost the whole sustenance of his life.

It was approaching Christmas, and he suddenly realized that
the representation of paintings through figures in the round
must have derived from the cribs, from the pious presentations*
dedicated at this holy time to the Mother of God and the child,
when in their apparent lowliness they are worshipped by
shepherds and soon after by kings.

He had a perfect conception of the possibility of such a
tableau. A beautiful baby boy had been found; nor would there
be any shortage of shepherds and shepherdesses; but they could
not carry it through without Ottilie. In his thinking the young
man had made her the Virgin Mary, and if she refused there
was no question for him but the whole enterprise must founder.
Ottilie, half embarrassed by his plea, directed him to Charlotte.
She gladly gave him permission and also, in a friendly fashion,

overcame Ottilie's reluctance to presume to impersonate that holy figure. The Architect worked day and night so that nothing should be wanting on Christmas Eve.

And indeed literally day and night. He had in any case few needs, and Ottilie's presence seemed to serve him for all refreshment. Working for her sake it was as if he needed no sleep, and being occupied with her, no food. Thus for that evening, for that solemn and festive hour, everything was finished and ready. He had managed to put together a small ensemble of wind instruments whose melodious playing served as introduction and produced an appropriate mood. When the curtain rose Charlotte was in truth astonished. The picture offered her had been seen so many times before that one could scarcely expect it to have any novel effect. But on this occasion reality itself, making up the tableau, enjoyed some particular advantages. The whole scene was more night than twilight, but in its component details nothing was unclear. By a clever arrangement of the lighting, which was concealed by the figures in the foreground, themselves in shadow and lit only glancingly, the artist had succeeded in giving expression to the incomparable idea that all light emanates from the child. Joyful girls and boys stood round, their fresh faces sharply lit from below. There were angels too, whose own radiance seemed dimmed by that of the divinity and whose ethereal bodies seemed, in the presence of the divinely human, somehow more solid and in need of light.

Fortunately the child had fallen asleep, and as prettily as could be wished, so there was no distraction when the eyes rested on the figure of his mother who, with infinite grace, had lifted back a veil to reveal the hidden treasure. In that instant the picture seemed held and frozen. Dazzled in the body, astounded in the soul, the ring of common people seemed to have moved a moment since to avert their smitten eyes and then to stare again in curiosity and delight and with more wonder and joy than admiration and reverence; though these were not lacking either but were expressed in one or two of the older faces.

But Ottilie's pose, bearing, expression, and looks excelled anything a painter has ever depicted. Any sensitive connoisseur, seeing this sight, would have been fearful lest anything move; would have been alarmed by the thought that perhaps nothing would ever please him so much again. Unhappily there was no one present quite able to appreciate the effects in their entirety. Only the Architect, who in the person of a tall, slim shepherd was looking in from the side over the heads of those kneeling, though his perspective was not the very best, nevertheless his enjoyment exceeded everybody else's. And indeed how shall anyone describe Ottilie's appearance as the newly created Queen of Heaven? Purest humility, the sweetest modesty in the receipt of a great and undeserved honour and of an inconceivably immeasurable happiness, were pictured in her face, such being her own feelings as well as her conception of what she was acting.

Charlotte was delighted by the beautiful tableau, but what most affected her was the child. The tears streamed down her face, and with great intensity she dwelled on her hopes of soon having such a sweet infant in her lap.

The curtain had been lowered, in part to give the performers some relief and in part to change the subject of the tableau. The artist had had the idea of transforming the first image, one of night and lowliness, into one of daylight and glory, and to that end had assembled on all sides the means of a vast illumination and in the interval put them into service.

Ottilie's chief solace in her half-theatrical state had been that, apart from Charlotte and a very few members of the household, nobody had been watching this pious and sophisticated dumb show. She was then somewhat perturbed to hear during the interval that a stranger had arrived in the room and had been warmly welcomed by Charlotte. Who it was nobody could tell her. She submitted, not wishing to spoil the performance. Candles and lamps were burning and a truly infinite brightness was all about her. The curtain rose, the spectators were amazed by what they saw: the whole tableau was all light, and in the place of the shadows, now entirely abolished, only the colours remained and they, being skilfully selected, produced a sweet, mellow effect. Looking up from under her long lashes Ottilie noticed a male figure seated next to Charlotte. She could not make out who it was, but thought she recognized the voice of the Assistant from her school. A strange sensation took hold of her. How much had happened since she last heard the voice of that loyal teacher! As in a thunderflash the succession of her joys and sorrows passed rapidly before her soul, and she asked herself how much of it all she would dare admit to him. 'Then how little right I have,' she thought, 'to appear before him in this sacred guise and how strange he must find it to see me, whom he has only ever seen as nature made me, now behind a mask.' There followed at once a hurried to-ing and fro-ing in her thoughts and feelings. Her heart was constrained, her eyes filled with tears, as she forced herself to continue in the appearance of a frozen image; and how glad she was when the child began to stir and the artist was obliged to signal for the curtain to fall again.

Added to Ottilie's other feelings in the last moments had been the painful sense that she could not hasten to greet an estimable friend, but now she was in a still greater trouble. Should she go to him in this strange costume and finery? Should she change? There was no question: she did the latter and sought in the meantime to take hold of herself, calm herself, and had just regained her balance and composure when finally she met the new arrival and greeted him in her accustomed clothes.

CHAPTER SEVEN

In so far as the Architect wished the best for the ladies to whom he owed so much he was glad, when he finally had to depart, to know that a man as admirable as the Assistant would be keeping them company; but when he thought of himself as the object of their favour it did pain him somewhat to see himself replaced so swiftly and, as it seemed to him in his modesty, so well, indeed so completely. He had been putting off the moment, but now he was in haste to leave; for he wished to spare himself at least the present sight of things he would have to accept once he was gone.

His half-unhappy mood was brightened considerably at the moment of departure when the ladies presented him with a waistcoat which for a long time he had watched them both working at and envied in silence whoever it was intended for. A gift of that sort is the most pleasing a man full of love and reverence can receive; for thinking of the tireless play of a woman's fingers over it he will be bound to flatter himself that from a work of such duration the heart itself will not have been entirely absent.

The women now had another man to look after, whom they were well disposed towards and wished to make welcome. The female sex has its own inner immutable interest which nothing in the world will cause it to desert; but in outward, social relations they gladly and easily let themselves be determined by the man currently engaging their attention; and thus refusing and accepting, resisting and yielding, in fact they rule, and no man in the civilized world dares disobey.

The Architect had used and demonstrated his talents for the amusement and benefit of his friends pretty much as his own inclinations moved him, and it was in that spirit and with such intentions that their activities and entertainments had been organized; but now through the presence of the Assistant a new mode of life soon established itself. His great gift was speaking well and discussing human relations, especially in the context of the education of young people. And thus arose a quite palpable contrast with their previous way of life, and all the more so since the Assistant did not entirely approve of what had latterly been their exclusive occupation.

He said nothing at all about the *tableau vivant* that had greeted him on his arrival. But when they showed him, with some satisfaction, the church, the chapel, and related things, he could not refrain from expressing his opinion and his sentiments. 'For myself,' he said, 'I do not at all like this *rapprochement* and mingling of the sacred and the sensuous; and that certain special rooms should be set aside and consecrated and decorated, and that only in them should feelings of piety be preserved and nourished, is not to my liking either. No surroundings, not even the meanest, should disturb the sense of the divine in us, for that sense can accompany us everywhere and make any place a temple. I like to see family prayers conducted in the room where people eat, come together, and enjoy themselves playing games and dancing. The highest and the best in man is formless, and one ought to be wary of giving it form except in noble acts.'

Charlotte, in a general way already acquainted with his sentiments and soon getting to know them in more detail, was quick to engage him in his professional capacity, and had her young gardeners, whom the Architect had mustered just before leaving, march into the great hall and be presented. Their clean, bright, cheerful uniforms, orderly movements, and lively and natural ways made a very good impression. The Assistant examined them after his particular method, and by means of a variety of questions and strategies had very soon brought out their personalities and abilities and, without seeming to, in the space of less than an hour, had quite significantly instructed and advanced them.

'How ever do you do it?' Charlotte asked as the boys withdrew. 'I listened very carefully, the things that came up were not in the least extraordinary, but to utter them in such good order in so short a time when the talk was going backwards and forwards all the while, would be quite beyond my power.'

'One ought perhaps to make a mystery of one's professional successes,' the Assistant replied. 'But I will give you a simple rule for achieving what you have just seen and much more besides. Seize hold of your subject, your material, your idea, or whatever, and keep tight hold of it. Make sure you have understood it with perfect clarity in all its parts. Then when you talk to a group of children you will easily discover what of your subject has already been developed in them, what needs further encouragement, and what there is still to impart. Their answers to your questions may be as inappropriate as can be, may lead entirely away from the point, but so long as your next question reintroduces sense and meaning, so long as you do not allow yourself to be moved from your own position, in the end the children will be obliged to think, understand, and be persuaded of the truth of only those things the teacher wishes, and only as he wishes it. His greatest mistake is to let himself be carried away by his pupils, if he fails to hold them fast to the one point he is presently dealing with. Try it yourself when you can, you will be greatly entertained.'

'How nice!' said Charlotte. 'Good practice in teaching is entirely the opposite of good manners. In company one should never dwell on anything, whereas it seems that in the classroom the first commandment is to combat any changing of the subject.'

'Variety without distraction would be the best motto, in education as in life, if such commendable equilibrium were that easy to achieve,' said the Assistant, and was about to continue when Charlotte called out to him to look at the boys again, who were at that moment moving in a cheerful procession across the courtyard. He said how pleased he was to see that the children were required to wear uniforms. 'Men', he said, 'ought to wear uniforms from childhood onwards since they must accustom themselves to acting in concert, losing themselves among others of their kind, obeying as a mass, and working for the whole. Then every sort of uniform encourages a military sense and a brisker, smarter bearing, and all boys are in any case born soldiers—look at their games of battle and combat and how they are forever storming this and climbing that.'

'But you will not chide me,' said Ottilie, 'for not making my little girls all wear the same. I hope that when I present them it will give you pleasure to see such a colourful mixture.'

'Quite right,' he replied. 'Altogether, women should dress with great variety, each in her own manner and style, so that each may learn to feel what suits her best and is appropriate for her. And a further reason, and a more important one, is this: that women are fated to stand alone all their lives and to act alone.'

'That seems to me very paradoxical,' said Charlotte in reply. 'Surely we almost never act for ourselves?'

'Indeed you do,' the Assistant replied, 'and most certainly in your relations with other women. Consider a woman when she is in love, or engaged to be married, or as a wife, housewife, and mother, she is always isolated, always alone, and wishes to be alone. Vain women are just the same. Every woman excludes all other women, by her very nature, since it is incumbent upon every woman to do everything that the whole sex is required to do. With men it is different. Men need men. A man would create another man if none existed, a woman might live an eternity without it ever occurring to her to bring forth another of her kind.'

'Only let the truth appear strange,' said Charlotte, 'and before long what is strange will appear true. We shall put the best complexion we can upon your remarks and hold together as women despite them, and work together too, or we give men too great an advantage over us. And you must not mind us feeling a certain satisfaction, which will be all the keener in future, when we see the gentlemen too falling out among themselves.'

With close attention then, in his sensible fashion, the Assistant examined how Ottilie was managing the children in her charge, and expressed decided approval. 'You do very well,' he said, 'having this authority over them, to aim only at making them immediately useful. Cleanliness makes children feel pleased with themselves, and once they are prompted to do things cheerfully and with some self-esteem, then the battle is won.'

He was besides especially pleased to see that nothing was being done for outward appearance only, but for what lies within and for the children's real needs. 'Why,' he cried, 'the whole business of education might be summed up in a very few words, if anyone had ears to hear.'

'Will you try whether I have?' said Ottilie with a smile.

'Gladly,' he replied. 'But you must keep it a secret. Educate the boys for service and the girls for motherhood, and all will be well.'

'For motherhood,' said Ottilie, 'women might let that stand, since whether they become mothers or not they must always expect to have to look after somebody. But as for being servants, our young men would consider themselves far too good for that. You can see it in every one of them that he thinks he should be the one to give the orders.'

'Precisely why we keep it a secret from them,' said the Assistant. 'We flatter ourselves about our chances in life, and life soon undeceives us. But how many people will concede willingly what they will be forced to concede in the end? Now enough of these thoughts. They do not concern us here.

'I think you fortunate that you are able to proceed correctly with your charges. If your littlest girls run around with their dolls and fasten a few bits of rag together for them, if older sisters look after the younger children and the household looks after itself through its own members and helps itself along, then to start in life after that is not a very big step, and such a girl will find in her husband's house what she left behind at her parents'.

'But in the educated classes the task is very complicated. We have to take higher, finer, and subtler relations—and especially social relations—into account. There as teachers we must shape our pupils for an outward life. It is necessary, it is indispensable, and may well be a good thing, always providing we do not go too far. For as we endeavour to shape a child for the wider world it is easy to push him to where there are no boundaries at all and to lose sight of what his inner self actually requires. That is the task, and the educators succeed or fail at it in varying degrees.

'I am alarmed by a good deal of what we provide our girls with in the boarding-school, because experience tells me that it will be of very little use to them in future. How much a young woman discards and consigns to oblivion as soon as she becomes a mother and the mistress of a household!

'Nevertheless, having dedicated myself to this profession, I still cherish hopes that one day, with a loyal companion at my side, I shall fully develop in my pupils the qualities they will need when they enter into their independence and the sphere of their own endeavours; that I should then be able to say to myself: in this sense their education is complete. Admittedly, education of another kind will continually ensue, in almost every year of our lives, if not by our own doing then through circumstances.'

Ottilie felt the truth of this last remark. How much had been brought on in her by an unforeseen passion in the past year! And what trials she saw approaching if she looked only a very little way ahead!

It was not unintentionally that the young man had mentioned a helpmeet, a wife; for, however diffident he might be, he could not help giving some remote hint of his intentions. Indeed, several factors and occurrences had prompted him to try to get a little closer to his goal in the course of this visit.

The Principal of the school was already elderly, for some time she had been casting about among her male and female colleagues for one who would in practice enter into partnership with her, and had at length put to the Assistant, in whom she had good cause to have every confidence, the proposition that he should continue the running of the establishment in tandem with her, co-operate in it as in a thing of his own, and come into it as heir and sole owner after her death. The chief consideration in all this seemed to be that he must find himself a wife of the same mind. Though he said nothing, Ottilie was before his eyes and in his heart. Doubts arose, but were then countered by certain favourable events. Luciane had left the school; it would be easier for Ottilie to return; there were rumours about her relationship with Eduard, it is true, but like other cases of its kind the matter was not taken very seriously, and it might indeed help bring Ottilie back. No decision would have been taken, however, and nothing would have been done, if here too an unexpected visit had not given added impetus. But the arrival of people of importance in a particular circle will never be without some effect.

The Count and the Baroness, who were often asked about the relative merits of different boarding-schools, since almost everyone finds the education of his children a problem, had decided to acquaint themselves particularly with this one, which was so well spoken of, and in their new circumstances could now undertake such an enquiry together. But the Baroness had a further purpose. When she was last at Charlotte's they had gone over the whole matter of Eduard and Ottilie in every detail. She insisted again and again that Ottilie must be sent away. She sought to give Charlotte, still fearful of Eduard's threats, the courage to act. Various expedients were discussed, and when the school was mentioned the Assistant's fondness for Ottilie was mentioned also, and the Baroness became all the more determined to pay the intended visit.

She arrived, met the Assistant, they were shown the school, and they spoke of Ottilie. The Count himself was glad to talk about her, having got to know her better during their recent stay. She had drawn nearer to him, indeed she was attracted by him, because in his conversation, which was so rich in matter, she seemed to see and recognize things which previously had been quite unknown to her. And whereas in her dealings with Eduard she forgot the world, through the Count's presence the world seemed to her for the first time truly desirable. Every attraction is mutual. The Count felt a fondness for Ottilie, such that he liked to think of her as his daughter. Here too, and more than on the first occasion, she was an irritation to the Baroness. Who knows what she might have engineered against Ottilie in more violently passionate times! Now she contented herself with seeking to render her less harmful to married women by marrying her off.

Cleverly then, but also discreetly, she prompted the Assistant to take a trip to the Hall and there move nearer the accomplishment of his plans and wishes, which he had not kept secret from her, without further delay.

And so, with the Principal's full support, he set off on his journey and his hopes were high. He knew that Ottilie was not ill-disposed towards him, and though a little mismatched socially, modern ways of thinking would help them over that. Besides, the Baroness had more than hinted that Ottilie would always be poor. Being related to a wealthy family was no advantage, she said; for however large the fortune they will never feel they ought to deprive their closer relatives, who have more obvious claims, of any large part of it. And indeed it is curious how very rarely we use the great privilege of being able to dispose of our goods even after death to the advantage of those we love best, and that we, out of respect for tradition as it seems, only benefit those who would inherit from us whether we had any say in the matter or not.

In his feelings, as he travelled towards her, the Assistant became Ottilie's complete equal. A warm welcome raised his hopes. It is true, Ottilie did not seem quite so open with him as she had been; but she was more adult, more formed and, it might be said, in a general way more communicative than he had known her. He was made privy to things which concerned him particularly in his capacity as Ottilie's teacher; but whenever he wished to get nearer to his purpose a certain inner shyness held him back.

But then on one occasion Charlotte gave him the opportunity when, though Ottilie was with them, she said: 'Well, now you have been the examiner of most things that are growing up around me, how do you find Ottilie? I am sure you can tell me in her presence.'

The Assistant's reply was calmly delivered and full of insight. He found her, he said, much changed for the better, her manner less constrained, more at ease in her conversation, and with a more developed view of the world that expressed itself in her actions at least as much as in her words; but still he believed she might benefit very greatly by returning to the school for a while, so as to assimilate in proper order thoroughly and for ever the things which the world imparts only brokenly and more confusingly than satisfyingly, and often, indeed, too late. But he need not labour the subject; Ottilie herself would know what interconnected studies she had been torn from.

Ottilie was bound to agree; but she could not admit what she felt at his words, since she could hardly make sense of it herself. When she thought of the man she loved nothing in the world seemed unconnected any longer, and without him she could not see how things would ever connect again.

Charlotte's response to the Assistant's suggestion was kindly and also shrewd. She said that both she and Ottilie had for some time thought a return to the school desirable; but latterly she would not have been able to manage without her dear friend and helper; in the future, however, she would not object if it remained Ottilie's wish to return for as long as was necessary to complete what had been begun and to assimilate entirely what had been interrupted.

This proposal delighted the Assistant; Ottilie was in no position to say anything against it, though she shuddered at the thought. What Charlotte wanted was to gain time. First let the fact of a happy fatherhood return Eduard to his senses and bring him home; after that, so she believed, everything would fall into place again and Ottilie too would be taken care of in one way or another.

After a serious conversation, when all parties have been given food for thought, it usually happens that a sort of stand-still is reached, which rather resembles a general embarrass-ment. They walked up and down in the room, the Assistant glanced at a book or two and eventually lit upon the folio that was still lying about from the time of Luciane's visit. When he saw that there was nothing in it but monkeys he shut it again at once. This incident may, however, have given rise to a conversation of which traces are to be found in Ottilie's diary.

From Ottilie's Diary

'How can anyone bring himself to do such careful pictures of those horrible monkeys? We debase ourselves even by looking at them as animals; but there is a greater evil still in giving in to the temptation to look for people we know behind those masks.

'Altogether it requires a certain perversity to enjoy looking at caricatures and grotesques. I can thank our excellent Assistant that I was spared the torment of studying natural history. I never could get on with worms and beetles.

'On this occasion he admitted that he felt the same. "We should know nothing about the natural world," he said, "except what we have as our immediate living surroundings. With the trees that blossom, leaf, and bear fruit around us, with every plant along our way, every blade of grass we walk on, we have a real relationship, they are our true compatriots. The birds hopping to and fro on our branches and singing in our greenery belong to us, speak to us, have done so since we were children, and we have learned their language. Is it not the case that every foreign creature, torn from its own environment, fills us with a sort of uneasiness which only familiarity will relieve? We should have to live very tumultuous and colourful lives to bear the company of monkeys, parrots, and blackamoors."

'Whenever a curiosity and longing for exotic things came over me I used to envy the traveller who sees such wonders in a living and daily connection with other wonders. But even he becomes another person. Nobody lives among palm trees unpunished, and it is certain one's sentiments alter in a country where elephants and tigers are at home.

'A naturalist only deserves respect if he can depict and present the most strange and foreign things in their locality, with all their neighbouring circumstances, always in their own peculiar element. How I should love to hear Humboldt* talk.

'A natural-history cabinet can seem like an Egyptian tomb with the different animal and plant gods standing around embalmed. No doubt it would be right for a mysterious priesthood to busy itself with such things in semi-darkness; but they should not be let into our general education, particularly since they can easily keep out something closer to home and worthier of respect.

'A teacher who can arouse our feelings over a single deed or a single poem does more than one who gives us the whole series of inferior forms of life with all their names and structures; for the end-result is what we may know already: that the best and nearest likeness of divinity is worn by man.

'Let each retain the freedom to occupy himself with what he finds attractive, what gives him pleasure, what seems to him useful; but the proper study of mankind is man.'*

CHAPTER EIGHT

Few people are capable of concerning themselves with the most recent past. Either the present holds us violently captive, or we lose ourselves in the distant past and strive with might and main to recall and restore what is irrevocably lost. Even in the great and wealthy families who owe their ancestors so much it is very often the case that the grandfathers are remembered more than the fathers.

Thoughts such as these were prompted in our friend the Assistant when, on one of those beautiful days that raise false hopes of the end of winter and the beginning of spring, he had walked through the extensive old grounds of the Hall and admired the tall avenues of lime trees and the formal gardens that went back to Eduard's father's time. They had come on superbly, just as the man who planted them had intended, and now, when by rights they should have been saluted and enjoyed, nobody ever mentioned them; they were scarcely visited; instead, money and enthusiasm went elsewhere, towards a greater liberty and spaciousness.

He made this observation to Charlotte on his return, and she did not disagree. 'As life hurries us along,' she replied, 'we suppose ourselves to be the authors of our actions, and that what we undertake and how we amuse ourselves are matters of our own choosing; but looked at closely, of course, they are only the plans and tendencies of the times, in whose execution we are obliged to co-operate.'

'Indeed,' said the Assistant, 'and who can resist the trend of his surroundings? Time hurries on, and with it our own sentiments and opinions, our prejudices and our hobbies. If the son grows up in a time of change you can be sure he will have nothing in common with his father. If in the father's time the mood was for acquiring things, securing their possession, reining in, delimiting, and affirming one's own pleasure by cutting oneself off from the world, the son will seek to spread himself, give out, expand, and open up what was enclosed.'

'Whole epochs', said Charlotte in reply, 'resemble the father

and son you are describing. We can nowadays scarcely imagine the times when every little town had to have its walls and
ditches, every manor was set in a marsh, and every tiny chateau
had to be entered over a drawbridge. Now even the larger
towns are doing away with their walls, even the royal palaces
are filling in their moats, the towns are wide open, and when
you travel and see these things you would think a general peace
were here for good and the Golden Age very near. No one feels
comfortable in a garden unless it looks like the open country;
there must be nothing that makes us think of art or rules; we
want room to breathe, and no constraints at all. Do you think
it possible we might ever quit this state for another one, for the
old one perhaps?'

'Why not?' said the Assistant in reply. 'There are difficulties
in every condition, in restraint and in unrestraint. The latter
presupposes superfluity, and leads to waste. Let us keep to your
example, which is striking enough. As soon as there is a
shortage self-restraint is reimposed. People obliged to put their
land to use wall in their gardens again so they can be sure of
keeping what they produce. That gradually gives rise to a new
view of things. Usefulness gets the upper hand again, and even
the man who owns a great deal in the end, like everyone else,
feels bound to make use of it all. Take my word for it, your son
may want nothing to do with the new park, and may well
withdraw behind the solemn walls and beneath the tall lime
trees of his grandfather instead.'

Charlotte was secretly delighted to have a son foretold, and
so pardoned the Assistant his rather pessimistic view as to what
might happen one day to her beautiful and beloved park. She
answered him therefore in perfectly friendly terms: 'Neither of
us is old enough to have experienced such reversals more than
once; but if we think back into childhood and remember what
we used to hear older people complaining about, and if we
consider different regions and cities too, then there is probably
no denying the truth of your observation. But should we do
nothing to counter such a process of nature? Should it not be
possible to establish some agreement between fathers and sons,
parents and children? You were kind enough to prophesy a son
for me. Must he then necessarily contradict his father and

destroy what his parents have built, instead of completing it and raising it higher, as he might if he continued in their spirit?'

'There is indeed a sensible rule for ensuring precisely that,' said the Assistant in reply, 'but people seldom follow it. The father should promote his son into co-ownership, they should build and plant together, he should allow him, as he does himself, a harmless freedom of action. One activity may be woven into another, but not simply tacked on to it. A young shoot will graft very easily and gladly on to an old stem, but a grown branch never will.'

The Assistant was glad that, just as he was obliged to leave, he had happened to say something Charlotte was pleased to hear, for thus he kept her well-disposed towards him. He had been away too long already, but could not bring himself to leave until he was entirely convinced that he must wait out the period of Charlotte's confinement, now imminent, before he could hope for any decision concerning Ottilie. Then he bowed to the circumstances, and with those prospects and hopes returned to the Principal.

Charlotte's confinement approached. She kept more to her rooms. The women who had gathered around her were more and more the only company she kept. Ottilie looked after the house, and scarcely dared think what she was doing. True, her acceptance was total; she wished that in future too she might serve Charlotte, the child, and Eduard in every helpful way; but she did not see how that would be possible. She was saved from complete confusion only by carrying out her duties day after day.

A son came safely into the world, and all the women agreed that he was the living image of his father. Only Ottilie, though she said nothing, could not see the likeness when she went to offer her congratulations to the mother and her first heartfelt greetings to the child. Charlotte had been grieved by the absence of her husband during the preparations for her daughter's wedding; and now the father was not present at the birth of his son either, and would not decide what name he should be called by in the future.

The very first friend to come with congratulations was Mittler, who had sent out his spies so as to have word of the event at once. He arrived, and was all complacency. Barely concealing his triumph from Ottilie he expressed it loudly to Charlotte and set about dispelling all anxieties and removing every present difficulty. They must hurry ahead with the christening. The old parson, one foot in the grave, would unite past and future with his blessing; the child must be called Otto; he could have no other name but the name of the father and the friend.

It took all Mittler's determined bullying to overcome the thousand-and-one doubts, objections, hesitations, falterings, better ideas, other ideas, and the dithering, and the thinking one thing, then another, then the first again; since on such occasions whenever a worry is removed more and more spring up, and wishing to spare everybody's susceptibilities we always wound a few.

Mittler saw to all the notices and letters to godparents; he wanted them done without delay, for it was to him a matter of the utmost importance that a happiness in his view so significant for the family should be made known to the wide world too where not everyone was kind in what they thought and said. And the recent passionate events had of course been noticed by a public in any case convinced that whatever happens happens in order that they shall have something to talk about.

The christening ceremony was to be dignified, but limited and brief. They assembled; Ottilie and Mittler were to act as sponsors. The old parson approached, his steps were slow, he was supported by the verger. Prayers had been said, the child laid in Ottilie's arms, and looking down fondly at him she was more than a little startled by his open eyes, for she seemed to be looking into her own. Anyone would have been astonished by such likeness. Mittler, taking the child next, was similarly shocked, for he saw in its features a resemblance, but to the Captain, that was more striking than anything he had ever seen of the kind before.

The old clergyman's frailty had prevented him from accompanying the baptism with more than the usual liturgy. Mittler meanwhile, full of the occasion, remembered the times he had himself officiated. It was altogether his way in every situation to imagine what he would say and how he would phrase things, and on this occasion he was even less able to restrain himself because the gathering was only a small one and only of friends. Accordingly, towards the end of the proceedings, he usurped the parson's place and began with cheerful self-satisfaction to list the hopes and duties that were his as a sponsor, and dwelled on them at length, reading an encouragement to do so in Charlotte's contented looks.

Forging ahead, the speechmaker failed to notice that the poor cleric would have liked to sit down, and still less did he realize that he was about to be the cause of something much worse. For having, with considerable emphasis, described the relationship of everyone present to the child, thereby putting Ottilie's composure severely to the test, he turned last to the old man himself, with these words: 'And you, the respected patriarch among us, can say with Simeon, "Lord, now lettest thou thy servant depart in peace, for mine eyes have seen the salvation of this house." '*

He was rising now to a glorious peroration, but soon saw that the old man, to whom he was holding out the child, though he first seemed to bend towards it, then at once fell back. Scarcely kept from sinking to the floor he was got to a chair, and notwithstanding every effort at first aid, was there pronounced dead.

To see birth and death, coffin and cradle, so immediately side by side, to envisage them thus, to connect these colossal opposites not just in the imagination but with their very eyes was a hard task for those assembled, it was put to them so abruptly. Only Ottilie gazed at the parson, now gone to his rest and still amiable and kindly in his appearance, with a sort of envy. The life of her soul had been killed, why should her body be preserved?

But if in this way unpleasant events of the day quite often turned her thoughts towards transience, parting, and loss, she had wondrous night-time apparitions for comfort, and by them she was reassured of the existence of the man she loved and her own existence was affirmed and enlivened. When she lay down at night and was floating in the sweet sensation between sleep and waking, she seemed to have a view into a room that was at once perfectly bright and yet lit gently. In this room she saw Eduard quite distinctly, clothed not as she was used to seeing him but for war, each time in a different posture which was, however, always entirely natural and had nothing fantastic about it: standing, walking, lying, or riding. The figure, depicted in every detail, moved willingly before her without her having to do the least thing herself, without her volition, without her having to strain her imagination. Sometimes she also saw him surrounded, especially by something in motion which was darker than the light background; but the most she could distinguish was shadows, which might appear to her variously as people, horses, trees, or mountains. Usually she fell asleep while the apparition lasted, and waking next morning after a peaceful night she was refreshed, comforted, she felt convinced: Eduard was still alive, she stood with him still in the closest possible relationship.

CHAPTER NINE

Spring had arrived, later but also more suddenly and more joyfully than usual. In the garden now Ottilie was rewarded for her foresight. Everything budded, leafed, and blossomed at its proper time; things brought on carefully under glass and in the beds now lifted quickly to meet Nature herself working in the open air again at last; and everything that needed doing and seeing to was no longer, as it had been, a hopeful labour but became a cheerful pleasure.

She had to console the Gardener however for the gaps that Luciane's wildness had caused among the pot-plants and the damage done to the shapes of some of the trees. Ottilie urged him to take heart, it would right itself again before very long; but he had too deep a sense and too pure a conception of his work to be much comforted by her arguments. Just as the gardener himself must not be distracted by other hobbies and passions, so there must be no interruption of the tranquil process by which a plant attains a lasting or a transient perfection. Plants are like obstinate individuals—entirely amenable if you treat them their way. The gardener, more than anyone else perhaps, needs a steady eye and a quiet steadiness of purpose to do exactly what is appropriate in every season and in every hour.

These were qualities he possessed in a high degree, which was why Ottilie enjoyed working with him; but for some time now he had not had the contentment of doing what he was really best at. For although he was perfectly competent in everything concerning fruit-growing and the kitchen garden and could manage an old-style ornamental garden too (and it is generally the case that different people do well at different things), and although what he did in the orangery and with bulbs, carnations, and auriculas was a challenge to Nature herself, he had never entirely got to like the new ornamental trees and fashionable flowers, and the limitless world of botany then opening up and all the foreign names buzzing around in it filled him with a sort of timidity, which made him cross.

What the lord and lady had begun sending away for in the previous year he regarded as useless expense and downright waste, particularly since quite a few of the plants that cost so much then came to nothing, and his dealings with the suppliers, whom he thought less than honest, were not of the happiest.

After several attempts he had devised a sort of plan to answer these circumstances, and Ottilie supported him in it, the more so since its real premiss was the return of Eduard, whose absence in this as in so many matters was daily more grievously felt.

As the plants rooted deeper and sent forth more and more shoots Ottilie likewise felt the tightening of her attachment to that place. Exactly a year before she had arrived as a stranger and person of no consequence; how much she had acquired since then! And since then lost again, alas! She had never been so rich, and never so poor. Feelings of each alternated in her by the minute, indeed were very deeply intermixed, so that her only recourse, again and again, was to put her sympathies, her passions, into whatever things were nearest.

Naturally she was most attentive to all the things Eduard loved best. For why should she not hope he would soon return and notice with a present gratitude how carefully she had served him in his absence?

But in a quite different way besides she had cause to be active on his behalf. The baby was now principally in her care, and that care was all the more immediate because it had been decided not to give him to a wet nurse but to bring him up on milk and water. In that lovely season he was to enjoy the fresh air; and she much preferred to take him out herself and carried him sleeping and oblivious among the flowers and the blossom that would in time smile kindly on his childhood, and among the shrubs and plants which seemed intended, being in their infancy, to accompany his growing with their own. When she looked around her she saw how ample was the condition the child had been born to enjoy; for almost everything as far as the eye could see would be his one day. Given so much then, how desirable it was that he should grow up under the eyes of his father and mother and be the confirmation of their renewed and joyful union.

Ottilie felt all this in such purity that she thought of it as a decided reality and felt nothing on her own account. Under those clear skies, in that bright sunshine, it was suddenly clear to her that her love, to be perfected, must become wholly unselfish; indeed, there were moments when she believed she had already attained those heights. All she wanted was her friend's well-being; she believed herself capable of giving him up, even of never seeing him again, if she could be sure he was happy. But for herself she was quite decided never to belong to anyone else.

Care had been taken that the autumn should be as magnificent as the spring. All the summer annuals, everything that will not give up flowering in autumn but pushes on bravely into the coming cold, asters especially, had been sown in abundance and great variety and, transplanted now into all four corners, would make, when the time came, a starry sky over the earth.

From Ottilie's Diary

'If in a book we come across a good idea or hear something striking in conversation we very likely copy it into our diaries. But if we also took the trouble to excerpt characteristic remarks, original opinions, fleeting witticisms from the letters of our friends, we should be very rich. We keep letters, but never read them again; then finally one day we burn them, to be discreet; and thus the loveliest and most immediate breath of life disappears irrevocably for us and for others. I have resolved to make good this omission.

'So the fairy tale of the seasons begins again at the beginning. Here we are once more now, thankfully, in the prettiest chapter. Violets and lilies of the valley are like captions or vignettes in it. We are always pleased when we open the book of life at their page again.

'We scold the poor, and especially the youngsters among them, when they loiter at the roadside and beg. We seem not to have noticed that they are busy again just as soon as there is something for them to do. Scarcely has smiling Nature displayed her gifts again than the children are after them, to begin a trade; then no child begs, every one offers you a bouquet; it was plucked before you woke, and the supplicant looks at you as smilingly as the gift itself. No one looks wretched who feels he has some right to ask.

'Why is the year sometimes so short and sometimes so long, and why does it seem so short, and yet so long when we look back on it? That is how I feel about the year which has passed, and nowhere more acutely than in the garden where fleeting things and lasting things go hand in hand. And yet nothing is so fleeting that it leaves no trace and no continuation of its kind.

'We can enjoy the winter too. We seem to extend ourselves more freely when the trees stand before us so ghostly and transparent. They are nothing, but they hide nothing either. But once the buds and the blossom come then we are impatient for all the foliage to be there and for the landscape to become substantial again and the trees to press towards us each in its own shape.

'Everything which is perfect in its kind must exceed its kind and become something else, something incomparable. In some of its sounds the nightingale is still a bird; then it goes beyond its class, as though to show every feathered thing what singing is really like.

'A life without love, without the presence of the beloved, is only a *comédie à tiroir*,* a thing all in little episodes. You pull out one after the other and push them back in again and hurry to the next. What there is in it of any value and meaning scarcely hangs together. Everywhere you have to begin again, and everywhere you feel like ending it.'

CHAPTER TEN

Charlotte for her part was cheerful and well. Her thriving boy was a delight to her, she dwelled on him, so full of promise, constantly with her eyes and in her thoughts. He had given her a new relationship with the world and with the estate. Her old energy revived; wherever she looked she saw the many things that had been done in the previous year, and was pleased by them. On a strange impulse she climbed up to the summer-house with Ottilie and the child, and laying him on the little table, as on a household altar, and seeing two places empty, she remembered times past and was filled with a new hope for herself and for Ottilie.

A girl herself may cast a modest look at the young men around her perhaps, and secretly consider whether she would like this one or that for a husband; but whoever has to make provision for a daughter or a female ward looks further afield. Charlotte was doing so at that moment, and a union of the Captain and Ottilie, who had sat side by side in that very place, now seemed to her not impossible. She had learned that the Captain's prospects of an advantageous marriage had come to nothing.

Charlotte climbed higher, Ottilie carrying the child. She gave herself up to a host of reflections. There are shipwrecks on dry land too; the proper and laudable thing is to recover and recuperate from them as quickly as possible. Life is a matter of profit and loss after all. How often we make provision and are thwarted! How often we set off only to be diverted! How often we are distracted from a goal clearly sighted, in order to achieve a higher one! A traveller, to his vast annoyance, breaks a wheel, and through this disagreeable accident he makes acquaintances and relationships of a most delightful kind which have an influence on the rest of his life. Fate grants us our wishes, but in its own way, so as to be able to give us something beyond our wishes.

Thinking these and similar thoughts Charlotte made her way to the new house on the ridge, and there they were entirely confirmed. For the surroundings were far more beautiful than one could have imagined. On all sides everything trivial and distracting had been removed; all the good in the landscape, all that Nature and time had done to it, appeared cleanly and was evident; and where new planting had been done, to fill out a few gaps and pleasantly connect the separated parts again, there was already some greenness.

The house itself was almost habitable; the views, especially from the upper rooms, were extraordinarily various. The longer one looked, the more beauties were discovered. What effects the different times of day and sun and moonlight would bring forth! It was a place one longed to live in, and how quickly the desire to build and be busy awoke in Charlotte when she saw that all the rough work was complete. A joiner, an upholsterer, a painter who could manage stencils and do a little gilding—they were all that was needed, and in no time the building was ready. Cellar and kitchen were rapidly fitted out, for at that distance from the Hall all the necessities of life had to be on hand. So now the women lived up there with the child and from this dwelling-place, as from a new mid-point, unexpected walks were opened up for them. There in a higher region they savoured the fresh open air in beautiful weather.

Ottilie's favourite walk, sometimes alone, sometimes with the baby, was down to the plane trees on an easy path which then led further to where one of the boats was moored that were used for crossing over. She enjoyed going on the water sometimes; but without the child, since at that Charlotte showed some anxiety. But Ottilie was sure to go to the Hall every day, to visit the Gardener and take a friendly interest with him in the numerous young plants now all enjoying the fresh air.

In this beautiful season Charlotte had a very welcome visitor. It was an Englishman who had got to know Eduard whilst travelling, had met him on a few occasions, and was now curious to see the grounds whose attractions he had so often heard praised. He brought with him a letter of introduction from the Count, and himself introduced a quiet but very agreeable gentleman as his travelling companion. Then as he explored the estate—sometimes with Charlotte and Ottilie, or with the garden staff, the gamekeepers; often with his companion, but sometimes alone—it was obvious from his remarks that he was a lover and connoisseur of such parkland and gardens and had doubtless laid out more than one himself. Although getting on in years he took part cheerfully in all the things by which the beauty and significance of life may be enhanced.

It was in his company that the women first fully appreciated their surroundings. His practised eye took in every effect with a complete freshness, and his pleasure in what had come into being was all the greater since he had not known the landscape beforehand and could scarcely distinguish the things that had been done to it from those that Nature had supplied herself.

It could indeed be said that through his observations the park grew and was enriched. He saw in advance what a place newly planted and only now coming on would one day be like. Wherever some beautiful feature could be accentuated or a new one added, he spotted it. Here he drew their attention to a spring which, if it were cleaned out, might be the ornament of a whole area of shrubbery; and here a cave which, if it were cleared and extended, would make a very desirable place to sit, since from it, after the removal of only a few trees, they would have magnificent rock formations towering in their sight. He congratulated the proprietors on having so much still to do, and urged them not to be in a hurry but to store up some of the pleasant work of creation and design for future years.

Nor did he ever mind being left to himself, since for most of the day he was busy taking picturesque views of the park in a portable camera obscura* and sketching them so that he, and others, should have something beautiful and profitable from his travels. He had been doing this for several years now wherever the surroundings merited it, and had put together a most agreeable and interesting collection as a result. He showed the ladies the large portfolio he carried with him and entertained them with the pictures and also with his commentary. They were delighted to be able to travel the world so comfortably and to see shores and harbours, mountains, lakes and rivers, cities and fortresses, and many places famous in history pass before them in their solitude.

Each of the women had her own particular interest: Charlotte's the more general, wherever there was something historically remarkable; whilst Ottilie dwelled especially on the regions Eduard had been most used to speak about, places he liked being in and to which he often returned. Every man has particular localities, near home and far away, which attract him and are, after his character, peculiarly dear and exciting to him, for the first impression they make, for certain circumstances attaching to them, and for their accustomedness.

Ottilie asked the English lord where he liked being best and where he would make his home now if he had to choose. He mentioned several beautiful regions, and with obvious pleasure, in his peculiarly accented French, he spoke of the experiences in those places which had made them so precious to him.

When asked, however, where he usually resided and where he was happiest to return to he replied quite straightforwardly but, for the women, surprisingly:

'I have accustomed myself to being at home everywhere and have come to feel it the best possible arrangement that others should build, plant, and exert themselves domestically on my behalf. I have no longing to return to my own estates, partly for political reasons but principally because my son, for whom, in the end, all the work I did was done, to whom I hoped to bequeath it all, with whom I hoped for a time still to enjoy it, takes no part in any of it but has gone to India like many another to lead a more useful life there or, for all I know, to waste himself completely.

'It is certain that we spend far too much time and money merely preparing to live. Instead of settling down at once in a moderate condition of life we go on and on expanding, to our greater and greater discomfort. Who has any pleasure in my buildings now, and in my park and gardens? Not I, nor even my own kith and kin: only visiting strangers, sightseers, restless travellers.

'Even the very wealthy are only half at home, especially in the country where things we are used to in town are missing. The book we desire to read above all others is not to hand, and what we need most we have left behind. We are forever settling in only to depart again, and if we do not do it to suit our own whims and wishes then circumstances, passions, accidents, necessity, and whatever else will force it anyway.'

The Englishman had no idea how deeply the two friends were affected by his observations. And indeed how often any one of us may run that risk by making a general observation even when we mainly know the circumstances of the company we are in. Being accidentally hurt thus, even by people who were sympathetic and meant well, was nothing new to Charlotte; and the world in any case lay in such clarity before her that she felt no particular pain when somebody thoughtlessly and carelessly obliged her to gaze upon this or that unpleasant place. Ottilie on the other hand, who in her half-conscious youthfulness sensed more things than she saw, and might, indeed had to, avert her eyes from what she did not wish to and was not supposed to see, Ottilie was thrown by these confidences into the cruellest state: the agreeable veil before her eyes was torn asunder and it seemed to her as if everything done till then for the house, the garden, the park, and the whole environment was in fact for nothing, because the man to whom it all belonged had no joy of it since he, like their present visitor, was wandering the world, and in the most dangerous fashion, having been driven to do so by those who were closest in his love. She had grown used to listening in silence, but her situation now was painful in the extreme, and was made worse rather than better by what their guest, with peculiar gravity and serenity, then went on to say.

'It seems to me,' he said, 'that I do best to think of myself as a perpetual traveller, giving up a great deal in order to enjoy a great deal. I am used to change, indeed I find it necessary, just as at the opera we are always waiting for a scene-change precisely because there have already been so many. I know what I can expect of the best inn and the worst. It can be as good or as bad as it likes, I am never in one place long enough to grow accustomed, and what does it matter in the end whether our lives are determined entirely by fixed habits or entirely by the most casual accidents? At least I no longer have the irritation of misplacing or losing things, or of not being able to use my living-room because it has to be decorated, or of somebody breaking my favourite cup and nothing tasting right out of any other for an age. I am free of all that, and if the place goes up in flames the servants will calmly pack my bags and load my carriage and I leave town. And with all these advantages, when I reckon it up I have not spent more by the end of the year than it would have cost me at home.'

In this description Ottilie saw no one but Eduard, saw him too now deprived and suffering hardships, travelling the unmade roads, lying under the stars in want and in danger, and amid so much precariousness and risk accustoming himself to being homeless and friendless and to throwing away everything so as to have nothing to lose. Fortunately then the company broke up for a while. Ottilie found space to weep in solitude. None of her dull griefs had been so hard on her as this clarity which she now strove to make even clearer, as people will indeed torment themselves once they have begun to be tormented.

Eduard's condition seemed to her so poor, so pitiable, that she decided, cost what it might, to do everything in her power to bring about his reunion with Charlotte, then in some quiet place to hide her grief and love and cheat them with some sort of work.

In the meantime the English lord's companion, a sensible, tranquil, and observant man, had noticed the *faux pas* in the conversation and had pointed out to his friend the similarity of his and Eduard's lives. He for his part knew nothing about the family circumstances; but the companion, whom, as he travelled, nothing interested more than the strange things which are caused to occur by natural and artificial circumstances, by the conflict of law and unrestraint, pragmatism and reason, passion and prejudice, had in advance, but then especially when arriving in the house, made himself acquainted with all that had happened and was still happening.

His Lordship was sorry, but not seriously embarrassed. To avoid such errors it would be necessary to say nothing whatsoever in society; for not only serious observations but even the most trivial remarks may happen to chime badly with the interests of those present. 'We shall put things right this evening,' he said, 'and avoid all conversation of a general kind. I suggest you give them one or two of the curious anecdotes and stories with which you have so enriched your portfolio and your memory on our travels.'

But despite the best of intentions the visitors still did not manage to cause the women no distress with the entertainment.

For when the companion, through a series of strange, instruct-
ive, cheerful, moving, and terrible stories, had excited their
attention and roused their interest to the highest degree, he
thought to close with an admittedly odd but none the less
gentler happening, and did not guess how near it was to his
listeners.

STRANGE NEIGHBOURS
A NOVELLE

'Two children of wealthy neighbouring families, a boy and a
girl, similar in age, were brought up together in the pleasant
expectation that they would one day be man and wife, and
their parents looked forward joyfully to this eventual union. But
before long it began to be apparent that what they had planned
would be unlikely to come about, for a strange antipathy arose
between the characters, both excellent, of the two children.
Perhaps they were too alike. Both self-absorbed, clear in their
wishes, firm in their intentions; both loved and respected by
their play-fellows; always opponents when they came together;
each separately creative, but mutually destructive when they
met; not competing after a distant goal, but forever fighting for
some immediate purpose; entirely good-natured and lovable,
and only full of hatred, indeed wicked, in their dealings with
one another.

'This strange relationship was already manifest in their childish games, and thereafter as they grew older. And as boys play
at war and divide into sides and fight battles, so the proud and
spirited girl once set herself at the head of one of the armies
and fought with such fierceness and force that the other would
have been shamefully routed if her sole real opponent had not
stood his ground and in the end disarmed her and taken her
prisoner. But even then she defended herself with such ferocity
that he, to save his eyes and so as not to harm his enemy, had
to tear off the silk kerchief he wore around his neck and use it
to tie her hands behind her back.

'She never forgave him this, indeed she went to such secret
lengths to harm him that the parents, who had for some time
been keeping a watchful eye on these bizarre passions, con-

ferred together and agreed to separate the hostile pair and to
abandon the hopes they had been cherishing.

'The boy soon excelled in his new circumstances. He took in
everything he was taught. His patrons as well as his own
inclinations directed him towards the army. Wherever he might
be he was loved and respected. His good qualities seemed to
promote only well-being and contentment in others; and in
himself, without fully realizing it, he was glad to have lost the
one opponent Nature had given him.

'The girl on the other hand now suddenly entered into a
changed condition. Her years, her increasing culture, and
more, a certain inner sense, drew her away from the rough
games she had been used to playing in the boys' company.
Altogether, she seemed to be lacking something. There was
nothing around her fit to excite her hatred, and no one had
come her way yet who was worthy of being loved.

'A young man, older than her former neighbour and enemy,
a man of rank, wealth, and consequence, well liked in society,
sought after by women, bestowed upon her his entire affection. It was the first time that a man had approached her as
friend, lover, and devoted servant. She was greatly flattered to
be thus preferred by him over many others older, more
cultured, more brilliant, more sophisticated than herself. His
sustained attentions, that were never importunate, his faithful
support in various contretemps, the candid yet—since she was
still very young—temperate and no more than hopeful expression of his sentiments to her parents, all this inclined her towards him, and the accustomedness of the situation, its outward form becoming known and accepted in the world, this
also played a part. She had been spoken of so often as a
bride-to-be that in the end she thought of herself as one, and
neither she nor anybody else thought any further trial necessary when she exchanged rings with the man so long thought
of as her future husband.

'The placid course which the whole business had taken was
not accelerated by the engagement either. Both sides simply let
things carry on. They took pleasure in one another's company
and wished to enjoy the pleasant time of year really as a
springtime before the more serious life that was to come.

'The younger man meanwhile, away from home, had developed as well as anyone could have wished. He had achieved a deserved advancement in his career, and was given leave to visit his family. In a quite natural and yet strange fashion he stood again now face to face with his beautiful neighbour. Latterly all her feelings had been kindly ones, having to do with her family and with matrimony, she was at one with everything that surrounded her; she thought herself happy, and was so in a certain sense. But now for the first time in years something again confronted her—and not something fit to be hated, she had become incapable of hatred; rather that childish hatred, really only an obscure acknowledgement of inner merit, expressed itself now in a joyful astonishment, a glad contemplation, a pleased admission, and in a half-willing, half-involuntary, and yet inevitable drawing near; and all that was mutual. Their long separation gave rise to long conversations. Even their childish unreasonableness was now, as they remembered it in their more enlightened state, a source of amusement, and it was as if they must make up for that teasing hatred at least by friendly and attentive dealings now, as if that violent mistaking must now be countered by explicit recognition.

'On his side everything kept a sensible and desirable measure. His rank, his circumstances, his wish to advance, preoccupied him abundantly, so that to have the friendliness of this beautiful bride-to-be was a grateful extra which he was well pleased to receive, without then viewing her in any connection with himself or begrudging her fiancé, with whom moreover he was on excellent terms, the possession of her.

'But for her things looked very different. It seemed to her that she had woken from a dream. The battle against her young neighbour had been her first passion and that violent fighting, under the guise of resistance, was only, after all, a violent and, as it were, inborn affection. And now as she remembered things she had no other sense than that she had always loved him. She smiled at those hostile searchings with a weapon in her hand; she seemed to remember the pleasantest possible sensation when he disarmed her; she imagined she must have felt the intensest bliss when he tied her hands, and everything she had ever undertaken to harm and annoy him seemed to her now only innocent means by which she might attract his attention. She cursed their separation, she rued the sleep she had fallen into, she damned the slow and dreamy process of habit which had betrothed her to such an insignificant man; she was changed, doubly changed, forwards and backwards, according to how one views it.

'If anyone had been able to untangle and share her feelings (which, however, she kept to herself), he would not have blamed her; for it had to be admitted that in any comparison of the two men her husband-to-be came off much the worse. Though he could be said to inspire a certain confidence, his rival called forth the completest trust; though he was good company, the latter was a man you might want for a lifelong companion; and in exceptional circumstances, were there ever a need for a higher understanding and sympathy, you might have had doubts about the one but felt an entire certainty about the other. Women have a particularly fine feeling, inborn in them, for these distinctions, and have reason, as well as opportunity, to develop it.

'The more the lovely bride-to-be nourished such sentiments secretly in her heart, the less she liked hearing, from anyone at all, what her fiancé had in his favour, what circumstances and duty seemed to recommend and dictate, indeed what an unalterable necessity seemed irrevocably to require, all the more did her feelings favour their own beautiful one-sidedness; and being on the one hand indissolubly bound by the world and family, by her fiancé and her own consent, and since on the other the youth, going his ambitious way, made no secret of his sentiments, plans, and prospects and behaved towards her only like a faithful and not even very loving brother, and when there was even talk of his imminent departure, then it seemed as if her early childish spirit awoke again with all its ploys and violence and now on a higher level of life armed itself in dudgeon, to act with more consequence and with more dire effect. She decided to die, to punish the man she had hated and now so passionately loved for his indifference, and, since she could not have him, at least to marry herself for ever to his imagination and his remorse. She wanted him never to be able to rid himself of her dead image, never cease reproaching himself that he had not recognized, explored, and valued her feelings.

'This strange madness went with her everywhere. She hid it under all manner of outward appearances; and though people thought her odd no one was attentive or shrewd enough to discover the true inner cause.

'Meanwhile friends, relatives, and acquaintances had been exhausting themselves in the staging of numerous festivities. Scarcely a day went by without something novel and unexpected being put on. There was hardly a beauty spot around that had not been decorated and made ready for the reception of crowds of happy guests. And our young homecomer too wished to play his part before leaving again and invited the bridal couple and a few close family for an outing on the river. They boarded a large, beautiful, well-fitted ship, one of those yachts that offer rooms and a small suite and aim to transpose on to the water all the comforts of the land.

'They sailed, with music, down the great river; the company had gone below out of the heat and were amusing themselves with quizzes and games of chance. The young host, never able to remain inactive, had seated himself at the helm to relieve the elderly captain, who had fallen asleep at his side; and thus, left as the one awake, he needed precisely then to use all possible care since he was approaching a place where two islands narrowed the bed of the river and their flat pebble shores, extending now from the one side and now from the other, made a dangerous rapids. Steering cautiously, staring intently ahead, he was almost tempted to wake the skipper, but trusted his own ability and headed for the narrows. At that moment his beautiful enemy appeared on deck wearing a wreath of flowers in her hair. Removing the wreath she flung it at the helmsman. "Take this to remember me by," she cried. "Get out of my way!" he cried, catching the wreath. "I need all my strength and concentration." "I shall," she cried. "You will never see me again." Those were her words, then she hurried to the bows and jumped into the water. "Oh, save her, save her!" voices cried. "She is drowning!" He was in the most frightful dilemma. The noise woke the old captain, who made to take over the helm and the younger man to give it him; but there was no time to change command: the ship stranded, and at that moment, throwing off the more encumbering of his clothes, he dived into the water and swam after his beautiful enemy.

'Water is a friendly element for whoever knows it well and is able to manage it. It bore him up, and being a good swimmer he mastered it. He had soon reached the girl carried away ahead of him; he seized her, raised, and bore her; both were then carried away by the violent force of the water until the islands and the shoals were far behind them and the river again began to flow with breadth and ease. Now at last he took heart and revived from the first pressing danger in which he had acted without thought and only mechanically. Keeping up his head he looked around him and steered then with all his strength towards a flat and bushy place which ran out prettily and conveniently into the water. There he brought his beautiful catch ashore; but could discern no breath of life in her. He was in despair, when his eyes lit upon a well-trodden path through the bushes. Again he took up his precious burden, soon saw an isolated dwelling, and reached it. There he found good people, a young married couple. The misadventure, the grave danger were soon uttered. What, after a moment's reflection, he asked, was done. A bright fire burned; woollen blankets were laid upon a bed; furs and fleeces and whatever else they had in the house that was warming, were quickly fetched. Now the intense desire to save overrode every other consideration. Nothing was left undone that might bring the beautiful, stiffening, naked body back to life. It worked. She opened her eyes, she saw her friend, she fastened her wonderfully beautiful arms around his neck. So she remained for a long while; tears flowed from her eyes, which completed her recovery. "Will you leave me now?" she cried—"Now that I have found you again like this?" "Never!" he cried—"Never!" and knew neither what he said nor what he did. "But now be still," he added, "be still. Think of yourself, for your sake and for mine."

'She did think of herself, and only now became aware of the condition she was in. Before her rescuer, before the man she loved, she could not feel any shame; but she was content to let him go so that he could see to himself, for what he had on was still dripping wet.

'The young married couple conferred: he offered the youth and she the girl their wedding clothes which still hung ready to dress two people through from head to toe. Before long the two adventurers were not only dressed but they stood in finery. They looked delightful, gazed at one another in astonishment when they met, and with immoderate passion and yet half laughing at their disguises violently embraced. Youthful strength and the quickness of love very soon restored them entirely, and had there been music they would have danced.

'To have come from the water to dry land, from death to life, from the circle of the family into a wilderness, from despair to ecstatic happiness, from indifference to affection, to passion, all in the space of a moment—the mind would not be adequate to comprehend it, the mind would burst or lapse into confusion. Then the heart must do most if such a wondrous reversal is to be borne.

'Being entirely lost in one another it was some time before they could give any thought to the anxiety and the fears of those they had left behind; and they were themselves almost not able to think without fears and anxiety of how they should ever confront them again. "Shall we flee? Shall we hide?" the young man asked. "We will stay together," she said, her arms around his neck.

'The countryman, having heard from them the story of the stranded ship, hurried without further questions to the river-bank. The vessel was coming safely by; with a great deal of effort it had been got off again. They had sailed on in all uncertainty, in the hope of finding the lost pair. When therefore the countryman attracted the attention of those on board by shouting and waving, and ran to a place where it was safe to land, and kept on with his shouting and waving, the ship bore in towards the bank, and what a spectacle that was when they came ashore! The parents of the betrothed couple hurried off first; the husband-to-be was almost distracted with grief. Scarcely had they learned that the two beloved children were safe when the couple themselves came out of the bushes in their strange costumes. Nobody knew them until they came up close. "Who are you?" the mothers cried. "What are you?" cried the fathers. The two now safe threw themselves down at their feet.

"Your children," they cried. "Two joined as one." "Forgive us," the girl cried. "Give us your blessing," cried the boy. "Give us your blessing," they cried together, when for astonishment nobody spoke. "Your blessing," it came again for the third time, and who could have refused it?'

CHAPTER ELEVEN

The story-teller paused, or rather had already finished before he noticed that Charlotte was greatly agitated; indeed, she rose and with a gesture of apology left the room. She knew the story. Those things had happened in reality to the Captain and the daughter of a neighbouring family, not entirely as the Englishman had described them, it is true, but in the chief features there was no distortion, only in the details it had been developed and embellished, as is usually the case when stories of that kind pass from mouth to mouth and finally through the imagination of an intelligent and sensitive story-teller. In the end scarcely anything and almost everything is as it was.

Ottilie followed Charlotte, being urged to do so by the two visitors. And now it was the nobleman's turn to remark that perhaps once again a *faux pas* had been committed and a story told that was known to the household or even intimately associated with it. 'We must beware', he continued, 'of doing yet more harm. We seem to have given these ladies very little pleasure in return for all the kindness and enjoyment we have had here. We must look for a tactful way of taking our leave.'

'I have to confess,' his companion replied, 'that there is something else holding me here, and without an explanation and closer knowledge of it I should be very loath to leave. Yesterday, my lord, when we were in the park with the camera obscura, you were busy choosing the very best perspective and did not notice what was going on besides. You left the main path to get to a place by the lake, one not much visited, with a charming view across. Ottilie, who was with us, seemed reluctant to follow and asked if she might make her way there in the boat. I got in too. Her beauty and her skill with the oars were a great delight. I assured her that not since Switzerland (for there too the most charming girls do the ferryman's job) had I had such an agreeable ride across the water, but could not resist asking why she had not wanted to take that little path. For really there was a kind of anxious embarrassment in her avoiding it. 'If you promise not to make fun of me,' she answered with a smile, 'I can give you a sort of explanation, though even for me it is something of a mystery. I have never gone that way without feeling a quite peculiar cold shudder such as I never feel anywhere else and which I cannot explain. I prefer not to expose myself to such a sensation, especially since I at once then get a headache on the left side, which is something I do suffer from occasionally.' We landed, Ottilie talked to you, and I went and examined the place which she had pointed out to me quite distinctly in the distance. How great was my amazement when I found very clear traces of coal there, so that I am certain that with some digging a rich seam might be discovered in the depths.

'Forgive me, my lord—I see you smiling and am well aware that you indulge my passionate interest in these things, to which you yourself do not give any credence, only as a wise man and a friend—but I cannot possibly leave here without having that beautiful child try the oscillations too.'

Invariably when this matter was discussed the English lord repeated the reasons for his scepticism, the companion listened to them with all patience and deference, but in the end abided by his own opinion and his wishes. He also reiterated the consideration that one ought not to give up the business merely because such experiments did not succeed with everybody, indeed one ought rather to pursue it all the more seriously and thoroughly, since many more relationships and affinities of inorganic entities among themselves, of organic entities with them and also among themselves, at present unknown to us, would surely be revealed.

He had already set out his apparatus—the golden rings, marcasites,* and other metallic substances which he always carried with him in a handsome box—and now laid out certain metals and lowered others over them, on threads, to make a trial, saying as he did so: 'I see it amuses you, my lord, that nothing will move for me nor in me either, and I do not begrudge you your amusement. My procedures however are only a subterfuge. When the ladies return I intend them to be curious to know what strange things we are up to.'

The women came back. Charlotte knew immediately what was going on. 'I have heard a good deal about such things,' she

said, 'but never seen it done. Since you have everything so
nicely ready here, let me try if it will work with me.'

She took the thread in her hand, and being serious in her
desire she held it steadily and without emotion; but not the
slightest oscillation was to be observed. Then Ottilie was
bidden to try. She held the pendulum even more calmly and
with even less inhibition and conscious intention over the
metals. But at once the dangling metal was seized, really as if
in a whirlpool, and veered to one side or the other, according
to what new substances were placed below, now in a circle,
now in an ellipse, or swinging in straight lines, just as the
gentleman's companion might have hoped, indeed in a way
exceeding all his hopes.

The gentleman himself was somewhat taken aback, but his
friend's delight and avidity were such that he would not cease
and begged again and again for the experiments to be repeated
and varied. Ottilie was accommodating enough to do as he
wished, until at last, in the nicest way, she asked him to let her
desist, since her headache was coming on again. Amazed,
indeed delighted, he assured her with great enthusiasm that he
would entirely cure her of this malady if she would entrust
herself to his treatment. There was a moment's hesitation; but
Charlotte, who soon realized what he had in mind, declined
the well-intentioned offer, being unwilling to permit in her
presence something she had always felt gravely apprehensive
about.*

The visitors had departed, and although their impact had
been a strange one still, when they left, a desire to meet them
again somewhere remained behind. Charlotte now took advantage of the fine weather to repay visits in the neighbourhood, but could scarcely get to the end of them since everyone
for miles around, some out of real kindness, others only as a
matter of custom, had been diligently solicitous of her welfare.
At home she was enlivened by the sight of the child; and
certainly he deserved every love and care. They thought him a
wonderful child, indeed a wonder, in his size and shapeliness,
his strength and good health, a delight to behold, and even
more astounding was that double likeness which developed
more and more. In his features and in the whole shape of his

body the child more and more resembled the Captain, and his eyes were less and less distinguishable from Ottilie's.

Led by this strange relatedness and perhaps even more by the beautiful inclination a woman feels to lavish affection on the child of a man she loves though it is not her own, Ottilie became as good as a mother to the growing boy, or rather she became another sort of mother. When Charlotte went away Ottilie was left alone with the child and his nurse. Nanni had left her some time ago, in pique, and had gone home to her parents, being jealous of the boy on whom all her mistress's affection now seemed to be bestowed. Ottilie continued taking the child into the fresh air, and got used to longer and longer walks. She had the feeding bottle with her, to give the child his milk whenever necessary. Almost always she had a book with her too and made thus, the child in her arms, reading and taking her walks, a very charming *penserosa*.*

CHAPTER TWELVE

The main aim of the campaign had been achieved and Eduard, decorated for his services, had been honourably discharged. He returned at once to his little estate and there was given precise news of those at home whom, without their noticing or knowing it, he had kept under close surveillance. His quiet dwelling-place was a joy to enter again; for there had been many alterations and improvements and much progress in the meantime according to his instructions, so that now the gardens and the grounds made up in intimacy and in the immediacy of their amenities for what they lacked in extensiveness.

Eduard, accustomed by the quicker pace of his recent life to acting more decisively, now resolved to do what he had had time enough to think about doing. And first he summoned the Major.* Their joy at seeing one another again was great. Youthful friendships, like blood relationships, have the considerable advantage that aberrations and misunderstandings of whatever kind never fundamentally harm them and after a while the old dealings are restored.

Thus warmly welcoming the Major Eduard asked about his present circumstances, and learned how completely in accordance with his wishes fortune had treated him. Half-teasingly then, but in the tones of intimacy, Eduard enquired whether any romantic engagement were not also under way. 'None,' said his friend with meaningful seriousness.

'I cannot be devious,' Eduard continued. 'It would be wrong. I must at once reveal to you my feelings and intentions. You know my passion for Ottilie, and have long since understood that it was she who drove me into these wars. I do not deny that I had wished to be rid of a life that without her was no longer any use to me; but I must also at once admit to you that I could not bring myself to despair completely. Happiness with her was so beautiful, so desirable that I remained unable to renounce it fully. There were many consoling hints and many cheering signs which strengthened me in the belief, in the delusion, that Ottilie could be mine. A glass marked with our initials thrown into the air when the foundation stone was laid, instead of smashing to pieces it was caught and is in my hands again. "Well then," I cried to myself, having spent many uncertain hours in this solitude, "I will make myself into a sign in the place of that glass, to see whether our union shall be possible or not. I will go and seek my death, and not as a madman but as one who hopes to live. Ottilie shall be the prize I am fighting for, and she will be what I hope to win and to conquer behind the enemy lines on every battlefield and behind every fortification and in every siege. I will perform miracles, in the wish to be spared and in the intention to win Ottilie and not to lose her." These feelings guided me, they stood by me in all the dangers; but now I feel like a man arrived at his goal, all obstacles overcome and nothing now in my way. Ottilie is mine, and what still lies between that thought and its execution is not, as I see it, of any significance.'

'With a few strokes,' the Major replied, 'you cancel out everything that might and ought to be said on the other side; but said it must be nevertheless. It is not for me to remind you of your relationship with your wife and of what that is worth; but you owe it to her and to yourself not to be in any doubts. And I cannot bring to mind that a son has been given you without at the same time telling you that you belong to one another eternally, that you owe it to the child to live united so that unitedly you may see to his upbringing and his future good.'

'It is only the parents' conceit,' Eduard replied, 'if they imagine their children to have any such need of them. All living things find nourishment and succour, and if the father dies young and the son's early years are not so favoured and not so comfortable as a consequence, that itself might equip him all the more quickly for the world by making him realize betimes that he has to fit in with others; a thing we all have to learn sooner or later. But that is not the issue here: we are rich enough to look after several children, and it is certainly neither a duty nor a kindness to heap so many goods upon one head.'

When the Major began to say something about Charlotte's worth and about Eduard's long-lived attachment to her, Eduard broke in abruptly: 'We were foolish,' he said, 'as I now see only too well. Anyone in middle age who seeks to realize the hopes and wishes of his youthful past is always a dupe, for every decade in a person's life has its own happiness and its own hopes and prospects. Woe betide the man whom circumstances or his own delusions cause to reach forwards or back! We made a foolish mistake: must it be for the rest of our lives? Shall we, because of doubts of whatever kind, deny ourselves something that the morals of our times do not forbid? People so often go back on their intentions and their deeds: why should not we whose case is the whole, not an individual part, and not one particular requirement of life but life in its entirety?'

The Major did of course set out before Eduard, in a way that was as tactful as it was emphatic, all the different considerations relating to his wife, the families, society, and the estates; but Eduard was quite unmoved.

'All this, my dear friend,' he said in reply, 'passed before my soul in the chaos of battle when the earth was shaken by a constant thunder, when musket balls whined and whistled, to right and left my comrades fell, my horse was hit, my hat shot through; it hovered before me at nights by the quiet fire under the starry vault of heaven. Then all my attachments presented themselves to my soul; and in my thinking and in my feelings I went through them all; I made them truly mine, I was reconciled, again and again, and now for ever.

'At such times, why should I hide it from you, you too were present, you too belonged in my circle; and have we not for many years belonged to one another? If I have got into your debt at all I am now in a position to pay you back with interest; and if you are in my debt in any way you are enabled now to make it up to me. I know you love Charlotte, and she deserves your love; I know she has feelings for you in return, and why should she not recognize your worth? Take her as a gift from me, bring me Ottilie, and we are the happiest people on earth.'

'Precisely because you are bribing me with such precious gifts,' the Major replied, 'I must be all the more cautious and all the more severe. Your proposal, which in my heart I honour and respect, instead of easing the matter renders it more difficult. For now what concerns you also concerns me, and it is not just a matter of the destiny but also of the reputation, of the honour of two men who have come thus far uncensured, but who now through this strange drama, not wishing to call it by any other name, run the risk of appearing before the world in a most peculiar light.'

'The very fact that we are uncensured,' said Eduard in reply, 'gives us the right to be for once. If a man is sound all his life that lends soundness to things he does which would appear equivocal if done by others. For my part I feel justified by the ordeals to which I have lately submitted myself and by the difficult and dangerous things I have done for others in doing something for myself as well. For yourself and Charlotte, let the future decide; but neither you nor anyone else will hold me back from doing what I have resolved to do. Offer me your hand and I will again be entirely amenable; but if I am left to myself, or worse if I am opposed, then certainly, whatever the outcome, it will be extreme.'

The Major thought it his duty to resist Eduard's intention for as long as possible, and now he employed a skilful tactic against his friend by seeming to give in and by turning to the formalities, the official procedures which would be necessary to bring about this separation and these unions. Then so much surfaced that was unpleasant, onerous, and distasteful that Eduard's humour was made worse and worse.

'It is clear to me,' he cried at last, 'that a man must take what he wants by storm from friends as well as foes. What I want, what I cannot do without, never leaves my sight. I shall seize hold of it, and that before long, you may be sure. I know very well that relationships of this kind are neither annulled nor formed unless things fall that are at present standing and unless things shift that only desire to stay. Such matters will never be settled by reflection, all rights are equal when the reason views them and on the rising scale you can always lay a counter-weight. Therefore, my friend, decide to act on my behalf and on your own, decide for my side and for yours to unravel, dissolve, and fasten anew these relations. Do not let any considerations hold you back. We have in any case already made ourselves talked about, we shall be talked about again and then, like everything when it loses its novelty, we shall be forgotten and left to get on with our lives as best we can and nobody will mind us.'

The Major's arguments were at an end. Eduard, beyond any possibility of a change of view, was treating the matter as a decided fact, and had moved on to discuss in detail how it might all be arranged, and in the cheerfulest manner, even jestingly, was expatiating upon the future.

Then becoming serious and thoughtful he said: 'Were we to trust to the hope or the expectation that everything will work itself out and that chance will guide and favour us, we should be criminally deluding ourselves. We cannot possibly save ourselves that way, nor restore a communal peace of mind; and how will I ever console myself, having innocently caused it all? I pestered Charlotte into inviting you to live with us, and Ottilie only came as a consequence of that change. We cannot undo what ensued, but we can render it harmless and direct our circumstances for our own happiness. If you will not contemplate the smiling prospects I have opened up for us, if you impose on me, impose on us all, a sad renunciation, in so far as you think that possible and in so far as it might really be possible, surely in that case also, if we resolve to return to our former conditions, much unpleasantness, inconvenience, and bitterness will return there with us, and still nothing good or cheerful ever come of it. Would your present happy situation give you any pleasure if you were prevented from visiting me and living in my house? And after what has happened it would be bound to be always painful. Charlotte and I, with all our wealth, would be in a poor state. And if like other men of the world you are inclined to think that absence and the passage of the years will dull such feelings and expunge such deeply graven marks, then, precisely, it is those years we are speaking of, and we wish to spend them not in pain and doing without but in well-being and joy. And lastly let me put to you the most important consideration of all. Though we, our inner lives and our material lives being what they are, might at a pinch be able to bear these things, what will become of Ottilie who would have to leave our house and in society do without our loving care and make shift pitiably in the cold and wicked world? Describe to me any circumstances in which Ottilie might be happy without me, without us, and then you will have uttered a stronger argument than any other and one which, even if I cannot concede it, cannot bow to it, I will nevertheless very gladly add to the debate.'

This was no easy task, at least no sufficient answer occurred to Eduard's friend, and all he could do was insist again and again how serious, worrying, and in many senses dangerous the whole enterprise was, and that at the very least they must consider with all possible earnestness how best to manage it. Eduard agreed, but on condition that his friend would not leave him until they were entirely of one mind in the matter and had taken the first steps.

CHAPTER THIRTEEN

Even people who are entirely strange and indifferent to one another will exchange confidences if they live together for a while, and a certain intimacy is bound to develop. All the more then is it to be expected that our two friends, being side by side, daily and hourly in each other's company, kept nothing back. They revived the memory of their earlier circumstances, and the Major revealed that Charlotte had intended Ottilie for Eduard when he came back from his travels, that it had been her intention to marry the beautiful child to him when the time was right. Eduard, beside himself with delight at this disclosure, spoke without any restraint now about the mutual affection of Charlotte and the Major, depicting it, since it suited and favoured him, in the liveliest colours.

The Major could neither entirely deny nor entirely concede it; but Eduard only grew firmer and more definite. Everything seemed to him not merely possible but already achieved. All parties only needed to agree to do what they in fact wished to do; a divorce could certainly be got; soon after there would be a marriage, and Eduard would leave with Ottilie.

None among all the mind's sweet fantasies are sweeter than those of lovers and persons newly married when they look forward to the enjoyment of their fresh new relationship in a fresh new world and to the testing and confirmation of a lasting union in circumstances that are forever changing. The Major and Charlotte, meanwhile, were to have complete authority over everything concerning property, wealth, and all other things desirable and needful in the world, and make such arrangements and fairly and properly initiate such courses of action as would leave all the parties satisfied. But the thing Eduard seemed to take more than any other as his basis and from which he seemed to be promising himself the greatest advantage was this: since a child ought to remain with its mother, the Major would be able to bring the boy up, guide him according to his lights, and develop his gifts. Not for nothing then had he been christened with the name they shared: Otto.

This had all become so decided in Eduard's mind that he was reluctant to linger even one more day before beginning to make it a reality. On their way towards the estate they arrived in a small town where Eduard owned a house, and there he would stay and wait for the Major to return. But he could not bring himself to halt, and accompanied his friend further, through the town. They were both on horseback and, being involved in serious conversation, they rode on together, further still.

Suddenly in the distance they saw the new house on the ridge, saw for the first time its red tiles catch the light. Eduard was seized by a longing he could not withstand; it must all be settled the same evening. He would remain in hiding in a village very close by; the Major would put the matter to Charlotte with every degree of urgency, overwhelm her cautiousness, and force her by the unexpected proposition into the frank revelation of her sentiments. For Eduard, transferring his own desires on to her, fully believed that he was answering her own decided wishes, and hoped to have her agreement so rapidly because he was incapable of wishing for anything else.

A happy outcome shone before his eyes, and so that it should be speedily announced to him lurking there, a few cannon shots were to be fired off and, if it were already dark, a few rockets sent up.

The Major rode towards the Hall. He did not find Charlotte; on the contrary, he learned that at present she was living in the new house on the ridge, but was just then visiting in the neighbourhood and might be some time yet before returning home. He went back to the inn where he had left his horse.

Eduard meanwhile, driven by an impatience he could not master, crept from his hiding-place, on remote paths known only to fishermen and hunters, in the direction of the park and towards evening had arrived among the bushes near the lake whose surface he saw now for the first time pure and entire.

That afternoon Ottilie had walked out to the lake. She was carrying the child and reading as she walked in her usual way. She reached the oaks at the crossing-point. The boy had fallen asleep; she sat down, laid him beside her, and went on reading. The book was one of those that draws a tender-hearted reader in and will not let go. She forgot time and the hour and that over land she would have a long way back to the new house; but she sat lost in her book, in herself, such a sweet sight that the trees and the bushes around her ought to have been given life and eyes to admire her and take delight in her. And at that moment a warm light from the setting sun shone in behind her and gilded her shoulder and her cheek.

Eduard, having made his way so far unseen, finding his park empty and the whole vicinity deserted, was emboldened to advance even further. Finally he emerged from among the bushes near the oak trees; he saw Ottilie and she him; he ran to her and lay at her feet. After a long silence, in which both struggled to compose themselves, he explained to her briefly why and how he had come. He had sent the Major to Charlotte, the course of all their lives was perhaps being decided at that very moment. He had never doubted her love and she, he was sure, had never doubted his. He begged her to consent. She hesitated, he besought her; he was ready to assert his former rights and enfold her in his arms; she pointed to the child.

Eduard looked, and was amazed. 'Dear God,' he cried, 'if I had any reason to be suspicious of my wife and my friend this living shape would tell against them terribly. Is he not the image of the Major? I never saw such a likeness.'

'No, no,' said Ottilie in reply, 'everyone says he is like me.'

'Can that be possible?' said Eduard, and at that moment the child opened its eyes, two large, black penetrating eyes, profound and affectionate. The boy already viewed the world so understandingly; he seemed to know them both standing there before him. Eduard threw himself down by the child, then again he knelt before Ottilie. 'It is you!' he cried. 'Those are your eyes. But yours, your own, are the only ones I want to look into. Let me cast a veil over the ill-fated hour that gave this creature life. Shall I frighten your pure soul with the unhappy thought that a man and wife, estranged, in their embraces may defile a legal union by their real living desires? Or since we have come so far, since my relationship with Charlotte must be brought to an end, since you will be mine, why should I not say it? And I will, though it is harsh: this child was begotten and conceived in a double adultery! It severs me from my wife and my wife from me when it ought to have united us. May it be a witness against me, and may those beautiful eyes tell yours that in the arms of another woman I belonged to you, and may you feel, Ottilie, truly feel, that only in your arms can I expiate that error, that crime.

'Hark!' he cried, and sprang up, believing he had heard a shot, the sign the Major had agreed to give. It was a hunter, shooting, on the hills nearby. Nothing followed; Eduard was impatient.

Only now did Ottilie notice that the sun had sunk behind the mountains. Its light still shone a moment off the windows of the house on the ridge. 'Go now, Eduard,' Ottilie cried. 'We have done without one another so long and have been patient so long. Think what we owe Charlotte, both of us. She must decide, do not let us pre-empt her. I am yours if she allows it; if not I must give you up. Since you think the decision will be very soon, let us wait. Go back to the village where the Major thinks you are. There may be any number of things that need to be explained. Is it likely he will fire off a gun? That would be a very crude way of announcing the success of his negotiations. He may be looking for you at this very moment. I do know that he has not seen Charlotte. He may have gone to meet her, they knew where she went to. But how many things might have happened! Leave me now! She must be back any minute. She will be expecting me up there with the child.'

Ottilie spoke in haste. She was imagining all the possibilities. She was happy there with Eduard and felt that now she must make him go away. 'I beg you, my love, I beseech you!' she cried. 'Go back and wait for the Major.' 'I shall do as you ask,' Eduard cried, first gazing at her full of love and clasping her tightly in his arms. She enfolded him in hers and pressed him lovingly against her heart. Hope, like a star falling from heaven, soared above their heads and away. It seemed to them they belonged to one another, they believed it; for the first time ever they gave and received kisses that were sure and free, and when they parted it was like an act of violence and they suffered pain.

The sun had gone down, it was getting dark, there were damp scents around the lake. Ottilie stood confused and agitated; she looked across to the house on the hill and thought she saw

Charlotte's white dress on the balcony. The detour round the lake was a long one; she knew how impatiently Charlotte would be waiting for the child. She could see the plane trees opposite, only a stretch of water was between her and the path which climbed directly to the house. In her thoughts she was already over, as she was with her eyes. The risk of going on the water with the child vanished in her urgency. She hurried to the boat, was unaware that her heart was pounding, her feet unsteady, her senses threatening to desert her.

She sprang into the boat, seized an oar, and pushed off. It was hard, she had to push again with some force, and the boat rocked and glided a little way out on to the lake. She had the child on her left arm, the book in her left hand, the oar in her right and she unbalanced herself, with the rocking, and fell into the boat. She lost the oar on one side and, as she sought to steady herself, the child and the book on the other, all overboard. She managed to seize hold of the child's clothing; but her awkward position prevented her from getting up. Her free right hand was insufficient to help her turn and rise; when at last she succeeded and dragged the child out of the water its eyes were closed and it had ceased to breathe.

At that moment all her good sense returned to her, but her anguish, correspondingly, was all the greater. The boat was drifting near the middle of the lake, the oar was far away, she could see no one on the land and how would it have helped her had she seen anyone? Cut off from everything, she drifted on the faithless element as its prisoner.

She sought her own help. So often she had heard of the resuscitation of the drowned. She had witnessed it on the evening of her birthday. She undressed the child and dried him with her own muslin skirt. She tore open her bodice and for the first time showed her breasts uncovered under the open sky; for the first time ever she pressed something living against her pure and naked bosom, alas!—not living at all. The cold limbs of the unfortunate creature chilled her bosom through into her innermost heart. Tears welled without end from her eyes and cast over the stiffened form a semblance of warmth and life. She would not let up, she wrapped him in her shawl, and thought by caressing him and pressing him close and breathing on him and by her kisses and her tears to compensate for all the remedies denied her where she was, cut off.

All in vain! The child lay motionless in her arms, and the boat motionless on the surface of the water; but even then her sweet spirit did not give her up to helplessness. She looked for help above. She fell on her knees in the boat and with both hands lifted up the stiffened child above her innocent bosom which in its whiteness and also, alas, in its coldness was like marble. Tearfully she looked up and cried for help from where a feeling heart will always hope to find abundance when the lack of it is all around.

And nor was it in vain that she appealed to the stars which one by one were now beginning to shine. A breeze arose and drove the boat towards the plane trees.

CHAPTER FOURTEEN

She hurried to the new house, called for the Surgeon, handed him the child. Never unprepared, he treated the infant corpse step by step according to his accustomed method. Ottilie aided him in everything; fetched, carried, saw to whatever was needed, existing in another world, it is true, for the greatest unhappiness, like the greatest happiness, changes the appearance of all things; and only when the Surgeon, at the end of his efforts and his science, shook his head and answered her hopeful questions first with silence then with a gentle 'No', only then did she leave Charlotte's bedroom where all this had taken place, and scarcely had she entered the living-room than, unable to reach the sofa, she fell exhausted headlong, face-down on the carpet.

They heard Charlotte draw up. The Surgeon begged those present to keep back, he would meet her, prepare her; but she had already entered the room. She found Ottilie on the floor, and a maid rushed towards her screaming and in tears. The Surgeon entered and she learned everything at once. But how should she give up every hope at once? Experienced, skilled, and wise, he begged her not to look at the child; he withdrew, pretending there was more he might try. She sat on the sofa, Ottilie still lay on the floor, but raised now to her friend's knees, her beautiful head resting there. The Surgeon came and went, seemed to be seeing to the child, but was seeing to the women. So it came to midnight, and the stillness of death grew deeper and deeper. Charlotte no longer pretended that the child would come back to life; she asked to see him. He had been laid in clean, warm, woollen wraps, in a cradle, which they set next to her on the sofa, only the little face uncovered; he lay there at peace, beautiful.

The accident had soon excited the village and word of it at once reached the inn. The Major had taken the familiar path up the hill; he went round the house and, catching a servant who was running to fetch something from the annex, he informed himself more fully, and asked that the Surgeon be sent out to him. The Surgeon came, and was astonished to see his old protector there; he told him how things stood, and undertook to prepare Charlotte for his appearance. He went back in, began to speak of things that would lead her thoughts away, and led her thus from one subject to another and at last brought her friend to mind, and to her spirit and to her feelings made his certain sympathy, his presence, palpable, and so from there soon passed to the reality. In short, she learned that her friend was at the door, knew everything, and desired to be admitted.

The Major entered; Charlotte greeted him with a painful smile. He stood before her. She lifted the green silk coverlet which concealed the corpse, and in the dark light of a candle he saw, with a thrill of horror which he managed to conceal, his frozen image. Charlotte pointed to a chair and so they sat, in silence, facing one another, all night through. Ottilie still lay quietly, her head in Charlotte's lap; she was breathing gently; she slept, or seemed to sleep.

It began to get light, the candle went out, the two friends seemed to wake from a heavy dream. Charlotte looked at the Major and said composedly: 'Explain to me, my dear friend, what fate brings you here to share in this spectacle of grief?'

'This is no time,' the Major replied, as softly as he had been asked, as though they were afraid of waking Ottilie, 'this is neither the time nor the place to hold back or lead in gently. The situation I find you in is so monstrous that my reasons for coming here, important though they are, lose their value by comparison.'

Thereupon he disclosed to her, very calmly and simply, what the purpose of his mission was, in so far as Eduard had sent him; and what the purpose of his coming was, in so far as his own free will and his own interest were concerned. He presented both very gently, but honestly; Charlotte listened, kept her composure, and seemed neither surprised nor angered.

When the Major had finished Charlotte replied, so softly that he was obliged to move his chair nearer. 'I have never been in such a situation before,' she said, 'but in situations at all resembling this I have always asked myself: "How will it be tomorrow?" I feel very keenly that I hold the fates of a number of people in my hands, and there is no doubt in my mind as to what I should do. It is soon said. I agree to a divorce. I ought to have agreed to it sooner; by hesitating, by resisting, I have killed the child. There are certain things which Fate determines on very obstinately. Reason and virtue, duty and everything holy stand in its way in vain. Something is set to happen as Fate sees fit but which to us does not seem fit; and at length it will accomplish its own end however we behave.

'But what am I saying? Really, all Fate is doing is to set my own wishes and my own intentions on course again, when I was foolish enough to work against them. Did I not myself think Eduard and Ottilie the best possible couple and join them in my thoughts? Did I not seek to bring them together? And were you not yourself, my dear friend, my accessory in this plan? And why could I not distinguish mere insistency from true love? Why did I accept his hand in marriage when as his friend I should have made him and another wife happy? And only look at this unhappy sleeper here. I tremble to think of the moment when she will wake out of this sleep which is almost a death and be conscious again. How shall she live, how shall she be comforted, if she may not hope through her love to give back to Eduard what she, as the instrument of the strangest chance, has robbed him of? And she can give him back everything, seeing how devotedly and passionately she loves him. Love can bear anything, but it can do much more than that: make good everything. There must be no thought of my own position at this time.

'Go now while it is quiet, my dear Major. Tell Eduard I agree to a divorce and that I leave it to him, you, Mittler, to initiate it; that I am easy in my mind as regards my future situation, and in every sense have reason to be. I will sign any paper you bring me; but please do not ask me to play any active part or give any thought to it or offer an opinion.'

The Major rose. She gave him her hand across the sleeping Ottilie. He pressed it to his lips. 'And for myself,' he whispered, 'what am I permitted to hope?'

'Do not oblige me to give you an answer now', said Charlotte in reply. 'We have not done anything to deserve unhappiness, but nor have we deserved to be happy together either.'

The Major left. Though he felt the deepest sympathy for Charlotte he could not grieve over the poor departed child. Such a sacrifice seemed to him necessary for the happiness of them all. He thought of Ottilie with her own child in her arms as the best possible compensation for what she had caused Eduard to lose; he thought of a son in his own lap who would be the image of himself with more right than the one who had died.

Such flattering hopes and images were passing through his soul when on his way back to the inn he met Eduard, who had spent the whole night out of doors waiting for the Major, with never any sign of fire or noise of thunder announcing the success. He had heard of the unhappy accident and he too, instead of grieving over the poor creature, saw this event, though he would not quite admit it to himself, as an act of providence by which everything in the way of his happiness was instantly removed. Thus he was easily persuaded by the Major, who lost no time in telling him of his wife's decision, to return to the village and from there to the little town where they would consider and initiate what needed doing next.

When the Major had gone Charlotte sat only a few moments longer sunk in her own thoughts, for then Ottilie sat up, looking at her friend with wide eyes. First she raised herself from Charlotte's lap, then from the floor, and stood before her.

'It has happened again'—so the extraordinary child began with an irresistible seriousness and grace—'the same thing has happened to me again. You said to me once that similar things often happen to people in their lives in a similar way, and always at important moments. Now I see that what you said is true, and I feel impelled to confess something. Shortly after my mother's death, when I was a little child, I had pushed my stool up close against you. You were sitting on the sofa as you are now; my head was on your knees, I was not asleep, I was not awake, I was between the two. I could hear everything that was going on around me, and especially everything that was being said, very clearly; and yet I could not stir, or speak, or indicate, even if I had wanted to, that I felt conscious of myself. You were talking with a friend about me at the time; you were pitying me, being left a poor orphan in the world; you were describing my condition of dependence, and how doubtful my prospects were unless some particular lucky star came and shone over me. I comprehended everything you seemed to be wishing for me and everything you seemed to be asking of me, I comprehended it all perfectly and exactly, only perhaps too strictly. And on the basis of my limited insights I made rules for myself concerning all those things; for a long time now I have lived in accordance with those rules, have done things or not done things as they dictated, in the days when you loved me and cared for me and when you took me into your house and for some time after that.

'But I went off course, I broke my rules, I have even lost my sense of them, and after a terrible occurrence again you have enlightened me about my situation, which is more wretched than the first one was. Lying in your lap, half-stricken, again, as out of another world, I heard you speaking softly above my ear. I heard what my situation appears to be, I shuddered at my own self; but as on the previous occasion so too on this, in my sleep that was half like death I have set out my new course for myself.

'I have decided, as I did then, and what I have decided I must tell you at once. I will never be Eduard's. In a terrible fashion God has opened my eyes to the crime in which I am caught up. I will atone for it; and do not anybody seek to dissuade me from my intention. Dearest friend, take what steps you must in the light of that. Have the Major come back; write to him that nothing must happen. What anguish I felt that I could not move or stir when he was leaving. I wanted to jump up and cry out that you must not let him go with such criminal hopes.'

Charlotte saw Ottilie's condition, and felt it; but she hoped that in time and by argument she would be able to sway her. But when she said one or two words that suggested a future, a lessening of grief, some hope—'No,' cried Ottilie in exalted tones. 'Let none of you try to move me or cheat me. The moment I hear you have agreed to a divorce, in that selfsame lake I will atone for my offence and crime.'

CHAPTER FIFTEEN

When people are living peacefully and happily together more time is spent than is necessary or proper in discussing things that have happened or ought to happen; relations, friends, others in the house are forever swapping plans and the details of their projects and occupations, and without exactly ever taking advice from one another they do nevertheless go through the motions of seeking it on every occasion. At times of crisis, on the other hand, when it might be thought that a person would be most in need of assistance and support, the individuals all withdraw into themselves, everyone tries to act for himself, everyone in his own way, and the particular means all being thus concealed, only the outcome, the ends, the thing achieved, become common property again.

After so many wondrous and unhappy events a certain quiet seriousness had come over the two friends, expressing itself as a sweet regard for one another's feelings. With all secrecy Charlotte had removed the child to the chapel. It rested there as the first victim of the fate still lowering over them.

Charlotte, so far as she was able to, turned her attention to living again, and found Ottilie the first in need of her support. She paid her very particular attention, without letting it appear so. She knew how much the heavenly girl loved Eduard; little by little, partly from Ottilie herself and partly from the Major in letters, she had learned every detail of what had happened before the calamity.

Ottilie for her part did much to lighten Charlotte's immediate life. She was open, even talkative, but there was never any mention of the present nor of the recent past. She had always been attentive, always observant, she was knowledgeable; all that became apparent now. She entertained and diverted Charlotte, who still secretly hoped to see the union of two people so dear to her.

But Ottilie had a different sense of things. She had disclosed to her friend the secret of how she lived; she was released from her earlier constraints and subservience. By her remorse, by her decision, she also felt freed from the weight of her misfortune and offence. She needed no further law over herself; in the depths of her heart she had forgiven herself, but on one condition, which was complete renunciation; and there could be no release from that condition, ever.

So a little time passed, and Charlotte felt how much the house and the park, the lakes, the rocks and trees daily renewed in both of them only sadness. It was clear they must leave the place, but how was not so easy to decide.

Should the two women remain together? Eduard's earlier wishes seemed to demand it, his declaration, his threat, to make it necessary; but there could be no disguising the fact that the two women, for all their goodwill, their reasonableness, and their efforts, were in a painful situation being together. Their conversations were evasive. Sometimes they were content to only half-understand a thing, but often an expression might be misinterpreted nevertheless, if not by the mind then by the feelings. They were fearful of hurting one another, and precisely in that fear they were most likely to be hurt, and also to hurt.

If they were to move from there and also, for a time at least, lead separate lives, the old question arose: where should Ottilie go? That great and wealthy house already mentioned had tried in vain to find girls to live in with the promising young heiress, to entertain her and compete with her. When the Baroness had last visited, and recently again in letters, Charlotte had been urged to send Ottilie there; now Charlotte mentioned it herself. But Ottilie refused categorically to go where she would encounter what we call society.

'My dear aunt,' she said, 'so that I shall not seem narrow-minded and obstinate, let me say something which in other circumstances it would be one's duty to keep quiet about and conceal. Any peculiarly unhappy person, even if he is blameless, is marked in a terrible way. His presence excites a sort of horror wherever he is seen and noticed. Everyone searches his appearance for traces of the monstrous fate which has been laid upon him; everyone is curious and at the same time fearful. In the same way a house or a town in which something monstrous has happened remains frightful to anyone entering it. Daylight is not so bright there and the stars seem to lose their radiance.

'How great, and yet perhaps excusable, are the indiscretion, the silly intrusiveness, and clumsy goodwill shown towards unhappy persons of that kind. Forgive me for speaking like this; but I suffered unbelievably with that poor girl when Luciane fetched her out of her secluded rooms, took a friendly interest in her, and with the best intentions tried to make her join in the dancing and the games. When the poor child grew more and more anxious and in the end fled and fainted, when I held her in my arms and people were alarmed, excited, and everyone more than ever was curious to look at the unfortunate girl, I never thought a fate like that awaited me. The pity I felt then, which was true and intense, is still alive. Now I can apply that pity to myself and see to it that I am never the occasion of such a scene.'

'But my dear child,' said Charlotte in reply, 'where could you go and not be seen by people? We have no nunneries nowadays where feelings such as yours used to be able to find sanctuary.'

'It is not solitude which gives sanctuary, my dear aunt,' said Ottilie in reply. 'Sanctuary of the most valuable kind is to be found in places where we can be busy. Penance and deprivation, in whatever amount, are not at all the best way to escape a fate we feel is determined to hunt us down. Only if I have to be idle and be on show to people are they antipathetic and frightening to me. But if I can be cheerfully busy and tirelessly doing my duty then I do not mind what human eyes are looking at me, because then I can face the eyes of heaven too.'

'Unless I am very much mistaken,' said Charlotte in reply, 'you are inclined to go back to the school.'

'Yes,' Ottilie replied, 'I do not deny it. I think it would be a very happy calling to educate others along the usual ways when my own education has been along the strangest. And has it not happened in history that people who, on account of grievous moral accidents, have gone into the wilderness were by no means hidden and shielded there as they had hoped? They were called back into the world to lead the lost on to the proper paths again, which they could do better than anybody else, being themselves already initiated into the errors of life. They were called to help the unfortunate, and could do so supremely well, having themselves already met with every earthly misfortune.'

'That is a strange choice of vocation,' Charlotte replied, 'but I shall not oppose you. So be it, if only, as I hope, for a short time.'

'I am very grateful to you,' said Ottilie, 'for allowing me this trial, this experience. I may be deluding myself, but I do think it will work. In that place I shall remember the ordeals I went through, and how small, how negligible they were compared with those I have had to go through since. I shall contemplate the youngsters' difficulties quite serenely, smile over their childish griefs, and lead them with a gentle hand out of all their little confusions. Happiness is no qualification for a person in charge of happy people. Whoever has received a great deal will ask a great deal of himself and of others. That is human nature. Only an unhappy person, who is recovering, knows how to nourish for himself and for others the sense that even a moderate good should be enjoyed with intense delight.'

'Let me say one more thing against your plan,' said Charlotte at last, after some thought, 'and it seems to me the most important thing of all. I am not thinking of you but of another person. The Assistant, who is a good, sensible, and pious man, has feelings which are known to you. Proceeding as you intend to, you will become more precious and indispensable to him every day. Since already, his feelings being what they are, he is unhappy living without you, he will in future, having grown used to your working at his side, no longer be able to do his job without you. Being first a source of strength to him in his work, you will finish by making him hate it.'

'Fate has not dealt kindly with me,' said Ottilie in reply, 'and perhaps whoever loves me cannot expect much better. But since our friend is so good and sensible he will, I hope, in his feelings develop a pure relationship with me. He will see in me somebody consecrated, who has a hope of countering a monstrous evil for herself and others only if she dedicates herself to that holy power which, invisibly all around us, can alone protect us against the monstrous forces that are pressing in.'

All this, uttered by the sweet child with such conviction, Charlotte took in, to reflect upon it quietly later. In various ways, but always very gently, she had tried to ascertain whether any rapprochement of Ottilie and Eduard were thinkable; but even the gentlest mention, the faintest expression of a hope, the smallest suspicion seemed to agitate Ottilie to the depths; indeed, on one occasion, when she could not avoid doing so, she spoke her mind on the subject quite unequivocally.

'If your decision to give up Eduard is so firm and unalterable,' Charlotte said to her, 'then only beware of ever seeing him again. Away from the person we love, the intenser our feelings are the more we seem to gain mastery over ourselves, because we turn inwards the whole violence of the passion, which formerly extended outwards from ourselves; but how soon, how rapidly we are undeceived when the person we thought ourselves able to do without suddenly stands before us again, and doing without him is impossible. Do what you think most suitable to your situation. Be sure. Indeed, it would be better to change your mind, but of your own accord, of your own free volition and inclination. Do not let yourself be dragged back into the earlier state of affairs by accident or by surprise, for then there really will be a division in your soul, and one that will not be bearable. As I have said, before you take this step, before you go away from me and begin a new life which will lead you who knows where, ask yourself once again whether you can really give up Eduard for ever and ever. But if you say you can then let it be agreed between us that you will have nothing to do with him, will not even speak with him if he should come looking for you and force his way into your presence.' With not a moment's further thought Ottilie gave Charlotte the promise she had already given herself.

But now Charlotte was mindful of the threat Eduard had made that he could only be without Ottilie so long as she stayed with Charlotte. Admittedly their circumstances had changed since then, so much had happened that those words forced from him by the moment were to be thought of as annulled by subsequent events; nevertheless she did not care to risk doing anything that might conceivably offend him, and so Mittler was asked to ascertain what Eduard's feelings would be.

Since the death of the child Mittler had often visited Charlotte, if only briefly. The accident, which made the reunion of man and wife seem to him extremely improbable, had troubled him greatly; but it was in his nature to be always hopeful, always striving for the best, and privately now he was delighted by Ottilie's decision. He trusted to the soothing passage of time, still thought he might hold husband and wife together, and saw these passionate agitations only as trials of marital love and fidelity.

At the outset Charlotte had informed the Major by letter of Ottilie's first declaration, and implored him to persuade Eduard to take no further steps; rather they should keep calm and wait and see whether the beautiful child's spirits might recover. And she had also told him all he needed to know about events and feelings since then, and now Mittler had been given the difficult job of preparing Eduard for a change in the situation. But Mittler, knowing that it is easier to get acceptance of an accomplished fact than the agreement to accomplish it, persuaded Charlotte that it would be best to send Ottilie to the school at once.

Accordingly, as soon as he had gone, they made preparations for the journey. Ottilie packed her things, but Charlotte noticed that she intended taking neither the beautiful box nor anything out of it. She said nothing, and let the girl, who also said nothing, do as she wished. The day of her departure arrived; Charlotte's carriage was to convey Ottilie on the first day as far as a place they knew where she would spend the night, and on the second as far as the school; Nanni was to accompany her, and remain as her maid. The passionate little girl had made her way back to Ottilie immediately after the death of the child, and by nature and affection was as attached to her now as ever; indeed, she seemed in her entertaining garrulousness to be seeking to make up for what she had missed and to devote herself to her beloved mistress utterly. She was quite beside herself with joy at going on the journey and seeing new places, since she had never left home before, and ran from the Hall to the village, to her parents, her relatives, announcing her happiness and saying goodbye. Unfortunately in so doing she went into rooms where children were sick with the measles and was at once infected. They did not wish to postpone the journey; Ottilie herself insisted on going, she had done it before, knew the people who kept the inn where she would stay, the coachman from the Hall was driving her; there was nothing to worry about.

Charlotte made no objection; in her thoughts she was herself already hurrying away from the surroundings of her home; only she first wanted to put the rooms Ottilie had lived in back as they were before the arrival of the Captain, for Eduard. Hopes of restoring a former happiness will rise in a person again and again, and once more now Charlotte had a right to such hopes, indeed a need for them.

CHAPTER SIXTEEN

When Mittler arrived to discuss the matter with Eduard he found him alone, leaning on the table and pressing his right hand against his head. He seemed to be in great pain. 'Is your headache troubling you again?' Mittler asked.

'It is troubling me,' Eduard replied, 'but I cannot hate it for doing so, since it reminds me of Ottilie. Perhaps she is in pain herself at this very moment, leaning on her left arm, and doubtless more in pain than I am. And why should I not bear it as she does? The pain is good for me, I can almost say I am glad of it, it brings the image of her patience, accompanied by all her other virtues, ever-more intensely, clearly, vividly into my soul. Only in suffering do we feel with perfect completeness all the great qualities necessary to bear it.'

Finding his friend so resigned Mittler did not hold back with what he had come to say, but he delivered it stage by stage, as a narrative: how the thought had occurred to the women, how gradually then it had ripened into an intention. Eduard made almost no objection. What little he said seemed to imply that he would leave it all to them; the pain he was in seemed to have made him indifferent to everything.

But as soon as he was alone he stood up and paced the room. He no longer felt his pain, he was entirely preoccupied outside himself. Even during Mittler's narrative his imagination, the imagination of a man in love, had been intensely at work. He saw Ottilie, alone or as good as, on a route he knew well, in a familiar inn whose rooms he had so often entered; he thought, he pondered, or rather he did neither; all he did was desire and want. He had to see her, speak to her. To what end, why, what could come of it? No matter. He did not resist, he had to.

His valet was taken into his confidence, and had soon found out the day and the hour of Ottilie's journey. The morning dawned; without delay Eduard set off alone on horseback to where Ottilie would spend the night. He arrived far too early; the astonished landlady greeted him joyfully; she owed him thanks for a great good fortune in her family. He had got her son decorated for bravery in the field by making a particular mention of his deed, which he alone had been present at, and by vigorously bringing it to the attention of the commander-in-chief and overcoming the objections of a few ill-wishers. She hardly knew where to begin in her efforts to please him. Quickly she tidied up as well as possible in her best parlour, which was also, it must be admitted, her cloakroom and pantry; but he announced that a young lady would be arriving, and got her to prepare a room for him, in a rough-and-ready way, on the corridor at the back of the house. The landlady thought it mysterious, and was delighted to do something for her bene-factor, who clearly had an interest in the matter and was very busy about it. He himself, in what emotion he spent the long long time till evening! He looked about the room in which he would see her; in all its domestic strangeness it seemed to him a heavenly abode. He thought and thought: whether he should surprise Ottilie or prepare her first. In the end the latter view prevailed; he sat down and wrote. She was to receive this letter.

Eduard to Ottilie

'Dearest, when you read this letter I shall be near to you. Do not be frightened, do not be horrified, you have nothing to fear from me. I shall not force myself upon you. You will not see me until you allow it.

'First think of your position and of mine. How grateful I am to you that you are not intending to take any conclusive step; but what you have in mind to do is serious enough. Don't do it. Here, at a sort of crossroads, think again: Can you be mine, will you be mine? Oh, you would do us all a great good, and me an immeasurable one.

'Let me see you again, see you again joyfully. Let me put my beautiful question to you with the words of my mouth and you answer it with the beauty of your person. Come into my arms, Ottilie, where I have held you once or twice and where you belong always.'

As he wrote he was seized by the feeling that now what he longed for more than anything was approaching, would at any moment be there, present. 'She will come in at this door,' he said to himself, 'she will read this letter, she will be really here, as she used to be, after all my longing for her to appear. Will she still be the same? Will she look the same? Have her feelings changed?' He was holding the pen in his hand and was about to set down what he was thinking; but the carriage rolled into the yard. In haste he added: 'I hear you arriving. Farewell, but only for a moment.'

He folded the letter and wrote her name on it; there was no time to seal it. He hurried into the bedroom from where he knew a way on to the corridor, and at once it occurred to him that he had left his watch and seal on the table. He did not wish her to see these things first; he hurried back, and retrieved them. In the hall he could hear the landlady, she was already approaching the room, to show the guest in. He ran to the door of the bedroom, but it had closed. He had caused the key to fall out as he ran through, it lay on the other side, the lock had sprung shut, he stood as if in a trance. With some violence then he pressed against the door; it would not give. How he wished he were a ghost and could slip through the crack! All in vain. He hid his face against the doorpost. Ottilie came in, the landlady, seeing him, withdrew. Not for one moment could he remain hidden from Ottilie either. He turned to her, and so the lovers faced one another again, in the strangest fashion. She looked at him calmly and earnestly, neither advancing nor retreating, and when he made a move to approach her she stepped back a few paces as far as the table. He too then stepped back. 'Ottilie,' he cried, 'let me break this terrible silence. Are we only shades that we face one another thus? But listen at least. It is an accident that you have come upon me here immediately. There you have a letter which was to have prepared you. Read it, I beg you, read it. And then decide what you can.'

She looked down at the letter, thought for a while, then took it up, opened it, read it. Her expression did not change as she was reading, and likewise she laid it gently aside; then, raising her hands and pressing the palms together, she brought them to her breast, inclining herself very slightly, and looked with such a look at the impassioned and demanding man that he was obliged to desist from demanding or desiring anything. That gesture rent his heart. He could not bear how Ottilie looked nor the posture of her body. It seemed certain that she would fall to her knees if he persisted. He ran from the room in despair and sent the landlady in to the solitary girl.

He paced up and down in the hall. It had grown dark, there was silence in the room. At last the landlady appeared and took the key out of the lock. The woman was moved, embarrassed, she did not know what she should do. In the end, as she was leaving, she offered the key to Eduard, who refused it. She left the light burning and went away.

Eduard in deepest grief threw himself down on the threshold of Ottilie's room, and wept. Perhaps lovers in such proximity have never spent a sadder night.

Dawn broke; the coachman hustled, the landlady unlocked the room and went in. She found Ottilie asleep fully clothed. She went back and signalled to Eduard with a smile of sympathy. Both then approached the sleeping girl; but this sight too was more than Eduard could bear. The landlady did not have the heart to wake the child from her rest, she sat down opposite. At last Ottilie opened her beautiful eyes and stood up. She refused any breakfast, and then Eduard came in to her. He begged her to speak, to explain what she wanted. He swore he wanted only what she wanted; but she remained silent. Again, full of love and urgently, he asked would she be his. In the sweetest way, her eyes cast down, she shook her head in a gentle refusal. He asked did she want to go on to the school. She signified no, with indifference. But when he asked whether he might conduct her back to Charlotte, then with relief, inclining her head, she agreed. He hurried to the window to give the coachman orders; but behind him like lightning she had left the room, and was down the stairs and in the carriage. The coachman set off for home, Eduard following on horseback at a little distance.

CHAPTER SEVENTEEN

Charlotte was greatly surprised to see Ottilie draw up in the courtyard and Eduard dash in on horseback immediately after her. She hurried to the door. Ottilie got out and approached with Eduard. With a violent eagerness she took hold of the hands of the man and wife and pressed them together, then ran to her room. Eduard flung himself into Charlotte's arms, and wept; there was no explanation he could give, he begged her to be patient with him, look after Ottilie, help her. Charlotte hurried to Ottilie's room, and went cold as she entered: it had already been entirely cleared, there were only the bare walls. It looked as vast as it did cheerless. Everything had been taken away, only the box was left, since nobody knew where to put it, left standing in the middle of the room. Ottilie lay on the floor embracing the box, her head on it. Charlotte knelt down by her, asked what had happened, and received no answer.

She left her maid, bringing refreshments, with Ottilie, and hurried to Eduard. She found him in the drawing-room; but he would tell her nothing either. He fell on his knees before her, bathed her hands in tears, fled to his rooms, and when she sought to follow him she was met by the valet who gave her what explanation he could. The rest she pieced together herself, then at once determinedly put her mind to what needed doing forthwith. Ottilie's room was restored with all speed. Eduard had found his own as he left them, down to the last scrap of paper.

The three seemed to resume their relations with one another, but Ottilie still would not speak and Eduard could do nothing but beg his wife to be patient, whilst seeming himself incapable of patience. Charlotte sent messengers to Mittler and to the Major. The first could not be found; the Major came. To him Eduard poured out his heart, confessed every least detail, and so Charlotte learned what had happened, what had altered the situation so strangely and caused such a turmoil of the emotions.

In the gentlest way she spoke about it with her husband. Her one request was that for the present the girl should not be subjected to any more persuasion. Eduard felt his wife's worth, her love, her reasonableness; but his passion possessed him exclusively. Charlotte urged him not to lose hope, she promised to agree to a divorce. He did not believe it; he was in such a sickness that hope and faith were deserting him in turn. He demanded that Charlotte should promise to marry the Major; he was in the grip of an insane discontent. Charlotte, to soothe him, to keep him from collapse, did as he asked. She promised to marry the Major in the event of Ottilie's agreeing to a union with Eduard, but only under the express condition that for the time being the two men would go away together. The Major had some business to conduct in another part of the country for the court he was at, and Eduard promised to go with him. They made their preparations, and grew a little calmer since at least something was being done.

Meanwhile it was noticeable that Ottilie was scarcely eating or drinking as she continued in her refusal to speak. They sought to persuade her, she became distressed; they let her be. And is it not a weakness in most of us that we shy away from tormenting a person even for his own good? Charlotte cast around for a remedy and at last hit upon the idea of sending for the Assistant from the school since he had a good deal of influence over Ottilie and had made friendly enquiries after her failure to arrive—without, however, receiving a reply.

They spoke of this intention when she was present, so that she should not be surprised. She seemed not to agree to it; she thought for a while; finally she appeared to have reached some decision, she hurried to her room, and before it was evening sent the following note to the others who were still together.

Ottilie to her Friends

'Dear ones, why must I say outright what is self-evident? I have left my proper course and am not to be allowed to resume it. Even if I were at one with myself again, still in the world outside a malevolent spirit has me in its power and seems to be thwarting me.

'My intention to give up Eduard and go away from him was quite unqualified. I hoped I would not meet him again. It happened otherwise; he appeared before me even against his own will. Perhaps I took and interpreted my promise too literally that I would never have any conversation with him. But as my feeling and my conscience at that moment prompted me I fell silent, I became dumb before my friend, and now I have nothing more to say. The vows I have taken are very strict, and perhaps they would worry a person who had thought about them first; but I submitted to them on the spur of the moment, forced by my feelings. Let me persist in them as long as my heart commands. Do not call in anyone to negotiate with me. Do not press me to speak or to take more food and drink than I absolutely need. Help me over this time by your indulgence and your patience. I am young, young people recover quite unexpectedly. Let me be in your company, give me the joy of your love and the benefit of your conversation; but leave my inner self to me.'

The men's departure, long prepared for, was put off, because of delays in the business on which the Major was to be sent. This pleased Eduard. Ottilie's note had roused him again, her words, which gave both comfort and some hope, had encouraged him, he felt he had reason to go on steadfastly waiting, and suddenly declared that he would not leave. 'How foolish', he cried, 'to throw away deliberately and prematurely what we can least do without, what we need most, when, though its loss does threaten, we might still be able to preserve it. And why do such a thing? Really only so that a man may seem to have a will of his own and to be free to choose. In that ridiculous conceit I have often torn myself away from friends hours and even days too early, only so as not to be under the duress of the last, implacable moment. But this time I will stay. Why should I go away? Has she not already gone away from me? There is no likelihood that I will take her hand or hug her to my heart; I must not even think of it, I go cold at the thought. She has not gone away from me, she has risen above me.'

And so he stayed, as he wanted to and had to. But nothing could equal his well-being when he was in her company. And in her too the same feeling had remained; she was no more able than he was to escape that blessed necessity. Now as before they exerted an indescribable, almost magical power of attraction over one another. They were living under one roof; but even without exactly thinking of one another, busy with other things, pulled this way and that by the company they were in, still they drew near to one another. If they were in a room together before long they were standing or sitting side by side. Only complete nearness could make them tranquil, but then utterly tranquil, and this nearness was enough; neither a look, nor a word, nor a gesture, nor any contact was necessary, only a pure being together. Then they were not two people but only one in an unthinking and complete well-being, content with themselves and with the world. Had one of them been held fast at the far end of the house the other, little by little, involuntarily would have been impelled thither. Life was a mystery to them, and they found its solution only in each other's company.

Ottilie was altogether serene and calm, so that their minds could be entirely at rest on her account. She rarely left them, except that she had got their permission to eat alone. Only Nanni served her.

There is more repetition in a person's life than we suppose. His own nature is the immediate cause of it. Character, individuality, disposition, bent, locality, surroundings, and habits make up an entirety in which each person lives, as in an element, an atmosphere, and only in that element does he feel himself contented and at ease. And so we find human beings, about whose changeability there is so much complaint, after many years, to our amazement, not changed at all, and after an infinite number of inner and outward stimuli in fact unchangeable.

Thus now in our friends' daily lives together almost everything had resumed its former course. Still Ottilie, never speaking, expressed her helpful nature in many an act of kindness; and everyone likewise, after his or her own fashion. In this way their domestic round was the illusory image of their former lives, and it was forgivable that they should delude themselves into thinking things were still the same.

The autumn days, equal in length to those of spring, brought the company back indoors at exactly the same hour. The seasonal beauty of fruits and flowers was such that they could think this the autumn of that first spring; the time in between had fallen into oblivion. For now the kinds of flowers in bloom were those they had sown in those first days also; now fruits were ripening on the trees which then they had seen in blossom.

The Major came and went; Mittler too appeared from time to time. Their evening sessions mostly had the same pattern. Usually Eduard read aloud, and with a greater liveliness, with more feeling, better, indeed, as one might say, more cheerfully than before. It was as if he were seeking through gaiety as well as through passion to reanimate Ottilie out of her stone-coldness and to melt her silence. He sat as he had done formerly in such a way that she could read over his shoulder, indeed he was uneasy, distracted, if she were not doing so, if he were not certain that she was following the words with her eyes.

The disagreeable and uncomfortable feelings of their middle period had been entirely extinguished. No one had any grudge against anyone else; no bitterness of any kind remained. Charlotte played the piano, the Major accompanied her on the violin, and Ottilie's particular management of the keys came into unison, as formerly, with Eduard's flute. So they drew near to Eduard's birthday, whose celebration they had missed the previous year. This time it was to be celebrated quietly, by friends at ease, without festivities. That was the understanding they had arrived at, half tacitly, half expressly. But as the day approached so the solemnity of Ottilie's being, more felt than noticed till then, grew ever greater. In the garden it was often as though she were making an assessment of the flowers. She had directed the Gardener to spare all of the late summer blooms, and spent most time among the asters, which that year more than any other were flowering in extreme abundance.

CHAPTER EIGHTEEN

But most significantly, as the friends continued their silent observation of Ottilie, they saw that for the first time she had unpacked the chest, taken different things out of it, and cut them up to make an outfit of clothes, only one, but that full and complete. When with Nanni's help she tried then to pack the rest back in again she could hardly manage it. The space was overfilled even though a part had been taken out. The young girl gazed and gazed. She was desperate to have something for herself, especially when she saw that all the smaller items of an outfit were provided too. Shoes and stockings, embroidered garters, gloves, and numerous other things remained. She begged Ottilie to give her something from these. Ottilie refused, but at once opened a drawer in her dressing-table and let the child take what she liked. She did so, hastily and clumsily, and ran off with her booty to announce her good fortune to everyone else in the house and show them what she had got.

At last Ottilie managed to put everything back, in careful layers; then she opened a secret compartment let into the lid. There she had hidden Eduard's little notes and letters, a few dried flowers as reminders of earlier walks, a lock of her beloved's hair, and other things besides. Now she added one more thing—it was the portrait of her father—and locked the whole box, hanging the tiny key on its golden chain around her neck again, in her bosom.

All sorts of hopes meanwhile had been awakened in her friends. Charlotte was convinced that on the day itself she would begin to speak again; for there had been an air of secret busyness about her and of serene self-contentment, and she wore a smile such as shows on the face of a person harbouring something good and joyful for the ones he loves. Nobody knew that Ottilie was spending many hours in a condition of great weakness, and only by strength of spirit lifted herself out of it for the times when she appeared in company.

During this period Mittler had quite often called, and had stayed longer than formerly. Never one to give up, he knew he must not miss his chance if it presented itself. Ottilie's silence and refusal seemed to him auspicious. So far no steps had been taken towards a divorce; he hoped he might determine the poor girl's fate in some other and more favourable way. He listened, he made concessions, or he let it be thought that he had, and in his own fashion he acted sensibly enough.

But again and again it got the better of him if ever he had occasion to deliver an opinion on subjects he held to be very important. He lived a good deal in himself and when he was with other people his dealings with them mostly took the form of actions. If words burst forth from him in the company of friends then, as we have seen more than once already, they rolled on heedlessly, they hurt or healed, brought benefit or harm, just as it happened.

On the evening before Eduard's birthday Charlotte and the Major were sitting together waiting for Eduard who had ridden out. Mittler was walking up and down the room; Ottilie had remained in hers laying out her clothes for the next day and giving various directions to her maid, who understood her perfectly and did her silent bidding in a trice.

Mittler had just got on to one of his favourite topics. He was given to asserting that in the education of children, as in the government of peoples, nothing is more out of place and more barbaric than prohibitions, than laws and regulations which forbid. 'Human beings are born doers,' he said, 'and for anyone who knows how to manage them they will set to work at once and busy themselves and get things done. For my part I would rather put up with mistakes and failings around me until such time as I have the opposing virtues at my command, than get rid of the failings and have nothing proper to put in their place. People are very glad to do what is right and useful if they only can; they do it in order to have something to do, and think no more about it than about the stupidities they commit out of idleness and boredom.

'I have never liked listening to children being made to repeat the Ten Commandments. The fifth is fine and sensible, being a commandment to do something: "Honour thy father and thy mother." If the children really take that to heart they can spend all day practising it. But the sixth! I ask you: "Thou shalt do no murder." As though anyone had the slightest desire to murder anyone else. You might hate someone, grow angry, grow hasty, and as a consequence of one thing and another it might indeed happen that on occasion you strike somebody dead. But is it not a barbarous practice to forbid a child to commit an act of murder? Now if it said: Take care of your neighbour's life, put out of his way whatever might be harmful to him, save his life even at the risk of your own, if you harm him consider that you are harming yourself—those are commandments such as obtain among cultured and rational peoples, and all we have of them in our catechism is the poor addendum: "What dost thou learn by this?"*

'And then the seventh! Really quite abominable! All it does is cause the wondering minds of children to lust after dangerous secrets, it excites their imaginations with such peculiar images and ideas that the very thing we are seeking to remove is brought forcibly into view. Far better to have things of that sort punished arbitrarily by secret courts than to have them gossiped about in front of the whole congregation.'

At that moment Ottilie came in. ' "Thou shalt not commit adultery," ' Mittler continued. 'How coarse, how very indecent! Now would it not sound quite different if it said: Show reverence for the marriage bond. Seeing a loving man and wife, be glad, take pleasure in it as you do in the happiness of a sunny day. Should any cloud come over their union, seek to dispel it, strive to appease and soothe them, make clear to them what advantages they have in one another, and with a beautiful selflessness further the good of others by making them sensible of the happiness that derives from every duty done and especially from this which binds a man and a woman together indissolubly.'

Charlotte sat in torment, all the worse since she felt sure that Mittler did not realize what he was saying and where he was saying it, and before she could interrupt him she saw Ottilie, altered in appearance, leave the room.

'You will spare us the eighth commandment,' said Charlotte with a forced smile. 'And all the others too,' said Mittler in reply, 'so long as I save the one on which all those others rest.'

There was a terrible scream. Nanni rushed in, crying: 'She is dying! Miss is dying! Oh, come quick!'

When Ottilie, staggering on her feet, had returned to her room, her fine clothes for the next morning lay all spread out across several chairs and the little girl, passing from one piece to the next in a wondering contemplation, exclaimed triumphantly: 'Oh, Miss, do look. It's a wedding outfit, and just right for you!'

Ottilie heard these words and sank down on the sofa. Nanni saw her mistress turn pale and stiffen. She ran to Charlotte, they came. Their friend the Surgeon was soon on the scene; he thought it only exhaustion. He had them fetch some beef tea; Ottilie refused it with disgust, indeed she almost fell into convulsions when the cup was brought to her lips. He asked then gravely and quickly, as the circumstances prompted him to, what Ottilie had eaten that day. The little girl hesitated; he repeated his question, the girl confessed that Ottilie had eaten nothing.

There was something suspicious in the degree of Nanni's distress. He hurried her next door, Charlotte followed, the girl fell on her knees, confessed that Ottilie had been eating almost nothing for some considerable time. Urged to by Ottilie, Nanni had eaten the meals herself; she had kept quiet about it because, with gestures, her mistress had pleaded and threatened, and also, she added innocently, because it tasted so good.

The Major and Mittler came in, they found Charlotte busy in the company of the Surgeon. The pale, ethereal girl sat, self-possessed as it seemed, in the corner of the sofa. They begged her to lie down; she refused, but indicated that they should bring her box. She placed her feet on it and, half-recumbent then, was comfortable. She seemed to want to say goodbye, her gestures expressed the tenderest affection for those around her, love, gratitude, a plea for forgiveness and the most heartfelt farewell.

Eduard, dismounting, learned of her condition, rushed into the room, threw himself down beside her, seized her hand and, never speaking, wetted it with his tears. So he remained a long while. At last he cried: 'Am I not to hear your voice again? Will you not come back into life with a single word for me? Well then, I shall follow you over. There we will speak with other tongues.'

She pressed his hand, hard, looked at him full of life and full of love, and after a deep breath, after a heavenly, silent moving of the lips: 'Promise me you will live!' she cried out, sweetly and tenderly expending her strength, and at once fell back.

'I promise,' he answered, but he was already calling after her. She had departed.

After a night of weeping it fell to Charlotte to see to the burial of the beloved remains. The Major and Mittler supported her. Eduard's condition was pitiable. Once he was able to lift himself at all out of despair and compose his mind somewhat he insisted that Ottilie should not be removed from the Hall, she must be tended, cared for, treated like a living woman, for she was not dead, she could not be dead. They did as he wished, at least in the sense that they forbore to do what he had forbidden. He did not ask to see her.

There was a further shock, a further worry for the friends. Nanni, severely scolded by the Surgeon, brought to confess by threats and then reproached, abundantly, after her confession, had fled. After much searching she was discovered; she seemed beside herself. Her parents took her back. The kindest treatment seemed without effect, she had to be locked up since she threatened to run away again.

Step by step they managed to retrieve Eduard from the most violent level of despair, but only into unhappiness, for it was clear to him, it was a certainty, that he had lost his life's happiness for ever. They plucked up the courage to suggest to him that if Ottilie were buried in the chapel she would still be among the living and would still have a friendly and quiet dwelling as her own. It was hard to get his agreement, and only on condition that she would be carried out in an open coffin and in the chapel itself should have at most a glass lid over her, and that a lamp be donated to be kept always alight, did he at last give his consent and seemed then to have acquiesced in everything.

They dressed the precious body in the fine clothes she had prepared for herself; they wreathed her head with asters that shone like stars, sadly and full of portent. To decorate the bier, the church, the chapel, all the gardens were stripped of what had decorated them. They lay like a waste, as though winter had already erased the joy from all the beds. Very early in the morning she was carried out of the Hall in an open coffin, and the rising sun gave the flush of life again to her ethereal face. Those accompanying her crowded around the bearers, nobody wanted to go ahead or follow behind, everyone wanted to be around her and enjoy her presence for the last time. Among the boys, the men, the women, no one was unmoved. The girls were inconsolable, feeling the loss of her the most immediately.

Nanni was absent. They had kept her away, or rather they had kept the day and the hour of the funeral a secret from her. She was locked up at her parents' house in a little room overlooking the garden. But when she heard the bells she knew at once what was happening and when the woman in charge of her, being curious to see the procession, left her alone she escaped through a window on to a passageway, and from there, since she found the doors all locked, on to the roof.

At that very moment the cortège was swaying through the village down the clean street strewn with leaves. Nanni saw her mistress clearly below her, more clearly, more perfectly, in a greater beauty than any who were following in the procession. She seemed no longer earthly, but to be borne along on clouds or waves, and seemed to be beckoning to her maid and she, in confusion, swaying, tottering, fell.

With a terrible scream the crowd dispersed in all directions. In the press and tumult the bearers were obliged to set down the bier. The child lay near it; all her limbs seemed shattered. They lifted her up; and by chance or by some intervention of fate they rested her across the corpse, indeed with the life that remained to her she seemed herself to be trying to reach her beloved mistress. But no sooner had her shaking limbs touched Ottilie's dress and her nerveless fingers Ottilie's folded hands than the girl sprang up, first raised her arms and her eyes to heaven, then fell on her knees by the coffin and in ecstatic reverence gazed up at her mistress.

At last she leapt to her feet as if inspired, and with a religious joy cried out: 'Yes, she has forgiven me. What no human being could forgive me, what I could not forgive myself, God has forgiven me through her look, her gesture, and her mouth. Now she is lying down again so quiet and gentle, but you saw how she sat up and opened her hands and blessed me and how she looked at me and smiled. You all heard it, you are my witnesses that she said to me: "You are forgiven." Now I am not the murderess among you any more, she has forgiven me, God has forgiven me, and nobody can have anything against me any more.'

The crowd was pressing round; they were astonished, they listened, looked this way and that, and scarcely knew what to do next. 'Carry her to her rest now,' said the girl. 'She has done and suffered all her share and can no longer dwell among us.' The bier moved on, Nanni immediately behind it, and they reached the church and the chapel.

Thus Ottilie's coffin lay now, at her head the coffin of the child, at her feet the little chest, and around all a stout enclosure of oak. They had arranged that for a period there should be a woman who would watch over the body lying so sweetly under the glass cover. But Nanni would not let anyone have this office but herself; she wished to be there alone, without any companion, and diligently look after the lamp now for the first time lit. She requested this so eagerly and so insistently that they let her, in order to prevent any worsening of her state of mind, which there was reason to fear.

But she was not alone for long. Just as night fell and the hanging lamp, coming into its own, cast a brighter light, the door opened and the Architect entered the chapel whose piously decorated walls, now in so mild a radiance, pressed forward to meet him more full of the past and heavier with futurity than he would ever have believed.

Nanni was sitting on one side of the coffin. She recognized him at once; but without a word she pointed to her dead mistress. And so he stood on the other side, in youthful strength and grace, thrown back upon himself, stiff, inward looking, his arms hung down, his hands clasped, wrung in pity, bowing his head, lowering his gaze upon the lifeless girl.

Once before he had stood like that in front of Belisarius. Involuntarily now he assumed the same posture; and how natural it was on this occasion too. Here too something inestimably valuable had fallen from its height; and if in the former case courage, intelligence, power, rank, and wealth were lost irrevocably and lamented in the person of one man, if qualities necessary at critical times to the nation and its prince had there been disregarded, indeed rejected and repudiated, here a like number of other, quiet virtues, brought forth by Nature out of her abundant depths only a short time since, had now been quickly erased again by her indifferent hand; rare, beautiful, and lovable virtues whose peaceable influence the needy world at all times welcomes with delighted satisfaction and laments the loss of with longing and grief.

The young man said nothing, nor the girl for a while; but when she saw the tears start frequently from his eyes, when he seemed to be utterly dissolved in grief, then she spoke to him, and with so much truth and power, with so much kindness and certainty, that he, astonished at her eloquence, was able to compose himself, and his beautiful friend hovered before him living and working in a higher region. His tears ceased, his grief was less; kneeling he said goodbye to Ottilie, and to Nanni, warmly pressing her hands, and that same night rode away, having seen no one besides.

The Surgeon, unbeknown to the girl, had spent the night in the church, and visiting her next morning he found her cheerful and comforted. He was prepared for all sorts of delusions; he expected her to tell him of conversations with Ottilie during the night and of other such phenomena; but she was normal, calm, and entirely self-possessed. She remembered earlier times and circumstances all perfectly well and with great exactness, and nothing in her talk left the usual course of what is true and real except the happening at the funeral, and that she often recounted with delight: how Ottilie had sat up, blessed her, forgiven her, and in so doing set her mind at rest for ever.

The continuing beauty of Ottilie's state, more like sleep than death, attracted numbers of people. Those who lived there or nearby wanted to see her while they could and everyone was eager to hear Nanni's incredible story from her own lips; some then made fun of it, most were sceptical, and there were a few whose attitude towards it was one of belief.

Every need denied its real satisfaction perforce engenders faith. Nanni, all broken by her fall in full view of everyone, was made whole again by touching the virtuous corpse. Why should not a similar benefit be vouchsafed others from it? Loving mothers brought their children, at first in secret, if they were afflicted with any ill, and believed they discerned a sudden improvement. Belief in this grew, and in the end even the oldest and the weakest came looking for some refreshment and relief. The numbers grew, and it became necessary to close the chapel; indeed, except for services, to close the church itself.

Eduard never had the heart to visit the departed girl. He lived by rote, seemed to have no more tears, to be incapable of any more grief. His participation in the talk, his appetite for food and drink, lessened daily. He imbibed some comfort still, a little, so it seemed, only out of the glass, for all it had been a false prophet to him. He still took pleasure in contemplating the entwined initials, and his look then, solemn and serene together, seemed to suggest that even now he was still hoping for reunion. And just as a happy man seems favoured by every trivial circumstance and raised up high by every chance, so the littlest occurrences will easily combine to distress and bring to perdition the unhappy man. For one day, as Eduard was raising the beloved glass to his lips, he set it down again in horror; it was the same and not the same, he missed one small identifying mark. They confronted the valet, who admitted that the real glass had been broken recently and a similar one, also from Eduard's boyhood, had been put in its place. Eduard could not be angry, his fate was spoken by the deed—why should the symbol move him? And yet it pressed him down. Thenceforth he seemed to find it repugnant to drink; he seemed to be purposely abstaining from food and from conversation.

But from time to time he became restless. He called for something to eat again, began speaking again. 'Alas,' he said on one occasion to the Major, who rarely left his side, 'it is my deep misfortune that all my striving remains an imitation and a false exertion. What was blessedness for her is a torment to me; and yet for the sake of that blessedness I am obliged to take on that torment. I must go after her, and along this way. But my own nature holds me back, and my promise. It is a terrible task to imitate the inimitable. Now I understand that genius is necessary for everything, even martyrdom.'

In this hopeless condition why dwell on the efforts in which, as wife, as friend, as doctor, Eduard's loved ones for a while exhausted themselves? At last he was found dead. It was Mittler who made the sad discovery. He called the Surgeon and took note, in his customary fashion, of the exact circumstances in which the deceased was found. Charlotte rushed to the scene; she suspected suicide; she was ready to blame herself and the others for an unforgivable negligence. But the Surgeon, with reasons in nature, and Mittler, with reasons in morality, were soon able to convince her she was wrong. It was quite obvious that Eduard had been surprised by his end. At a quiet moment he had taken out of a little box, and out of his pocket-book, all the things left him by Ottilie, things he had previously been careful to conceal, and had laid them all out before him: a lock of her hair, flowers plucked in an hour of happiness, all the notes she had written him, from that first one which his wife had so casually and with such consequence, handed over to him. He would not intentionally have exposed all that to chance discovery. And so he too, whose heart until a moment since had suffered a ceaseless agitation, lay now in peace, unassailably; and since he had gone to his rest in thinking of that saintly girl, surely he could be called blessed. Charlotte gave him his place next to Ottilie and ordered that no one else should be buried under that roof. On that condition she made sizeable bequests for the benefit of the church, the school, the clergyman, and the schoolteacher.

So the lovers are side by side, at rest. Peace hovers over their dwelling-place, cheerful images of angels, their kith and kin, look down at them from the vaulted ceiling, and what a sweet moment it will be for their eyes when on some future day they wake together.

EXPLANATORY NOTES

15   *Mittler*: the name means 'mediator'. Considering his role in the novel I was tempted to translate him as 'Meddler'.

17   *Let us make a trial of it*: the German ('den Versuch machen') may mean either 'make a trial' or 'carry out an experiment'.

18   *name-days*: the day sacred to the saint whose name a person bears. In several European countries these days may be celebrated as well as birthdays.

     both called Otto?: Eduard has a second name: Otto. Hence the initials E and O on the glass (in Part One, Chapter Nine and Part Two, Chapter Eighteen). Eduard, the Captain, Charlotte, and Ottilie may be said to have the name Otto in common. Then the child is christened Otto.

27   *strange and momentous intervention*: see the interpolated Novelle in Part II, Chapter 10. If the Captain really was one of the male protagonists in that *Novelle* he must surely be the one who loses.

29   *relations between things . . . my relations*: in the discussion here the characters are playing on the word *Verwandtschaft*, which means a relationship (or affinity) in science and in human affairs. The English term 'elective affinity', current in science from the late eighteenth century onwards, was given wider currency in its human and emotional sense by Goethe's novel, by the title alone perhaps. Hazlitt, for example, in 1821, before the novel had been translated into English, writes thus in his essay 'On Genius and Common Sense': 'The imagination gives out what it has first absorbed by congeniality of temperament, what it has attracted and moulded into itself by elective affinity, as the loadstone draws and impregnates iron.'

32   *skilled in the art of separation*: the German word is *Scheidekünstler*. *Scheiden* is also the usual word for marital separation and divorce.

41   *a solace to the eye*: Saint Odilia is traditionally associated with cures for maladies of the eye.

59   *lime*: *Kalk*, here used in lime-mortar to bind, is of course a substance in the equation cited in Part One, Chapter Four.

75   *the Sarmatians*: a nomadic tribe closely related to the Scythians. In classical times they moved north from the Black Sea as far as the Baltic coast.

76   *sons of Anak*: a race of giants whom the Israelites fought against.
     See Numbers 13: 33.

107 *the Carthusians*: a monastic order which had famous nurseries
     near Paris.

112 *Tears are a sign of goodness in a man*: the Greek proverb is *aridakrues
     anepes esthloi*, and means literally: 'Men rich in tears are good
     men.'

118 *Philemon with his Baucis*: Philemon and Baucis are the very type
     of the faithful and contented old married couple. Their story is
     told by Ovid in the *Metamorphoses*.

135 *nixie*: the German is *Saalnixe*. A musical drama of that name,
     adapted by Christiane Vulpius's brother from one called *Das
     Donauweibchen*, was staged in Weimar in 1805. The Saale is the
     river that flows through nearby Jena, but in the title, at least as
     Goethe uses it here, there may be a pun on the word for
     drawing-room.

     poses plastiques: Goethe saw Emma Hart (later Emma Hamilton)
     perform such things at Caserta, outside Naples, in March 1787.
     The art she began was continued by, among others, Johanna
     Hendel Schütz, who performed in Weimar in 1810.

     improvisatori: poets who compose and recite their verses on the
     spur of the moment, often on a topic suggested to them. It was
     a traditional art in Italy especially.

     Artemisia: queen of Caria, in Asia Minor, in the fourth century
     BC. She married her own brother Mausoleus, and when he died
     drank his ashes in her wine and raised to his memory a
     mausoleum that was one of the Seven Wonders of the World.
     She died inconsolable two years after him.

136 *Lombard*: the Lombards, being an ancient Germanic tribe, are
     more in the Architect's own line of interest.

     widow of Ephesus: the story of the Widow of Ephesus—her drastic
     failure to remain faithful to the memory of her husband—is told
     by La Fontaine in his *Contes et Nouvelles*.

138 *Incroyables*: outrageously fashionable Parisians at the time of the
     Directory (1795–9). This reference locates the story in post-
     revolutionary times.

147 *van Dyck*: Flemish painter (1599–1641). Belisarius was a general
     under the Emperor Justinian. He died, after a glorious career,
     disgraced, in AD 565. He is said to have had to beg for charity.

The engraving of Van Dyck's painting has the caption: *Date obolum Belisario* ('Give a penny to Belisarius').

Poussin's . . . Esther: Nicolas Poussin, French painter (1594–1665). The story of Esther before King Ahasuerus is told in the Old Testament, in the Book of Esther.

148 *Paternal Admonition, by Ter Borch*: this painting by the Dutch painter Gerard Ter Borch (1617–81) is sometimes known as 'The Satin Gown', that being its most striking feature. It actually depicts a brothel. The 'fatherly' figure is offering a sum of money for the girl. But in Goethe's day (the coin in the client's hand having by that time been expunged) the picture had the sense given here. Johann Georg Wille (1715–1808) was an engraver from Hessen.

156 *derived from . . . pious presentations*: the Architect's explanation of the origin of *tableaux vivants* reappears in Goethe's *Italian Journey*, 1816–17.

169 *Humboldt*: Alexander von Humboldt (1769–1859) was an explorer and natural scientist. Goethe got to know him in 1795.

     the proper study of mankind . . . is man: Alexander Pope, *Essay on Man*, II. 2.

174 *Lord, now lettest thou . . . house*: Luke 2: 29–30, slightly altered.

179 *comédie à tiroir*: literally 'a play made up of drawers'. It is a play whose plot is complicated by sub-plots and digressions which are, so to speak, fitted into it like drawers.

182 *camera obscura*: 'an instrument consisting of a darkened chamber or box, into which light is admitted through a double convex lens, forming an image of external objects on a surface of paper, glass, etc., placed at the focus of the lens' (*OED*). Robert Boyle, or his assistant Robert Hooke, invented the portable camera obscura in the 1660s.

195 *marcasites*: the crystallized form of iron pyrites.

196 *gravely apprehensive about*: doubtless the English visitor is offering to cure Ottilie by hypnotism.

197 *penserosa*: 'the thoughtful one'. A man or woman deep in thought or contemplation was a popular figure in earlier painting, and here Goethe may also be remembering Milton's poem 'Il Penseroso'.

198 *the Major*: this of course is the Captain after the honorary promotion promised him in Part One, Chapter Fourteen.

233 *What dost thou learn by this?*: see the Catechism in the Book of Common Prayer. The German Lutheran Catechism has above each part the question: *Was ist das?*

The Oxford World's Classics Website

www.worldsclassics.co.uk

- Browse the full range of Oxford World's Classics online

- Sign up for our monthly e-alert to receive information on new titles

- Read extracts from the Introductions

- Listen to our editors and translators talk about the world's greatest literature with our Oxford World's Classics audio guides

- Join the conversation, follow us on Twitter at OWC_Oxford

- Teachers and lecturers can order inspection copies quickly and simply via our website

www.worldsclassics.co.uk

American Literature

British and Irish Literature

Children's Literature

Classics and Ancient Literature

Colonial Literature

Eastern Literature

European Literature

Gothic Literature

History

Medieval Literature

Oxford English Drama

Poetry

Philosophy

Politics

Religion

The Oxford Shakespeare

A complete list of Oxford World's Classics, including Authors in Context, Oxford English Drama, and the Oxford Shakespeare, is available in the UK from the Marketing Services Department, Oxford University Press, Great Clarendon Street, Oxford OX2 6DP, or visit the website at www.oup.com/uk/worldsclassics.

In the USA, visit www.oup.com/us/owc for a complete title list.

Oxford World's Classics are available from all good bookshops. In case of difficulty, customers in the UK should contact Oxford University Press Bookshop, 116 High Street, Oxford OX1 4BR.